HANDBOOK ON PLANNING AND POWER

RESEARCH HANDBOOKS IN PLANNING

This important and timely series brings together critical and thought-provoking contributions on the most pressing topics and issues within the field of planning. Comprising specially commissioned chapters from leading academics these comprehensive *Research Handbooks* feature cutting-edge research, help to define the field and are written with a global readership in mind. Equally useful as reference tools or high-level introductions to specific topics, issues, methods and debates, these *Research Handbooks* will be an essential resource for academic researchers and postgraduate students in planning and related disciplines.

Titles in the series include:

Handbook of Planning Support Science
Edited by Stan Geertman and John Stillwell

Handbook on Planning and Complexity
Edited by Gert de Roo, Claudia Yamu and Christian Zuidema

Handbook on Planning and Power
Edited by Michael Gunder, Kristina Grange and Tanja Winkler

Handbook on Planning and Power

Edited by

Michael Gunder

Formerly School of Architecture and Planning, The University of Auckland, New Zealand

Kristina Grange

Professor of Urban Planning and Design Theory, Department of Architecture and Civil Engineering, Chalmers University of Technology, Sweden

Tanja Winkler

Associate Professor of City and Regional Planning, School of Architecture, Planning & Geomatics, University of Cape Town, South Africa

RESEARCH HANDBOOKS IN PLANNING

Edward Elgar
PUBLISHING

Cheltenham, UK • Northampton, MA, USA

Published by
Edward Elgar Publishing Limited
The Lypiatts
15 Lansdown Road
Cheltenham
Glos GL50 2JA
UK

Edward Elgar Publishing, Inc.
William Pratt House
9 Dewey Court
Northampton
Massachusetts 01060
USA

A catalogue record for this book
is available from the British Library

Library of Congress Control Number: 2023934083

This book is available electronically in the **Elgar**online
Geography, Planning and Tourism subject collection
http://dx.doi.org/10.4337/9781839109768

Printed on elemental chlorine free (ECF)
recycled paper containing 30% Post-Consumer Waste

ISBN 978 1 83910 975 1 (cased)
ISBN 978 1 83910 976 8 (eBook)

Printed and bound in the USA

This book is dedicated to Michael Gunder

*After Michael's untimely passing, a former student had a star with
the co-ordinates of Libre 21h58m22s +12˚38'44 registered and named
Michael Gunder with the following message:
'a star lecturer and best mentor'.*

*As you all know, Michael was very involved with this book and enjoyed
immensely the discussion with you. I am sure he would have been grateful to
you all to have seen this project to conclusion.*

I said goodnight, but I never had a chance to say goodbye.

*RIP Michael; we send our love.
Adriana Gunder and Huia*

Contents

Contributors

Ernest R. Alexander is Emeritus Professor of Urban Planning at the University of Wisconsin-Milwaukee, USA. He has practised architecture and/or planning in Israel, Ghana, the UK and the USA and currently practises in Israel. Alexander's research interests in planning theory include rationalities, organisations, planning processes and institutions, and institutional design.

Leonora C. Angeles has been the Director of the University of British Columbia's (UBC) Institute for Gender, Race, Sexuality, and Social Justice, Canada, since July 2022. A cross-appointed to the UBC School of Community and Regional Planning, she is also faculty research associate at the UBC Centre for Human Settlements (CHS) and the Centre for Southeast Asian Research (CSEAR). She has worked on a number of applied research and capacity-building research projects in Brazil, Vietnam, Thailand and the Philippines. Her continuing research and interests are on community and international development studies and social policy, participatory planning and governance, participatory action research, and the politics of transnational feminist networks, women's movements and agrarian issues, particularly in Southeast Asia. She is President of the Board of the National Pilipino Canadian Cultural Centre (NPC3) and the Canadian Council on Southeast Asian Studies (CCSEAS, 2019–2021).

Ozlem Atalay is a fifth-year PhD candidate in Urban and Regional Planning at Florida State University, USA. Their research focuses on queer spaces and the involvement of LGBTQ communities in the local decision-making processes. They are interested in space making and everyday resistance strategies of LGBTQ individuals across the globe.

Elham Bahmanteymouri is a Senior Lecturer at the School of Architecture and Planning (Te Pare), the University of Auckland (Waipapa Taumata Rau), New Zealand. Elham is co-founder and co-director of the History and Theory Hub. She has a bachelor's degree in economics, a master's degree in urban and regional planning and urban design and a PhD in planning. She worked as a senior planner in both the public and private sectors for sixteen years. The focus of her research is on land use planning, urban economics, digital platform economy, behavioural economy, alternative approaches to planning theory and practice, and urban critical theories such as the Lacanian post-Marxist approach.

Elena Besussi is a Lecturer at The Bartlett School of Planning, University College London, UK. Her research focuses on urbanisation and the capitalist city, the financialisation of urban planning and local government, and the regulation of land policy and development.

Raoul Beunen is Associate Professor of Environmental Governance at the Open University, the Netherlands. His research explores the potentials and limitations of environmental policy and planning from the perspective of adaptive governance and sustainability. It focuses on innovation and evolution in governance, paying attention to the dynamics of policy implementation and integration, multi-level governance, stakeholder involvement, and the performance of institutional structures.

Camillo Boano is Full Professor in Urban Design and Critical Theory at The Bartlett Development Planning Unit (DPU) and Full Professor in Architecture and Urban Design at the Politecnico di Torino, Italy. He is co-director of the UCL Urban Laboratory. Camillo's research has centred on the interfaces between critical theory, radical philosophy, and urban design processes. He is working on a series of interconnected research projects in Latin America, Southeast Asia, and the Middle East on urban infrastructures, habitability, and the urban project. He is the author of *The Ethics of Potential Urbanism: Critical Encounters between Giorgio Agamben and Architecture* (Routledge, 2017) and *Progetto Minore: Alla ricerca della Minorità nel Progetto Archiettonico ed Urbanistico* (LetteraVentidue, 2020) and, with Cristina Bianchetti, of *Lifelines Politics, Ethics, and the Affective Economy of Inhabiting* (Jovis, 2022).

Petra Doan is Professor Emerita at Florida State University, USA. She remains active and conducts research on planning and the LGBTQ community. In addition to numerous journal articles, her most recent co-edited book with Lynda Johnston is titled *Rethinking Transgender Identities: Reflections from Around the Globe* and was published by Routledge in 2022.

Martijn Duineveld is Associate Professor at the Cultural Geography Group Wageningen University, the Netherlands and co-director of the Centre for Space, Place and Society. He is co-founder and active contributor to the emerging body of literature on Evolutionary Governance Theory. Martijn has been involved in many international research and consultancy projects situated in Argentina, Uganda, Georgia and Russia. On a more conceptual level his research is focused on three themes: democratic innovation in governance; conflicts and power in governance; and materiality and object formation in governance.

James Duminy is Lecturer in Human Geography at the University of Bristol, UK and an honorary research associate at the African Centre for Cities, University of Cape Town. His work examines the governance of urban change in Africa and the Global South, with a focus on planning, food systems, demography and health.

Mona Fawaz is a Professor of Urban Studies and Planning at the American University of Beirut, Lebanon, where she co-founded the Beirut Urban Lab, a regional research centre working towards more inclusive, just, and viable cities. Mona's research and teaching span urban history and historiography, social and spatial justice, informality and the law, land, housing, property, and planning theory. In addition, Mona has been closely engaged in influencing Beirut's ongoing transformations, advocating for the right to the city for the urban majorities.

Linda Fox-Rogers is Assistant Professor within the School of Architecture, Planning and Environmental Policy at University College Dublin. Her research is guided by her interest in exploring the uneven power dynamics in the planning process. The current focus of her works centres on power and politics in the planning system, the neoliberalisation of planning, and stakeholder perceptions of planning.

Kristina Grange is Professor of Urban Planning and Design Theory at Chalmers University of Technology, Sweden. She has an interest in poststructuralist theory and its implications for planning theory and practice. Her current research focuses on migration, homelessness and spatial inequalities.

Jean Hillier is Emeritus Professor at RMIT University, Melbourne, Australia. Research includes engagement with Deleuze and Guattari's ideas for poststructural theory and methodology for strategic practice and planning with non-human animals. Publications include *Deleuze and Guattari for Planners* (2013), with Gareth Abrahams; 'On Planning For Not Having A Plan?', *Planning Theory and Practice* (2017); 'Make Kin, Not Cities! Multispecies Entanglements and "Becoming-world" in Planning Theory', with Diana MacCallum, Wendy Steele, Donna Houston and Jason Byrne, *Planning Theory* (2017); 'Towns within Towns: From Incompossibility to Inclusive Disjunction in Urban Spatial Planning', with Jonathan Metzger, *Deleuze and Guattari Studies* (2021).

Andy Inch is a Senior Lecturer in Urban Studies and Planning at the University of Sheffield, UK. His research interests include the politics of planning and the contested ways planning seeks to govern futures.

Crystal Legacy is an Associate Professor of Urban Planning at the University of Melbourne, Australia, where she is also the Deputy Director of the Informal Urbanism Research Hub. She resides on Wurundjeri Country where she writes, teaches and works with communities on issues related to urban transport politics, public participation and the post-political city. She publishes in a range of academic journals, provides critical commentary on local and national media outlets, and works in solidarity with a range of community-based groups seeking climate-just outcomes in transport planning. Crystal is an editor of two journals *Planning Theory and Practice* and *Urban Policy and Research.*

Jaime Lopez is a PhD candidate of urban planning at USC, USA. He has degrees in film and history, and has served as a Planning Commissioner. His research focuses on environmental justice, participatory planning, and media. Jaime has recently directed two short documentaries (*Hex Chrome and the Community*; *Crisis and Campaign*).

Ernesto López-Morales is a Researcher at the Faculty of Engineering, Architecture and Design, Universidad San Sebastián, Chile. His research interests cover urban capitalism and its inequalities, land and housing markets, neoliberal governance and gentrification. He has conducted several case studies in Latin America, Europe and Asia, collaborating with local researchers and activists. His work has been published in Spanish, English and Portuguese.

Hilary Malson is a PhD student in Urban Planning at UCLA, a Ford Foundation Predoctoral Fellow, and a Researcher with the UCLA Luskin Institute on Inequality and Democracy, USA. Her research examines grassroots planning histories, Black life, housing justice, migration and displacement, suburban inequalities and community building.

Raine Mäntysalo is Full Professor of Strategic Urban Planning and Head of Department at Aalto University Department of Built Environment, Finland. In addition, he has the title of Docent in University of Oulu in the thematic of planning theory and communicative planning. He has also been visiting professor in Politecnico di Milano, University of Amsterdam, University of Newcastle and University of Aalborg.

Marlyana Azyyati Marzukhi is an Associate Professor in the College of Built Environment at the Universiti Teknologi MARA, Selangor, Malaysia. She obtained her Bachelor of Urban and Regional Planning from International Islamic University Malaysia, Master in Land Administration from Universiti Teknologi Malaysia and PhD in planning from the University of Auckland, New Zealand. She worked as a senior planner in both the private and public sectors for more than fifteen years. Marlyana is a Registered Town Planner of the Board of Town Planners Malaysia and a Council Member of the Malaysian Institute of Planners. Her main research interest is not limited to, but includes areas in sustainable development, urban governance, planning law, theory and practice, and psychological aspects in urban planning.

Katie McClymont is an Associate Professor and programme leader in Urban Planning at UWE, Bristol, UK. Her teaching and research interests include community participation and planning theory. Recent projects include UK and international research council funded work that uses creative methods to explore cemeteries in multifaith and multicultural urban settings, the unspoken and intangible values community assets, health/well-being in community-led housing and post-consent regulation in planning practice.

Mohsen Mohammadzadeh is a Senior Lecturer at the School of Architecture and Planning (Te Pare), the University of Auckland (Waipapa Taumata Rau), New Zealand. Mohsen is an urban planner and designer with twelve years of professional experience in Iran and then New Zealand. He completed his bachelor's in civil engineering, Master of Urban and Regional Planning and Master of Urban Design, and PhD in planning. Mohsen's research interests include, but are not limited to, urban automation, disruptive mobility, decolonising planning theory and practice, planning in the emerging global cities, and planning and urban conflicts.

Enda Murphy is Professor of Planning within the School of Architecture, Planning and Environmental Policy at University College Dublin, Ireland, where he is also Director of the Masters of Regional Urban Planning (MRUP) programme. His research interests are broad in scope but currently centre on the areas of neoliberalism/neoliberalisation, transport and spatial organisation, and urban and regional sustainability. He has published widely in the international scholarly literature and is co-author of two books.

Lina Olsson is Assistant Professor in Urban Studies at the Department of Urban Studies, Malmö University, Sweden. Her research focuses on justice issues, uneven development and the political economy of urban planning, urban governance, land policy, city regionalism, regional development policy and lately also transport policy.

John Pløger is Professor Emeritus at the Department of Global Development & Planning, University of Agder, Norway. He has published widely on agonism and planning, planning theory, and urban studies. His focus is currently on participation, governing by process, and planning as the micro-physics of power. He also works as a consultant on urban planning with architects and anthropologists in Denmark and Norway.

Libby Porter is a scholar in planning and urban geography, based at the Centre for Urban Research, RMIT University, Melbourne, Australia. Her work is about displacement and dispossession in cities.

Nikolai Roskamm is Professor for Planning Theory, History of Urbanism and Urban Design at the University of Applied Sciences Erfurt, Germany. He lives in Berlin and works at the interface of critical urban studies and political theory. He is concerned with historiographies of knowledge in urban planning.

Yvonne Rydin is Professor of Planning, Environment and Public Policy in The Bartlett School of Planning, University College London, UK. She has researched and published widely on planning policy and practice. With R. Beauregard, L. Lieto and M. Cremaschi, she co-edited *Regulation and Planning: Practices, Institutions, Agency* published by Routledge in 2022. Other single-authored books include *The Purpose of Planning* (2011) and *The Future of Planning: Beyond Growth Dependence* (2013) both published by Policy Press. She is currently working on elaborating planning approaches which do not rely on growth for their effectiveness.

Lisa Schweitzer is Professor of Urban Planning and Spatial Analysis and Gender and Sexuality Studies at the University of Southern California.

Eric Sheppard is a Research Professor Emeritus and former Alexander von Humboldt Chair of Geography at the University of California, Los Angeles, USA. He holds an honorary Doctor of Laws from the University of Bristol, served as President of the American Association of Geographers, and has co-edited the journals *Antipode*, *Environment and Planning A* and *Area, Development and Policy*. His scholarship embraces geographical political economy and socio-spatial theory, currently focusing on uneven geographies of capitalist globalisation, more-than-capitalist practices, southern urban theory, urban social movements and southern urban land transformations in and beyond Jakarta. His publications include thirteen books, most recently *Spatial Histories of Radical Geography*, *Urban Studies Inside-Out*, *Limits to Globalization*, and *The Wiley-Blackwell Companion to Economic Geography*, and some 200 refereed journal articles and book chapters. He has supervised over fifty PhD and MA students and served on the committees of over 200 other graduate students.

Bjørn Sletto's research focuses on environmental and social justice, informality, and insurgent and decolonial planning. His work engages with intersections of race, gender, class and other markers of difference, drawing on ethnographic and arts-based approaches in order to foster transformative research, pedagogy, and plan-making in marginalised communities. He has lived and worked in indigenous villages and border cities in Venezuela, investigating environmental conflicts and land rights struggles and conducting participatory mapping projects with the Pemon in the Gran Sabana and Yukpa in the Sierra de Perijá. For the past fifteen years, he has conducted activist research accompanied by his students in Santo Domingo, Dominican Republic, focusing on the role of critical pedagogy for insurgent planning in informal settlements.

Kristof Van Assche is interested in evolution and innovation in governance with focus areas in spatial planning and design, development and environmental policy. Kristof has worked in various countries, often combining fieldwork with theoretical reflection: systems theories, interpretive policy analysis, institutional economics and post-structuralism. Adaptive governance, resilience and especially strategy at community level are recent interests, building on our theory of evolutionary governance, while methodological work explores the implications of our perspective for research strategies and trans-disciplinary collaborations.

Chuan Wang is a Lecturer at the School of Architecture, Southeast University, People's Republic of China. His academic interest aims to answer how post-structuralist planning and urban design theories facilitate urban practice, with a focus on Lacan, language and discourse. His recent publications include an AESOP-sponsored booklet *Jacques Lacan: Introducing Thinkers for Planners – a Narrative and Conversation* (co-authored with Michael Gunder) and articles on post-structuralist analyses of planning practice in *Planning Theory*, *Habitat International* and *Urban Geography*.

Vanessa Watson (deceased) was Emeritus Professor of City and Regional Planning at the University of Cape Town, South Africa.

Tanja Winkler is an Associate Professor in the School of Architecture, Planning & Geomatics at the University of Cape Town, South Africa. Her pedagogical approach is geared towards engaged scholarship, while her research interests include spatial justice, planning ethics and decoloniality.

Acknowledgements

Funding from Genie, The Gender Initiative for Excellence at Chalmers University of Technology, contributed towards Tanja Winkler's research visit at Chalmers University of Technology, and funding from Iris Jonzén-Sandblom and Greta Jonzén's Foundation contributed towards Kristina Grange's research visit at University of Cape Town.

Introduction to the *Handbook on Planning and Power*

Kristina Grange and Tanja Winkler

It has been said that power resides everywhere, and that it is, above all else, productive. Power is found in every social relation, embedded in all our institutions, and even in every utterance made through the ways we attach meaning to certain values, articulate knowledge claims, and negotiate discourses. The field of planning is no exception. It is a field defined by its power relations between different actors, institutions, market players, states, non-governmental organisations and the public. But how, exactly, are the productive aspects of power played out in planning? Through which mechanisms and to what ends? Can one conclude that planners have power to make a difference when power increasingly seems to be consolidated in powerful elites; when exclusion, marginalisation and segregation have become systematic, leading to greater socio-economic and spatial injustices; when basic human needs such as housing are not defended as human rights; and when different practices of racial, gendered and religious oppression continue to be played out in so many corners of our society? Indeed, whose truth claims are valued in planning processes, and on behalf of whom do planners hope to *speak truth to power*?

This *Handbook on Planning and Power* argues that there is a deep-rooted need for a greater awareness of how power plays out in the field of planning. It presents thirty-six authors' insightful and critical analyses of how power can be both *theorised* and *situated* in planning contexts in many different parts of the world, and what, potentially, ought to be done if planning hopes to make a difference. By drawing on diverse thinkers in planning research, this book reveals the cutting edge of contemporary understandings about power so as to identify the current state of knowledge about planning and power, as well as this scholarship's new emerging trajectories. Planning, and its many roles in relation to agency and governance, has changed profoundly over the last few decades; and so too have the theories of and about power in planning, from both a critical and an explanatory standpoint. The wider world and the planning discipline will undoubtedly change even further over the next few decades. Nevertheless, this book provides the reader not only with key insights into contemporary planning theories about power – and the myriad interconnections between planning and power – it also demonstrates the effects of power within planning itself and on those who are shaped and impacted positively and negatively by its diverse practices.

REVISITING ASPECTS OF THE TERRAIN

More than two decades ago, David Booher and Judith Innes (2002: 221) suggested that 'power is an elusive concept; [and] when [scholars] use the term, they typically assume others know what they mean'. Booher and Innes (2002: 221, 222) go on to lament, 'whatever power is, planners [either] do not have it; [or they] typically do not recognize the power they do have'. For Booher and Innes this unrecognised power resides in the democratic potential of 'network power' that could serve to minimise the conventional distortions and corruptions often attributed to power. Fast-forward to the present day and we might find some comfort in the transformative power of platform urbanism including, for example, the role that social media played in mobilising action during the Arab Spring (Wolfsfeld et al., 2013). Yet, contemporary platforms of collaboration and networking are also beset by exclusionary practices, fake news, alternative facts, algorithmic violence, and participatory methods have their own limitations especially under a governmentality of neoliberalism. Thus, and in contrast to Booher and Innes' more hopeful assessment of planning and power, Bent Flyvberg's (1998) sobering publication, *Rationality and Power: Democracy in Practice*, convincingly demonstrates how planning strategies, frameworks and policies are almost always trumped by the *realrationalität* of powerholders regardless of planners' well-intentioned deliberations that contain technically optimal solutions and socially desirable outcomes. Flyvberg (1998) therefore maintains that if planners hope to promote socio-economic and spatial justice, they have no choice but to engage with the tactics of power that are integral to the arenas in which planning operates. In 1961, Edward Banfield presented a similar argument in his classic book *Political Influence*. This text revealed how Chicago's then powerful mayor, Richard J. Daley, accommodated private capital interests at the expense of socio-economic and spatial justice, thereby setting in motion the idea that planners have limited influence in the face of powerful elites who, invariably, dominate political decision-making processes.

Ambe Njoh (2009), however, questions the longstanding claim that planners have limited power. Rather, 'urban planners proved invaluable [to] European powerholders in realizing their twin objectives of domination and socio-political control in colonial Africa' (Njoh, 2009: 301). And while one might assume that 'colonial Africa' is a thing of the past, Njoh (2009: 301) reminds us that many planning policies and land laws promulgated during the colonial era 'continue to guide spatial development projects in Africa'. The same can be said of other Southern contexts (see Bhan et al., 2018). Njoh (2009) usefully distinguishes between 'power over' and 'power to' in his detailed analysis of how planning was – and continues to be – used as a tool of control and exclusion via seemingly neutral technical regulations. Njoh draws on Max Weber's (1978) definition of power in order to analyse 'power over' someone or something. This type of power, he argues, is easy to identify and rebuke. By contrast, the 'power to' enforce values, behaviour and conformity is far more subtle, subversive and insidious in nature. It involves the co-optation and remaking of subjects in accordance with coloniality's established norms, and, as such, it often faces less resistance than more overt power tactics. Amin Kamete (2012) equates this form of power with 'pastoral power' which, in turn, has its roots in the evangelical fervour of nineteenth-century missionaries that accompanied European colonialism. And for Kamete, 'pastoral power' is as violent and repressive as overt forms of disciplinary power. Still, a focus on 'power over' and 'power to' alone might negate the emancipatory categories of 'power with' and 'power within' that encompass aspects of Anthony Giddens' (1984: 14) conceptualisation of power as 'the capacity to make a difference'.

'Power with', as Lisa VeneKlasen et al. (2007) explain, resembles a type of shared power based on mutual support, solidarity and collaborative decision making that leads to collective action. This conceptualisation of power corroborates aspects of John Forester's (1989) seminal text: *Planning in the Face of Power*. And while Forester desists from explicitly using 'power with' as an analytical or normative tool, he, nevertheless, calls on planners to exercise their 'legitimate power' that resides in their frequent communications and engagements with citizens, politicians, planning commissioners, developers and the like via processes of active listening and learning through dialogue. For Forester (1989), a deliberate consensus-building approach serves not only to facilitate collective actions, but also to counter 'illegitimate power' that is exercised and maintained as a result of distorted communication. *Planning in the Face of Power* however desists from examining the workings of power per se, and focuses, instead, on how planners might become more effective in negotiating power, conflict and powerlessness.

'Power within', on the other hand, is predicated on an individual's or a group's sense of self-worth and self-knowledge (VeneKlasen et al., 2007). It serves as a form of emancipatory power that challenges asymmetrical power relations and the silencing strategies of the privileged (Roy, 2021). It also generates resistance to planning's disciplinary and unjust forms of control by, for example, celebrating 'the voices from the borderlands' (Sandercock, 1998), or by celebrating grassroots mobilisations and collective actions (Beard, 2003; Castells, 1983; Friedmann, 1987, 2011; Holston, 2008; Miraftab and Wills, 2005; Sandercock, 1999; Swyngedouw, 2018). Here, individuals or groups are viewed as active agents for themselves, thereby expanding the traditional planning field from professional practitioners alone to include civil society organisations, activists and citizens as *planners*. And in this framework, planning is no longer 'only that professional domain that constitutes the field of city-building, but [it is] also that form of collective action [and shared power] which we might call community-building' (Sandercock, 1999: 39).

SITUATING PLANNERS WITHIN THIS TERRAIN

Power is, indeed, an elusive concept, as argued by Booher and Innes (2002). For this reason, Patsy Healey and Jacky Underwood (1978) equally concluded – as Banfield (1961) and later Flyvberg (1998) concluded – that planners have limited powers. And since at least the 1960s, planners have raised concerns about their role and mandates (Davidoff, 1965). Some have gone as far as to raise doubts about the value of planning in itself (Campbell, 2010), thereby suggesting that there is no longer any need for a planning profession (Evans, 1993; Wildavsky, 1973). Whereas others seem reluctant to engage in value discussions, and have chosen, instead, to describe their role as neutral (Campbell and Marshall, 2005). Some planners even argue that their role necessitates working at a distance from values they would otherwise identify with (Inch, 2009). These worrying testimonies highlight the urgent need to rethink the relationship between planning and power, since what futures do we hope to contribute to if these are shaped by values that planners do not believe in?

In response to this, some scholars are calling for a decolonialisation of power in planning practices (see, for example, Barry and Thompson-Fawcett, 2020; Porter, 2010; Porter et al., 2017; Winkler, 2018); whilst others have emphasised a growing need to situate planning within its wider discursive context (see, for example, Flyvbjerg, 1998; Grange, 2017; Huxley, 2018; Huxley and Yiftachel, 2000; Richardson, 2002). Some of the latter contributions have drawn on Foucault and as such they have contributed to a growing body of research on governmentality. These scholars describe and critically assess a shift in governing modes, from governing through strong welfare states, to new forms of neoliberal governing. And via these critical assessments, power has increasingly come to be seen as part of a regulating discourse which often operates through different mechanisms for self-governing. These mechanisms typically work at a distance, and have been described as techniques of subjectivity (Dean, 2010; Miller and Rose, 2008). According to Miller and Rose (2008: 71), these self-governing mechanisms have contributed to a new form of relationship between expertise and politics, namely a relationship defined by the unfortunate but 'constant registration of "failure"', as well as 'the constant injunction to do better next time'. A potential outcome of such a relationship is perhaps the gradual distancing from values as maintained by some planners and described above.

Foucault (1983) understood governing as the capacity to structure the possible actions of others, or what he often termed *the conduct of conduct*. Drawing on Foucault, Laclau and Mouffe (1985) argued that such discursive fields of possible actions ought to be understood as spaces of hegemony. Much like Foucault, they argue that all spaces are discursively constructed. In order to build on this argument, they outlined an ontology of the social in which they claimed that openness is society's constitutive ground. The fact that society is interpreted as fundamentally open, and never fixed, is what guarantees that there will always be conflicts and struggles over meanings (Laclau, 1996); otherwise, they claimed, there would be nothing to hegemonise. Indeed, for Laclau and Mouffe (1985), the stabilisation of a relationship between a signifier and a signified is what they term as hegemony. Consequently, interventions to fix meaning will always be political. What Foucault, Laclau and Mouffe can teach us is that there will always be attempts to construct society as if it is closed, when, in fact, it is always open and contingent. Discursive fields, like the field of planning, or even the relationship between expertise and politics, are therefore always open for productive articulations of new meanings. Professional values do contribute to shaping new futures, but they need to be expressed. Interpreting the role of the planner as neutral will not assist us in destabilising current hegemonies.

Another way of understanding power is through the concept of ideology. Within the field of planning, Michael Gunder was perhaps the one voice who most persistently argued for the need to critique taken-for-granted ideologies (see, for example, Gunder 2005a; 2010; 2011a; 2011b). Gunder primarily drew on Lacanian theory, in which fantasy and desire are essential. Gunder authored several articles in which he argued that a greater awareness of how power and desires are embedded in political ideologies, such as neoliberalism, might allow planners to reimagine signifiers that structure society.

In Lacanian theory the subject is understood as split. On the one hand, the subject consists of different, but conscious, ego-ideals. On the other hand, it consists of unconscious desires. An important aspect of Lacanian theory, and emphasised by Gunder (2005c: 174), is that our strongest beliefs often stem from that which 'resides outside of symbolic language'. Consequently, many of society's ideological manifestations are shaped by a desire for completeness (Gunder, 2005a; 2005b). In several articles, Gunder showed how planning ought to be understood as an institutionalised activity that is aimed at generating narratives, or even fantasies, about a desirable future. Gunder (2010; 2011a) persistently argued that current planning practices, via the implementation of plans and policies, help 'determine and establish the ideology of contemporary neoliberal space' (Gunder, 2011a: 327). He also convincingly demonstrated how planning has become a scapegoat for neoliberalism's many failures (Gunder, 2015). Drawing on Žižek, Gunder (2011a: 330) argued that the subject does not always believe in what it does and sometimes 'fakes ideological belief'. What Gunder helps us to see is that the productive aspects of power are not only structured by discourses and hegemonic articulations imposed on us, but also by, and to a large extent, our own desires, or even by our faked ideological beliefs. Hence, his critique of ideology compels us, as planners, to critically scrutinise the consequences of our actions, as opposed to simply faking belief in unattainable futures, or silently concluding that our role is a neutral role.

However, where there is power there is always resistance, as Foucault famously stated. According to Foucault (2007: 75), resistance, or a critical attitude, stems from 'the will not to be governed thusly, like that, by these people, at this price'. In this respect, Foucault (2007: 75) understood critique as 'the art of voluntary insubordination':

> I will say that critique is the movement by which the subject gives himself [*sic*] the right to question truth on its effects of power and question power on its discourses of truth. Well then!: critique will be the art of voluntary insubordination, that of reflected intractability. Critique would essentially insure the desubjugation of the subject in the context of what we could call, in a word, the politics of truth. (Foucault, 2007: 47)

It has been argued elsewhere that such a critical mode of being implies a commitment to 'expose oneself as a subject' (Lemke, 2012: 70). Such exposure not only implies giving an account of oneself before others, but also requires an agonistic relationship towards the self (Foucault, 1985: 67). Indeed, Foucault underlined that new forms of democratic subjectivity can only come about through desubjugating processes. During his later phase he emphasised the ethical and empowering aspects of the subject's relationship to itself, which he referred to as *the care of the self* (Foucault, 1985, 1986, 2001, 2005).

Via his interest in ethics, Foucault returned to the ancient Greek and Roman concept of *parrhesia*, which means fearless speech (Foucault, 2001, 2005, 2011). According to Foucault, a *parrhesiastes* is a person who speaks what they know to be true, regardless of the potentially dangerous consequences of parrhesia that always involves risks (Foucault, 2001: 13). Parrhesia is not exercised in self-interest, but, as Foucault (2011: 179) emphasised, in the interest of the city. What drew Foucault (2001: 169; see also Foucault 1985: 6–7) to investigate the concept of parrhesia was an urge to understand 'the problem of the truth-teller'. In an interview from 1984, Foucault (1996: 443) expressed that 'it seems to me that contemporary political thought allows very little room for the question of the ethical subject'. He warned that without critique, democracy will be reduced to consensus – to the voice of the majority – or even to passivity.

That democracy is under threat in current times is not an understatement. Planners have a role to uphold democratic perspectives. With this *Handbook on Planning and Power*, we argue that there is a need within the field of planning to nurture a critical ethos in order for planners to create democratic spaces where the political can play out in new and alternative ways, where the consequences of the ideological narratives we construct about the future can be identified and discussed, where there is room for fearless speech, and where greater awareness of how power plays out in the field of planning might lead to socio-economic and spatial justice.

THE STRUCTURE OF THE BOOK

There are countless other ways of *theorising* and *situating* power in planning, as evidenced by the succeeding chapters of this *Handbook*. Power is, after all, central to our understanding of how planning and its practices function and are constantly evolving. The twenty-six chapters of this book are structured as two parts: *theorising power in planning* and *situating power in planning*. The first part – which focuses on the manifold onto-epistemological lenses used to explain, analyse and critique power in planning – begins, in Chapter 1, with Enda Murphy and Linda Fox-Rogers' assessment of the ongoing relevance of a Marxist analysis of political and economic systems if we hope to understand the power dynamics that shape planning outcomes. Aspects of Murphy and Fox-Rogers' argument resonate with Lina Olsson and Elena Besussi reading of Henri Lefebvre's *right to the city*, his radical concept of urban citizenship, and his vision of a *renewed urban society*. These readings are presented in Chapter 2; and both Chapters 1 and 2 conclude with critical reflections on planning's potential role as a radical praxis. In Chapter 3, Raine Mäntysalo expands on this critical enquiry by demonstrating not only the values but also the limitations of Stephen Lukes' influential theory of power for planning research and practice. Thereafter, in Chapter 4, John Pløger tackles the monumental impact of Michel Foucault's scholarship on planning. This influence dates back to Foucault's publication, in 1966, of *Le mots et les choses* (Words and Things). Remaining within the genre of twentieth-century philosophy, Jean Hillier draws our attention, in Chapter 5, to both the subtle nature of power found in Gilles Deleuze and Félix Guattari's work, and their explicit engagements with 'power over' (*pouvoir*) and 'power to' (*puissance*) concepts. Here, Hillier demonstrates how *pouvoir* is associated with dominance, whereas *puissance* presents us with creative opportunities. This chapter sets up a useful segue into Chuan Wang's assessment, in Chapter 6, of Jacques Lacan's account of power found in language and desire. Lacanian perspectives in turn corroborate Ernesto Laclau and Chantal Mouffe's conception of hegemony, as Nikolai Roskamm demonstrates in Chapter 7, and, like Wang, Roskamm concludes this chapter by arguing for a more sobering awareness of power's everyday impact on planning. The final chapter that explicitly draws on continental philosophy as an approach towards *theorising power in planning* is Camillo Boano's exploration of Jacques Rancière's 'destituent power'. Thus, in Chapter 8, Boano posits *destituent power* as a means to radically break with the modern logic of sovereignty for the purpose of promoting a politics beyond power.

The next four chapters of Part I shift gears into the terrain of planning theory. In Chapter 9, Crystal Legacy outlines the potential power of communicative planning from a transformed standpoint, namely one grounded in citizen-led and reflexive practices. This standpoint corroborates aspects of Bjørn Sletto's insurgent planning project found in Chapter 10, despite the oft maintained incompatibility between collaborative/communicative and insurgent/radical planning. Legacy and Sletto add a fresh dimension to theorising power by arguing for renewed attentions to co-productions that foster counterhegemonic knowledges, imaginaries and actions. Calls to foster counterhegemonic knowledges, imaginaries and actions are equally engendered by Libby Porter's chapter on decoloniality. Porter begins Chapter 11 by arguing that conceptualisations of power are, in themselves, shaped by histories and structures of violence, colonialism and imperialism before positing pluri-versal understandings of knowledge and ethics. Katie McClymont's focus on how normative ethics either support or unsettle the less visible structures of power in planning serves as the final chapter of Part I (namely, Chapter 12). McClymont employs Lukes' power analysis to reframe grounds for judgement and decision making in planning processes and outcomes.

Part II – which focuses on *situating power in planning* – begins with Andy Inch's suggestion that any attempt to renew the idea of 'the public good' in planning necessitates reclaiming the overlooked role of 'promissory power'. Promissory power, as Inch demonstrates in Chapter 13, is often ceded to developers under neoliberal planning regimes. In Chapter 14, Hilary Malson expands on this situated power dynamics by defining and tracing an abolitionist tradition of housing justice. Malson's multi-dimensional analysis demonstrates how abolition emerges as a counterhegemonic praxis that enables marginalised residents to cultivate their own power by imagining alternatives beyond systems that perpetuate subjugation. Within a similar ontological framework, Mona Fawaz sets out to demonstrate, in Chapter 15, how the disjuncture between planning's imagined order and informality results in a top-down, exclusionary adoption of power by the state, which, in turn, fuels a counter power dynamic by excluded residents. Fawaz goes on to argue that while both analytical frameworks might be deemed relevant, expanded readings of power beyond state/citizen relations might, in fact, be more useful if planners hope to recognise and address power struggles among unequal actors, where the legislation tends to favour the formal and 'the included'. The final chapter in this cluster of housing concerns – namely, Chapter 16 – is Ernesto López-Morales's chapter on the rent gap that epitomises the intersectional relation between uneven development, planning and power.

The next three chapters that speak of *situating power in planning* are James Duminy and Vanessa Watson's Southern planning perspective; Petra Doan and Ozlem Atalay's application of queer theory to examine the relationship between planning, power and LGBTQ communities in Atlanta and Istanbul; and Leonora Angeles' feminist analyses of power in the planning field. In Chapter 17, Duminy and Watson identify three distinctive yet interrelated lines of critical inquiry associated with Southern planning research, and they conclude the chapter by reflecting on the limitations of the Southern perspective in confronting Northern epistemological hegemony. In Chapter 18, Doan and Atalay highlight the powerful attributes associated with queer-insurgency and queer-theory that serve to transform discourses of redevelopment and gentrification. And in Chapter 19, Angeles argues for an intersectional feminist thinking that might enable planners to imagine multiple centres of intersecting power relations of oppression and privilege affecting practice in the face of complex realities and identities.

The themes discussed in the final seven chapters of Part II are undisputedly shaped by the current moment in history. Thus, in Chapter 20, Marlyana Marzukhi presents the tension created for planning as a consequence of neoliberalism's hegemonic power and global impact. A more celebratory embrace of the contemporary era allows Elham Bahmanteymouri and Mohsen Mohammadzadeh to explore, in Chapter 21, the advancement of cybernetic technologies in relation to planning and power, while Yvonne Rydin's chapter (Chapter 22) demonstrates how planning regulations operate as powerful connections between socio-material assemblages. This chapter concludes with pertinent reflections pertaining to the reform of regulatory processes. In Chapter 23, Kristof Van Assche, Raoul Beunen and Martijn Duineveld reflect on the ways in which planning and power are intertwined by distinguishing between power *in* planning (namely, the power dynamics within the planning domain), power *on* planning (societal influences on the planning system), and the power *of* planning (the impact planning has in society). This argument serves as a viable launching pad for Ernest Alexander's post-postmodern approach to situating power in planning (see Chapter 24). Alexander's argument begins with the established critique of modernist planners as professionals who are empowered to plan rationally, comprehensively and in the interest of an homogenous public good. Postmodernists, by contrast, reject these metanarratives, whilst post-postmodernists are neither technocrats nor communicators, nor do they aspire to become social-change agents. Rather, they are experts in their fields, and, as such, they contribute to the social co-construction of knowledge, which, as posited by Alexander, is the essence of planning. The final two chapters of the book present more sobering accounts of the contemporary era. In

Chapter 25, Jaime Lopez and Lisa Schweitzer de-tangle the complex power relations between media and planning by arguing for new norms and practices, whilst simultaneously warning planners and built environment practitioners against the pitfalls that may further proliferate within an already noisy and authoritarian environment of mis- and disinformation. Failing to achieve a more refined appreciation of media's power threatens to prevent planning from delivering equitable outcomes. Similarly, Eric Sheppard concludes the part and the book with a poignant chapter on the current 'post-truth' moment that is not new but that is, nevertheless, accommodating ardent right-wing truth claims that bend the arc of knowledge production away from social and environmental justice (see Chapter 26). But instead of ending on a note of despair and utter dysfunctionality, Sheppard reminds us that planning is a political process with ends and means up for grabs. He therefore urges planners to face the future from a position of engaged pluralism.

HOW THIS BOOK CAME ABOUT

This book grew out of an invitation from Michael Gunder to both of us to collaborate on a *Handbook on Planning and Power*. All three of us were, at the time, editorial board members of *Planning Theory:* the same journal for which Michael served as the Managing Editor from 2011 to 2015. We therefore knew Michael as an experienced editor, an inspired theorist and above all else, an exceptionally caring and supportive person. With this in mind, neither of us needed much convincing to accept Michael's invitation to collaborate on a fascinating – but broad and complex – 'planning and power' project.

We started the joint work by deciding that a *Handbook* on power must, by necessity, include many different voices. We knew we wanted to attract authors from diverse parts of the world, and to celebrate both emerging and experienced scholars. For this reason, we reached out to colleagues with whom we had collaborated in the past, as well as colleagues with whom no prior connections had been established. The outcome, as evidenced in the succeeding chapters, is inspiring; and this can be said despite the fact that we were limited to working only with scholars who write and publish in the English language. While we were unable to secure authors for some of our original chapter themes, this forced us to rethink and craft new themes. Looking back, this rethinking and recrafting contributed to some of the most valuable aspects of our planning and power understanding.

A year and a half into the project – when we were starting to receive the first chapter drafts, and when the three of us were in contact with each other almost on a daily basis – we received the heart-breaking news of Michael's death. After the initial shock, we – in collaboration with all the contributing authors – decided to continue the project in honour of Michael's work and unwavering dedication to planning scholarship. If it wasn't for Michael, the two of us would not have met and we would not have been given the fantastic opportunity to discuss so many different aspects about power and planning with all the chapter authors of this book. For all the new insights these chapters have given us we are immensely thankful, and we can only hope readers of this *Handbook on Planning and Power* will feel the same. With gratitude we dedicate this book to Michael.

REFERENCES

Banfield, E.C. (1961), *Political Influence: A New Theory of Urban Practice*, New York: Free Press.

Barry, J. and M. Thompson-Fawcett (2020), 'Decolonizing the Boundaries between the "Planner" and the "Planned": Implications of Indigenous Property Development', *Planning Theory and Practice*, 21 (3): 410–425.

Beard, V. (2003), 'Learning Radical Planning: The Power of Collective Action', *Planning Theory*, 2 (1): 13–35.

Bhan, G., S. Srinvas and V. Watson (2018), *Companion to Planning in the Global South*, London, New York: Routledge.

Booher, D. and J. Innes (2002), 'Network Power in Collaborative Planning', *Journal of Planning Education and Research*, 21, 221–236.

Campbell, H. (2010), 'The Idea of Planning: Alive or Dead – Who Cares?' *Planning Theory & Practice*, 11 (4): 471–475.

Campbell, H. and R. Marshall (2005), 'Professionalism and Planning in Britain', *Town Planning Review*, 76 (2): 191–214.

Castells, M. (1983), *The City and the Grassroots*, Berkeley: University of California Press.

Davidoff, P. (1965). 'Advocacy and Pluralism in Planning'. *Journal of the American Institute of Planners*, 31 (November): 227–297.

Dean, M. (2010), *Governmentality: Power and Rule in Modern Society*, 2nd edition. London: SAGE.

Evans, B. (1993), 'Why we no Longer Need a Town Planning Profession', *Planning Practice and Research*, 8 (1): 9–16.

Flyvberg, B. (1998), *Rationality and Power: Democracy in Practice*, Chicago, IL: University of Chicago Press.

Forester, J. (1989), *Planning in the Face of Power*, Berkeley: University of California Press.

Foucault, M. (1983), 'The Subject and Power', in H.L. Dreyfus and P. Rabinow (eds) *Michael Foucault: Beyond Structuralism and Hermeneutics*, 2nd edition, Chicago, IL: University of Chicago Press, 208–226.

Foucault, M. (1985), *The Use of Pleasure: The History of Sexuality*, vol. 2. London: Penguin Books.

Foucault, M. (1986), *The Care of the Self: The History of Sexuality*, vol. 3. London: Penguin Books.

Foucault, M. (1996), 'The Ethics of the Concern for Self as a Practice of Freedom', in S. Lotringer (ed.), *Foucault Live: Michel Foucault. Collected Interviews, 1961–1984*. New York: Semiotext(e), 432–449.

Foucault, M. (2001), *Fearless Speech*. Los Angeles, CA: Semiotext(e).

Foucault, M. (2005), *The Hermeneutics of the Subject. Lectures at the Collège de France 1981–82*. New York and Basingstoke: Palgrave Macmillan.

Foucault, M. (2007), *The Politics of Truth*. Los Angeles, CA: Semiotext(e).

Foucault, M. (2011), *The Government of Self and Others. Lectures at the Collège de France 1982–83*. New York; Basingstoke: Palgrave Macmillan.

Friedmann, J. (1987), *Planning in the Public Domain: From Knowledge to Action*, Princeton: Princeton University Press.

Friedmann, J. (2011), *Insurgencies: Essays in Planning Theory*, London, New York: Routledge.

Giddens, A. (1984), *The Construction of Society: Outline of the Theory of Structuration*, Cambridge: Polity.

Grange, K. (2017), 'Planners – A Silenced Profession? The Politicisation of Planning and the Need for Fearless Speech', *Planning Theory*, 16 (3): 275–295.

Gunder, M. (2005a), 'Lacan, Planning and Urban Policy Formation', *Urban Policy and Research*, 23: 87–107.

Gunder, M. (2005b), 'Obscuring Difference through Shaping Debate: A Lacanian View of Planning for Diversity', *International Planning Studies*, 10: 83–103.

Gunder, M. (2005c), 'The Production of Desirous Space: Mere Fantasies of the Utopian City?' *Planning Theory*, 4: 173–199.

Gunder, M. (2010), 'Planning as the Ideology of (Neoliberal) Space', *Planning Theory*, 9: 298–314.

Gunder, M. (2011a), 'A Metapsychological Exploration of the Role of Popular Media in Engineering Public Belief on Planning Issues', *Planning Theory*, 10: 325–343.

Gunder, M. (2011b), 'Fake it Until You Make it, and Then ...', *Planning Theory*, 10: 201–212.

Gunder, M. (2015), 'Planning's "failure" to Ensure Efficient Market Delivery: A Lacanian Deconstruction of this Neoliberal Scapegoating Fantasy', *European Planning Studies*, 24 (1): 21–38.

Healey, P. and Underwood, J. (1978), 'Professional Ideals and Planning Practice: A Report on Research into Planners' Ideas in Practice in London Borough Planning Departments', *Progress in Planning*, 9 (2): 73–127.

Holston, J. (2008), *Insurgent Citizenship: Disjunctions of Democracy and Modernity in Brazil*, Princeton, NJ: Princeton University Press.

Huxley, M. (2018), 'Countering "the Dark Side" of Planning: Power, Governmentality, Counter-Conduct', in M. Gunder, A. Madanipour and V. Watson (eds), *Routledge Handbook of Planning Theory*, Chapter 17, 207–220, London and New York: Routledge.

Huxley, M. and Yiftachel, O. (2000), 'New Paradigm or Old Myopia? Unsettling the Communicative Turn in Planning Theory', *Journal of Planning Education and Research*, 19 (4): 333–342.

Inch, A. (2009), 'The New Planning, and the New Planner: Modernisation, Culture Change and the Regulation of Professional Identities in English Local Planning', unpublished doctoral thesis, Oxford Brookes University, UK.

Kamete, A. (2012), 'Interrogating Planning's Power in an African City: Time for Reorientation?' *Planning Theory*, 11 (1): 66–88.

Laclau, E. (1996), 'The Death and Resurrection of the Theory of Ideology', *Journal of Political Ideologies*, 1: 201–220.

Laclau, E. and Mouffe, C. (1985), *Hegemony and Socialist Strategy: Towards a Radical Democratic Politics*, London: Verso.

Lemke, T. (2012), *Foucault, Governmentality, and Critique*, London: Paradigm Publishers.

Miller, P. and Rose, N. (2008), *Governing the Present: Administering Economic, Social and Personal Life*, Cambridge: Polity Press.

Miraftab, F. and S. Wills (2005), 'Insurgency and Spaces of Active Citizenship: The Story of Western Cape Anti-eviction Campaign in South Africa', *Journal of Planning Education & Research*, 25: 200–217.

Njoh, A. (2009), 'Urban Planning as a Tool of Power and Social Control in Colonial Africa', *Planning Perspectives*, 24 (3): 301–317.

Porter, L. (2010), *Unlearning the Colonial Cultures of Planning*, London: Routledge.

Porter, L., H. Matunga, L. Viswanathan, L. Patrick, R. Walker, L. Sandercock, D. Moraes, J. Frantz, M. Thompson-Fawcett, C. Riddle, T. Jojola (2017), 'Indigenous Planning: From Principles to Practice', *Planning Theory and Practice*, 18 (4): 639–666.

Richardson, T. (2002), 'Freedom and Control in Planning: Using Discourse in the Pursuit of Reflexive Practice', *Planning Theory & Practice*, 3 (3): 353–361.

Roy, A. (2021). 'Planning on Stolen Land', in L. Porter, A. Roy and C. Legacy, C. (eds), 'Planning Solidarity? From Silence to Refusal', *Planning Theory & Practice*, 22 (1): 111–138.

Sandercock, L. (1998), *Towards Cosmopolis*, Chichester: John Wiley & Sons.

Sandercock, L. (1999), 'Translations: From Insurgent Planning Practices to Radical Planning Discourses', *Plurimondi*, 1 (2): 37–46.

Swyngedouw, E. (2018), *Promises of the Political: Insurgent Cities in a Post-political Environment*, Boston: MIT Press.

Weber, M. (1978), *Economy and Society. An Outline of Interpretative Sociology*, translated by G. Roth and C. Wittich, Berkeley: University of California Press.

Wildavsky, A. (1973), 'If Planning is Everything, Maybe it's Nothing', *Policy Sciences*, 4 (2): 127–153.

Winkler, T. (2018), 'Black Texts on White Paper: Learning to See Resistant Texts as an Approach Towards Decolonising Planning', *Planning Theory*, 17 (4): 588–604.

Wolfsfeld, G., E. Segev and T. Sheafer (2013), 'Social Media and the Arab Spring: Politics Comes First', *International Journal of Press/Politics*, 18 (2): 115–137.

VeneKlasen, L., V. Miller, D. Budlender and E. Clark (eds) (2007), *A New Weave of Power, People and Politics: The Action Guide for Advocacy and Citizen Participation*, Warwickshire: Practical Action Publishing.

PART I

THEORISING POWER IN PLANNING

1.　Marxian understandings of power

Enda Murphy and Linda Fox-Rogers

INTRODUCTION

This chapter considers historical and contemporary understandings of the Marxian interpretation of power. This is an understanding which highlights the structural relations that govern how power is distributed in society. For Marx, power is a resource largely concentrated within the ruling class and the state; it has its origins primarily in the economic sphere and this, in turn, wields influence in the political sphere. Thus, Marxist scholarship is particularly interested in analysing the political economy changes within the economic sphere of society as well as within the state (as the enabling arm of power) and its associated institutions. It is from this critical vantage point that Marxist political economy analysis can demonstrate its powerful analytical and explanatory power in and for understanding changes in the planning process and wider planning practice.

Under the capitalist mode of production power is wielded over the working-class population via the capital accumulation process and the materialisation of ideas that shape social reality – everyday life – to preserve dominant class interests. Central to the accumulation process is the illusion of fair exchange of wages for workers' 'labour power' in the production process. However, from a Marxian perspective, the surplus value that workers generate via this process is exploited by the ruling class (who control the means and instruments of production) enabling a circular process of capitalist accumulation. The role of the state in preserving these exploitative class relations is central to Marxian conceptions of power. This is because Marxist scholars trace the material origins of class relations to the emergence of the state whose function was (and continues to be) centred on serving dominant class interests.

This chapter examines how Marxian conceptions of power and the state have been drawn upon in more or less explicit ways by a range of critical planning theorists. In doing so, emphasis is placed on Marxist interpretations of planning as an activity of the capitalist state that necessarily serves powerful interests while the inherent power disparities that are reproduced and exacerbated by the planning system itself is also outlined. Finally, the chapter reflects more broadly on why this theoretical perspective appears to have lost momentum in recent decades and explores its relevance to more contemporary debates in planning.

POWER RELATIONS UNDER THE CAPITALIST MODE OF PRODUCTION

Although Marxism does not explicitly theorise about power *per se*, Marxist theory is predominantly concerned with issues of power in society. Indeed, Hearn (2012: 49) points out that while Marx offers one of the most 'strenuous critiques' of exploitative power relations that exist in capitalist society, he never systematically defines what he means by power. Nevertheless, power remains the central tenet for Marx's core ideas on social labour, the mode of production, class conflict and alienation (Hearn, 2012), all of which will be explored throughout this chapter.

Drawing on classic enlightenment ideas, Marx considered the essence of human nature to be rooted in a person's desire to be a 'free and conscious producer' (Marx, 1844 in Tucker, 1978: xxv). Building on this basic principle, Marxist theory draws attention to the fact that under capitalism, people are *driven* to produce by engaging in paid labour (which they have no control over) for their own subsistence. More specifically, the capitalist mode of production is underpinned by exploitative class relations between capitalists (the bourgeoisie) and wage workers (the proletariat) on the basis of the former's ownership and control over the means of production. This enables capitalists to generate profits by extracting surplus value (the value generated by labour in the productive process over and above their wages) from workers, who are forced to sell their labour power into the labour market for survival (Murphy and Mercille, 2019). Through this capital accumulation process, the capitalist class can preserve and reinvent itself as well as reinforce 'its domination over labour' (Harvey, 1989: 59).

Because the social relations of production that exist under capitalism prevent wage workers from engaging in spontaneous action and free enquiry, Marx considers their labour to be involuntary and thereby 'estranged' or 'alienated' from human nature (Tucker, 1978: xxv). In this regard, Marxism can be aligned to classical liberal assumptions about the innate 'human need for liberty, diversity and free association' unbound by external force or coercion (Chomsky, 2005: 123). While several analysts associate Marx's humanist concerns about the alienation of man under the capitalist economic system with his earlier works (such as his Economic and Philosophic Manuscripts of 1844), Tucker (1978) rightly points out that there is evidence of these elements throughout Marx's work as a whole. For instance, concerns about man's alienation from his labour are inherent within the concept of the 'division of labour' which describes how technological advances adopted by capitalists (in order to increase the relative surplus value generated), leads to increasingly routinised operations for workers. Marx's later works can thus be considered as remaining power focused by elucidating (albeit implicitly) the power relations that emerge between a dominant capitalist class and a subordinate class of labourers under the capitalist mode of production. Marx's contribution in this regard is important as the exploitative relationship between capitalists and workers is not always obvious as 'workers are not tied to any particular capital owner but must be employed' (Tucker, 1978: 207). Power relations under capitalism are therefore less visible when compared to other historical forms of domination (for example landlord and serf) (Dunleavy and O'Leary, 1987) but exist, nevertheless.

There are several contradictions within the capitalist system which threaten its survival. These revolve around two central issues, namely the class struggle between the capitalist class and wage workers, and the inherent crisis tendencies within the capital accumulation process itself. With regard to the former, Marxism posits that relations of exploitation create class struggles, which under capitalism are rooted in the capitalist's generation of profit from the exploitation of labour (Scott and Roweis, 1977). In the continuous drive for accumulation, capitalists are 'forced into inflicting greater and greater violence upon those whom they employ', yet labourers are relatively 'powerless to resist this onslaught' as they are forced to compete with each other in the labour market for employment (Harvey, 1978: 103).

The second threat confronting the capital accumulation process is rooted within capitalism's own inherent crisis tendencies. This is because the continuous drive for expansion and accumulation requires capitalists to maximise profits primarily by reducing the wages of the working class in order to extract more surplus value from workers. However, in doing so, the purchasing power of the masses is diminished, which in turn reduces the market to which capitalists supply creating a problem of effective demand (Fraser et al., 2013). The shrinking of the market (a key precondition to capital accumulation), inevitably results in over-production and crisis of accumulation occurs. As put by Harvey (2001: 239), 'as capitalism creates the conditions necessary for its own existence, it too creates the barriers and as such, crises are considered endemic to the capital accumulation process'. For Marx, these challenges mean that capitalist society is unable to ensure the conditions for it owns existence without some form of intervention. It is here where Marxists look towards the role of the state as playing a fundamental role in preserving the power imbalances that underpin capitalist society. This is where our attention now turns.

THE ROLE OF THE STATE

Contrary to conventional views of the state as a neutral institution that guards the 'public interest', Marxist political economy perceptions view the state's role as being necessarily supportive of capitalist class interests based on its historical origins and the social conditions 'that gave it birth' (Paul, 1917: 1). The more conventional view is typically associated with classical democratic theory which assumes that the state arose out of individuals wishing to establish a sovereign power that would safeguard their common interests. Marxist materialist interpretations of the state, on the other hand, focus on the class relations that emerged with the rise of private property, contending that the state emerged as a direct result of such class divisions (see Paul, 1917; Held, 1989). To illustrate this point, Marxists look backwards to the earliest forms of social organisation such as the clan/tribal system where lands were held in communal ownership in a system of economic equality, rather than the current system of private ownership (see Paul, 1917). However, as annual land divisions were extended from three- to five-year periods in order to facilitate the adoption of more modern agricultural practices, 'users began to look upon the land as their own property', and inequalities gradually arose as some families were allocated slightly larger or more fertile plots than others (Paul, 1917: 23). Stressing a similar point, Held (1989: 35) outlines that class divisions only arise when surpluses are generated 'such that it becomes possible for a class of non-producers to live off the productive activity of others'. The emergence of such inequalities naturally generated conflicting class interests as those with greater resources sought to safeguard their material welfare, while those with fewer resources sought a more just redistribution. In the absence of any means for settling class disputes under tribal systems 'a new method had to be devised' (Paul, 1917: 41). The wealthy class thus created a new social institution of government – the political state – in order to maintain order and crush revolts or any challenges which may be raised against it. It is on this basis that Marxist materialist interpretations of the state maintain that the state arose organically out of competing individual and community interests in order to 'preserve the privileges of property and to suppress the clamorous demands of the propertyless' (Paul, 1917: 41).

From this vantage point, the state cannot be considered a neutral arbitrator standing above class struggles; rather, it is 'deeply engaged in them' (Carnoy, 1984: 47) and is considered the 'weapon of class rule' (Paul, 1917: 41) and the repressive apparatus of the bourgeoisie (Carnoy, 1984). This view is summarised in an infamous statement within The Communist

Manifesto: 'the executive of the modern state is but a committee for managing the common affairs of the whole bourgeoisie' (Marx and Engels, 2010: 11). However, as rightly pointed out by Carnoy (1984: 48) 'it should not be inferred from this that the state is a class plot'. Rather, it evolves in order to 'mediate contradictions between individuals and community, and since community is dominated by the bourgeoisie, so is the mediation by the state' (Carnoy, 1984: 48). It is on this basis that Marxist political economy perspectives of the state consider the economic and political spheres to be inextricably linked as 'those who are able to gain control of the means of production form a dominant or ruling class both economically and politically' (Held, 1989: 32). Power, from a Marxist perspective, is thus structurally determined. In contrast to other theorists who consider power to be multi-dimensional and widely distributed throughout society, Marxists emphasise the importance of class (i.e. one's relationship to the means of production) as a key determinant of relative economic and political power.

Although the state has taken various forms throughout history, Marxists argue that its inherent function remains the same from its origins through ancient state systems, feudal society and right up to industrial capitalism. As put by Engels (1968: 155–157 in Carnoy, 1984: 49) 'the ancient state was, above all, the state of slave owners for holding down the slaves, just as the feudal state was the organ of the nobility for holding down the peasant serfs and bondsmen, and the modern representative state is the instrument for exploiting wage labour by capital'. From this perspective, the state ultimately exists to 'perpetuate the mode of exploitation which is in the best interests of the economically dominant class during any period' (Paul, 1917: 55).

As capitalist society is unable to ensure the successful conditions for its own survival, the state must out of necessity perform 'certain basic minimum tasks in support of a capitalist mode of production' (Harvey, 2001: 269). Indeed, Scott and Roweis (1977: 1102) warn that 'without the presence of an agency capable of maintaining social balance, capitalist society would rapidly disintegrate'. The state must therefore guarantee and legitimise existing capitalist social and property relations in order to mediate class conflict and facilitate the continued social and economic domination by capital (MacLaran and McGuirk, 2003). As put by Edel (1981: 28), 'the state must provide a framework for exchange, a guarantee of capitalist's property rights and some degree of control to keep workers in their subordinate class positions'.

However, Harvey (2001: 277) warns that 'bourgeois democracy can survive only with the consent of the majority of the governed while it must at the same time express a distinctive ruling interest'. He identifies two strategies whereby allegiance of the working class can be achieved. The first is to represent dominant interests as the illusory general interest 'by universalising ruling class ideas as the only universally valid ones'. As put by Milliband (1977: 66), the idea that the state can serve the common good 'is part of the ideological veil which a dominant class draws upon the reality of class rule, so as to legitimate that rule in its own eyes as well as in the eyes of subordinate classes'. The second way in which the capitalist state gains popular consent is by providing the appearance of neutrality in its operations through the provision of certain social goods such as social housing, education, transport or welfare payments. The fact that such goods are prerequisites to facilitate the continued survival of the capitalist mode of production, but lie beyond the logic of individual capitalists to provide, is not made explicit (Sandercock, 1998; Harvey 2001; MacLaran and McGuirk, 2003). In return for such concessions, the state receives 'an allegiance of the subordinate class' and an ideology of the 'common good' is established which disguises the inherent interests of the capitalist state as a facilitator of the capitalist system (Harvey, 2001: 277). For Marxists, these strategies negate class conflict and prevent challenges being brought to bear on the power structure governing capitalist society.

It is important at this juncture to highlight that the mainstream Marxist position as set out above has been subject to a series of variations and revisions throughout the twentieth century, many of which have attempted to address the pitfalls of classical Marxism. In this regard, many have questioned why the working class remains 'unrevolutionary' in the face of economic crises, and why communist states developed in the way they did (Carnoy, 1984: 45). Such critiques are commonly levelled at Marx's theory of the state but should instead be considered more of a critique of socialism as it developed in the Soviet Union (Chomsky, 2005). Indeed, it seems that the experiences of Bolshevism or what some believe to be Marxism in practice (Chomsky, 2005), have led to the adoption of more conservative positions which advocate a transition to socialism via political reform and reorganisation while others advocate more radical forms of libertarian Marxism. The debate essentially stems from the ambiguities that exist within Marxism on the issue of state autonomy, an issue which underpins many of the conflicting opinions about the role of the state in the transition from capitalism to socialism.

MARXIST POLITICAL ECONOMY PERSPECTIVES OF PLANNING

Marx wrote very little specifically about the planning system or the wider state-planning nexus. Indeed, despite the very important implications of his scholarship for urban processes, he also had little comment to make on urbanisation. But, as highlighted by Holgersen (2020), he did write on many issues of crucial relevance to understanding urban planning and related processes such as capital accumulation, exploitation, different forms of rents, (labour) alienation, relations with nature and social reproduction. In addition, Marx's key collaborator – Frederick Engels – did write specifically about urban issues in publications such as the *The Housing Question* (1942) and *The Condition of the Working-Class in England in 1844* (2013). Teasing out the implications of Marx's work for contemporary planning was undertaken by a rage of scholars who applied Marx's theories to urban and regional planning questions. Most of this work emerged in the 1970s and 1980s via key scholars such as Henri Lefebvre, David Harvey and Manuel Castells, among others.

Perhaps the most important implication of Marx's work for planning lies in its critique of the nature and origins of the state and the implication of the state-planning relationship for planning practice and the urbanisation process more widely. Just as the state intervenes to facilitate the continuation of the capital accumulation process at the general level, planning (as an arm of the state) is considered a form of state intervention which necessarily functions to serve dominant class interests. In this regard, power lies at the heart of Marxist political economy perceptions of planning, although this is often rather implicit within the broad body of Marxist-inspired planning literature. From a Marxist perspective, planning is an institution of the capitalist state which is compelled to intervene to manage the contradictions of capitalism that become manifested spatially (Fainstein and Fainstein, 1982) (e.g. land-use conflicts, underinvestment in collective goods and services, etc.). In doing so, the planning system takes on the dual facilitatory and ideological role of the state, whereby it functions to facilitate the accumulation of capital, whilst also legitimising the capitalist economic system (McDougall, 1982; Yiftachel, 1989).

With regard to the former, Marxist perceptions of planning contend that planning must intervene in the production of the built environment to ensure that it remains useful for capitalist production, circulation, exchange and consumption (Harvey, 1985). The central ways in which it facilitates the capital accumulation process is through the 'development of physical infrastructure, land aggregation and development, containment of negative environmental externalities, and the maintenance of land values' (Fainstein and Fainstein, 1982: 148). Marxist scholars point towards the post-war public housing programmes, the construction of underground railway systems in major cities, and land-use zoning matrices as examples of the state providing social goods that capital requires, yet fails to deliver privately (see Scott and Roweis, 1977; Kirk, 1980; Fainstein and Fainstein,1982). In this sense, the state (and by implication the planning system) is viewed as a 'direct active agent in creating urban form and socialising many of the expenses of production' (Fainstein and Fainstein, 1982: 161). In terms of ameliorating the negative externalities accruing from the emergence of conflicting land uses (including declining land values, nuisance, congestion, etc.), planning, through the implementation of development plans and zoning objectives and policies, facilitates the interests of private capital as it not only protects (and indeed enhances) land values, but also reduces the emergence of conflicts from adversely affected members of society which may subsequently threaten the status quo.

This latter point leads us to the second aspect of planning's 'dual role', which is the argument that the ideology of planning supports capital by depoliticising the state's intervention in the urbanisation process. Gramscian interpretations of planning argue that planning ideology legitimises planning as a form of state intervention that essentially works to safeguard the continuation of the capitalist economic order, thereby preserving the existing power base in society. As explained by Mäntysalo and Saglie (2010: 327) 'power in public planning relies on legitimacy'. For Chomsky (2002: 11), the standard way that power protects itself is by instituting ideological filters and terms of political discourse which mask and obscure the true manner in which power operates (by, for example, the use of terms such as the 'common good', 'national interest', democratic decision making, etc.). Chomsky (2003: 147) also outlines that what constitutes the common good 'will be articulated by those who control the central economic and political institutions'. Such ideas are inherent within Marxist political economy perceptions of planning whereby planning is considered to be one such filter that disguises and legitimises the role of the state 'by providing a semblance of intervention and public interest while in reality making little, if any, difference' (Allmendinger, 2002: 81). This is achieved through the rhetoric of technical, rational, and professional planning that purportedly operates in a neutral capacity to serve the 'common good' and 'public interest', as well as the casting of planners in purely technical terms (as opposed to political agents) thereby legitimising the planning activities of the state. In doing so, planners themselves play a key part in fulfilling the ideological role of planning, and further universalise the legitimising ideology by 'bolstering justification in the name of the public interest with arguments ostensibly based on scientific rationality' (Fainstein and Fainstein, 1982: 149; see also Murphy and Fox-Rogers, 2015). In a similar vein, scholars have highlighted that the rhetoric of participatory planning approaches legitimise the status quo and diffuse attention towards the process of planning rather than the outcomes being arrived at and in doing so, 'capital gets what it needs' (Purcell, 2009: 147).

Furthermore, scholars such as Scott and Roweis (1977) and Harvey (1985) highlight that planning theories and ideologies arise and evolve in response to the changing needs of capital. More specifically it seems that periodic crises can be ameliorated through shifting the imperatives (goals, emphases and theories, etc.) of planning in a manner that serves the needs of private capital (Allmendinger, 2002: 78). In this regard, the planner's world view can alter with changing circumstances in such a way that it continues to support the existing capitalist power structure. For instance, Harvey (1985) explains that policies of dispersal in the 1960s developed in response to the urban riots of that period, whilst the rhetoric of 'community improvement' was adopted by planners to control civil strife in urban areas, a phenomenon now referred to as 'guilding the ghetto'. Others have pointed towards the adoption of Enterprise Zones in the UK and Strategic Development Zones in Ireland (Fox-Rogers et. al., 2011) as means of creating the conditions for private capital accumulation in response to market conditions through the rhetoric of 'efficiency' and 'streamlined approaches' to planning. Whatever the rhetoric used, the planner as an agent of the state must contribute to the requirements for the reproduction of the capitalist social order. As argued by Harvey (1985: 184), the 'commitment to the ideology of harmony within the capitalist social order remains the still point upon which gyrations of planning ideology turn'.

The ideological role fulfilled by planning has meant that the regressive outcomes brought about through the urbanisation process are typically not viewed as manifestations of the capitalist social order, but instead are interpreted as bad planning decisions. In doing so, planning has been charged with depoliticising the capitalist mode of production, while politicising planning and the failures of the state (Allmendinger, 2002). This explains why planning and particularly planners are so often blamed for the inequities brought about by capitalism at the urban level, thereby 'distracting attention from the "problem" itself' (Allmendinger, 2002: 81–82). While giving the impression that 'the impacts and injustices of the market are being treated … planning is actually helping to perpetuate those symptoms' (Allmendinger, 2002: 79). In this sense planning can be viewed as a smokescreen for powerful interests, rather than a neutral institution working to serve the public interest.

Planning theorists of a Marxian persuasion thus highlight that the role of planning is to support capital by facilitating accumulation and legitimising planning interventions as rational and non-political. The overarching result is that the planning outcomes arrived at reflect dominant class interests and not only lead to the 'perpetuation of inequality, but in many cases to the enhancement of inequality' (McDougall, 1982: 259). Marxist political economy approaches to planning have been widely regarded as a vital development in revealing the structural drivers shaping planning practice. These approaches have demystified the idea that planning can operate as a politically neutral institution which serves some notion of the 'common good', instead emphasising the capitalist nature of the state and the planning system (see Scott and Roweis, 1977; Kirk, 1980). As Harvey (1985: 184) has noted, drawing on this theoretical framework helps us understand why 'the high-sounding ideals of planning theory are so frequently translated to grubby practices on the ground'.

THE RELEVANCE OF MARXIST THEORY TO CONTEMPORARY PLANNING DEBATES

Despite its strengths as a theoretical perspective, Marxism has fallen out of favour with planning theorists over the past three decades relative to its height in the 1970s and 1980s. This is somewhat curious given its recent rise to prominence in other disciplinary settings across the social sciences and humanities, particularly in the aftermath of the 2008 economic crisis when

Marxist political economy critiques became a powerful lens for understanding global political economic upheaval (Holgersen, 2020). In this sense, recent planning research and related theory deserves some focused attention and critique, particularly with regard to the relative absence of more radical critical discourse and related suggestions for planning practice. While the reasons for this change are undoubtedly complex, it seems clear that planning research and theory has been heavily influenced by alterations in global political economy over the last three decades. These changes have coincided with the rise of neoliberalism and related experimental projects and frameworks which have had wide-ranging impacts on social, economic and political life (Mercille and Murphy, 2019). Planning, in particular, has been moulded and shaped considerably by neoliberalism and neoliberalisation to the point that the fundamental principles underpinning planning theory are barely recognised in planning practice (Murphy and Fox-Rogers, 2015). Indeed, many of the most important critiques of neoliberalism, its rise and prevalence are underpinned by Marxist scholarship (see Jessop, 2002; Harvey, 2007) and this body of literature has been important for understanding transformations in state-planning relationships, urban governance and planning practice.

Within the context of these wider political economy shifts, one might have expected more significant engagement and discourse on these issues within planning theory. However, as Holgersen (2020: 808) has noted 'rather than engaging in the political economy, the opposite happened' with planning theory turning inwards '… focusing more on process and the procedural, and advocating for communicative theory'. The communicative turn in planning theory has had a significant impact on the evolution of consensus-based participatory collaborative planning approaches to planning theory and practice. Despite being the dominant theoretical position within the discipline, it has failed to advocate appropriately for altering the power imbalances inherent in the urban planning process; rather, (economic) power has found ways to by-pass process-driven participatory planning measures. Indeed, Holgersen (2020: 809) has pointed out that 'the communicative turn has removed planning theory even further from the messy world of political economy'. The result has meant that redistribution in the planning process has been only marginal and the pursuit of better outcomes for local communities has been circumvented to the detriment of less powerful interests (see Fox-Rogers and Murphy, 2015).

Another part of the explanation surely relates to perceived shortcoming of classical Marxist approaches and related critiques that have been levelled at its nihilistic tendencies. In this regard, Sorenson (1982: 184) outlines that whilst Marxist perspectives provide valuable insights into the underlying processes which create urban problems, they fail to specify alternatives and provide 'no signpost to the future'. Fainstein and Fainstein (1982: 168) echo similar concerns arguing that because Marxist approaches lead 'intellectually alive radical planners to conclude that system change lies in the mode of production', the theory leaves 'little room for progressive action by planners'. Despite this charge, Marxist perspectives on power and planning have continued relevance to contemporary debates in planning and critical urban theory such as those surrounding the 'right to the city' (see McCann, 2002; Harvey, 2003; Marcuse, 2009; see also Chapter 2 by Olsson and Besussi), the financialisation of the economy and housing (Aalbers, 2016; Bryan et al., 2009; Fine, 2013; Lapavitsas, 2013; Van der Zwan, 2014), the neoliberalisation of the state and planning (Fox-Rogers and Murphy, 2014), and accumulation by dispossession amongst others.

To elaborate, Marxist perspectives of the state and planning can be applied within the broad body of literature surrounding the 'right to the city' in ways which largely address the perceived nihilistic tendencies traditionally associated with Marxist scholarship. The 'right to the city' is a phrase first popularised by Henri Lefebvre in the late 1960s but has since been widely used to expresses much wider 'concerns with the alienation of modern urban life and the ability to live life fully' (McCann, 2002: 77). Here we see an immediate connection with the ideas associated with the 'right to the city' and Marx's own preoccupation with the alienation of man under the capitalist economic system. The right to the city is about active urban citizenship and the right to be included in decision making, as well as the transition to an ideal city where there is broad participation, enfranchisement, unalienated labour and a 'triumph of use value over exchange value' (McCann, 2002: 78). As Harvey (2003: 939) notes, more than thirty years of neoliberalism has taught us that freer markets result in greater inequalities and so the right to the city 'is not merely a right of access to what already exists, but a right to change it after our heart's desire'. Indeed, there are some who already claim their right to the city including powerful financiers, real estate owners, politicians, and the owners of large business enterprises (namely capitalists). However, there are many more who do not include those who are directly oppressed or alienated under existing conditions. It is within this context then that the right to the city must be understood as 'both a cry and a demand, a cry out of necessity and a demand for something more' (Marcuse, 2009: 190).

Moving beyond traditional Marxist views which identify the proletariat as the key driver of change, Marcuse (2009: 192) argues that the push for the right to the city will be led by the deprived and the discontented involving 'a convergence of all groups, coalitions, alliances, movements, assemblies around a common set of objectives, which see capitalism as the common enemy and the right to the city as their common cause'. In this regard, Marxist perspectives of power, the state and planning can lend support to contemporary critical urban theory in terms of exposing and revealing the root causes of inequality, injustice, alienation and deprivation which is central to developing useful responses to address those issues. Marcuse (2009) argues that what is required is a fundamental rejection of the prevailing capitalist system which relies on power disparities, deprivation and alienation in order to survive. Others advocate less radical and deterministic approaches. For instance, McCann (2002: 78) offers an alternative strategy that involves capitalising on the contemporary rise of participatory decision-making processes which can offer opportunities for making claims for new rights to the city which 'may occasionally provide opportunities for the articulation and realization of new visions of urban life'. There are avenues, therefore, for the identification of advocacy and change in planning.

In a similar vein, Marxian understandings of the state and power can also be contemporaneously applied to the proliferation of literature on the financialisation of the economy which centres on analysing the growing influence of financial services and markets within the overall economy and across virtually all sectors (Bryan et al., 2009; Fine, 2013; Lapavitsas, 2013; Van der Zwan, 2014). In essence, this body of scholarship highlights how capitalist economies have become increasingly financialised over the past thirty years (Lapavitsas, 2013). Specifically, scholars make the distinction between classical nineteenth-century capitalism (to which Marxist theory specifically relates) and contemporary financialised capitalism, the latter being much more complex due to a diverse range of factors including the growth of transnational enterprises, the deregulation of labour and financial markets, but most notably the general rise of finance that has taken place since the late 1970s. During this time the dramatic development of the financial sector has brought with it a rapid expansion of financial profits, whilst growth in the productive sector has remained relatively modest resulting in rising unemployment and wealth inequality, as well as broader asymmetries between 'the sphere of production and the ballooning sphere of circulation' (Lapavitsas, 2013: 793). From a Marxian perspective, the shift from production to the sphere of finance circulation emerged in direct response to the crisis tendencies that Marx identified as being inherent within the capitalist system. In this regard, Marxist political economy has cast 'considerable light on financialization' (Lapavitsas, 2013: 798) by explaining how the growth of finance has emerged to facilitate the absorption of surplus value from the productive sphere in new and alternative ways that continue to generate profit, namely through the realm of finance (Baran and Sweezy, 1966; Lapavitsas, 2013). This is the general view held by regulationists who contend that a new regime of accumulation centred on finance has replaced more traditional forms of accumulation that emerged during the Fordist crisis. In recent years, scholarship has increasingly focused on the relationship between financialisation practices and urbanisation processes, with some focusing particular attention on the financialisation of housing as 'new financial instruments and regulatory experimentation are used to transform spatially fixed housing into highly liquid investment products' (Waldron, 2019: 687; see also Aalbers, 2016; 2017). In essence, these debates demonstrate how the exchange value rather than use value of housing has increased under contemporary financialised capitalism and critically analyses the financialisation of the urban development process, specifically the interactions between the 'real estate–financial complex' (Aalbers, 2012).

Another broad area of Marxist-inspired scholarship in the planning field relates to the concept of accumulation by dispossession, a term coined by Harvey (2003, 2007) to update Marx's original concept of 'primitive accumulation'. In its original form (Marx's primitive accumulation), the concept denotes the absorption and conversion of non-capitalist spaces, places, and practices into the capitalist system. The concept therefore refers to the range of processes that contribute to this transformation including marketisation, liberalisation, and privatisation (see Mercille and Murphy, 2017). The classic example of primitive accumulation is when peasants living outside the capitalist system are dispossessed and their land expropriated, thereby turning them into wage labourers. On the empirical side, the range of studies assessing the process of accumulation by dispossession is relatively narrow with most studies focused on the developing world and concerned primarily with land grabs or water (Adnan, 2013; Arrighi et al., 2010). Nevertheless, there are a number of studies with an explicitly urban focus which relates either directly or indirectly to the role of the planning system. These include studies on urban gentrification (Ortega, 2016), urban space (Gillespie, 2016), housing (Kappeler and Bigger, 2011), public services (Huws, 2012), and urban resistance to dispossession (Latorre et al., 2015). The concept and related studies have made Marx's work useful for analysis of contemporary capitalism and its relationship with urban and rural planning processes.

THE FUTURE FOR MARXISM AND PLANNING

The Marxist political economy perspective goes beyond other theories by emphasising the structural constraints and power imbalances that are inherent within capitalist society. Rejecting any notion of the state being a neutral arbitrator or a vehicle for reform, the Marxist position highlights that the state must necessarily serve the interests of capital or the dominant class and holder of power of any period given its historical origins. This is the classical Marxist position. It is on this basis that the political and economic spheres are considered interdependent; those with the greatest levels of economic power have considerable power and influence in the political arena. Thus, rather than advocating reformist solutions to the inherent inequalities that are generated in a class-based society, Marxism looks towards a classless society where the eventual need for a state will no longer remain. The analytical power of the Marxist political economy approach offers penetrating insights from which to explore issues surrounding how power arises, is exerted and ultimately operates within the state and its associated institutions such as the planning system.

However, it is important to note that the future of Marxism and its continued relevance to planning theory will likely require Marxist scholars to engage more with and address contemporary political economy issues which it has done only sparingly over the past three decades. This is particularly important to the issue of power in the planning system. Power finds a whole series of means by which to influence the planning system for its own ends (see Olesen, 2014). In this regard, the rise of neoliberalism and its impact on planning has surely not been studied closely enough by planning theorists. This is important because neoliberal experiments have been embraced by powerful interests in the planning process and across a variegated range of public policies (see Mercille and Murphy, 2019).

Furthermore, the intersection of political economies via a range of neoliberal experiments in the planning process and Marxist political economy critiques of such changes is well placed to reveal the underlying nature of broad-based changes in planning systems. In planning practice, Marxist political economy frameworks have provided evidence that theoretical approaches such as communicative action (or collaborative planning) have been co-opted to marginalise, nullify and sideline the potential effectiveness of any power redistribution within participatory processes (Fox-Rogers and Murphy, 2014; 2015) and Sager (2005: 7) has cautioned planning theorists against ignoring critiques '… suggesting that their well-intentioned reforms are being transformed and perverted by economic-political forces only to end up making society less rather than more democratic'. Indeed, the previous section has highlighted the extent of the influence of Marxist political economy scholarship on wider debates relevant to planning. The implication of Sager's aforementioned comment is that Marxist political economy understandings of power in the planning system need to be embraced to a more significant degree in contemporary planning theory and practice debates than is currently the case.

While there is a tendency to think of Marxist scholarship in terms only of radical planning interventions and solutions, there is a need for Marxist political economy frameworks to assist with producing more progressive outcomes in the planning process. In this sense, Fainstein and Fainstein (1982) have emphasised that less determinist positions can be employed to highlight the possibilities for planners to be progressive, even if they legitimise the system in the short run. This position is common in other political economy analysis. For example, Chomsky (2002: 345) notes that it is 'completely realistic and rational to work within structures to which you are opposed, because by doing so you can help to move to a situation where then you can challenge those structures'. Of course, this does not negate the need for Marxist political economy scholarship to adapt and demonstrate its continued relevance for planning in the future, and particularly for understanding systems of power. There is little doubt that such a project will need to focus more on advocacy in planning (Davidoff, 1965), and for planners to take an opposing (rather than neutral) position to the interests of power, one more focused on issues of human well-being, reducing inequality and promoting environmental and ecological sustainability (Rydin, 2013). As Holgersen (2020: 3) rightly asserts: 'We need to embrace what previous Marxist discourse did not manage to include, something that is necessary if a Marxist discourse on planning is going to have an impact – the greatest promise of Marxism: a call for social change'.

REFERENCES

Aalbers, M.B. (ed.) (2012) *Subprime Cities: The Political Economy of Mortgage Markets*. Wiley-Blackwell, Chichester.

Aalbers, M.B. (2016) *The Financialization of Housing: A Political Economy Approach*. Oxon: Routledge.

Aalbers, M.B. (2017) The Variegated Financialization of Housing, *International Journal of Urban and Regional Research*, 41(4): 542–544.

Adnan, S. (2013) Land Grabs and Primitive Accumulation in Deltaic Bangladesh: Interactions Between Neoliberal Globalization, State Interventions, Power Relations and Peasant Resistance, *Journal of Peasant Studies*, 40(1): 87–128.

Allmendinger, P. (2002) *Planning Theory*. Hampshire: Palgrave.

Arrighi, G., Aschoff, N. and Scully, B. (2010) Accumulation by Dispossession and its Limits: The Southern Africa Paradigm Revisited, *Studies in Comparative International Development*, 45: 410–438.

Baran, P.A. and Sweezy, P.M. (1966) *Monopoly Capital*. New York: Monthly Review Press.

Bryan, D., Martin, R. and Rafferty, M. (2009) Financialization and Marx: Giving Labor and Capital a Financial Makeover, *Review of Radical Political Economics*, 41(4): 458–472.

Carnoy, M. (1984) *The State and Political Theory*. New Jersey: Princeton University Press.

Chomsky, N. (2002) *Understanding Power: The Indispensible Noam Chomsky*. London: Vintage Books.

Chomsky, N. (2003) *Chomsky on Democracy and Education*. New York: Routledge Falmer.

Chomsky, N. (2005) *Chomsky on Anarchism*. West Virginia: AK Press.

Davidoff, P. (1965) Advocacy and Pluralism in Planning, *Journal of the American Planning Association*, 31(4): 331–338.

Dunleavy, P. and O'Leary, B. (1987) *Theories of the State: The Politics of Liberal Democracy*. New York: New Amsterdam Books.

Edel, M. (1981) Capitalism, Accumulation and the Explanation of Urban Phenomena. In M. Dear and A.J. Scott (eds), *Urbanization and Urban Planning in a Capitalist Society*, New York: Methuen & Co. Ltd, pp. 19–44.

Engels, F. (1942 [1872]) *The Housing Question*. London: Martin Lawrence.

Engels, F. (2013 [1845]) *The Condition of the Working-Class in England in 1844*. Mansfield: Martino.

Fainstein, N. and Fainstein, S. (1982) New Debates in Urban Planning: The Impact of Marxist Theory within the US. In C. Paris (ed.) *Critical Readings in Planning Theory*. Oxford: Pergamon Press.

Fainstein, S. (2009) Planning and the Just City. In P. Marcuse, J. Connolly, J. Novy, I. Olivo, C. Potter and J. Steil (eds) *Searching for the Just City*. Oxford: Routledge, pp. 19–39.

Fine, B. (2013) Financialization from a Marxist Perspective, *International Journal of Political Economy*, 42 (4): 47–66.

Fox-Rogers, L., Murphy, E. and Grist, B. (2011) Legislative Change in Ireland: A Marxist Political Economy Critique of Planning Law, *Town Planning Review*, 82(6): 639–668.

Fox-Rogers, L. and Murphy, E. (2014) Informal Strategies of Power in the Local Planning System, *Planning Theory*, 13(3): 244–268.

Fox-Rogers, L. and Murphy, E. (2015) From Brown Envelopes to Community Benefits: The Co-option of Planning Gain Agreements under Deepening Neoliberalism, *Geoforum*, 67: 41–50.

Fraser, A., Murphy, E. and Kelly, S. (2013) Deepening Neoliberalism Via Austerity and 'Reform': The Case of Ireland, *Human Geography*, 6(2): 38–53.

Gillespie, T. (2016) Accumulation by Urban Dispossession: Struggles Over Urban Space in Accra, Ghana, *Transactions of the Institute of British Geographers*, 41(1): 66–77.

Harvey, D. (1978) The Urban Process Under Capitalism: A Framework for Analysis. *International Journal of Urban and Regional Research*, 2: 101–131.

Harvey, D. (1985) *The Urbanisation of Capital*. Oxford: Basil Blackwell Ltd.

Harvey, D. (1987) Flexible Accumulation through Urbanization: Reflections on 'Postmodernism' in the American City, *Antipode*, 19: 260–286.

Harvey, D. (1989) From Managerialism to Entrepreneurialism: The Transformation of Urban Governance in Late Capitalism, *Geografiska Annaler*, 71B: 3–17.

Harvey, D. (2001) *Spaces of Capital: Towards a Critical Geography*. Edinburgh: Edinburgh University Press.

Harvey, D. (2003) The Right to the City, *International Journal of Urban and Regional Research* 27(4): 939–994.

Harvey, D. (2007) *A Brief History of Neoliberalism*. Oxford: Oxford University Press.

Healey, P. (1997) *Collaborative Planning: Shaping Places in Fragmented Societies*. Basingstoke: Macmillan Press Ltd.

Hearn, J. (2012) *Theorizing Power*, Basingstoke: Palgrave Macmillan.

Held, D. (1989) *Political Theory and the Modern State: Essays on State, Power and Democracy*. Oxford: Polity Press.

Holgersen, S. (2020) On Spatial Planning and Marxism: Looking Back, Going Forward, *Antipode*, 52(3): 800–824.

Huws, U. (2012) Crisis as Capitalist Opportunity: The New Accumulation through Public Service Commodification, *Socialist Register*, 48: 64–84.

Jessop, B. (2002) Liberalism, Neoliberalism, and Urban Governance: A State–theoretical Perspective, *Antipode*, 34(3): 452–472.

Kappeler, A. and Bigger, P. (2011) Nature, Capital and Neighborhoods: 'Dispossession without Accumulation'?, *Antipode*, 43(4): 986–1011.

Kirk, G. (1980) *Urban Planning in a Capitalist City*. London: Croom Helm Ltd.

Lapavitsas, C. (2013) The Financialization of Capitalism: 'Profiting without Producing', *Cities*, 17(6): 792–805.

Latorre, S., Farrell, K.N. and Martínez-Alier, J. (2015) The Commodification of Nature and Socioenvironmental Resistance in Ecuador: An Inventory of Accumulation by Dispossession Cases, 1980–2013, *Ecological Economics*, 116: 58–69.

Marcuse, P. (2009) From Critical Urban Theory to the Right to the City, *City*, 13(2–3): 185–197.

MacLaran, A. and P. McGuirk (2003) 'Planning the City. In A. MacLaran (ed.), *Making Space: Property Development and Urban Planning*. London: Arnold, pp. 63–94.

Mäntysalo, R. and I. Saglie (2010) Private Influence Preceding Public Involvement: Strategies for Legitimizing Preliminary Partnership Arrangements in Urban Housing in Norway and Finland. *Planning Theory and Practice*, 11(3): 317–338.

Marx, K. and Engels, F. (2010) *The Communist Manifesto*. London: Vintage.

Mercille, J. and Murphy, E. (2019) Market, Non-market and Anti-market Processes in Neoliberalism, *Critical Sociology*, 45(7–8): 1093–1109.

Mercille, J. and Murphy, E. (2017) What is Privatization? A Political Economy Framework, *Environment and Planning A*, 49(5): 1040–1059.

McCann, E.J. (2002) Space, Citizenship, and the Right to the City: A Brief Overview, *GeoJournal*, 58: 77–79.

McDougall, G. (1982) Theory and Practice: A Critique of the Political Economy Approach to Planning. In P. Healey, G. McDougall and M.J. Thomas (eds) *Planning Theory: Prospects for the 1980s*. Oxford: Pergamon Press, pp. 258–271.

Milliband, R. (1977) *Marxism and Politics*. Oxford: Oxford University Press.

Murphy, E. and Fox-Rogers, L. (2015) Perceptions of the Common Good in Planning, *Cities*, 42: 231–241.

Murphy, E. and Mercille, J. (2019) (Re)Making Labour Markets and Economic Crises: The Case of Ireland, *The Economic and Labour Relations Review*, 30(1): 22–38.

Olesen, K. (2014) The Neoliberalisation of Strategic Spatial Planning, *Planning Theory*, 13(3): 289–303.

Ortega, A.A.C. (2016) Manila's Metropolitan Landscape of Gentrification: Global Urban Development, Accumulation by Dispossession and Neoliberal Warfare against Informality, *Geoforum*, 70: 35–50.

Paul, W. (1917) *The State: Its Origin and Function*. Glasgow: Socialist Press.

Purcell, M. (2009) Resisting Neoliberalization: Communicative Planning or Counter-Hegemonic Movements?, *Planning Theory*, 8(2): 140–165.

Rydin, Y. (2013) *The Future of Planning: Beyond Growth Dependence*. Bristol: Policy Press.

Sager, T. (2005) Communicative Planners as Naïve Mandarins of the Neo-liberal State?, *European Journal of Spatial Development*, December 2005. Available at: https://archive.nordregio.se/Global/Publications/Publications%202017/Debate_Sager(2005).pdf (accessed 19 March 2021).

Sandercock, L. (1998) *Towards Cosmopolis*. Chichester: John Wiley.

Scott, A.J. and Roweis, S.T. (1977) Urban Planning in Theory and Practice: A Reappraisal, *Environment and Planning A*, 9: 1097–1119.

Tucker, R.C. (1978) *The Marx-Engels Reader* (2nd edn). New York: Norton.

Van der Zwan, N. (2014) Making Sense of Financialization, *Socio-Economic Review*, 12(1): 99–129.

Waldron, R. (2019) Financialization, Urban Governance and the Planning System: Utilizing 'Development Viability' as a Policy Narrative for the Liberalization of Ireland's Post-Crash Planning System, *International Journal of Urban and Regional Research*, https://doi.org/10.1111/1468-2427.12789.

Yiftachel, O. (1989) Towards a New Typology of Urban Planning Theories, *Environment and Planning B: Planning and Design*, 16: 23–39.

2. Lefebvre's right to the city and a radical urban citizenship: struggles around power in urban planning

Lina Olsson and Elena Besussi

INTRODUCTION

In recent times, local decision-makers, activists, and academics, have paid increasing attention to how the shaping of urban space could be framed in justice terms. This has come to expression, not least through the growing popularity among activists and grassroots of invoking a 'right to the city' – a notion first used by Henri Lefebvre – as a normative framework and vision for their struggles for more equitable living conditions in cities (Mayer, 2009; Rolnik, 2014). In institutional urban policy, we can see a notable growth of interest in adopting human rights language to mobilise and reformulate ideas about citizens' rights to non-discrimination and wellbeing. In some places, this has led to initiatives for institutionalising such rights, for instance by adopting local rights charters (Oomen et al., 2016). There are also examples, however few, of blending human rights concepts with notions of a right to the city, which is commonly regarded as more radical and transformative compared with the former, in policy and legislation (e.g. the Brazilian City Statute and Mexico City's Charter for the Right to the City) (Gerlofs, 2020; García Chueca, 2016). At the same time as these initiatives are recognised as demands rising from lived experiences of marginalisation and inequality, there are concerns that the inscription of rights not only risks depoliticising, but also diluting and de-radicalising them (Purcell, 2014; Gerlofs, 2020). For instance, in their studies of human rights adoption in urban and local policy in so-called Human Rights Cities, Grigolo (2019) observes that rights promotion are adapted to, and can even be facilitative for, neoliberal urban agendas (see also Mayer, 2009).

These observations express similar concerns found in the planning and urban research, which detects the prioritisation of economic growth and branding agendas, and narrowed democratic influence over political decision-making, as key features of contemporary neoliberal urban policy (Baeten, 2017). While it has been debated to what extent contemporary planning practice is dominated by neoliberal hegemony (Sager, 2015), such observations have placed a scepticism around the outlooks of forming radical ideas and initiatives in and through planning practice (Metzger, 2017). As Baeten (2017) points out, more hopeful perspectives on planning are added to the debates by those who see potential in insurgencies in planning (Friedmann, 2011; Miraftab, 2017) and 'fearless speech' for action by planners (Grange, 2017). Some have illustrated examples of how planners act as organic intellectuals bringing activism into planning practice (Stefanelli, 2020). Others have called planning theorists to delve into Lefebvre's notion of a right to the city in search of a vision to advise a renewed, radical planning ethos (Leary-Owhin, 2018).

This chapter provides a reading of Lefebvre's ideas of a right to the city, his radical concept of urban citizenship, and his vision of a 'renewed urban society', by relating these notions to his analysis of 'the crisis of the city' as well as his theory on the production of space (Lefebvre, 1991; 1996b). We discuss how Lefebvre sought to contribute to renewing Marxian theorisation on the reproductive power of capitalist modernity by not only expanding on its dominating and exploiting mechanisms – in particular on how space is dominated to sustain and form new types of capitalist social relations – but also by elaborating on practices that carry the potential to alter and replace it (see also Chapter 1 by Murphy and Fox-Rogers). This is the baseline for how power is addressed in Lefebvre's works. Lefebvre, thus, deploys a Marxian vocabulary that does not always use the term 'power' directly, but nevertheless very much 'talks' about the practice of power in its dominating as well as liberating capacities (which most of the time are inseparable), using terms such as exploitation, alienation, appropriation and struggle. As we argue in this chapter, for Lefebvre it was important to combine analysis and critique of capitalist modernity with a dialecital utopian envisioning and practice. By elaborating on his call for a right to the city, a radical urban citizenship and a renewed urban society, we seek to illuminate how Lefebvre sought to combine a critique of power within capitalist modernity with a reinvigoration of a radically liberating practice of power. Recognising that bringing the right to the city into the current urban context necessitates a continuously renewed analysis and theorisation (Lefebvre, 1996b: ch. 4), this chapter also reflects briefly on contemporary urban crises before turning to discuss Lefebvre's adoption of rights language in his vision for a radical transformation of social space. Differences and overlaps between the right to the city and human rights in cities are discussed and problematised. The chapter ends with a discussion of the potential of planning to be a social field where struggles for a right to the city and dialectical utopian visioning to counteract the global domination of capitalist socio-spatial relations and concentrations of economic and political power may take place. As we argue, Lefebvre's call for a right to the city can be conceived to include a 'right to planning' based on a radical notion of urban citizenship.

LEFEBVRE'S CRITIQUE OF EVERYDAY LIFE IN 'THE URBAN'

Lefebvre's thinking has undoubtedly had a large impact on the study of cities and the socio-spatial process of capitalist modernity within humanities and social sciences. Over several decades, his pioneering theoretical works have provided a vital source for the analysis and understanding of 'the urban', everyday life and the role of space and time for the experience and reproduction of modernity and capitalism. In more recent times, his fusing of a critique of capitalist urbanisation with experimental thinking and imagining around radical alternative futures and emancipation has gained increased attention (Purcell, 2014; Gerlofs, 2020). Yet, Lefebvre has so far had limited influence on planning theory (Leary-Owhin, 2018). This is rather surprising considering that his theoretical contributions directly address a core matter of urban planning – the spatial shaping of societies – and also considering his involvement in conceptualising urban planning practice, and his visionary participation in collaborative planning projects, competition juries, and different fora for urbanists, planners and architects (Pinder, 2015). As Leary-Owhin (2018: 2) argues, Lefebvre's work could provide a powerful conceptual framework for planners to challenge neoliberal planning practice.

Lefebvre presented his vision for a radically renewed urban society in a series of essays, which were first published in the book *The Right to the City* (*Le droit à la ville*) in 1968. The book came out just before the eruptive events occurring that same year, and the 'cry and demand' for a right to the city that Lefebvre intended to provoke was picked up as a slogan within the movement. In *A Right to the City*, Lefebvre presents not only a critique of the contemporary state of capitalist urbanisation – which he termed 'the crisis of the city' (Lefebvre, 1996b) – but also explored a vision of how cities and urban everyday life could be transformed. His analysis of the crisis of the city – which he elaborated on further in the book *The Urban Revolution* (*La révolution urbaine*) (2003: 3) and which built on his earlier works on rural sociology and everyday life – depicted the dissolving of town and countryside and predicted the spread of a dispersed and fragmented 'urban fabric' that would leave no space on earth untouched. These ongoing urban transformation processes, argued Lefebvre, could not be adequately grasped with the hitherto established notions of urbanisation. Explorations into 'the urban phenomenon' – in short, 'the urban' – Lefebvre claimed, called for an epistemic change (Kofman and Lebas, 1996).

A question that preoccupied Lefebvre, and many of his radical contemporaries, was the continuously shifting reproduction of capitalist modernity. An aspect that appears to especially attract the attention of a diversity of scholarships to Lefebvre's work is his heterodox approach to this question. Together with the epistemic exploration on 'the urban', his conceptual elaborations on everyday life and space offer a critique of political economy and modernisation reaching beyond the structuralist episteme, which dominated the time of his writings (Elden, 2004; Kipfer et al., 2008). Lefebvre's approach to the reproduction of capitalist modernity is a proposal of an epistemic transition in Marxism whereby *the industrial* is replaced by *the urban* to illustrate what role the production of (urban) space plays for the reproduction of capitalist modernity, and for colonising and reconditioning everyday life (Prigge, 2008). Lefevre did not thereby suggest that industrial production was of lesser importance to capitalist accumulation; rather, he saw industrialisation and urbanisation as dialectically intertwined (Lefebvre, 1996b, ch. 3 and 11).

In Lefebvre's works, 'the urban' captures a particular form of sociability that emerges along the profound reconfiguration of space occurring globally, and unevenly, in the twentieth century. The main driver of this spatial restructuring, which at this moment had transformed the so-called natural environment entirely into a second nature, and made 'the production of space' premised on the prioritisation of exchange value over use value in capitalist modernity (Kofman and Lebas, 1996). The urban entails the conditioning of everyday life on the treatment of space primarily as raw material and as a commodity and financial asset (Harvey, 2013: ch. 1–2). Materially and ideologically, the spatial restructuring process manifesting the urban is the industrious spread of the modernist city, modelled on a functionalist, productivist and consumerist conception of space. The standardisation and functional division of space in the modernist city resembles an industrial production model that conceives space as a mass product and the whole city as an accumulation mechanism (Lefebvre, 1991: 344–347). The zoning and specialisation of space into residential areas, central business districts, industrial zones, and so on, make space at the one and the same time condensed and dispersed (Lefebvre, 1996b: 123). This turns the urban landscape into a hierarchal and strongly programmed, yet fragmented and disintegrated, space where the spatialities and temporalities of everyday life are profoundly transformed.

For Lefebvre (1991: 130), it is 'the temporal process which gives rise to, which produces, the spatial dimension – whether we are concerned with bodies, with society, with the universe or with the world'. The urban, argues Lefebvre, represents the domination of space over time. Lefebvre's conceptual spatial triad – presented at length in *The Production of Space* (1991) – seeks to capture the working of the urban condition where, as he claims, space is both product and producer. The spatial triad is, however, not limited to this analysis; it also intends to be a general theory about space as a product and producer of social relations. The power of space lies in its capacity to structure social practices, both spatially and temporally. Social practices, in turn, reproduce space. Space is a social product and as such it 'contains – and assigns (more or less) appropriate places to – (1) the social relations of reproduction, i.e. the bio-physiological relations between the sexes and between age groups, along with the specific organization of the family; and (2) the relations of production, i.e. the division of labour and its organization in the form of hierarchical social functions' (Lefebvre, 1991: 32–33). Since space has the capacity to communicate, represent and materialise symbolic orders in society Lefebvre insisted that political-economic analyses of the reproductive power of capitalist modernity need to go beyond the economic (Elden, 2010: 806; Soja, 1996). This is what he sought to do with his theory of production of space, building on his understanding of power as omnipresent: 'It [power] is everywhere *in space*. It is in everyday discourse and common-place notions, as well as in police batons and armoured cars. It is in *objets d'art* as well as in missiles. It is in the diffuse preponderance of the "visual," as well as in institutions such as school or parliament. It is in things as well as in signs (the signs of objects and object-signs). Everywhere, and therefore nowhere .... [P]ower has extended its domain right into the interior of each individual, to the roots of consciousness, to the "topias" hidden in the folds of subjec-tivity' (Lefebvre cited in Soja, 1996: 31–32). As Lefebvre saw it, the production of space is realised through three dialectically integrated moments, which could be understood as: *spatial practices*, *representations of space*, and *spaces of representation*; corresponding to *perceived spaces, conceived spaces, and lived* spaces (Lefebvre, 1991; Soja, 1996).[1]

Spatial practices encompass 'production and reproduction, and the particular locations and spatial sets characteristic of each social formation' (Lefebvre, 1991: 33). Each historical urban formation produces its own spatial practice, which ensures continuity and cohesion of its social formation. According to Lefebvre, the exhibitive spatial practices of the post-war city were its dispersed spatial structure, built for automobile transport rather than walking, and the functionalised, repetitive, and sprawling housing areas. *Representations of space* are concepts of space, or conceived spaces, that is spaces produced from simulations of space, such as maps, plans, and scientific spatial models. Such representations of space – which are always both abstract and concrete – are produced and used by scientists, planners, and other types of bureaucrats and analysts to predict and control space; thus, they 'are tied to the relations of production and to the "order" which those relations impose, and hence to knowledge, to signs, to codes, and to "frontal" relations' (Lefebvre, 1991: 33). Representations of spaces are, in other words, not only (abstract) desktop products, and (concrete) spaces produced according to these. Representations of spaces encompass representations of social relations, and as such they contribute to reproducing them. Therefore, they could be used as tools of power seeking to dominate and control; this is indeed how plans, maps and scientific models have been, and still are, used within and through bureaucratic forms of planning. In contrast to representa-tions of spaces stands *spaces of representation*, which are 'complex symbolisms, sometimes coded, sometimes not, linked to the clandestine or underground side of social life, as also to art' (Lefebvre, 1991: 39). Spaces of representation are produced, associated, and symbolised through appropriation of space, that is, through the lived experiences and spatial practices of so-called inhabitants. In Lefebvre's words, spaces of representation are 'dominated', but as the loci of symbolism and imagination, they also reside a liberating power (ibid.).

The epistemic transition proposed by Lefebvre entails an understanding of exploitation and alienation not only in terms of relations of labour and production. Alienation occurs not only as a result of labour exploitation. As Kristin Ross (1995: 37) points out, one of Fordism's major accomplishments was 'that of transforming its workers into the consumers of the products they make'. A striking, and contradicting, feature of the modernist mid-twentieth century urban landscape was that while a fast-growing number of people worldwide could acquire the modern 'living standards' associated with it – access to electricity and running water, car ownership, a household equipped with various appliances – their everyday lives had also become dominated by it. Everyday life – the lived spaces of difference, the collective and individual rhythms, spatial practices, and imaginings of inhabiting – had been substituted, argued Lefebvre, with a trivial everydayness (Elden, 2004: 112). This is signified not only by spatially and temporally programmed ways of living, but also by the colonisation of desire by consumerist images and imaginaries of modern life produced by the so-called culture industries (Ross, 1995).

Looking at how the French post-war urbanisation was depicted in media, Kristin Ross illustrates how the imaginaries of modernisation, centred on two types of mass consumption objects – cars and home appliances for cleaning – recurrently analysed in Lefebvre's writings, reflected the evolution of a new genderised and racialised spatial order. Together with suburban housing, the car – constructed as a masculine object – was the mass-market product that most of all contributed to reproducing a decentralised and privatised urban landscape. Associated with myths of speed and spatial liberty, it symbolised the acceleration of commodity circulation and increased labour mobility in this period. In the sprawling space, the modern home was not only made commodity in itself; it was a space that supported the creation of a mass market for various home appliances. The homogenising and privatising character of the post-war urban landscape, depicted and critiqued by Lefebvre, was, in Ross' (1995: 11) words, 'a movement echoed on the level of everyday life by the withdrawal of the new middle classes to their newly comfortable domestic interiors, to the electric kitchens, to the enclosure of private automobiles, to the interior of a new vision of conjugality and an ideology of happiness built around the new unit of middle-class consumption, the couple, and to depoliticization as a response to the increase in bureaucratic control of daily life'. Alienation, emphasises Lefebvre (1996b: ch. 3, 14), occurs also in the form of an everyday life deprived of difference and communal life.

In this context, imaginaries of class are replaced with those of national identity. Communicated in media and through consumption, the commonly feminised appliances for cleaning, argues Ross (1995: 74), represented the creation of 'a desire to be clean'. The notion of cleanness was not only a selling point targeting women, especially; it also established a particular modernised notion of French national identity. Acquiring a modern living standard, and pursuing a privatised and sanitised 'lifestyle', is made equivalent to being French. At the city level, this is articulated through the spread of suburban single-family housing developments and the 'sanitation' – the demolition and redeveloping – of inner-city areas regarded as unmodern, and which lead to the expulsion of workers, many with origins in the French colonies, to *banlieus*. Through this restructuring of space, a spatially and symbolically racialised interior–exterior boundary is established between on the one hand inner-city areas, populated mostly by white upper and middle-class groups, and the *banlieus*.

A RIGHT TO THE CITY

Over the past couple of decades, the revival of interest in Lefebvre's ideas about a right to the city has generated a wide stream of scholarly debates. A search on 'right to the city' with the Google Scholar search engine in 2021 shows that the phrase occurs in no fewer than 16,900 publications between 2010 and 2020. The proliferating engagement in the right to the city is perhaps not only encouraged by a perceived need to (re)conceptualise spatial and social justice in the context of the contemporary urban landscapes. The attraction to the right to the city may also lie in the flexibility of the notion, coming from Lefebvre's open and indicative, rather than complete, formulation of it. At the same time as it may be perceived as vague, it allows flexibility for adoption and reformulation. As Pinder (2015) points out, the right to the city is a utopic vision of what everyday life could be, but not communicated through the kind of concrete ideals that socialist and communitarian utopians of the nineteenth and early twentieth centuries formulated. Lefebvre's approach is a conscious avoidance of such positive formulations since – regardless of how radical they appeared in their historical context – they represent spatial imaginaries around hierarchal and fixed social relations.

If we look at the definitional openness of the right to the city in combination with the depiction of the modernist city as the antidote to what the right to the city aims for, we find a rather rich conceptual material in Lefebvre. As underlined in the previous section, it is in the context of all the forms of suppressions of post-war urbanisation, and the uprisings they triggered in the late 1960s, that Lefebvre formulated his call for a right to the city. With this in mind, Lefebvre's right to the city should not be reduced to mere critique. He emphasised that to go 'beyond the horizon of the most classical philosophical rationalism, that of liberal humanism', the crisis of the city and the urban phenomena need to be theorised with a notion of a possible alternative, that is, with an idea of the possibility of radical transformation (Lefebvre, 1996b: 129). The right to the city exercises the power of both critique and utopic conceptualisation. Despite his critique of the urban, Lefebvre maintains that the possibility for liberation and appropriation is found in it, this because contradictions, conflicts, and struggle are at its core. The everyday life in the urban is, at the same time, revealed as a sphere of alienation and liberation (Kipfer et al., 2008). 'The form of a new urban society' can be spotted in the subversive elements that 'survives in the fissures of the planned and programmed order'; transformation is a possibility residing in the lived spaces of everyday life in the urban fabric (Lefebvre, 1996b: 129). This is an aspect of Lefebvre's dialectical materialism: the fusion of idealism and materialism (Elden 2004: 16–17; Kofman and Lebas, 1996: 9–19).

As far as Lefebvre specifies the right to the city, he does it around the notion of the city as a collective work of art, as an *oeuvre*. In this, we find the utopic and transformative power of the urban episteme. Lefebvre's aim was to replace the narrow Marxist concept of labour with a concept for liberated human creative force (Ronneberger, 2008). Grasping the possibilities of counteracting homogenisation, instrumentalisation and commodification of space, the concept represents a view of the city 'as an end, as place of free enjoyment, as domain of use value' (Lefebvre, 1996b: 126). As a collective oeuvre, the city evolves through *autogestion*, that is via decentralised, bottom-up management and production of space. The form of the collective oeuvre evolves through appropriation in and through lived spaces; through a permanently unfolding process generated from below, not from above (Elden, 2004: 157; Purcell, 2014: 147–148). Lefebvre paid much attention to the power and potentiality of the supposed non-productive parts of everyday life, where practices of appropriation and creativity expressed through artistic creation, play, and festive socialisation can be found. In these, Lefebvre not only saw the yearnings, but also the seeds, for metamorphosis.

Remaining within dialectical thinking, Lefebvre adopts an additive approach to defining the right to the city. His elaboration on the notion can be found scattered in several texts subsequent to *The Right to the City* and *The Urban Revolution* (cf. Lefebvre, 1996a: 185). Additional rights aspects are elaborated on, to various extents, but they are not always announced with reference to the actual slogan. In one passage, he specifies the (plural) right to the city in the following way:

> The right to the city manifests itself as a superior form of rights: right to freedom, to individualisation in socialisation, to habitat and to inhabit. The right to the oeuvre, to participation and appropriation (clearly distinct from the right to property), are implied in the right to the city (Lefebvre, cited in Elden, 2004: 152).

Among the (overlapping) rights that Lefebvre discusses, besides those mentioned in the quote, are the right to difference, the right to urban life, the right to autogestion, the right to participation, the right to centrality, the right to information, and the right to public services (Lefebvre, 1996b; Elden, 2004: 231). Lefebvre adds these to the rights conceptions that he saw were evolving in the twentieth century: 'the rights of ages and sexes (the woman, the child and the elderly), rights of conditions (the proletarian, the peasant), rights to training and education, to work, to culture, to rest, to health, to housing' (Lefebvre, 1996: 157). Lefebvre's notion of right differs, however, from established liberal rights concept, and to this we return below.

To summarise, the various rights specified for pursuing the right to the city as a collective oeuvre aim for liberation from the oppression of urbanisation under capitalist modernity. The right to difference, put briefly, seeks to embrace the plurality of identity and lived space, including rhythms, customs, cultures and aesthetic expressions, at the level of the individual and at the level of the collective (Elden, 2004: 226–231; cf. Lefebvre, 1996b: ch. 8). This right is a part of the right to urban life as well as of the right to autogestion. These suggest a right to lived spaces characterised by difference, appropriation, encounter and (political) socialisation. Proximity and assemblage are central aspects of this, and it calls for a right to centrality (Elden, 2004). This right is also a call against the exclusion and expulsion from the urban centres of those groups that, by economic means and/or association, are denied the possibility of inhabiting them. This is not only a right not to be deprived of space one has appropriated and lived. The displacement from centres, observed by Lefebvre, brought these groups away from the privileged places of political decision-making and public services. Thus, the right to centrality links to the right to (political) participation, the right to information, and the right to public services (Elden, 2004: 231, Kofman and Lebas, 1996: 34). As Prigge (2008) highlights, the right to centrality also has a symbolic dimension. It entails the re-establishing of a (radical) symbolic link between the city – and the collective – and its inhabitants. In the dispersed urban landscape, this is lost or replaced by symbols of power and privilege.

In relation to this, a comment on how the right to the city applies, or relates, to rural areas ought to be made. It may appear that the right to the city, with the emphasis on a right to centrality and a right to urban life, contains an urban bias overlooking places beyond the metropolitan areas. Lefebvre spent much time studying rural areas before he turned to theorise the urban. His work on this was not a neglect of the countryside. On the contrary, he observed and critiqued how urbanisation transformed and in some places destroyed rural areas. Into the right to the city, Lefebvre weaves the idea of a moment where society has been completely urbanised. At the time of his writings, he saw that the urban had, in fact, already absorbed much of the countryside. Thus, the right to the city ought not to be viewed through the lens of a city–countryside dichotomy. Bearing in mind that Lefebvre formulated his vision in and against the post-war moment, in the next section we discuss the actuality of his notion of a right to the city by looking, briefly, at how cities have changed and at some examples of contemporary struggles in the urban landscape.

STRUGGLES OF POWER IN 'THE URBAN' TODAY

Salient in Lefebvre's texts is the epochal moment of post-war urbanisation against, and within which he formulated his call. A recurring theme in publications on Lefebvre's right to the city concerns the use and validity, as well as the need for adapting and expanding the concept, for capturing and contesting oppressions in/of the contemporary urban landscapes. Over the more than five decades that have passed since Lefebvre wrote his manifesto for a right to the city, urban landscapes across the world have undergone many changes. From the 1980s onwards, inequalities have grown along with the broad regulatory shift through which Keynesian redistributive policies for collective consumption have been replaced by neoliberal policies and state regulation that prioritise economic growth in select places over equalising policy. Urban space has been continuously restructured in various ways under the pressures of capital, and 'the urban fabric' has been expanding evermore through extractivist and productivist activities. Over the past twenty years, the urban has been characterised by more pronounced social polarisation, which has deepened social segregation. In many places, homelessness and housing precarity have grown profoundly along with the increasing financialisation of housing. The use of urban public spaces has been restricted and programmed as they have been placed under private commercial control to an increasing degree. Exclusion and discrimination expressed through escalation of violence targeting racialised groups and militarisation of public spaces are also marks of the urban in the contemporary. Some places have seen a distressing increase in gender violence (Fuentes, 2020), and in many places, LGBTQI+ people cannot feel safe in their homes and in public spaces. Globally, and recurrently, these developments are counteracted through acts of everyday resistance, uprisings and demonstrations, as witnessed for instance by the global expansion of the social movements Black Lives Matters, the Women's March movement, and the Fridays for Future school strikes. The upswing of both radical and reformist demands for greater justice are not simply expressions of fashionable policy or trendy experimentation. They are responses to perceived and lived experiences of increasingly unequal living and working conditions in cities and city-regions. The COVID-19 pandemic has also highlighted the impacts of social inequalities and the unequal responses that cities provide to basic needs such as access to clean air and housing. All these ongoing developments demonstrate that the call for a right to the city is continuously pressing.

LEFEBVRE'S NOTION OF RIGHTS AND CITIZENSHIP

An aspect discussed in the scholarly debates regards the multiple ways Lefebvre's right to the city is deployed today. As mentioned earlier, the right to the city slogan is increasingly used by social movements, grassroots organisations, NGOs, and, in some places, even by public authorities. While the ample and creative engagement with Lefebvre's notion of a right to the city is acknowledged to be productive, the various ways by which it is deployed have also generated certain concerns. In academic contexts, Purcell (2002; 2014) observes that the right to the city has often been used without careful examination of Lefebvre's original vision. Purcell (2014) also notes that along with the popular elaboration on the notion of a right to the city, is a tendency of using it in ways that make it increasingly indistinct. His concern is primarily the risk of diluting Lefebvre's ideas about a radical and renewed form of citizenship with liberal-democratic ones. David Harvey takes a different approach in this regard. For him, the notion of a right to the city is an open signifier that acquires meaning primarily through practice, that is, by those who appropriate and use it (Harvey, 2013: xv). Pointing at the potential weakness of adopting a discourse of rights, according to Harvey (2013: xv) the notion of a right to the city (and the power dimensions it enables) can be claimed not only by the excluded and exploited but also by powerful groups such as financiers and developers. If we, with Marcuse (2009) see the right to the city as empowering the excluded and oppressed, especially, Harvey's message may seem a bit disheartening. However, what Harvey points at is that the meaning and practice of the right to the city depends on the outcome of struggle. This approach clearly follows Lefebvre's insistence on the evolving of urban society as a contradictory and conflictual process from below (Elden, 2004: 151–157, 226–231). Yet, we may still ask why Lefebvre adopted the notion of right, and how he conceived of rights.

As Purcell (2014: 146) has underlined, Lefebvre's vision of a right to the city is accompanied by the proposal of a renewed citizenship; a citizenship that is not based on a liberal-democratic idea of the social contract. Lefebvre's proposal for a renewed social contract is, instead, based on the idea of autogestion. In line with Harvey, Purcell (2014: 146) argues that Lefebvre conceived of rights as outcomes of struggle; '[t]hey are the end result of collective claims made by mobilized citizen'. As such, they are reshaped by further struggle. To energise this continuous struggle is, proposes Purcell, Lefebvre's goal with formulating a new set of rights and a new social contract. Thus, Lefebvre's dialectical approach to rights entailed both a dismissal and a claim of them (Gerlofs, 2020: 67). From here, we could bring in Lefebvre's dialectical materialism and illuminate the notion of right in Lefebvre further.

Dialectical materialism places concepts and practices, form and content – the abstract and the concrete – in a dialectical relation. This is at the core of Lefebvre's notion of right and contract. One central feature of the contract as a 'form', argues Lefebvre (1996b: 134, italics in original), is '*reciprocity* in a socially constituted and instituted engagement'. He goes further and says, 'each engages himself [sic] vis-a-vis the other to accomplish a certain sort of action explicitly or implicitly stipulated. One knows that reciprocity entails some *fiction*, or rather, that as soon as it is concluded, it reveals itself to be *fictional*, inasmuch as it does not fall into contractual stipulation and under the rule of law' (Lefebvre, 1996b: 134, our italics). The contract and its content are concrete abstractions. Lefebvre says that the abstract – the contract, or narrated right – has no meaning without content, yet it may be detached – as representations of spaces – from the concrete, from 'the real', to which it relates dialectically. Not only are the narrative contents of rights (re)shaped through struggle; as abstractions (fictions) rights influence the (ideas of) direction and outcome of struggles. This is how the power of abstractions operates. Formulated by Lefebvre (1996b: 134, italics in original), 'these fictions have a social existence and influence. They are the various contents of a general juridical *form* with which jurists operate and which become the codification of social relations: the civil code'. Purcell suggests that Lefebvre did not imply that the new sets of rights that he proposed were necessarily to be codified as law. As (concrete) abstractions, rights could appear in other narrative forms, for instance, charters and declarations. In whatever abstract form they appear, they are necessarily tied dialectically to the concrete – material and embodied – social reality.

THE RIGHT TO THE CITY VS HUMAN RIGHTS (IN) CITIES

Over recent decades, the notion of rights has been increasingly adopted in urban policy around the world. This has occurred largely through calls and initiatives from 'below'; by activist networks, NGOs, and local authorities, sometimes acting in alliance (Darling, 2016; Grigolo, 2019). Many of these calls and initiatives are claims for social justice articulated around the notion of human rights. An increasing number of local authorities have made local human rights charters and/or ratified declarations for human rights. Some actively participate in the spread of human rights under the emerging brand of Human Rights Cities (Grigolo, 2019). Some of the rights-based initiatives, instead, refer to the right to the city, sometimes with direct reference to Lefebvre (Global Platform for the Right to the City, 2021). In other calls and initiatives, references to human rights and to the right to the city are merged; see for example the Mexico City Charter for the Right to the City (Mexico City, 2010) and the European Charter for the Safeguarding of Human Rights in the City (United Cities and Local Governments, 2012). Despite the reference to the right to the city in the latter charter, human rights claims rather than the right to the city have been the primary focus of local rights-based policy in Europe. So far, most examples of institutional adoption and adaption of a notion of a right to the city – emphasising democratic management and cities' social functions – are found in Latin America (García Chueca, 2016).

Following the growth of rights-based urban policy, there has been a surge of academic analyses and interpretations of the mixes and differences of, on the one hand, notions of human rights in cities and, on the other, notions of the right to the city (Oomen et al., 2016). In line with Purcell's argument, the former are commonly regarded as less radical than the latter. Glancing, for instance, at the UN Universal Declaration of Human Rights, which establishes the right to private property as a human right, we can see a clear example of how notions of human rights may depart from Lefebvrean ideas of a right to the city. Lefebvre's call for a right to the city is an explicit repudiation of the right to private property. Critically oriented legal scholarship has since long criticised the notion of human rights for being Western-centric, anthropocentric, and modelled on male heterosexual bodies as legal persons (Grear, 2011). Human rights are also critiqued for individualising the notion of rights as well as having contributed little to advance redistributive justice (Moyn, 2018).

In the literature on 'human rights cities', the adoption of human rights discourses in urban policy is seen as representing a shift in the use and meaning of international human rights. Soohoo (2016) claims that the 'innovation' of localising human rights is the development of methods to locally adapt and implement human rights in governance and service provision (see also Oomen and Baumgärtel, 2018). Whether the invocation of human rights by grassroots activists and urban policy-makers risks falling short or have the potential to advance social justice has been a recurring point of discussion (Darling, 2016; Grigolo, 2019). While the literature on human rights cities generally highlights the potential of human rights claims in urban policy and law for strengthening social justice and expanding notions of citizenship, it also points at potential pitfalls of employing human rights. One highlighted aspect is that human rights are centred on the idea that rights are granted by institutions to individual rights subjects (García Chueca, 2016). In his book, *The Human Rights City*, Grigolo (2019) presents empirical research illustrating how human rights have been gradually institutionalised in urban policy and statute via routes of struggle by activists and grassroots mobilising around human rights claims to demand reforms for justice. He observes that as these processes have contributed to institutionalise human rights, there are also tendencies of adapting local human rights policies and charters in ways that fit neoliberal urban governing (see also Mayer, 2009). As a global 'brand' associated with diversity, liberalism, and tolerance, human rights promoted by local authorities, notes Grigolo, may lie well in line with efforts of promoting tourism and attracting the middle-class groups that Richard Florida has termed the creative class. In some places, for instance in Barcelona, which is known for its human rights advocacy, human rights promotion has been increasingly oriented towards emphasising law and order. While human rights-based policy has advanced work against discrimination and contributed to expanding social services, obligations of good citizenship have, at the same time, made vulnerable groups dependent on using public spaces for work and living targets for penalties (Grigolo, 2019: 122–126).

Grigolo, like Purcell and Harvey, emphasise that the meaning and usage of human rights are shaped through political struggle. In empirical research, it has been shown that inscribing human rights into law is rarely enough to generate social change, demonstrating limitations of the power of rights. For this to happen, mobilisation and invocation of human rights in politics is essential (Langford, 2018). The outcomes of struggle may be uneven and momentary, and may even result in setbacks for social justice. García Chueca (2016) notes that the adoption and implementation of human rights-based policy often tend to be rather uneven. In Europe, for instance, few cities have adopted and implemented urban policy based on human rights, even though over 400 municipalities have ratified the European Charter for the Safeguarding of Human Rights in the City (García Chueca, 2016). Even when changes to policy and law are achieved, over time and with institutionalisation, their radical content may be diluted or replaced. A recent example of this is the revisions and reversals of human rights commitment in Brazil occurring under the right-wing leadership (Morais de Sá e Silva, 2020).

Still, in the context of neoliberal urbanism, struggles originating in human rights claims witness that these are regarded as having the potential – if not starting a process of radical transformation – to contribute to taking steps towards strengthening justice, or at least resisting the further spread of poverty, discrimination, exclusion and other kinds of social harms. Pointing at both the potential shortcomings and possibilities of human rights, Langford (2018: 71) states that '[t]he shadow of populism, illiberal democracy, and authoritarianism may be evidence of the failure of human rights, or it may very well confirm or remind us of its enduring importance, including for sustainable forms of social justice'. As Grigolo (2019: 17) and Morais de Sá e Silva (2020) point out, in politics the advocacy of human rights is often seen as a tool for implementing radical – centre and left-wing – agendas. Over recent decades, human rights discourse has provided an impactful vocabulary for advancing moral and political claims. There are also academic studies that point at concrete examples where human rights policy and claims have contributed to step changes.

Notwithstanding the progressive changes these efforts have generated, their results are far from resembling Lefebvre's utopian vision. Nevertheless, they can illustrate the concrete abstract – and dialectical – character of rights. The interpretation, formulation, and implementation of (human) rights are not necessarily static as their content is only (and necessarily) momentarily fixed.

THE POSSIBILITIES AND POTENTIALITIES OF DIALECTICAL UTOPIANISM WITHIN PLANNING AS A SOCIAL FIELD OF UNEVEN POWER RELATIONS

To illuminate how struggles for a right to the city, and a renewed urban society, can take place, or even expand, in and through planning it is necessary to discuss what limitations and possibilities planning places on such struggles. To do this we could combine Lefebvre's conceptualisation of power with a Bourdieusian (cf. Grigolo, 2019, see also Porter, 2010; 2014) understanding of planning as a social 'field' where power is omnipresent, yet operates unevenly. That is, planning is a social field where the actions of various agents and actors are situated unevenly within the social and spatial hierarchies of capital accumulation processes, institutional structures and various forms of knowledge production. With this approach, we can analyse the conditions and potential promises that planning offers as a social field where rights claims and dialectical utopian visions are and may be shaped with the goal of counteracting domination and uneven power relations.

Since the time of Lefebvre's writings, planning has undergone successive changes. Compared to the conditions in the late 1960s and early 1970s, in many places, the right to democratic participation in planning has been expanded as, at least, a formal procedural right. Even though planning takes place through governance processes with the involvement of multiple private actors, and to various degrees also citizens, governmental decision-making and state-led coordination within the framework of a capitalist liberal democracy constitution still constitute a decisive part of planning. Planning continues to be a social field through which space is dominated and controlled. The state-led coordination task of planning both enables and limits democratic participation. Planning is not only structured by pre-established procedural rights to participation but also determines them concretely. Similarly, planning is not only structured around property rights and public (including human) rights, but actively determines and regulates their meaning and content in concrete space. As a social field of contested production of space, planning articulates the relationships between different rights and translates them into the articulation of space production and structures of decision-making. As such, planning is a process of selecting which rights to uphold and which to dismiss. That is, planning shapes rights as concrete abstractions.

How these selection processes play out is determined also by the exclusionary and selective nature of the notions and models of democratic participation that underpin both planning practice and planning theory today. Selective exclusionary practices are embedded, for instance, in the assumptions made about ethnicity and other aspects of difference within planning. These assumptions affect the design of participation practices in planning (Beebeejaun, 2006; 2012). Claims for the recognition of diversity are often regarded, not as questions on planning's normative notions of equality, but as particularist and separated from the mainstream (Young, 2002). Selective practices that aim to restrict the participation in planning as a social field are also embedded in technologies of government (see Clarke and Cochrane, 2013) that, while they appear to expand the role of citizens' participation through devolution and decentralisation of planning powers, remain dictated by an interpretation of the urban as space for accumulation and allow for debating contradictions and conflicts over space production only insofar as the participants to those debates have already subscribed to pre-existing hegemonic notions of public interest. This means that when planning recognises rights and right-holders, not only is it selective, but it effectively shapes the qualities of all political and technical actors involved, and constructs political identities which might not have existed previously (see Clifford and Tewdwr-Jones, 2013; Inch, 2015).

In the context of contemporary capitalist liberal democracy, struggles for recognition (of rights) are captured in a planning and democratic regime that 'ignores the more radical and fundamental claims of the right to space and reduces what should be properly political questions to regulation through procedure' (Porter 2014: 390). The possibility for planning to be a field of radical alternative to capitalism's neoliberal form is dependent on who gains access to planning and what and whose rights are recognised in planning as a space where the contradictions and conflicts on the use and production of urban space, which Lefebvre placed at the centre of the struggle for the right to the city, are articulated. Thus, we argue that the right to participation can be understood as a 'right to planning', conceptualised as the right to access and form the space-shaping social field of planning where a struggle for the right to the city in a Lefebvrian sense, not in a liberal sense based on notions of citizenship founded on social contract or property (Gray, 2018; Purcell 2014: 146), takes place. Because planning, as a social field of action and as a state apparatus, is permeated by uneven power relations, the notion of the right to planning allows us to conceive a planning practice of continuous and permanent challenge and reorganisation of such relations. That is to say, struggles to expand inclusion and participation in planning necessarily take place within it. Practising a right to planning, thus, seeks to change planning as a social field of uneven power relations; it is a struggle to create the discords and disruptions and that lead to socio-spatial change and the creation of new, yet only temporarily fixed, power relations and concrete abstractions of rights. Struggles around a right to planning, thus, contribute to a continuous struggle towards shaping a radical and enacted urban citizenship.

Progressive alternatives to mainstream planning practices take their form at different scales and formats from neighbourhood-level appropriation of space in the face of institutional disinvestment (e.g. Can Batllo in Barcelona and Al-Ashqariya in East Jerusalem discussed in Cohen-Bar and Ronel, 2013), or in response to the threat of displacement brought about by profit-seeking investments in the built environment (e.g. Ward's Corner in London, in Vardy, 2019); to progressive practices of civic participation and community organising (e.g. REDWatch in Sydney in Rogers, 2013, and Just Space in London, in Just Space, 2021). They are grounded in the principle that access to the democratic processes that establish the public interest in planning must not be dependent on a commitment to a predefined hegemonic conception of values and public good but must remain an open field of social struggle. The civic claim for a more open and democratic process of plan-making, can be seen as a search for a legitimate position in the social field that constitutes planning from those who are more often excluded by it. Such claims recognise the importance of the concrete abstraction of the urban plan as the document that condenses the distribution of rights in property and in public goods into a social contract and demands that their voices are written into and not out of the plan.

NOTE

1.   In the English 1991 version of The Production of Space, 'espaces de représentation' is translated to 'representational spaces'. Soja, however, uses the translation 'spaces of representation', which has been preferred by many other authors. Thus, we use this translation instead of the former.

REFERENCES

Baeten, G. (2017) 'Neoliberal planning', in Gunder, M., Madanipour, A. and Watson, V. (eds), *The Routledge Handbook of Planning Theory*. London, UK: Taylor & Francis Group, pp. 105–117.

Beebeejaun, Y. (2006) 'The Participation Trap: The Limitations of Participation for Ethnic and Racial Groups', *International Planning Studies*, 11(1), pp. 3–18. doi: 10.1080/13563470600935008.

Beebeejaun, Y. (2012) 'Including the Excluded? Changing the Understandings of Ethnicity in Contemporary English Planning', *Planning Theory & Practice*, 13(4), pp. 529–548. doi: 10.1080/14649357.2012.728005.

Clarke, N. and Cochrane, A. (2013) 'Geographies and Politics of Localism: The Localism of the United Kingdom's Coalition Government', *Political Geography*, 34, pp. 10–23. doi: 10.1016/j.polgeo.2013.03.003.

Clifford, B. and Tewdwr-Jones, M. (2013) *The Collaborating Planner? Practitioners in the Neoliberal Age*. Bristol: Policy Press.

Cohen-Bar, E. and Ronel, A. (2013) 'Dynamic Planning Initiated by Residents: Implementable Plans for the Informal Built Urban Fabric of the Palestinian Neighbourhoods of East Jerusalem', *Planning Theory & Practice*, 14(4), 538–541. doi: 10.1080/14649357.2013.853470.

Darling, J. (2016) 'Defying the Demand to "Go Home": From Human Rights Cities to the Urbanisation of Human Rights', in Oomen, B., Davis, M.F. and Grigolo, M. (eds), *Global Urban Justice: The Rise of Human Rights Cities*. Cambridge: Cambridge University Press, pp. 121–138.

Elden, S. (2004) *Understanding Henri Lefebvre*. London; New York: Continuum.

Elden, S. (2010). Land, Terrain, Territory, *Progress in Human Geography*, 34(6), 799–817. doi: https://doi.org/10.1177/0309132510362603.

Friedmann, J. (2011) *Insurgencies: Essays in Planning Theory*. New York: Routledge.

Fuentes, L. (2020) '"The Garbage of Society": Disposable Women and the Socio-Spatial Scripts of Femicide in Guatemala', *Antipode*, 52(6), pp. 1667–1687. doi: https://doi.org/10.1111/anti.12669.

García Chueca, E. (2016) 'Human Rights in the City and the Right to the City: Two Different Paradigms Confronting Urbanisation', in Oomen, B., Davis, M.F. and Grigolo, M. (eds), *Global Urban Justice: The Rise of Human Rights Cities*. Cambridge: Cambridge University Press, pp. 103–120.

Gerlofs, B. (2020) 'Dreaming Dialectically: The Death and Life of the Mexico City Charter for the Right to the City', *Urban Studies*, 57(10), pp. 2064–2079. doi: 10.1177/0042098019868102.

Global Platform for the Right to the City (2021) *Global Platform for the Right to the City*. Available at: www.right2city.org/ (accessed: 26 February 2021).

Grange, K. (2017) 'Planners – A Silenced Profession? The Politicisation of Planning and the Need for Fearless Speech', *Planning Theory*, 16(3), pp. 275–295. doi: 10.1177/1473095215626465.

Gray, N. (2018) 'Beyond the Right to the City: Territorial Autogestion and the Take Over the City Movement in 1970s Italy', *Antipode*, 50(2), pp. 319–339. doi: https://doi.org/10.1111/anti.12360.

Grear, A. (2011) 'The Vulnerable Living Order: Human Rights and the Environment in a Critical and Philosophical Perspective', *Journal of Human Rights and the Environment*, 2(1), pp. 23–44. doi: 10.4337/jhre.2011.01.02.

Grigolo, M. (2019) *The Human Rights City: New York, San Francisco, Barcelona*. New York: Routledge, 2019. doi: 10.4324/9781315628530.

Harvey, D. (2013) *Rebel Cities: From the Right to the City to the Urban Revolution*. London; New York: Verso Books.

Inch, A. (2015) 'Ordinary Citizens and the Political Cultures of Planning: In Search of the Subject of a new Democratic Ethos', *Planning Theory*, 14(4), pp. 404–424. doi: 10.1177/1473095214536172.

Just Space (2021) *Just Space*. www.justspace.org.uk (accessed: 9 March 2021).

Kipfer, S., Goonewardena, K. Schmid, C. and Milgrom, R. (2008) 'On the Production of Henri Lefebvre', in Goonewardena, K., Kipfer, S., Milgrom, R. and Schmid, C. (eds), *Space, Difference, Everyday Life: Reading Henri Lefebvre*. London; New York: Routledge, pp. 1–24.

Kofman, E. and Lebas, E. (1996) 'Lost in Transposition', in Kofman, E., Lebas, E. and Lefebvre, H. (eds), *Writings on Cities*. Translated and edited by Eleonore Kofman and Elizabeth Lebas. Oxford: Blackwell Publishing, pp. 3–60.

Langford, M. (2018) 'Critiques of Human Rights', *Annual Review of Law and Social Science*, 14(1), pp. 69–89. doi: 10.1146/annurev-lawsocsci-110316-113807.

Leary-Owhin, M.E. (2018) 'Henri Lefebvre, Planning's Friend or Implacable Critic?', *Urban Planning; Lisbon*, 3(3), pp. 1–4. doi: http://dx.doi.org/10.17645/up.v3i3.1578.

Lefebvre, H. (1991) *The Production of Space*. Translated by Donald Nicholson-Smith. Oxford: Blackwell Publishing.

Lefebvre, H. (1996a) 'Space and Politics', in *Writings on Cities*. Translated and edited by Eleonore Kofman and Elizabeth Lebas. Oxford: Blackwell Publishing, pp. 183–215.

Lefebvre, H. (1996b) 'The Right to the City', in *Writings on Cities*. Translated and Edited by Eleonore Kofman and Elizabeth Lebas. Oxford: Blackwell Publishing, pp. 61–181.

Lefebvre, H. (2003) *The Urban Revolution*. Minneapolis, MN: University of Minnesota Press.

Mayer, M. (2009) 'The "Right to the City" in the Context of Shifting Mottos of Urban Social Movements', *City*, 13(2–3), pp. 362–374. doi: 10.1080/13604810902982755.

Marcuse, P. (2009) 'From Critical Urban Theory to the Right to the City', *City*, 13(2–3), pp. 185–197. doi: 10.1080/13604810902982177.

Metzger, J. (2017) 'Postpolitics and Planning', in Gunder, M., Madanipour, A. and Watson, V. (eds), *The Routledge Handbook of Planning Theory*. London: Taylor & Francis Group, pp. 180–193.

Mexico City (2010) *Mexico City Charter for the Right to the City*. Mexico: Mexico City. Available at: www.hlrn.org/img/documents/Mexico_Charter_R2C_2010.pdf (accessed: 26 February 2021).

Miraftab, F. (2017) 'Insurgent Practices and Decolonization of Future(s)', in Gunder, M., Madanipour, A. and Watson, V. (eds), *The Routledge Handbook of Planning Theory*. London: Taylor & Francis Group, pp. 276–288.

Morais de Sá e Silva, M. (2020) 'Once Upon a Time, a Human Rights Ally: The State and its Bureaucracy in Right-Wing Populist Brazil', *Human Rights Quarterly*, 42(3), pp. 646–666. doi: 10.1353/hrq.2020.0036.

Moyn, S. (2018) *Not Enough: Human Rights in an Unequal World*. Cambridge, MA: The Belknap Press of Harvard University Press.

Oomen, B. and Baumgärtel, M. (2018) 'Frontier Cities: The Rise of Local Authorities as an Opportunity for International Human Rights Law', *European Journal of International Law*, 29(2), pp. 607–630. doi: 10.1093/ejil/chy021.

Oomen, B., Davis, M.F. and Grigolo, M. (eds) (2016) *Global Urban Justice: The Rise of Human Rights Cities*. Cambridge: Cambridge University Press.

Pinder, D. (2015) 'Reconstituting the Possible: Lefebvre, Utopia and the Urban Question', *International Journal of Urban and Regional Research*, 39(1), pp. 28–45. doi: 10.1111/1468-2427.12083.

Porter, L. (2010) *Unlearning the Colonial Cultures of Planning*. Farnham, UK and Burlington, VT: Ashgate Publishing Co.

Porter, L. (2014) 'Possessory Politics and the Conceit of Procedure: Exposing the Cost of Rights under Conditions of Dispossession', *Planning Theory*, 13(4), pp. 387–406. doi: 10.1177/1473095214524569.

Prigge, W. (2008) 'Reading the Urban Revolution: Space and Representation', in Goonewardena, K., Kipfer, S., Milgrom, R. and Schmid, C. (eds), *Space, Difference, Everyday Life: Reading Henri Lefebvre*. London and New York: Routledge, pp. 46–61.

Purcell, M. (2002) 'Excavating Lefebvre: The Right to the City and its Urban Politics of the Inhabitant', *GeoJournal*, 58(2–3), pp. 99–108.

Purcell, M. (2014) 'Possible Worlds: Henri Lefebvre and the Right to the City', *Journal of Urban Affairs*, 36(1), pp. 141–154. doi: 10.1111/juaf.12034.

Rogers, D. (2013). 'REDWatch: Monitory Democracy as a Radical Approach to Citizen Participation in Planning'. *Planning Theory & Practice*, 14 (4), 538–541. doi:10.1080/14649357.2013.853470.

Rolnik, R. (2014) 'Place, Inhabitance and Citizenship: The Right to Housing and the Right to the City in the Contemporary Urban World', *International Journal of Housing Policy*, 14(3), pp. 293–300. doi: 10.1080/14616718.2014.936178.

Ronneberger, K. (2008) 'Henri Lefebvre and Urban Everyday Life: In Search of the Possible', in Goonewardena, K., Kipfer, S., Milgrom, R. and Schmid, C. (eds), *Space, Difference, Everyday Life: Reading Henri Lefebvre*. London and New York: Routledge, pp. 134–146.

Ross, K. (1995) 'Fast Cars, Clean Bodies: Decolonization and the Reordering of French Culture'. Cambridge, MA: The MIT Press.

Sager, T. (2015) 'Ideological Traces in Plans for Compact Cities: Is Neo-liberalism Hegemonic?', *Planning Theory*, 14(3), pp. 268–295. doi: 10.1177/1473095214527279.

Soja, E.W. (1996) *Thirdspace: Journeys to Los Angeles and Other Real-and-imagined Places*. Cambridge, MA: Blackwell.

Soohoo, C. (2016) 'Human Rights Cities: Challenges and Possibilities', in Oomen, B., Davis, M.F. and Grigolo, M. (eds), *Global Urban Justice: The Rise of Human Rights Cities*. Cambridge: Cambridge University Press, pp. 257–275.

Stefanelli, A. (2020) 'Beyond the Organic Intellectual: Politics and Contestation in the Planning Practice', *City & Society*, 32(3), pp. 649–669. doi: 10.1111/ciso.12340.

United Cities and Local Governments (2012) *European Charter for the Safeguarding of Human Rights in the City (CISDP)*. Available at: https://www.uclg-cisdp.org/sites/default/files/CISDP%20Carta%20Europea%20Sencera_baixa_3.pdf (accessed: 11 September 2020).

Vardy, S. (2019) 'Urban Dissensus: Spatial Self-Organisation at Wards Corner', in Fisker, J.K. et al. (eds), *Enabling Urban Alternatives: Crises, Contestation, and Cooperation*. Singapore: Springer, pp. 65–81. doi: 10.1007/978-981-13-1531-2_4.

Young, I.M. (2002) *Inclusion and Democracy*. Oxford: Oxford University Press.

3. Lukes and power: three dimensions and three criticisms

Raine Mäntysalo

INTRODUCTION

Steven Lukes (born 1941) is a British political and social theorist, whose 'radical view of power', presented in a small book in 1974, has been highly influential among political scientists. However, towards the turn of the century his theory of power received remarkable criticism, too, with the rise of postmodernist and Foucauldian ideas of power (see Chapter 4 by Pløger). Thus, his notion of 'real interests', focus on agency, and approach to power as domination were challenged by a relativist view of interests, and emphasis on the structural and productive sides of power. In 2005, Lukes revisited his theory with an expanded edition of his book, defended it especially against the popular Foucauldian view, but made some crucial corrections to it, too. While a new generation of Lukes' followers emerged, much of the criticism was maintained. In this chapter, I will present Lukes' three-dimensional view of power, first as he originally formulated it (1974), and then the revisions he made to it (2005). Then I will discuss the main criticisms of it. Before concluding remarks, I will briefly review the applications of Lukes' theory of power in planning research, and make some initial suggestions for resolving the limitations and dilemmas in his theory.

LUKES' THREE-DIMENSIONAL THEORY OF POWER

Lukes' concept of power emphasizes analytical clarity, empirical applicability and critical normativity. For Lukes, power is exercised when *an actor 'A' affects another actor 'B' in a manner that is contrary to the latter's interests.* According to him, this basic definition is workable in research, 'that is, empirically useful in that hypotheses can be framed in terms of it that are in principle verifiable and falsifiable' (Lukes, 2005: 14). In addition, Lukes claims that the concept of power is unavoidably *value-dependent*: 'both its very definition and any given use of it, once defined, are inextricably tied to a given set of (probably unacknowledged) value-assumptions which predetermine the range of its empirical application' (Lukes, 2005: 30). Therefore, for Lukes (2005), power is an analytical concept, which is at once value-laden too.

This definition narrows the use of the concept of power crucially. In Lukes' terms, power is about control, domination and restraint – not about capacity, ability and enablement. Thus, Lukes conceives power as 'power over', not as 'power to'. In his 1974 book *Power: A Radical View*, he argues against Hannah Arendt's and Talcott Parsons's 'power to' approaches by claiming that their 'revisionary persuasive redefinitions of power' (Lukes, 2005, 34) are not in line with how power is traditionally understood and with the concerns usually associated with power. Thereby, 'the conflictual aspect of power – the fact that it is exercised *over* people

– disappears altogether from view' (Lukes, 2005: 34). In Lukes' terminology, the 'power to' instances of co-operative activity, where individuals and groups enable each other and gain shared capacities, are identified as instances of 'influence', not of 'power' (Lukes, 2005: 35).

The main target of Lukes' criticism, however, is the behaviourist approach to power, held by the so-called pluralists in American political science in the 1960s and early 1970s, fronted by the work of Robert A. Dahl. But instead of dismissing the behaviourist approach as incompatible with his, as in the case of Arendt and Parsons, Lukes is merely criticizing it as too shallow a view of power. In this, he draws on Peter Bachrach and Morton S. Baratz, who in their influential article, *The Two Faces of Power* (1962), argue that behind the 'face of power' that is directly observable in decision-making behaviour, there is a second, 'hidden' face of power. Beyond asking, 'who gets to decide', Bachrach and Baratz ask, who gets to set the agendas in terms of which decisions are made. Controversial interests may thereby be advanced by removing them from the horizons of those opposing them. However, Lukes argues that there is an even 'deeper', third face of power. Beyond manipulating decision agendas and thereby un-addressing the interests of those subjected to such power, power can be exercised by shaping the very wants and desires of those subjected to it. There are then cultural, ideological and institutional influences in place that shape the interests of those worse off in society – resulting in their assent to, and sometimes even support for, the circumstances unfavourable to them, against their 'real interests'.

Thus, the radical theory of power that Lukes developed in his 1974 book is, in his terms, 'three-dimensional' (Lukes, 2005: 15). He perceived the pluralists' view of power as one-dimensional, and Bachrach and Baratz's (1962) 'two-face view' two-dimensional. Through critically reflecting on these two views, Lukes built his own three-dimensional view. Next, I will review Lukes' account of each view in turn. Then, I will review how Lukes elaborated and corrected his theory in the revised edition of his book, published in 2005.

One-dimensional View

In explaining the one-dimensional view of power, Lukes draws mainly on the work of Dahl. He basically agrees with Dahl's concept of power: 'A has power over B to the extent that he can get B to do something that B would not otherwise do' (Lukes, 2005: 16). So, the exercise of power is observable, when A gets B to act against its own interests. But how should the exercise of power be observed, and how should the actors' interests be understood?

Dahl and other pluralists focused in their observations on behaviours in actual situations of political decision-making, such as city council meetings. The actors having power were identified as those who had succeeded in initiating proposals that had finally been adopted, or had vetoed proposals by other actors, when the actors had had conflicting interests. The actors having the largest share of successes were observed to be the most powerful.

Further, the pluralists understood interests as policy preferences. A conflict of interests is thereby understood as a conflict of policy preferences that are revealed in concrete decision-making situations. As Lukes (2005) notes, the pluralists were against the possibility that interests might be less articulate and observable in the behaviour of the participants in decision-making, not to mention the possibility that they might be unaware of their own interests.

Lukes' (2005: 19) conclusion of the one-dimensional view of power is that it 'involves a focus on behaviour in the making of decisions on issues over which there is an observable conflict of (subjective) interests, seen as express policy preferences, revealed by political participation'.

Two-dimensional View

As mentioned above, Bachrach and Baratz are critical of the one-dimensional view. Firstly, it 'takes no account of the fact that power may be, and often is, exercised by confining the scope of decision-making to relatively "safe issues"' (Bachrach and Baratz, 1962: 948). Secondly, it 'provides no *objective* criteria for distinguishing between "important and unimportant issues arising in the political arena"' (Bachrach and Baratz, 1962: 948). Bachrach and Baratz are against the idea that a sound concept of power could be built on the assumption that power would be fully embodied and reflected in the actions involved in the making of concrete decisions (Bachrach and Baratz, 1962: 948). In the view of Bachrach and Baratz (1962: 948),

> Power is also exercised when A devotes his energies to creating or reinforcing social and political values and institutional practices that limit the scope of the political process to public consideration of only those issues which are comparatively innocuous to A. To the extent that A succeeds in doing this, B is prevented, for all practical purposes, from bringing to the fore any issues that might in their resolution be seriously detrimental to A's set of preferences.

A may exercise power by participating in decision issues in the public domain (one-dimensional view), but also by working to keep certain issues from entering the public domain in the first place (two-dimensional view). When most successful, the latter is non-identifiable in the public processes of political decision-making.

To illustrate this, Lukes draws on Matthew Crenson's comparative study of policy-making in two neighbouring cities in Indiana, USA, which applied Bachrach and Baratz's (1962) approach. In the post-World War II decades, both cities had similar populations and suffered from similar levels of air pollution, but one of them, East Chicago, had adopted a policy to clear its air already in 1949, whereas for the other, Gary, it took thirteen years longer to adopt a similar policy. Crenson seeks an explanation for the delay in Gary from the fact that the prosperity of the city was dependent on one company, US Steel, which had a strong party organization. In turn, when East Chicago adopted its air pollution control policy, there were a number of steel companies without a strong party organization. With convincing use of documentation, Crenson builds a case of US Steel having prevented the air pollution issue from even being raised in Gary. To achieve this, no concrete action in the political arena had been necessary for US Steel; its mere reputation as a powerful actor had been sufficient to inhibit critical voices on the local air quality (Lukes, 2005).

Bachrach and Baratz call this *nondecision-making*: limiting decision-making 'to relatively non-controversial matters, by influencing community values and political procedures and rituals' (Bachrach and Baratz, 1962: 949). They draw on Schattschneider's (1960: 71) concept of *mobilization of bias*: 'All forms of political organization have a bias in favor of the exploitation of some kinds of conflict and the suppression of others, because organization is the mobilization of bias. Some issues are organized into politics while others are organized out'. Bachrach and Baratz (1962: 949) conclude: 'to the extent that a person or group – consciously or unconsciously – creates or reinforces barriers to the public airing of policy conflicts, that person or group has power'.

Hence, from this two-dimensional viewpoint, both decision-making between alternative choices and nondecision-making of preventing controversial issues from entering the decision-making arena, are to be included in the analysis of power in politics and policy-making. Regarding the analysis of nondecision-making, it is crucial for Bachrach and Baratz that the analysis is able to identify those potential issues that are prevented from becoming actualized.

Lukes, however, criticizes this view of power as being limited to the presumption of an actual, identifiable conflict of interests, whether overt or covert. Despite expanding critically the approach to power from that of the pluralists, Bachrach and Baratz's approach still shares with them the idea of connecting power to conflict. Moreover, Lukes (2005) claims that Bachrach and Baratz, too, view interests as policy preferences that are consciously articulated and observable. Lukes, in turn, argues that there is an even 'deeper' dimension of power that prevents the 'real interests' of those subjected to it from being articulated as policy preferences, and thereby prevents the identification of a conflict between preferences. 'The most effective and insidious use of power is to prevent such conflict from arising in the first place' (Lukes, 2005: 27).

Three-dimensional View

Lukes further criticizes Bachrach and Baratz for following the pluralists' Weberian approach in adopting a view of power that is methodologically too individualist. In Lukes' view, the 'actor' in question may be an organization (a group, a party, a corporation, a government, etc.), and hence no particular individuals exercising power may be identified. How, then, do these organizations exercise power? According to Lukes, there is more to it than decisions and choices made by individuals within these organizations. In explaining this, he returns to Schattschneider's idea of mobilization of bias. As exercise of power, the mobilization of bias ought to be understood as embodied in the constitution and purpose of the organization or system given. There is thus power that results from organizational or systemic effects, which cannot be attributed to individuals making decisions within these organizations or systems (Lukes, 2005). 'Decisions are choices consciously and intentionally made by individuals between alternatives, whereas the bias of the system can be mobilized, recreated and reinforced in ways that are neither consciously chosen nor the intended result of particular individuals' choices' (Lukes, 2005: 25).

According to Lukes, the bias of the system is sustained by deeper influences than by the mere choices made by individuals. Crucially, it is sustained 'by the socially structured and culturally patterned behaviour of groups, and practices of institutions, which may indeed be manifested by individuals' inaction' (Lukes, 2005: 27). A may exercise power over B by getting him to do what he does not want to do, but he also exercises power over him by 'influencing, shaping or determining his very wants' (Lukes, 2005: 27). Ultimately, such shaping of wants is part of processes of socialization.

Lukes argues that his three-dimensional view of power 'allows for consideration of the many ways in which potential issues are kept out of politics, whether through the operation of social forces and institutional practices or through individuals' decisions' (Lukes, 2005, 28). This may be realized, and most effectively so, without any conflict of interests in place. According to Lukes, there is always a potentiality for a conflict to actualize, but that may never happen. 'What one may have here is a latent conflict which consists in a contradiction between the interests of those exercising power and the *real interests* of those they exclude' (Lukes, 2005, 28). This notion of 'real interests' rests on Lukes' (2005: 38) position that 'people's wants may themselves be a product of a system which works against their interests, and, in such cases, relates the latter to what they would want and prefer, were they able to make the choice'.

The difficulty is how can the researcher identify these real interests, if they are not identified by the actors themselves? This is a question to which Lukes gives considerable thought, bearing in mind his ambition of developing an analytically and empirically applicable theory of power. According to Lukes (2005), the identification of real interests would ultimately have to rest on hypotheses, but such research designs are needed that would enable testing these hypotheses empirically. 'It is not impossible to adduce evidence – which must, by nature of the case, be indirect – to support the claim that an apparent case of consensus is not genuine but imposed' (Lukes, 2005: 49).

When studying what it is that the exercise of power prevents people from doing, and even from thinking, Lukes (2005) suggests that researchers should examine how people in subordinate positions react to perceived opportunities when they occur in societal hierarchies. Evidence can be presented of relevant counterfactuals that are implicit under the domination of three-dimensional power: 'One can take steps to find out what it is that people would have done otherwise' (Lukes, 2005: 52). But Lukes (2005) admits that such evidence cannot be conclusive, and justifying the relevant counterfactual may sometimes be extraordinarily difficult. Although the comparative case research approach of Brenson, discussed above, was more akin to studying two-dimensional power, Lukes sees it as an example of how three-dimensional power, too, could be examined. Providing a comparative lens to the air clean-up policy development of East Chicago enabled the identification of what had been suppressed in Gary (Lukes, 2005: 48–49).

An equal difficulty concerns the other end of the three-dimensional power relationship. How can evidence be found that a certain actor exercises three-dimensional power, when such an exercise may (1) be more about inaction than observable action, when it may (2) be unconscious, and when it may (3) be organizational or systemic? (Lukes, 2005: 52.) Lukes tackles each point in turn:

1. Inaction does not mean that we have a non-event with no features. If, in a given situation, an actor fails to make a certain choice, the consequences of this failure may become evident to the researcher, if s/he has hypothesized what the consequences could have been, had the actor made that choice. When hypothesized further, this inaction may be found to have led to further inaction, such as the non-appearance of a political issue, which would have emerged if an alternative course of action would have taken place. For Lukes (2005), a case in point is the 'causal nexus' between the inaction of US Steel and the public silence over air pollution in Gary.
2. How can one exercise power if one is doing it unconsciously? According to Lukes, there are many ways of being unconscious of what one is doing, but from the point of view of power analysis, the most problematic way is being unconscious of the consequences of one's action. 'Can A properly be said to exercise power over B where knowledge of the effects of A upon B is just not available to A?' (Lukes, 2005: 53). Lukes' answer depends on whether A can be expected to have had the means to find out the potential consequences of its action beforehand. For example, had gathering further data and making further tests

been ignored, when a drug company had brought a new drug to the market that was later on found to have dangerous side effects? If so, this would be a case of the drug company's power over the public. However, such an analysis needs to be critically aware of the trap of unfair hindsight wisdom, as in making posterior judgments on what culturally determined limits to cognitive innovation there had been in a certain historical situation. (Lukes, 2005: 53–54.)

3. The difficulty with organizations or systems exercising three-dimensional power is how to tell the difference between exercise of power and structural determination (Lukes, 2005: 54). This links to the age-old debate in sociology and political science between voluntarism and determinism, or agency and structure. In any organization or social system, the relationships between voluntary action and structural determination are complex. For Lukes, to speak about power is to speak about *human agency*: the choices that humans individually or collectively make or miss in their social contexts, and the constraints imposed and opportunities afforded by these contexts. 'In speaking thus, one assumes that, although the agents operate within structurally determined limits, they none the less have a certain relative autonomy and could have acted differently' (Lukes, 2005: 57). To the degree there is room for agency, there is room for power – and 'within a system characterized by total structural determinism, there would be no place for power' (Lukes, 2005: 57).

> To identify a given process as an 'exercise of power', rather than as a case of structural determination, is to assume that it is in the exerciser's or exercisers' power to act differently. In the case of a collective exercise of power, or the part of a group, or institution, etc., this is to imply that the members of the group or institution could have combined or organized to act differently. (Lukes, 2005: 57)

Following Lukes (2005: 58), as power is about human agency, it is also about *responsibility*: 'an attribution of power is at the same time an attribution of (partial or total) responsibility for certain consequences'. Thus, an actor that exercises power through its action or inaction is to be held responsible for the consequences thereby brought.

As we will see later on in this chapter, the notions above that Lukes attaches to his three-dimensional view of power – the postulation of real interests and the attribution of power to human agency – have been subjects of notable criticism. In the 2005 revision of his book he responds to his critics and refines his theory further. His response, however, did not silence his critics, and the refinements he made to his theory aroused some further criticism.

Lukes' Theory Revised

The revised edition of *Power: A Radical View* (2005) included the original book as its first chapter, and two new chapters, making the book three times longer than the original fifty-page version. In the new chapters Lukes comments on the newer research discourses on power, especially around Michel Foucault, responds to commentaries on his work and makes some refinements to his own theory of power.

Most crucially, Lukes redefines his concept of power, announcing that the theory he had previously developed is not, after all, about power *per se*, which he now sees as a broader concept. Instead of 'power', he now speaks of 'domination', arguing that his three-dimensional view is concerned with 'securing of compliance to domination' (Lukes, 2005: 109). In turn, his notion of power as a broader category now receives attributes in the sense of 'power to': 'Power is a capacity not the exercise of that capacity (it may never be, and never need to be, exercised); and you can be powerful by satisfying and advancing others' interests: (the original book's) topic, power as domination, is only one species of power' (Lukes, 2005: 12).

With such narrowing down of the focus of his theory, as dealing with how the powerful secure the compliance of those they dominate, Lukes largely maintains its argumentation, although he acknowledges its view of power relations as too simplistic. Power relations are more complex than binary relations (A and B) between actors, each possessing unitary inter-ests. The relations between actors are usually more multiple, and the actors' own interests are also multiple, differentiated and conflicting (Lukes, 2005). In defending his concept of real interests as necessary for identifying domination, Lukes turns to Baruch Spinoza. People are free when enabled to live according to their 'dictates of nature', and domination is about rendering them less free, 'by restricting their capabilities for truly human functioning' (Lukes, 2005: 118). Lukes suggests that the human 'dictates of nature' have an objective, transcultural basis, relying further on the 'capabilities approach' by Amartya Sen and Martha Nussbaum. The idea is that there are certain functions that characterize life as distinctively human, so that their absence also means the absence of human life. Furthermore, human beings are self-directed, shaping their lives in mutual cooperation and reciprocity. The assumption is that there are certain human capabilities that are central to any human life across cultures. While humans have all sorts of pursuits, these central capabilities are not instrumental to them but have value in themselves in making life human (Lukes, 2005).

For Lukes (2005), the concept of 'interests' refers to what is important in people's lives. Interests may be conceived as necessary conditions of human welfare. 'Here I have in mind what political philosophers variously call 'primary goods' (Rawls) or 'resources' (Dworkin) that satisfy basic needs … or else endow people with basic human capabilities (Sen) or 'central capabilities' (Nussbaum)' (Lukes, 2005: 81). They include 'such basic items as health, ade-quate nourishment, bodily integrity, shelter, personal security, an unpolluted environment, and so on' (Lukes, 2005: 82). Which of these basic welfare interests are to be treated as generally valid human interests, and which are to be seen as specific to particular regions of culture? Rather than answering this question, Lukes (2005: 82) points to the importance of approaching welfare interests in this manner, which leads to treating them as objective instead of preference-dependent: 'conditions that damage your health are against your interests, in this sense, whatever your preferences, and even if you actively seek to promote them'.

For Lukes, real interests thus understood provide an external objective standpoint for identifying domination and its consequences. If domination is about constraining actors' real interests, to the extent of inducing 'false' and 'distorted' ideas of what their real interests are, an objective standpoint is needed to tell the 'false interests' apart from the 'true interests' (Lukes, 2005: 121).

At the core of human real interests is to be self-directed, to be able to make independent judgements and live accordingly – and this is what domination restricts. This notion is also the main source of Lukes' criticism of Foucault. In Lukes' reading, Foucault sees no escape from domination. By imposing regimes of truth, domination prevails everywhere in Foucault's world, and there is no state available to humans for more self-directed living (Lukes, 2005). With such a Nietzschean rhetoric, Foucault undermines 'the model of the rational, autonomous moral agent', in Lukes' view (Lukes, 2005: 92). 'If Foucault is right, then we must abandon "the emancipatory ideal of a society in which individuals are free from the negative effects of power" and the conventional view that power can be based on the rational consent of its subjects' (Lukes, 2005: 92).

Lukes is much more sympathetic to Pierre Bourdieu's sociological theory and its rootedness in ethnographic studies of social practices. Lukes especially views Bourdieu's concept of 'symbolic violence' as similar to his own idea of domination in the third dimension – in how agents' dispositions in stratified social spaces become embodied and 'naturalized in their habituses', in processes of socialization and cultural production of knowledge (Lukes, 2005: 141). Similarly to Lukes' own idea of domination being most successful when exercised unconsciously, Bourdieu's (1987: 31) symbolic violence is conducted unconsciously by 'strategies of distinction', which Bourdieu saw as the best of strategies, as they are not recognized as strategies at all. What remains unclear, however, is the degree of determination of this unreflective socialization and enculturation, and where, when and how cracks can be opened for actors' 'discursive' learning and self-transformation (Lukes, 2005: 143).

THREE CRITICISMS

There are three main criticisms of Lukes' theory of power. The first concerns his concept of real interests, and the related assumption of an objective standpoint for the analyst. The critics ask, is the analyst thereby taking a superior position, assuming that they know better what people's interests are than they themselves? A further critical question follows as to whether the researcher is thereby mixing analysis and normative critique.

The second criticism concerns Lukes' view of power as being exercised by human agents who should be assigned responsibility for the consequences of their exercise of power. While Lukes acknowledges the limitations of human agency within organizations and systems, the critics ask, whether he undermines the role of structural power, and whether focusing on actors' responsibilities obscures appropriate structural analysis.

The third criticism concerns Lukes' redefinition of power that he made in the revised edition of his book. Here, the critical debate concerns the plausibility of Lukes' distinction between 'power over' and 'power to', and the very foundations of his approach to power.

In this section, I will review all these main criticisms by drawing on Lukes' commentaries, as well as on later work by Lukes himself.

Real Interests: Analysis or Critique?

As discussed above, the very idea of power in the third dimension requires that the analyst assumes an external standpoint, a position for separating people's real interests from those preferences that they are led to support (Lukes, 2005: 146). According to Colin Hay (1997: 47), Lukes thereby turns the analyst into a 'supreme arbiter of the genuine interest of the "victim"'. In his criticism to Lukes' original book, Hay (1997: 47) notices that with his concept of real interests Lukes thus 'resurrects the spectre of false consciousness which many had thought exorcised from contemporary social and political theory'. Lukes (2005: 149) openly acknowledges this in the revised edition of his book:

> False consciousness is an expression that carries a heavy weight of unwelcome historical baggage. But that weight can be removed if one understands it to refer, not to the arrogant assertion of a privi-

leged access to truths presumed unavailable to others, but rather to a cognitive power of considerable significance and scope: namely, the power to mislead.

In a later article, Lukes (2011) further defends the plausibility of the Marxist concept of false consciousness (see Chapter 1), and the critical approach implied in it. As an example of false consciousness, he mentions the 'illusion of free markets', referring to Bernard Harcourt's work. Harcourt has traced the origins of perceiving market processes as 'natural' and government interventions as 'artificial' to Physiocrats in the eighteenth century. It involves the 'illusion' that market transactions, if left undisturbed, would achieve equilibrium – an illusion, which matured in the nineteenth and twentieth century into a doctrine of the inherent efficiency of the markets. Such 'naturalization' of markets is a powerful notion against normative judgments on the stark wealth distribution effects that are brought by them. Further, it masks the legal coercion involved, in providing the necessary legal and regulatory frameworks for the supposedly free markets to operate (Lukes, 2011).

In Lukes' view, an analyst allowing him/herself to make such critical reflections on false consciousness, or on the inhibition of one's real interests, does not entail assuming any epistemic privilege. The aim, after all, is 'to specify the various sources of these failures of reasoning and understanding and to ascertain to what extent they are irremediable and to what extent rectifiable' (Lukes, 2011: 28). Such a normative task could not be undertaken, if the analyst would take a Foucault-inspired position of perceiving each thought construct as belonging to equally valid 'regimes of truth', determined by power (Lukes, 2011: 19).

However, Lukes' approach makes it difficult to tell the difference between analysis and normative critique. This is another point of Hay's criticism, as he argues that for Lukes already the identification of a power relationship is, in effect, to engage in critique (Hay, 1997). 'Within such a schema power is not so much an analytical category as a critical category' (Hay, 1997: 49). In Hay's (2011) view, Lukes is close to confusing analysis and critique, as sometimes Lukes is aware of the value-laden nature of the concept of power, and thereby the unavoidability of being evaluative when identifying domination; but then, in turn, he also argues for developing an empirical basis for the identification of real interests, thereby emphasizing the approach to power as an analytical concept.

Hay (1997: 49) argues that conflating the identification of power and the critique of its exercise leads to perceiving power as 'a purely pejorative concept by a definitional fiat'. Power thus defined cannot be legitimately and responsibly exercised. 'The essence of power is negative, the purpose of critique to expose power relations as a potential means to their elimination' (Hay, 1997: 49). Lukes responds to this criticism in his 2005 revision by broadening his concept of power to include legitimate and capability-building forms of power, while reframing the subject of his earlier theory to be merely about 'one species' of power, that is, domination.

However, Clare Heyward (2007) and Keith Dowding (2006) argue that the actual problem of Lukes' theorizing is not the conflation of analysis and normative critique. Heyward (2007: 54) claims: 'If we are to move towards a complete analysis of all political issues, we must accept the normative aspects of any theoretical framework and its most central political concepts, including the conception of power'. Dowding (2006: 137) agrees: 'Lukes, just like anyone else, can analyse and evaluate the situation of others. To suggest that people are always the best judge of their own interests and have privileged moral status over their own preferences is to deny any sort of normative social analysis.'

The problem, they both argue, is Lukes' focus on agency at the expense of structure, especially in the original version of his theory. Neglecting structural power leads to deeming all those who gain at the expense of others as dominant, and viewing everyone who loses as being dominated by someone (Dowding, 2006). Peter Morriss (2006) speaks of 'paranoid fallacy'; of assuming that if people lack power, this must be a result of them being dominated by someone – a criticism which Lukes acknowledges in his revised edition (Lukes, 2005: 68). Dowding (2006: 137) appropriately asks: 'Must the dominant need to know what they are doing or can their privilege be a by-product of forces they do not understand?' Dowding (2006) suggests an alternative approach, pointing towards structural power analysis. He proposes breaking down values to the component parts of *beliefs* and *desires*. In Dowding's view, domination is about beliefs contradicting desires. People have certain desires, but they may have been socialized or indoctrinated into holding certain beliefs that work against these desires, or lead astray from them (Dowding, 2006).

> Given someone's desires, their false beliefs may lead them to act in ways which do not further those desires … So we have two ways of explaining objective interests, one based on false belief, and one based upon the (contingent) structure of the situation someone faces. However, Lukes wants a further notion of objective interest than those suggested here. He not only wants to look at the situation of people and their beliefs: he also wants to criticise their desires. (Dowding, 2006: 138)

The 'illusion of free markets', discussed above, could be approached as a deep-seated cultural belief that, at least to a degree, brings undesirable outcomes, when exceedingly applied in various realms of society – such as real estate markets – the freedom of which is conditioned by various structural factors, irrespective of whether the public sector intervenes in them or not (see next section). But is there anyone to be held responsible for these undesirable outcomes?

Actors or Structures?

Lukes associates power with responsibility. It means that power concerns human agency, either individual or collective (Hayward and Lukes, 2008). According to Lukes, power is exercised by agents, albeit within the constraints of their structural circumstances. Understanding social life thus requires approaching it 'as an interplay of power and structure, a web of possibilities for agents, whose nature is both active and structured, to make choices and pursue strategies within given limits, which in consequence expand and contract over time' (Lukes, 2005: 68–69).

Lukes claims that depending on the structural constraints and their complexity at play, the powerful agents' responsibility may be *moral* but often also *political*. We can place the *moral* blame on discriminatory landlords and corrupt planning officials – but, at different levels of governance, we place *political* responsibility on planners, decision-makers and other key actors who, individually or jointly, we perceive as having a capacity to make a difference in the face of societal problems, but who fail to do so (Lukes, 2005). 'We can and often do hold agents responsible for consequences they neither intend nor positively intervene to bring about' (Hayward and Lukes, 2008: 7).

In an article constructed in the form of dialogue, Lukes and Clarissa Hayward discuss the example of the poor and racially oppressed who are denied access to decent and affordable housing. Lukes claims: 'Insofar as this problem is due to the action or inaction of identifiable individuals or groups or institutions, that, by acting otherwise, could have made a difference, then it makes sense to see the latter as powerful because responsible' (Hayward and Lukes, 2008: 7). Yet, he admits that often it is very difficult and sometimes even impossible to trace where particular contributions and responsibilities lie (Hayward and Lukes, 2008).

Hayward, in turn, provides a reminder that neither deindustrialization, nor the flight of well-to-do whites from the older American cities to the suburbs, was an intentional coordinated process. The combined effects on those 'left behind' were not caused by some 'bad men, but structural forces' (Hayward and Lukes, 2008: 9–10). Hayward argues that 'if the aim is not to wag a moralizing finger, but to criticize and inform efforts to change relations of power and domination, then it is necessary to examine the structural constraints that help shape those relations' (Hayward and Lukes, 2008: 10–11). Such a structural examination of power leads one to address, not only moral, but also political responsibility.

Morriss (2006), in turn, argues that evaluative critique of societal structures is qualitatively very different from distributing responsibility to agents, even if it were of political nature. It demands a distinction between *being powerless* and *being dominated*, which Lukes blurs, in Morriss' (2006) view. While indeed there are people who lack power because of being dominated by identifiable actors, there are also people who are powerless *without* being dominated, but because of structural incapacitation. If this powerlessness is to be viewed as injustice, then the focus should be on how to change the social set-up reproducing such powerlessness. This does not require identifying certain agents that could be assigned with responsibility:

> Many Marxists used to argue that capitalism is unjust *even though* (or, perhaps, *particularly because*) no blame could attach to any individuals; that was thought to be precisely why the whole system had to be swept away. That position may (or may not) have been factually inaccurate, but it was certainly not logically incoherent. Hence, we do need to keep social evaluation separate from individual responsibility; it is a fault of Lukes' analysis that such a gap seems impossible within it. (Morriss, 2006: 130)

Morriss argues that Lukes' difficulties in locating power in the agency–structure interrelationship follow from his insistence on working with the 'power-over' approach. The structural dimension falls out of its grasp: 'structural power' appears paradoxical, or structures have to be assigned responsibility for exercising power over people. But, in Morriss' view, this dilemma fades away when the approach is shifted to *power to*, and when evaluation of social structures is relieved from the burden of attributing responsibility: 'for there is no difficulty in saying that structures limit the ends that people can obtain (and should, for that reason, be altered)' (Morriss, 2006: 130).

Power Over or Power To?

In Morriss' (2006: 126) view, the essence of power is 'power to: the ability to effect outcomes – not the ability to affect others'. In his revised book, Lukes (2005: 65) admits this: a better definition of power in social life than that offered (in the original book) is in terms of 'agents' abilities to bring about significant effects'. A local government, for example, exercises power over people in making decisions on zoning plans; yet it does so not for the purpose of dominating people, but more likely for the purpose of attaining certain outcomes (such as well functioning and sustainable built environment, management of estimated population growth, fair treatment of land-owners' property rights, attractiveness and competitiveness of the municipality for investors and developers, etc.). The local government's 'power over' is thereby exercised as a means for achieving certain ends ('power to'). The intention is not to dominate the constituents of the local government subjected to its authority, but to empower them. Unlike domination, such form of power over can be seen as legitimate authority.

What Lukes ended up doing in his revision was that he reframed his theory to concern only a sub-set of power: 'power over'. Actually not even that, since by rearticulating his theory as one about 'securing of compliance to domination', his concern was only on a sub-set of 'power over' – bypassing the type of 'power over' that is exercised as instrumental to 'power to' (Morriss, 2006: 131), such as legitimate authority of public planning and decision-making. Thereby Lukes' 'domination' misses what he himself understood power to be about fundamentally: the ability to bring about significant effects – not about securing compliance. Hence Morriss (2006: 134) concludes: 'He can separate his concept of domination altogether from that of power and retain intact the three-dimensional view – although it will not, of course, now be a three-dimensional view of *power*'.

LUKES AND POWER IN PLANNING RESEARCH: A WAY FORWARD?

Besides political science, Lukes has been influential in planning research, too, although – similarly to political science – his impact has been overshadowed by that of Foucault. Most probably, it is through John Forester's influential work on *planning in the face of power* (Forester, 1982; 1989) that Lukes has been introduced to the community of planning researchers. Forester applied Lukes' theory in elaborating the difference between structural and voluntary misinformation in planning. Regarding the latter, he distinguished different types of misinformation available for planners in their interactions with stakeholders, by using Jürgen Habermas' criteria of validity of claims in communication (managing comprehension, trust, consent or knowledge) (Forester, 1989).

However, only a few planning researchers have used Lukes' three-dimensional view explicitly, in analysing power in planning. These include Mhairi Aitken's (2010) case study of how public participation on a planning proposal for wind power development in Scotland was managed; and John Sturzaker's (2010) case study of how power was exercised by rural elites in the English countryside, to prevent new housing development. Additionally, Lukes' approach has been used in combination with other approaches. With Mark Shucksmith, Sturzaker added the perspective of Bourdieu's 'symbolic violence', in studying further how the rural elites in England, by their discursive uses of 'sustainability', warded off new housing (Sturzaker and Shucksmith, 2011). In turn, Raine Mäntysalo and Inger-Lise Saglie combined Lukes' three dimensions of power and Fritz Scharpf's types of political legitimacy, in investigating how power was exercised in different dimensions to legitimize preliminary partnership arrangements in urban housing planning in Norway and Finland. With Kaisa Schmidt-Thomé, Mäntysalo associated Lukes' theory of power with Gregory Bateson's theories of power and learning, coming up with an analytical framework where Lukes' three dimensions of power are combined with Bateson's three levels of learning (Schmidt-Thomé and Mäntysalo, 2014). With a case study of public resistance and empowerment against a massive development project in the Stuttgart railway station area in Germany, Schmidt-Thomé and Mäntysalo sought to reveal the value of Bateson's theoretical work in complementing Lukes' limited view of power.

Indeed, in view of the main criticisms against Lukes' theory, discussed above, Bateson's (1987) approach to power, outlined in his theory of alcoholism, offers a promising broader perspective of power. Firstly, the view of 'power over' as a sub-set of 'power to', is understood, in a Batesonian reading, as a subsystem of the broader ecosystem of 'power to' of human activity. The application of Bateson's view in Cultural-Historical Activity Theory, outlined by Yrjö Engeström (1987; Engeström et al., 1999), expands the focus on human activity to historically and culturally evolved 'activity systems' of organisations. In these activity systems, 'power over' is a necessary form of power, in divisions of roles, authority relations and institutional rules applied, being instrumental to their 'power to'. But this 'power over' is inclined to lead to contradictions where this instrumentality is lost, turning to domination that threatens the sustained performance of the activity system. These contradictions may lead to systemic *double binds* – a key concept in Bateson's work, also adopted by Bourdieu (see Bourdieu and Wacquant, 1995). An alcoholic may be faced with a double bind situation – 'hit the bottom' – upon realizing that his/her repeated attempts of gaining 'power over' the 'bottle' have led him/her to a state of mental and/or physical incapacity, loss of 'power to'. An organization, in turn, may be faced with a double bind situation, when some of the core beliefs that inform its operations cease to reflect its present-day operational contexts, either due to becoming outdated or overly stretching the realm of their applicability. Then a cultural-historical analysis of these core beliefs and their contextual implications is needed, to build critical reflectivity on the repeated mismatches between core beliefs and contemporary contexts in the organizational activity.

In my view, the concept of double bind can be explained by referring to Dowding's idea of values as consisting of beliefs and desires. As discussed above, in Dowding's explanation, unreasonable conditions result when the beliefs generally held determine living and working arrangements in ways that are contradictory to the more profound desires held. When unreasonable beliefs are maintained by domination in an activity system, the more profound ecosystemic desires connected to the sustenance of the activity system are threatened. Take the belief in the infallibility of the free market. Associate this belief with a realm, where markets are dominated at the outset, the goods to be traded are unique and bound to their sites, access to them is unevenly distributed and historically determined, and the very functioning of the market in this realm is dependent on public interventions via *planning*. Generally real estate markets are such structurally constrained realms. Treating them as infallible free markets might threaten their sustenance as market systems (see Alexander, 2001; Klostermann, 1985; Moore, 1978; Virtanen, 1991). When this happens, analysing the double bind of the dysfunctional real estate market inappropriately treated as free market requires a cultural-historical analysis of the origins of the belief of the free market and the societal circumstances implied in it – in relation to the rules, arrangements and conditions actually at play in a given real estate market. Hence, a *structural* analysis is needed, to offer the *actors* insights that are necessary for generating more appropriate beliefs, in guiding the performance of real estate markets and taking part in them.

Moreover, postulating an external real interest is not necessary when the analysis is focused on the subsystem/ecosystem double binds within the studied activity system itself – such as the subsystemic 'free market' belief recurrently contradicting the ecosystemic desire for the sustained functioning of the real estate market. The incapacitating effects of domination, deteriorating the ecosystemic 'power to' of the given activity system, can be analysed by examining the inner contradictions and double binds of the system itself – whether we are interested in the real estate market system or any other activity system.

CONCLUDING REMARKS

As the critical discussion around Lukes' theory reveals, the theory is rather about domination as exercised in three dimensions, dismissing a broader view of power regarding its capability-building aspects. While the criticisms on Lukes' theory of power reveal its limitations and shortcomings, there are some important insights to be gained in planning research from both Lukes' theory and its criticisms. Firstly, take Lukes' (2005: 82) approach to 'interests', as including 'such basic items as health, adequate nourishment, bodily integrity, shelter, personal security, an unpolluted environment, and so on'. With such an understanding of interests, 'real interests' represent for Lukes that of taking an analytical 'objective' standpoint for identifying domination and its consequences – rather than assuming the necessity of determining real interests in transcendental terms. The correlation to the concept of 'public interest' in planning is evident. The concept of public interest is controversial, the approaches to it are varying (such as utilitarian, unitary, rights-based and dialogical) with even contradictory derivations, but, nonetheless, the concept is still found necessary in evaluating and legitimizing public planning (e.g. Alexander, 2002; Campbell and Marshall, 2002; Moroni, 2004). When associating Lukes' concept of real interests with the concept of public interest in planning research interested in domination, the implication would be to draw on the standpoint of public interest negatively in the sense of identifying domination that does *not* correspond with the public interest; while the normativity of one's research interest for arriving to this 'objective' standpoint would have to be openly revealed.

Secondly, the distinction between domination and legitimate authority is crucial when studying the limitations and resources for the justification of public planners' exercise of 'power over'. Lukes' theory, and Forester's application of it, sensitize planning researchers to planners' varying possibilities for exercising domination over other actors involved in and subjected to planning. But public planners' 'power over', provided to them through their societal and institutional positions and professional expertise, is also unavoidable and indeed societally necessary. In Habermasian terms, it is part of the necessary rationalization of society (Habermas, 1984), which in its appropriate forms is instrumental to communal and societal 'power to'. This would warrant legitimacy of the authority of the public planner.

Thirdly, despite Morriss' claim that focusing on political responsibility might obscure appropriate structural analysis, when reasons for powerlessness of certain groups are structural and not the outcome of certain actors' domination, identification of political responsibility is still necessary *after* the structural analysis has been made. Structures, public institutions and governmental policies, are not immutable, but may be subjected to reforms when revealed to produce unjust and unsatisfactory outcomes. Then it is the political decision-makers, and public planners on whose advice they rely, to be identified as responsible for making and managing such revisions. For *normative* planning research interested in structural power, a sufficient research result may not be the structural analysis as such. There may well be a further motivation of gaining insights on what public planners, having a degree of power and thereby *responsibility* to amend the structures, *can do*, when the structures are found to lead to unjust powerlessness.

REFERENCES

Aitken, M. (2010), 'A Three-dimensional View of Public Participation in Scottish Land-use Planning: Empowerment or Social Control?', *Planning Theory*, 9 (3), 248–264.

Alexander, E.R. (2001), 'Why Planning vs. Markets is an Oxymoron: Asking the Right Question', *Planning and Markets*, 1 (1), www-pam.usc.edu/volume4/v4i1a2print.html (accessed 28 November 2015).

Alexander, E.R. (2002), 'The Public Interest in Planning: From Legitimation to Substantive Plan Evaluation', *Planning Theory*, 1 (3), 226–249.

Bachrach, Peter and M.S. Baratz (1962), 'Two Faces of Power', *The American Political Science Review*, 56 (4), 947–952.

Bateson, G. (1987), *Steps to an Ecology of Mind*, Northvale, NJ: Jason Aronson.

Bell, J.P.W. and A. Stockdale (2016), 'Examining Participatory Governance in a Devolving UK: Insights from National Parks Policy Development in Northern Ireland', *Environment and Planning C: Government and Policy*, 34 (8), 1516–1539.

Bourdieu, P. (1987), *Sosiologian kysymyksiä*, Tampere: Vastapaino.

Bourdieu, P. and L.J.D. Wacquant (1995), *Refleksiiviseen sosiologiaan*, Joensuu: Joensuu University Press.

Campbell, H. and Marshall, R. (2002), 'Utilitarianism's Bad Breath? A Re-evaluation of the Public Interest Justification for Planning', *Planning Theory*, 1 (2), 163–187.

Dowding, K. (2006), 'Three-dimensional Power: A Discussion of Steven Lukes' Power: A Radical View', *Political Studies Review*, 4, 136–145.

Engeström, Y. (1987), *Learning by Expanding*, Helsinki: Orienta-konsultit.

Engeström, Y., R. Miettinen and R.-L. Punamäki (1999), *Perspectives on Activity Theory*, Cambridge: Cambridge University Press.

Forester, J. (1982), 'Planning in the Face of Power', *Journal of the American Planning Association*, 48 (1), 67–80.

Forester, J. (1989), *Planning in the Face of Power*, Berkeley, CA: University of California Press.

Habermas, J. (1984), *The Theory of Communicative Action. Volume 1 – Reason and the Rationalization of Society*, Boston, MA: Beacon Press.

Hay, C. (1997), 'Divided by a Common Language: Political Theory and the Concept of Power', *Politics*, 17 (1), 45–52.

Hayward, C. and S. Lukes (2008), 'Nobody to Shoot? Power, Structure, and Agency: A Dialogue', *Journal of Power*, 1 (1), 5–20.

Heyward, C. (2007), 'Revisiting the Radical View: Power, Real Interests and the Difficulty of Separating Analysis from Critique', *Politics*, 27 (1), 48–54.

Hutchings, K. (2005), 'Book Review: Steven Lukes, Power: A Radical View 2nd ed.', *Millennium: Journal of International Studies*, 33 (3), 889–891.

Klostermann, R.E. (1985), 'Arguments For and Against Planning', *Town Planning Review*, 56 (1), 5–20.

Lukes, S. (2005), *Power: A Radical View*, second edition, Houndmills, UK and New York: Palgrave Macmillan.

Lukes, S. (2011), 'In Defense of "False Consciousness"', *University of Chicago Legal Forum*, 2011/3, 19–28.

Mäntysalo, R. and I.-L. Saglie (2010), 'Private Influence Preceding Public Involvement', *Planning Theory and Practice*, 11 (3), 317–338.

Moore, T. (1978), 'Why Allow Planners to Do What They Do? A Justification from Economic Theory', *Journal of the American Institute of Planners*, 44 (4), 387–398.

Moroni, S. (2004), 'Towards a Reconstruction of the Public Interest Criterion', *Planning Theory*, 3 (2), 151–171.

Morriss, P. (2006), 'Steven Lukes on the Concept of Power', *Political Studies Review*, 4, 124–135.

Schattschneider, E.E. (1960), *The Semisovereign People: A Realist's View of Democracy in America*, New York: Holt, Rhinehart & Winston.

Schmidt-Thomé, K. and R. Mäntysalo (2014), 'Interplay of Power and Learning in Planning Processes: A Dynamic View', *Planning Theory*, 13 (2), 115–135.

Sturzaker, J. (2010), 'The Exercise of Power to Limit the Development of New Housing in the English Countryside', *Environment and Planning A: Economy and Space*, 42 (4), 1001–1016.

Sturzaker, J. and M. Shucksmith (2011), 'Planning for Housing in Rural England: Discursive Power and Spatial Exclusion', *Town Planning Review*, 82 (2), 169–193.

Virtanen, P.V. (1991), Kiinteistömarkkinoiden ominaisuuksia ja erityispiirteitä, Espoo: Teknillinen korkeakoulu, Maanmittaustekniikan laitos, Kiinteistöoppi, julkaisu B 57.

4. Michel Foucault, power and planning

John Pløger

INTRODUCTION

Michel Foucault (2000: 284; Metzger et al., 2017) insisted throughout his life that 'power is what needs to be explained'. This is not least because power is everywhere, 'in the smallest elements', and human beings are thus always placed within power–knowledge relations (Foucault, 1986a: 209; see also Elden, 2016, 2017).

Foucault's understanding of power revolted against a structural perspective on power as owned, hierarchical, repressive, and fixed. Rather than looking for power as the effect of institutional structures, rules, and regulations, we should look for how power circulates, how it is exercised, how it is productive, how power is configured to knowledge, and the effects of the micro-powers of power. He explored how power–knowledge relations became part of the governing of life from mechanisms like discipline, truth, reason, advice, and discourse. Psychiatry, medicine, science, and architecture are forces of governing working as knowledge apparatus' acting 'in' the body rather than 'on' the body.

We must look for 'the mesh of power' (Foucault, 2012) – how power is a mesh connecting governing and forms of knowledge constitutive of certain kinds of discipline, procedures, and techniques. We have to be nominalists on power; it is a name and not a substance, and we have to be pluralists on understanding power. There is no single power.

Starting from outlining how power and knowledge are conditions of possibility, the chapter moves into three entrances to understand how planning as power is exercised. The first area is the apparatus (governing, governmentalization, governmentality). The second area is power as a mode of praxis and an effect (*techne*, discipline, ethos). This includes exploring space as policing and planning as a *techne*. The third area is the micro-physics of power (security, discipline) and power as subjectification (norm, normation). The next section discusses how the concept *dispositif* is crucial to an understanding on this issue, and how power–knowledge relations are generative and become micro-powers. Before concluding, there is a section briefly introducing some recent research on Foucault.

THE HOW OF POWER: CONDITIONS OF POSSIBILITY

> Power is nothing more than a certain modification, or the form, differing from time to time, of a series of clashes which constitute the social body, clashes of the political, economic type etc. Power, then, is something like the stratification, the institutionalization, the definition of tactics, of implements and arms which are useful in all these clashes. (Foucault, 1989: 188)

There is no such thing as power; there is only power exercised and clashes (e.g., resistance). The 'how' of power is its mechanisms, elements, and 'net-like organisations' (Foucault, 1980: 98) that differ in their capacity to produce effects. Rather than being the effect of institutionalized structures such as the law, economy, politics, the army, or police (Foucault, 1980: 88), power ascends from local relations and mechanisms invested in a certain problematic responding to 'an urgent need' (Foucault, 1980: 195). Relations of power emerge because they are useful to specific reasons or tactics and advantageous at a given moment or in specific conjunctures. This makes power an 'extremely complex configuration of realities' (Foucault, 1980: 217), not only because of the many (in)visible forces at play, but also because it means power is 'exercised … through and by means of conditions of possibility' (Colin Gordon in Foucault, 1980: 237).

The condition of possibility points, first, to the fact that relations of power are not static, but 'elaborated, transformed, organized' (Foucault, 1986a: 224). Power is emerging rooted in different types of events and relations of forces and will always become rooted in a 'system of social networks' (Foucault, 1986a: 224). Second, there is always 'a specificity to power relations, a density, an inertia, a viscosity, a course of development, and inventiveness which belonged to these relationships' from the immediacy and simultaneity of multiple forces constitutive to the possibility (Foucault, 1989: 184).

Foucault (1986a: 223–224)) suggested certain points of mapping of how the 'conditions of possibility' at a given time and in a certain conjuncture are rooted in a configuration of forces and elements:

- *The systems of differentiation* that condition the operation of 'acting upon others', such as the law, economic difference, knowledge, and culture.
- *The types of objectives* pursued, such as profit, authority, trade, or privileges.
- *The means of bringing power relations into being*, such as 'threat of arms', economic differences, control and surveillance, rules, and technologies.
- *Forms of institutionalization*, such as legal structures, customs of ruling, the military, school, asylums, or imprisonment.
- *The degree of rationalization*, which may depend on the field of possibilities, the effectiveness of instruments, and/or the certainty of a particular result.

The condition of possibility has a genealogy, but the configuration of a possibility is not objective to a past but related to the configuration of forces that emerges from the rationality of knowledge, aims, and ends-supporting strategies, tactics, or clashes – or better, the strategic developments, the tactics, and the interdependent specificity, complementarity, or blockages of forces (Foucault, 1980: 188).

Foucault for instance referred to the Classical period, where he saw 'a new "economy" of power' developing. This was a thinking about an 'economization' of forces, which allowed 'the effects of power' to circulate more or less 'uninterrupted' and '"individualised" throughout the entire social body' (Foucault, 1980: 119). In order to administrate, control, and direct the productive 'accumulation of men', society and cities needed to get access to people's 'acts, attitudes, and modes of everyday behaviour' (Foucault, 1980: 125).

Power always includes this kind of discourse–knowledge formation, but a power–knowledge relation can strengthen, support, make, or displace aims and strategies of governing. Power relations work discretely, anonymously, and indefinitely on the body and mind through representations, signs, language, statements, norms, and reason that are forces applied to the body as a 'procedure of individualization' (Foucault, 2006: 15).

Foucault (2013: 197) came to look at power as a power–knowledge relation by following Friedrich Nietzsche's claim that 'behind the will to know there is … the will to power'. The first volume of the *History of Sexuality* is an example of how Foucault analysed the transformative force of certain power–knowledge relations, including the usefulness of alliance forces such as the law, possession, rituals, and norms to make a hegemonic power–knowledge relation on marriage and sexuality. Such connectivities, alliances, and strategies of power must be studied in their specificity, mutations, and (inter)dependencies to understand their normalizing effect (Foucault, 1978: IV).

Power is a relation of procedures and mechanisms that connect and establish a certain effect to governing. Governing is to 'lead others', 'the conduct of conduct' of others (Foucault, 1986a: 220), and towards this endeavour, knowledge is a force and mechanism to 'act upon the behaviour of individuals'; to discipline or modify 'their way of conducting themselves' (Foucault, 1998: 463). Knowledge produces reason or truth to be 'effectively incorporated into the social whole' (Foucault, 1980: 101).

Power comprises generative forces formative to the exercise of effect from a specific ensemble of knowledge, strategies, tactics, institutions, discourses, schemes of signification, tactics, bodies, etc. responding to an urgent problem (Foucault, 1980: 194–195). The rationality of a power–knowledge relation to this urgent problem is its 'local cynicism', that is, how tactics, knowledge, and mechanisms reciprocally make, support, or displace each other and become 'installations in a whole' milieu (Foucault, 1978: 107).

Some crucial points emerge from this: first, power is nothing more and nothing less than the effect of the coalesced elements and the relative strength of forces connected in place and put into practice. Power is interwoven with social and spatial forces like sexuality and housing as well as governing institutions used as a force of domination. Second, power is subject-less, because 'individuals are the vehicles of power, not its points of application'. Power passes through individuals, making them 'relays' to power relations (Foucault, 1980: 98). Third, there is no escape from power. It is everywhere and ubiquitous (Foucault, 1980: 142). Fourth, relations of power have a genealogy, being part of 'a chain' of power–knowledge relations invisible on the surface (Foucault, 2003: 29). Fifth, power is invisible-visible. Power happens (visible), but its outcome is immanent to the relative strength between forces at play (invisible).

WHAT IS KNOWLEDGE TO POWER?

Two statements from Foucault indicate why it is crucial to focus on power–knowledge relations. First, any culture has its fundamental cultural codes that rule or 'govern its language, its meaning patterns, its exchanges, its technics, its values, its hierarchy of practices', the 'empirical orders' people will meet (Foucault, 2003: 29). And second, 'power and knowledge directly imply one another', and there is 'no power relation without the correlative constitution of a field of knowledge, nor any knowledge that does not presuppose and constitute at the same time power relations' (Foucault, 1995: 27, 1977: 27).

Cultural codes, thinking, what one knows, interpretations, significations, and subjectification are encircled by an ordered space of knowledge: the epistemological field or the *épistème*. The épistème is the ordering of a space of recognition. It is the space of what can be known, said, and thought within a certain culture. The épistème is subconscious to the statement itself, and there is an epistemological field of language and knowledge prior to what is perceived (perception), which becomes meaning and experience. The épistème enables recognition and experience. It is not static but is a changing field of knowledge from the 'play of rules, of transformation, of thresholds, of remanences' (Foucault, 1991: 55) within the discourse itself. It is possible to analyse this constitutive process by exploring the following (Foucault, 1991: 54):

- 'Criteria of *formation*', that is, 'the set of rules of formation' for modes of objectification, conceptualization, and theory building.
- 'Criteria of *transformation* or of threshold', from which the discourse is possible at a certain moment in time.
- 'Criteria of *correlation*', or the discourse relations to other discourses and nondiscursive contexts ('institutions, social relations, economic and political conjuncture').

Seen epistemologically, knowledge is thus on one hand 'that which can be talked about within a discursive practice and thus being specified', and on the other hand it is 'the space within which the subject can take a position to speak about the objects' (Foucault, 1972: 203) – the presentation and representation of the objects.

Understanding and recognition, however, are not only a consequence of the historic concordance between language, words, and thought, but any statement is always and already 'inscribed in a play of power' and 'linked to certain coordinates of knowledge' (Foucault, 1980: 196). The 'new archivist', as Deleuze called Foucault, shows how any statements are encircled by three realms constitutive to the possibility of meaning. They are the *collateral space* of statements, or the 'associate or adjacent domain formed from other statements that are part of the same group'; the *correlative* space linked to the statements' connection to other 'subjects, objects, and concepts'; and the statements' *complementary space* of nondiscursive formations, 'instructions, political events, economic practices and processes' (Deleuze, 1986: 5–9).

So there is no 'real' knowledge, only constructed knowledge from within a dominant *epistème*. 'The being of knowledge is to lie' (Foucault, 2013: 213), because there is no a priori 'real' to knowledge. Within 'a circle of reality, knowledge and lie' (Foucault, 2013: 213), the power–knowledge relation orders knowledge through the *epistème*, classifications of words and things, and a system of representation and meaning (Foucault, 2003). The ordering rationalizes the possible diversity of experience and knowledge, and the epistemic field is thus a historical, not universal, a priori construct that makes the 'unthought precondition' to understanding, thinking, and doing. The *epistème* is in a state of change (Krause-Jensen, 1983: 14), and a power–knowledge regime compensates this problem by speaking of 'truth', 'reason', or 'the normal' constructed within 'the nature of connection that can exist between … heterogeneous elements' (Foucault, 1980: 194).

Foucault reflected knowledge from the interconnection between two meanings of the word in French: *savoir* and *connaissance*. These words are untranslatable to English and ambiguous to the French language itself (Foucault, 1998: xxviii). *Savoir* is 'a knowledge' (Foucault, 1998: 324), 'to know' (Foucault, 1998: xxviii), which is the knowledge from experience (discourses and practices) and from having 'a will to knowledge' (Foucault, 2013: 17). *Connaissance* is 'the sum of scientific knowledge' and a 'set of elements' constitutive to a discourse formation (Foucault, 1998: 324). It is the knowledge we find in archives, the *epistème*, written texts of the time, and in hegemonic institutional or professional discourses.

Foucault (2013: 16; also Doron, 2021: 329) could thus say that 'a single subject goes from desire to know (*savoir*) to knowledge (*connaissance*)'. A power–knowledge relation defined as apparatus is *connaissance*, while the effect of the hegemonic discourse is dependent on the strife between *savoir* and *connaissance* – knowledge experienced (learning) and knowledge institutionalized, or as expressed by Foucault (2007b: 70), 'knowledge as such, took on the form of a power (*pouvoir*) or a potency (*puissance*), while on the side of power, always defined as a *savoir-faire*, a certain way of knowing'.

Knowledge thus involves several things: (a) it constitutes *discursive formations* for what can be talked about, from which position and perspective, and from which concepts and theories; (b) it is a *discursive praxis*, which is not only a way of talking about things but also constitutive to a mode of relating to things; and (c) any culture has a management of knowledge and its *norms of knowledge* (what can count as knowledge).

ENTRANCE (A): POWER AS GOVERNING, GOVERNMENTALIZATION, GOVERNMENTALITY

To govern is to have technologies and mechanisms to conduct others. Foucault (1986a: 221) showed how there is a change from feudal repressive power to the appearance of a modern mode of governing 'to structure the possible field of action of others', in part, as Dean (1999:11) argues, by working through 'desires, interests and beliefs'.

Foucault saw a text from 1555 by Guillaume de La Perrière as a prefiguration of a modern government of a population. To Perrière, government is 'the right disposition of things' (Foucault, 2007: 96), which relate for example to wealth, resources, ways of acting, habits, accidents, epidemics, and death. The 'right of arranging (*disposer*) things in order to lead (*conduit*) them' [human beings] (Foucault, 2007: 99) should not be a matter of imposing 'obedience or order by law', but 'of employing tactics' to arrange things to reach a certain aim and end. Governing is meant to direct (*diriger*) through the 'perfection, maximization, or intensification' of the processes (Foucault, 2007: 99) and is meant to build on the 'wisdom' of how to make the right 'disposition (*disposition*)' of things. Governing is a governing based on knowledge rather than the law (Foucault, 2007: 100).

The Perrière text represents a shift from the belief in governing by institutional structures or violence towards a governing through the body, the soul, and behaviour. To impose a regime of forces able to have a conductive effect on a population in their lives must enhance its will to have knowledge on 'customs, habits, ways of acting and thinking' (Foucault, 2007: 96) in order to govern more rationally and specifically (Foucault, 1977: 154–160, 1995: 170–176). Instead of using bare force, the focus became the social body, 'the conduct of souls' (Foucault, 2007: 193).

The objectives of governing shifted from being about territory, law, and the use of judicial mechanisms to having the 'complex of men and things' in their lives as its object (Foucault, 2000: 324). This conduct of a population not only applies to governing in 'a moral sense of the term' but also concerns 'movement in space, material subsistence, diet', care, and health as mechanisms for self-control and self-governing (Foucault, 2007: 121–122).

Foucault argued that it is a move from a managing state to a steering and controlling state of security. The seventeenth-century sovereign who governs moved into the eighteenth-century 'governmentalization of the state' (Foucault, 2007: 109), a governmentalization 'intended to rule them [the population] in a continuous and permanent way' (Foucault, 2000: 300). Bio-politics (biological features as 'the object of a political strategy') became vital to this endeavour (Foucault, 2007: 1), supported by a political anatomy (turning human bodies into 'objects of knowledge') (Foucault, 1977: 30, 1995: 28). The aim of the 'political anatomy' is *discipline* (*dressage*) developed and implemented by institutions like the school and the military, and the aim of 'bio-politics' is a *population control*, a regulation of the population, based for instance on statistics and demography.

Foucault once said that his lectures on 'security, territory, population' should have been called 'a history of governmentality'. We live in 'the era of governmentality', he added (Foucault, 2007: 109).

The term *governmentality* was Foucault's effort to say that there is a change of 'mentality' on 'how to govern' to the historic development of new modes of governing. Although Foucault (2007: 116) admitted that governmentality is a vague and insubstantial domain to study, he said he invented the term because he wanted to move away from an 'institutional centric' approach and to focus on the function of power and its technologies as practice. Power is not connected to institutions or structures, but to power–knowledge relations supporting the exercise of power in practice.

A governmentality is (a) the ensemble formed by 'institutions, procedures, analyses and reflections, calculation and tactics' that allows the exercise of a power targeting the population, using political economy as form, and using the 'apparatus of security' as technology; (b) the historical development of 'a series of specific governmental apparatuses (*appareil*)' and a 'series of knowledge (*savoirs*)'; and (c) the result of the process from an administrative state to a governmentalization of society (Foucault, 2007: 108–109). This society is 'controlled by the apparatuses of security' (Foucault, 2007: 110) and its 'juridico-legal' and 'disciplinary techniques' (Foucault, 2007: 9). The focus is no longer (only) the administration of a territory but the discipline of a population.

A govern-*mentality* is thus about how generative power technologies and mechanisms such as knowledge, procedures, and regulations intertwine with and support power relations in the development of a dynamic strategic field of discursive and mental dispositions and practices. A governmentality is a force to 'the art of governing, that is to say, the reasoned way of governing best' and 'reflections on the best possible way of governing' (Foucault, 2008: 2). It is concerned with the way people act and react linked to others (Foucault, 1988b: 15), and to govern thus needs both knowledge and a hegemonic epistème, as well as an ethos to govern from (Dean, 1999: 18).

In using the word 'governmentality', Foucault wanted to stress that a governmentality emerges from the dynamic relation between conditions of possibility and of potentiality, *puissance*.

ENTRANCE (B): SPACE AS DISCIPLINE AND POWER AS *TECHNE*

Foucault (1986b: 252) once said that 'space is fundamental in any form of communal life, space is fundamental in any exercise of power'. He added that 'all power is physical, and there is a direct connection between the body and political power' (Foucault, 2006: 14). The spatialization of life is a technique to increase a detailed and fine-grained exercise of 'the conduct of conduct' of human beings (see first and foremost Foucault 1977, 1995). Urban planning and bio-politics are closely related in that endeavour, where planning represents a knowledge and practice on how to spatialize 'the right way' of living (Foucault, 1986b: 273–290).

An 1836 text in the newspaper *La Phalange* argued that 'the perfect urban plan' should be a concentric physical plan of combined functions (inner city for hospitals; then a ring of court, police, and military; and a third ring of trade, industry, brothels, and gambling houses). Although the text may be seen as an 'imaginary geo-politics', the text also saw the city as built on 'a net of walls, space, institutions, rules, ways of speaking' to 'fabricate the disciplinarian individual' (Foucault, 1977: 272, 1995: 307). Urbanism became a reflection on how urban planning could be a tool to exercise 'the conduct of conduct' and produce the disciplined individual (Foucault, 1986b: 240).

Early industrialization made local conditions (e.g., soil, density, excessive living, housing) an object of concern (Foucault, 1980: 150–151) to the government of human beings. Foucault repeatedly turned to urban planning to show how societies at that time developed a governmentality of security and discipline by using space as a mechanism. The seventeenth–eighteenth-century contagious and epidemic city emerged as a problem of security, and this 'pathogenic city' had 'an urgent need' of 'techniques to prevent urban revolt' (Foucault, 2008: 18). The bourgeoisie feared social uprising, and up against this threat they thought society needed a population with a disciplined life as part of securing society against social riots. In several cities around Europe, a philanthropic bourgeoisie decided to intervene within poor social milieus to improve the living conditions of (some of the) people living there.

The intervention in the habitat was exercised by a new form of 'policing' that, according to notes from Nicolas Delaware (1705), should concern 'religion, morals, health and subsistence, public peace, the care of buildings, squares, and highways … the care and discipline of the poor'; 'the goodness of life', 'the preservation of life', 'convenience of life', and the 'pleasures of life' (Foucault, 2007: 334). The intervention was to be done within 'the reality of fluctuations' of economic, political, and social events (Foucault, 2007: 37), but essentially it was to be operative as 'procedures of normalization' to secure the control of space (Foucault, 2007: 49).

Foucault (2007: 2, see also Foucault, 1980: chapter 9) mentioned the German *Medicinische Polizei* as an example of how 'the basic biological features of the human species became the object of a political strategy'. The *Medicinische Polizei* was an administrative apparatus (Foucault, 2000: 140–141) made to establish a *system of observation* of disease, and it included medical officers to register medical observations at locations. From the systematization of this knowledge, the police should make directives on action. The standardization of the socio-medical knowledge from surveys turned into a bio-political tool and advanced as 'a necessary correlate to the state' praxis (Foucault, 2000: 350), because it was a knowledge apparatus that could be used in the 'regulation of a larger, constantly changing social milieu' (Wright and Rabinow, 1982: 16).

When 'order rules, everyone is prescribed his place, body, illness and death, his property' (Foucault, 1977: 178).[1] The police and urban planning were apparatuses used in the process of normalization (Foucault, 1980: 107), 'to foster civil respect and public morality', using a spatial intervention in the social milieu (Foucault, 1988b: 154). To change everyday life habits and hygiene, spatial planning efforts were supported by a discursive strategy using magazines, newspapers, and posters to inform citizens about 'the right way of living'. This paternalism made women responsible for the family's hygiene and proper moral living.

The knowledge complex emerging around the 'pathogenic city' inscribed a new 'art of the government of men' (Foucault, 1980: 240) and responded not only to the dangers of social uprising but also to a mercantilism that became aware that the population is a source of wealth if it is effectively 'trained, divided up, distributed, and fixed by disciplinary mechanisms' (Foucault, 2007: 69).

Foucault used urban planning to exemplify how cities operate in the exercise of power by using space to handle with contingence (Wright and Rabinow, 1982: 16). Urban planning connected 'government to problems of rules' (Huxley, 2007: 192) to be complied with through the spatial management of life (hygiene, housing, zones, common facilities, etc.) and a normalization of the population through space (circulation in space, habits, informal surveillance, communication). Space stood out as a potential force 'to teach, to mould conduct, to instil forms of self-awareness and identities' (Colin Gordon, here Foucault, 2000: xix)[2] to benefit 'the disposition of space for economical political reasons' (Foucault, 1980: 148).

The 'treatment of space' (Foucault, 2007: 12) was a targeting of 'the notion of habitat' rather than poverty and unemployment, and by this move the cities had the urban population 'constituted as an object of administration and political intervention' (Elden, 2017: 176). Urbanism became part of 'a practical rationality governed by a conscious goal' (Foucault, 1986b: 255) that supported the politics of security by making possible a disciplined space and a surveyed and predictable milieu (Foucault, 2007: 11), making an immanent force to shape a milieu of virtue (Osborne and Rose, 1999: 1). The police, registration, collective equipment, and the building plan were tools and mechanisms to develop a micro-physical normalizing effect (Foucault, 2007: 17) and to discipline life for instance by giving citizens an economic commitment to work by having bank loans and insurance.

Foucault's *Discipline and Punish* (1977, 1995) discussed 'distribution in space' (enclosing, placing), 'ordering in time' (schedules, programming), and 'composition in space-time' (constituting a productive force) (Deleuze, 1986: 71). Space became part of 'the *dressage*' of the population (Foucault, 1980: 161) and urban planning a *techne* to this endeavour.

The meaning of the concept *techne* can be traced back to Aristotle, who used it as a concept for reasoned praxis such as for instance the art of building (Flyvbjerg, 1991: 71). The Greek *techne* pointed at 'a practical rationality governed by a conscious goal' (Foucault, 1986: 255). *Techne* is thus both 'a certain systematic set of action and a certain mode of action' (Foucault, 2017: 251), and it includes the *techne of life* – the techniques of 'how to live'. These *tekhnai* (techniques) not only had life as its object but also saw life as 'ordered procedures, considered ways of doing things' (Foucault, 2017: 251).

Planning is a *techne*. Collective equipment like transport, railways, public laundry, and other structures of public service are used to order – systematize and direct – life by working on people's habits and praxis in time and space. Intertwined with advice on proper use, collective equipment works as a constitutive force to 'the social unconscious' of life by staging a collective 'normal' acting and body experience (Foucault, 1996: 108–109). Habits became a technique of 'the art of government of men' (Foucault, 1986a: 240) and part of the 'apparatus (*dispositif*) of security' (Foucault, 2007: 6).

The history of town planning shows 'the role of knowledge as useful and necessary to the exercise of power' (Foucault, 2000: xvi), and Foucault (2000: xxiv) showed how spatial planning is the use of micro-physical power 'focused on individuals, and the details of their behaviour and conduct' using architecture and urban design.

ENTRANCE (C): MICRO-PHYSIC POWER

Institutions and apparatus are part of the political body technology and an effort continuously to improve the management of life. The apparatus is about 'a kind of micro-physics of power that different kinds of institutions put in circulation, but whose field of validity is situated between the great functionings of the societal machines and the body itself with their materiality and forces' (Foucault, 1978: 29).[3] The micro-physics of power is a level where government is partial and incomplete, because it is a milieu where 'uncertain elements unfold' (Foucault, 2007: 20).

The micro-physics of power, and its disciplinary mechanisms, is about how power works on bodies – on 'acts, attitudes, and modes of everyday behaviour' (Foucault, 1980: 125). We cannot understand this power by only looking for the apparatus implementing the strategies, because the effect depends on how the mechanism 'runs through the whole body' (Foucault, 1980: 119). Micro-physical power is a multiplicity of forces that support each other and gradually give form to 'a social *anatomy*' (Eliassen, 2016: 128) composed of spatial, disciplinary, and discursive elements inciting and inducing self-governance. The effect depends on 'a multiplicity of organisms, forces, energies, materials, desires, thoughts etc' (Foucault, 1980: 97), and to address this complex is to address how a net of forces becomes linked to a micro-physical strategy of domination exercised through the 'dispositions, manoeuvres, tactics, techniques, functions' (Foucault, 1980: 26), which are invested to form and discipline human being and life.

Foucault (2006: 41) explored how the abstract idea of the panopticon by Jeremy Bentham was taken as a 'Columbus egg' providing 'the most general political and technical formula of disciplinary power'. The panopticon – a circle of prison cells with a central guard tower from where all prisoners are visible, but the prisoners never know when they are seen – shows an 'architectural apparatus', 'a machine' that creates and bears the effect of domination 'independent of who practice it' (Foucault, 1977: 180, 1995: 201).[4]

The panopticon form may in itself have power by making a physical, visible organization of people and its use, but the micro-physical effect is uncontrollable to the individual. The effect of 'everyday life panoptism' (Foucault, 1977: 197, 1995: 223), or this 'physical-politico technique' (Foucault, 1977: 198, 1995: 223) of governing everyday life by space, is to induce, produce, and traverse the body. Panoptism can be read as something like a utopia about how power can have normalizing, disciplinary, and moral effects anonymously and tacitly.

It is what happens micro-physically that reveals how power operates and has effect. The micro-power of power is a subject placed within power–knowledge relations that incite the subject to a way of doing and a mode of thinking, which should perform certain forms of behaviour (Foucault, 1977: 29, 1995: 26).

There is thus a double aspect of the micro-physics of power that remained in focus throughout Foucault's writings: first, the micro-physics of power is a field of 'schemes, disposition, manoeuvre, tactical acts, techniques, modes of function' transmitted by knowledge and communication within a targeted social milieu (Foucault, 1977: 29, 1995: 26), and second, the micro-power of power is about normation; 'procedures, processes, and techniques of normalization' including the effect of the law, disciplines, and training (*dressage*) (Foucault, 2007: 56–57). A norm is related to 'the normal', and power is therefore basically related to 'normation' (e.g., reason) rather than normalisation alone (e.g., of behaviour) (Foucault, 2007: 57).

POWER AS A DISPOSITIF

The dispositif of power is 'a productive instance of discursive practices' producing 'statements, discourses, and, consequently, all the forms of representation that may then derive from it' (Foucault, 2006: 13). A dispositif can thus be described as a 'heterogenous ensemble consisting of discourses, institutions, architectural forms, regulatory decisions, laws, administrative measures, scientific statements, philosophical, moral, and philanthropic propositions – in short, the said as much as the unsaid' (Foucault, 1980: 194).

The dispositif, the English translation says, is 'the system of relations' (Foucault, 1980: 194) that can be established between the elements, while the German translation, correctly, translates it as '*das Netz*'; a net (Foucault, 1978b: 120). Foucault disregarded the concept apparatus as mechanistic ('a system') and pointed out that the formative forces to power constitute a changing and generative connection of elements (a 'net'). It is not a matter of 'order', but 'the nature of connection' from the 'interplay of position and modification of function' (Foucault, 1980: 194–195).

The translation of dispositif to the mechanistic 'apparatus' thus misses seeing 'the play' (*le jeu*) of interchanging positions of discursive and nondiscursive forces, and it fails to acknowledge the conjunction of positions that configure or displace a power–knowledge effect. A dispositif ensemble is a configuration from how the elements involved affect each other, and a dispositif establishes a relation between institutions, knowledge, and practice (procedures), and it is not a permanent order (Eliassen, 2016: 97, 103).

A dispositif is not an apparatus, a machine, a structure, a system, or an organism (Lambert, 2020: 47), but an effect of the conjunction of generative forces that emerge from 'strategies of relations of forces supporting, and supported by, knowledge' (Foucault, 1980: 196).[5] A dispositif is not an emerging deterministic but answers to an urgent need, and we might say that it develops rhizomatic connections (a multilinear network of changing connections) (Deleuze and Guattari, 1982: 9–22), according to the understanding of the urgent need, strategies, or tactics.

A dispositif ensemble is thus never final or closed, and it has an effect as a temporal 'functional overdetermination' (Foucault, 1980: 195) supporting a strategic elaboration of a praxis. A dispositif establishes 'particular relations between the discourse and its "object"', which makes it useful as a force that 'directs (*dirigèr*) … the process it directs' (Foucault, 2007: 99). A dispositif perspective identifies the principles, positions, and relations of forces, mechanisms, and technologies directed towards forming and managing people, spaces, and behaviour. A dispositif effect is not produced by telling how reality *is*, but by making a certain 'reality' *becoming* 'real' through truth, reason, normality, or spatial design.

A dispositif ensemble in fact makes a power–knowledge relation 'begin to appear' (Lambert, 2020: 50). Gilles Deleuze (2006: 338) stated that a dispositif is 'a skein' of forces that disperse and connect in space through a net of discourses and regulatory installations. A space is not only a materialization, and architecture is not just a 'disciplinary form'. Both space and architecture become useful. Foucault explored how panoptism was seen as 'a new mode of obtaining power, *of mind over mind*' (Foucault, 2006: 74), supporting an art of governing, where 'the invisible eye' could be used to exercise 'a power of normalization' (Foucault, 1995: 308; see also Huxley, 2006).

A spatial form turned into a body politics by giving 'a set of material elements and techniques' to exercise domination by the appropriation of a fictive eye (Foucault, 1995: 28). The disciplinarian strength of the panoptic form is that it has the 'collective at its centre' (prisoners, population), but it is 'always individual at the point where it arrives' (Foucault, 2006: 75). The *dressage* of people through 'institutions, praxis, and documents' (Eliassen, 2016: 103) turns bodies into objects, and the panoptic utopia 'promised' an informal and invisible surveillance constitutive to a self-disciplined subject: mind over mind.

A *dispositif* apparatus to Foucault is thus a composition of elements that are deployed as an apparatus (organization, structure, domain of action, hegemonic knowledge) to make a significative intervention into space, praxis, or meaning making. A dispositif ensemble thus manifests a certain but unstable and shifting connection of elements. It is *both* 'an always-modulating network of positions (of subjects) and relations (of forces)' (Crano, 2020: 8) *and* a particular and uncertain connection between the said and the unsaid, the discursive and nondiscursive. A dispositif ensemble is contingent, affected by an exchange of positions, modifications of knowledge, strives on knowledge, forces involved, etc. But at a certain (tactical, strategic) point it becomes a configuration of power–knowledge forces that gets a position to be 'an embodied dimension of one's existence' (Rabinow, 2003: 10).

FOUCAULT AND PLANNING RESEARCH

If, following Foucault, one of the intriguing problematics to planning studies is how the spatialization of life builds on a power–knowledge regime, from where the body and life are made an object to planning, planning is part of 'a series of strategies of governmentalisation … to convert the unsociable sociability of the city to the ends of government' (Osborne and Rose, 1999: 758). Using Moroccan planning as his study object, Rabinow (1989) found that the intersection of the macro-planning and micro-physical effect was clear from the eighteenth-century housing schemes and onwards (see also Gromark, 1987). Housing, collective equipment, urban design, infrastructures, landscape, etc. all represent a *disposer*, a force of 'the disposition of things' (Foucault 2007: 99), constitutive to micro-physical effect: ways of doing, ways of thinking about doing, and the normal.

The how of power in late-modern planning was exemplary, and it is still uniquely demonstrated in Bent Flyvbjerg's (1991) study on transport planning in Aalborg, Denmark. Flyvbjerg showed how a power analysis 'simply involves investigating where and how, between whom, between what points, according to what processes, and with what effects, power is applied' (Foucault, 2007: 2). Flyvbjerg performed a discourse ensemble study using policy documents, institutional communication and tactics, and political arguments made through the planning process. His research revealed how mechanisms like notes, research, information gathering, knowledge, informal alliances, and intimidation of planners secured a hegemonic power relation between politics and business.

In the last three or four decades we have seen a great many planning studies using Foucault. There have been studies of the *discursive* staging and wording of public participation, including how the planning law and regulations, architecture, and planning's hegemonic discourses direct what can be said and counted as legitimate knowledge according to the agenda or plan. This perspective has been used to look for a kind of *institutionalization* of (public) planning other than the power-ridden decisional hierarchy that forms many planning systems around the world (e.g., Bäcklund and Mäntysalo, 2010; Bond, 2011; Mouat et al., 2013).

Within the participatory planning studies as such, a focus on agonistic planning has emerged as a suggestion on how to empower participants within the planning system. One line of such studies is to understand 'how governing dispositifs emerge in contextualised, situated practice', thus emerging in specific arrangements and done with interventions around the issue (McGuirk and Dowling, 2020: 4). McGuirk and Dowling (2020: 14–16) found that the governance dispositif on the Sydney office market included inducement, persuasion, negotiation, and authority as forces that configured the process.

Looking at how dispositifs relate to 'the conduct of conduct' by ordering space may lead to looking at its opposite: planning as *improvisation* (Hillier, 2017; Oesch, 2020). Studying the nonplanning or improvised planning in the Al-Hussein refugee camp in Jordan, Lucas Oesch found a planning outside the law of urban regulation, but still tacitly accepted. The camp is a 'making of urban planning invisible', although there is a need for an upgrading of physical infrastructure and the building of new houses authorities need to know about (Oesch, 2020: 358). This constitutes planning as a response to an urgent need. Planning the camp is done by an illegal force that works provisionally as needs emerge, and this kind of planning is possible only as bottom-up planning.

A camp is what Oren Yifthacel defined as a politics of 'displaceability' done by technocratic states, making 'grey spaces' where citizens are regarded as 'unrecognized, illegal, temporary or severely marginalized'. It is a 'creeping apartheid' (Yiftachel, 2015: 5, 10). Some of the dispositif forces supporting this displaceability are tactical policy making, legal systems, the building of dividing spaces, and the occupation of land, and these forces illustrate the use of planning as a tool of political suppression and subjugation of ethnicities.

In his late work and lectures, Foucault looked back to the Greek philosophy on *parrhèsia:* 'free speech' or 'fearless speech' (Foucault, 2001). A few scholars have used this perspective to look at planning as part of a governing and governmentality problematic (Grange, 2016). Speaking in the interests of the city, *parrhèsiastes* use 'the reflexive exercise of freedom' (Grange, 2016: 7), but within the Swedish planning system planners must work from a political demand for loyalty, and planners are experiencing being 'corrected' in public by politicians. Kristina Grange's analysis of Swedish politics showed how politics are aiming at making planning loyal to neoliberal politics, and this endangers planners as 'freely' speaking and democratic planning based on 'a professional commitment to problematise truth claims', if needed (Grange, 2016: 16).

FOUCAULT IN PERSPECTIVE

The three areas outlined above highlight how Foucault reconnoitred critical thresholds of how the power–knowledge relation is constitutive to subjectification, normalization, and praxis. Foucault (1977: 30, 1995: 28) showed how planning is involved in (at least) three fundamental power–knowledge relations emerging from the sixteenth century onwards: *a political anatomy,* the body 'politics' of subjugating human bodies by 'turning them into objects of knowledge', *the panoptic society*, making the disciplinary society invisible but effecting a self-governing mentality; and *the disciplinarian society*, building on a generalized surveillance and the (in) formal micro-physical and spatial discipline of human beings (Krause-Jensen, 1983: 133–134).

The histories of knowledge and power formations are discontinuously affected by events and ruptures (Foucault, 1998: 279–297), but any discourse, any statement, any understanding, any meaning are always points in a power–knowledge net of tactics and strategies to have an embodied effect. This includes the use of 'the discourse of true and false, by which I mean the correlative formation of domains and objects, and of all the verifiable, falsifiable discourses that bear on them' (Foucault, 1991: 85).

Foucault was looking for the 'real history' of power, the exercise and effect, or what is done. Power is subject-less but a permanent folding of power–knowledge forces that is constitutive to ever new compositions of political, systemic, discursive, nondiscursive, and spatial power–knowledge relations. Foucault's archival and genealogical studies on how certain discourse formation in a certain historical time and conjuncture became 'useful' to certain power–knowledge relations are to him in fact a perspective on our present mode of thinking, speaking, and acting.

As Foucault says, 'power is not possessed, it acts in the very body and over the whole surface of the social field according to a system of relays, modes of connection, transmission, distribution etc. Power acts through the smallest elements; the family, sexual relations, but also: residential relations, neighbourhoods etc. As far as we go in the social network, we always find power as something which "runs through" it, that acts, that bring about effects' (Foucault, 1979: 59).

Power is exercised 'through a net-like organization', and Foucault explored different dispositif nets such as sexuality, psychiatry, bio-politics, the prison, and (occasionally) the spatial dispositif of urban planning. A dispositif is thus a net of forces where both actors and power–knowledge forces become 'the element of its articulation' (Foucault, 1980: 98).

This is one reason why Foucault lacked interest in Power with a capital P. Power is everywhere and in every minor and macro relation between human beings as well as between forces. Power constitutes mechanisms 'co-extensive with the body' (Foucault, 1980: 142), and critical planning studies should try to grasp planning as both subjection in its material instance and as a constitutive power to subjectification through space. The conduct of conduct has its apparatus, its institutions, and its practices, and planning is one *techne* meant to have an effect on the 'immediate social *entourage*' (Foucault, 1980: 101).

Planning as a tool and mechanism of governing unfolds in two main ways: first, the effect of planning is the folding of a specific configuration of forces: (a) a net of power–knowledge relations (hegemonic discourses, *savoir*, *connaissance*), (b) an apparatus of government (politics, law, institution), and (c) semiotics, text performances: the performative language of meaning and signification. Second, planning is a power–knowledge apparatus of discursive and nondiscursive practices constitutive to a mode of doing and thinking (a governmentality) and a conditional force to a micro-physical effect (normalization, normation).

There is, however, no power without resistance; 'at the very heart of the power relationship, and constantly provoking it, are the recalcitrance of the will and the intransigence of freedom' (Foucault, 1986: 221–222). So up against the mechanisms that ensure institutions' 'own preservation' (Foucault, 1986: 222) there is always the counter force of the agonistic provocation inherent to social existence. We should not forget that there is also a potential pleasure to subordination for power to play on:

Once you admit that the function of power is not essentially to prohibit, but to produce, to produce pleasure, at that moment you can perfectly understand how we are able to obey order and find pleasure in this obedience, which isn't necessarily masochistic (Foucault, 2012: 14).

NOTES

1. The English translation says, 'it lays down for each individual his place, his body, his disease and his death, his well-being' (1995: 197).
2. *Technologies* are operative on a macro-level, for instance the law on punishment. *Mechanisms* are directed towards specific practices (e.g., learning by curriculum) and function (e.g., procedures, rules).
3. English translation (1995: 26) slightly changed to stress that to Foucault, the state apparatus 'circulates' the micro-physics of power, it does not 'operate' it.
4. Foucault (1995: 201) is changed.
5. In Foucault (2017: 289), he ends his lectures on 'subjectivity and truth' by saying that the 'relationship of self to self' has transformed from 'developed, organized, and distributed in an apparatus (*dispositif*) that was first that of the flesh before becoming, much later, that of sexuality'. A dispositif is here a power–knowledge complex distributed by different 'apparatus'/institutions, but the dispositif itself is a power–knowledge relation to be identified from its discourse–knowledge relations, before turning into an institutionalized idea of let's say sexuality. Most translations miss this generative aspect of the dispositif concept.

REFERENCES

Althusser, Louis (2000) *Machiavelli and Us*, London: Verso.

Bäcklund, Pia and Mäntysalo, Raine (2010) Agonism and Institutional Ambiguity: Ideas on Democracy and the Role of Participation in the Development of Planning Theory and Practice – The Case of Finland, *Planning Theory* Vol. 9, No. 4, 333–350.

Bond, Sophie (2011) Negotiating a 'Democratic Ethos': Moving Beyond the Agonistic-Communicative Divide, *Planning Theory* Vol. 10, No. 2, 161–186.

Bussolini, Jeffrey (2010) What is a Dispositive? *Foucault Studies* No. 10, 85–107.

Cisney, Vrenon W. and Morar, Nicolae (2015) *Bio-power: Foucault and Beyond*, Chicago: University of Chicago Press (Open access book: https//cupola.gettysburg.edu/books/91).

Crano, Ricky (2020) *Dispositif* (https://doi.org/10.1093/acrefore/9780190201098.013.1026) (published online: 27 August 2020).

Dean, Michell (1999) *Governmentality. Power and Rule in Modern Society*, London: Sage.

Deleuze, Gilles and Guattari, Felix (1982) *Kafka for en mindre litteratu* (*Kafka – pour une littèrature mineure*), Viborg: Sjakalen ørkenserie.

Deleuze, Gilles (1986) *Foucault*, Minneapolis: University of Minnesota Press.

Doron, Claude-Olivier (2021) Course Context, in Michel Foucault (ed.) *Sexuality. The 1964 Clermont-Ferrand and 1969 Vincennes Lectures*, New York: Columbia University Press, 299–359.

Dreyfus, Hubert L. and Rabinow, Paul (1986) What is Maturity? Habermas and Foucault on 'What is Enlightenment?', in D. Couzens Hoy (ed.) *Foucault: A Critical Reader*, Oxford: Blackwell, pp. 109–122.

Elden, Stuart (2016) *Foucault's Last Decade*, Cambridge: Polity.

Elden, Stuart (2017) *Foucault. The Birth of Power*, Cambridge: Polity.

Flyvbjerg, Bent (1991) *Magt og rationality* (*Power and Rationality*), Copenhagen: Akademisk Forlag.

Foucault, Michel (1972) *Vetandets arkeologi* (*The Archaeology of Knowledge*), Köthen: Bo Caverfors Förlag.

Foucault, Michel (1977) *Overvåkning og straf*, København: Rhodos Forlag.

Foucault, Michel (1978) *Seksualitetens historie 1. Vilje til viden* (*Histoire de la sexualité 1, La volonté de savoir*), Copenhagen: Rhodos Bibliotek.

Foucault, Michel (1978b) *Dispositive der Macht*, Berlin: Merve Verlag.

Foucault, Michel (1979) *Power, Truth, Strategy* (eds Meaghan Morris and Paul Patton), Sydney: Feral Publications.

Foucault, Michel (1980) *Power/Knowledge: Selected Interviews and Other Writings 1972–1977* (ed. C. Gordon), New York: Pantheon.

Foucault, Michel (1986a) The Subject and Power, in H.L. Dreyfuss and P. Rabinow (eds) *Michel Foucault: Beyond Structuralism and Hermeneutics*, New York: Harvester Press, pp. 208–226.

Foucault, Michel (1986b) *The Foucault Reader* (ed. Paul Rabinow), London: Penguin Books.

Foucault, Michel (1988) *The Final Foucault* (eds James Bernauer and David Rasmussen), Cambridge, MA: The MIT Press.

Foucault, Michel (1988b) *Technologies of the Self. A Seminar with Michel Foucault* (eds Luther H. Martin, Huck Gutman and Patrick H. Hutton), London: Tavistock Publications.

Foucault, Michel (1989) *Foucault Live*, New York: Semiotext(e).

Foucault, Michel (1991) Politics and the Study of Discourse, in Graham Burcell, Colin Gordon and Peter Miller (eds) *The Foucault Effect: Studies of Governmentality*, Hemel Hempstead, UK: Harvester Wheatsheaf.

Foucault, Michel (1995) *Discipline and Punishment: The Birth of the Prison*, New York: A Vintage Book.

Foucault, Michel (1996) *Foucault Live: Collected Interviews, 1961–1984*, New York: Semiotext(e).

Foucault, Michel (1998) *Aesthetics, Method, and Epistemology*, New York: The New Press.

Foucault, Michel (2000) *Power: Essential Working of Foucault 1954–1984*, New York: The New Press.

Foucault, Michel (2001) *Fearless Speech* (ed. Joseph Pearson). Los Angeles: Semiotext(e).

Foucault, Michel (2003) 'Society Must Be Defended'. *Lectures at Collège de France 1975–1976*, New York: Picador.

Foucault, Michel (2003b) *Abnormal: Lectures of the Collège de France 1974–1975*, New York: Picador.

Foucault, Michel (2003c) *Ordene og Tingene* (*The Order of Things/Les mots et les choses*), Copenhagen: Akademisk Forlag.

Foucault, Michel (2006) *Psychiatric Power: Lectures at the Collège de France 1973–74*, New York: Palgrave Macmillan.

Foucault, Michel (2007) *Security, Territory, Population: Lectures at the Collège de France 1977–78*, New York: Palgrave Macmillan.

Foucault, Michel (2007b) *The Politics of Truth*, New York: Semiotext(e).

Foucault, Michel (2008) *The Birth of Biopolitics: Lectures on the Collège de France 1978–1979*, London: Palgrave Macmillan.

Foucault, Michel (2010) *The Government of Self and Others: Lectures at the Collège de France 1982–1983*, London: Palgrave Macmillan.

Foucault, Michel (2011) Socialmedicinens fødsel, *Distinktion: Scandinavian Journal of Social Theory*, Vol. 2, No. 3, 11–23.

Foucault, Michel (2012) The Mesh of Power, *viewpointmag.com*, 1–17 (viewpointmag.com/2021/09/12/the-mesh-of-power/) (accessed 22 March 2021).

Foucault, Michel (2013) *Lectures on the Will to Know: Lectures at the Collège de France 1970–1971*, London: Palgrave Macmillan.

Foucault, Michel (2017) *Subjectivity and Truth: Lectures at the Collège de France 1980–1981*, New York: Picador.

Foucault, Michel (2021) *Sexuality: The 1964 Clermont-Ferrand and 1969 Vincennes Lectures*, New York: Columbia University Press.

Grange, Kristina (2016) Planners – A Silenced Profession? The Politicisation of Planning and the Need for Fearless Speech, *Planning Theory*, Vol. 16, No. 3, 275–295.

Gromark, Steen (1987) *Fänglande Arkitektur* (*Prisoning Architecture*). Gothenburg: Bokförlaget Korpen.

Hillier, Jean (2007) *Stretching beyond the Horizon: A Multiplanar Theory of Spatial Planning and Governance*, Aldershot, UK: Ashgate.

Hillier, Jean (2011) Strategic Navigation Across Multiple Planes: Towards a Deluzian-Inspired Methodology for Strategic Spatial Planning, *Town Planning Review*, Vol. 82, No. 5, 503–527.

Hillier, Jean (2017) On Planning for Not Having a Plan, *Planning Theory & Practice*, Vol. 18, No. 4, 668–675.

Huxley, Margo (2006) Spatial Rationalities: Order, Environment, Evolution and Government, *Social & Cultural Geography*, Vol. 7, No. 5, 771–787.

Huxley, Margo (2007) Geographies of Governmentality, in Jeremy W. Crampton and Stuart Elden (eds) *Space, Knowledge and Power. Foucault and Geography*, Aldershot, UK: Ashgate, pp. 185–204.

Krause-Jensen, Esbern (1983) *Nomade Filosofi* (*Nomad Philosophy*), Aarhus: Sjakalens ørkenserie.
Lambert, Gregg (2020) *The Elements of Foucault*, Minneapolis: The University of Minnesota Press.
Lemke, Thomas (2019) *A Critique of Political Reason: Foucault's Analysis of Modern Governmentality*, London: Verso.
McGuirk, Pauline and Dowling, Robert (2020) Urban Governance Dispositifs: Cohering Diverse Ecologies of Urban Energy Governance, *Environment & Planning C: Politics & Space*, Vol. 39, No. 4, 1–22.
Metzger, Jonathan, Soneryd, Linda and Hallström, Kristina Tamm (2017) 'Power' is that which Remains to be Explained: Dispelling the Ominous Dark Matter of Critical Planning Studies, *Planning Theory*, Vol. 16, No. 2, 203–222.
Mouat, Clare, Legacy, Crystal and March, Alan (2013) The Problem is the Solution: Testing Agonistic Theory's Potential to Recast Intractable Planning Disputes, *Urban Policy and Research*, Vol. 31, No. 2, 150–163.
Nealon, Jeffrey T. (2008) *Foucault Beyond Foucault: Power and its Intensifications Since 1984*, Stanford: Stanford University Press.
Nicolic, Mirko (2018) Apparatus x Assemblage, *New Materialism*, 28 March, https://newmaterialism.eu/almanac/a/apparatus-x-assemblage.html, 1–4.
Nilsson, Jakob and Wallenstein, Sven-olov (eds) (2013) *Foucault, Biopolitics and Governmentality*, Södertörn Philosophical Studies 14, Stockholm (E-print: www.sh.se/publications).
Oesch, Lucas (2020) An Improvised Dispositif: Invisible Urban Planning in the Refugee Camp, *International Journal of Urban and Regional Research*, Vol. 44, No. 2, 349–365, DOI:10.1111/1468-2427.12867.
O'Leary, Timothy (2009) *Foucault and Fiction: The Experience Book*, London: Continuum.
Osborne, Thomas and Rose, Nikolas (1999) Governing Cities: Notes on the Spatialisation of Virtue, *Environment & Planning D: Society & Space*, Vol. 17, 737–760.
Pløger, John (2008) Foucault's Dispositif and the City, *Planning Theory*, Vol. 7, No. 1, 51–70.
Rabinow, Paul (1989) *French Modern: Norms and Forms of the Social Environment*, Chicago: The University of Chicago Press.
Rabinow, Paul (2003) *Antropos Today. Reflections on Modern Equipment*, Princeton, NJ: Princeton University Press.
Yiftachel, Oren (2015) Epilogue – From 'Gray Space' to Equal Citizenship? Reflections on Urban Citizenship, *International Journal of Urban and Regional Research*, Vol. 39, No. 4, 726–737, DOI:10.1111.1468-2427.12263.
Wright, Gwendolyn and Rabinow, Paul (1982) A Discussion of the Work of Michel Foucault, *Skyline*, March, 14–16.

5. Deleuze, Guattari and power
Jean Hillier

INTRODUCTION

John Friedmann (1998, p. 252) once commented on the reluctance of planning theorists to incorporate dimensions of power into their work. Over twenty years later, conceptualisations of power are mainstreamed in many contributions, as the chapters in this volume testify. My concern here is with the work of Gilles Deleuze and Félix Guattari, whose projects sought to undermine the constructions of power, to decentre patriarchy, anthropocentrism, racism, fascism and so on. However, Deleuze and Guattari wrote very little directly about power *per se*. Power is a difficult, and often implicit, issue in their thought as it evolves over a multi-decade time frame via several other concepts. This presents myself, as chapter author, with two problems: first, which of the multitude of intertwined concepts to introduce in order to assist planning theorists and practitioners to encounter and make sense of Deleuze and Guattari's thought; and second, how to present an understanding of Deleuze and Guattari's ideas without approaching their work as a body of 'knowledge', transformable into academic dogma. I potentially 'betray' Deleuze and Guattari (1987, pp. 125ff), therefore, to creatively enable the fabrication of new readings, concepts and procedures in the spirit in which I believe the authors intended. I seek to destabilise the too-common idea of power as an 'in-itself all-covering explanation of societal events' (Metzger et al., 2017, p. 204) – a 'thing' to be possessed and wielded or a 'product' of action – and present power as relational, immanent and processual, inseparable from its effects.

I offer a 'provisionary map' (Kedem, 2011: 3) of concepts that may be appropriate to planning. Since Deleuze's close friendship with Foucault inevitably affected their thinking, I engage briefly with similarities and differences of selected conceptualisations, including Deleuze and Guattari's critique of Foucault's preference for the fundamental significance of power rather than desire. Deleuze and Guattari claim that power is not transcendent but immanent. 'There is no external reference to power, no force imposing itself from the outside to consider, only the sets of relations and circumstances that one finds oneself within. *Power does not show itself because it is implicated in all that we are and all that we inhabit*' (Allen, 2003: 65, emphasis added). This lack of conceptual means of capturing and expressing the immanent capacities of power suggests to Deleuze and Guattari that the machinic function of power is desire.

Like Foucault, Deleuze and Guattari refer to power as both *pouvoir* – power over – and *puissance* – power to. *Pouvoir* is associated with dominance and capture, including concepts such as territorialisation, striation, signifying regimes, order-words, control societies and faciality. *Puissance*, in contrast, is creative, with the political configured not as resistance, as by Foucault, but as generation, via lines of flight, nomads and war machines. Deleuze, Guattari and Foucault emphasise the inherent interconnection of concepts: 'in all things, there are lines of articulation or segmentarity, strata and territories; but also lines of flight, movements of deterritorialisation and destratification' (Deleuze and Guattari, 1980 [1987]: 3).

Having outlined these concepts, I demonstrate ways in which they might be engaged in planning practices. I allude to the idea of planning as fabulation, 'the means whereby a creative future may be generated' (Bogue, 2011: 77). I conclude by emphasising the importance of relationality and how it is not land *per se*, but particular relations to land that account for the various logics of spatial planning. I argue the need to challenge the over-conditioned presuppositions of many institutions associated with spatial planning and to think from the outside in order to prevent continued domination of *pouvoir* and offer opportunities for creative *puissance*.

DELEUZE, GUATTARI AND FOUCAULT

In Deleuze and Guattari's work, the concept of power is not easily disentangled. The authors' material on force relations (Deleuze, 1962 [1983]; Deleuze and Guattari, 1977 [1984]) is often referenced alongside Foucault's work on power relations, explored earlier in this volume (see Chapter 4 by Pløger). For instance, for all three scholars, power is not a 'thing' to be owned, but rather a relational process. Deleuze, nevertheless, engaged in debate about power with his friend, Michel Foucault, exemplified by their 1972 interview, in which Deleuze states that 'theory is by nature opposed to power' and expresses his preference for desire rather than power as such (Foucault and Deleuze, 1977, p. 208).[1]

For Deleuze and Guattari, desire is a plane of immanent relations – the pre- or unconscious – separate from want, need and interest, all of which are products of desiring machinic social arrangements. Desire is repressed or transformed when its immanence is disrupted by other forces, such as power.[2] Whilst a power-formation is also composed of immanent relations, its essence, nevertheless, persists through states of disruption (a genetic code, a value or ideal, a language, religion and so on). Power, then, is concerned with strategies for production and transformation of relations, whereas desire is concerned with the driving force *behind* creation and relation (Goodchild, 1996). Desire is part of the infrastructure of power (Deleuze and Guattari, 1972 [1984]).

In a footnote to *A Thousand Plateaus* (1980 [1987]: 531, n. 39), Deleuze and Guattari state their only points of disagreement with Foucault as:

1. To us the assemblages seem fundamentally to be assemblages not of power but of desire (desire is always assembled) and power seems to be a stratified dimension of the assemblage;
2. The diagram and the abstract machine have lines of flight that are primary, which are not phenomena of resistance or counterattack in an assemblage, but cutting edges of creation and deterritorialisation.

Whilst I explore the concepts of territorialisation and lines of flight below, it is appropriate to insert a brief comment on the diagram at this point.

In Deleuze's commemorative book, *Foucault* (1986 [1988]), he suggests that the diagram constitutes the foundation of Foucault's conceptualisation of power. Although Deleuze quotes Foucault's own definition of diagram – 'functioning, abstracted from any obstacle … or friction [and which] must be detached from any specific use' (Deleuze 1986 [1988]: 34, from Foucault 1975 [1995]: 205), he, nevertheless, reads the diagram in his own way. He (1986

[1988]: 72–74) summarises Foucault's diagram of power as possessing four, distinctively Deleuzian, characteristics:

> It is the presentation of the relations between forces unique to a particular formation; it is the distribution of the power to affect and the power to be affected; it is the mixing of non-formalized pure functions and unformed pure matter ... it is always local and unstable ... not 'localized' at any given moment, ... a strategy, an exercise of the non-stratified; not a determinate form – power relations are therefore not *known*, [but remain] almost mute and blind, [exterior to forms].

Deleuze reads Foucault's diagram as a way of understanding how discursive and visual operations of power fold together in the constitution of and acting out of subjectivity. Despite being 'almost mute and blind', therefore, a diagram 'makes others see and speak' (Deleuze, 1986 [1988]: 34).

While Foucault's (1975 [1995]) diagram generalises the spatial practices and techniques of power suggested by Bentham's diagram of the Panopticon into the imposition of various forms of disciplinary conduct and subjectivation through space and time, Deleuze's reading emphasises Foucault as the self-confessed '*un cartographe, un releveur de plans*' (Foucault, 1994: 1593) which highlights the open relationality of forces as an abstract machine, developed in Deleuze and Guattari's emergence-oriented cartography or pragmatics (1980 [1987]).[3]

Both Deleuze and Foucault were influenced by the work of Nietzsche. They co-edited and co-authored the Introduction to the *Œuvres complètes de F. Nietzsche* (Foucault and Deleuze, 1967). Deleuze builds upon Nietzsche's (1886 [1966]) concept of the will to power, explaining that the will to power does not imply wanting power or to dominate (Deleuze, 1962 [1983]: 79). Rather, it is an internal, creative cause of being; the active principle of the organisation of relations between dominant and dominated, active and reactive, affirmative and negative forces.[4]

Power, as explicated in Deleuze and Guattari's question 'what is a power centre?' (1980 [1987]: 224), is internal to what it can do; the outcome of its immersion in organisational forms where 'all manner of reinterpretation, fluid negotiation and translation hold sway' (Allen, 2003: 83). No wonder, then, that for Deleuze, the State is 'not at all the master of its plans' (Deleuze and Parnet, 1977 [2002]: 145). Key analytical questions are thus 'which will to power has taken hold of the forces in this thing to make it what it is?' (Bignall, 2008: 132); what relations of forces have been/are in play?; can they be diagrammed?

POWER: *POUVOIR* AND *PUISSANCE*

Deleuze and Guattari (1980 [1987]: 106) make a crucial distinction between power in French as *pouvoir* – instituted power of domination or coercive power – and *puissance* – the capacity to form emergent unities which respect the heterogeneity of their components, immanent forces/capacities of becoming, capacity to act/be acted upon rather than to dominate another. *Pouvoir* may be regarded as a power of antiproduction (Deleuze and Guattari, 1972 [1984]), in which affirmative relations are prevented from forming and negative relations dominate; an asymmetrical relation of power. *Puissance*, in contrast, is a power of autoproduction, a creative capacity in which a relation emerges by connecting heterogeneous elements.

Deleuze and Foucault both distinguish between *pouvoir* and *puissance*, deriving the distinction from Spinoza's (1677 [1985]) discussion of *potestas* and *potentia*. But whereas Foucault's analytics of power tend to be concerned with processes of *pouvoir*, Deleuze and Guattari are more interested in *puissance*. In this section, I concentrate on Deleuze and Guattari's contribution. For ease of reading in a necessarily linear document, I explore selected concepts under the subheadings of *pouvoir* and *puissance*. As Deleuze and Guattari (1991 [1994]: 35) explain, however, concepts are 'not pieces of a jigsaw puzzle', although they resonate into a powerful whole. The power of a concept emerges when it joins others on a plane, limiting or enhancing each other and working together. Interpreting Deleuze and Guattari is nigh on impossible. What follows is, therefore, inevitably a 'monstrous' offspring (Deleuze, 1990 [1995]: 6) of their work.

Pouvoir

Deleuze and Guattari use *pouvoir* in a similar manner to Foucault, as 'an instituted and reproducible relation of force, a selective concretization of potential' (Massumi, 1987: xvii). It is often easy to discern the power of *pouvoir* in relation to planning practice. For example, the construction, in South Australia, of the bridge at Hindmarsh Island, known to Indigenous Aboriginal people as Kumarangk, demonstrates the privileging of colonial, rational, documented, adversarial systems of spatial planning-related law over Indigenous oral, spiritual knowledges about sacred sites (Hillier, 2007). The story illustrates how *pouvoir* restricted the potential for *puissance* of the local Ngarrindjeri women to respect their heritage.

Researchers investigating processes of *pouvoir* may find the following DeleuzoGuattarian concepts of interest, recognising their dynamic entanglement.

Territorialisation is a concept frequently engaged in Deleuze and Guattari's work. Processes trace flows of materialities and expressivities that come together for various reasons of territorialisation at particular times, as coded and stratified assemblages of dynamic, heterogeneous elements. Territorialisation produces order, functionally organising sets of elements into groups with common features (such as species taxa, land use zones, use classes and so on), using certain signs to mark fixed borders between them. It involves 'an activity of selection, elimination and extraction' (Deleuze and Guattari, 1980 [1987]: 311). In this way, territorialisation is linked with production of identity, subjectivity and naming.

Deleuze and Guattari (1980 [1987]) describe space according to its degree of smoothness and *striation*. Smooth and striated spaces are tendencies or modes of organisation which can be physical (as in cities) or mental (psychological). Smooth space is seemingly undifferentiated space (Deleuze and Guattari offer the example of felt cloth, with fibres matted together) in contrast to striated space (woven cloth, with fibres ordered in a delimited, gridded system) which is regular, ordered and closed. In striated space, relationships are linear cause and effect, and the observer has a god's-eye view, able to see the order of things by deterministic laws. Smooth space consists of points as relays between lines; striated space consists of lines between points (Deleuze and Guattari, 1980 [1987]: 480–481).

Regarding the world in terms of striated space sees it in terms of a set of categories, 'formed and perceived things' and properties (Deleuze and Guattari, 1980 [1987]: 479). It is the space made of things as opposed to space as process (Somers-Hall, 2018: 244). However, what is important is not the structure of the world *per se*, but the process by which a certain structure is used to investigate the world and to demarcate space. Deleuze and Guattari (1980 [1987]: 377) suggest that counting is a frequent method of dividing space; such as the number of voters in an electorate, the number of rare species in a plot of land, the number of residential units per hectare.

Striated space is fixed. It 'bounds, structures, frames and locates action; and practices of discipline, regulation, subjection take place inside these spaces' (Osborne and Rose, 2004: 218). Yet, striated space is always lacking. There is a constitutive outside or lack: people rebel, plans go awry, things change. 'Striated spatialization, precisely because it aspires to a certain rigour or rigidity, is vulnerable to forces that would turn its lines into points, open up its intervals, redistribute its surfaces' (Osborne and Rose 2004: 218). Striated space tends to be associated with the State: 'one of the fundamental tasks of the State is to striate the space' (Deleuze and Guattari, 1980 [1987]: 479) (through local zoning schemes, land use classes and so on). Smooth space is created by war machines along lines of flight (such as anti-wind farm lobbies, civil liberties organisations). Both spaces, nevertheless, cannot be completely actualised, opening up opportunities for the counter form of space. Forces at work within space are constantly attempting to striate it whilst in the course of striation other forces are smoothing. The two exist in complex, mixed forms in agonistic relation which Deleuze and Guattari (1980 [1987]: 481) exemplify through the sea and the city: 'the sea is a smooth space fundamentally open to striation, and the city, is the force of striation that reimparts smooth space'.

The story of Antony Gormley's art installation, *Another Place*, illustrates how planners have striated the sea and beach at Crosby Beach, Liverpool, England (Hillier, 2012). It demonstrates how the 'smooth space par excellence' (Deleuze and Guattari, 1980 [1987]: 479) of the sea and the random placing of 100 cast iron statues of Gormley's naked body were striated by requirements to comply with a multiplicity of planning, health and safety, environmental and other policies and regulations. After two years of heated debate the iron men, the beach, human visitors, fishers, jet skiers, sailors, dogs, and the sea were acceptably striated for permissions to be granted. Several iron men were relocated to afford lifeboat passage, a by-law requires dogs to remain on-lead, signage and ranger patrols warn visitors of safe areas to walk and fish. Powerful, managerial discourses of territorialization and striation demanded the iron men be gridded along lines of fixed orientation, mapped on maritime and coastguard agency charts and fitted with numbered identity bracelets.

Deleuze and Guattari call any specific formalisation of expression, such as the above, a regime of signs, in which 'patterns of power relations interconnect via discursive and non-discursive assemblages' (Bogue, 2007: 147). The authors present four, always mixed, regimes of signs (1980 [1987]: 111ff).[5] The *signifying regime* is applicable to all 'hierarchical, centred groups' (1980 [1987]: 116). Signs are regarded as discrete constants linguistically coded by a bureaucracy in imposition of power relations as sets of rules, permitted discourses and so on. The power of signifying regimes to define, classify and rank in a hierarchy 'is an act which is based not on the quality or essence of an entity but on the powers which constitute the capacity to define' (MacCormack, 2014: 2).

Deleuze and Guattari regard language as one of the strongest vehicles to transmit a set of rules and to produce territorial codes. As Deleuze and Guattari write: 'language is made not to be believed but to be obeyed and to compel obedience' (1980 [1987]: 76). What Deleuze and Guattari term *order-words* include commands: 'stop!'. But the authors go beyond such explicit statements, suggesting that every word or every statement has implicit presuppositions. Questions, promises and so on are order-words which compel belief in a particular ordering of the world. 'Let people say' (Deleuze and Guattari, 1980 [1987]: 76).

Let people say, for instance, that *Planning Makes it Happen* (WAPC, 2009). This Western Australian 'Blueprint for Planning Reform' opens with the statement that 'the planning system has to be supportive of economic development and job creation while offering lifestyle choice, urban amenity and a sustainable future to a growing population' (WAPC, 2009: 1). The Minister for Planning comments that this represents 'a strong message to simplify the approvals process, cut red tape, reduce timelines and have greater certainty and accountability in the process', requiring 'the betterment of the planning system in its totality' (WAPC, 2009: 1). Order-words (verbs – simplify, cut, reduce; nouns – red tape, certainty, accountability, betterment) both give orders and establish order by determining relations between the planning system, economic development, job creation, lifestyle choice, urban amenity and so on, and presupposing networks of statements that can be made about the planning system. This enacts many types of implicit obligations (including the planning system to the development industry) and preset directions (urban development and resource development are good; streamlined and simplified planning is good). 'The order-word begins and sustains chains of signifiers that are presupposed and somewhat predetermined' (Hargraves, 2018: 189), expressing 'a possible world as if it were the only and inevitable world' (Gatens, 2000: 71).

Order-words effect an incorporeal transformation which changes the status of a body in its relations to other bodies. Deleuze and Guattari (1980 [1987]: 80–81) offer the example of the word 'guilty' uttered by a judge in a courtroom transforming an accused body into a convict. Statements, such as 'guilty', and its immanent implications for the respective body, reflect the semiotic order of the social field in which 'guilty' is uttered. In this manner, planning policy and regulations become 'red tape', reduction becomes 'betterment'. For Deleuze and Guattari, 'the order-word is a death sentence; it always implies a death sentence' (1980 [1987]: 107). In my example above, the death sentence hangs over non-human ecosystems and habitat deemed 'in the way' of urban growth and economic development, possibly even of the planning system 'in its totality'.

Order-words are instruments of control. In his 1985–86 lectures on Foucault and the 'Postscript on Control Societies' (1990 [1995]), Deleuze develops and updates Foucault's work on biopower and biopolitics, identifying *control societies* as taking over from disciplinary societies. Deleuze (1990 [1995]: 179) explains: 'in disciplinary societies you were always starting all over again (as you went from school to barracks, from barracks to factory), while in control societies you never finish anything – business [the corporation], training [education], and military service being coexisting metastable states of a single modulation'. The confining institutions of the disciplinary regime have not disappeared, but are relocated within broader regimes of power, continuous monitoring and control, such as electronic tags for persons on bail, CCTV, GPS tracking devices and so on. Control power works on the calculation of probabilities: of a bail subject absconding, a person entering an exclusion zone, for instance.

Foreseeing the future, Deleuze (1990 [1995]: 181–182) tells us that 'Foucault has imagined a town where anyone can leave their flat, their street, their neighbourhood, using their (dividual) electronic card that opens this or that barrier; but the card may also be rejected on a particular day, or between certain times of day; it doesn't depend on the barrier but on the computer that is making sure everyone is in a permissible place'. This scenario has become familiar across the globe during the COVID-19 pandemic, with the international use of mobile phone apps which 'contact trace' users' encounters and locations, awarding green, orange or red 'traffic lights' of permissibility to leave home and enter particular places.

Algorithms control people's lives based on calculated probability of some future behaviour occurring, from security screening at transit hubs, surveillance in department stores and so on. Algorithms have been used in planning practice for some time, with regard to transport modelling, anticipating demand for residential construction, infrastructure provision, modelling behaviours in stakeholder participatory strategies and so on (Davis et al., 2019; Wagner and de Vries, 2019). 'Smart cities' are of the present. The 2019 trial of algorithmic face-recognition software in Perth, Australia, was partly justified on the basis of providing data 'which will assist planning and urban decision-making such as the placement of infrastructure or enhancing the development of transport solutions' (Thomas, 2019, online). However, such software is particularly susceptible to reifying power relations as many algorithms embody specific ontological views of space, humans and non-humans and/or epistemological approaches. What Deleuze and Guattari term *faciality* comprises a universal reference point of identity and subjectivity which channels social perception, stratifying elements such as belonging or not belonging, normal and deviant. Faciality operates through power-laden binarisation of acceptability and non-acceptability. One's face must 'fit'.

Faciality comprises white walls of signification and black holes of subjectification. However, as Deleuze and Guattari (1980 [1987]: 180) point out, 'there is no signifiance without a despotic assemblage, no subjectification without an authoritarian assemblage'. The white wall/black hole faciality machine constitutes the face and organises faces in relation to a standard or norm. For instance, a masterplanned residential estate 'brand' often white walls a specific discourse and materialities of delimited construction materials, paint colours, turf and shrub species, mailboxes and so on. All purchasers of lots in such estates must submit their design details for the developer's approval prior to lodging a planning application with the local municipality. 'Deviance' in the form of individualism or experimentation is not permitted. Faciality thus creates the 'resigned, docile and neurotic subjects needed for capitalist assemblages to govern' (Widder, 2018: 130).

Puissance

Michel Foucault summarised a key principle of Deleuze's and Guattari's thought as 'do not become enamoured of power' (in Deleuze and Guattari, 1972 [1984]: xiv); particularly the power of capitalist societies. As such, Deleuze and Guattari's work may be read as offering an 'array of concepts, tools and practices to critique strategy, combat capitalism and develop alternative forms of life' (Munro and Thanem, 2018: 70).

The concepts outlined below relate to *puissance*, a DeleuzoGuattarian capacity for existence and to form assemblages, a capacity to affect and be affected. *Puissance* signifies a range of potential (Massumi, 1987: xvii). It is not directly concerned with resistance (as for Foucault), but more with generation, reflecting Nietzsche's affirmative will to power. It tends to be micro or 'molecular' in nature, relating to strife and flux, in contrast with the more macro or 'molar' relations of *pouvoir* described above. Typical concepts include lines of flight, war machines and the nomad, all of which deterritorialise molar functions and structures, and are movements of creative resistance.

A *line of flight* is a vector of escape, or trajectory, of transformation from what has been towards a direction which is unknown. It marks a threshold of lowered resistance to something, a change in desire or the intensity of desire: 'you can no longer stand what you put up with before' (Deleuze and Parnet, 1977 [2002]: 126). Protest groups using social media, for example, may challenge state power by speaking outside of the normal institutional boundaries of citizen participation. Lines of flight may be born from resistance, but they are creative and generative: 'it's along this line of flight that things come to pass, becomings evolve, revolutions take shape' (Deleuze 1990 [1995]: 45). They are not necessarily positive for all concerned, however. The line of flight of Boko Haram in Nigeria negatively affects women's rights and opportunities. State power may act to block and capture lines of flight with which it does not agree or feels threatened, such as homeless people using public places or the Occupy movement.

Lines of flight are deterritorialising. Grids, codes, systems which confer fixed meaning are disrupted and destroyed. Deleuze and Guattari argue in *Anti-Œdipus* (1972 [1984]) that capitalism is defined by deterritorialising lines of flight. Absolute deterritorialisation, however, would generate its collapse. Capitalism thus develops a network of reterritorialising forces to moderate or capture the extent and nature of deterritorialisation and effectively save itself from itself, demonstrated by the response to the 2008 financial crisis. Deterritorialisation is always accompanied by some form of reterritorialisation and the establishment of new rules.

Although Deleuze distinguishes between 'sedentary' (in pre-established categories) and 'nomadic' (non-hierarchical and emergent) distributions of elements in *Difference and Repetition* (1968 [1994]), it is in Plateau 12 of *A Thousand Plateaus*, '1227: Treatise on Nomadology – the War Machine', that Deleuze and Guattari introduce the linked concepts of *nomad* and *war machine* as an alternative to State organisation. It is important to note that war machine does not refer to war as armed fighting, but to forms of spatialisation and distribution within space, which Deleuze and Guattari relate to philosophical, political, technical and artistic thought processes and practices.

The opposition between nomad and State is central for Deleuze and Guattari (1980 [1987]: 380): 'either nomos or polis'. Whereas State space is striated, sedentary space, 'the points of which are distributed between its different occupants in a stable and regulated way' (Antonioli, 2017: 431) and characterised by 'walls, enclosures and roads between enclosures' (Deleuze and Guattari, 1980 [1987]: 381), nomadic space is inhabited according to the dynamic laws of its own movement; a smooth space, populated by entities inserting themselves into the continually shifting nature of the land (Lundy, 2013). The State and the nomad, therefore, are characterised by their differing spatial relations; distribution *in* space and *of* space. Nomadism denotes adaptability, shifting patterns of behaviour, non-linearity, self-organisation and so on. It is the 'subversion of set conventions' (Braidotti, 1994: 5), linked with the concept of lines of flight, of reacting against microfascist dominant systems of thought and social conditions: not of running away, but of runoffs (Deleuze and Guattari, 1980 [1987]: 204). Nomadism thus shifts the focus from a rationality-driven consciousness to an ontological relationality of *puissance* in which 'other' or 'minor' values and elements are affirmed and capacitated.

Allegedly the invention of nomads (Deleuze and Guattari, 1980 [1987]: 380), the war machine is exterior to the State, resisting coding by the State as much as possible. A key issue is, therefore, that of analysing and understanding the nature of interaction between 'war machines of metamorphosis and State apparatuses of identity' (Deleuze and Guattari, 1980 [1987]: 361). Yet nomos and polis are not truly independent. They are, Deleuze and Guattari (1980 [1987]: 367, 385) point out, 'ontologically a single field of interaction' in which the State attempts to 'vanquish' or appropriate nomadic anexact essence, and nomads attempt to 'cut loose' State scientific thinking by problematising it in a different way. Olkowski (2017: 82) suggests that 'the war machine is not necessarily seeking war or revolution – only displacement'. Examples of war machines may include guerrilla gardening, design activism and so on, demonstrating that 'it is possible to live smooth even in the cities, to be an urban nomad' (Deleuze and Guattari, 1980 [1987]: 482).

Deleuze (1968 [1994]) wrote that the power (*pouvoir*) of a classic or dogmatic image of thought renders it impossible to think about problems 'authentically' because problems are defined through their solutions. Yet, far from disappearing beneath the solution, the problem persists (Deleuze, 1968 [1994]: 163), often in another form. A toll-freeway may divert traffic onto a rat-run through residential streets, saving time for those willing and able to pay the toll, but the 'solution' is problematic for those living along the rat-run who suffer increased noise and fumes, reduced property value and so on. It is important that planners do not allow solutions to define problems (such as only considering projects for which private sector funding is available, or what 'best practice' manuals suggest). Solutions are actual, real identities, whereas problems are virtual, inexhaustible. It is easy to allow a solution to determine how a problem is framed. In this way, many potential virtuals may be ignored, succumbing to the power of an overdetermined solution. *Puissance* would entail the capacity to think outside the proverbial box, to deterritorialise standard planning 'solutions' and follow experimental lines of flight.

AND SO TO PLANNING

Whilst Deleuze and Guattari do not write much about planning (architecture is discussed in *What is Philosophy*, 1991 [1994]), they did participate with Michel Foucault and other researchers in a number of projects under the auspices of the Centre d'Études, de Recherche et de Formation Institutionelle (CERFI) on urban planning-related topics. In the early 1970s, the research group was involved in five funded projects on new towns, mining towns, green spaces and urban planning.[6] The projects are concerned with collective social organisation and infrastructure in urban areas, grouped together as *Les équipements de pouvoir*, where *équipement* translates roughly as technical, social and moral system infrastructure (Rabinow, 1989) or as collectively used infrastructure or amenities.

The research stresses the importance of understanding the powerful axiomatics underlying provision of *équipement*. Although the city de- and re-territorialises flows, it tends to be a totalising structure; 'a form of territorialization, of blockage' (Fourquet and Murard, 1973: 44), where the function of collective *équipement* is to produce the socius, its expressive and material logics, internal orderings and so on. The group claim that provision of collective *équipement* represents the State interpretation of needs of subjects not conscious of what they need. 'Needs' thus become normalised (Fourquet and Murard, 1973: 153–156), characterised by relations of power (as argued by Foucault: 46) and control (by Deleuze: 217).[7] The funded projects further develop these ideas, with Deleuze heading a group researching the emergence of collective *équipement*, Guattari on green spaces and Foucault on *équipements* of normalisation, especially health and education, and *équipement* in urban planning as an administrative colonisation of the territory (Elden, 2017: 173–175).

Deleuze and Guattari's body of work might be engaged by planning researchers and practitioners as enhancing understanding and analysis of planning processes and outcomes, especially the multiple ways in which desire and power processes oppress and constrain, stimulate resistance or generate capacities for action. One might examine, for instance, whether state planning practices function as a DeleuzoGuattarian 'power centre' (1980 [1987]: chapter 9) situated between striated lines and flows of multiplicities. Power centres are defined 'not by an absolute exercise of power within its domain but by the relative adaptations and conversions it effects between the line and the flow' (Deleuze and Guattari, 1980 [1987]: 217). Planning as a power centre would function as a logical regulatory device, converting or territorialising a flow into a line, differences into identities (such as unzoned to zoned land, landowners into development applicants, plans and elevations into an approved design, local residents into a citizen jury). Yet something always escapes along a line of flight to create something new, to 'reshuffle and stir up its segments' (Deleuze and Guattari, 1980 [1987]: 218): a new use class, a design precedent, an alternative way of thinking, perhaps.

Strategic spatial planning attempts to articulate contingencies. However, contingencies are non-articulable 'potential relational modulations of contexts that are not yet contained in their ordering as possibilities that have been recognised and can be practically regulated' (Massumi, 2002: 240). Planning practices thus constitute the indeterminate potential for possibilities to be added to particular context situations: 'a fiction at the heart of the real' (Deleuze, 1985 [1989]: 144). Practices address a more-than-human community to come; a not-yet. It could be argued that a becoming-democratic of the more-than-human lends itself to a form of fabulation: a 'conceptual groping towards potential-to-be' (Massumi, 2002: 242).

Deleuze (1990 [1995]: 174) politicises Henri Bergson's (1932 [1986]) notion of fabulation into a creative process in which 'the writer and the people [*sic*] go toward one another' (Deleuze, 1985 [1989], in Lambert, 2002: 137) in inclusionary co-production to make new possibilities visible. Fabulations are visions of yet to be explored possibilities (Bogue, 2006: 220) which break historical continuities and disrupt conventional narratives. This would be a vision radically different (a line of flight) from that familiar to planning practitioners; a vision with capacity to 'falsify orthodox truths in the process of generating emergent truths' (Bogue, 2011: 81). As Bogue (2011: 81) explains:

> Fabulation does not presume an ideal, nor does it have an external goal as its motivation. It is its own end, an irreducibly temporal process of becoming-other that is open-ended, and if it is a process of summoning forth a future people [*sic*], it is one that cannot move beyond itself without involving the participation of a collectivity in its action.

Fabulation could provide stimulation for 'an experiment which exceeds our capacities to foresee' (Deleuze and Parnet, 1977 [2002]: 48) and seeds future processes, pushing futurity into presentness by imagining 'what if …'.

Like all lines of flight, fabulation commences with resistance because 'to create is to resist' (Deleuze and Guattari, 1991 [1994]: 110). It resists a pre-formed blueprint of the future in favour of reference points of landmarks for a pragmatic cartography. Not utopian, but 'a creative experimentation with what reality can become' (Stenner, 2018: 158), which sits somewhere along a spectrum from dependence on epistemic norms and planes of scientific reference to a creative imagination of new becomings, bringing the unthinkable to the table.

Would this be possible, or would such 'plans-that-are-not-plans' – or non-plans[8] – be captured and reterritorialised by the State? Co-design activists around the world are inclusively engaging generally marginalised participants in activities which permit subtle redirections of collective assessments of situations and for speculative actualisations of desires toward possible futures (Lenskjold et al., 2015). Such actions may, nevertheless, be criticised for remaining within the dominant system rather than rupturing it, regarding 'the marginal' as 'little more than a resource to be co-opted, harnessed and exploited for purposes of organizational creativity' (Munro and Thanem, 2018: 71).

Mark Purcell (2013: 1) suggests that Deleuze and Guattari's advocacy of lines of flight and *puissance* should 'force us to ask both existential questions about what planning is and normative questions about whether we should be planning at all'. These are important questions and ones which should include explicit consideration of both negative and positive forms of power: *pouvoir* and *puissance*. But it is also important not to focus on planning alone, as planning is but part of a much larger belief system, the problematisation of which forms the focus of Deleuze and Guattari's *Anti-Œdipus* (1972 [1984]). An ethical response is necessary, not one based on a transcendent framework, but one which gives voice to, and listens to, the problem itself, rather than to its solution.

CONCLUSIONS: SHADES OF POWER

'When any kind of convention, procedure, guideline, suggestion, influence or provocation is deemed to count as a technique of power, there comes a moment when … everything begins to shade into power' (Allen, 2003: 99). Is spatial planning, then, 'a powerful tool for the implementation of capital', so powerful that it becomes blocked 'from perceiving power other than in the distorted mirror of its own autonomy' (Wallenstein, 2016: xxix)? But there may be dangers of seeing power-plays in everything, losing sight of what is specific to the different relational processes or modalities of power and lacking the capacity to engage relevant strategies of resistance and disruption.

Spatial planning, as a land-based practice, is a site where unevenly positioned worlds entangle. Powerful enactments of land-based expertise, by agents of the State and private sectors, render some futures more or less possible for these worlds. Land is increasingly recognised as ontologically plural – as relation, as geospatial object, as lived experience, as speculative practice and so on – as a 'particularly fraught semiotic object' (Shoffner and Reisman, 2020: online). Yet, it is not land *per se*, but agents' particular relation to the land which explains the cultural logics of practices such as planning and development. For instance, the same piece of peri-urban land, once called a swamp, too difficult for farming or urbanisation, may now be termed a wetland or lake for drainage purposes or curated as an aesthetic centrepiece of a residential estate. Landowners, planners and developers exert power over (*pouvoir*) the swamp ecosystem, creating a novel ecosystem, often with very different assemblages of plants and animals.

If, as Deleuze and Guattari (1980 [1987]) suggest, power is internal to what it can do, and what it can do relates to its immersion in organisational forms (spatial planning systems, capitalist systems, political systems …), where interpretation and reinterpretation, translation and retranslation, negotiation, coercion and so on, are important, there should be locatable cracks in those configurations of power such that lines of flight of disruption, mutation and transformation are possible. These cracks may be prised open by human and non-human agents. In my wetland/lake example above, agents might include environmental professionals and/or activists, or non-humans, such as cyanobacteria, phragmites, cattails and mosquitoes. These actors may generate capacities for *puissance*, to deterritorialise and 'rewild' the waterbody.[9] This would be an affirmative will to power, a *puissance* which actively destroys the human-coded structure.

Control may have become the cultural logic of our time, with its signifying regimes and order-words, striations/codings and technologies of *pouvoir*. Yet perhaps there will be opportunities for lines of flight for more-than-humans to be positive. Perhaps a crack may be opened if planning practitioners 'betray' the system by 'anticipat[ing] and detect[ing] the powers (*puissance*) of the future rather than applying past and present powers (*pouvoirs*)' (Deleuze and Guattari, 1980 [1987]: 124). The question for planning is not how to find a resolution or to impose a solution. It is how to enable and nurture the positive capacities of future more-than-human encounters.

Deleuze and Guattari (1980 [1987]: 422–423) state that a scientific or artistic movement can be a potential war machine if it maps or diagrams a plane of immanence, a creative line of flight and a smooth space in which to move. Might spatial planners be nomadic? It is possible to read Deleuze and Guattari as suggesting that the power (*puissance*) of minorities/nomads is not to be measured by their capacity to overthrow or reverse the system, but to bring to bear the force of a 'supplement' or 'synthetic relation' of an alternative kind of organising which makes 'war' by creating something else.

Becoming-nomad may enable us as planning theorists and practitioners to think through and move across established categories and conventional ways of thinking and acting, to consider the effects of power (both *pouvoir* and *puissance*) that our actions are likely to have upon human and non-human worlds. To do so requires critical analysis of oneself and one's part in the planning system. We need to begin by acknowledging that we are part of the problem, rather than its solution.

I conclude with the words of Félix Guattari (2013: 57, my translation):

> The complexity of the position of the architect and the town planner is intense but exciting from the moment they take into consideration their aesthetic, ethic and political responsibilities. Immersed at the heart of the consensus of the democratic city, it is their concern to navigate, through their plan and their design, decisive bifurcations of the destiny of the subjective city.
>
> Either humanity, with their help, will reinvent its urban future, or it will be condemned to perish under the weight of its own immobility which today threatens to render it impotent in the face of the extraordinary challenges which … confront it.

NOTES

1. Deleuze regards desire as creating relations through which power might actualise and operate: 'there are investments of desire that mould and distribute power, that make it the property of the policeman [*sic*] as much as of the prime minister' (Foucault and Deleuze, 1972 [1977]: 215).
    Many commentators (including Bignall 2008; Grace 2009; Morar et al. 2016; Rabouin 2000; Schönher 2015) have examined differences in understandings of desire and power between Deleuze and Foucault. Several authors also indicate the convergences between Foucault's, Deleuze's and Guattari's ideas of power as a productive, heterogeneous, variable process which can be either positive or negative (Cisney, 2014; Morar and Gracieuse, 2016; Patton, 2000; 2016; Penfield, 2014; Protevi, 2015). Debates are often passionate, with Nail (2016: 257) complaining that scholarly arguments 'have largely hinged on interpretive comparisons based on what Deleuze or Foucault did *not* say' rather than what they said or wrote.
2. Deleuze utilises the term 'force' in two distinctive ways. The first derives from his reading of Nietzsche (1962 [1983]) and relates to force as an abstract, relational form of energy. This form of force should not be confused with power. Power is the domestication of force; a network of forces operating in an impelling mode (Massumi, 1992). In his work with Guattari, Deleuze expresses force as a form of *puissance*, or capacity.

3.   While Deleuze offers several different conceptual interpretations of diagram throughout his work and that with Guattari, my concern in this chapter is Deleuze's engagement with Foucault's diagram of power. For detailed discussion of the diagram as engaged by Foucault and Deleuze, see Wallenstein (2009) and Hetherington (2011).
4.   Active and reactive forces are closely affiliated to, and complicit with, but not the same as, affirmative and negative wills to power. Action and reaction are like 'instruments of the will to power which affirms and denies' (Deleuze, 1970 [1988]: 50). Affirmation and negation 'go beyond' action and reaction. As qualities of becoming, affirmation expresses active forces becoming dominant and negation expresses forces in their becoming reactive.
5.   These are a pre-signifying regime (of polyvocality operating in 'primitive' regimes), a counter-signifying regime (nomadic, warrior bands), a signifying regime and a post-signifying regime.
6.   For more information regarding these projects see Elden (2016; 2017).
7.   Here Foucault's concept of biopower and Deleuze's control societies come together.
8.   In the 1960s, *Non-Plan: An Experiment in Freedom* (Banham et al., 1969: 436) asked 'what would happen if there were no plan?' *Non-Plan* explored ways of circumventing planning bureaucracy to involve people in the co-design of their living and working environments. Critics, however, claimed that absence of planning control power would give free rein to market capitalism with dire social and environmental consequences.
9.   Of course, human agents may consequently capture and reterritorialise the waterbody by spraying with herbicide and insecticide.

REFERENCES

Allen, John (2003), *Lost Geographies of Power*, Oxford: Blackwell.
Antonioli, Manola (2017), 'Urban war Machines', in Paulo de Assis and Paulo Guidici (eds), *The Dark Precursor*, Vol. 2, Leuven: Leuven University Press, pp. 431–436.
Banham, R., P. Barker, P. Hall and C. Price (1969), 'Non-plan: An Experiment in Freedom', *New Society*, 13(338), pp. 435–443.
Bergson, Henri (1932), *The Two Sources of Morality and Religion,* trans. R. Audra and C. Brereton (1986), Notre Dame, IN: University of Notre Dame Press.
Bignall, S. (2008), 'Deleuze and Foucault on Desire and Power', *Angelaki*, 13(1), pp. 127–147.
Bogue, Ronald (2006), 'Fabulation, Narration and the People to Come', in Constantin Boundas (ed.), *Deleuze and Philosophy*, Edinburgh University Press, Edinburgh, pp. 202–223.
Bogue, Ronald (2007), *Deleuze's Way*, Aldershot, UK: Ashgate.
Bogue, R. (2011), 'Deleuze and Guattari and the Future of Politics: Science Fiction, Protocols and the People to Come', *Deleuze Studies*, 5(Supp.), pp. 77–97.
Braidotti, Rosi (1994) *Nomadic Subjects*, Cambridge: Cambridge University Press.
Cisney, V. (2014), 'Becoming-other: Foucault, Deleuze, and the Political Nature of Thought', *Foucault Studies*, 17, pp. 36–59, accessed 12 May 2020 at https://rauli.cbs.dk/index.php/foucault-studies/article/view/4252.
Davis, Paul, Angela O'Mahony and Jonathan Pfautz (eds) (2019), *Social-Behavioral Modeling for Complex Systems*, New York: Wiley.
Deleuze, Gilles (1962) *Nietzsche and Philosophy*, trans. H. Tomlinson (1983), London: Athlone Press.
Deleuze, Gilles (1968), *Difference and Repetition*, trans. P. Patton (1994), London: Athlone Press.
Deleuze, Gilles (1968), *Expressionism in Philosophy: Spinoza*, trans. M. Joughin (1990), New York: Zone Books.
Deleuze, Gilles (1970), *Spinoza: Practical Philosophy*, trans. R. Hurley (1988), San Francisco, CA: City Light Books.
Deleuze, Gilles (1985), *Cinema 2: The Time-image*, trans. H. Tomlinson and R. Galeta (1989), Minneapolis, MN: University of Minnesota Press.
Deleuze, Gilles (1986) *Foucault*, trans. S. Hand (1988), London: Athlone Press.
Deleuze, Gilles (1990) 'Postscript on Control Societies', in Gilles Deleuze, *Negotiations 1972–90*, trans. M. Joughin (1995), New York: Columbia University Press, pp. 177–182.

Deleuze, Gilles (1990) *Negotiations 1972–90*, trans. M. Joughin (1995), New York: Columbia University Press.

Deleuze, Gilles and Claire Parnet (1977), *Dialogues*, trans. by H. Tomlinson and B. Habberjam (2002), London: Athlone Press.

Deleuze, Gilles and Félix Guattari (1972) *Anti-Oedipus: Capitalism and Schizophrenia*, trans. R. Hurley, M. Seem and H. Lane (1984), London: Athlone Press.

Deleuze, Gilles and Félix Guattari (1980) *A Thousand Plateaus: Capitalism and Schizophrenia*, trans. B. Massumi (1987), London: Athlone Press.

Deleuze, Gilles and Félix Guattari (1991) *What is Philosophy?*, trans. H. Tomlinson and G. Burchill (1994), London: Verso.

Elden, Stuart (2016), *Foucault's Last Decade*, Cambridge: Polity Press.

Elden, Stuart (2017), *Foucault: The Birth of Power*, Cambridge: Polity Press.

Foucault, Michel (1975) *Discipline and Punish: The Birth of the Prison*, trans. A. Sheridan (1995), New York: Vintage Books.

Foucault, Michel (1994) '"Sur la sellette": An Interview with J.-L. Ezine', *Dits et écrits 1*, Paris: Gallimard, pp. 1588–93.

Foucault, Michel and Gilles Deleuze (1972), 'Intellectuals and Power: A Conversation between Michel Foucault and Gilles Deleuze', trans. D. Bouchard and S. Simon, in Donald Bouchard (ed.) (1977), *Michel Foucault: Language, Counter-Memory, Practice*, Ithaca, NY: Cornell University Press, pp. 205–217.

Foucault, Michel and Gilles Deleuze (eds) (1967) *Œuvres complètes de F. Nietzsche*, Paris: Gallimard.

Fourquet, F. and L. Murard (1973), 'Les équipements du pouvoir', *Recherches*, 13.

Friedmann, J. (1998), 'Planning Theory Revisited', *European Planning Studies*, 6(3), 245–253.

Gatens, M. (2000), 'Feminism as "Password": Rethinking the "Possible" with Spinoza and Deleuze', *Hypatia*, 15(2), pp. 59–75.

Goodchild, Philip (1996), *Deleuze and Guattari: An Introduction to the Politics of Desire*, London: Sage.

Grace, W. (2009), 'Faux amis: Foucault and Deleuze on sexuality and desire', *Critical Inquiry*, 36(3), pp. 52–75.

Guattari, Félix (2013), 'Pratiques écosophiques et restauration de la cité subjective', in Stéphane Nadaud (ed), *Guattari: Qu'est-ce que l'écosophie?*, Paris: Lignes, pp. 31–57.

Hargraves, Vicki (2018), 'The Posthuman Condition of Ethics in Early Childhood Literacy: Order-in(g) Be(e)ing Literacy', in Candace Kuby, Karen Spector and Jaye Johnson Thiel (eds), *Posthumanism and Literacy Education*, New York: Routledge, pp. 187–200.

Hetherington, K. (2011), 'Foucault, the Museum and the Diagram', *Sociological Review*, 59(3), pp. 457–475.

Hillier, Jean (2007), *Stretching Beyond the Horizon: A Multiplanar Theory of Spatial Planning and Governance*, Aldershot, UK: Ashgate.

Hillier, J. (2012), 'Liquid Spaces of Engagement: Entering the Waves with Antony Gormley and Olafur Eliasson', *Deleuze Studies*, 6(1), pp. 132–148.

Kedem, N. (2011), 'Introduction: Prophetism and the Problem of Betrayal', *Deleuze Studies*, 5(Supp.), pp. 1–6.

Lambert, Gregg (2002), *The Non-Philosophy of Gilles Deleuze*, New York: Continuum.

Lenskjold, T., S. Olander and J. Halse (2015), 'Minor Design Activism: Prompting Change from Within', *Design Issues*, 31(4), pp. 67–78.

Lundy, C. (2013), 'Who are our Nomads Today? Deleuze's Political Ontology and the Revolutionary Problematic', *Deleuze Studies*, 7(2), pp. 231–249.

MacCormack, Patricia (2014), 'Introduction', in Patricia MacCormack (ed.), *The Animal Catalyst*, London: Bloomsbury, pp. 1–12.

Massumi, Brian (1987), 'Notes on the Translation', in Gilles Deleuze and Félix Guattari (1980), *A Thousand Plateaus: Capitalism and Schizophrenia*, trans. B. Massumi (1987), London: Athlone Press, pp. xvi–xix.

Massumi, Brian (1992), *A User's Guide to Capitalism and Schizophrenia*, Cambridge, MA: MIT Press.

Massumi, Brian (2002), *Parables for the Virtual*, Durham, NC: Duke University Press.

Metzger, J., L. Soneryd and K.T. Hallström (2017), '"Power" is that Which Remains to be Explored: Dispelling the Ominous Dark Matter of Critical Planning Studies', *Planning Theory*, 16(2), pp. 203–222.

Morar, Nicolae and Marjorie Gracieuse (2016), 'Against the Incompatibility Thesis: A Rather Different Reading of the Desire-pleasure Problem', in Nicolae Morar, Thomas Nail and Daniel Smith (eds), *Between Deleuze and Foucault*, Edinburgh: Edinburgh University Press, pp. 232–246.

Morar, Nicolae, Thomas Nail and Daniel Smith (eds) (2016), *Between Deleuze and Foucault*, Edinburgh: Edinburgh University Press.

Munro, I. and T. Thanem (2018), 'Deleuze and the Deterritorialization of Strategy', *Critical Perspectives on Accounting*, 53, pp. 69–78.

Nail, Thomas (2016) 'Biopower and Control', in Nicolae Morar, Thomas Nail and Daniel Smith (eds), *Between Deleuze and Foucault*, Edinburgh: Edinburgh University Press, pp. 247–263.

Nietzsche, Friedrich (1886), *Beyond Good and Evil*, trans. W. Kaufmann (1966), New York: Vintage.

Olkowski, D. (2017), 'Serious Fun? Deleuze's *Treatise on Nomadology*', *PhænEx*, 12(1), pp. 71–84.

Osborne, T. and Rose N. (2004) 'Spatial Phenomenotechnics: Making Space with Charles Booth and Patrick Geddes', *Environment and Planning D, Society & Space*, 22, pp. 209–228.

Patton, Paul (2000), *Deleuze and the Political*, London: Routledge.

Patton, Paul (2016), 'Deleuze and Foucault: Political Activism, History and Actuality', in Nicolae Morar, Thomas Nail and Daniel Smith (eds), *Between Deleuze and Foucault*, Edinburgh: Edinburgh University Press, pp. 160–173.

Penfield, C. (2014), 'Toward a Theory of Transversal Politics: Deleuze and Foucault's Block of Becoming', *Foucault Studies*, 17, pp. 134–172, accessed 12 May 2020 at https://rauli.cbs.dk/index.php/foucault-studies/article/view/4257.

Protevi, J. (2015), 'Resonance with Deleuze', accessed 12 May 2020 at http://blogs.law.columbia.edu/foucault1313/2015/12/08/foucault-713-john-protevi-on·resonance-with-deleuze.

Purcell, M. (2013), 'A New Land: Deleuze and Guattari and Planning', *Planning Theory and Practice*, 14(1), pp. 20–38.

Rabinow, Paul (1989), *French Modern*, Chicago: University of Chicago Press.

Rabouin, D. (2000), 'Entre Deleuze et Foucault: le jeu du désir et du pouvoir', *Critique*, 637–638, pp. 475–490.

Schönher, M. (2015) 'Deleuze, a Split with Foucault', *Le foucaldien*, 1(1), accessed 12 May 2020 at https://foucaldien.net/articles/abstract/10.16995/lefou.8/.

Shoffner, E. and E. Reisman (2020), 'Knowing the Land: Ontological Plurality, "Experts", and Struggles over Space', *Pesoemails*, 8 May, accessed 8 May 2020 at https://listserv.utep.edu/mailman/listinfo/pesoemails.

Spinoza, Baruch (1677), *The Collected Writings of Spinoza*, Vol. 1, trans. E. Curley (1985), Princeton, NJ: Princeton University Press.

Somers-Hall, Henry (2018), 'The Smooth and the Striated', in Henry Somers-Hall, Jeffrey Bell and James Williams (eds), *A Thousand Plateaus and Philosophy*, Edinburgh: Edinburgh University Press, pp. 242–259.

Stenner, P. (2018) 'The Risky Truth of Fabulation: Deleuze, Bergson and Durkheim on the Becomings of Religion and Art', *Annual Review of Critical Psychology*, 14, pp. 149–173.

Thomas, E. (2019), 'Perth Council Facial Recognition Trial Greeted with Concern and Skepticism', *The Guardian*, 12 June, accessed 12 May 2020 at www.theguardian.com/technology/2019/jun/12/perth-councils-facial-recognition-trial-accused-of-blanket-surveillance.

Wagner, M. and W.T. de Vries (2019), 'Comparative Review of Methods Supporting Decision-making in Urban Development and Land Management', *Land*, 8(123), accessed 12 May 2020 at www.mdpi.com/2073-445X/8/8/123/pdf.

Wallenstein, Sven-Olov (2009), 'Diagrams of the Mind', in Warren Neidich (ed), *Lost Between the Extensivity/Intensivity Exchange*, Eindhoven: Onomatopee, pp. 8–13.

Wallenstein, Sven-Olov (2016), *Architecture, Critique, Ideology: Writings on Architecture and Theory*, Stockholm: Axl Books.

Western Australian Planning Commission (WAPC) and Department of Planning, Western Australia (DOPWA) (2009), *Planning Makes It Happen: A Blueprint for Planning Reform*, Perth: WAPC.

Widder, Nathan (2018) 'Year Zero: Faciality', in Henry Somers-Hall, Jeffrey Bell and James Williams (eds), *A Thousand Plateaus and Philosophy*, Edinburgh: Edinburgh University Press, pp. 115–133.

6. A Lacanian perspective on power in planning
Chuan Wang

INTRODUCTION

Planning practitioners work in political environments, since planning outcomes that pertain to land use and property rights are undoubtedly the result of political power (Forester, 1982). Planning might then be defined as 'an institutional set of ideas and practice' (Inch and Shepherd, 2020: 64). Furthermore, 'more than a passive recipient of the political ideas of the powerful' (Shepherd et al., 2020: 13), planning is a space of political contestation for different priorities in spatial arrangements and environmental conservation. It therefore also has the potential to challenge and transform power.

However, power analysis in planning research often regards power as enforcing relations amongst social actors (e.g. Albrechts, 2003; Metzger et al., 2017; Njoh, 2009; Sanli and Townshend, 2018). As a result, both the subjective and intersubjective dimensions of power – that concern how we become attached to, and sometimes resist, our own subjective and inter-subjective powers – lack more nuanced explanations (Newman, 2004). The often-complex relations in planning needs an approach to examine this intersubjective exchange of power between individuals and groups. From a Lacanian perspective, 'power is a relation which exists whenever a difference (real or symbolic) is created … as a social relationship' (Millot, 1988: 675). By exploring the ideological and symbolic dimensions of power, Lacanian analysis provides an explanatory approach for understanding how language exercises power in human affairs from both subjective and intersubjective dimensions (Bracher, 1988). Above all else, this approach allows us to examine the ultimate impulse of power, namely desire (Millot, 1988).

For Lacan, most human agency involves resolving a deficiency about something and the desire that this lack induces. Through planning policies, mottos and even buzzwords – such as 'urban resilience', 'sustainable development' and 'smart city' – politicians and planners execute their power by surreptitiously imposing their desire onto others for the purpose of constructing a common shared social reality. Although often without clear meanings, these buzzwords – or master signifiers in Lacanian terms – loosely fill the majority's lack of imagination to promote better urban futures through the creation of 'sublime objects of ideology' (Žižek, 1989). This sublimation process, which can be understood as a short-circuit 'between socially valorised objects and [individuals'] direct drive satisfactions', serves as a 'self-initiating and self-regulating form of power' (Hook, 2010: 859). When it comes to practice, the failure to satisfy the desired planning objectives thus tends to produce 'a subject that always already eludes the grasp of power' (de Vries, 2007: 38). By contrast, the Lacanian perspective on power allows us to discover its subjectifying function and 'the processes by which the subject comes to resist this subjectification' (Newman, 2004: 166).

This chapter firstly links power with desire and ideology as the entry point to employ a Lacanian power analysis. It then contends that the unconscious ideological dimension of power can be studied through the Lacanian account of 'the symbolic'. After arguing that master signifiers are the key medium of the master's power, and after demonstrating the endless power-seeking process found in the inherent divided subject – with both conscious and unconscious needs and wants – and the inherent unattainability of many objects of desire, this chapter then turns to Lacan's four discourses to elucidate four types of power relations in planning. This chapter also provides a Lacanian perspective on how subjects are attached to power through the use of numerous buzzwords that are found in contemporary planning policies and practices, and how always-divided subjects attach to or resist this subjectification of power.

POWER, DESIRE AND IDEOLOGY

Power analyses, particularly those of a Foucauldian nature, face difficulties in explaining the actual mechanisms as to how subjective passions are attached to objects of power: how we are willing to be gripped by power and how this can maintain and sustain our subjectivity and intersubjectivity (Butler, 1997; Hook, 2010; Newman, 2004). For planning – the discipline of shaping urban futures – many practical actions are driven by the profession's passionate beliefs in powerful ideas. These have the magic to maintain power in subjects seeking the goals of future-oriented stories, beyond their mere degrees of innovation and rationality (Throgmorton, 2003). In fact, 'every power structure is necessarily split inconsistent … in short, the foundation of power can be shaken because the very stability of its mighty edifice hinges on an inconsistent and fragile balance' (Žižek, 1996: 3). This fundamental instability raises questions of how power is anchored in subjectivity and operated through conscience and unconsciousness identifications via emancipation and resistance (Butler, 1997; Newman, 2004). A Lacanian perspective has the potential to uncover the psychic, symbolic and ideological dimensions of power, allowing us to observe unwitting collusions with it, as Roberts (2005: 638) stated:

> Identification collapses the space for resistance for it is through such identification that we inscribe the power relation within the self. But resistance is also integral to the operation of disciplinary power, in part through the felt necessity to defend our imagined autonomy against the intrusion of others.

Jacques Lacan was a French psychoanalyst and philosopher who extended Freud's theory to a new era and changed the institutional face of psychoanalysis. He is arguably one of the most important modern thinkers with a significant influence on intellectual life in the humanities (Gunder, 2005). His yearly seminars in Paris between 1953 and 1979 were some of the most influential intellectual activities of the time, attracting the active participation of leading French intellectuals. Along with Lacan's (2006) book *Écrits*, the published transcripts of these spoken seminars are the core material comprising Lacanian theory. This chapter employs these published seminars as a key resource. Many of these published transcripts have been translated into English texts over the past half century (Lacan, 1998, 1999, 2006, 2007).

If we look at it from a Lacanian perspective, power is understood as a force that emerges in intersubjective relationships, and these relationships form the subject. The processes of subjectification offer confirmation of our existence in the 'self'-defining process as evidence of the worthiness of our existence. The Lacanian real – the 'leftover' in the process of symbolisation – suggests that 'the very identity of power is itself incomplete' (Newman, 2004: 157). The fragile connection between desire and the Symbolic causes the instability of power in discourse (Hook, 2010). Lacan's work is an explanatory analytic tool for understanding power relations (Milovanovic, 1992; Ragland-Sullivan, 1986).

For Lacan, as stated in the introduction to this chapter, most human agency involves resolving a deficiency about something and the desire that this lack induces. Humans are easily manipulated through their desires. 'Lack stimulates desire, and thus, necessitates the constitution of every identity through processes of identification with socially available objects of identification such as political ideologies, patterns of consumption and social roles' (Stavrakakis, 2008: 1041). A promise to fulfil a lack, perhaps a politician's claim to solve an urban housing problem, constitutes the use of power as it may manipulate our desires and consequential agency. This mechanism induces constant pressure – power – on subjectivities for their resultant perceptions and actions. Indeed, the lacking subject desires its subjection to these various forms of powers that have emerged in society. The unconscious form of difference – desire – is the ultimate impulse of power (Millot, 1988). 'This lack in the structure of power is what constitutes power's identity as "power" and it cannot function without it. It differentiates power from other signifiers. Yet, paradoxically, this lack makes resistance to power possible' (Newman, 2001: 142). In planning, a desiring subject is a response to the lack in the existing urban order that a subject aims to grasp and resolve and which power supports (de Vries, 2007). The dominant claims in planning that can create lack in planners and their polity's residents' perceptions become powerful arguments to impel planners in the pursuit of ideal cities.

This ideological dimension of power is a form of recognition from the other: 'a power made more forceful by the difficulty of discerning quite what it is that the other wants and therefore what one must be in order to exist' (Roberts, 2005: 631). The subjectivity that is supposed to be the self-awareness of resisting the external power 'is actually formed by, and is dependent upon, one's very subordination to power' (Newman, 2004: 152). Paradoxically, when the subject looks for the other's obedience for confirming his/her power, this attention given to the other seemingly acquires the power but in fact reduces its powerfulness and accepts the existence of resistance. Žižek (1989: 32) uses the idea of 'cynical distance to power' as an example of how power shapes subjectivity: 'cynical distance is just one way to blind ourselves to the structuring power of ideological fantasy; even if we do not take things seriously, even if we keep an ironical distance, *we are still doing them*'.

Ideology has a power of making us conform to how we think we are expected to act. In the end, even if we do not personally believe in something, but our public actions believe for us, at least we appear to believe in something to others. As a consequence, while we may 'no longer believe in ideological truth … the fundamental level of ideology … [is] that of an (unconscious) fantasy structuring our social reality itself' (Žižek, 1989: 30). Planners may not fully comprehend, or even doubt, the historical and ongoing debates on new concepts in engineering, environmental and social sciences, but they still claim how we should act so that these actions can create more resilient, more ecological or smarter cities for the public good. But 'eco' for whom? Where is resilience? Why smartness? (Anthopoulos, 2017; Caprotti et al., 2015; Meerow et al., 2016). With numerous unanswered questions, planners' actions still tend to follow their imaginary fantasies for the 'better' city, rather than any scientifically tested truth. The power behind our ideals for better urban futures generates our attachment or resistance to the ongoing trajectory of planning debates and practice.

LACAN, SYMBOLIC AND POWER ANALYSIS

How can we analyse power in planning from a Lacanian perspective? Lacanian analysis acknowledges the complexity of the power–language–subject relations (Contu et al., 2010) and provides an approach to analyse how ideology shapes social reality (Glynos, 2001), through the unconscious and the agency of the letter[1] (Clarke, 2015; Hook, 2013; Parker, 2005). Part of the desire from the subject that cannot be put into the Symbolic remains in the Real.[2] The endless loop between the Symbolic, the Real and the Imaginary opens a new perspective to interrogate the actors' behaviours and their power relations in planning discourse. Lacan's innovation on symbolic subjectivity has more contributions to social theory than to its original discipline – psychoanalysis (Dean, 2000: 2), and is further employed in the analysis of complex social relationships in planning (Gunder, 2005, 2010, 2016; Hillier and Gunder, 2005).

Rather than simply a traditional function of communication, language is also seen as a manifestation of power, a representation of desire and a medium of political and social practice. Language is one of the most important manifestations of power in the social sphere, as a tool of action with definite effects upon social relations (Bourdieu, 1991). The exercise of power relations is represented in the use of signs and symbols, since the Symbolic generates power through legitimating meanings by imposing or inculcating knowledge and ideology in discourse (Millot, 1988). Language and the material world are inseparable, since the former allows people to 'constitute and integrate our perceptions of social reality' (Gunder and Hillier, 2009: 13). The planning discipline is one of the approaches that humans use to materialise their ideas from language into the real world, through policy-making, public debates, planning applications and legislation. For planning, 'language does not simply mirror or picture the world but instead profoundly shapes our view of it' (Fischer and Forester, 1993: 1).

The discourses of planning ideas and concepts matter 'because they have the power to shape the terms by which political and social reality is understood, articulated and (re)shaped through planning practice' (Shepherd et al., 2020: 5). In this process, numerous new concepts, revived ideas or outdated thoughts are infused into the symbolic system, particularly when it pertains to non-professional conversation: for example, 'let us build a twenty-first century *New Town*' or 'we need *resilient cities* to tackle the uncertainty after the disaster'! Indeed, '[w]hat creates the power of words and slogans, a power capable of maintaining or subverting the social order, is the belief in the legitimacy of words and of those who utter them' (Bourdieu, 1991: 170).

Lacanian discourse analysis provides a perspective to 'identify and analyse the crucial factors through which language exercises power in human affairs' (Bracher, 1988: 32). For Lacan, 'discourse is central to human being – to life, love, politics, power and death' (Clarke, 2015: 74). The Lacanian approach contends that we can never say exactly what we want, for we must adopt a pre-existing language of the other to express ourselves. Consequently, we can only adopt inherently ill-fitting words to describe what we specifically desire. It means that the political and professional powers are constantly in conflict for legitimation and priorities in spatial configurations. A Lacanian theoretical framework can help planners achieve a better understanding of both individual and societal desires for urban futures and to analyse the exercise of complex power relations behind planning policy and practice through discourse.

POWER-INFUSED MASTER SIGNIFIERS

'The symbol of power would be, in a Lacanian analysis, a "master signifier" – that is a primary structural interdiction that brings the symbolic order into being' (Newman, 2004: 158). The popular buzzwords in spatial planning such as 'urban resilience', 'sustainable development' and 'smart city', are Lacanian master signifiers, which are the primary nodes of the symbolic order of knowledge and power. Via master signifiers, the master imposes his/her non-justified, dogmatic, arbitrary power into knowledge (Fink, 1998). The master's assertions shape all before it, as 'one reads or hears such a discourse, one is forced, in order to understand the message, to accord full explanatory power and/or moral authority to the proffered master signifiers and to refer all other signifiers (objects, concepts, or issues) back to the master signifiers' (Bracher, 1993: 64). Even if you do not believe in these new concepts, your repeated resistance to them ultimately enhances their powerfulness in the planning discourse. Through debates and policies, the power of master signifiers is ultimately executed from planning discourse to planning practice.

The question here is: how does the power behind planning sustain the planners' beliefs? 'We are not expected to believe in or identify with ideological messages [but] our actions believe for us' (Newman, 2004: 164). Whether you believe in a master signifier or not, your actions ultimately passionately attach to its claims after repeated use. For instance, when everyone talks about 'urban resilience', planners unconsciously begin to use this signifier in their planning work, even if they are still confused about the exact meaning of resilience in cities (Meerow et al., 2016). The power behind 'urban resilience' is ultimately exercised through planning policy, graphics and mottos and these motivate and justify diverse planning actions.

Moreover, master signifiers can unify the antagonistic forces between conflicting social positions. Laclau (1996, 2006) argued that the antagonistic powers cannot reach a full consensus concerning their own identities since both sides cannot objectively present the clash between the forces. The production of an empty signifier (roughly a synonym to Lacan's master signifier) 'signifies a totality which is literally impossible' (Laclau, 2006: 107; see also chapter 7 by Roskamm). 'These "empty" signifiers have given up explicit, concise, significance to secure multifarious points of view, or unique interpretations pertaining to particular situations, under one common label' (Stavrakakis, 1999: 80). Many flexible but vague planning concepts are powerful in practice, since they are empty signifiers that can be filled with any desires of public officials and private developers in planning practice (Hatuka et al., 2018). For instance, although there are many contested interpretations, the signifier 'ecocity' can smooth the antagonism between the environmentalist movement and the growth-oriented development, which conflict with each other in planning practice (Wang, 2016). As Žižek (2002: 58) asserts:

> The master signifier that guarantees the community's consistency is a signifier whose 'signified' is an enigma for the members themselves – nobody really knows what it means, but each of them somehow presupposes that others know it, that it has to mean 'the real thing', and so they use it all the time.

Many high-profile planning concepts are misinterpreted or even hijacked when they become significant and powerful. When deployed perniciously, the justification for 'sustainable cities' may provide the power to develop land that consumes enormous energy and resources while generating acute environmental effects (Parr, 2012; Vojnovic, 2014). Similarly, 'resilient cities' grip the power of adjusting residents' life when this concept diverges from residents' discontent and anger on socio-environmental inequality (Kaika, 2017). In the name of master signifiers, urban projects consist of numerous planning ideas but only implement on the points that powerful stakeholders aim to execute. These magical words are powerful in planning discourse as the fundamental promises of what Žižek (1989) calls 'sublime objects of ideology', and eventually shape the ideology itself in planning practice (Gunder and Hillier, 2009). From a Lacanian perspective, the underlying narratives pertaining to these emotive and powerful words makes them key tools of power.

DIVIDED SUBJECT, *OBJET PETIT A* AND POWER-SEEKING

The pair of Lacanian concepts – the divided subject and *objet petit a* – explains why the subject can often emotionally align itself with the execution of power. For Lacan, the subject is inherently divided between the conscious (the Symbolic articulation) and the subject's own unconscious drives and desires (Gunder, 2003). As the object is the final desire of desire, there is an irrevocable loss of *jouissance*, which is the motivation to keep our communication ongoing in perpetuity. The seeking of this loss of *jouissance* is the *objet petit a*. The inherent division of the subject is always seeking the power to confirm itself, while the *objet petit a* creates a constant desire for the subject to pursue. Similarly in planning, its nature is society's fundamental desire for harmony and security in 'better' urban futures, which can never be fulfilled in reality (Gunder and Hillier, 2009).

When master signifiers intervene in the already constituted field of the other signifiers, the divided subject emerges (Lacan, 2007: 15). The failure to identify the right one is the divided subject (Bracher, 1988; Lacan, 2007): if one thinks, the subject has changed according to his/her thinking; if one knows where the place is, he/she cannot think anymore. The subject is not only embedded in language, but also structured 'through its encounter with language' (Malone and Roberts, 2010). Therefore, the power that is attached to master signifiers cannot easily be sustained but is always in the status of seeking, since the subject is undetermined and fragile in the execution of power.

Jouissance is the nature of enjoyment. Although it means 'enjoyment' in French, with an obvious sexual-related connotation, Lacan (1998: 184) considered that 'there is a *jouissance* beyond the pleasure principle', 'a seeking of enjoyment that transcends the pleasure principle' (Gunder, 2003: 96). It compels the divided subjects to break the prohibitions that constantly hinder his/her enjoyment. 'I have the right of enjoyment … I will exercise this right, without any limit stopping me in the capriciousness of the exactions that I might have the taste to satiate' (Lacan, 1989: 58). *Objet petit a* is the object of desire that we seek in the other. It is the unattainable object of desire, or the object cause of desire. Lacan elucidated this concept as *plus-de-jouir*, which literally means a surplus of enjoyment (Verhaeghe, 1995). It is the *jouissance* beyond the necessary one pursued on the way to search for the designated *jouissance*. These desires in motions are the drives that we cannot attain but rather keep circling around (Lacan, 1998).

Therefore, our desire for the better urban environment driven by *jouissance* behind 'a forgotten or repressed keyword, phrase, memory, image or belief, i.e., a master signifier' creates an unconscious force that makes us passionately follow the master's power (Gunder, 2003:

97). Urban policies with the master signifiers of 'sustainability', 'eco', 'smart' and so on are all good examples of *objet petit a*: if we build ecotowns, our metropolises will be sustainable; if we use smart transport strategies, cities' traffic jams will disappear; if we build creative urban clusters, our industry will be diverse and prosperous. Even though the goals behind these powerful keywords look difficult to fully achieve, planners still seek the altered versions behind these buzzwords to empower themselves in the planning discourse.

ANALYSING POWER RELATIONS THROUGH THE FOUR DISCOURSES

In Lacan's theory, discourse is 'a necessary structure … beyond speech' and 'subsists in certain fundamental relations which would literally not be able to be maintained without language' (Lacan, 2007: 12–13). He proposed four types of discourse to represent 'a number of social relations "beyond" actual utterances (French: *énonciations*)' (Lacan, 2007: 13). Indeed, Lacan contends that we speak not to simply pass on information, rather we fundamentally speak to induce a product, or change, on the part of the other (Verhaeghe, 2001: 41). Therefore, Lacan's four discourses inherently illuminate power relations along the symbolic formation and open up a critique of ideology from the perspective of subjectivity and undesirability (Vighi and Feldner, 2007). Each discourse is associated with one specific type of social relation (Bracher, 1988): the master's discourse for indoctrinating; the university discourse for legitimating; the hysteric's discourse for resisting/protesting; and the analyst's discourse for subverting.

Furthermore, Lacan invented his schematic structure of the four discourses to 'identify and analyse the crucial factors through which language exercises power in human affairs' (Bracher, 1988: 32). There are four fixed positions in the diagram namely agent, other, production and truth (Lacan, 2006, as shown in Figure 6.1). The first position in the top left, agent, is the starting point of dominating each discourse. The top right one, other, is called to take actions through the discourse. The top two positions are usually the explicit part of the speaker and the receiver in the discourse and the arrow '→' denotes the direction of the information. By contrast, the bottom positions are usually latent factors that are unconscious to the speaker and the receiver. The production, in the bottom right, is the real effect produced by the discourse. The truth in the bottom left is the hidden motivation that underlies and supports the dominant position of the agent.

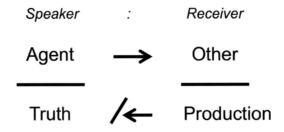

Source: Wang (2022a); reproduced with permission.

Figure 6.1   *Schematic structure of the Four Discourses*

The schemata contain four variables: master signifier (S1), knowledge (S2), divided subject ($) and the *objet petit a* (*a*) (Lacan, 2006). These four variables follow a clockwise loop of S1 → S2 → $ → *a* in the schematic structure in each type of discourse. While the four positions stay in their fixed locations in each type of discourse, the movement of variable-loop changes the type of discourse being deployed (Figure 6.2) and creates different power relationships behind the discourse. The following sections will explain how each type of discourse generate, attach to or resist the master's power as well as the power relations behind, with brief examples in planning.

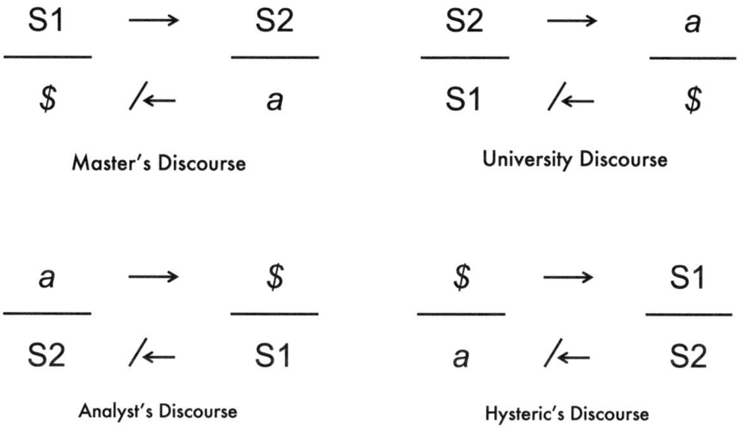

$$\frac{S1}{\$} \xrightarrow{\quad} \frac{S2}{a} \qquad\qquad \frac{S2}{S1} \xrightarrow{\quad} \frac{a}{\$}$$

Master's Discourse   University Discourse

$$\frac{a}{S2} \xrightarrow{\quad} \frac{\$}{S1} \qquad\qquad \frac{\$}{a} \xrightarrow{\quad} \frac{S1}{S2}$$

Analyst's Discourse   Hysteric's Discourse

Source: Wang (2022a); reproduced with permission.

Figure 6.2   *Diagrams of the Four Discourses*

Master's Discourse: Imposing Power through Master Signifiers

The master's discourse is one of indoctrination asserted by the master – who must be obeyed – through their master signifiers (S1). Through its non-justified, dogmatic, arbitrary power, the masters want the receivers to reorganise their own knowledge to maintain the unquestionable master signifiers (Fink, 1998; Gunder and Hillier, 2009). Knowledge is placed in the other position, implying that knowledge has to sustain the master's will in his/her own illusion in the master's discourse (Verhaeghe, 1995). The receivers of this discourse are there to 'learn and organise their belief', and repress other knowledge, desires and fantasies that go against the master's (Bracher, 1994: 121). It is a discourse to mould the receiver's ego-ideal[3] (Gunder and Hillier, 2009). Driven by the divided subject between the conscious and the unconscious ($), the master attempts to unify the divided subject with master signifiers (S1).

Although master signifiers are imposed on the existing knowledge system of the receivers, the abstract concepts often cannot completely persuade the latter to adopt the ideas attached to the former into their own knowledge system. The other's production is the receivers' interpretation based on their own understandings of the master signifiers. Therefore, the master's expectation is never fully achieved. The real production of this discourse is the unattainable object of desire rather than the desire pursued by the master. When discussing the May 1968 events in France, Lacan said, '[the master's discourse] embraces everything, even what thinks itself as a revolution, or more exactly as what is romantically called Revolution, with a capital R' (Lacan, 2007: 87). The master's discourse 'accomplishes its own revolution in the other sense of doing a complete circle' (Lacan, 2007: 87). Instead of a military or governmental phenomenon, this revolution merely revolves around the variables in the discourse schemata signifying that master signifiers are dominant, and the other variables cannot disrupt their dominance (Bracher, 1994: 119).

In planning, the master's discourse is typically made by authorised bodies such as government officials, political elites and influential scholars to exercise power on the public and spread their own beliefs. The masters face fewer disputes when they propose master signifiers, such as 'resilience', 'sustainability' and 'smartness', which sounds unquestionable for future cities (Gunder and Hillier, 2009). When an influential political leader or an urban-policy guru proposes a 'resilient city', few people raise questions about the necessity or orthodoxy of this fashionable concept, as no one knows what the term really means. Indeed, the master can reorganise his/her ideal to further explain what the 'resilient city' denotes in his/her own way (Vale, 2014). Without a clear definition, a master signifier can exist beyond current human knowledge and experience (Gunder and Wang, 2019). Politicians often appropriate well-established planning concepts without fully acknowledging their definitions, history and development, but can infuse their power to motivate local governments to transfer it from policy to practice (Biddulph, 2016). This explaining power behind popular keywords offers the master the chance to attract subjects to believe in his/her transcendental ideals for urban futures.

University Discourse: Legitimising the Master's Power through Knowledge

The university discourse is one seeking to legitimise the master's power by imposing systemic knowledge (S2) onto the one seeking the unattainable object of desire (*a*), the surplus of the others' *jouissance*. This discourse rationalises or legitimises the abstract and arbitrary signifiers, and makes them become a supplement to knowledge (Fink, 1995: 132). Rather than political-neutral or interest-free systems, the knowledge in this discourse is motivated by a network of master signifiers created or developed by the master in power. The master signifier (S1), the motivation of this discourse is the command to 'keep on knowing' about what the powerful master signifier is (Lacan, 2007: 105). It is impossible, as Lacan observed, not to obey the power within master signifiers because humans 'always continue to know more' (Lacan, 2007: 105).

Lacan used the discourse of science as an example to elucidate this type of discourse (Lacan, 2007; Verhaeghe, 2001). Although many regard science as a more progressive understanding of the world, Lacan argued that science 'surpasses anything that could result from just an effective understanding (French: *connaissance*) of things' (Bracher, 1994: 107–108). Instead, science rather involves the construction of realities that we previously had no awareness of, since they 'did not in any way exist at the level of our perception' (Lacan, 2007: 158). Planning professional education is a typical way of the university discourse, which divert students from their original desires and beliefs to the institutional knowledge due to the imposition of the planning education system (Gunder, 2004; Gunder and Hillier, 2009).

In planning practice, the dissemination (publication, workshops, initiatives etc.) of technical standards, design handbooks and planning policy is a form of the university discourse. The distribution of knowledge is an approach of legitimising the master's power through creating an ideology that planners are willing to follow. This discourse emphasises the rightness of master signifiers via a network of related knowledge, such as the 'necessity' to build 'smart cities', the 'right timing' to construct 'resilient infrastructures' or the 'benefits' of developing 'sustainable communities'. Through publishing comprehensive programmes and guidelines around the powerful master signifiers, planning authorities, public think-tanks or professional organisations persuade planning professionals or even the public to believe in their ego-ideals. For legitimising the master's power, there is no need to verify that a new master signifier is more progressive than the old concept. It is in the end politicising and its ultimate purpose is to seduce planners to passionately attach themselves to the power behind this master signifier.

Analyst's Discourse: Deliberately Subverting the Master's Power

The analyst's discourse is opposed to the will of the master, 'engaging in a continuous flight from meaning and closure' (Bracher, 1988: 46). The analyst, the agent of this discourse, 'interrogates the subject in his/her own division' (Fink, 1998: 37). Derived from Lacan's background of psychoanalysis, the analyst in this discourse attempts to draw out the fundamental truth from the conversations with the analysand, aiming to get her/him to talk about any traumas experienced and to reveal the true desires of the divided subject that is analysed (Gunder and Wang, 2019). This discourse is not limited to just individuals but also may be deployed to the whole of society. Through producing a new signifier against the powerful and dominating master signifiers, this discourse attempts to trigger revolution to subvert the master's power (Lacan, 2007). In a seminar during the May 1968 events, Lacan said: 'What you aspire to as revolutionaries is a master. You will get one' (French: *vous voulez un maître, vous l'aurez*), as his response to the student riots (Lacan, 2007: 207). The analyst's discourse offers 'the only ultimate effective means of countering the social tyranny exercised through language' (Bracher, 1988: 45).

   In planning, the analyst's discourse is the fierce criticisms that attempt to counter the controlling power – political elites, celebrity scholars or renowned planners. It raises questions of the social hegemony of unsuitable or divergent concepts in the planning discourse. Biddulph (2016: 123) questioned a series of new concepts for urban communities in the UK and argued that the repetition of similar concepts is just 'an apparent celebration of wilful ignorance'. Kaika (2017) contended 'resilient city' merely vaccinates citizens from inequality and degradation and warned: 'don't call me resilient'. The analyst's discourse in planning reveals the deep problem of hegemonic power in policy and academic discourse, and deliberately subverts the master's power through their own analysis.

Hysteric's Discourse: Dissolving Power through Questioning Master Signifiers

The hysteric's discourse[4] is one of resistance, protest, and complaint. The agent in this discourse – the hysteric speaker – seeks a response from the master to offer 'a secure meaning that will overcome anxiety and give a sense of meaningful, and respectable identity' (Bracher, 1993: 53). The receiver of the discourse is a master signifier, which is a form that aims to satisfy all the desires of the divided subject(s). This agent-other relationship indicates that this discourse questions the validity of master signifiers (S1). Through this process, the hysteric's discourse produces a system of knowledge/beliefs around the master signifiers to stabilise the hysterical subject (Bracher, 1988: 45). Lacan associated this discourse with real scientific activities, arguing that the hysteric's discourse questions the powerful master signifiers and produces ever-increasing real knowledge (Fink, 1998; Verhaeghe, 1995).

For urban planning, this discourse raises questions 'against the ideological environment' (Hillier, 2003: 159) by questioning popular planning concepts: 'so what?' or 'but what about?' This discourse serves as a critical review of the existing power relations sustained around master signifiers. The agent in this discourse is the urban scholar, planner, or even member of the public, who refuses to follow the existing planning discourse that sustained the master's command and raises questions on the meaning of master signifiers. Is the 'zero-carbon city' a feasible goal for our common urban futures (Cugurullo, 2015)? Does the 'urban village' denote the same connotation in a global context (Wang, 2022b)? These critical questions lead more comprehensive reviews of these new concepts and their attached ideas, policies and practice, and eventually generate more authentic knowledge about how to plan urban futures. Different from the fierce rejection of everything in the analyst's discourse, this one gradually dissolves the master's hegemonic power through challenging and then developing new knowledge around the current master signifier based on the scholars' own interpretations as well as their own power to challenge the power of the master.

CONCLUSION

Facing the difficulties in explaining intersubjective relations of power, this chapter draws on Jacques Lacan's psychoanalytical theory to explore the ideological and symbolic dimensions of power. It opens interrogation into desire and ideology in the power exercise of planning practice and explores how subjects can passionately attach or reluctantly resist the hegemonic power of the master. In particular, Lacan's account on the power–language–subject relations provides a unique perspective to understand how power is exercised and resisted around popular planning concepts. Many of these concepts are Lacanian master signifiers that encapsulate a perceived solution to identified deficiencies in a polity or, perhaps, merely provide a positive feeling about the potential for better urban futures. As demonstrated in this chapter, these powerful concepts are often fuzzy without clear meanings so that many people can adopt these concepts as a 'good' thing. They can loosely fill everyone's perceived lack of community security and/or wholesomeness, thus providing collective *jouissance* to a polity's residents.

This chapter further explains four different types of power relation in planning discourse. The Lacanian schemata of the four discourses are 'an attempt to identify and analyse the crucial factors through which language exercises both formative and transformative power in human affairs' (Bracher, 1994: 107). Influential politicians, celebrity planners or academic gurus (masters) impose their power to the planning community through unquestionable master signifiers. Bearing the master's pressure, knowledge (urban policies, planning proposals, technical guidance, etc.) is generated to legitimise this power for a wider audience to passionately believe in and follow the master's will. However, the inherently divided subject and the unattainable object of desire in the four discourses indicate that the attachment and resistance to power are an endless loop in seeking human security and completeness free from further want and need. Critics want to deliberately subvert the master's power with denial of their dominating concepts; scholars and planners dissolve the master's power and blend in their own ideals into the extended discourse and practice. This Lacanian exploration on power and planning provides a complementary perspective to explain the often-ignored ideological and symbolic dimensions of power in the planning discipline.

NOTES

1. The agency of the letter is one of the foundations of Lacan's interpretation of Freud with the linguistics, denoting the inherent gap between the signifier and the signified. Lacan (2006: 412–441) contended that the subject is implicated in language from one's birth and the letter can only express a part of what the subject aims to tell.
2. As core concepts in Lacanian theory, the triad of the Symbolic-Real-Imaginary registries explain how we perceive and understand the world. Developed during Lacan's lectures in the 1950s, these three registries derive from Freud's theory of Oedipal phase and infantile sexuality: an infant emerges into the Real when it was born and then enters into the Imaginary and the Symbolic when it receives the influence of culture and language constituting social reality (see details in Gunder and Wang, 2019). Žižek (2006: 8–9) explains these three registries using the analogy of chess: the Symbolic is the rules of chess, the Imaginary is the shape of the pieces (knights, bishops etc.), and the Real is everything outside of the actual board but affecting the game, such as the players' ability, playing atmosphere and audience.
3. For Lacan, the ego-ideal is a symbolic introjection of the subject's ideal point to look at himself/herself. Lacan (2006) distinguishes the ego-ideal from the ideal-ego which is an imaginary projection of oneself. Therefore, the ego-ideal is internalised aims of laws, plans, rules and guidance that the subject positions in the symbolic order.
4. The hysteric's discourse is not necessarily associated with any hysteric symptoms. Rather, it is a unique way to question the power behind the existing knowledge systems.

REFERENCES

Albrechts, L. (2003), 'Planning and Power: Towards an Emancipatory Planning Approach', *Environment and Planning C: Government and Policy* 21 (6), 905–924.

Anthopoulos, L. (2017), 'Smart Utopia VS Smart Reality: Learning by Experience from 10 Smart City Cases', *Cities* 63, 128–148.

Biddulph, M. (2016), 'Should We Build a Garden City? Politicising Knowledge and Concepts in Planning Policy and Practice', *Town Planning Review* 87 (2), 117–124.

Bourdieu, Pierre (1991), *Language and Symbolic Power*, Cambridge, MA: Harvard University Press.

Bracher, M. (1988), 'Lacan's Theory of the Four Discourses', *Prose Studies* 11 (3), 32–49.

Bracher, Mark (1993), *Lacan, Discourse, and Social Change: A Psychoanalytic Cultural Criticism*, Ithaca, NY: Cornell University Press.

Bracher, M. (1994), 'On the Psychological and Social Functions of Language: Lacan's Theory of the Four Discourses', in Mark Bracher, Marshall W. Alcorn and Ronald J. Corthell (eds) *Lacanian Theory of Discourse: Subject, Structure and Society*, New York: New York University Press, pp. 107–128.

Butler, Judith (1997), *The Psychic Life of Power: Theories in Subjection*, Stanford, CA: Stanford University Press.

Caprotti, F., Springer, C. and Harmer, N. (2015), '"Eco" for Whom? Envisioning Eco-urbanism in the Sino-Singapore Tianjin Eco-city, China', *International Journal of Urban and Regional Research* 39 (3), 495–517.

Clarke, M. (2015), '"Knowledge is power"? A Lacanian Entanglement with Political Ideology in Education', *Critical Studies in Education* 56 (1), 71–85.

Contu, A., Driver, M. and Jones, C. (2010), 'Editorial: Jacques Lacan with Organization Studies', *Organization* 17 (3), 307–315.

Cugurullo, F. (2015), 'Urban Eco-modernisation and the Policy Context of New Eco-city Projects: Where Masdar City Fails and Why', *Urban Studies* 53 (11), 2417–2433.

de Vries, P. (2007), 'Don't Compromise your Desire for Development! A Lacanian/Deleuzian Rethinking of the Anti-politics Machine', *Third World Quarterly* 28 (1), 25–43.

Dean, Tim (2000), *Beyond Sexuality*, Chicago, IL: University of Chicago Press.

Fink, Bruce (1995), *The Lacanian Subject: Between Language and Jouissance*, Princeton, NJ: Princeton University Press.

Fink, B. (1998), 'The Master Signifier and the Four Discourses', in Dany Nobus (ed.) *Key Concepts of Lacanian Psychoanalysis*, New York: Other Press, pp. 29–47.

Fischer, Frank and Forester, John (eds) (1993), *The Argumentative Turn in Policy Analysis and Plan*, Durham, NC and London: Duke University Press.

Forester, J. (1982), 'Planning in the Face of Power', *Journal of the American Planning Association* 48 (1), 67–80.

Glynos, J. (2001), 'The Grip of Ideology: A Lacanian Approach to the Theory of Ideology', *Journal of Political Ideologies* 6 (2), 191–214.

Gunder, M. (2003), 'Planning Policy Formulation from a Lacanian Perspective', *International Planning Studies* 8 (4), 279–294.

Gunder, M. (2004), 'Shaping the Planner's Ego-ideal', *Journal of Planning Education and Research* 23 (3), 299–311.

Gunder, M. (2005), 'Lacan, Planning and Urban Policy Formation', *Urban Policy and Research* 23 (1), 87–107.

Gunder, M. (2010), 'Making Planning Theory Matter: A Lacanian Encounter with Phronesis', *International Planning Studies* 15 (1), 37–51.

Gunder, M. (2016), 'Planning's "Failure" to Ensure Efficient Market Delivery: A Lacanian Deconstruction of this Neoliberal Scapegoating Fantasy', *European Planning Studies* 24 (1), 21–38.

Gunder, Michael and Hillier, Jean (2009), *Planning in Ten Words or Less: A Lacanian Entanglement with Spatial Planning*, Aldershot, UK and Burlington, VT: Ashgate.

Gunder, Michael and Wang, Chuan (2019), 'Jacques Lacan: Introducing Thinkers for Planners – A Narrative and Conversation', AESOP YA Network, accessed 8 May 2021 at www.aesop-planning .eu/uploads/lacan-introducing-thinkers-for-planners-a-narrative-and-conversation.pdf.

Hatuka, T., Rosen-Zvi, I., Birnhack, M. et al. (2018), 'The Political Premises of Contemporary Urban Concepts: The Global City, the Sustainable City, the Resilient City, the Creative City, and the Smart City', *Planning Theory & Practice* 19 (2), 160–179.

Hillier, J. (2003), 'Puppets of Populism?', *International Planning Studies*, 157–166.

Hillier, J. and Gunder, M. (2005), 'Not Over your Dead Bodies! A Lacanian Interpretation of Urban Planning Discourse and Practice', *Environment and Planning A* 37 (6), 1049–1066.

Hook, D. (2010), 'The Powers of Emptiness', *Theory & Psychology* 20 (6), 855–870.

Hook, D. (2013), 'Tracking the Lacanian Unconscious in Language', *Psychodynamic Practice* 19 (1), 38–54.

Inch, A. and Shepherd, E. (2020), 'Thinking Conjuncturally about Ideology, Housing and English Planning', *Planning Theory* 19 (1), 59–79.

Kaika, M. (2017), '"Don't call me resilient again!": the New Urban Agenda as Immunology … or … What Happens when Communities Refuse to be Vaccinated with "Smart Cities" and Indicators', *Environment and Urbanization* 29 (1), 89–102.

Lacan, J. (1989), 'Kant with Sade', *October* 51, 55–75.

Lacan, Jacques (1998), *The Four Fundamental Concepts of Psycho-Analysis*, London: Vintage.

Lacan, Jacques (1999), *The Seminar of Jacques Lacan, Book XX: On Feminine Sexuality, the Limits of Love and Knowledge*, New York: Norton.

Lacan, Jacques (2006), *Écrits: the First Complete Edition in English*, New York: Norton.

Lacan, Jacques (2007), *Seminar XVII: The Other Side of Psychoanalysis*, New York: Norton.

Laclau, Ernesto (1996), *Emancipation(s)*, London: Verso.

Laclau, E. (2006), 'Ideology and post-Marxism', *Journal of Political Ideologies* 11 (2), 103–114.

Malone, K.R. and Roberts, J.L. (2010), 'In the World of Language but not of it: Lacanian Inquiry into the Subject of Discourse Psychology', *Theory & Psychology* 20 (6), 835–854.

Meerow, S., Newell, J.P. and Stults, M. (2016), 'Defining Urban Resilience: A Review', *Landscape and Urban Planning* 147, 38–49.

Metzger, J., Soneryd, L. and Tamm Hallström, K. (2017), '"Power" is that which Remains to be Explained: Dispelling the Ominous Dark Matter of Critical Planning Studies', *Planning Theory* 16 (2), 203–222.

Millot, B. (1988), 'Symbol, Desire and Power', *Theory, Culture & Society* 5 (4), 675–694.

Milovanovic, D. (1992), 'Rethinking Subjectivity in Law and Ideology: A Semiotic Perspective', *The Journal of Human Justice* 4 (1), 31–54.

Newman, Saul (2001), *From Bakunin to Lacan: Anti-Authoritarianism and the Dislocation of Power*, Lanham, MD and Oxford: Lexington Books.

Newman, S. (2004), 'New Reflections on the Theory of Power: A Lacanian Perspective', *Contemporary Political Theory* 3 (2), 148–167.

Njoh, A.J. (2009), 'Urban Planning as a Tool of Power and Social Control in Colonial Africa', *Planning Perspectives* 24 (3), 301–317.

Parker, I. (2005), 'Lacanian Discourse Analysis in Psychology: Seven Theoretical Elements', *Theory & Psychology* 15 (2), 163–182.

Parr, Adrian (2012), *Hijacking Sustainability*, Cambridge, MA: MIT Press.

Ragland-Sullivan, Ellie (1986), *Jacques Lacan and the Philosophy of Psychoanalysis*, Champaign, IL: University of Illinois Press.

Roberts, J. (2005), 'The Power of the "Imaginary" in Disciplinary Processes', *Organization* 12 (5), 619–642.

Sanli, T. and Townshend, T. (2018), 'Hegemonic Power Relations in Real Practices of Spatial Planning: The Case of Turkey', *European Planning Studies* 26 (6), 1242–1268.

Shepherd, E., Inch, A. and Marshall, T. (2020), 'Narratives of Power: Bringing Ideology to the Fore of Planning Analysis', *Planning Theory* 19 (1), 3–16.

Stavrakakis, Yannis (1999), *Lacan and the Political: Thinking the Political*, Abingdon, UK: Routledge.

Stavrakakis, Y. (2008), 'Subjectivity and the Organized Other: Between Symbolic Authority and Fantasmatic Enjoyment', *Organization Studies* 29 (7), 1037–1059.

Throgmorton, J.A. (2003), 'Planning as Persuasive Storytelling in a Global-scale Web of Relationships', *Planning Theory* 2 (2), 125–151.

Vale, L.J. (2014), 'The Politics of Resilient Cities: Whose Resilience and Whose City?', *Building Research & Information* 42 (2), 191–201.

Verhaeghe, P. (1995), 'From Impossibility to Inability: Lacan's Theory on the Four Discourses', *The Letter: Lacanian Perspectives on Psychoanalysis* 3, 91–108.

Verhaeghe, Paul (2001), *Beyond Gender: From Subject to Drive*, New York: Other Press.

Vighi, F. and Feldner, H. (2007), 'Ideology Critique or Discourse Analysis? Žižek against Foucault', *European Journal of Political Theory* 6 (2), 141–159.

Vojnovic, I. (2014), 'Urban Sustainability: Research, Politics, Policy and Practice', *Cities* 41, S30–S44.

Wang, Chuan (2016), 'Ecocity – A New Creative Ambiguity or An Adopted Fashion?', in Chris Younès and Céline Bodart (eds) *Encore l'architecture Encore la philosophie*, Paris: Éditions Hermann, pp. 83–96.

Wang, C. (2022a), 'Do Planning Concepts Matter? A Lacanian Interpretation of the Urban Village in a British Context', *Planning Theory* 21 (2), 155–180, DOI: 10.1177/14730952211038936.

Wang, C. (2022b), 'Urban Village on a Global Scale: Diverse Interpretations of One Label', *Urban Geography* 43 (2), 184–205, DOI: 10.1080/02723638.2020.1842097.

Žižek, Slavoj (1989), *The Sublime Object of Ideology*, London: Verso.

Žižek, Slavoj (1996), *The Indivisible Remainder: An Essay on Schelling and Related Matters*, London: Verso.

Žižek, Slavoj (2002), 'The Real of Sexual Difference', in Suzanne Barnard and Bruce Fink (eds) *Reading Seminar XX: Lacan's Major Work on Love, Knowledge, and Feminine Sexuality*, Albany, NY: SUNY Press, pp. 57–75.

Žižek, Slavoj (2006), *How to Read Lacan*, London: Granta.

7. Filling the empty place: Laclau and Mouffe on power and hegemony

Nikolai Roskamm

INTRODUCTION

In 1985, Ernesto Laclau and Chantal Mouffe published *Hegemony and Socialist Strategy* and they obviously hit a nerve with it. Few books in political theory have polarised the academic community more in recent decades and led to such passionate debates. The controversies are still ongoing. Laclau's and Mouffe's stated aim was to update and reformulate the idea of socialism. To do this, they bring two meta-narratives into conversation with each other – post-structuralist and Marxian thought. The result is a concept of radical and plural democracy. Central to this is the question of power relations. This is taken from Marxian thinking and grounds the postmodern and rather abstract approach of the two authors. In the field of planning (or planning theory), Laclau's and Mouffe's writings are important and much-discussed inspirations for a reflection on one's own entanglement in social and political power relations and for the question of what produces such relations and what holds them together.[1]

Both Mouffe and Laclau came to the UK in the 1970s. Chantal Mouffe studied philosophy and literature at the University of Louvain, Belgium, and continued with a Master of Arts in Politics at the University of Essex. She then taught and researched at various universities in Europe, North America and South America. In Paris, she led a program at the Collège International de Philosophie. Since 1995, she has been based in London at the Centre for the Study of Democracy, in the School for Social and Policy Sciences at the University of Westminster. Ernesto Laclau emigrated from Argentina, where he studied history at the University of Buenos Aires. Laclau was an active supporter of Peronism. Shortly after his appointment as a professor at the Universidad Nacional de Tucumán, Laclau, like many other left-wing academics, was dismissed from the university after General Onganía's coup d'état. In 1969, he accepted an invitation from Eric Hobsbawm to Oxford University. In 1973 he moved to the Department of Government at the University of Essex, where he taught until his retirement in 2003. Laclau was the founder of the Centre for Theoretical Studies in the Humanities and Social Sciences and the Graduate School in 'Ideology and Discourse Analysis', both known today as the 'Essex School' (see Marchart 2018; Anderson 2017).

In this chapter, I give an overview of the theories of Laclau and Mouffe. I start with taking a glance at the conception of hegemony, which is central to their understanding of power. From here, I reconstruct some of the key issues in Laclau and Mouffe's work as the constitutive outside, the relation of sedimentation and dislocation, the concept of equivalential chain and the empty signifier. I then switch to Claude Lefort's edict of the empty place of power, for two reasons: first, because it is a central reference for Laclau's and Mouffe's understanding of power and secondly, because it can be used to create a transition to a reflection on planning. Thereafter, I consider Mouffe's advances in thinking about antagonism/agonism and Laclau's variant thereof. I then report on how Laclau and Mouffe use the concept of ideology to extend another version of their anti-essentialist thinking and also discuss how ideology and planning are related to one another and how a critique of ideology of planning informed by Laclau and Mouffe's theories might proceed. The last part of my chapter provides a general reflection on the relationship between power and planning.

HEGEMONY – POWER IS NEVER FOUNDATIONAL

Laclau and Mouffe's key concept for exploring and reflecting on power is the notion of hegemony. This notion – a basic concept of Marxist social analysis – is quite close to the concept of power. Both have in common their difficult tangibility and their ubiquitous presence. Both are from the same provenance. Hegemony can be considered as a form of power; power can be considered as a form of hegemony.

What is hegemony? The history of the notion is ancient.[2] In Greek antiquity, the word *hegemonia* – in addition to, or to distinguish from, *arkhe* (domination) – was used for indicating leadership of a certain *polis* (as Athens or Sparta) against an external enemy (i.e. the Persian army). The way to hegemony in the Greek sense was not fighting each other but based on solidarity and consensus. The hegemonic position of power therefore did not result from submission, but from conviction. This made the leadership role negotiable: if the arguments and convictions changed, the hegemonic position also changed.

In modernity, the concept of hegemony appears in the nineteenth century. The endeavour by the Prussian kingdom to become the leader within the German confederacy was labelled by contemporary rapporteurs – in the tradition of the Greek usage of the concept – as an attempt to achieve hegemony. Again, we have a state-confederation-leadership-question and again the way to it is persuasion. Then, the concept underwent a certain change, particularly in the Russian context. Most famously in the writings of Vladimir Ilyich Lenin, hegemony turned to the internal domestic level: at stake in that new understanding was not the hegemony *of* a nation but rather the hegemony *in* the nation. Lenin (1962, p. 79) wrote about the hegemony of the proletariat and he argues, how the working class can assume power in Russia. Hegemony changed therefore from a strategic goal of the leadership of a state to the strategy of how to come into power. According to Lenin, in order to come to power, it is first necessary to convince and unite the working class – here we first find the familiar attributes of the classical understanding of hegemony. The second step in the socialist striving for hegemony, however, then deviates from the previous interpretations: now it is a matter of taking power in the state through revolution. The united proletariat stands up against the ruling classes and seizes power. In Lenin's writings, hegemony thus becomes an attribute of the working class. In the socialist understanding, hegemony is just that: a virtue of the proletariat and a strategy to overcome the ruling power relations. Both features are interwoven and lend pathos and emotion to the term. In the socialist context, hegemony is not neutral or objective, it is always partisan, and it is always political.

In that context the best known and arguably the most relevant thinker on hegemony, Antonio Gramsci, then intervenes. Gramsci (1992, 1996, 2007) was a leader of the Italian Communist party and in the 1930s he wrote his famous prison notebooks as a detainee of the Italian fascist state. Gramsci, a non-dogmatic Marxist thinker, follows the socialist understanding and comprehends hegemony as a position of power to be striven for (by socialist forces). The effort to achieve hegemony thus takes place even before governmental power is achieved. Hegemony is what has to be won in order to overthrow an existing government (Gramsci, 1992: 137). The goal of socialist politics in the fascist state (which is the historical context in which Gramsci's thought intervenes) is to achieve hegemony. Gramsci develops a theory of hegemony as an extended concept of power. In Gramsci's understanding, hegemony is both a fact and a concept and he argues – with reference to Lenin – for understanding hegemony as an epistemological and philosophical form of analysis (Gramsci, 2007: 183). Gramsci's thinking opens up the question of power relations. According to Gramsci (1992: 179), hegemony is a multifaceted conglomerate consisting of economic power, cultural interpretative sovereignty and intellectual leadership and the possession of the more convincing political arguments. Not only is the content of hegemony pluralistic in this concept, but even the actors in the hegemonic struggles for power are too. Gramsci examines the shifts that are necessary before a change of power takes place. Hegemony becomes a contingent concept in that approach. Gramsci (1996: 187) historicises power relations, makes them dependent on different influences and explicitly opposes a purely economistic analysis. Moreover, Gramsci's arguments scratch away at the idea that only the working class can be the agent of socialist politics and thus softens the traditional Marxist concept of class. In addition to the proletariat, he introduces the concept of 'subaltern classes' (Gramsci, 1996: 91), which encompasses all those classes that do not (yet) hold a hegemonic position.

Laclau and Mouffe (2001 [1985]) drew on Gramsci's understanding of hegemony to refresh the formulation of socialist ideals, while outlining the project of a radical and plural democracy. In doing so, they opposed dogmatic Marxism while emphasising the constitutive role of pluralism. From that angle hegemony broke with a linear and one-directional understanding of history and imported pluralism into the socialist question of power relations. At the same time, however, the concept of hegemony works in the opposite direction and counters the postmodern liberalist interpretation of pluralism, as is often personified by the diversity of identity politics. For Laclau and Mouffe hegemony was an anti-dogmatic and anti-postmodern concept that did not give up the (socialist) question of power; rather it places power right at the forefront. Such an approach recognises the existence of power relations as much as it emphasises the urgent need to transform them. Laclau and Mouffe – and this is perhaps the decisive further development of Gramsci's thinking – describe hegemony not only as the act of producing power, but also and precisely as the preliminary collapse of power and, additionally, as the impossibility of retaining power forever. That thinking has consequences. The path Laclau and Mouffe take is to implement a radical break with all forms of essentialism and social objectivity. Every objectivity, according to Laclau and Mouffe, is on the one hand constituted by acts of power and on the other hand based on the exclusion of something else. Objectivity and power do not simply exist, but are always produced and the result of transformations. Hegemony means that 'power is never foundational' (Laclau and Mouffe, 2001: 142).

CONCEPTS AND CATEGORIES

Laclau's and Mouffe's theory of hegemony includes a number of abstract and theoretical categories that make up the conceptual tools of their approach. Among them are the idea of a constitutive outside, the opposite movements of sedimentation and dislocation, the concept of equivalential chains and the empty signifier. Some of these concepts are introduced here.

Laclau introduces the concept of the 'constitutive outside', a radical outside that is nonetheless conceived as the goal and driving force for all social constitutions (Laclau 1990: 84; see also Roskamm 2015; 2019). The basic idea is that every system of meaning is constituted by an outside, every discourse, every identity and every structure: all systems of meaning have an outside as a founding condition. According to Laclau (1990: 18), it is not possible for such systems of meaning (discourses, identities, systems, societies) to fully stabilise themselves. All insides inherently push towards the constitutive outside (Laclau, 1990: 35). The result is, on the one hand, that the constitutive outside becomes the cause for the meaning systems to strive for stabilisation; but, on the other hand, it is also the reason that a complete stabilisation of the system is impossible. The constitutive outside thus sparks the driving forces that bring about any social constitution in different ways. First, the outside is the goal of every social identification – albeit a goal that is impossible to achieve. Second, the outside makes possible the efforts to strive for the impossible goal. This double movement – triggering an effort and making it impossible – is the source and reason for all hegemonic efforts (cf. also Laclau, 2012: 111).

The resulting forms of stabilisation and destabilisation are described by Laclau as 'sedimentation' and 'dislocation'. The constitution of the inside, which is impossible in the long term, can be successful for a short time: in the form of sedimentations (Laclau,1990: 35). Sedimentations are discursive and/or material settlements, deposits that arise through repetition and routinisation. They are (temporarily) successful fixations of meaning and thus also the name for the result of such fixations, that is, of (supposed, claimed) objectivity. 'Sedimentations' are what is considered objective in a discourse.[3] The forces directed against the sedimentations (which de-solidify the fixations) are given the name 'dislocation' (Laclau, 1990: 21). Dislocations endanger every stability, they reactivate the connection to the outside, make identity impossible, but at the same time create the reason for the next attempt (that is once again doomed to failure). They destroy systems of interpretation and at the same time create space, air and room for the constitution of new identities and new sedimentations. Sedimentation and dislocation are now given further names by Laclau, namely 'politics' (sedimentation) and 'the political' (dislocation). Politics is the attempt at stabilisation and closure, establishment and consolidation; it is the sphere of 'real politics', of state organs, administration, planning, statistics. Opposite the sedimentational realm of 'politics' there is dislocated sphere of 'the political'. In Laclau's model of stabilising and destabilising forces, 'the political' is the counter-movement to sedimentation; it de-fixes meaning, questions positions that were thought to be secure, brings forward the uncertain and torpedoes routines. The political is disruption, interruption, event. For Laclau and Mouffe, the concept of hegemony integrates both sides of the theory (inside/outside, sedimentation/dislocation, politics/the political). Hegemonic action aims on the one hand to become politics, to be inside of power, to sediment its own agenda. On the other hand, and at the same time, it is concerned with dislocating the validity of existing power (orders and systems of meaning) and plays in the register of the political.

One question that Laclau and Mouffe repeatedly pose is how and on what basis hegemonic aspirations can form and develop in the first place. This point leads to the concept of equivalence. With equivalence, Laclau and Mouffe propose a structural principle with which the production of commonality or community can be thought without resorting to traditional concepts of identity. The basic consideration is that any orthodox idea of community is built on concepts of identification that emanate from an objectivist and essentialist worldview. A worldview based on the rejection of such foundations requires a different principle of establishing community. And this is not least to ensure that goals such as solidarity or emancipation are possible even if the world is based on contingent and non-objectivist foundations. The concept of equivalence thus pursues the intention (and that is why it is so important) of thinking the possibility of how common positions can be taken in a non-objectivist world. The solution that Laclau and Mouffe outline with their concept of equivalence is that here commonality is not established directly and in relation to something positively shared, but through a different mechanism.

Equivalence is the radicalised counterpart of difference, it is the name of the subversion that prevents closure, undermines the production of social objectivity and introduces the substance of pure negativity. Equivalence is both *negating identification* and *negative identity*. Unlike difference, equivalence is conceived as a structure in which, first, the individual components are constructed as contingent and empty elements and in which, second, these components are not formed in terms of a positive whole, but solely through demarcation from something external. What holds things together, the non-identity based and anti-positive form of community, is what Laclau and Mouffe call an equivalential chain. In an equivalential chain, elements gather by aligning themselves against something. An equivalence chain consists of particular 'unfulfilled demands' that become solidary with each other (Laclau, 2005a: 120). The elements of an equivalential chain are always constituted in common reference to such an externality, which itself cannot be something positive. In this case, if it were itself something positive, the relationship between the two poles could be established in a direct and positively identity-based way. The abstract and theoretical concept has at least two important consequences: by assigning a special position to negativity, the positivism and essentialism that is at least latently inherent in all social theoretical concepts (even Marx's) is to be exorcised. Additionally, it is relevant to answer the complex question 'how a common political position is possible' without taking the bait of thinking identity and last truth (social objectivity).

Finally, we should look at a concept that Laclau in particular discusses again and again in his writings: the empty signifier. This reveals another line of tradition, namely the psychoanalytical philosophy of Jacques Lacan (see Chapter 6 by Wang). A basic condition in Laclau and Mouffe's theory of hegemony is the experience of a lack, the noticing of a gap that opens up in the harmonious flow of 'the social'.[4] What is missing, in Laclau's words, is the wholeness of society. The initial experience of lack is the counterpart to what is at the bottom of the social: the unfulfilled/unfulfillable desire for completeness. Laclau (2005a: 125) calls this desire, which is represented in terms such as 'freedom', 'justice' and 'equality', a 'democratic demand'. Such demands, in this interpretation, are not abstractions for something positive and concrete, but they primarily represent the absence itself, the impossibility of being complete, the emptiness that manifests itself in this impossibility. They are what Laclau (2005a: 127) calls 'empty signifier'. On the one hand, an empty signifier represents a real emptiness, namely the founding lack. It designates a place in the sign system that is constitutively unrepresentable, an empty space in the meaning whole. Only this lack of fulfilment (i.e. the impossibility of closing a system of meaning), gives desire its material as well as its discursive presence. On the other hand, the empty signifier points to another gap, specifically the gap between the particular and the universal. Without empty signifiers such as 'justice' and 'freedom', Laclau and Mouffe argue, social demands (such as for higher wages, for more rights, for lower rents) would remain entrenched in their particularism and therefore ineffective. Only because of the 'radical investment' (Laclau, 2005a: 115), with which the universal is striven for, is something of the emptiness represented in the expressions 'justice' and 'freedom' shifted into the particular demand. The gap between the individual and the total is not closed by such an investment, but the particular is given a share in the universality (Laclau and Mouffe, 2001: 5). However, this also means that particularity remains (Laclau, 2005a: 97): the tension between the two poles is not lost in the efforts to achieve a hegemonic position – which is precisely what a radical investment is about (Laclau, 2005a: 120) – and creates the framework for political action.

THE EMPTY PLACE OF POWER

To understand of the relation between hegemony and power one reference of Laclau and Mouffe is crucial: the theory of Claude Lefort about the empty place of power. Whenever Laclau and Mouffe explicitly discuss the nature and locality of power, they refer to Lefort's edict of the empty place of power (Laclau and Mouffe, 2001: 186; Laclau, 2012: 102; 2005a: 164; 2005b: 69; Mouffe, 1993: 11).[5] The connection to the discussion of hegemony is clear and direct. Laclau (1990: 259) himself explains the matter of the empty place as a crucial supplement to the theoretical apparatus of hegemony. In the context of this anthology, the thesis of the empty place is highly relevant, not least because of the location of power there (in an empty place): planning sciences are often counted among the spatial sciences, in which things as places and locations traditionally play a major role.

Lefort's thesis is based on an analysis of the transition from monarchy to democracy in the French Revolution. The starting point is a historicising image of the body, which is used to describe the power of the king. In the body of the king, this is the context of Lefort's thesis, 'the principle of the emergence and order of the kingdom is condensed' (Lefort, 1990: 292). Strictly speaking, however, it is not just one body, but two. Referring to the study *The King's Two Bodies* by Ernst Kantorowicz (1997 [1957]), Lefort distinguishes between a natural mortal body and a supernatural body that (comparable to the angels) never dies. The king is mortal, but in terms of his dignity and his 'political body' (Kantorowicz, 1997: 268) he is immortal. This use of language, Kantorowicz shows, stems from the late Middle Ages, where, according to the interpretation of Elizabethan Crown lawyers, the monarch was allowed to switch back and forth between two bodies and thus between divine and earthly responsibility. In this image, the king becomes the connecting link between human beings and God, represented in the division into the body on this side and the body on the other side. What is important here is that the assertion of immortality introduced with the image is at the same time an 'objectification of the [...] body politic' (Kantorowicz, 1997: 502). The body generalises and reifies itself, it becomes an object.[6]

Lefort illustrates the empty place of power with a second image: with the story of the king's severed head. The empty place is created by a historical event, namely the execution of Louis XVI, the last monarch of the Ancien Régime, who was deposed following the French Revolution in 1792 and sentenced and guillotined in 1793 at Robespierre's instigation. The 'link between the man-made and the transcendent ground of legitimation of society' is definitively broken at the moment of the beheading (Marchart, 2010: 133). What is decisive here is that not only the king's earthly body, but also his mystical and transcendent body is decapitated (there is no new king). For Lefort (1986: 303), the beheading of Louis XVI is therefore the execution of the 'democratic revolution' or the inscription of the democratic invention. The capping of power from the royal body leads to the empty, unoccupied and non-occupiable place that can only be partially and temporarily filled in democracy. The place of power that has become empty, as Lefort (1990: 293) puts it, is the 'revolutionary and unprecedented trait of democracy'. And it brings about a paradox: the empty place is 'non-occupiable precisely in the sense that the testing of the impossibility of establishing oneself there proves constitutive of the processes of socialisation' (Lefort and Gauchet 1990: 101). The inability to occupy becomes the actual driving force. The un-occupied and non-occupiable place is an external goal, a place that is outside of the sphere we can influence, 'but precisely because of this absence' unfolds its effect and organises the entire field (Lefort and Gauchet, 1990: 101).

Lefort particularly emphasises the founding negativity of the democratic invention. Not only the decapitation itself, but also and above all the destruction of the organic social totality represented in the body image is a decidedly negative founding prerequisite of democracy. In Lefort's thesis, on the one hand, the 'institutionalisation of the conflict' is accomplished and a division between the 'social inside and outside' is affected, which 'at the same time establishes their relationship' (1990: 293). The conflict over the occupation of the empty place of power – an occupation that cannot succeed completely in the last instance – is the central functional principle of democracy. Secondly, the impossibility and absence of complete causality is the very basis of Lefort's theoretical design. The destruction of the monarchy and the disintegration of the natural determinacy inscribed in the person of the king produce a vacuum in the place where the substance of society was formerly represented by the body of the king. Lefort explains that democracy 'institutes and sustains itself precisely by dissolving the foundations of all certainty' and thus a 'supernatural principle' has become impossible (1990: 296).

Laclau's and Mouffe's theory of hegemony ultimately revolves around explaining the endless efforts to fill the empty place of power, and to illuminate how and why these attempts do not and cannot succeed in the long run. That is perhaps the shortest way to define their approach: hegemony is nothing other than the name for the failing struggle to fill the empty place of power. Laclau explicitly discusses the connecting lines between the two structurally similar concepts of his empty signifier and Lefort's empty places of power. In doing so, he points out that for him the emptiness is not so much a structural location, but above all a type of identity (Laclau, 2014: 177). As Laclau (2014: 177) puts it, it is crucial that the 'occupation of an empty place is not possible without the occupying force itself becoming, to some extent, the signifier of emptiness'.

At this point, at the latest, it becomes clear that Lefort's empty place is not only helpful for an understanding of hegemony as a term for the ultimately unsuccessful efforts to occupy the empty place, but that it is also appropriate to think about planning from this point. Planning, it might be said, is a technique in the hegemonic effort to occupy the empty space: Planning is an occupying force. If we follow this argument and Laclau, then it turns out that planning – as an occupying force – is itself *a signifier of emptiness*. I come back to this idea in the last section.

THINKING AGONISM, THINKING ANTAGONISM

After *Hegemony and Socialist Strategy*, Mouffe and Laclau went their own and independent ways in further developing the jointly elaborated theoretical model. While Laclau focuses on the formulation of a theory of antagonism, Mouffe turns to the concept of agonism.

Mouffe's conception derives from the Greek agon, a term in which both Hannah Arendt (1958) and Friedrich Nietzsche (1872) were strongly interested. Agon refers to a struggle that is conceptualised not as war but as a contest in which there are rules and no destruction (Mouffe, 2013: 4). The central reference for her approach (Mouffe, 2005: 11) is Carl Schmitt's text on *The Concept of the Political* (2007 [1932]). The catchy formula Schmitt (2007: 44) uses to answer 'the question as to the specific content of the political' is the equation of the political with the opposition of friend and foe: 'Political thought and political instinct prove themselves theoretically and practically in the ability to distinguish friend and enemy' (Schmitt, 2007: 67). Schmitt defines first and foremost what the enemy is: the other, the stranger. He explains with ominous style that it must be determined 'whether the adversary intends to negate his opponent's way of life and therefore must be repulsed or fought in order to preserve one's own form of existence' (Schmitt, 2007: 27). Mouffe adopts Schmitt's approach and defines the political as a sphere of antagonistic forces.

However, unlike Schmitt, Mouffe wants to establish a democratic political theory. Therefore, at a certain point she has to distance herself from Schmitt's theses. Schmitt, Mouffe argues (1993: 133), constitutes pluralist democracy as a 'contradictory combination of irreconcilable principles': on the one hand, deliberative consensus as the goal of democratic politics, on the other, antagonistic forces as the essence of the political; for Schmitt, the contradiction between these two principles would lead to the conclusion that 'liberal democracy is a non-viable form of government'. Mouffe (1993: 133) reverses this argument and explain that it is precisely the tension between a 'logic of identity' (of consensus) and a 'logic of difference' (of antagonism) that constitutes democracy. Therefore, Mouffe argues, such a tension should not be lamented, but both logics should be welcomed along with their contradictions. The aim should be to defend both approaches in their contradictions, not to eliminate them. The basic tension produced by the relationship between consensus and antagonism is the 'best guarantee that the project of modern democracy is alive' (Mouffe, 1993: 133).

In Mouffe's interpretation, agon stands between the two poles of 'harmonious agreement' and 'irreconcilable struggle'. Agonism thus becomes the link between antagonism and consensus (i.e. between the two main explanations of the nature of the social). Contrary to the post-political ideal of consensus, Mouffe wants to preserve and anchor the dimension of conflict as a fundamental principle of the social, but without setting them as absolute. The agonistic conflict is supposed to function as a competition in which there are opposing and perhaps also irreconcilable positions and interests, but in which the opponents adhere to common rules and insofar as accept they each other, recognise the legitimacy of the other's position. Mouffe (1999: 752) claims that the real challenge of democracy is not to achieve a general rational consensus – that would be impossible. Instead, the task is to recognise the fact of antagonism as the basis of the social and to defuse this fundamental antagonism, to tame it and transform it into rule-accepting agonism.[7]

The concept of agonism can be used to explain and describe efforts at the level of the social to repress contingency and domesticate antagonism in politics and planning. The agon sublimates the fundamental antagonism and thus becomes (in this activity) a structural basis of the social. Antagonism is always present in the agon; agonism is the name for the effort to tame antagonism. Such taming is necessary for the attempt to build an orderly society, a social structure where everything is in its place. Politics in general and planning in particular are the main instruments for establishing such an order. The production of an agon as a tamed antagonism is therefore a good description of how planning works. Politics and planning always aim to contain (control, suppress) antagonism. In fact, the concept of agon can thus be used to signpost a theory of planning and it is true that planning is always an agonistic attempt (Hillier, 2002: 268).

While planning theory often works with the concept of agonism, for Laclau the concept of antagonism is central. According to Oliver Marchart (2018: 47), a student of Laclau, antagonism is the 'ungroundable "ground"', a kind of inverted horizon where every social and political foundation is built on. Antagonism is a core term in post-foundational thinking, one theoretical trend that substantially refers to Laclau and in recent times have become prominent in critical urban studies and geography (see Landau et al., 2021). Generally speaking, post-foundational thinking claims that – within the social and historic fabric – ultimate reasons are not possible. Nothing determines with final necessity the course of things. Post-foundational theory states that precisely this impossibility is the ground for all social and historical events.

Originally, antagonism was the Marxian term for the contradiction between the working and the owning class, which could be overcome only through revolution. Marchart imports the Marxian concept – and that imports a large helping of Marxian tradition; it is responsible for attributing post-foundational thinking as post-Marxian theory – and transforms it via Laclau to the final ground of post-foundationalism. Antagonism is the political ontology of post-foundational thinking condensed in one word. Sailing close to the wind of tautologies, post-foundational theory has found a valid focus with antagonism. Antagonism – and this is perhaps the clue to that thinking – is the substance of the social. The latter, as Marchart (2018: 96) puts it, is 'antagonistic by nature'. However, it is usually a latent antagonism which is inherent to all social identity. As compared to other post-foundational concepts of contingency as 'event', 'ambivalence', 'hybridity' or 'undecidability', antagonism has two advantages: the inherent link to the absence of the last ground (antagonism needs at least two elements to be antagonistic) and the closeness to conflict as the mode of every social articulation (Marchart, 2013: 360).

Assuming that antagonism is a constitutive element of any society helps to explain what we may call the 'planning paradox': Planning usually comes with the aim of resolving conflicts and establishing consensus. In this endeavour, however, planning fails again and again – and this is due antagonism being inherent to the social.

LET'S TALK ABOUT IDEOLOGY

Laclau's theory of ideology is based on a critique of the criticism of ideology. Criticism of Ideology deals with systems of ideas (doctrines, structures, rituals) and recognises and names them as ideologies. What are the conditions for such a critique? Critique of ideology, Laclau argues, must always find a point that is located outside the ideological. Only when such a point is found can ideology be recognised as ideology. If critique were to remain within the system, it would itself be part of ideology. Going outside ideology is the decisive step in any critique of ideology. But this step has a prerequisite. The assertion of an extra-ideological reality, as Laclau's argument goes, itself only functions as ideology. This is well illustrated by Marx and Engels, who famously defined ideology as a false consciousness that obscures power structures and distorts the representation and perception of real economic relations. The problem Laclau explains is that immanent in the denunciation of a false consciousness or a distortion is the assertion that there is – outside of the ideology – a true consciousness or an undistorted perspective. This assertion, i.e. the assumption that one is in possession of true consciousness, is for Laclau (2014: 13) the actual ideological moment, it is what he calls 'the ideological illusion par excellence'.

A further development of ideology theory, Laclau argues, must start precisely here. First, it is a matter of recognising that there is not and cannot be an extra-ideological point and that therefore the classical form of critique of ideology is not possible. Everything in this world is discursively mediated and this means that nothing can be outside the ideological. This eliminates the possibility of criticising ideology from the outside, i.e. a 'critique of ideology as such' (Laclau, 2014: 13). Everything is ideological and a critique of ideology must therefore take a different path.

Laclau proposes starting with the concept of distortion. Similar to false consciousness, the concept of distortion also presupposes something, namely that there is something that is not distorted. So this again imports a bit of an essentialist perspective, which claims that there would be the extra-discursive and extra-ideological and thus undistorted representation/perception. Laclau proposes incorporating the concept of distortion into the theory and make it the cornerstone of a more developed theory of ideology. He proposes considering distortion as constitutive. Distortion is a form of misrecognition: the true character is misrecognised, and therefore reality is perceived and represented in a distorted way – this is the narrative of classical critique of ideology. Opposite to misrecognition is the principle of closure. Symbolic and social systems have closure of their own system as their structural principle – everything demands closure, coherence and objective meaning. Identities, states, spaces, etc. – all these are systems that strive for such a closure. Recognition, as Laclau puts it, has to do with closure. Indeed, all closure requires misrecognition and distortion, and this is because it (closure) is impossible. This impossibility must be misrecognised. The very idea of closure is in fact the highest form of misrecognition. Distortion and misrecognition are 'part of universal misrecognition' and this means that 'what presents itself as the opposite of misrecognition belongs to the essence of the latter' (Laclau, 2014: 14). In this process, misrecognition contaminates closure and penetrates to its very core. Distortion is constitutive of social objectivity. Conversely, the proclamation of objective meaning is the basic form of distortion/recognition through which every identity acquires a fictive coherence. Distortion and distortion are universal principles whose main form is closure.

Distortion and misrecognition are necessary and impossible in this theory. To distort and to misrecognise is precisely the fact that any original (not distorted, not misrecognised) meaning is illusory. The distortion is there to create this illusion and to suggest original meaning. This is what ideologies do: they create an illusion of social objectivity and originality. And this is also where a renewed contemporary critique of ideology can start: it can recognise and identify the distorting operation of closure and the assertion of objectivity as an illusory practice.

Such a theory of ideology can be a starting point for thinking about planning. In his brilliant essay 'Planning as the ideology of (neoliberal) space' (2010), Michael Gunder argues, with reference to Laclau and Mouffe, that planning is always ideological. An ideology is always inherent in the concept of 'planning', even if it is not made explicit. With 'planning', ideas are structured and processed according to fixed procedures. Gunder (2010: 298) suggests examining how these ideas are 'ideologised', how they unfold as 'sublime ideals of a better future'. He argues for a resumption of ideology critique in the field of planning theory. Gunder also links the two basic elements of institutional planning: ideology and space. Planning, he argues, has the task of controlling spatial relations – of permitting or excluding certain uses in certain spaces. Therefore, planning is the ideology of how space is defined and used (Gunder, 2010: 308).

Generally speaking, planning is a symbolic system of meaning that strives for closure and social objectivity. It is not uncommon for planning to attempt to present itself as pragmatic, neutral, apolitical and unideological. With Laclau's theory of ideology, precisely this attempt can be worked out as the distorting operation itself and understood as the ideological core of planning.

HEGEMONY, IDEOLOGY AND PLANNING

How does Laclau's and Mouffe's abstract thought and theory building help us to gain an understanding of planning? To what extent is it possible to work with the conceptual tools outlined here in planning theory?

It is important to note that such thinking about planning with the help of Laclau and Mouffe is already being done extensively. In planning theory and its environments there are many attempts to grasp the conditions and effects of planning by this means. Laclau's and Mouffe's theories have been reflected comprehensively in research on planning: Legacy et al. (2019: 273) explore 'the problematique of the consensus and conflict binary' referring to Mouffe's critique on the narrative of the post-political. McClymont (2019: 282) contributes to 'post-foundationalist critiques of planning practice' and discusses 'the reassertion of disagreement as fundamental to democratic politics'. Jabareen and Eizenberg (2020) write on 'a new theoretical perspective for understanding urban social spaces' with references to Laclau and Mouffe's model of the logic of equivalent chains. McAuliffe and Rogers (2019: 300) consider 'the role of value pluralism in theorising urban development and the politics of participatory planning' with reference to Mouffe's agonism and its concept of productive conflicts. Jon (2020: 147) addresses 'normativity and political solidarity within the postmodern paradigm' and emphasises Laclau and Mouffe's argument of the historicity of all social relations. Grange (2014: 2670) tries to 'understand some of the ideological mechanisms at work' in the recent debates on the crisis of planning, drawing explicitly on the theory by Laclau and Mouffe. Trapenberg Frick (2021: 62) theorises the 'coalition formation' between citizens and communities outside of formal planning processes as agonistic situations. White (2021) proposes an 'alternative formulation of agonism' with embracing the 'idea of the moral equality of voice'. Asenbaum (2020: 86) studies disidentification as a possible radical democratic practice. Finally, Palonen (2021) elaborates on the distinction between democracy and demography considering recent post-foundational approaches.

The contributions to this list, which is of course not exhaustive, show that thinking about ideology, hegemony, the empty signifier and the other concepts of Laclau and Mouffe can be enormously inspiring for a fundamental reflection on the conditions and on the essence of planning.

However, the writings from Laclau and Mouffe probably do not directly contribute to planning differently and better or to providing a different and/or better self-understanding for planners. But their theory proves to be helpful in different ways: it provides a theoretical vocabulary to analyse politics, planning and power. Attention to the embeddedness of planning in hegemonic power processes is necessary to understand and situate current planning processes and controversies. Moreover, planners are political actors. Planning is always political, hegemonic and ideological, and it is therefore always necessary for planners to position themselves within the realm of politics and within the realm of the political. For such efforts, Laclau and Mouffe's reflections continue to be topical and inspiring offers, and they are also helpful to look at (or even do) planning from a radical democratic, non-dogmatic and leftist point of view.

Planning is not isolated or single, it is always part of a political agenda and embedded in a social and historic context – this is perhaps the main lesson that can be drawn from the writings of Laclau and Mouffe. They demonstrate how power emerges in hegemonic disputes, and argue that the aim of these disputes is to fill the empty space of power. The empty space is both the goal and the impetus for hegemonic interventions. Emptiness and unoccupiability guarantee that the hegemonic game can never come to an end. Planning is inscribed as a technique of power in this game. It is part of hegemonic political events. In this capacity, planning tries in various ways to occupy the empty space and to secure the partial successes that are achieved along the way. Ultimately, however, if one follows the theory of Laclau and Mouffe, this filling of the void is never permanently successful. For planning theory and its reflection on planning, this also means that it is more important to look at this failure of planning than to try to trace planning successes and create planning manuals.

NOTES

1. Over the past twenty years, Laclau and Mouffe have both gained some attention in planning theory ([Hillier 2002, 2003; Gunder 2003; Purcell 2009). Mouffe's approach emerged in many scholarly debates as 'agonistic planning theory' (Mäntysalo 2011; Bond 2011; Bäcklund/Mäntysalo 2010; Roskamm 2015). Laclau's writings form part of the ongoing debates on the general nature of politics, planning and space, and they are influential especially within post-Marxist arguments pertaining to political theory, culture studies, critical geography and urban studies.
2. A detailed history of the notion of hegemony is Anderson's *The H-Word* (2017). At the same time, the book is a good example for the strong emotions emerging from Laclau and Mouffe's approach until today.
3. Results of formal planning are excellent examples for sedimentations.
4. The question of what constitutes 'the social' and how it is distinguished from politics cannot be discussed in detail here. One suggestion is to grasp the social as the 'echo room of the political', which, however, 'is not in itself politics' (Marchart, 2010: 299).
5. The importance of Lefort's empty place is also regularly elaborated in the secondary literature on the work of Laclau and Mouffe (Dyrberg, 1997: 113; Marchart, 2010: 131; 2007: 86; Critchley, 2004: 115; Roskamm, 2017; the list could be extended at will); it is only in the contributions from the field of planning theory that the reference to Lefort's thesis has, interestingly, been found only sporadically so far – in my view, another good reason to discuss it somewhat more explicitly here.
6. Jacques Derrida (2006: 8) puts the issue in this way: 'King is a thing, Thing is the King, precisely where he separates from his body which, however, does not leave him'.
7. For a critique on Mouffe's concept of agonism from a post-foundational point of view see Roskamm (2015) and Marchart (2013).

REFERENCES

Anderson, Perry (2017), *The H-Word. The Peripeteia of Hegemony*, London and New York: Verso.
Arendt, Hannah (1958), *The Human Condition*, Chicago: The University of Chicago Press.

Asenbaum, H. (2020), 'The Politics of Becoming: Disidentification as Radical Democratic Practice', *European Journal of Social Theory*, 24(1), 86–104.

Bäcklund, P. and R. Mäntysalo (2010), 'Agonism and Institutional Ambiguity', *Planning Theory*, 9(4), 333–350.

Bond, S. (2011), 'Negotiating a "Democratic Ethos". Moving Beyond the Agonistic – Communicative Divide', *Planning Theory*, 10(2), 161–186.

Critchley, Simon (2004), 'Is there a Normative Deficit in the Theory of Hegemony?', in Simon Critchley and Oliver Marchart (eds), *Laclau: A Critical Reader*, Abingdon, UK: Routledge, pp. 113–122.

Derrida, Jacques (2006), *Specters of Marx: The State of the Debt, the Work of Mourning and the New International*, New York and London: Routledge.

Dyrberg, Torben Bech (1997), *The Circular Structure of Power: Politics, Identity, Community*, London and New York: Verso.

Gramsci, Antonio (1992), *Prison Notebooks: Volume 1*, trans. by Joseph A. Buttigieg and Antonio Callari, New York: Columbia University Press.

Gramsci, Antonio (1996), *Prison Notebooks: Volume II*, trans. by Joseph A. Buttigieg, New York: Columbia University Press.

Gramsci; Antonio (2007), *Prison Notebooks: Volume III*, trans. by Joseph A. Buttigieg, New York: Columbia University Press.

Grange, K. (2014), 'In Search of Radical Democracy: The Ideological Character of Current Political Advocacies for Culture Change in Planning', *Environment and Planning A*, 46(11), 2670–2685.

Gunder, M. (2003), 'Passionate Planning for the Others' Desire: An Agonistic Response to the Dark Side of Planning', *Progress in Planning*, 60(3), 235–319.

Gunder, M. (2010), 'Planning as the Ideology of (Neoliberal) Space', *Planning Theory*, 9(4), 298–314.

Hillier, J. (2003), 'Agon'izing over Consensus – Why Habermasian Ideals cannot be "Real"', *Planning Theory*, 2(1), 37–59.

Hillier, Jean (2002), *Shadows of Power. An Allegory of Prudence in Land-Use Planning*, London and New York: Routledge.

Jabareen, Y. and E. Eizenberg (2020), 'Theorizing Urban Social Spaces and their Interrelations: New Perspectives on Urban Sociology, Politics, and Planning', *Planning Theory*, Online First, https://doi.org/10.1177/1473095220976942.

Jon, I. (2020), 'Reframing Postmodern Planning with Feminist Social Theory: Toward "Anti-Essentialist Norms"', *Planning Theory*, 19(2), 147–171.

Kantorowicz, Ernst H. (1997), *The King's Two Bodies. A Study in Mediaeval Political Theology*, Princeton, NJ: Princeton University Press.

Laclau, Ernesto (1990), *New Reflections on the Revolution of our Time*, London and New York: Verso.

Laclau, E. (1995), 'Subject of Politics, Politics of the Subject', *Differences* 7(1), 146–164.

Laclau, Ernesto (1996), 'Why do Empty Signifiers Matter to Politics?', in Ernesto Laclau, *Emancipation(s)*, London and New York: Verso, pp. 36–46.

Laclau, E. (2001), 'Democracy and the Question of Power', *Constellations* 8(1), 3–14.

Laclau, Ernesto (2005a), *On Populist Reason*, London and New York: Verso.

Laclau, Ernesto (2005b), 'Deconstruction, Pragmatism, Hegemony', in Chantal Mouffe (ed.), *Deconstruction and Pragmatism: Simon Critchley, Jacques Derrida, Ernesto Laclau and Richard Rorty,* London and New York: Routledge, pp. 49–70.

Laclau, Ernesto (2012), 'Antagonism, Subjectivity and Politics', in Ernesto Laclau (2014), *The Rhetorical Foundations of Society*, London and New York: Verso, pp. 101–125.

Laclau, Ernesto and Mouffe, Chantal (2001), *Hegemony and Socialist Strategy: Towards a Radical Democratic Politics*, London and New York: Verso.

Landau, Friederike, Pohl, Lucas and Roskamm, Nikolai (eds) (2021), *[Un]Grounding. Post-Foundational Geographies*, Bielefeld: Transcript.

Lefort, Claude (1982), 'Démocratie et avénement d'un "lieu vide"', in Claude Lefort (2007), *Le temps présent: Écrits 1945–2005*, Paris: Belin, pp. 461–469.

Lefort, Claude (1986), *The Political Forms of Modern Society*, Cambridge, MA: MIT Press.

Lefort, Claude (1988), *Democracy and Political Theory*, Cambridge: Polity Press.

Lefort, Claude (1990), 'Die Frage der Demokratie', in Ulrich Rödel (ed.), *Autonome Gesellschaft und libertäre Demokratie*, Frankfurt am Main: Suhrkamp, pp. 281–297.

Lefort, C. and M. Gauchet [1967] (1990), 'Über die Demokratie: Das Politische und die Instituierung des Gesellschaftlichen', in Ulrich Rödel (ed.), *Autonome Gesellschaft und libertäre Demokratie*, Frankfurt am Main: Suhrkamp, pp. 89–122.

Legacy, C., Metzger, J., Steele, W. and Gualini, E. (2019), 'Beyond the Post-political: Exploring the Relational and Situated Dynamics of Consensus and Conflict in Planning', *Planning Theory*, 18(3), 273–281.

Lenin, Vladimir Ilyich (1962), *Collected Works, Vol. 8*, London and Moscow: Lawrence and Wishart.

Mäntysalo, R. (2011), 'Planning as Agonistic Communication in a Trading Zone: Re-examining Lindblom's Partisan Mutual Adjustment', *Planning Theory*, 10(3), 257–272.

Marchart, Oliver (2007), *Post-foundational Political Thought: Political Difference in Nancy, Lefort, Badiou and Laclau*, Edinburgh: Edinburgh University Press.

Marchart, Oliver (2010), *Die politische Differenz: Zum Denken des Politischen bei Nancy, Lefort, Badiou, Laclau und Agamben*, Berlin: Suhrkamp.

Marchart, Oliver (2013), *Das unmögliche Objekt: Eine postfundamentalistische Theorie der Gesellschaft*, Berlin: Suhrkamp.

Marchart, Oliver (2018), *Thinking Antagonism: Political Ontology after Laclau*, Edinburgh: Edinburgh University Press.

McAuliffe, C. and D. Rogers (2019), 'The Politics of Value in Urban Development: Valuing Conflict in Agonistic Pluralism', *Planning Theory*, 18(3), 300–318.

McClymont, K. (2019), 'Articulating virtue: Planning Ethics Within and Beyond Post Politics', *Planning Theory*, 18(3), 282–299.

Mouffe, Chantal (1993), *The Return of the Political*, London and New York: Verso.

Mouffe, Chantal (1999), 'Deliberative Democracy or Agonistic Pluralism?' *Social Research*, 66(3), 745–758.

Mouffe, Chantal (2002), *The Democratic Paradox*, London and New York: Verso.

Mouffe, Chantal (2005), *On the Political*, London and New York: Routledge.

Mouffe, Chantal (2013), *Agonistics. Thinking the World Politically*, London and New York: Verso.

Nietzsche, Friedrich (1872), 'Homer's Wettkampf', in *Nietzsche Werke (1973), Kritische Gesamtausgabe: Dritte Abteilung, Zweiter Band. Nachgelassene Schriften 1870–1873*, Berlin: Walter de Gruyter, pp. 277–286.

Palonen, E. (2021), 'Democracy vs. Demography: Rethinking Politics and the People as Debate', *Thesis Eleven*, Online First, https://doi.org/10.1177/072551362098366.

Purcell, M. (2009), 'Resisting Neoliberalization: Communicative Planning or Counter-hegemonic Movements?' *Planning Theory*, 8(2), 140–165.

Roskamm, N. (2015), 'On the Other Side of "Agonism" – "the Enemy", the "Outside" and the Role of Antagonism', *Planning Theory*, 14(4), 384–403.

Roskamm, Nikolai (2017), *Die unbesetzte Stadt: Postfundamentalistisches Denken und das urbanistische Feld*, Berlin: de Gruyter.

Roskamm, N. (2019), 'The Constitutive Outside of Planetary Urbanization: A Post-Foundational Reading', Online Publication, www.nikolairoskamm.de, 1–21.

Schmitt, Carl [1932] (2007), *The Concept of the Political*, Chicago: The University of Chicago Press.

Trapenberg Frick, K. (2021), 'No Permanent Friends, No Permanent Enemies: Agonistic Ethos, Tactical Coalitions, and Sustainable Infrastructure', *Journal of Planning Education and Research*, 41(1), 62–78.

White, S.K. (2021), 'Agonism, Democracy, and the Moral Equality of Voice', *Political Theory*, Online first, https://doi.org/10.1177/0090591721993862.

8.   The destituent power of Rancière's radical equality

Camillo Boano

INTRODUCTION

Jacques Rancière (born 1940) – Emeritus Professor of Philosophy at the Université de Paris, VIII – is one of the most influential philosophers of our time, whose figure and thoughts occupy a vast and rising body of literature (Davis, 2010, 2013; Rockhill and Watts, 2009; May, 2008; 2010; Bowman and Stamp, 2011; Deranty and Ross, 2012; Quintana, 2020). As one of the contemporary thinkers who has re-interrogated the tasks and challenges of critical theory, Rancière offers analytics for the many mechanisms of injustice, exclusion and domination in our late capitalist societies and, at the same time, conceptualizes an agenda for society's liberation (Bingham and Biesta, 2010; Biesta, 2010; Rancière, 2017b; Quintana, 2018).

Bringing to the fore the relationship between the political and the aesthetic (Rancière, 2002, 2006, 2013; Tanke, 2011; Gage, 2019), Rancière develops reflections on the equality of citizens in the face of power and knowledge, questioning the dominant position of the intellectual who speaks truth to the world.

Recentring politics as aesthetics, Rancière provides a critical theory that makes visible the many mechanisms that configure power and keep 'bodies trapped in the reiteration of their subjections, instead of delving into the affective territories that circulate among them and the unforeseeable ways in which they could be transformed' (Quintana, 2020: 2). Tracing the practices of emancipation in their singularity and their aesthetic-political (experiential, corporeal, affective) dimension (Quintana, 2020), Rancière positions politics as the disruption of accounts that premise politics on certain conditions or capacities (Huzar, 2021).

This chapter introduces Rancière's key motif of equality and how it helps us to rethink the notion of power. For Rancière it is the absent presence of 'equality' that both enables social order and allows its hierarchy of power relations to be challenged. Elaborating on equality, the chapter frames Rancière's politics and power in a way that is never static and pure, but characterized in terms of division, conflict and polemics that allow the invention of the new, the unauthorized and the disordered.

Particular attention will be given to the tension within the politics of aesthetics. Rancière called this *le partage du sensible* to describe the many procedures by which forms of experience – broadly understood as the domains of what can be thought, said, felt or perceived – are divided up and shared between legitimate and illegitimate bodies and forms of activity.

Acknowledging the relevance of Rancière's body of work in planning discourses (Dikeç, 2005, 2007; Raco, 2014; Metzger et al., 2015) framed as conflictive (Pløger, 2004; Grange and Gunder, 2019) or emancipatory and revolutionary (Purcel, 2009, 2014) or discussed within democracy and community formation (Sonderegger, 2002; Inston, 2019), this chapter is suggesting a complementary reflection reframing power as destituent, an an-archic power. Without tracing a comprehensive genealogy of the term,[1] it appears for the first time by the

Colectivo Situaciones in Buenos Aires to describe the original features of the Argentine *piqueteros* movement of 2001 capable of bringing about a real change in Argentina by del-egitimizing existing political forces (Laudani, 2016). More recently, the concept has been found in Giorgio Agamben, a figure who expresses the full force of its political meaning in *The Use of Bodies* (2016) where suggesting that a destituent power is one that 'deactivate[s] something and render[s] it inoperative – a power ... without simply destroying it but by liber-ating the potentials that have remained inactive in it in order to allow a different use of them' (Agamben, 2016: 273).

Contemporary planning and other post-positivistic disciplines are caught in the wake of multiple overlapping crises that question in essence their theories and modes of practice. These crises include global climate change, hegemonic neoliberalism, growing inequalities, the surge of a fascist and far-right extremism; all of which overlap with the structural complicities of racial capitalism, settler colonial global apartheid and the other diverse issues of globalisation (Porter, 2010; Cohen, 2012; Brown, 2019; Besteman, 2020; Harcourt, 2020).

Therefore, a reflection on a radical alternative to constituent power able to offer multiple and plural instances of liberation is both necessary and urgent.

In the wake of Trump's election in the United States, Roy (2017: np) had posited that 'we must think critically and historically about this specific infrastructure and its alliances with various forms of power ... complicit with colonialism and imperialism'. This urgent call to arms 'will require relinquishing the cherished myths of neutrality and innocence and instead deploying the power of knowledge and expertise for the purposes of civil disobedience ... being in opposition to state power rather than seeking its patronage' (Roy, 2017: np). Inspired by radical black scholars, Roy sees a sort of destituent power, that she calls a 'double agent' as 'one who is embedded in systems of power and yet is able to stage moments of rebellion against and within such systems' (Roy, 2017: np). Not a return to the foundations of the dis-cipline – fully compromised in the current crisis-making – but a series of liberatory practices, without an *archè*, intended both as origin and command/intention (Metzger et al., 2015). It is not the rejection of the planning subject and its strategic intention, but rather an acknowledge-ment that such practices exclude and oppress. More recently, Roy (2021, np) posits again that the complex present 'demands that we divest from the protocols of neutrality that have kept planning on the sidelines of freedom struggles, making liberal excuses for its role in the repro-duction of racial harm'. Bélanger (2020: 127), reframes these distituent words as an undoing:

> to undress this carceral landscape requires the unmapping of settler urbanism. It means destroying the dispossessive categories that sanction exclusion, exploitation, extraction and erasure. Dismantling the structures that obviate the legal landscape of treaties and that are constructed to sever relations between lands, waters, beings, cycles and communities. Unplanning oppressive policies. Unnaming colonial place names. Debasing base maps. Debunking benchmarks. Redrawing legends. Retroceding lands.

Following Roy, there is the necessity to think of planning not as an ontology of disciplinary, geographical or methodological power, but one that is able to offer and bring out a 'power of not' (Agamben, 2016: 283) an undoing, a 'non-projecting imagination' as Glissant (1997) would say.

While the first part of the chapter outlines Rancière's key concepts, the second frames some reflections on power that dislocates politics in a territory without foundations and serves to establish an initial qualifying point of destituent power. Importantly, this chapter is not intended to be a collection of references on Rancière-ways-of-planning, but neither is it an overview of his theories. More precisely, it poses itself as thoughts in movement, thoughts that look at praxis without directly descending from it. Earlier reflections were emerging in some of my engagement with the design actions of community architects and everyday citizens in South East Asia (Boano and Kelling, 2013; Boano and Hunter, 2018; Boano and Talocci, 2018) to which I briefly refer as illustration. Thinking on power and planning with Rancière helps to reflect on a destituent politics (Tarì, 2017; Laudani, 2016; Boano, 2020). A politics with a limited but precise task: to create the conditions, so that another politics – the one that today seems impossible – can happen 'to unleash a politics of the event, the event of politics nests in a singular desertion from what is, to break the normal course of history and produce a multiple, ecstatic, plurality' (Di Cesare, 2020: 16).

RANCIÈRE IN CONTEXT

Rancière's power cannot be understood, either theoretically or politically, without taking into account the context in which it emerged – the struggle in France in the second half of the twentieth century, the reception of German philosophy from the First World War to the Second, the Resistance to May 1968, and from the election of Mitterrand to the onset of neoliberalism to the more recent revolt of the *gilets jaunes* (Rancière, 2019). His thoughts emerge outside of a Habermasian deliberative theory that cannot accept the idea of an a-conflictual consensus, letting Cesarale (2019: 135) call Rancière's politics 'born from dissent', and centred on 'the class struggle that generates the conditions of politics' (Cesarale, 2019: 135–136).

Rancière offers an account of politics in relation to a dominant order that is marked by its members' possession of reasoned capacity of speech. He also highlights the problematic aspects in which such dominant frames 'prevent us from considering the unforeseeable and incalculable ways in which bodies can reinvent themselves from the positions, roles, and practices they are subjected to' (Quintana, 2020: 2). In such situations he analyses the 'interruptive force of forms of existence that were previously insensitive and that, via their demonstration of their reasoned speech, transform' (Huzar, 2021: 1): he calls this 'distribution of the sensible' (Rancière, 2010: 36), making themselves understood as speaking beings when they previously could not be heard in this way. The conceptual distancing from the structural Marxism of Althusser (Rockhill and Watts, 2009; May, 2008) and the refusal of the ideology of the scientific status of theory and its dominant linguistic paradigm, brings Rancière into direct engagement with the material, the concrete and the sensory dimension of experience (Rancière, 1994; Rockhill and Watts, 2009).

POLICE AND POLITICS: UNFOLDING OF DISSENSUS AND THE EMERGENCE OF EQUALITY

Recalling the Aristotelian *polis*, Rancière used the word *police* to refer to the established social order of governing where the political problem is drastically reduced to assigning individuals their place and position through the administration of the conflicts between different parties by a government funded on juridical and technical competences. In contrast, Rancière's *politics* is constituted by *dissensus*, by disruptions of the police order through the dispute over the common space of the *polis* and the common use of language (Rancière, 1999; 2010). With such an approach, politics is not about identifying the *excluded* and trying to include them as such logic of identification belongs to the police. Politics *proper* is to question the *given* order of police that seems to be the *natural* order of things and to verify the equality of any speaking being to any other speaking being (Rancière, 1999). Police, therefore, is an order of bodies that are organized with specific allocation of ways of doing, ways of being, ways of saying. Police, not politics, assign bodies by name to a particular place and task in the order of things. For Mecchia (2009: 71) his essential aspect of politics is 'the affirmation of the equality in the speech of people who are supposed to be equal but who are not counted as such by the established policing of the democratic community'. This is the true political principle of 'agonistic claim to equality, as defined in humans, primarily by the sharing of speech as logos: that is not the mere voice, but reason' (Mecchia, 2009: 74). The centrality of equality is to be found in *The Ignorant Schoolmaster* (1991), where Rancière criticises any distributional approach to ethics and governance. Alternatively, in the words of May 'where there is a distribution, there is a distributor … the claim of equality, then, is a claim directed at governing institutions on behalf of the individual those institutions govern … equality is a debt owed to the individuals by the governing institution of a society or a community' (May, 2009: 109).

Illustrating the story of Joseph Jacotot (a French pedagogue forced to move to Flanders in the early nineteenth century, without speaking Flemish, but nevertheless able to get a position as a teacher, practicing with the aid of only one dual-language edition of *Telemachus* in French and Flemish), Rancière draws a very important and scandalous conclusion: 'what stultifies the common people is not the lack of instruction, but the belief in the inferiority of their intelligence' (Rancière, 1991: 39). This reflection brings out a crucial element in Rancière's concept of equality: the presupposition of equality that should be the basis for any democratic politics; the presupposition that people are, in some sense, equally intelligent. To presuppose that people are equally intelligent is not to presuppose that they are capable of the same. Rather, it is to presuppose that each person, anyone and everyone as Rancière puts it, is capable of speaking to one another, understanding one another, and reasoning with one another. The equality of intelligence, then, is not a numerical or quantitative equality. Nor is it a conclusion to an argument, but rather a starting point for politics. He clarifies that 'our problem isn't proving that all intelligence is equal. It's seeing what can be done under that presupposition. And for this, it's enough for us that the opinion be possible – that is, that no opposing truth be proved' (Rancière, 1991: 46).

In *Disagreement* (1999) Rancière expands this point beside the pedagogical implication orienting his thought to a radically egalitarian understanding of politics as the enactment of such equality, writing that 'what makes an action political is … the form in which confirmation of equality is inscribed in the setting up of a dispute' (Rancière, 1999: 32). Equality becomes therefore a condition of the possibility of Rancière's conception of agonistic politics, never pacified, restricted and simply organized in space and time.

By equality, Rancière does not mean something that can be stated independently of a particular social dispute, confrontation, agonistic discourse, or assemblage of power. Instead this implies 'the pure empty quality of equality between anyone and everyone' (Rancière, 1999: 35). When seen in this light 'emancipation is neither a movement toward illumination, in which we manage to see what did not let itself be seen, nor a process of knowledge and acknowledgment of what we did not know, nor the reappropriation of a capacity that had become separated from itself' (Quintana, 2020: 3). In challenging the emancipatory potential of critical theory (Rockhill and Watts, 2009; Cesarale, 2019), Quintana (2020: 4) suggests that such arrangements are 'always affective, corporeal forms of awareness' and therefore an 'emancipatory movement is, above all, an affective movement that pushes one to "seek another way of life" different from the habitual one, on the basis of the affirmation of the power of bodies to reconfigure themselves, of their plasticity'.

With this, we can say that for Rancière there is politics only when there are no foundations. For him, politics consists of the process that takes away any foundation – *archè* Di Cesare (2020b) would have said – from any social order. Since an order always tends to stabilize itself and represent itself as complete, rational and absolute, politics shows its conditional and fragile character. In fact, it takes place in the interruption of an order, its presumed naturalness; as itself intermittent, politics is not always there, indeed it never exists, it does not exist, but is carried out here and there as the disruption of an effective order. Such a perspective, in such an intractable form, poses more 'political' questions than it answers. Patton argues that 'politics is commonly thought in terms of struggles over power institutions, public reasons and public opinions. By contrast for Rancière (2012: 129), 'politics is a matter of conflicts over the very existence of this stage as well as the make-up status of the performers who are entitled or able to appear'. Without a terrain, a specific area, a surface and an object whether in the form of the state, the government, the territory or the law, politics is also deprived of a subject whether in the form of people, nation or class who can guide an emancipatory process.

In this interpretation of politics, equality gives rise to politics in a unique way as it becomes a continuous polemical expression of it, never fixed and assumed even if presupposed in any social order. As May (2008: 40) puts it, 'voting, writing to elected representatives, even attending a demonstration, are not by themselves matters of politics. Politics concerns something else: it concerns equality'. The rare event of politics happens only when 'the traditional mechanisms of what are usually called "politic" are put into question' (May, 2008: 40) and equality emerges.

POLITICS AND RECONFIGURATION OF BODIES: THE *PARTAGE*

Jacques Rancière's rupture with the linguistic structural Marxism towards a material, sensorial and concrete formulation of politics and its possible emancipation are the centre of a new politics of aesthetics and the aesthetics of politics (Rancière, 2002, 2006, 2013; Highmore, 2011; Davis, 2013b). Rancière's *le partage du sensible* describes the procedures by which forms of experience – broadly understood as the domains of what can be thought, said, felt or perceived – are divided up and shared between legitimate and illegitimate persons and forms of activity. The double meaning of the French term *partage* as both 'to share, to have in common', and also 'to divide, to share out' (Mechoulan, 2004: 3) which refers to the fact that, 'the affirmation of something in common is at the same time the repartition of authorized positions' (Mechoulan, 2004: 3). For Rancière, proper order is always interrupted by impropriety which, despite being focused on critical writing and 'literality' served to set the stage for his provocative conception of politics and his constant and insistent defence of democracy as *dissensus*, as scandalous (Rancière, 2010, 2017).

Therefore, Rancière (2010: 35) views politics as a refusal to properly determine what constitutes politics: 'the essential object of political disputes is the very existence of politics itself'. For Rancière (1999: 30), 'political activity is whatever shifts a body from the place assigned to it or changes a place's destination'. Politics disrupts 'ways of doing, ways of being, and ways of saying' (Rancière, 1999: 29) that are allocated 'within a dominant, extant order' (Rancière, 1999: 29). This is a position that has been criticized by Huzar (2021: 14), because 'an insistence on politics demonstrating equality ignores the fugitive politics proper of the black tradition and the politics of those subject', thereby endangering 'what constitutes politics by linking politics with making oneself visible in the transformation of the aesthesis of a dominant order' (Huzar, 2021: 3).

Huzar's critique is an important reflection on the power of invisibility and fugitivity we do not have space to explore in detail, however, it does not modify the central idea of politics as reconfiguration of places. Rancière's (1999: 30) central spatial reference remains a reconfiguration of a space 'where parties, parts or lack of parts have been defined … making visible what had no business being seen and makes heard a discourse where once there was only place for noise'. This reconfiguration of a space remains heavily illustrative for a newly conceptualized version of power that is not static, transformative and always contested and that in some extreme, includes a fugitive strategy One of the ways in which police avoid the disturbance of politics is to name phenomena and assign them to their 'proper places' in the established order, thereby de-politicising them (Dikeç, 2005). In Rancière's approach, this is not a question of politics; it is about alterations in a police order. Politics, therefore, is not about identifying the 'excluded' and trying to include them. The logic of identification belongs to the police. Politics is not, furthermore, about the negotiation of interests by previously identified groups. Politics proper is to question the 'given' order of police that seems to be the 'natural' order of things, to question the whole and its partitioned spaces, and to verify the equality of any speaking being to any other speaking being (Rancière, 1999). Therefore, genuine political activities always involve forms of innovation that tear bodies from their assigned places and prevent free speech and right of expression from being reduced to mere functionality (Rancière and Corcoran, 2010). With Quintana (2020: 4) this produces 'a rupture with a corporeality, with a way of experiencing the body, which brings about a transformation of its position, that is, an inscription in another sensible universe, other than the one assigned to it'. Thinking with what she coined a 'politics of bodies', emancipatory potentials and new realities are emerging, manifesting 'in other economies of affective forces, in other forms of gesturality and in practices of corporeal reflectivity that also produce another way of seeing the world, of being affected by it, and of judging it' (Quintana, 2020: 4). For Quintana (2020: 4) this is really the manifestation of what Rancière's *partage du sensible* as 'alteration of the way in which bodies take on what they can, in the way they experience their capacities and incapacities'. This happens when *dissensus* emerges. Dissensus introduces new subjects and heterogeneous objects into the fields of perception. Such emergent distribution sets the divisions between what is visible and invisible, speakable and unspeakable, in Rancière's words – audible and inaudible. It determines what can be thought, made or done (Porter, 2010), that 'define[s] the 'modes of perception' that make that order visible and sayable in the first place' (Rancière, 2010: 20).

AESTHETICS AS POLITICS

Since the early 1990s, Rancière's work has increasingly focused on aesthetics. He has written a series of works on film and literature in which he stresses the political dimension of aesthetics, and a number of works of political theory in which he argues that an aesthetic dimension is inherent in politics (Conley, 2005; Rancière, 2017). In an interview with Mark Foster Gage (2019: 10), Rancière posited that

> aesthetics is not the theory of art, appreciation of art, or so on … It is not art, but it is what constitutes the sensible experience. It is about the experience of a common world. The aesthetic problem is not at all about beauty. It is about the experience of a common world and who is able to share this experience.

As elaborated earlier, the *sensible* is an aesthetic order in a broad sense centred on a particular kind of speech situation which is often litigious and conflictive, inventing new ways of being, seeing and saying, that emphasize both an order of intelligibility and a share-out or order of distribution. An order of intelligibility makes sense but is intimately related also to an order of distribution. An order of distribution derives from an order of sense and, in addition, constitutes social division.

Any *partage* is open to polemical egalitarian challenge, establishing a setting for the creation of new subjectivities, and new forms of collective enunciations (Rancière and Corcoran, 2010: 7). Such partition serves to draw together Rancière's political-philosophical apparatus and acts as lynchpin to his interests in aesthetics when he states that 'aesthetic is at the core of politics' (Rancière, 2006: 13). He defines aesthetic as 'a delimitation of spaces and time, of the visible and the invisible, of speech and noise' (Rancière, 2006: 13) where partitions 'define[s] the "modes of perception" that make that order visible and sayable in the first place' (Rancière, 2001: 20). Politics in this formal sense necessarily takes the form of aspect-change. Following the recent exchange between Rancière and Honneth (2016), we can put this point another way: a police order is an order of recognition; politics is a struggle over recognition.

Rancière's work is illuminating as it clarifies the call to see the political as aesthetics and politics in aesthetic terms. More importantly, this approach is not anti-materialist. In contrast, it is essential to see that aesthetic transformation involves not only a change of consciousness but also material social changes. For Rancière, the idea of the distribution of the sensible is best explained by Gage (2019: 17), in that this idea implies that

> an art always does something else than its proper business. At this point, it may meet the paths of emancipation, since emancipation means that you stop doing just your 'own business'. The aesthetic is not the same as the artistic. The artistic is about the implementation of an idea. It implies some kind of anticipation of the result, which may be put to the extreme in the case of political art. Instead, the aesthetic means that you don't exactly know what will be the effect of what you are doing.

Central here is the process of becoming a political subject, in which those who have no recognized part in the social order, who are invisible or inaudible in political terms, assert their egalitarian claim – a collective claim to exist as political subjectivity. Such a process has three different dimensions. First, it is an argumentative demonstration, second, a heterologic disidentification, and third, a theatrical and spectacular dramatization. Space is crucial to this, as it becomes the creative and dramatic stage for visibility. In the words of Holloway (2005), this process is 'theatrocratic' as it is creative and constructive and involves not only the manifestation of a new subject but also the construction of common space or 'scenes' of relationality which did not exist previously. This dimension of theatrical dramatization thus goes beyond the single perception of visibility/audibility – the stage – in that it constructs new ways in which parts of society relate to each other and reconfigures the way in which subjects are heard and seen. '[S]pace … becomes an integral element of the interruption of the 'natural' (or, better yet, naturalized) order of domination through the constitution of a place of encounter by those that have no part in that order' (Dikeç, 2005: 172). Aesthetics – rethought as 'the invention of new forms of life' – becomes a critical break with common sense and opens up possibilities of new commonalities of sense. Here, politics changes the fundaments on which judgements about what makes sense are based and thus destabilizes the 'aesthetic regime' that renders occurrences sensible or not. This is important for planning and design as it 'is not only supposed to construct units for inhabiting, but really constructing new senses of seeing, working, acting, and feeling' (Gage, 2019: 18). Yet what Rancière offers ultimately is a power of moments, rather than a politics of movements. As other critics have noted, there is little sense in his writing of how one gets from one moment of political disagreement to another, and little interest in social change – in how a better order might be established. However, the strength and originality of Rancière's philosophy of the political remain.

POLITICS THAT IS NOT POWER: TOWARDS A DESTITUENT POLITICS

Rancière's body of work has been a reference for several disciplines, including architecture and planning. His work was used to unpack the planning/resistance interface (Dikeç, 2005, 2007; Raco, 2014; Nicholls and Uitermark, 2017), the urban post-political (Davidson and Iveson, 2015; Swyngedouw, 2008; 2009, 2011), the conflictive dimension of planning (Pløger, 2004), the complex praxis of social movements and urban democracy (Purcel, 2009, 2014; Bassett, 2014; Meyer, 2020), and the urban scale (Bassett, 2016; Blakey, 2020). It was mobilized as a critique of planetary urbanization (Grange and Gunder, 2019), as well as a renewed political aesthetic engagement with architecture (Sandin, 2013; Boano and Kelling, 2013; Oommen and Pal, 2015; Gage, 2019). In this variegated territory for the aim of the chapter, it is important to mention Pløger's work (2021) on the homeless and the occupy movement. In this work he sees very clearly that planning and politics cannot be neutralized and depoliticized. For Pløger 'planning is politicized through policies and de-politicized through regulations, plans, guidelines, and the hegemony of zoning' (2021: 2) becoming de facto agonistic (Mouffe, 2013) and dissensual (Rancière, 2010) as a practice that challenges the normal distribution of power building new, undisciplined and enabling alliances, capable of producing new subjectivities and triggering actions capable of destitution of its own power. Such work is echoed by Metzger et al. (2015: 3) who again recentred politics away from the drive of managerial governance aiming to 'highlight and grasp the glaring democratic deficits that appear to be generated in these contexts'. Situating their reflections with Rancière's post-foundational political thought adapted to cities in Europe, they refer to 'the fundamental distinction between society as an instituted social order and the impossibility of finding a definite foundation for any social order' (Metzger et al., 2015: 3). The authors read planning politics as 'the ultimate ungovernability of the heterogeneous and multifarious bundles of entanglements and partial connections that we choose to label as "societies", as well as the related necessary limits in space (Euclidean as well as relational) and time of any governance arrangement' (Metzger et al., 2015: 4). What is important in this post-foundational thinking – one without an *archè*, intended both as origin and command/intention – is not the rejection of the planning subject and its strategic intention, but is an acknowledgement that such practice (Metzger et al., 2015: 13)

> always excludes a part and hence stands to be disrupted from time to time. It does not at all preclude or reject spatial planning interventions, as these are as inevitable as the establishment of a police order, but argues for an awareness of the lack of definite foundations for such strategies.

In other words, planning process is somehow 'unfinished' (Pløger, 2021: 2) where 'to see action as a work in progress, having new knowledge, change of lifeforms, ongoing dilemmas and conflicts – is to be unable to make a final decision, but to have the potential to strengthen critique' (Pløger, 2021: 9).

Such a view, situating planning practice in the contingency of order and away from perfect consensual solutionism, allows for a dissensus and therefore for an alternative, a different imagining, a visioning and projection. In other words, such approach recentres immanence and brings back the discussion on themes of domination, control, commodification and communication typical of architecture and urbanism, 'advancing a speculative claim that in the eyes of the majority could only appear naïve' (Ronchi, 2017: 11) and makes reflections on planning as not an homogeneous practice but an heterogenous one, caught between fixed and overly determined futures and open and experimental transformative potentials; 'whilst planning involves the search for a spatial plan, the current and dominant approach to planning displaces the 'search for a plan' with the 'search for consensus on the plan. This is a subtle distinction but one that goes to the heart of the post-foundationalist political critique' (Metzger et al., 2015: 14; see also Chapter 7 by Roskamm).

To illustrate such political modality, I will briefly recall some work that emerged from my engagement with the Baan Mankong housing and community upgrading practice and its regional expansion by the Asian Coalition for Housing Rights (ACHR) first in Bangkok and more recently in Myanmar.[2] In this complex territory, the focus was to highlight the fragmented attempt to scale the claim to justice and inclusion at the city level, while acknowledging the different spatial practices developed by multiple groups of urban poor who have no part in city-making and speculate on a radical definition of active equality that is 'presumed in the now' (Davis, 2013: 5) and connecting to the conventional conception of distributive equality (May 2008) with Rancière's radical politico-aesthetic.

As stated earlier, Rancière's political struggle occurs when the excluded seek to establish their identity by speaking for themselves and striving to get their voices heard and recognized so that the many marginalized communities struggling for space, resources and nature can leverage their collective resources. The participants of the Baan Mankong programme and the ACHR upgrade funding programme, mirror Rancière's idea of presupposition of equality as they locate the agency of change to the excluded, thereby creating a radical break from conventional participatory development practice and the environmental justice debate, both distribution-focused and recognition-centred. The Baan Mankong were exemplifying design politics (Boano and Kelling, 2013; Boano and Talocci, 2018) with a two-fold function, involving the material improvement of the urban poor as well as fostering confidence in marginalized groups by enhancing and encouraging their capacities, individually and collectively. Such visible actions illustrate Rancière's ethics and politics of recognition. The Baan Mankong programme represents one of the most successful examples of urban upgrading at the scale of the city, making effective use of the available resources and enacting potentials by using the power of the networks and collective savings, to spark off a new mode of urban production. At the same time, it is grounded in the aspirations of the new political collective subjects, manifesting and making visible alternative development pathways through design and architectural practices born in communal ethos and aesthetics of collective and environmental respects. A new aesthetics is put forward by the activity of Baan Mankong, one not belonging to the existing order; it is neither an 'aesthetics of poverty', nor a nostalgic vernacular one. The physical upgrading of informal houses and sites has a two-fold function for this historically marginalized group: improving the material reality of the urban poor; and beyond that, fostering confidence in their skills and capacities, individually and collectively (Boano and Kelling, 2013). The specific pathways of production of spaces through community architecture have several potentials. By re-composing contemporary, constructed ways of developing cities, the urban poor are emerging as actors of their own development, making their own history and enacting their own change.

Communities are not just simply invited to participate but become equal actors in the process. In this way, their inherent resilience is tested and verified allowing them to 'create a new political identity that did not exist in the existing order' (Rancière, 1999: 30). What clearly emerges in the presupposition of inclusion in the Baan Mankong programme is a critique of numerical teleology. Unlocking people's energy is achieved through strategic reconfiguration by taking existing identities and subjects and presupposing their equality. This drastically changes the status of individuals and communities, who are no longer simply invited to participate but whose power and agency are redistributed, thereby impeding the simple reproduction of police order that contributed to their marginalization in the production of cities and urban environments. The Baan Mankong programme offers a reconfiguration of collective struggles and mobilization, contesting the spatial ordering that assigns everyone and everything its proper place and highlights the importance of Rancière's thoughts on planning and power.

Similarly – but in a less organized and pacified manner – everyday practices of resistance of urban dwellers in peripheral Yangon – through incremental occupation, trespassing and building on vacant land – organized groups challenge the spatial order established by post/colonial regimes. These groups do not simply enact a repossession of the urban fringe to shape their own power over the urban neoliberal expansion process of international corporations and aggressive military industries, they literally contribute to the restoration of the commons in a gesture of inversion – whereas the commons can never be expropriated or appropriated but can only be used. In Yangon. I had engaged with Women for the World, a city-wide network of women's savings groups, supported by ACHR. From the mid-2000s, they started to collectively purchase large plots of farmland to build houses. As a collective, they managed to afford loans and obtain credit from banks. The fact that purchased land continues to belong to the government or farmers even after the purchase, resulting in ambivalent regimes of ownership, does not halt the housing process.

Individuals usually resort to leasing small plots of land through village leaders or other individuals who are managing the land. In some cases, minimal infrastructure already exists; in every other case the individuals of a household are responsible for acquiring materials and commencing the building process. Usually, people start out by constructing their unit with cheap and unstable materials that are gradually replaced by more stable ones, once the residents can afford to purchase them. This is a form of incrementality that is not linear, as it is often halted by a lack of certainty about the future, the continuous threat of eviction and resettlement, and the lack of secure tenure. Women's mobilization in Yangon is not only aimed at securing resources. Collective savings develop financial and social capital (Astolfo and Boano, 2020) and enable a different relationship with government agencies in the hope of influencing planning and policy in the long term. What is interesting to note now is the changing relationship between state and communities as a result of the current transition, and how this is reflected in social mobilization and women's networks which are currently shifting from a quietly revolutionary encroachment (Bayat, 2000) towards more complex forms of co-management, co-implementation, co-financing and co-learning even if in a very precarious national transition.

Reflecting, briefly, on planning practices in Bangkok and Yangon, a different constellation of Rancière's ideas make evident a reconfiguration of power: far away from sovereignty, dominion and administration of bodies and their practices and close to space of struggle, *sensible*, a kind of savoir-faire, through equal voice when fighting any kind of exception caused by the police order in the public space and discourses. In Bankok and Yangon, Rancière's politics arises in the irruption, on the scene, of those who are generally without a part in the world. Such practices, as many others ranging from revolt, manifestation and occupation to (Di Cesare, 2020) to proposition and participation (Grange and Gunder, 2019) define a 'topography' of resistance to police violence that 'conquers space, acquires power over bodies, examines and experiments with a new legality, redefines the limits of what is possible' (Di Cesare 2020: 12) and 'unveils the immunopolitics of public space'.

Those were the same spaces and practices Rancière sought to reflect on a new *partage* of the sensible, a new organization of bodies, speeches in a new configuration of spaces. Di Cesare (2020: 20) sees them as places where 'the politics of the state, of the institutions is questioned whether democratic or despotic, secular or religious, it brings to light its violence, it deprives it of its sovereignty'. In an intricate assemblage of motivations of 'an imprecise malaise, the manifestation of a nagging unease, disappointed expectations ... the abyss of inequality, the logic of profit, the plundering of the future, the spectacular arrogance of the few in the face of the impotence of the many' (Di Cesare, 2020: 21). Such events are where politics is. A specific 'politics of bodies' (Quintana, 2020) that manifest

> injustice within the guarded confines of public space, reconfiguring it; a practice of irruption, which, coming from the edges, embarrasses governmental politics, exposes its police function that ... structures space, assigns parts, establishes competences in having, doing and saying. It fixes places to be occupied and regulates the faculty of appearance (Di Cesare 2020: 22).

TOWARDS A DESTITUENT POWER

Rancière's politics of interruption could be *destituent*, as power is not anti-political or proto-political or even post-political. Rather, it takes us outside the traditional trajectories of the conceptualization of modern politics, outside the modern construct of the coincidence of politics and power, and therefore between politics and state. Destituent is a politics beyond the question of power, or rather not founded by power nor founded on power. It is a politics that

> follows the opposite path, moving from the edges, breaking barriers, escaping the police function, and redeems its own name ... it shares the wrong, manifests dissent, and shines lights on the invisible and the unwelcomed. It also takes the part of those who do not have parts, denies the distribution, shows

the contingency of order, breaks the police hierarchy of the *archè*, which wants the monopoly of the beginning, which claims to have established the command (Di Cesare, 2020:23).

Destituent was used for the first time by the *Colectivo Situaciones* in Buenos Aires to describe the original features of the Argentine *piqueteros* movement of 2001 capable of bringing about real change in Argentina by delegitimizing the existing political forces (Laudani, 2016). More recently, the concept has found in Agamben a figure who expresses the full force of its political meaning. In his last instalment of the Homo Sacer project, *The Use of Bodies*, Agamben (2016: 273) suggests that a destituent power is one that 'deactivates something and renders it inoperative – a power … without simply destroying it but by liberating the potentials that have remained inactive in it in order to allow a different use of them' and that 'while remaining heterogeneous to the system, had the capacity to render decisions destitute and suspend them' (Agamben, 2016: 274). Destituent power is configured as a way of practising and thinking about politics that radically breaks with the modern logic of sovereignty. Consequently, it can be seen as a radical alternative to constituent power in a time that is not that of control and sovereignty, but that of the immanent permanence, albeit in a potential form, of multiple and plural instances of liberation that do not find a solution in state institutions and somehow remain in *écarts* with respect to dominant forms.

This dislocates politics in a territory without foundations and serves to establish an initial qualifying point of destituent power – one that, as noted earlier, does not disregard the myriad subjectivities that reject political power. In other words, social movements do not simply position themselves against power, but at a distance from it: they dodge it. It is clear that in a certain type of demonstration and struggle over the last twenty years, that is, from the Los Angeles riots to the Arab Spring, to Fergusson and now in Yangon which have in common the desire to avoid any direct conflict with the established power, the dynamic of refusal is crucial, of absence, of the non-negative force of the negative, of the affirmative dimension of destruction, as a critique of everything that exists, according to that link between nihilism and politics. Destituent subjectivities are linked to an idea of politics without foundation (a politics without *arché*, that is, which feeds a conception of democracy as excess: democracy is always a democratic excess; what every democratic regime today intends to suffocate in the name of democracy), are a people (they are the people). They are the (im)popular, unexpected, uncounted, event of the people. An unexpected, unforeseen people, without conscience (there is no project), without head nor tail, which emerges unexpectedly in the struggle. Only a power that aggregates in this way can be a democratic power that escapes its democratic capture (democracy is never a matter of numbers). A destituent politics has a limited but precise task: to create the conditions, that is, the vacuum, so that another politics, the one that today seems impossible, can happen. It indicates the first movement to be made: to unleash a politics of the event, the event of politics nests in a singular desertion from what is, to break the normal course of history and produce a multiple, ecstatic plurality.

For Rancière there is politics only when there is no foundation, when radically egalitarian understanding of power is the enactment of equality. Destituent politics consists, rather, in the process that removes the foundation from a social order. And since an order always tends to stabilize itself and to represent itself as complete, rational and absolute, politics shows its conditional and fragile character. It takes place, in fact, in the interruption of an order, of its presumed naturalness: intermittent itself, politics is not always there, indeed it never is, it does not exist, but it takes place here and there as a disruption of an effective order.

A perspective of this kind poses many problems for political reflection; without soil, without a specific garment, be it the state, the territory, or power itself, it also lacks a subject in the form of a class, a people, or an individual that can guide an emancipatory process. Rancière does not rely on other disciplines but simply revives politics in its specific absence of content, seeking, in this absence, the virtuous efficacy of difference, of discard, of emptiness.

Rancière's power can be thought of as the power of emptiness. It is a void where references are not given but elusive, where coherence emerges but is not already given, where the arrogance of the canon, of the authorial, of the major is vulnerable and requires new forms of narration and subjectification (Boano 2020). Rancière helps us to think of and see power not only as conflictual and confrontational but as backlash, an (un)emptying that creates space for the possible. It is not another project that survives planning in order to deactivate and depose them but coincides with its own destitution for new plural instances of liberation, without synthesis of liberation, without synthesis or composition, questioning its very possibility.

NOTES

1. This chapter was originally written in late 2020. Since then, several publications have expanded on the notion of destituent power that have not been included here: for example, Esposito and Giannuzzi (2022), Wainwright (2022), Fusco (2023) and Aarons and Robinson (2023).
2. This was part of a learning partnership between ACHR and DPU (UCL) within the BUDD MSc Program. The empirical reflections celebrated in this chapter are indebted to colleagues, students and partners who allow such multi-year and multi-sited opportunity.

REFERENCES

Agamben, Giorgio (2016), *The Use of Bodies*, trans. by Adam Kotsko, Stanford, CA: Stanford University Press.

Aarons, Kieran and Idris Robinson (eds) (2023), 'Destituent Power', Special Issue, *The South Atlantic Quarterly*, 122 (1), January.

Astolfo, G. and C. Boano (2020), 'Unintended Cities and Inoperative Violence: Housing Resistance in Yangon', *Journal of Planning Theory and Practice*, 21 (3), 426–449.

Badiou, Alain (2009), 'The Lessons of Jacques Rancière: Knowledge and Power after the Storm', in Gabriel Rockhill and Paul Watts (eds), *Jacques Rancière: History, Politics, Aesthetics*, Durham, NC: Duke University Press, pp. 30–54.

Bassett, K. (2014), 'Rancière, Politics, and the Occupy Movement', *Environment and Planning D: Society and Space*, 32 (5), 886–901.

Bassett, K. (2016), 'Event, Politics, and Space: Rancière or Badiou?', *Space and Polity*, 20 (3), 280–293.

Bayat, A. (2000), 'From "Dangerous Classes" to "Quiet Rebels": Politics of the Urban Subaltern in the Global South', *International Sociology*, 15 (3), 533–557.

Bélanger, P. (2020), 'No Design on Stolen Land: Dismantling Design's Dehumanising White Supremacy', *Architectural Design*, 90 (1), 121–127.

Besteman, Catherine (2020), *Militarised Global Apartheid*, Durham, NC: Duke University Press.

Biesta, G. (2010), 'A New Logic of Emancipation: The Methodology of Jacques Rancière', *Educational Theory*, 60 (1), 39–59.

Bingham, Charles and Gert Biesta (2010), *Jacques Rancière: Education, Truth, Emancipation*, London: Bloomsbury.

Blakey, J. (2020), 'The Politics of Scale through Rancière', *Progress in Human Geography*, 45 (4), 1–18. DOI: 10.1177/0309132520944487.

Blesznowski, B. (2012), 'In Defence of the Political: The Crisis of Democracy and the Return of the People from the Perspective of Foucault and Rancière', *Polish Sociological Review*, 179, pp. 331–348.

Boano, Camillo (2020), *Progetto Minore: Alla ricerca della minorità nel progetto urbanistico ed architettonico*, Siracusa: LetteraVentidue Edizioni.

Boano, C. and W. Hunter (2018), 'Activating Equitable Landscapes and Critical Design Assemblages in Bangkok', in Ed Wall and Tim Waterman (eds), *Landscape and Agency: Critical Essays*, London: Routledge, pp. 164–176.

Boano, C. and E. Kelling (2013), 'Towards an Architecture of Dissensus: Participatory Urbanism in South-East Asia', *FOOTPRINT*, 7, 41–62.

Boano, C. and G. Talocci (2018), 'Inoperative Design: "Not Doing" and the Experience of the Community Architects Network', *CITY*, 21 (6), 860–871.

Bowman, Paul and Richard Stamp (2011), *Reading Rancière*, London: Continuum.

Brown, Wendy (2019), *In the Ruins of Neoliberalism: The Rise of Antidemocratic Politics in the West*, New York: Columbia University Press.

Cesarale, Giorgio (2019), *A Sinistra: Il Pensiero Critico dopo il 1989*, Bari-Roma: Laterza.

Cohen, Tom (ed.) (2012), *Telemorphosis: Theory in the Era of Climate Change*, Open Humanity Press, University of Michigan.

Conley, T. (2005), 'Cinema and its Discontents: Jacques Rancière and Film Theory', *SubStance*, 34 (3), 96–106.

Davidson, M. and K. Iveson (2015), 'Recovering the Politics of the City: From the "Postpolitical City" to a "Method of Equality" for Critical Urban Geography', *Progress in Human Geography*, 39 (5), 543–559.

Davis, Oliver (2010), *Jacques Rancière*, Cambridge: Polity Press.

Davis, Oliver (2013), *Rancière Now: Current Perspectives on Jacques Rancière*, Cambridge: Polity Press.

Davis, Oliver (2013b), 'The Politics of Art: Aesthetics Contingency and the Aesthetic Effect', in *Rancière Now: Current Perspectives on Jacques Rancière*, Cambridge: Polity Press, pp. 155–168.

Di Cesare, Donatella (2020), *Il Tempo della Rivolta*, Torino: Bollati Borlinghieri.

Di Cesare, Donatella (2020b), 'Anarchia', *Aut*, 388, 87–97.

Dikeç, M. (2005), 'Space, Politics, and the Political' *Environment and Planning D: Society and Space*, 23 (2), 171–188.

Dikeç, Mustafa (2007), *Badlands of the Republic: Space, Politics and Urban Policy*, Oxford: Blackwell.

Dillon, M. (2005), 'A Passion for the (Im)possible: Jacques Rancière, Equality, Pedagogy and the Messianic', *European Journal of Political Theory*, 4 (4), 429–452.

Deranty, Jean-Philippe and Alison Ross (2012), *Jacques Rancière and the Contemporary Scene: The Philosophy of Radical Equality*, London: Continuum.

Elden, Stewart and Jeremy W. Crampton (2007), 'Space, Knowledge and Power: Foucault and Geography', in Jeremy W. Crampton and Stewart Elden (eds), *Space, Knowledge and Power: Foucault and Geography*, Aldershot, UK: Ashgate, pp. 1–18.

Esposito, R. (2020) 'Immunitas: Oltre le feconde contraddizioni di Foucault', *Micromega*, 8, 34–55.

Esposito, Roberto and Mariaenrica Giannuzzi (2022), 'Instituting Thought: Three Paradigms of Political Ontology', *Cultural Critique*, 115, 75–92.

Fusco, Gian Giacomo (2023), *Form of Life: Agamben and the Destitution of Rules*, Edinburgh: Edinburgh University Press.

Gage, Mark Foster (ed.) (2019), *Aesthetics Equals Politics: New Discourses across Art, Architecture and Philosophy*, Cambridge, MA: MIT Press.

Galli, C. (2020), 'Il doppio volto della biopolitica', *Micromega*, 8, 94–105.

Grange, K. and M. Gunder (2019), 'The Urban Domination of the Planet: A Rancièrian Critique', *Planning Theory*, 18 (4), 389–409.

Harcourt, Bernard E. (2020), *Critique and Praxis: A Critical Philosophy of Illusions, Values and Actions*, New York: Columbia University Press.

Highmore, Ben (2011), 'Out of Place: Unprofessional Paining, Jacques Rancière and the Distribution of the Sensible', in Paul Bowman and Richard Stamp (eds), *Reading Rancière*, London: Continuum, pp. 95–110.

Huzar, T.J. (2021), 'Toward a Fugitive Politics: Arendt, Rancière, Hartman', *Cultural Critique*, 2021 (110), 1–48.

Inston, K. (2019), 'Improper Communities in the Work of Roberto Esposito and Jacques Rancière', *Contemporary Political Theory*, 19 (4), 621–641.

James, Ian (2012), *The New French Philosophy*, Cambridge: Polity.

Kelly, Mark G.E. (2009), *The Political Philosophy of Michael Foucault*, London: Routledge.

Laudani, Raffaele (2016*), Il Movimento della Politica. Teorie critiche e potere Destituente*, Bologna: Il Mulino.

May, Todd (2008), *The Political Thought of Jacques Rancière: Creating Equality*, Edinburgh: Edinburgh University Press.

May, Todd (2009), 'Rancière in South Carolina', in Gabriel Rockhill and Paul Watts (eds), *Jacques Rancière: History, Politics, Aesthetics*, Durham, NC: Duke University Press, pp. 105–119.

May, Todd (2010), *Contemporary Political Movements and the Thought of Jacques Rancière*, Edinburgh: Edinburgh University Press.

Mecchia, Giuseppina (2009), 'The Classics and Critical theory in Postmodern France: The Case of Jacques Rancière', in Gabriel Rockhill and Paul Watts (eds), *Jacques Rancière: History, Politics, Aesthetics*, Durham, NC: Duke University Press, pp. 67–82.

Mechoulan, E. (2004), 'Introduction: On the Edges of Jacques Rancière', *SubStance*, 33(1), 3–9.

Mechoulan, E. (2009), 'Sophisticated Continuities and Historical Discontinuities or, why not Protagoras?', in Gabriel Rockhill and Paul Watts (eds), *Jacques Rancière: History, Politics, Aesthetics*, Durham, NC: Duke University Press, pp. 55–66.

Metzger, Jonathan, Philippe Allmendinger and Stijn Oosterlynck (eds) (2015), *Planning against the Political. Democratic Deficits in European Territorial Governance*, London: Routledge.

Meyer, J.M. (2020), 'The Politics of the "Post-political" Contesting the Diagnosis', *Democratization*, 27(3), 408–425.

Mouffe, Chantal (2013), *Agonistics: Thinking the World Politically*, London: Verso.

Nicholls, W.J. and J. Uitermark (2017), 'Introduction: Planning/resistance', *Urban Geography*, 38 (4), 512–520.

Oommen, T. and S. Pal (2015), 'Politics of Architecture', *Economic & Political Weekly*, l (16), 16–19.

Patton, Paul (2012), 'Rancière's Utopian Politics', in Jean-Philippe Deranty and Alison Ross (eds), *Jacques Rancière and the Contemporary Scene*, London: Continuum, pp. 129–144.

Pløger, J. (2004), 'Strife: Urban Planning and Agonism', *Planning Theory*, 3 (1), 71–92.

Pløger, J. (2021), 'Conflict, Consent, Dissensus: The Unfinished as Challenge to Politics and Planning', *Environment and Planning C: Politics and Space*, 39 (6), 1–16, DOI: 10.1177/2399654420985849.

Purcell, M. (2009), 'Resisting Neoliberalization: Communicative Planning or Counter-Hegemonic Movements?', *Planning Theory*, 8 (2), 140–165.

Purcell, M. (2014), 'Rancière and Revolution', *Space and Polity*, 18 (2), 168–181.

Porter, Libby (2010), *Unlearning the Colonial Cultures of Planning*, Farnham, UK: Ashgate.

Raco, Mike (2014), 'The Post-Politics of Sustainability Planning: Privatization and the Demise of Democratic Government', in Japhy Wilson and Erik Swyngedouw (eds), *Post-Political and its Discontents: Spaces of Depoliticisation, Spectres of Radical Democracy*, Edinburgh: Edinburgh University Press, pp. 25–47.

Rancière Jacques (1991), *The Ignorant Schoolmaster: Five Lessons in Intellectual Emancipation*, trans. by Kristin Ross, Stanford, CA: Stanford University Press.

Rancière Jacques (1994), *The Names of History: On the Poetics of Knowledge*, Cambridge: Minnesota University Press.

Rancière Jacques (1999), *Disagreement: Politics and Philosophy*, trans. Julie Rose, Minneapolis: University of Minnesota Press.

Rancière, J. (2002), 'The Aesthetic Revolution and its Outcomes', *New Left Review*, 14, Mar/Apr, 39–44.

Rancière, Jacques (2006), *The Politics of Aesthetics: The Distribution of the Sensible*, trans. Gabriel Rockhill, New York: Continuum.

Rancière, Jacques (2010), *Dissensus: On Politics and Aesthetics*, trans. Steven Corcoran, London: Continuum.

Rancière, Jacques (2013), *Aisthesis: Scenes from the Aesthetic Regime of Art*, London: Verso.

Rancière, Jacques (2016), *Film Fables*, London: Bloomsbury.

Rancière, Jacques (2017), *Dissenting Words: Interviews with Jacques Rancière*, ed. and trans. by Emiliano Battista, London: Bloomsbury.

Rancière, Jacques (2017b), *Democracy, Equality, Emancipation in a Changing World*, accessed 13 January 2021 at www.versobooks.com/blogs/3395-democracy-equality-emancipation-in-a-changing-world.

Rancière, Jacques (2019), *Jacques Rancière on the Gilets Jaunes Protests*, accessed 13 December 2020 at, www.versobooks.com/blogs/4237-jacques-ranciere-on-the-gilets-jaunes-protests.

Roy, A. (2017), 'The Infrastructure of Assent: Architecture in the Age of Trump', *Metropolis Magazine*, accessed 3 March 2021, at: www.metropolismag.com/ideas/infrastructure-assent-architecture-age-trump/.

Roy, A. (2021), 'Planning on Stolen Land', in Libby Porter, Ananya Roy and Crystal Legacy (eds), Planning Solidarity? From Silence to Refusal, *Planning Theory & Practice*, 22 (1), 111–138, DOI: 10.1080/14649357.2021.1872952.

Rockhill, Gabriel and Paul Watts (2009), *Jacques Rancière: History, Politics, Aesthetics*, Durham, NC: Duke University Press.

Sandin, G. (2013), 'Democracy on the Margin: Architectural Means of Appropriation in Governmental Alteration of Space', *Architectural Theory Review*, 18 (2), 234–250.

Sonderegger, R. (2002), 'On the Construction of a Community of Equals', *OnCurating*, 17, 16–17.

Stavrides, S. (2016) 'Toward an Architecture of Commoning', *ASAP/Journal*, 1 (1), 77–94.

Swyngedouw, Erik (2008), 'The Post-political City', in BAVO (ed.), *Urban Politics Now: Re-imagining Democracy in the Neoliberal City*, Rotterdam: NAi Publishers, pp. 59–76.

Swyngedouw, E. (2009), 'The Antimonies of the Postpolitical City: In Search of a Democratic Politics of Environmental Production', *International Journal of Urban and Regional Research*, 33 (3), 601–620.

Swyngedouw, E. (2011), 'Interrogating Post-democracy: Reclaiming Egalitarian Political Spaces', *Political Geography*, 3 (7), 370–380.

Tanke, J.J. (2011), 'What is the Aesthetic Regime?', *Parrhesia*, 12, 71–81.

Tarì, Marcello (2017), *Non esiste la Rivoluzione Infelice*, Rome: DeriveApprodi.

Quintana, L. (2018), 'Jacques Rancière and the Emancipation of Bodies', *Philosophy and Social Criticism*, 45 (2), 212–238.

Quintana, Laura (2020), *The Politics of the Bodies: Philosophical Emancipation with and beyond Rancière*, London: Rowman and Littlefield Publishers.

Wainwright, Joel (2022), 'Praxis', *Rethinking Marxism*, 34 (1), 41–62.

Wilson, Japhy and Swyngedouw Erik (eds) (2014), *Post-Political and its Discontents: Spaces of Depoliticisation, Spectres of Radical Democracy*, Edinburgh: Edinburgh University Press.

9. Communicative planning and the transformative potential of citizen-led participation

Crystal Legacy

INTRODUCTION

Communicative planning is a theory that is unfinished. While critics argue that communicative planning possesses little transformative power as a technology of government and its formalisation can be highly coercive, it remains one of the key pathways through which citizens engage in the planning of their cities and regions (Calderon and Westin, 2021; Innes and Booher, 2015), especially in transport planning (Vigar, 2017, Tornberg and Odhage, 2018). Critiques directed at communicative planning reveal how it privileges consensus-making over engagement that acknowledges difference, and under explores issues that may generate conflict (Huxley, 2000; McGuirk, 2001; Hillier, 2003). The extent to which communicative planning is viewed as a coercive practice lies in the way the prevailing structures foreclose from these spaces the kind of citizen-led participation that exposes how power is mobilised and exclusions perpetuated. In other words, when communicative planning is used by the power-elite to maintain the status quo and it can establish the power conditions to prevent transformational change into the future. In democratic planning contexts, when opportunities are granted to citizens to participate, these opportunities can be guided by prevailing discourses, practices and processes that further condition what counts as citizen participation in those spaces, as well as outside those spaces.

In those efforts to understand the limits and potential of communicative planning lies a focus on the participating citizen. Here Inch (2015) explores two possible forms of participatory action. One potential form is becoming a citizen-actor that engages in formal processes that are structured upon principles of deliberation and consensus-making. By comparison, the other is a citizen acting agonistically and seeking to challenge the prevailing discourses as they are revealed across contexts and structures of power (Inch, 2015). Also examining the practices of participation, van Wymeersch et al. (2019) show how political subject-formation, as a process through which citizens become participating actors, may allow citizens to dis-identify from formal communicative planning. In other words, participation is explicitly political as it seeks to detach from the dominant logics, practices and processes that make up the 'status quo'; that is the formal system of planning and participation. Dis-identification sets the ground for participation to be performed differently, and it possesses the potential to help evolve the way planning theorists and planners understand communicative planning.

The dis-identification or 'un-binding' described by post-foundational scholars, such as Badiou (2005), and also Jacques Rancière (1995, 1999), and to a lesser extent by Chantel Mouffe (2000, 2005, 2013) and others can take many forms. One such form is through citizen-led participation that exposes what does not get counted in formal communicative planning spaces. Exposing what counts (and what does not) in these spaces also helps to reveal the structure of participation, and how those structures are dictated by the state and prevailing politics. Casting our attention to the structure of participation, Badiou's (2005) work is a useful frame to examine *what counts as communicative planning* and how what counts is the focus of the dis-identification of the participating citizen.

The aim of this chapter is to examine what counts as communicative planning, by seeking to expose the boundaries placed around what kinds of participatory actions are perceived as legitimate by the formal system, and how those boundaries are challenged by citizen-led participation which is comparatively more informal. Within the formal system of planning and of participation, the institutions that serve as the gatekeepers of this system influence what form participation may take (e.g. a citizen jury or panel), and when that participation is sanctioned (e.g. during strategic or project planning). Less is known about what counts as communicative planning when generated from the informal efforts of dis-identification taken by citizens, which ultimately occur outside the formal spaces of what is typically understood as planning or participation.

Guided by this aim, I will look to Habermas (1984), as well as planning theorists writing on participatory forms of planning to explore how the power of communicative planning can find new expression through these informal participatory pathways. To give this enquiry grounding, I consider Habermas' (1984: 171) statement that the potential of communicative action, as he described it, is the 'capacity to agree in un-coerced communication on some community action'. Heeding caution from the many critiques made of communicative planning and its own hegemonic power in planning, this chapter concludes with insights taken from four vignettes that illuminate the power of un-coerced, informal and citizen-led participatory action, and the pathways they establish to resist the coercive and hegemonic logics of formalised planning. Finally, I offer a few concluding remarks centred on calling for an advanced theory of communicative planning that gives space to the citizen-led and reflective community of practice that sees participation as constantly evolving, and always finding new foundations to meet the complex and changing needs of citizens and communities.

THE POWER OF COMMUNICATIVE PLANNING

Communicative action gained prominence in planning as a powerful departure from expert-led approaches to planning. Early theorisation of communicative planning is grounded in ideas that power can be forged through practices and processes of uncoerced argumentation. With tenets stretching back to the 1970s with transactive planning (Friedmann, 1993) and more widely taken up in planning theory as communicative planning (Innes, 1998), deliberative planning (Forester, 1999) and collaborative planning (Healey, 1997), the communicative 'turn' shifted planning practice from the domain of techno-rationalism into one that saw the tacit knowledge of citizens as a valued part of the planning process (Healey, 1992). In describing this 'turn' Healey (1992: 143) characterised planning as 'making sense together, while living differently' through which 'a democratic form of planning' could be realised (Healy, 1992: 144), ultimately challenging the Cartesian tradition of planning that otherwise dominated.

The communicative 'turn' helped lay the foundation for three decades of scholarship investigating the democratic nature of communicative planning, and the potential this form of participation possessed. Of focus were possibilities born by communicative planning to inform policy and planning decisions, and to also transform the very institutions tasked with the planning of cities democratically, inclusively and deliberatively. It was promised that communicative planning processes could become a vehicle for institutional capital – policies, practices, dominant discourses – to be exposed and then, hopefully, transformed in support of comparatively more just and equitable ends (Healey, 1999: 120). It is these promises of communicative planning's potential to serve cities and their people in just and equitable ways that continues to give this theory of citizen participation its power, both in theory and in practice, even when faced with considerable and sustained critique.

It is useful to offer a brief reminder of the philosophical basis that helped forge communicative planning into a dominant theory of urban planning. With roots in Habermas' (1983 [1990], 1984) communicative action and Giddens' (1984) structuration theory, communicative planning would establish grounds for discussion about changing the character of participation whilst possessing potential to influence institutional culture. Giddens overlayed an institutionalists lens when theorising communicative planning presenting ways for the citizen's tacit knowledge to inform what counts as knowledge in planning. Habermas grounded communicative planning in ideas of argumentation upon which a communicative action might form. For political theorists, communicative action could support enlarged thought (Benhabib, 1988, 1992). With connections to ideas of social learning through individual and collective reflexivity (Eckersley, 2000: 121), ostensibly, this enlarged thought is made possible when participants hear 'reasoned arguments' and are open and prepared to support decisions on the bases of those arguments. Dewey (1930: 194) describes this kind of inter-subjective exchange as the processes through which reasoned interrogation can produce imagined outcomes, and these outcomes are articulated and considered by diverse participating actors. At least in theory, this exchange supports the building of legitimacy for policy decisions, developed based on 'mutually justifiable reasons' (Gutmann and Thompson, 2004: 102).

The potential for social learning remains an important aspiration for communicative planning, yet there are considerable barriers standing in the way. As Tewdwr-Jones and Allmendinger (1998) and others point out, the orientation towards consensus-building can be a barrier for challenges to be mounted in a way that allows dominant power structures and relationships to be exposed. In consensus-based communicative planning, discourse structured around ideas of sustainability and livability, for instance, which have been critiqued for presenting as 'empty signifiers' (Swyngedouw, 2018), are normalised in planning processes leaving them unquestioned and concealing answers to questions that may explore the uneven ways 'sustainability' in planning is implemented, and the hegemonic power that structures possible policy pathways. An excellent example of this hegemonic power is neoliberalism and automobility. Both are so pervasive in many western democratic nation contexts that they can be difficult to detach from the ways we know, for instance, the challenges of transport and mobility, and how these ideologies have come to structure not only contemporary life in many western democratic societies, but also the available pathways to address challenges. Yet for many, especially for the most marginal of communities, this hegemony is what reinforces social, spatial, economic and political inequality and helps to bound how these issues are known and addressed.

In planning cultures structured under neoliberalism, power is wielded through the dominance of growth, economic rationality, privatisation, and commercialisation logics that are bounded by the prevailing politics of the state (see Chapter 20 by Marzukhi). The structure of this hegemony also gives structure to who are the gatekeepers of this system. Protection is given to these gatekeepers in the processes that depoliticise what is otherwise deeply political, and this is particularly the case in planning where formal planning is complicit in a culture of silence (Porter et al., 2021) and in the disciplining of planners from speaking out against injustices borne from the institutions of planning (Grange, 2017). In seeking to expose this hegemony, the political philosopher, Chantal Mouffe (2000) looks to agonistic pluralism to describe how citizen-led conflict can present as critical interjections, for instance in planning processes. In planning theory, the examination of conflict, and the disciplining logics of state practices and processes, has delivered insights into the depoliticising forces of consensus-based communicative planning processes (MacDonald, 2015; Haughton and McManus, 2019).

In the context of the conditions described above, communicative planning can be exercised by those in power in a way that turns these spaces into places of enclosure, rendering them coercive. What counts in these spaces is political, and disciplined by the parameters – agendas, resourcing, procedural rules – which sets expectations for what counts as participation, and importantly, creates the conditions for what is counted in these spaces. The coercion of communicative planning through post-political structures of power to reduce what counts in these spaces, presents an interesting theoretical challenge for planning scholarship. That is, how might communicative action be recast to reveal the power of un-coerced yet political forming communication as a pathway to resist the coercive hegemonic logics of contemporary planning. The dis-identification taken up with the emergence of political citizen-subjects performing participation is one-way politicisation is being studied in planning theory (see Van Wymeersch et al., 2020). Extending these debates further, a focus on how power is generated through the citizen-led participatory action that aids in solidarity formation may help reveal new insights into the power of communicative planning, as an informal citizen-led practice.

In the following section I draw from my work on community engagement in contested arenas of transport planning in Melbourne, Australia to provide four illustrations of communicative planning and its politics. Grounding the analysis in theories of post-political planning, to account for the neoliberal practice of participation where conflict is managed out of otherwise consensus-based participatory spaces, I argue how communicative planning is an unfinished project of capturing and challenging what counts in participation processes. The way the state moves in rhythm with informal political participation by citizens, over time, changes the formal structures of communicative planning. There is temporal exchange between the formal and informal dis-identification that demands our critical attention, and it is through these spaces that communicative planning is transforming, and new power is being ascribed to citizen-led communicative action. But first, I want to distinguish participation from communicative planning. The former speaks to the everyday engagement of citizens in their cities, and through this engagement the different ways encounter and activity shape how we know a city, its people and ourselves. The former is fluid, not structured and is informal. The latter is typically understood as formal, state-led, curated and with boundaries set upon it. The purpose of the following section is to work between the binary of the formal/informal and of communicative planning as state-led (formal) and of participation as citizen-led (informal). The hope is of a new imaginary for communicative planning that situates it as an unfinished project, and possessing the potential to evolve as the bounds that have constrained it become fully exposed revealing an untapped power embodied within it.

THE FORMAL/INFORMAL OF COMMUNICATIVE PLANNING IN MELBOURNE, AUSTRALIA

As Healey (2003) described nearly twenty years ago, context matters in shaping our understanding of communicative processes. Context determines the extent to which communicative planning wields power to influence change in the built environment, and to forge new social relationships. Like other western democratic contexts, neoliberal orthodoxy has led to the privatisation of planning and of participatory processes in Victoria. Planners work across public and private sectors, and this distribution is widely seen in the transportation sector in Melbourne where corporate actors work 'in partnership' with state governments to deliver infrastructure or manage and/or operate services through complex franchise agreements or through public–private partnerships (Ashmore et al., 2019). These shifts have created complex urban transport planning governance arrangements from which communicative planning is curated and participation opportunities are extended to citizens. Looking to the critical planning literature on the techno-managerialism as a governmental technology in urban governance, these structures tend to reduce the practice of 'doing politics' to 'a form of institutionalized social managements, whereby problems are dealt with through enrolling managerial technologies and administrative procedures' (Swyngedouw, 2018: 34). For instance, techno-managerialism poses restrictions on what counts to that which can emerge through consensus politics in processes of knowledge production in these spaces. As Swyngedouw (2018: 37) posits, whatever the efforts to achieve depoliticisation of what is counted in decision-spaces, these efforts are 'always incomplete', leaving 'a trace' for a return to politicisation and to make visible what has been made invisible in the processes of planning.

In the next section I reflect on eight years of research examining citizen-led participatory action in Melbourne, Australia (see also Legacy 2016, 2017 and 2018). The context established above in which the vignettes are set also includes a dominant programme of toll-road construction that started in 2012 and continues at the time of writing. This dominance has extended across two Victorian State Elections, the first in 2014 and the other in 2018, both won by a Labor Party Government. Battles against proposed road infrastructure have a long history in Australian cities (see Davison, 2004). Automobility remains hegemonic, even in the face of calls for more investment in public transport and as the country continues to experience some of the most devastating impacts of climate change, as seen most recently in the 2019–20 summer bushfires. The vignettes below are themselves examples of how citizen-led forms of participation were used to rail against successively proposed toll-road projects. However, the focus of these four vignettes is on how these citizen-led participatory efforts can also be viewed as interventions in the structure of communicative planning, and ultimately what counts as communicative planning.

Communicative planning has become a cornerstone of land use planning, and of transport planning. In Melbourne, Australia, public agencies such as Infrastructure Victoria and successive government parties emerging from across the political spectrum have embraced forms of communicative planning in their practice (Legacy, 2018). Whether to inform the development of a strategic land use plan, or infrastructure strategies communicative planning as practised in the form of citizen juries, panels and forums, for instance, are now commonly used to infuse decision-making processes. Despite efforts to engage widely and deliberatively, what counts as communicative planning is an area of considerable intrigue, particularly in deeply conflictual spaces such as urban toll-road infrastructure planning. The illustrations below are drawn from critical participatory action research, including interviews with state government planners, elected and former politicians, community engagement facilitators, planning consultants, sustainable transport advocates and participating citizens, and policy and media analysis. This research has guided me in my analysis of the temporal transformation of communicative planning in the spaces of transport planning in Melbourne.

Vignette #1 – What Counts in Communicative Spaces

The post-political planning environment has reduced communicative planning's transformative potential. As a state-led practice, communicative planning has failed in any real effort to inform the establishment of spaces where citizens can wage challenges against formal planning. On the other hand, when acting outside the formal structures of participation citizen action can lay the ground for political subject formation and then dis-identification, where citizen-led participatory spaces lead to the politicisation of what is foreclosed in more consensus-based formal settings. In Melbourne, Australia, an example of political formation of citizen-led participation was ignited by a resistance to urban toll-road building in 2012 (Legacy 2016, 2017). The object of the citizen-led contestation was the East West Link, a proposed underground 6km toll road. Its planning would involve fast-tracking citizen engagement and planning approval processes to ensure that contracts for this controversial project would be signed before the 2014 state election.

While the project was itself extremely controversial given that it would result in the construction of a new motorway in the inner-city neighbourhoods of Melbourne, the planning process in support of this project was also the object of protest. Information put forward for public comment was in concept design only, and the business case whereby the government articulates the benefits of the project, was not publicly available (Gordon and Toscano, 2014). Yet, the government at the time, led by a right of centre Coalition government were proceeding with contract signing with a private consortium to build the project that would ostensibly lock the state and its citizens into building the project regardless of the outcome of the election. The opposition Labor government could see that inner-city seats were under threat by the rising Greens Party. To minimise the electoral chances of Labor in those seats, a commitment was publicly announced that if elected into state parliament, the Labor party would cancel the East West Link contracts (Worrall, 2014). Pressure was being mounted by vocal communities who were affected by this project, and who were leveraging key media outlets to help reframe it from being one of state significance, to a frame that suggested that this was a 'dud' project designed through a bad planning process (Murphy, 2019). These pressures were effective. Along with the threat of losing inner-north seats to the Greens Party, at the eleventh-hour, the opposition Labor Party announced that if elected they would cancel the East West Link contracts and released the business case. Upon their election into power, Labor indeed cancelled the East West Link and released the project's business case for public viewing the very first day upon being in power.

Grassroot opposition that mounted was born out of a concern for this project. However, its ferocity was ignited by a failure of the communicative planning process. The failure was specific: the plan did not reflect the sentiments expressed and the knowledge generated in the eighteen-month communicative process informing the creation of Plan Melbourne (The State Government of Victoria, 2014). In response, the government-appointed chair stood down; while the controversially proposed East West Link toll-road project was inserted into the plan

(McAfee and Legacy, 2015). Upon attracting significant media attention, the now former chair of the plan-making exercise became a founding member of the newly formed Future Melbourne Network with the aim of drawing attention to the disconnection between communicative plan-making and the decisions governments were taking elsewhere. The response, was a citizen-led planning process, led by these disgruntled planning advisors and some academic planning colleagues and students, involving a five-part public forum culminating in the release of the free ebook, *Melbourne: What Next? A Discussion on Creating a Better Future for Melbourne* (Whitzman et al., 2014). This was an effort in citizen-led communicative planning. While imperfect, as it was led by highly networked academics and planning professionals, it was grounded in a community sentiment that planning was failing the state and its diverse populations.

The efforts of the Future Melbourne Network were but one space where discussions about the state's future were taking place. Citizen-led protests reimagined communicative spaces at the height of the oppositional forces against the East West Link. I will turn to discussion about those spaces in the second vignette.

Vignette #2 – Politicising What Counts as Participation

The controversial East West Link toll road prompted a significant citizen-led backlash. The formal planning panel hearings, themselves a poor example of communicative planning which limit engagement to questions about how to minimise, reduce or avoid negative impacts born from the project rather than providing an outlet for questions about the project's efficacy and potential alternative pathways, were the only available formal channel for citizen participation. The panel presenting as a limited space for citizens to express their discontent, informal spaces became the site for campaigning and other forms of politicisation. Some groups presented as single-interest groups, while others where long-standing advocates for public transport and sustainable cities (Legacy, 2016). The expression of their participation also varied. Some groups participated in forms of direct-action activism through street protests and the creation of human linked fencing to slow geotechnical drilling along the project's corridor. While other groups looked to citizen-led forms of participation to generate a debate and spaces to discuss the efficacy of the East West Link (Legacy, 2016). Some of these spaces focused on the project's value to the city, and became the sites for expressed concern of what it would mean for the future of Melbourne, and also what the process would mean for the future of transport planning. There were also groups seeking to model an alternative practice of communicative planning and consideration of how these spaces could support the reimagining of transport for Victoria.

The coercive limitation of these formalised communicative spaces, ignited a groundswell of community-organising which came in the form of neighbourhood meetings, street protests, festivals to celebrate community love for threatened public parks and space, as well as efforts in citizen-led planning (e.g. community visioning of alternative projects to the controversial East West Link) (see for instance, Yarra Campaign for Action on Transport, 2014). While the practice of community organising is a common way for contestation to take space in cities, it was the 'shadowing' of communicative planning by citizens that led to the politicisation of these processes (Legacy, 2017).

These citizen-led spaces renewed communicative planning, through citizen-led participatory action. The spaces were established by citizens, and they offered potential in the way they grounded the politics of transport planning that led to their ignition, into a set of processes changing the social relationship with toll road transport planning and of participatory planning as well. What was being left uncounted in the otherwise formal spaces, counted in these informal citizen-created spaces. While the community campaigners were responding to the narrow remit of the public engagement brief, their participation had to adapt to be 'effective' – which some campaigners described as stopping the project and changing the discourse on transport alternatives – but also exposing and drawing wider attention to the deficiencies of the participatory process.

Facing the prospect that any campaign mounted could not stand in the way of construction of the East West Link, campaigns still emerged beyond the formal spaces forging alternative spaces for citizen participation, against tremendous odds. As described earlier, in addition to any assertion offered by the government to deliver a project in the face of opposition, the formal processes of city planning will at the very least offer defined sites for citizen engagement, but the very design and existence of these spaces work to limit broader expressions of engaged citizenship.

Vignette #3 – Depoliticisation of Communicative Planning

The cancellation of the East West Link and the election of the left-centre Labor Party government into power, was met with jubilation from those citizens who fought to stop this project. From the time when the East West Link was placed on the government's agenda in 2012, in 2015 there was a mild sense, albeit fleeting, that the toll-road movement was thwarted. But in the weeks following the East West Link's formal cancellation, the newly elected Labor government announced the proposal of the A\$6.7b West Gate Tunnel project (Premier of Victoria, 2015), and then later again, in 2016, the \$16.5b North East Link (Redrup, 2016). Curiously, the programme of mega inner city toll-road construction expanded rather than contracted following the cancellation of the East West Link. But in setting to expand this controversial form of transport infrastructure through Melbourne, the government also deepened its commitment to public engagement with the creation of Infrastructure Victoria in 2015, an independent infrastructure advisory agency, tasked with engaging the community on future infrastructure projects, and in the establishment of delivery authorities tasked with undertaking community engagement through the use of community liaison groups and events (Infrastructure Victoria, 2021).

The timing associated with the creation of Infrastructure Victoria was widely embraced. In an interview, one senior planning consultant commented on the 'unfolding debacle over the East West Link' and noted that an 'independent umpire' was needed (see Legacy 2018). One of its first tasks was to produce a thirty-year Infrastructure Strategy to advise the government on its infrastructure investment decisions. The legislation behind Infrastructure Victoria states that it must undertake public consultation on its thirty-year strategy. To this end, Infrastructure Victoria looked to citizen juries as one method among others to engage the public (Infrastructure Victoria, 2015). One jury for the metropolitan area and the other for regional Victoria, the motivation was to demonstrate an open engagement style, and the citizen jury providing the added bonus of demonstrating the role of social learning as a legitimate and important practice in these communicative spaces (see Legacy, 2018), and demonstrating to the wider public a commitment by the state to undertake community engagement. The high production value of these juries, the resources directed into them, and the significant time commitment being made from the selected citizens to participate would go some way to help legitimise and give power to the knowledge and advice generated across these spaces.

Indeed, the kind of engagement offered by citizen juries can be seen by some techno-rationalists, bureaucrats and politicians as inherently risky, but it is in taking on such risk that governments are then able to convey its interest in more 'genuine' forms of participation, limiting the perception that decision-makers are pre-empting outcomes. Herein lies a potential criticism of citizen juries in terms of their post-political potential; there is an interest on the part of the State in using these processes to legitimise policy goals and to further de-politicise citizen's participation efforts. In turn, decisions can potentially be seen by some non-government actors as politically more palatable having been generated through this process. Equally, governments can lean on the jury process and the outputs generated by it and claim the process as evidence of having consulted widely (with a randomly selected number of lay citizens) and deeply over multiple days. Such a defence can prove helpful in the moments when project proposals become politicised.

Just two days following the publication of the final strategy that proposed a North East toll-way to complete the existing ring road, the Labor government released a media statement that it would fund studies to explore possible routes (Lucas and Carey, 2017). In this same media statement, the government also noted that the contracts for this project would not be signed until after the 2018 state election in Victoria. The Labor Government created Infrastructure Victoria to combine a strong orientation towards research and citizen engagement and it has been quick to demonstrate the dual role that public participation plays in transport planning. Citizen participation can be used to drive discussions around the identification of transport infrastructure needs (what kinds of infrastructure will meet the needs of a growing population) and the values used to evaluate those needs. Second, citizen participation can also be mounted in more overtly political ways to politicise projects and to draw attention to problems, including issues about process.

Vignette #4 – Repoliticising Communicative Planning through Citizen Action

Since the cancellation of the East West Link, the politicisation of communicative planning spaces in Victoria has cast attention on the role formal participatory spaces play in protecting the power of the state. This can be seen in the way the Government of Victoria doubled down to protect its politics using communicative spaces, as discussed in the above vignette. With the cancellation of the East West Link, came a continued programme of proposing and constructing controversial toll roads. In this landscape of controversial toll-road construction, there was an extension of formal communicative planning spaces, designed to curate support for an infrastructure-led approach to planning that remained mostly dominated by toll-road construction. Spaces such as Community Liaison Committees (State Government of Victoria, 2021a), as well as the panel hearings provided two significant ways that citizens could participate in the project delivery stages of the planning process. The former was an initiative used to establish a connection between the project proponent, and the different geographies of communities being impacted by the project. The panel hearings were attached to the planning approval process and would involve an examination of how to minimise, reduce or avoid any negative impacts of the proposed project on communities (State Government of Victoria, 2021b). This is not a space to oppose the project, nor was it a space to propose project alternatives such as public transport initiatives.

A new feature of infrastructure planning used in the case of the West Case Tunnel, was the market-led planning proposal scheme (State Government of Victoria, 2018). This instrument of planning is an opaque tool used by governments to assess unsolicited projects proposed by the private sector. One critique of the market-led proposal scheme is that is has the power to delay concerned citizens in their organisation of any grassroots resistance as they await the outcome of the assessment, with the potential to defuse the kind of well-coordinated citizen-led political participation seen in the previous East West Link (see Woodcock et al., 2017). In the early stages of assessment, some active residents sought to raise awareness of this project. But it was not until the announcement came in late 2017 that the project was approved and construction imminent that the need to intensify campaigning became more palatable. The lack of transparency up to the point of the public hearing, and throughout the market-led assessment period, meant that there was not yet a clear 'project', nor a clear proponent that would produce a set of clearly articulated impacts that grassroots campaigners could then leverage in their efforts to widen the resistance.

As the planning panel hearing commenced for this project, some citizen actors stepped outside the formal communicative planning process. With the leadership of a well-known environmental organisation in Victoria, a community-grounded transport plan was developed. Bringing together citizens affected by large-scale transport infrastructure projects being built across the state, a series of weekend workshops were organised to consider what a community-powered plan might look like (Sustainable Cities Collective, 2018). Bringing together long-standing community activists and campaigners who are seeking to see the delivery of better quality public transport, as well as planning academics, there was a sense that the participatory spaces established by the state were all but compromised in favour of growth led, and pro-road building agendas. A construction of an alternative space for citizen-led planning was deemed necessary.

There is a dis-identification being practised by citizens within these formal processes. In other words, the limits of the formal communicative planning process have had the effect of fuelling a transformation, or in other words, a political subjectification of concerned citizens. This is the creation of political citizen subjects who directed some of their energy to the repoliticisation of communicative planning in a way that recast it through citizen-led efforts. This recasting is seen in the efforts taken by citizens to generate spaces for creating dialogue that reimagines communicative spaces.

The formal efforts taken by the state can also been seen as a practice of preserving the status quo. In these spaces, hegemonic power can be left unaddressed, and the politics, which is usually hard to see, yet gives formal planning its structure, can remain entirely coercive. These formal spaces act in ways that respond to conflict, seeking to contain it by establishing new enclosures. It may seem that government is doubling down, or rather enhancing participation (see Haughton and McManus, 2019), in its expansion of communicative spaces, but on the terms set by the those with existing power. In response, there is an evolution of citizen-led participation, that is acting in concert with the setting and resetting of those enclosures that is always establishing new grounds to politicise formal communicative spaces, and extend citizen-led efforts. The temporality of the toll-road building programme lent itself to an analysis of the many informalities of citizen-led political participation against these projects.

DISCUSSION AND CONCLUSION: THE UNCOERCED POTENTIAL OF COMMUNICATIVE PLANNING

Communicative planning, as a formal and state-led practice, has coercive structures of politics deeply embedded within it. When citizens are invited to engage in a planning process, this invitation is typically determined by existing legislation, or by the key moments in the planning process whereby community input is seen as valuable. Plan-making efforts and project planning and delivery are two key 'moments' when citizens are typically invited into transport planning spaces. What counts in these participatory spaces is curated by agendas set by government and project proponents, or again, by the legislative standards set for spaces like planning hearings. In the case of the transport infrastructure projects explored in this chapter, citizen engagement at the project planning stages was limited to questions of minimising, reducing or avoiding negative impacts brought about by the project. These spaces were not available to those who were seeking to question the efficacy of the project, the problems it purports to solve, or the many other ways such mobility and transport problems might be addressed. The power is wholly in the hands of the gatekeepers of these spaces to utilise formal participation in ways that serve their needs. Using communicative planning to direct the community's attention to some discussions, but deem other discussions off the table, is a disciplining and coercive action.

The power of communicative planning lies in establishing the grounds for citizens to participate. As the critical research on communicative planning has shown, these spaces can also exist as coercive spaces designed to limit what counts as knowledge, and what counts as participation. In post-political planning landscapes such as the one described here communicative planning evolved in response to informal citizen-led participatory action that challenged the limits of formal processes provided by the state. What counts as communicative planning was being challenged by political and informal forms of participation, akin to the insurgent participation described by Hilbrandt (2017). The latter was a dis-identification of the state of participatory planning as it is commonly practised, which has the potential to generate new spaces of power and to evolve understandings of communicative planning. The efforts of dis-identification, however small, are also challenges to communicative planning. When observed in this way, dis-identification raises questions about how we count communicative planning and who is guiding participation, if not citizens themselves. Asking such questions helps expose the coercive power of formal processes of communicative planning as it responds to challenges from outside.

To carve spaces where challenges against the project in question can be mounted, informal citizen-led participatory spaces might be crafted. In the four vignettes, these spaces included the Future Melbourne Network five-part community discussion series and the community meeting and citizen-led deliberative spaces. Examining these spaces through a temporal lens, shows the evolution of formal practices of communicative planning as the state seeks to respond to, or anticipate, community resistance. In the wake of the cancellation of the East West Link in 2014, the state introduced two important initiatives in the form of Infrastructure Victoria and the citizen jury processes. They also looked to community liaison groups to set limits on community engagement in some spaces (early project assessment and evaluation) and in other spaces, compartmentalise community engagement into forms of liaising that splinter deliberation.

The political participation that mounted was a practice of dis-identification of formal structures of communicative planning. To a considerable extent, this dis-identification was subtle and grounded in exposing how the state had abandoned any commitment to rationally communicate the community-wide benefits of such transport infrastructure projects. Some publics wanted to be convinced that this project was necessary and were calling on government actors to justify this project with a business case, thereby opening this project to public scrutiny. What could be observed in these informal spaces, was a calling for a return to a kind of communicative planning that gave participating citizens access to the information and knowledge upon which such projects were grounded. There was an acknowledgement of the failings of the state's communicative spaces to be truly deliberative where social learning was possible, to a cautionary engagement in such spaces, and a wider detachment from expecting these spaces to deliver on community concerns.

The extent to which there was a dis-identification from the failings of the formal process of communicative planning in these vignettes can be questioned. Walking entirely away from spaces of formal engagement risks not 'being at the table' in at least in some capacity to have your concerns heard. Stepping outside those spaces to become active in your political engagement in planning risks being cast aside as engaging in nothing more than NIMBY (not-in-my-backyard) protests, or practising a form of participation that is not only informal but de-legitimate; not worth the state taking any real notice of, or paying any attention. Citizen-led forms of participation as seen across the four vignettes were dis-identifying from formal communicative planning, and it was also establishing the grounds for citizen-led forms of communicative planning that could influence formal planning in different ways. Informal participation that embraces the principles of communicative action – deliberation, inclusion and social learning to name a few – are practised by citizens in the spaces invented by them. The Future Melbourne Network series is one example, as is the citizen-led design of a community-powered transport plan. The latter emerged from an exercise of creating connections across differently affected communities by the extensive toll-road building programme led by the State Government of Victoria to collaborate on a citizen-designed plan. The result was a one-page declaration of community-inspired transport ambitions for the state, which had the potential to be a document that might help build a political constituency on alternative principles that could structure the politics of transport planning. These exercises in citizen-led participation, however political, also raised questions about how to understand the practice of communicative planning.

The issue of who is doing communicative planning is a live question that requires further attention. What the four vignettes show, at the very least, is the fluid nature of communicative planning to be both formal and informal, to occupy the spaces between (where citizens participate in the formal offerings, but gain their political subjectivity, in part from constructing alternative spaces for their engagement as well), and to disassociate from the structures dictating what counts as participation. The latter might present as rather ordinary examples of community discontent with planning. However, for planners it provides a rich foundation for rethinking communicative planning as both a formal and informal practice. The power communicative planning possesses is embodied in the way it can evolve and transform as new understandings of citizen-led participation emerge.

To conclude, this chapter explored dis-identification as an example of a political practice of citizen-led participation. Using four short vignettes, I showed how citizen-led participation responds to the coercive power of formal forms of communicative planning laying the groundwork for an evolution in ways of doing communicative action. At its core, the critique of communicative planning is that it is ill-equipped to address the complex social, spatial, political, ideological, economic and environmental challenges ahead. Part of the problem has to do with urban planning being an instrument of state power. Urban planning has lost its public purchase through successive rounds of neoliberal reform, particularly in western democratic contexts. In the case of the latter, what stands in the way are the institutional and ideological contexts that are recentring what communicative planning is and does.

The act of claiming communicative spaces is to expose the power wielded by the state and exercised through formal communicative planning. These acts of claiming through dis-identification help to politicise what formal communicative planning conceals from view, and produce new expectations for communicative planning as it changes over time. While imperfect, and certainly at risk of its own hegemonic logics and structures of power, what is occurring is an evolution of the participating citizen's relationship to communicative planning. These changes, in hopeful ways, seem to be grounded in connection-making and community organising that together contain their own intentional power.

REFERENCES

Ashmore, D.P., Stone, J. and Kirk, Y. (2019). The Need for Greater Transparency when Assessing the Performance and Prospects of Melbourne's Rail Franchise Contracts. *Urban Policy and Research*, *37*(1), 82–96.
Badiou, A. (2005). *Metapolitics*. Verso: London.
Benhabib, S. (1988). I. Judgment and the Moral Foundations of Politics in Arendt's Thought. *Political Theory*, *16*(1), 29–51.
Benhabib, S. (1992). *Situating the Self: Gender, Community and Postmodernism in Contemporary Ethics*. Cambridge, UK: Polity Press.
Calderon, C. and Westin, M. (2021). Understanding Context and its Influence on Collaborative Planning Processes: A Contribution to Communicative Planning Theory. *International Planning Studies*, *26*(1), 14–27.
Davison, G.J. (2004). *Car Wars: How the Car Won our Hearts and Conquered our Cities*. Crows Nest: Allen & Unwin.
Dewey, J. (1930). *Human Nature and Conduct*. New York: The Modern Library.
Eckersley, R. (2000). Deliberative Democracy, Ecological Representation and Risk: Towards a Democracy of the Affected. In M. Saward (ed.), *Democratic Innovation: Deliberation, Representation and Association* (pp. 117–132). London, UK: Routledge.
Forester, J. (1999). *The Deliberative Practitioner: Encouraging Participatory Planning Processes*. Cambridge, MA: MIT Press.
Friedmann, J. (1993). Toward a Non-Euclidian Mode of Planning. *Journal of the American Planning Association*, *59*(4), 482–485.
Grange, K. (2017). Planners – A Silenced Profession? The Politicisation of Planning and the Need for Fearless Speech. *Planning Theory*, *16*(3), 275–295.
Giddens, A. (1984). *The Constitution of Society: Outline of the Theory of Structuration*. Berkeley, CA: University of California Press.
Gordon, J. and Toscano, N. (2014) Victorian Government Failed to Prove Case for East West Link, Infrastructure Umpire Finds. *The Age*. 25 January 2014. Accessed: www.theage.com.au/national/victoria/victorian-government-failed-to-prove-case-for-eastwest-link-infrastructure-umpire-finds-20140124-31e9k.html.
Habermas, J (1983 [1990]). *The Moral Consciousness and Communicative Action*, Cambridge, MA: MIT Press.
Habermas, J. (1984). *The Theory of Communicative Action: Reason and the Rationalization of Society*, vol. 1, 2 vols, London: Heinemann Educational Books Ltd.

Haughton, G. and McManus, P. (2019). Participation in Postpolitical Times: Protesting Westconnex in Sydney, Australia. *Journal of the American Planning Association*, 85(3), 321–334.

Healey, P. (1992). Planning through Debate: The Communicative Turn in Planning Theory. *The Town Planning Review*, 63, 143–162.

Healey, P. (1997). *Collaborative Planning: Shaping Places in Fragmented Societies*. Basingstoke, UK and London: Macmillan International Higher Education.

Healey, P. (1999). Institutionalist Analysis, Communicative Planning, and Shaping Places. *Journal of Planning Education and Research*, 19(2), 111–121.

Healey, P. (2003). Collaborative Planning in Perspective. *Planning Theory*, 2(2), 101–123.

Hilbrandt, H. (2017). Insurgent Participation: Consensus and Contestation in Planning the Redevelopment of Berlin-Tempelhof Airport. *Urban Geography*, 38(4), 537–556.

Hillier, J. (2003). Agon'izing over Consensus: Why Habermasian Ideals Cannot be 'Real'. *Planning Theory*, 2(1), 37–59.

Huxley, M. (2000). The Limits to Communicative Planning. *Journal of Planning Education and Research*, 19(4), 369–377.

Inch, A. (2015). Ordinary Citizens and the Political Cultures of Planning: In Search of the Subject of a New Democratic Ethos. *Planning Theory*, 14(4), 404–424.

Infrastructure Victoria. (2021). Victoria's Draft 30-Year Infrastructure Strategy. State of Victoria. 2021: www.infrastructurevictoria.com.au/project/30-year-strategy/.

Infrastructure Victoria. (2015). From the Ground Up: Developing a 30-year Infrastructure Strategy for Victoria. Melbourne, State of Victoria.

Innes, J.E. (1998). Information in Communicative Planning. *Journal of the American Planning Association*, 64(1), 52–63.

Innes, J.E. and Booher, D.E. (2015). A Turning Point for Planning Theory? Overcoming Dividing Discourses. *Planning Theory*, 14(2), 195–213.

Legacy, C. (2016). Transforming Transport Planning in the Postpolitical Era. *Urban Studies*, 53(14), 3108–3124.

Legacy, C. (2017). Is there a Crisis of Participatory Planning? *Planning Theory*, 16(4), 425–442.

Legacy, C. (2018). The Post-politics of Transport: Establishing a New Meeting Ground for Transport Politics. *Geographical Research*, 56(2), 196–205.

Lucas, C. and Carey, A. (2017). North East Link Options Reveal New Road Could Cost as Much as $23 Billion. *The Age*, 7 August. Accessed October 2017: www.theage.com.au/national/victoria/north-east -link-options-reveal-new-road-could-cost-as-much-as-20-billion-20170807-gxqp6s.html.

McAfee, A. and Legacy, C. (2015). Community Deliberation as a Procedural Planning Tool. *Instruments of Planning: Tensions and Challenges for More Equitable and Sustainable Cities*. New York: Routledge, pp. 65–79.

MacDonald, H. (2015). 'Fantasies of Consensus:' Planning Reform in Sydney, 2005–2013. *Planning Practice and Research*, 30(2), 115–138.

McGuirk, P.M. (2001). Situating Communicative Planning Theory: Context, Power, and Knowledge. *Environment and Planning A*, 33(2), 195–217.

Mouffe, C. (2000). *The Democratic Paradox*. London: Verso.

Mouffe, C. (2005). *On the Political: Thinking in Action*. London: Verso.

Mouffe, C. (2013). *Agonistics: Thinking the World Politically*. Verso. London.

Murphy, J. (2019). 'The Making and Unmaking of East-West Link', PhD dissertation, Swinburne University of Technology, Melbourne.

Porter, L., Roy, A. and Legacy, C. (2021). Planning Solidarity? From Silence to Refusal. *Planning Theory & Practice*, 22(1), 111–138.

Premier of Victoria (2015) Western Distributor Projects gets the Green Light. Media Release, 8 December 2015: www.premier.vic.gov.au/western-distributor-project-gets-green-light.

Rancière, J. (1995). *On the Shores of Politics*. London: Verso.

Rancière, J. (1999). *Dis-agreement: Politics and Philosophy*, London: University of Minnesota Press.

Redrup, Y. (2016) Victoria Announces $10 billion North East Link. *Financial Review*, 11 December 2016. Accessed: www.afr.com/politics/victoria-announces-10-billion-north-east-link-20161211-gt8n 6y.

State Government of Victoria (2014). Plan Melbourne: Metropolitan Planning Strategy. Department of Transport, Planning and Local Infrastructure, Melbourne.

State Government of Victoria (2018). Market-led Proposals. Treasury and Finance, Melbourne. Accessed: www.dtf.vic.gov.au/infrastructure-investment/market-led-proposals.

State Government of Victoria (2021a). Victoria's Big Build: Community and Stakeholder Liaison Groups, 27 May 2021. Accessed: https://bigbuild.vic.gov.au/community/have-your-say/community -and-stakeholder-liaison-groups.

State Government of Victoria (2021b). Planning: Environmental Assessment. Department of Environment, Land, Water and Planning. Accessed: www.planning.vic.gov.au/environment -assessment/environment-assessment-home.

Sustainable Cities Collective (2018). #GetOnBoard. Friends of the Earth and Public Transport Users Association. Accessed www.getonboard.org.au/.

Swyngedouw, E. (2018). *Promises of the Political: Insurgent Cities in a Post-political Environment.* Cambridge, MA: MIT Press.

Tewdwr-Jones, M. and Allmendinger, P. (1998). Deconstructing Communicative Rationality: A Critique of Habermasian Collaborative Planning. *Environment and Planning A*, *30*(11), 1975–1989.

Tornberg, P. and Odhage, J. (2018). Making Transport Planning More Collaborative? The Case of Strategic Choice of Measures in Swedish Transport Planning. *Transportation Research Part A: Policy and Practice*, *118*, 416–429.

Van Wymeersch, E., Oosterlynck, S. and Vanoutrive, T. (2019). The Political Ambivalences of Participatory Planning Initiatives. *Planning Theory*, *18*(3), 359–381.

Van Wymeersch, E., Vanoutrive, T. and Oosterlynck, S. (2020). Unravelling the Concept of Social Transformation in Planning: Inclusion, Power Changes, and Political Subjectification in the Oosterweel Link Road Conflict. *Planning Theory & Practice*, *21*(2), 200–217.

Vigar, G. (2017). The Four Knowledges of Transport Planning: Enacting a More Communicative, Trans-disciplinary Policy and Decision-making. *Transport Policy*, *58*, 39–45.

Whitzman, C., Gleeson, B. and Sheko, S. (2014). Melbourne: What Next?, Research Monograph No. 1., Melbourne Sustainable Society Institute, The University of Melbourne.

Woodcock, I., Sturup, S., Stone, J., Pittman, N., Legacy, C. and Dodson, J. (2017). West Gate Tunnel: Another Case of Tunnel Vision? RMIT University Centre for Urban Research, Melbourne.

Worrall, A. (2014). Greens Campaigning Hard on East West Link in Melbourne Inner-city Seats. *The Age*, 18 October 2014. Accessed www.theage.com.au/national/victoria/greens-campaigning-hard-on -east-west-link-in-melbourne-innercity-seats-20141018-1183vv.html.

Yarra Campaign for Action on Transport (2014). Royal Park, Ross Straw Field, 1 March 2014: www .ycat.org.au/inaugural-royal-park-festival-ross-straw-field-saturday-1st-march-2014/.

10. Insurgent planning and power

Bjørn Sletto

INTRODUCTION: RADICAL INSPIRATIONS

Insurgent planning has emerged as a promising theoretical framework to conceptualize the power of community-based action in the face of increasing urban inequality, the persistence of urban informality, and the continuous, pernicious refusal to allow the urban poor genuine access to the decision-making that shapes the conditions of their everyday life. Emerging from a tradition of radical planning (Friedmann, 1987) and based in civil society in contradiction to capital and the state (see also Friedmann, 2002; Grabow and Heskin, 1973), insurgent planning foregrounds the everyday practices deployed by communities as they invent spaces for critical dialogue and pursue community-based planning through practices of 'resistance, resilience and reconstruction' (Sandercock, 1999; see also Beard, 2002; Miraftab, 2009; Miraftab and Wills, 2005; Sandercock, 1999; Sandercock ed., 1998; Sweet and Chakars, 2010).

To contend with social complexities and uneven relations of power within marginalized communities, recent work in insurgent planning increasingly engages with intersectionality, feminist epistemologies, and queer and critical race theories to bring a relational sensibility on power to bear on the conceptualization of insurgent practice and its counterhegemonic potential. A deeper consideration of relationality of bodies, minds, and material landscapes places agency in multiple sites while encouraging a broader understanding of insurgency and planning as situated in memory, sociality, and materiality. Such an ethnographic sensibility towards the micropolitics of practice also illuminates the role of professional planners and other allies in insurgent planning, as their positionality and access to power calls for critical reflexivity and humility, coupled with a need to attend to risks of misrepresentation and co-optation.

This critical perspective on the role of expert allies also invites more nuanced considerations of the potential of co-production, thus returning us to the original critique of expert-driven planning that inspired insurgent planning. By decentring knowledge production away from planners and other professionals to differently situated actors, all engaged in critical knowledge production and the imagining of alternative futures across complex epistemological and ontological landscapes, insurgent planning signals an ontological break with traditional forms of planning that are premised on reaching 'equilibrium' between competing interests through ideal speech (Huq, 2020; Miraftab, 2018: 277). This critical perspective on knowledge co-production points to the agency of everyday practice and its potential for innovating forms of engagement that bypass the normalizing participatory structures of the neoliberal state.

The following sections begin by contextualizing insurgent planning within prevailing forms of neoliberal governance, examining the ways in which the decentralization and fragmentation of the state has provided openings for radical practice in the face of opaque, networked forms of disciplinary power. This leads to a discussion of the conceptual heritage of radical and insurgent planning, focusing specifically on the conceptualization of power situated in praxis and communitive action characteristic of pragmatism and communicative planning theory.

The subsequent section takes a deeper look into emerging understandings of power that have spurred promising new directions in insurgent planning, including critical conceptualizations of relationality, materiality, and co-production, which point towards more nuanced and situated approaches to insurgent planning.

EXPLAINING STATE POWER AND ITS LIMITS

As a theory of practice, insurgent planning is premised on a set of assumptions of state power under current, prevailing forms of neoliberal governance. 'What insurgent planning does,' argues Friedmann (1987: 391), 'is to rework radical planning to reflect the selective definition and celebration of civil society and citizen participation and the challenges it poses to socially transformative planning practices in the specific context of neoliberal global capitalism.' That is to say, the neoliberal city is characterized by privatization of public services, decentralization, and the formation of governance networks of multiple, private, government, and civil society actors and institutions (Bayat and Biekart, 2009; Caldeira, 2008, Swyngedouw, 2005). Private sector interests are increasingly shaping urban development in rapidly growing cities in the Global South, leading to forms of 'market-centric urbanism' (Brites, 2017) premised on attracting private investment. By subordinating planning 'to the logic of profit and private property' (Arabindoo, 2009, p. 886), neoliberal governance has led to increasing polarization, a continued growth of underserved and informal spaces, and worsening socio-economic inequities (e.g. Graham and Marvin, 2001; Massey, 1996; Mele, 2011).

As these fluid assemblages of actors facilitate the retreat of state-centred governance and instead promote forms of governance-beyond-the-state (Rose et al., 2006; Bogaert, 2011), such networked and horizontal governance also serves to undermine the traditional influence of political parties, large and historically significant NGOs, and labour in urban politics and policy-making. By devolving authority for public services such as infrastructure provision to assemblages of public, private, and civil society actors, neoliberal administrations also shift more responsibility to households and individuals (Lemke, 2001: 202). Because of the lack of clear accountability in such networked governance arrangements, this devolution of responsibility to assemblages of state, civil society and private actors (e.g. Mitchell, 2002; Pagden, 1998) allows state agents to evade resistance in the face of urban infrastructure interventions (Bayat and Biekart, 2009; Swyngedouw, 2005: 202).

With this diffusion of the state into assemblage forms of governance, the imposition of state power relies less on violence and coercion and more on forms of neoliberal governmentality, leading to new technologies of surveillance and disciplining accompanied by a restructuring of relations of power in decision-making and urban regulation (Lemke, 2001; Mitchell, 2002; Swyngedouw, 2005). Networked governance under neoliberalism relies on discourses that rationalize such horizontal arrangements while deploying techniques of power designed to discipline and 'alter the modes of thought' among the urban poor (Tabulawa, 2003: 10; see also Foucault, 1982; Jessop, 2002; Peake and de Souza, 2010). In particular, the rationality of participation relies on the governmental technique of responsibilization to constitute the neoliberal subject, i.e. residents who accept responsibility for tasks previously assumed by government are considered entrepreneurial, autonomous, and 'reasonable' (Clarke, 2005). As power thus works on bodies under neoliberal governmentality (Foucault, 2003), the production of the neoliberal subject through the technology of responsibilization (Lacey and Ilcan,

2006: 36) is further strengthened by self-surveillance, self-assessment (Shore and Wright, 2011), and self-regulation by individual residents (Rose, 2000: 324).

From the perspective of insurgent planning, technologies of neoliberal governmentality such as responsibilization are operationalized through structures of participatory governance, or what Miraftab refers to as 'structures of inclusion' (Miraftab, 2009). These structures of inclusion assume various forms such as participatory budgeting processes, inter-departmental commissions, community engagement forums and the like, but at their heart they are premised on neoliberal notions of responsible citizenship (Gabay, 2011; Trnka and Trundle, 2014: 137) and serve to define who are included, excluded or partially incorporated into the sanctioned spaces of participatory governance (e.g. Freitas, 2019; Zérah 2009). Participatory processes thus become a medium for 'good governance' (Baiocchi and Ganuza, 2014: 31) that serve to produce docile and governable subjects (McKee, 2009) while excluding those who are defined as unruly and irresponsible (Comack and Bowness, 2010: 43). In this way, state power under networked governance arrangements relies on a rationality of participation to involve civil society groups in governance while fostering citizen responsibility for provision and management of basic services.

However, insurgent planning holds that the power of neoliberal governmentality is an incomplete project that is subject to counterhegemonic epistemologies and practices. The rationality of participation is not 'fixed or universal, but heterogeneous and historically contingent' (McKee, 2009: 468), and the techniques of neoliberal governmentality are unstable, incomplete, and subject to social processes and material relations. As some residents participate in their subjectification by performing in accordance with the discourse of personal responsibility others contest or reproduce the meaning of responsibility in situated ways. From this Gramscian perspective, governing is 'characterized by contradictions, complexities and inconsistencies, a gulf between policy rhetoric, implementation and practices and the fact that outcomes are often partial, uneven and unpredictable' (Flint, 2002: 621). Because of these Gramscian fractures in governance regimes, the urban poor and their allies take advantage of these inconsistencies and disconnects in the networked governance to contest their subjectification and create spaces for counterhegemonic knowledge production and action.

As state power under neoliberal governance is operationalized through networked and horizontal assemblages, the neoliberal city itself can productively be thought of as fluid and contingent, characterized by mobilities that challenge the spatialized imperatives of formal urban Planning. Despite the attempts to order the city through the deployment of technologies of urban governance, the 'informal' prevails as the dominant mode of urbanization. Although areas labeled as informal are constructed as pathological spaces (Kamete, 2012) and defined by their lack of infrastructure, economic opportunity and good governance, spaces deemed as informal in fact cover the majority of urban areas in the Global South (see also Chapter 15 by Fawaz, and Chapter 17 by Duminy and Watson). These informal spaces are in turn connected through dense socio-spatial networks that form what Simone (2004) refers to as 'people as infrastructure'. Cities thus can be thought of as metropolises in flux, characterized by movement of people in shifting and discontinuous ways (Mbembe and Nuttall, 2004: 360) that bedevil the control of neoliberal governance and its normalizing technologies of responsibilization. The heterogeneity and contingency of the neoliberal city thus result in an urbanity characterized by unstable and overlapping spaces of formality and informality (Schmidt, 2005), which in turn produce zones 'of social transition and possibility with the potential for new social arrangements and forms of imagination' (Crawford, 2005: 9).

Insurgent planning understands state power as situated in networked assemblages of agents of the state and capital, effected through modes of neoliberal governmentality and subjectifying rationalities of participation. These networked formations of power, in turn, are incoherent and fractured, providing opportunities for counterhegemonic imaginaries and action. While these governance regimes take advantage of a heterogenous urbanity that provides dispersed and decentralized opportunities for formation of assemblages that support private capital, at the same time, the very flux of the neoliberal city and the unstable mobilities of informal modes of urbanization serve to undermine state power and challenge the stability of governance arrangements.

THE PRAGMATIC AND COMMUNICATIVE INFLUENCES IN INSURGENT PLANNING

The communicative turn in planning theory emerged in the 1990s precisely during the emergence of participatory neoliberal governance, calling for attention to the ways in which those with instrumental power in participatory processes sought to distort communication for their own ends. By explicitly conceptualizing power in communicative rather than instrumental or structural terms, communicative planning theorists saw the potential for counterhegemony as situated in discourse. That is to say, planners exercise power when, through critical analysis, they uncover distortions in communication by authorities and 'create the possibility for genuinely democratic politics' (Hoch, 1984: 90) and 'a distinctively counterhegemonic or democratizing role for planning and administrative actors' (Forester, 1993: 6; see also Forester, 1989).

Communicative planning theory (see Chapter 9 by Legacy) has been critiqued for glossing over uneven relations of power among participants in participatory planning processes and overlooking the associations between planning rationalities and power (Flyvbjerg, 2003), while critics from the Global South have pointed out the limitations of this theory in the face of conflicting rationalities (Watson, 2003) and different epistemologies of planning (Porter, 2006) that fundamentally shape communicative processes. By focusing on speech acts from the perspective of Habermasian communicative rationality, communicative planning may be co-opted to justify inclusive planning processes that ostensibly support community engagement but instead serve to mollify opposition and expedite state power and interests. The response of insurgent planning is to take these critiques seriously and consider the limitations of structures of inclusion in neoliberal governance, but at the same time seek new spaces for decolonial dialogue and knowledge production within these same governance structures.

In an important contribution to this conceptualization of communicative engagement under neoliberal governance, Miraftab (2009) develops the concepts of 'invited' and 'invented' spaces of inclusion. In this formulation, invited spaces are normalized forms of engagement, established by authorities through the networked assemblages of neoliberal governance. These forms of engagement reproduce neoliberal rationalities of participation and serve as spaces of subjectification through technologies of neoliberal governmentality such as the discourse of responsibility. 'Invented' spaces, meanwhile, emerge in contradiction to these sanctioned spaces of engagement through innovative and transgressive practices. These unsanctioned, invented spaces of engagement 'respond to neoliberal specifics of dominance through inclusions' (Miraftab 2009: 32) by destabilizing comfortable governance arrangements and challenging normalized order and planning rationalities. At the same time, however, insurgent planning seeks to avoid a false binary between invited and invented spaces. Instead, insurgent action may include participation in scripted and sanctioned forms of participatory planning and urban management as well as innovative, counterhegemonic actions that forge new spaces and forms of engagement and knowledge production (Miraftab 2018).

As this thinking on counterhegemonic forms of communicative action has evolved in insurgent planning theory, there has simultaneously been a reconceptualization of planners and their agency of planning under neoliberal governance. This has been driven by a need to better comprehend the citizen role in the formation of invented, counterhegemonic spaces, which in turn has necessitated critical consideration of the meanings of citizenship and what exclusions and inclusions are derived from such citizenship formations. An important inspiration for this evolving thinking on citizenship in insurgent planning is Holston's (1999, 2008) work on the 'insurgent forms of the social' (Holston, 1999: 167) in planning and urban design. The 'insurgent forms of the social' refers to the production of an alternative notion of right to belong through subversive and antagonistic activities, which in turn disrupts prevailing relations between citizens and the state based on structures of inclusion. Sandercock's (1998 [ed.], 1999) work on what she termed insurgent historiographies in planning was an early, important contribution to such a reconceptualization of citizens as planners, fostering a deeper understanding of the ways in which mainstream histories of planning have reproduced the hegemony of white and male expert planners and technical rationality as drivers of human progress. The emergence of an insurgent, 'differentiated' (Holston, 1999: 167) citizenship thus articulates a new norm of engagement with the state that challenges and bypasses neoliberal governance structures, but which also foregrounds a new conceptualization of agency that situates citizen practices and subaltern knowledge production at the heart of planning. As insurgent planning thus draws inspiration from the thinking on communicative action as a source of counterhegemonic power in the face of the state, through its emphasis on citizen practices as a source of radical action the field is similarly inflected by a pragmatist tradition of thinking of praxis and power.

Pragmatist thinking has had a major influence on US planning theories, including various progressive strands of planning as well as work in communicative planning theory, and can similarly be understood to inform assumptions of power and agency in insurgent planning today. Most closely associated with the three early twentieth-century scholars Charles Peirce, William James and John Dewey, pragmatism was characterized by a shared sense of human potentiality, scepticism of the scientific method, the diversity of ways of thinking and knowing, and an understanding of the importance of social context in shaping people's values and assumptions. The early pragmatists celebrated practical judgement in specific contexts and knowledge production based on experience rather than totalizing theories and natural laws. Pragmatism thus 'emphasized a relational view of the world' (Healey, 2009: 281) long before the emergence of postmodernism, celebrating 'what we might now call the "power of agency," of human capacity to invent, create, and transform' (ibid.). In this way, pragmatism shaped what Friedmann (1987) referred to as the social learning tradition in planning, a greatly influential understanding of social change as emerging from practice, community engagement, and the development of good judgement which still remains at the core of radical and insurgent planning.

Although pragmatist thought has been critiqued for representing a naïve and indeterminate view of power in planning, it is more correct to understand the view of power in pragmatism as enabling rather than repressive (Allen, 2008). In pragmatist thought, power is not seen solely as the constraints of discourse, the techniques of governmentality, or the dominance of oppressive structures, but as intrinsic to human praxis (Wolfe, 2012). A pragmatist theory of power considers the ways in which human action in social contexts has generative potential for social change through critical reflection and social learning within a community of inquiry. Pragmatism acknowledges 'that the ability of an agent to act, to intervene in events so as to make a difference, is also a form of power' (Allen, 2008: 1614). In Arendt's (1958, 1970) formulation, this ability to act is strengthened through mutual action for a common purpose, thus underscoring the pragmatists' view that power should be thought of as something that is enabling and which can be strengthened through collaborative action (Allen, 2008).

Thus pragmatist thinkers and their neo-pragmatist interpreters in the communicative school of planning theory can be understood to have influenced the conceptualization of agency, citizenship, and power of praxis in insurgent planning, including the understanding of the potential of dialogue and critical learning for counterhegemonic planning practice. In particular, insurgent planning has brought forward and made more explicit the understanding of citizens as planning actors and planning as the activities of 'disenfranchised urban citizens aimed at transforming urban policies to meet their needs' (Freitas, 2019: 289). This, in turn, required critical attention to how such planning action emerges, what forms it takes, and what potential it has in forging transformative policies within the fragmented governance landscape of neoliberal cities (see also Grabow and Heskin,1973; Shrestha and Aranya, 2015).

Insurgent planning, then, focuses attention on human practice, especially that of marginalized populations, while decentring the role of technical rationality and traditional planning representation, including the sanctioned forms of participation under neoliberal governance. This leads to a conceptual shift from the expert planner to the citizen planner as the driver of change, and to a new view of planning as a contested domain populated by numerous planning agents, much as neoliberal cities are defined by unstable networks of governance actors (Miraftab, 2018). This conceptual shift, in turn, leads insurgent planning theorists to ask similar questions about the transformative and counterhegemonic potential of such citizenship practices as voiced by the pragmatist thinkers, considering to what extent grassroots actions under certain conditions and in certain contexts are sufficiently innovative and transgressive to effect positive change. By shifting the locus of knowledge production from planners and other professionals, insurgent planning thus opens the possibility for focusing on praxis in the pragmatic tradition as a source of counterhegemonic power.

EMERGING CONCEPTUALIZATIONS OF POWER IN INSURGENT PLANNING: RELATIONALITY, MATERIALITY, AND CO-PRODUCTION

Perhaps precisely because of these implicit influences of North American and European social thought and their invocation in dominant Western planning theories, scepticism towards insurgent planning has emerged, especially among writers in the Global South. This critique serves as a reminder of the risk of totalizing theories and their uncritical adaptation in different contexts and folds into an important strand on thinking in international planning theory focusing on the problematic, colonial heritage of dominant planning rationalities. By failing to account for differences in social, economic and historical context, adaptation of Western theories for action have been unable to contend with the 'stubborn realities' (Yiftachel, 2006) of cities in the Global South.

As communicative planning practices have been faulted for reproducing expert rationalities (Watson, 2009), insurgent planning has similarly been subject to productive critique. Shrestha and Aranya (2015: 425) have argued that insurgent planning primarily emerged from experiences of collective organizing and social learning in Latin America and post-Apartheid South Africa 'where social mobilization is very much part of the planning culture and citizens are more aware of the strength of political participation in general.' In particular, the historically situated heritage of insurgent planning theory, coupled with the influence of pragmatism and communicative action theory, has prompted commonly held conceptions of insurgency and collective action. These notions should not be deployed uncritically across different geographic contexts lest insurgent planning falls victim to 'the very same homogenizing of discourse as the hegemonic practices of neo-liberal planning it aims to destabilize' (Shrestha and Aranya, 2015: 425; see also Meth, 2010).

In their analysis of potential insurgent action in Kathmandu, Nepal, Shrestha and Aranya (2015) propose several context-specific contingencies for the counterhegemonic potential of insurgent planning. First, they suggest that the development of 'invented' spaces of engagement may require mature grassroots organizations and a diffusion of power relations, which in turn fosters social learning and knowledge sharing in networks. At the same time, vested interests and power relations shape citizen engagement even in insurgent processes, which in turn illuminates the need to avoid homogenizing the poor, their collective organizing, and their organizational forms. Second, the authors caution against the romanticizing of all forms of practice as insurgent and all actors as insurgent 'planners,' which calls for more conceptual clarity as well as practical consideration of the role of the mediating agent in struggles with authority. This is especially true in the context of neoliberal governance where state-centric planning has given way to fragmented governance arrangements, making it less clear what exactly insurgents are struggling against and how sustainable such actions are. Finally, the authors return to a call for contextual and situated analysis of community-based action, especially in locales without a tradition of insurgency in the specifically Brazilian vein which was described by Holston and subsequently deployed, perhaps uncritically, to conceptualize planning more broadly in the Global South (Watson, 2013).

The current reconceptualizations of power and insurgency draw inspiration in part from non-representational thinking on performativity and materiality. As a 'theory of practices' (Thrift, 2003, 2004, 2007), non-representational theory proposes that counterhegemonic action derives from the performative relationships between the material world and everyday knowledge production. Thus non-representational theory challenges the privileging of representation in social theory, instead suggesting that theories of practice should be concerned 'with the performative presentations, showings and manifestations of everyday life' (Thrift, 1997: 127). In so doing, non-representational theory 'depends upon understanding and working with the everyday as a set of skills which are highly performative' (Thrift and Dewsbury, 2000: 415). From a non-representational position, it is therefore important to focus on the fluidity and instability of socio-material relations and the ways in which meaning as well as counterhegemonic action are produced through performance (Anderson and Harrison, 2010; Lorimer, 2005). Thus by understanding everyday practice 'as a set of skills which are highly performative' (Thrift and Dewsbury, 2000: 415), the work in performativity provides an 'alternative to more static approaches to place and landscape' (Nash, 2000: 661).

While the non-representational emphasis on performativity as an explanatory framework for socio-material relations has been critiqued for presenting an indeterminate view of agency that ignores structures of race, class, and power (see e.g. Nash, 2000; Thien, 2005; Tolia-Kelly, 2006; Van Dyke, 2013), scholars in this vein argue that a greater attention to everyday performance in fact brings renewed attention to the intimate relations of power that sustain neoliberal dominance. As Thrift (2003: 2021–22) suggests,

> the avowed intent of most performance is exactly the opposite. It wants to make things more political, much more political, in that, above all, it wants to expand the existing pool of alternatives and corresponding forms of dissent. What the performative approach shows is in just how many registers the political and political action operate, even as it necessarily questions straitjacketed notions of what the political and political action consist of.

That is to say, performative thinking draws attention to the myriad of everyday practices and asks to what extent these are 'political' and hence may be considered counterhegemonic and 'insurgent.'

The non-representational thinking on performativity also provides a better understanding of how such everyday practices may foster invented spaces of engagement for insurgent planning action, in specific material and social landscapes. Performativity by necessity focuses on encounters between bodies but also between bodies and material things, asking how social relations, memories and affect shape and are influenced by such encounters, whether these be staged in sanctioned spaces of inclusive neoliberal governance or occur in unplanned ways in invented and unexpected spaces. From the perspective of non-representational theory, the outcomes of such 'unplanned and unaccountable … relational encounters' (Cloke et al., 2008: 246) between multiple beings and materials constitute ruptures in space and subjectivity which furnish possibilities for action. As Nash (2000) suggests, such performative encounters make change seem possible. This perspective, in turn, presents insurgent planning with a call to closely examine the communicative, 'linguistic interplay' that take place in such encounters (Thrift and Dewsbury, 2000: 415) and to what extent such encounters serve to translate everyday practice into counterhegemonic, sustainable insurgent action.

What this performative perspective on socio-material relations also does is to foreground situated, ethnographic readings of (insurgent) planning cases that account for material context, which may also limit the risk of reproducing the totalizing effect of planning theory stemming from an uncritical adoption of concepts of insurgency and citizenship. That is to say, the development of invited spaces of neoliberal governmentality as well as the invented spaces of insurgent planning *takes place* in concrete landscapes traversed by people within built and natural environments that are in turn imbued with memory and meanings. In her work on insurgent plaza occupations in Spain, García-Lamarca (2017: 43) demonstrates the importance of accounting for the materiality of landscapes where insurgent practices and movements are performed. She calls for insurgent planning research that examines 'new forms of knowledge, signs, symbols and codes … created through collective processes and practices, alongside physical appropriation, in terms of disrupting the "order" that existing relations of production and power impose.' Sletto (2021) similarly examines the role of socio-material relations in driving insurgent practices in the Dominican Republic, suggesting that the emotional resonance and productive necessity of household plant production were channelled into the development of a women-led community organization, which in turn prompted counterhegemonic action in the face of a stormwater development project. Thus by focusing on the 'strategic yet flexible attachment to material space' (Centner 2012: 338) which characterize insurgent citizenship practices, scholars will be better positioned to assess the social learning and citizenship formation fostered through performative encounters in concrete landscapes. This move, in turn, will serve to minimize the risk of generalizing the contingencies of agency, insurgence and citizenship across quite different geographic contexts in the Global South (Shrestha and Aranya, 2015; see also Watson, 2009, 2013).

The performative approach in social science theory is closely associated with feminist epistemology, which has furnished important inspiration for the critique of normalizing, modernist theories and planning practices and which has informed, in large part, the important emphasis on co-production of knowledge by and with citizen planners. Feminist epistemology provides the foundation for the centring of the subaltern as the producer of knowledge as well as the practitioner of counterhegemonic action. Inspired by feminist epistemology, performative thinking challenges the masculinist privileging of Enlightenment knowledge and the lingering heritage of instrumental and communicative rationality and instead reveals the importance of the emotional register for counterhegemonic knowledge production. By examining the 'imperceptibles elided by representation (which) forge the weight of our meaningful relation with the world' (Dewsbury, 2003: 1907), this focus on emotion lends important new insights to scholarship seeking to grapple with the multiple epistemologies that may inform counterhegemonic potential of everyday practice. In particular, research at the scale of the body has opened new ways of thinking about violence and conflict and the intersectional forms of oppression that shape oppositional practices.

In the work of Sweet and Escalante (2015: 1827) focusing on gender violence, they argue that 'planners must understand how bodies as geographic spaces feel and experience violence and fear' in order to forge more just planning processes. By positioning the body as the central geographical space of inquiry and paying attention to how bodies feel, planners and their collaborators may 'collect new data, mobilise community members, and initiate a process of empowerment and transformation.' In their work, they draw inspiration from research in visceral geographies to understand bodily experience through innovative methods such as body-mapping, which has the potential to foster difficult yet intimate dialogue about the lived experience of violence. In doing so, their work draws on important contributions to our understanding of repression and agency at the scale of the body, demonstrating that the body constitutes a critical site for negotiating relations of power and a source of resistance (e.g. Longhurst and Johnston, 2014; Perkins, 2000; Peterson, 2001). Sutton's (2010) work in Argentina, for example, has shown how women's bodies became loci of resistance to the dictatorship. By *poner el cuerpo* (putting their body on the line) during demonstrations in the Plaza de Cinco de Mayo and elsewhere, women challenged both gender constructions as well as patriarchal oppression. Women's bodies represented an anti-militaristic conception of female bodies that challenged the male–female dualism of militarism Guzman Bouvard (1994), which more broadly demonstrates that '[w]ounded bodies, tortured bodies, defiant bodies, bodies that confront repression, bodies that protest in surprising ways, and out-of-place bodies shape both the political landscape and the embodied consciousness of participants' (Sutton 2010: 130).

Such a focus on the body in the context of insurgent planning, in turn, provides an opportunity to engender deeper understandings of the broader political, social and economic structures that reproduce violence experienced by subaltern communities. A focus on everyday activities of bodies, Selimovic (2019) reminds us in her work with Palestinian inhabitants in East Jerusalem, provides an opportunity to understand the agential nature of micro-practices while simultaneously accounting for the work of disempowering and violent structures of power. Such a relational approach reminds us of the importance of situated, contextual understanding of what drives community action, but this perspective also illuminates the ways in which relations of power within community groups may hamper community-based insurgent planning or serve to empower some at the expense of others. In her work on the struggles of marginalized women for adequate housing and employment opportunities in the face of neoliberal retreat of the state in Durban, South Africa, Meth (2010) problematizes easy assumptions of insurgency as either transformative and emancipatory (Sandercock, 1998) or potentially repressive (Holston, 1998). Instead, Meth follows a deeply ethnographic approach to demonstrate the multiplicities of gendered natures of insurgency. This work demonstrates that neoliberal patriarchy indeed reaches widely and deeply to limit employment opportunities, prompting women to express their agency in a variety of ways, including through vigilantism to contend with violence in their communities (see also Chapter 19 by Angeles).

Ultimately, the relational perspectives brought forth by critical work in feminist epistemologies and visceral geographies coupled with the insistence on unravelling the performative dimensions on socio-material relations in non-representational theory, point toward the need to more carefully consider the *planner* in insurgent planning. This returns us to the previous discussion of agency and practice, calling for a more critical understanding of the multiple roles and relationships among those who do insurgent planning, and perhaps most importantly, how these relationships contribute, or not, to forms of social learning that are innovative, transgressive, and transformative. These questions are particularly important to address in such an avowed theory of practice as insurgent planning, which must account for both the political, normative and communicative dimensions of claims-making in invented spaces but also the everyday material dimensions of governance, i.e. what Putri (2020: 1847) refers to as the 'technical-political sphere of insurgency.' As insurgent planners perform the technical aspects of infrastructure management, housing provision and the like, they develop a new 'planning pedagogy' (Putri, 2020) that brings planning technologies to bear on a political project of citizen formation and social liberation. This, in turn, calls for a critical understanding of knowledge co-production that goes beyond celebrating the insurgent potentials of everyday practice.

Co-production of knowledge in insurgent planning assumes, of course, that valid knowledge is not merely the province of the technical planner but is situated in everyday practice as well as memory and critical thinking. As such, insurgent planning folds into the decolonial school of critical planning which calls on planners and subaltern communities to question the foundational rationalities that privilege technicist knowledge production. This perspective on knowledge production assumes that knowledge is co-produced in situated and socially contingent encounters, thus challenging the entrenched dualism between scientific-technical knowledge and local knowledge which has reproduced the dominance of Enlightenment rationalities in planning (see e.g. Haraway, 1991; Agrawal, 1995). From the perspective of feminist epistemology, 'democratic practices of engagement and knowledge production' (Peake and de Souza, 2010: 119) that occur in invented and transgressive spaces may foster subaltern agency and lead to social change (see also Blomley 2008; Kitchin and Hubbard 1999; Pain 2003).

The potential for counterhegemonic knowledge production and hence action hinges, of course, on critical consideration of relations of power that shape social learning in invented spaces and careful attention to the positionality and situatedness of the external planner, as we are reminded by scholars working in the area of critical pedagogy (see e.g. Boyle-Baise 1998,

Heyman 2001). However, feminist epistemology similarly holds that the researcher's identity – i.e. the identity to be situated – in fact exists 'only through mutually constitutive social relations, and it is the implications of this relational understanding of position that make the vision of a transparently knowable self and world impossible …' (Rose, 1997: 314). Instead, Rose suggests that research can productively be thought of as performance wherein subjects – including the researcher and the researched – are mutually constituted through a research process that is inherently relational. 'Thus the authority of the researcher can be problematized by rendering her agency as a performative effect of her relations with her researched others. She is situated, not by what she knows, but by what she uncertainly performs' (1997: 316).

This perspective does not negate the consideration of relations of power in insurgent planning process; instead, it suggests that the danger of the planning process cannot be adequately resolved through transparent reflexivity, since the dangers are always as unknowable as the landscape of social relations. Instead, the mutual co-production of knowledge in insurgent planning processes reminds us that knowledges are inherently partial, evolving, and contingent. This conceptualization of knowledge production as fundamentally performative and relational, then, suggests that partial knowledges 'leave opportunities to learn from other perspectives and ways of knowing, to engage in translation exercises across nonreducible knowledges' (Pratt, 2000: 642). Thus while insurgent planners and their community partners are always and 'inextricably bound up with questions of authority, communication and representations, and the positions generated by such questions are inherently political' (Radcliffe 1994: 28), such a relational perspective on research as performance also opens possibilities for 'joint learning' (Walsh, 2005; Cerwonka and Malkki, 2007: 14; Biehl, 2013) which may spark transformative action. Central to such critical perspectives on co-production is the importance of enabling contestation and in fact re-politicize rather the depoliticize knowledge production (Turnhout et al., 2020). Such re-politicization of the fraught process of knowledge production is necessary in order to avoid simplistic assumptions of open dialogue and equality, forestall the reproduction of planning rationalities and uneven relations of power through communicative planning processes, and facilitate the connection between knowledge co-production and action for change (Montana, 2019).

CONCLUSION

While insurgent planning has emerged as a popular and perhaps prevailing theoretical framework for planning scholarship and practice that seek to challenges the persistent inequities and marginalizing structures that characterize neoliberal governance, the conceptualization of power in insurgent planning is multifaceted, often obliquely articulated, and frequently paradoxical. While the field draws inspiration most directly from radical planning and its view of action as situated in civil society organizing coupled with a specifically Brazilian perspective on insurgent citizenship, the emphasis on community engagement and everyday practice is also informed by the neo-pragmatist tradition. This philosophical tradition, which emerged from a trio of American philosophers, influenced thinking on counterhegemonic action through open and reflective dialogue in communicative planning theory, which in turn has been critiqued as failing to account for the situated and contextual relations of power that prevent open and unfettered dialogue in the invited spaces of participatory neoliberal governance.

At the same time, however, as an evolving theoretical approach to conceptualizing a form of emancipatory, decolonial approach to urban planning and development, insurgent planning remains porous and inquiring, allowing for the deployment of critical conceptualizations of power to better understand the associations between theory and practice. Recent work on performativity and materiality in what can be loosely termed the non-representational turn in the social sciences, coupled with critical perspectives on the body, agency, and co-production of knowledge brought forth by scholars in feminist epistemologies, offers promising avenues for new critical thinking on power in insurgent planning. The relational attitude towards research and practice reflected in this work folds neatly into the persistent questions posed in insurgent planning about the decolonizing possibilities of everyday practice and emancipatory forms of knowledge production. A central quandary faced by insurgent planning is the messiness, opacity, and fractured nature of neoliberal governance and the decentralized disciplinary power of neoliberal governmentality. Work in insurgent planning has demonstrated that the very fracturing of neoliberal governance regimes provides opportunities for the formation of new alliances and new, transgressive spaces of engagement. The complex understanding of power vested in socio-material relations of the everyday, the body as a source of agency and contestation, and the radical potentials of research and knowledge co-production as performative and inherently political furnishes new opportunities for a more nuanced understanding of the relationship between power and practice in insurgent planning. A more nuanced, ethnographic understanding of what happens in the invented spaces of insurgent planning – how counter-hegemonic knowledge is produced by whom in specific contexts, under what conditions and through what sort of politics and forms of contestation, inclusions and exclusions – may serve to illuminate the potentials but also complex implications of community-based action.

REFERENCES

Agrawal, A. 1995. Dismantling the Divide between Indigenous and Scientific Knowledge. *Development and Change* 26 (3): 413–439.

Allen, J. 2008. Pragmatism and Power, or the Power to Make a Difference in a Radically Contingent World. *Geoforum* 39: 1613–1624.

Anderson, B. and Harrison, P. (eds) 2010. *Taking Place: Non-representational Theories and Geography*. Farnham, UK: Ashgate.

Arabindoo, P. 2009. Falling Apart at the Margins? Neighbourhood Transformations in Peri-urban Chennai. *Development and Change* 40 (5): 879–901.

Arendt, H. 1958. *The Human Condition*. Chicago and London: University of Chicago Press.

Arendt, H. 1970. *On Violence*. San Diego: Harvest.

Baiocchi, G. and Ganuza, E. 2014. Participatory Budgeting as if Emancipation Mattered. *Politics & Society* 42 (1): 29–50.

Bayat, A. and Biekart, K. 2009. Cities of Extremes. *Development and Change* 40 (5): 815–825.

Beard, V. 2002. Covert Planning for Social Transformation in Indonesia. *Journal of Planning Education and Research* 22 (1): 15–25.

Biehl, J. 2013. Ethnography in the Way of Theory. *Cultural Anthropology* 28 (4): 573–597.

Blomley, N. 2008. The Spaces of Critical Geography. *Progress in Human Geography* 32 (2): 285–293.

Bogaert, K. 2011. The Problem of Slums: Shifting Methods of Neoliberal Urban Government in Morocco. *Development and Change* 42 (3): 709–731.

Boyle-Baise, M. 1998. Community Based Service-learning for Multicultural Teacher Education: An Exploratory Study with Pre-service Teachers. *Equity and Excellence in Education* 31 (2): 52–60.

Brites, W.F. 2017. La ciudad en la encrucijada neoliberal. Urbanismo mercado-céntrico y desigualdad socio-espacial en América Latina. *Revista Brasileira de Gestão Urbana* 9(3), 573–586. https://doi .org/10.1590/2175-3369.009.003.ao14.

Caldeira, T. 2008. From Modernism to Neoliberalism in São Paulo: Reconfiguring the City and its Citizens. In A. Huyssen (ed.), *Other Cities, Other Worlds: Urban Imaginaries in a Globalizing Age.* Durham, NC: Duke University Press.

Centner, R. 2012. Microcitizenships: Fractious Forms of Urban Belonging after Argentine Neoliberalism. *International Journal of Urban and Regional Research* 36 (2): 336–362.

Cerwonka, A. and Malkki, L.H. 2007. *Improvising Theory: Process and Temporality in Ethnographic Fieldwork*. Chicago: University of Chicago Press.

Clarke, J. 2005. New Labour's Citizens: Activated, Empowered, Responsibilized, Abandoned? *Critical Social Policy* 25 (4): 447–463.

Cloke, P., May, J. and Johnsen, S. 2008. Performativity and Affect in the Homeless City. *Environment and Planning D: Society and Space* 26: 241–263.

Comack, E. and E. Bowness. 2010. Dealing the Race Card: Public Discourse on the Policing of Winnipeg's Innercity Communities. *Canadian Journal of Urban Research* 19 (1): 34–50.

Crawford, M. 2005. Everyday Urbanism. In *Everyday Urbanism: Margaret Crawford vs. Michael Speaks* (ed.) R. Mehrotra. Michigan Debates on Urbanism, Vol. 1. Ann Arbor, MI: University of Michigan.

Dawson, A. 2004. Squatters, Space, and Belonging in the Underdeveloped City. *Social Text* 22 (4): 17–34.

Dewsbury, J.-D. 2003. Witnessing Space: 'Knowledge without Contemplation.' *Environment and Planning A* 35 (11): 1907–1932.

Flint, J. 2002. Social Housing Agencies and the Governance of Anti-social Behavior. *Housing Studies* 17 (4): 619–638.

Flyvbjerg, B. 2003. 'Rationality and Power.' In *Readings in Planning Theory* (eds.) S. Campbell and S. Fainstein. Cambridge, MA: Blackwell.

Forester, J. 1989. *Planning in the Face of Power.* Berkeley: University of California Press.

Forester, J. 1993. *Critical Theory, Public Policy and Planning Practice: Toward a Critical Pragmatism.* Albany, NY: State University of New York Press.

Foucault, M. 1982. The Subject and Power, in *Michel Foucault: Beyond Structuralism and Hermeneutics* (eds) H. Dreyfus and P. Rabinow. Brighton, UK: Harvester, pp. 208–226.

Foucault, M. 2003. The Birth of Biopolitics. In *The Essential Foucault: Selections from Essential Works of Foucault 1954–1984* (eds) P. Rabinow and N. Rose. London: The New Press.

Freitas, C.S. 2019. Insurgent Planning? Insights from Two Decades of the Right to the City in Fortaleza, Brazil. *City* 23 (3): 285–305.

Friedmann, J. 1987. *Planning in the Public Domain: From Knowledge to Action.* Princeton, NJ: Princeton University Press.

Friedmann, J. 2002. *The Prospect of Cities.* Minneapolis and London: University of Minnesota Press.

Gabay, C. 2011. Consenting to 'Heaven': The Millennium Development Goals, Neo-liberal Governance and Global Civil Society in Malawi. *Globalizations* 8 (4): 487–501.

Gandy, M. 2008. Landscapes of Disaster: Water, Modernity, and Urban Fragmentation in Mumbai. *Environment and Planning A* 40 (1): 108–30.

García-Lamarca, M. 2017. From Occupying Plazas to Recuperating Housing: Insurgent Practices in Spain. *International Journal of Urban and Regional Research* 41 (1): 37–53.

Grabow, S. and Heskin, A. 1973. Foundations for a Radical Concept of Planning. *Journal of the American Planning Association* 39 (2): 106–114.

Graham, S., and Marvin, S. 2001. *Splintering Urbanism: Networked Infrastructures, Technological Mobilities and the Urban Condition.* New York: Routledge.

Guzman Bouvard, M. 1994. *Revolutionizing Motherhood: The Mothers of Plaza de Mayo.* Wilmington, NC: Scholarly Resources Inc.

Haraway, D. 1991. *Simians, Cyborgs, and Women: The Reinvention of Nature.* London: Free Association Books.

Harrison, P. 2000. Making Sense: Embodiment and the Sensibilities of the Everyday. *Environment and Planning D: Society and Space* 18: 497–517.

Healey, P. 2009. The Pragmatic Tradition in Planning Thought. *Journal of Planning Education and Research* 28: 277–292.

Heyman, R. 2001. Why Advocacy isn't Enough: Realising the Radical Possibilities of the Classroom. *International Research in Geographical and Environmental Education* 10: 174–178.

Hoch, C. 1984. Pragmatism, Planning, and Power. *Journal of Planning Education and Research* 4 (2): 86–95.

Holston, J. 1999. Spaces of Insurgent Citizenship. In *Cities and Citizenship* (ed.) James Holston. Durham: Duke University Press, pp. 155–173.

Holston, J. 2008. *Insurgent Citizenship: Disjunctions of Democracy and Modernity in Brazil*. Princeton, NJ: Princeton University Press.

Huq, E. 2020. Seeing the Insurgent in Transformative Planning Practices. *Planning Theory* 1–21.

Jessop, B. 2002. Liberalism, Neoliberalism and Urban Governance: A State-theoretical Perspective. *Antipode* 34 (2): 452–472.

Kamete, A. 2012. Missing the Point? Urban Planning and the Normalisation of 'Pathological' Spaces in Southern Africa. *Transactions of the Institute of British Geographers* 38: 639–651.

Kitchin, R.M. and Hubbard, P. 1999: Editorial: Research, Action and 'Critical' Geographies. *Area* 31 (3): 195–98.

Lacey, A. and Ilcan, S. 2006. Voluntary Labor, Responsible Citizenship, and International NGOs. *International Journal of Comparative Sociology* 47 (1): 34–53.

Lemke, T. 2001. The Birth of Bio-politics: Michel Foucault's Lecture at the College de France on Neo-liberal Governmentality. *Economy and Society* 30 (2): 190–207.

Longhurst, R. and Johnston, L. 2014. Bodies, Gender, Place and Culture: 21 Years On. *Gender, Place and Culture* 21 (3): 267–278.

Lorimer, H. 2005. Cultural Geography: The Busyness of Being 'More-than Representational.' *Progress in Human Geography* 29: 83–94.

McKee, K. 2009. Post-Foucauldian Governmentality: What Does it Offer Critical Social Policy Analysis? *Critical Social Policy* 29 (3): 465–486.

Massey, D. 1996. The Age of Extremes: Concentrated Affluence and Poverty in the Twenty-first Century. *Demography* 33 (4): 395–412.

Mbembe, A. and Nuttall, S. 2004. Writing the World from an African Metropolis. *Public Culture* 16 (3): 347–372.

Mele, C. 2011. Casinos, Prisons, Incinerators, and Other Fragments of Neoliberal Urban Development. *Social Science History* 35 (3): 423–452.

Meth, P. 2010. Unsettling Insurgency: Reflections on Women's Insurgent Practices in South Africa. *Planning Theory & Practice* 11 (2): 241–263.

Miraftab, F. 2009. Insurgent Planning: Situating Radical Planning in the Global South. *Planning Theory* 8 (1): 32–50.

Miraftab, F. 2018. Insurgent Practices and Decolonization of Future(s). In *The Routledge Handbook of Planning Theory* (eds) M. Gunder, A. Madanipour and V. Watson. New York: Routledge, pp. 276–288.

Miraftab, F. and Wills, S. 2005. Insurgency and Spaces of Active Citizenship: The Story of Western Cape Anti-eviction Campaign in South Africa. *Journal of Planning Education and Research* 25 (2): 200–217.

Mitchell, K. 2002. Transnationalism, Neoliberalism, and the Rise of the Shadow State. *Economy and Society* 30 (2):165–189.

Montana, J. 2019. Co-production in Action: Perceiving Power in the Organisational Dimensions of a Global Biodiversity Expert Process. *Sustainability Science* 14: 1581–1591.

Nash, C. 2000. Performativity in Practice: Some Recent Work in Cultural Geography. *Progress in Human Geography* 24: 653–664.

Pagden, A. 1998. The Genesis of 'Governance' and Enlightenment Conceptions of the Cosmopolitan World Order. *International Social Science Journal* 50 (155): 7–15.

Pain, R. 2003. Social Geography: On Action Orientated Research. *Progress in Human Geography* 27 (5): 649–657.

Peake, L. and de Souza, K. 2010. Feminist Academic and Activist Praxis in Service of the Transnational. In *Critical Transnational Feminist Praxis* (eds) Amanda Lock Swarr and Richa Nagar. Albany, NY: State University of New York Press, pp. 105–123.

Perkins, W. 2000. Protesting Like a Girl: Embodiment, Dissent and Feminist Agency. *Feminist Theory* 1 (1): 59–78.

Peterson, A. 2001. The Militant Body and Political Communication: The Medialization of Violence. In *Contemporary Political Protest: Essays on Political Militancy.* Aldershot, UK: Ashgate.

Porter, L. 2006. Planning in (Post)colonial Settings: Challenges for Theory and Practice. *Planning Theory & Practice* 7 (4): 383–396.

Pratt, G. 2000. Research Performances. *Environment and Planning D: Society and Space* 18: 639–651.

Putri, P.W. 2020. Insurgent Planner: Transgressing the Technocratic State of Postcolonial Jakarta. *Urban Studies* 57 (9): 1845–1865.

Radcliffe, S.A. 1994. (Representing) Post-colonial Women: Authority, Difference and Feminisms, *Area* 26: 25–32.

Rose, G. 1997. Situating Knowledges: Positionality, Reflexivities and Other Tactics. *Progress in Human Geography* 21 (3): 305–320.

Rose, N. 2000. Government and Control. *British Journal of Criminology* 40 (2): 321–339.

Rose, N., O'Malley, P. and Valverde, M. 2006. Governmentality. *Annual Review of Law and Social Science* 2: 83–103.

Roy, A. 2011. Slumdog Cities: Rethinking Subaltern Urbanism. *International Journal of Urban and Regional Research* 35 (2): 223–238.

Sandercock, L. (ed.) 1998. *Making the Invisible Visible: A Multicultural Planning History.* Berkeley, CA: University of California Press.

Sandercock, L. 1999. Translations: From Insurgent Planning to Radical Planning Discourses. *Plurimondi* 1: 37–46.

Schmidt, S. 2005. Cultural Influences and the Built Environment: An Examination of Kumasi, Ghana. *Journal of Urban Design* 10 (3): 353–370.

Selimovic, J.M. 2019. Everyday Agency and Transformation: Place, Body and Story in the Divided City. *Cooperation and Conflict* 54 (2): 131–148.

Shore, C. and Wright, S. 2011. Conceptualising Policy: Technologies of Governance and the Politics of Visibility. In *Policy Worlds: Anthropology and the Analysis of Contemporary Power* (eds) C. Shore, S. Wright and D. Però. Oxford: Berghahn Books.

Shrestha, P. and Aranya, R. 2015. Claiming Invited and Invented Spaces: Contingencies for Insurgent Planning Practices. *International Planning Studies* 20 (4): 424–443.

Simone, A. 2004. People as Infrastructure: Intersecting Fragments in Johannesburg. *Public Culture* 16 (3): 407–429.

Simone, A. 2008. Emergency Democracy and the 'Governing Composite'. *Social Text* 26 (2): 13–33.

Sletto, Bjørn. 2021. Informal Landscapes and the Performative Placing of Insurgent Planning. *Planning Theory* 1–18.

Sutton, B. 2010. *Bodies in Crisis: Culture, Violence, and Women's Resistance in Neoliberal Argentina.* New Brunswick, NJ: Rutgers University Press.

Sweet, E. and Chakars, M. 2010. Identity, Culture, Land, and Language: Stories of Insurgent Planning in the Republic of Buryatia, Russia. *Journal of Planning Education and Research* 30 (2): 198–209.

Sweet, E. and Ortiz Escalante, S. 2015. Bringing Bodies into Planning: Visceral Methods, Fear and Gender Violence. *Urban Studies* 52 (10): 1826–1845.

Swyngedouw, E. 2005. Governance Innovation and the Citizen: The Janus Face of Governance-Beyond-the-state. *Urban Studies* 42 (11): 1191–2006.

Tabulawa, R. 2003. International Aid Agencies, Learner-centred Pedagogy and Political Democratisation: A Critique. *Comparative Education* 39 (1): 7–26.

Thien, D. 2005. After or Beyond Feeling? A Consideration of Affect and Emotion in Geography. *Area* 37: 450–456.

Thrift, N. 1997. The Still Point: Resistance, Expressive Embodiment and Dance, in *Geographies of Resistance* (eds) S. Pile and M. Keith. London: Routledge, pp. 124–151.

Thrift, N. 2003. Performance and … *Environment and Planning A* 35: 2019–2024.

Thrift, N. 2004. The Political Challenge of Relational Space. *Geografiska Annaler B, Human Geography* 86 (1): 57–78.

Thrift, N. 2007. *Non-representational Theory: Space/Politics/Affect*. London: Routledge.

Thrift, N. and Dewsbury, J.-D. 2000. Dead Geographies – and How to Make them Live. *Environment and Planning D: Society and Space* 18: 411–432.

Tolia-Kelly, D. 2006. Affect – An Ethnocentric Encounter? Exploring the 'Universalist' Imperative or Emotional/Affectual Geographies. *Area* 38: 213–217.

Trnka, S. and Trundle, C. 2014. Competing Responsibilities: Moving Beyond Neoliberal Responsibilisation. *Anthropological Forum: Journal of Social Anthropology and Comparative Sociology* 24 (2): 136–153.

Turnhout, E., T. Metze, C. Wyborn, N. Klenk and E. Louder. 2020. The Politics of Co-production: Participation, Power, and Transformation. *Current Opinion in Environmental Sustainability* 42: 15–21.

Van Dyke, C. 2013. Plastic Eternities and the Mosaic of Landscape. *Environment and Planning D: Society and Space* 31: 400–415.

Walsh, A. 2005. The Obvious Aspects of Ecological Underprivilege in Ankarana, Northern Madagascar. *American Anthropologist* 107 (4): 654–665.

Watson, V. 2003. Conflicting Rationalities: Implications for Planning Theory and Ethics. *Planning Theory and Practice* 4 (4): 395–407.

Watson, V. 2009. Seeing from the South: Refocusing Urban Planning on the Globe's Central Urban Issues. *Urban Studies* 46 (11): 2259–2275.

Watson, V. 2013. Planning and the 'Stubborn Realities' of Global South–East Cities: Some Emerging Ideas. *Planning Theory* 12 (1): 81–100.

Wolfe, J. 2012. Does Pragmatism Have a Theory of Power? Pragmatism and the Social Sciences: A Century of Influences and Interactions, Vol. 2, Section II: Law, Power, and the Prospects of a Pragmatist Social Theory. *European Journal of Pragmatism and American Philosophy* 4 (1), https://doi.org/10.4000/ejpap.775.

Yiftachel, O. 2006. Re-engaging Planning Theory? Towards 'South Eastern' Perspectives. *Planning Theory* 5 (3): 211–222.

Zerah, M.-H. 2009. Participatory Governance in Urban Management and the Shifting Geometry of Power in Mumbai. *Development and Change* 40 (5): 853–877.

11. Decolonial approaches to thinking planning and power

Libby Porter

LOCATIONS

'I can feel the chainsaws tearing through my heart' was the cry from Djabwurrung woman Sissy Austin when a very significant law tree on her Country was cut down by government contractors in late 2020 (Wahlquist and Bucci, 2020). The tree was a centuries old towering yellow box with vast spreading branches, a 'directions tree' according to Djabwurrung knowledge and law. Her cries echoed those of the wider Djabwurrung community, and First Nations peoples around the world at the ongoing destruction of lifeworlds, territories, sacred places and connection by the violence of colonisation. For the tree, along with other ancient Djabwurrung law trees nearby, stands in the way of a highway realignment. To protect the trees and their Country from this proposed devastation, Djabwurrung people established a Sovereign Embassy in mid 2018 and lived in the company of the trees for 862 days (Austin, 2020) before being forcibly evicted by Victoria Police.

This contemporary event is connected to the much longer struggle of Djabwurrung and First Nations peoples against and in the face of settler-colonial violence and destruction for more than two centuries in the place now called Australia. Perhaps it looks like a familiar dispute – of a government exerting power over a minority and destroying something precious to a few, in the interests of a larger proclaimed public interest. Yet the death of this tree, the struggle of the Djabwurrung people and that of Indigenous, First Nations and colonised peoples in all places against colonisation, and for decolonial worlds, has much to teach us about the specific organisation, wielding and experience of colonial power and planning. The story shines a light on the ongoing brutality and violence of coloniality as a constant drive to take up and extract land, water, energy and place. This coordinates who can be seen as a legitimate political authority, what forms of knowledge (and knowers) will be included and on whose terms. By coordinating which lives and relationships are deemed unworthy, it is inherently death-making. And the story also has much to teach us as students of planning and power about decolonial imaginaries and practices. About how things could be different.

In writing this chapter and re-telling just a tiny part of the Djabwurrung story here, I acknowledge and honour Djabwurrung Ancestors, Elders, community and Country. Writing from Wurundjeri country, in Melbourne, I acknowledge Wurundjeri Woi Wurrung Ancestors and Elders as the sovereign people of the place I call home. As an uninvited guest here on Kulin lands, descended from early (un)settlers, I am a beneficiary of dispossession and attempted genocide and my privilege is sustained by intricate systems of colonial racialised power. These are uncomfortable truths. While I cannot fully undo them, they can be learned with and from. The privileges they afford can be refused for they are truths that should generate an understanding of responsibility. As Joanne Barker teaches (2018: 34), living honourably and in respectful reciprocity 'requires that we begin with a purposeful attention to where we are'. This is where I am.

This chapter draws from deep currents of intellectual work and praxis about how colonial power functions to demand a different, decolonial world. I begin in the next section by attending to the 'de' of decoloniality as a distinctive call and ethic beyond the 'post'colonial and charting some of the important conceptual terrain laid out by scholars of decoloniality. Then, the chapter brings these lines of thinking to the question of planning and power to examine how planning functions as a mode of coloniality that controls land, legitimises political authority, and organises knowledge in the service of colonial power. The last section lays out some of the current lines of debate both within and beyond planning scholarship offering ways to reach toward decoloniality as an ethic and praxis. Throughout the chapter, I keep returning to the story of the trees to help demonstrate the lived reality of planning's colonial power and the counter-power asserted by Djabwurrung people's praxis.

This is not a definitive account, and I do not claim either to have, or offer, a neat theorisation of decoloniality in relation to planning. Such a thing is likely completely anathema to a decolonial ethic. Instead, my hope in this chapter is to bring teachings from decolonial practitioners and intellectuals to our conversations and concepts about planning and power. I am uncomfortably aware of my own positionality in authoring this chapter, as someone who benefits from coloniality as an enduring condition. But I also see that my privilege, and the privilege that holds up the colonial power of western planning, is a loss. The purpose of this chapter is to unlearn that privilege as our loss (Spivak, 1990: 9), led by the intellectual and political work of Indigenous and Black scholars, activists and communities.

ATTENDING TO THE 'DE'

Decoloniality is both a way of thinking and a political praxis with many diverse lineages, roots and contours. At heart are two common commitments: an attention to the systems of knowledge that organise and coordinate colonial power; and the political praxis of prefiguring alternative, decolonial worlds. That political praxis must be grounded in the ongoing struggles, and practices of refusal, of and by those who bear the violent burden of coloniality. As Djabwurrung custodians teach us through their praxis, this requires sustained and energetic attention to the materialities and discursive formations of coloniality, at the same time as refusing to stay inside those formations. Djabwurrung Sovereign Embassy is a practice of, for and from a sovereign, self-determining position, grounded within already existing structures of law, kin and governance.

Decoloniality might be usefully distinguished from decolonisation in a way resonant with Quijano's important distinction between colonialism and coloniality. For Quijano (2007: 168) colonialism is the violent process, underway over at least the last 500 years, that has resulted in the 'concentration of the world's resources under the control and for the benefit of a small European minority – and above all, of its ruling classes'. What he identifies as 'political colonialism' in its institutional and formal sense is a phase that has largely ended. What endures is the 'specific colonial structure of power' (Quijano, 2007: 168), directly observable in the fact that the relationship between European/Western culture and all other cultures or social formations is one of colonial domination.

This is a vital distinction for it orients our attention to some important matters. First, it seriously troubles the idea of a postcolonial or 'decolonised' condition. Colonial relations of domination and power are not in the past – they endure. We are not 'after' colonialism even where formal political colonialism may have ended, such as where a nation has achieved independence from an imperial power. Second, is that the distinction draws our attention to critically examining how coloniality sustains itself, for coloniality is a shape-shifter of the most enduring and resilient kind. Third, coloniality has the capacity to hold together in view multiple and diverse colonialisms. There are many different expressions, manifestations, operations and structures of colonialism. Settler colonialism – where settlers go to 'new lands to appropriate them and to establish new and improved replicas of the societies they left' (Mar and Edmonds, 2010: 2) is a distinct expression of coloniality, different from other kinds of exploitation colonies. Fourth it points to a distinction between decoloniality and decolonisation. The latter suggests an end point or completed project. A final destination. Decoloniality instead offers ways of thinking, acting and being – forms of ongoing praxis – open to multiple and overlapping possible futures.

Decoloniality has important roots in thinking from Latin America and Africa, from radical Black scholarship in North America, and from critical scholarship in the Middle East. Key thinkers include: Walter Mignolo, Sylvia Wynter, Anibal Quijano, Achille Mbembe, Edward Said, Frantz Fanon among many others. In the diverse work of these intellectuals, decoloniality is conceived as an epistemic, political and material transformation seeking to provincialise European histories and undo Eurocentrism in knowledge, power relations and material realities. To do this work, these thinkers begin with critically understanding the project of coloniality and how the 'colonial matrix of power' (Mignolo, 2010) functions. Sylvia Wynter (2003), Anibal Quijano (2007), Walter Mignolo (2012), Edward Said (1993) and many others have mapped how the west came to invent itself as the universalised norm of human experience against which every other human society was cast as subordinate to others, where 'one local history, that of western civilization, built itself as the point of arrival and owner of human history' (Mignolo, 2012: x). The history of Europe came to stand in as the proper history of all peoples everywhere. The forms of knowledge the west considers important became the only worthy forms to be counted as proper knowledge. The development of racialised categories served to coordinate bodies and systems of thinking into a hierarchy with white and male western/European thinkers and bodies at the apex. Wynter (2003) calls this the 'central overrepresentation of Man' in Eurocentric thinking. Where Man (by which she means a white European male) comes to stand as a universal proper human experience. Those who fail to match this universalised ideal are deemed Other, lesser or even not real.

This is more than a merely symbolic or discursive supremacist coordination, though the symbolic and discursive are vital elements of how coloniality is produced and sustained as a world order. For this 'central overrepresentation' also organises and coordinates the 'large-scale accumulation of unpaid land, labour, and overall wealth expropriated by western Europe from non-European peoples' (Said, 1993; see also Wynter, 2003: 291), thus enabling the interests and lives of the majority human world to be subordinated to what Wynter identifies as the 'globally hegemonic ethnoclass world of Man' (Wynter, 2003: 262).

Focus on the coordination of this large-scale accumulation by the west has also long been where Indigenous thinkers, communities, scholars and activists have oriented attention to questions of power under settler-colonialism. The fields of Critical Indigenous Studies, and Critical Whiteness and Race Studies provide critical analyses of the categories of humanness that help coordinate the colonial matrix of power, pointing out that the category of 'Indigeneity' itself originates from the colonial experience. Key thinkers including Aileen Moreton-Robinson, Linda Tuhiwai Smith, Glen Coulthard, Audra Simpson, Joanne Barker, Chris Andersen, Leanne Betasamosake Simpson, Sarah Hunt, J. Kehaulani Kauanui, Martin Nakata, Heather Dorries, among many others maintain persistent observation of the ever-changing scope of how settler colonialism functions as a matrix of power that controls relations and identities, land and materialities, and systems of knowledge. This matrix of power continues to endure well beyond and past any break with an obviously 'colonial' period. Settler colonialism, by definition, has no 'post' colonial (Barker, 2017: 23) because settlers, as Patrick Wolfe (2006: 387) observed, 'come to stay'. Their intention is to replace existing societies by implanting a new social order, a process that inevitably involves seizing the lands, waters, resources and materialities of Indigenous peoples (dispossession) as well as attempting to erase Indigenous bodies, lives, cultures, knowledge systems and languages (genocide). Dispossession and genocide are thus foundational categories to settler colonialism. They are the specific intent, structure and operation of any settler colonial project. Thus, a decolonial approach demands ongoing critical attention to dispossession and genocide as enduring structures of logic and relations of power.

Underpinning each of these strands of decolonial thinking is a focus on the invention of race and the operation of racism. As Sylvia Wynter (2003) observes, race was important to how new projected spaces and social differences, of Otherness, in the colonial encounter could be organised. This Otherness 'mapped on phenotypical and religio-cultural differences' (Wynter, 2003: 296) and the new world order was defined, by the west, in terms of degrees of those differences. This 'by-nature' difference was and remains central to the legitimation of coloniality as a general condition as well as specific colonial projects of invasion and conquest.

As Ruth Wilson Gilmore (2002: 16) writes, racism is a 'practice of abstraction' whose 'practitioners exploit and renew fatal power-difference couplings'. The practice of racism organises and sustains hierarchies of racial categories that operate from the global to the intimate scale. These hierarchies coordinate control over global resources and power in the interests of those who already control global resources and power (Gilmore 2002). The language of discovery and conquest is emblematic of this organisation. Everywhere outside Europe was determined uninhabitable and uncivil until European conquest and occupation. This operates at the most intimate scale, that of the body, where 'particular kinds of bodies … are materially (if not always visibly) configured by racism into a hierarchy of human and inhuman persons' (Gilmore, 2002: 16). Such a configuration relies on the capacity to displace those bodies deemed inhuman persons, both figuratively in the sense of erasures of subjectivities, lived experiences, cultures and knowledges and materially through what Ananya Roy (2019) calls 'racial banishment'. Racism, as Gilmore (2002: 16) writes, is ultimately a 'death-dealing displacement'.

Observing the function of race and racism is imperative for analyses of coloniality as well as an understanding of decoloniality or decolonial praxis. This also demands a more precise critique of whiteness, for as Aileen Moreton-Robinson (2000: xxi) observes 'as long as whiteness remains invisible in analyses, "race" is the prison reserved for the "Other"'. A critical focus on race, therefore, requires not merely paying attention to the ways in which racism functions as anti-Blackness, though that is certainly vital, but also to the way that 'white racial difference shapes those on whom it confers privilege as well as those it oppresses' (Moreton-Robinson, 2000: xxi). Drawing these lines of connection is core to the project of decolonial thinking and praxis, for it helps reveal what Moreton-Robinson (2000) would call relations of ruling, and Mignolo (2010) names as the colonial matrix of power.

Cheryl Harris' (1993: 1714) work demonstrates the 'entangled relationship' of race and property showing how 'rights in property are contingent on, intertwined with, and conflated with race'. This entangled relationship has its roots in systems of domination experienced by Black and Indigenous peoples which 'created racially contingent forms of property and property rights' (Harris, 1993: 1714). Harris' work revealed the common premise shared by whiteness and property – the right to exclude. Whiteness is, in this sense a type of 'status property' that has been continuously asserted, ratified and legitimised through law. This is crucial for decolonial approaches to planning and power demonstrating the interaction between conceptions of race and property that create and sustain ruling relations with death-displacing consequences for Black and Indigenous peoples.

Moreton-Robinson (2004, 2015) develops this understanding of the intrinsic relationship between relations of property and ruling racial relations into the concept of the white possessive. Conceptualising possessive logics as a 'mode of rationalization' (2015: xii), Moreton-Robinson shows how white possessive logics are organised through three main categories: owning property, becoming propertyless, and being property. Through each, 'whiteness is the invisible measure of who can hold possession' (Moreton-Robinson, 2015: 6) – of who will be considered property, who will be rendered propertyless, and who will be considered an owner. Moreton-Robinson provides an expansive, yet precise, conceptualisation of possessive logics demonstrating how these logics organise subjects through discursive, legal and material regimes of power and then normalise patriarchal white ownership (Moreton-Robinson, 2004: 2). Indigenous feminist perspectives situate the body as ontologically in relationship to other kin and land, drawing a vital connection between environmental exploitation and gendered violence. The perpetuation of racial ownership is intimately linked to the violence against Indigenous women's (Holmes, Hunt and Piedalue, 2015; Dorries and Harjo, 2020) and trans people's bodies (Simpson, 2017). As planning is an activity that organises social relations in space, then it does so in ways that perpetually reconstitute coloniality and racialised orderings of space and bodies (Yiftachel, 2020; Rutland, 2018; McElroy, 2020; Williams, 2020).

The struggle of the Djabwurrung people exposes these underlying structures of colonial intent operationalised through the practices of colonial violence and state power. Coloniality has not 'gone away' from Djabwurrung Country. The settler state, as a matrix of private and public agencies that constitute settler spatial governance across Djabwurrung Country, is fully present here with a persistent intent to seize Djabwurrung Country and erase Djabwurrung identities, laws, knowledge and bodies. The road is part of a wider coordination of ongoing settlement by connecting settler cities together through carbon-intensive forms of transport that support growth logics, reassert the fault lines of private and state property, and destroy parts of Country, such as ancient trees, that might uncomfortably surface these operations of colonial power.

Decoloniality is thus a struggle about the 'politics of being' (Wynter, 2003: 320). It is a struggle over 'what is to be the descriptive statement of the human' (Wynter, 2003: 320) – over who counts as fully human and who does not. This struggle involves practices of disrupting and de-normalising taken for granted categories and assumptions of political authority, control of land and resources, and the politics of knowledge. Examining these diverse and overlapping coordinates of the colonial matrix of power is essential, as Patricia Noxolo (2017: 318) argues, because to acknowledge or examine only one may re-coordinate colonial power regimes. The next section examines planning as a function of the colonial matrix of power, considering how racial logics have wrested control of land and resources, coordinated specific forms of political authority and rested on a politics of knowledge that has only valued western (white) knowledge.

THINKING PLANNING THROUGH THE COLONIAL MATRIX OF POWER

The contemporary regulation and control of place and spatial relations that we call 'planning' is intricately involved in the activities of colonial domination. As Heather Dorries (2012: i–ii) has shown, planning's role is to 'aid in the narration of a political imaginary and the creation of a legal geography' that will perpetually affirm the 'territorial and moral coherence' of settler societies. Hirini Matunga (2017: 641) argues that the deep-rootedness of planning in its colonial past and present is well known 'but a form of soporific amnesia has airbrushed it out of existence, because confronting it requires facing up to its own history, its own complicity with the colonial project, and its ongoing marginalisation and dispossession of the very communities it actually needs to engage'. Similarly, Beebeejaun (2021: 1) argues there is a deliberate 'distancing of empire' from the history of the discipline. A decolonial approach to unpacking these matters demands grasping at the roots, to follow Angela Davis, of how planning functions in these ways and through what mechanisms.

Planning as Control of Land and Resources

At its most material, planning organises how to wrest, in perpetuity, use and control of lands, waters and resources that have been drawn into colonial regimes. In settler-colonial contexts, planning is no mere accomplice to land theft but the architect and machinery of that theft. Little wonder then that non-Indigenous planning theory and praxis has constructed itself as fundamentally 'inhospitable' (Barry and Thompson-Fawcett, 2020) to the existence, expression and practice of Indigenous political and economic sovereignty (Matunga, 2013; Porter et al., 2017).

This is a salient reminder that the contemporary spatial organisation of cities, towns and human settlements is profoundly shaped by practices of people–place relationships that have existed for thousands of generations. As Borrows (1997: 431) notes in the context of North America, 'we scarcely appreciate that the early possibility and pattern of settlement in North America often depended upon an appropriation or a systematic denial of Indigenous environmental use'. Contemporary urban forms, mobility and access routes, and gathering places often closely follow long-existing Indigenous place formations. And these too are the product, following scholars such as Matunga (2013) and Jojola (2008), of Indigenous practices and systems of planning. Bringing a decolonial way of thinking to planning requires opening up to pluriversal ways of knowing, being and doing (Graham, 2008; Grandinetti, 2019; Simpson, 2017; Winkler, 2018) and refusing the intellectual arrogance of western thought that presumes the only styles of governance and forms of knowledge that count are its own. I will return to some of those alternatives later in the chapter.

Cities and urbanisation processes are centrally important to thinking about how planning functions in the service of the colonial matrix of power, because of the racialised nature of capitalism itself. Cedric Robinson (1983) famously argued that capitalism emerged in a context already saturated with racialised logics. Thus, the creation of racialised subjects is intrinsic to the operation of capitalism, rather than a side or 'identity' issue as often cast in conventional accounts of capitalist exploitation. Racial capitalism operates through urban processes of capital accumulation and extraction as a 'differential valuing of lives' (Dorries, Hugill and Tomiak, 2019b: 6) along racialised lines that have sought to literally build imperial power into urban landscapes (Abu-Lughod, 1965; King, 1976, 1990; Said, 1993; Home, 1997; Legg, 2007).

Settler-colonial urbanism has been shown to organise the dispossession of Indigenous lands and then normalise the occupation of non-Indigenous people, systems and lifeworlds on those lands (Edmonds, 2010; Mar and Edmonds, 2010; Hugill, 2017; Porter and Yiftachel, 2019; Dorries, Hugill and Tomiak, 2019a and 2019b). These conditions are different from other kinds of colonial urban formation, because in settler-colonial cities the whole purpose is to coordinate and enrich local settler constituencies through an enduring structure of settler-colonial power from which Indigenous people are excluded (Hugill 2017). A decolonial approach to planning therefore brings into view the colonial spatial imaginary of planning (Koh and Freitas 2018) intimately linked to racialised logics of extraction and banishment (Bates 2018; Dorries, Hugill and Tomiak 2019b; Roy 2019).

The destruction of Djabwurrung Country for the highway widening shows this extractive exploitation logic at work. There are many dozens of very significant trees in this part of Djabwurrung Country, having survived the extensive clearing mainly for agriculture that was perpetrated by white colonists since the mid-1800s. Many of the trees are sacred women's law trees, including an 800-year-old birthing tree that has nurtured the births of generations of Djabwurrung people, knowledge that Djabwurrung people have been forced to share publicly as a result of the threat of destruction (Djab Mara cited in Jacks, 2019). As the words of Djabwurrung woman Sissy Austin that opened this chapter explained, the violence of extraction is not merely an environmental impact, but a felt and lived experience. This makes gendered and sexual violence vitally important to theorise as part of the structure of colonial land dispossession (Simpson, 2017).

Planning as Political Authority

Colonial planning is founded in a concept of political authority that can only see itself. This arises from racialised categorisations of political subjectivity, such as those that enable slavery – where Black and brown bodies are defined as property and utterly without subjectivity – and those that underpinned ideas of conquest and 'discovery'. The legacy of these categorisations and concepts are still present in contemporary planning, where the state is the singular presumed political authority and Indigenous political authority is denied. In recent decades, it has become commonplace to recognise, in limited ways, different forms of Indigenous political authority. These, too, are founded on a structure of denial, as what is offered by the state, usually after generations-long struggles by Indigenous peoples, are various mechanisms for becoming recognisable to, and included in, state procedures. Glen Coulthard (2014) calls this the 'liberal politics of recognition', where settler states reconstitute themselves as benevolent providers of inclusionary processes and sometimes material resources to Indigenous peoples on terms that the settler state controls.

There are many examples of this form of recognition and inclusion practiced especially by settler states in formerly British colonies such as Australia and Canada: land reparation mechanisms controlled by states, practices of apology and reconciliation, and processes for including Indigenous perspectives within state-based legislative and policy procedures. The latter especially abound in planning, where First Nations peoples are often cast as a 'stakeholder' who should have a voice in planning processes. One of these practices particularly important to planning and power is cultural heritage protection. Let us turn again to the situation of the Djabwurrung trees to examine in a more concrete way how this organisation of state-based political authority functions to obscure the existence of political authority and coordinate inclusionary practices that serve state ends.

The State of Victoria is widely regarded as having Australia's most progressive and inclusive legislative framework with regard to Aboriginal cultural heritage protection and management. Aboriginal communities can form organisations based on ancestral connections and apply to the Victorian Aboriginal Heritage Council to be recognised as the 'Registered Aboriginal Party' (RAP) for the protection and management of their cultural heritage. The registration process is arduous and requires meeting a threshold of proof of ancestry and connection determined by the state. Often, applications for RAP status are declined and often for reasons of disputed territory or disputed kinship and lineage. The state is the final arbiter, via the Victorian Aboriginal Heritage Council of who can be recognised as a RAP.

Once Registered Aboriginal Party (RAP) status is achieved, that organisation then becomes the single point of contact for development authorities to seek consultation on the management of cultural heritage. Importantly, the system generates an income stream for RAPs, as development proponents are required to pay a fee to the RAP to undertake required heritage impact assessments and prepare a Cultural Heritage Management Plan (CHMP). In theory, RAPs can withhold consent for development, though this rarely happens. Instead, cultural heritage is 'managed' by being removed from sites where development will proceed. Many people working on their Country as cultural heritage officers describe their job as giving consent to destroy their heritage. It is common practice that archaeologists along with Elders and community members dig up artefacts from sites that are proposed for development and remove those items in order to protect them from certain destruction. The artefacts recovered are quite often only a tiny portion of what is likely to be on the site, given that Aboriginal occupation and use of land and water across Australia was intensive and occurred for tens of thousands of years. Really, everywhere in Australia is a site of cultural heritage importance, as the evidence, tangible and intangible, of ancient occupation and practice is literally everywhere.

The history of colonialism in Victoria caused profound and deep dispossession, loss and trauma. In just a handful of years, invasion caused mass death, incarceration and removal. Every single Aboriginal person was removed from their Country either by death or displacement. Those who survived were forced onto mission and reserves, forbidden to undertake their normal economic, cultural and social practices and from speaking their languages. Laws controlling every aspect of life including marriage, employment and mobility were all part of a colossal colonial machinery bent, quite explicitly, on extermination.

It is from this context that today Aboriginal people in Victoria are expected by settler society to form neat, cohesive communities based on ancestry, in organisational forms recognisable to, and accountable to, the settler state. In reality, First Nations people in Victoria are often still finding their way back home to their Country, families and communities, and continue to face high rates of incarceration, targeted policing, removal of children and intense structural racism. A direct legacy of colonial violence and dispossession is the deep division that can at times exist within and between communities, a division actively exploited by the settler state.

The Registered Aboriginal Party for managing the consent to destroy the Djabwurrung trees was de-registered after having made the decision to approve the road-widening project. The RAP responsibilities were then passed to the Eastern Maar Aboriginal Corporation (EMAC). Not all Djabwurrung people are involved in EMAC, nor wish to be – there is a strong practice of refusal to participate in state-based recognition regimes. The Djabwurrung people who established the Djabwrrung Sovereignty Embassy are not a part of EMAC or the de-registered RAP. This division within the community was strategically deployed, just as it was strategically engineered, by Government at both State and Federal levels, to dismiss the Embassy and its protest in protection of the trees.

Decolonial ways of understanding what is happening here point immediately to the organisation of state power as the primary source of power and authority itself. Rights-based or inclusionary models rely solely on concepts of western law and settler state power. There is no space within such ways of thinking for encountering systems of law, governance and authority outside what is presumed a universal and totalising western system. The only remedies on offer are those available within that western legal system and usually tightly bound to questions of private property (see also Chapter 15 by Fawaz). As Jodi Byrd (2011: 39) states, when redress for colonisation is only framed 'by further inclusion into the nation-state, there is a significant failure to grapple with the fact that such discourses further re-inscribe the original colonial injury'.

The erasure, at least discursively, of Indigenous political authority by settler coloniality creates an absence of Indigenous sovereignty. But this is not, as Joanne Barker (2018: 24) identifies, an 'absence that can be fixed by presence ... as if inclusion can resolve the problem of erasure'. Instead, as she argues, this is a 'politic of epistemology' of what and who gets to count in the world and how.

Planning as a Politics of Knowledge

Sustaining the project of colonialism, its varied materialities and violences, is the organisation and codification of a western system of knowledge that will be the only system of knowledge that can count. As Linda Tuhiwai Smith (1999: 65) observes 'most of the 'traditional' disciplines are grounded in cultural world views which are either antagonistic to other belief systems or have no methodology for dealing with other knowledge systems'. This is by design, as the success of colonial projects in material terms, requires the rendering of 'particular epistemologies unthinkable' (Mignolo, 2015).

Questions of epistemology are centrally important to decolonial praxis (Spivak, 1999; Wynter, 2003; Nakata, 2007; Mignolo, 2009; Smith, 2015). These critiques presented by these and other authors profoundly challenge western knowledge systems because they expose how the presumption of universality and objectivity at the core of western knowledge is itself an operation of power. Decolonial approaches instead advance a philosophy of knowledge that always foregrounds the 'social relations within which we as "knowers" know' (Polhaus cited in Nakata, 2007: 214). All knowledge systems have ways of codifying and making sense of different kinds of phenomena. Western knowledge systems stabilise particular social categories that operate as signifiers around which the coloniality of knowledge production works its magic. Race is the foundational example where whiteness fades from view – becomes a category that is no longer a category – and blackness or Indigeneity are framed as different so as to open them to endless forensic examination and in the same moment cast them as deficient, even if exotic. These are the 'overarching governing codes that have created, maintained and normalized practices of exclusion' (Mignolo, 2015) that so much intellectual effort from decolonial thinkers has been at pains to show.

In organising western knowledge as the only true system of knowledge that counts, all other knowledge systems are thus subjugated and diminished. We can see this in something as simple as labels, such as 'Indigenous knowledge' or 'traditional knowledge'. The purpose of this coordination is to determine what will count as proper knowledge, what methods of knowing will count as proper methods, and who will count as a knower. This is not to claim that there is a 'better or more truthful truth' (Nakata, 2007) but to examine how coloniality operates by establishing western knowledge as the single point of reference in a kind of hall of mirrors (Rose, 2004), diminishing or erasing all other ways of knowing.

There is a geography to the organisation of knowledge production in the service of coloniality. Knowledge is produced by the west, from the centres of western imperial power (a power that is often shifting in its own geography), about other places and people that are cast as interesting case studies or empirical examples of categories conceived and invented elsewhere (Roy, 2016). Edward Said (1978) identified this, and the broader system of knowledge that codifies, belittles and diminishes non-western knowledge systems as Orientalism. This territorial organisation follows specific geopolitical lines of power coordinating the domination and control of territories, resources and bodies through the domination of knowledge and knowing.

Decolonial approaches also pay critical attention to examining how knowledge functions to create racialised, gendered and sexualised subjects of difference. This requires centring the lived experience and standpoint of those who experience colonialism as oppression and domination. Analysing coloniality must inevitably engender 'problems about knowledge itself, for these analyses do not generally arise, and are not comfortably contained, within the knowledge structures of the global metropole' (Connell, 2014: 215). This is an important reminder that the knowledge systems designed in the service of coloniality (mostly) refuse or deny critical examinations of the very coloniality they work to sustain. The operation of epistemological power here is therefore a kind of double move: an organisation of knowledge that excludes or renders unthinkable non-western epistemological frameworks and then renders unthinkable the need to critique that exclusion.

Winkler (2018: 267) has helpfully observed this to be an approach 'purposefully geared towards rethinking thinking itself'. There are some important distinctions to make here about the intent and praxis of decolonial thinking about knowledge. For this is not about superseding western knowledge and replacing it with something else (as that would be a colonialist endeavour), but instead, to 'undo the systems through which knowledge and knowing are constituted' (Mignolo, 2015: 122). This demands a delinking from dominant knowledge systems, and a refusal to participate in codifications and methods that presume a singular viewpoint. This 'epistemic disobedience' as Mignolo (2009) calls it is crucial for removing 'the right that an ethno-class attributed to itself to 'possess' or embody the truth of what Human is and means' (Mignolo, 2015: 122).

Central to the dispute about the Djabwurrung trees is a politics of knowledge that deliberately operates as a divide and conquer tactic wielded by the settler state. Much of this operates around whether or not (and according to whom) the trees that Djabwurrung people are seeking to protect display markings that demonstrate, in the words of the Federal Environment

Minister at the time, that they are 'Aboriginal modified trees' and thus 'significant Aboriginal objects according to the Act'. The system of cultural heritage management in Victoria requires that western-trained, usually white, archaeologists examine and verify the cultural provenance of artefacts and sites. Much has been written about archaeology as a discipline geared toward containing Indigenous connection to places, objects and practices to a static past in order to control land and resources for an eternally unfolding settler future (Langford, 1983; Smith, 2004; Porter, 2006). The Djabwurrung trees are, according to Djabuwurrung knowledge holders, fully incorporated into Djabwurrung law and knowledge systems. To be heard by the settler system of cultural heritage management, this knowledge has had to be codified and verified by white archaeologists to become legible to the state. One of the great injuries of this process is the requirement that Indigenous people make available for public consumption knowledge that has no place being shared outside the relationships within which it is known and practised (Graham, 2008).

To add insult to that injury, the Victorian Government also ignored the advice of white archaeologists who confirmed the significance of the trees. Instead, the Government chose to run a line of divisive community politics by siding with another section of the community who felt the trees were less significant and weaponising a competing report that questioned whether the trees were 'culturally modified'. The settler states has thus doubled down on the fracturing work of settler-colonialism, using the deep rifts caused by colonisation and ongoing trauma to pit factions against each other, where claims and counter-claims are what gets aired in the public debate to discredit the conception of the trees as sacred and diminish the people practising their sovereignty in relation to the trees.

DECOLONISING PLANNING?

If planning is vital to the operation and function of colonial power, then decolonising planning is both urgent and exceptionally challenging. And because coloniality is a slippery beast, all the tendencies and desires for co-opting and sanitising decoloniality into simply 'reform' are fully present in planning as in all other policy domains and scholarly disciplines. Decolonisation is not a new buzzword for white researchers to launch their careers. It is, as Waziyatawin and Yellow Bird (2005: 2) teach the 'intelligent, calculated, and active resistance to the forces of colonialism that perpetuate the subjugation and/or exploitation of minds, bodies and lands and it is engaged for the ultimate purpose of over-turning the colonial structure and realizing Indigenous liberation'. Such resistance is its own form of power.

Decoloniality as a way of thinking and a political praxis must have Indigenous and other colonised voices, practices, resistances, and intellectual traditions at the centre. This is not merely a citational practice, though that is important too. This centring must also demand we – that is, those of us not burdened by the violence of coloniality – do the challenging work of calling to account the 'unbearable whiteness' (Derickson, 2017) of planning and urban profes-sions (Roy, 2017). The overwhelming majority of people in the planning research and practice community (at least in the place from where I write, so-called Australia) are people like me: marked by white privilege, sustained by the intricate webs of colonial power that coordinate global resources in the service of bodies and lives like mine. This is a structural feature of the colonial matrix of power particularly in the knowledge economy of academic scholarship.

That I have been invited to author this chapter, and that I made a choice to accept, might be read as practices that sustain this matrix of power.

A role, then, for those situated as I am, is to heed the urgent call to reckon with the fact of planning as central to the enduring structure of coloniality. It is here, in conceiving decoloniality as a way of thinking, that we might best situate work that aims to expose planning as a disciplining tool in the colonial matrix of power (Roy, 2006; Watson, 2009; Porter, 2010; Rankin, 2010; Dorries, 2012; Miraftab, 2012; Porter and Barry, 2015; Yiftachel, 2017), calling planning to account through critical investigations of both historical and contemporary practices of planning in many contexts around the world (Peters, 2005; Stanger-Ross, 2008; Howitt and Lunkapis, 2010; Barry, 2012; Livesey, 2019; Hartwig, Jackson and Osborne, 2018; Jackson, Porter and Johnson, 2018; Barry and Thompson-Fawcett, 2020) including work that exposes the active erasure of knowledge systems (Walker, Jojola and Natcher, 2013; Matunga, 2017; Patrick, 2017; Winkler, 2018).

Ugarte (2014) has examined some of these strands of literature to distinguish within the debate an emphasis on ethics, often conceived as an individual practice, and rights, often conceived as a wider institutional effort. This is an important observation and reveals the gaping insufficiency of our current praxis. In planning, our first response is to address problems of structural power and injustice with reforms to institutions and rights-based, particularly procedural rights, mechanisms. Reforms inside the colonial system cannot address and unpick the coloniality of the system. Procedural rights and individual ethical practices are not unimportant, but they too often deepen the functioning of colonial power through symbols of redress (Porter, 2014; Blatman-Thomas and Porter, 2019; Barry and Thompson-Fawcett, 2020), and other 'moves to innocence' (Tuck and Yang, 2012). The extraordinary strength and staunch resistance of Djabwurrung people won some reprieve, when in March 2021 the Victorian Government announced it would allow for a new cultural heritage plan before finalising the development of the road. This is temporary relief, not decolonisation. Grappling with the ongoing intellectual task – the *ways of thinking* – for decolonising planning will require constantly attending to that proclivity. This is necessary, exhausting, unending work. It demands breaking apart and reorganising assumed categories, forms of governance, relations of power and lines of responsibility with a view to creating as Matunga (2017) puts it a 'third space' for planning to connect with Indigenous domains and pluriversal knowledge systems.

Decoloniality as a *political praxis* asks us to situate planning in a relation of accountability with the strong and growing movements of Indigenous resurgence and broader anti-colonial resistance. Dorries and colleagues (2019a: 7) identify resurgence as 'movements and embodied practices focused on rebuilding nation-specific Indigenous ways of being and actualizing self-determination' whereas resistance is the 'movements and embodied practices focused on addressing and fighting against settler colonial and state violence'. Often both are happening at the same time. Djabwurrung people in protecting their sacred Country are engaged in a staunch effort of anti-colonial resistance, fighting against colonial violence perpetrated against their Country and their lives. At the same time, they are defining and practising Djabwurrung being and sovereignty as 'protocols for lived social responsibilities' (Barker 2018: 21) defined within Djabwurrung epistemologies. Djabwurrung Country is at the centre of knowledge and social relationships of accountability, a living demonstration of land as pedagogy (Simpson 2014, 2017), or grounded normativity (Coulthard, 2014) in practice (see also Graham, 2008; Corntassel, 2012; Bawaka Country et al., 2016; Larsen and Johnson, 2016). Decoloniality as political praxis is not a space for whiteness to occupy, but of vital Indigenous-led resurgence.

To learn more about the Djabwurrung Sovereign Embassy see their website at: https://dwembassy.com or find Djab Wurrung Heritage Protection Embassy on Facebook. There are ways to learn, support and donate.

REFERENCES

Abu-Lughod, J. (1965), 'Tale of Two Cities: The Origins of Modern Cairo', *Comparative Studies in Society and History*, 7(4), 429–457.

Austin, S. (2020), 'The Destruction of a Sacred Tree on Djab Wurrung Country has Broken our Hearts', *The Guardian: Australian Edition*, 27 October.

Barker, J. (2017), 'Introduction: Critically Sovereign', in Barker, J. (ed.), *Critically Sovereign: Indigenous Gender, Sexuality and Feminist Studies*, Durham, NC: Duke University Press, 1–44.

Barker, J. (2018), 'Territory as Analytic', *Social Text*, 36(2), 19–39.

Barry, J. (2012), 'Indigenous-State Planning as Inter-institutional Capacity Development: The Evolution of "Government-to-Government" Relations in Coastal British Columbia, Canada', *Planning Theory and Practice*, 13(2), 213–231.

Barry, J. and M. Thompson-Fawcett (2020), 'Decolonizing the Boundaries between the "Planner" and the "Planned": Implications of Indigenous Property Development', *Planning Theory and Practice*, 21(3), 410–425.

Bates, L.K. (ed.) (2018), 'Race and Spatial Imaginary: Planning Otherwise', *Planning Theory and Practice*, 19(2), 254–288.

Bawaka Country, S. Wright, S. Suchet-Pearson, K. Lloyd, L. Burarrwanga, R. Ganambarr, M. Ganambarr-Stubbs, B. Ganambarr, D, Maymuru, and J. Sweeney (2016), 'Co-becoming Bawaka: Towards a Relational Understanding of Space/Place', *Progress in Human Geography*, 40(4), 455–475.

Beebeejaun, Y. (2021), 'Provincializing Planning: Reflections on Spatial Ordering and Imperial Power', *Planning Theory*, 21(3), 248–268, DOI:10.1177/14730952211026697.

Blatman-Thomas, N. and L. Porter (2019), 'Placing Property: Theorizing the Urban from Settler Colonial Cities', *International Journal of Urban and Regional Research*, 43(1), 30–45.

Borrows, J. (1997), 'Living between Water and Rocks: First Nations, Environmental Planning and Democracy', *University of Toronto Law Journal*, 47(4), 417–468.

Byrd, J.A. (2011), *The Transit of Empire: Indigenous Critiques of Colonialism*, Minneapolis: University of Minnesota Press.

Connell, R. (2014), 'Using Southern Theory: Decolonizing Social Thought in Theory, Research and Application', *Planning Theory*, 13(2), 210–223.

Corntassel, J. (2012), 'Re-envisioning Resurgence: Indigenous Pathways to Decolonization and Sustainable Self-determination', *Decolonization: Indigeneity, Education & Society*, 1(1), 86–101.

Coulthard, G. (2014), *Red Skins, White Masks: Rejecting the Colonial Politics of Recognition*, Minneapolis: University of Minnesota Press.

Derickson, K.D. (2017), 'Urban Geography II: Urban Geography in the Age of Ferguson', *Progress in Human Geography*, 41(2), 230–244.

Dorries, H. (2012), 'Rejecting the 'False Choice': Foregrounding Indigenous Sovereignty in Planning Theory and Practice', PhD thesis, Toronto: University of Toronto.

Dorries, H., D. Hugill, and J. Tomiak (eds) (2019a), 'Introduction', in *Settler City Limits: Indigenous Resurgence and Colonial Violence in the Urban Prairie West*, Winnipeg: University of Manitoba Press.

Dorries, H. and L. Harjo (2020), 'Beyond Safety: Refusing Colonial Violence Through Indigenous Feminist Planning', *Journal of Planning Education and Research*, 40(2), 210–219.

Dorries, H., D. Hugill, and J. Tomiak (2019b), 'Racial Capitalism and the Production of Settler Colonial Cities', *Geoforum*, doi: 10.1016/j.geoforum.2019.07.016.

Edmonds, P. (2010), *Urbanizing Frontiers: Indigenous Peoples and Settlers in 19th Century Pacific Rim Cities*, Vancouver: UBC Press.

Gilmore, R.W. (2002), 'Fatal Couplings of Power and Difference: Notes on Racism and Geography', *Professional Geographer*, 54(1), 15–24.

Graham, M. (2008), 'Some Thoughts about the Philosophical Underpinnings of Aboriginal Worldviews', *Australian Humanities Review*, 45, 181–194.

Grandinetti, T. (2019), 'Urban aloha 'aina: Kaka'ako and a Decolonized Right to the City', *Settler Colonial Studies*, 9(2), 227–246.

Harris, C.I. (1993), 'Whiteness as Property', *Harvard Law Review*, 106(8), 1709–1790.

Hartwig, L., S. Jackson, and N. Osborne (2018), 'Recognition of Barkandji Water Rights in Australian Settler-Colonial Water Regimes', *Resources*, 7(1), 16–42.

Holmes, C., S. Hunt, and A. Piedalue (2015), 'Violence, Colonialism, and Space: Towards a Decolonizing Dialogue', *Acme*, 14(2), 539–570.

Home, R. (1997), *Of Planting and Planning: The Making of British Colonial Cities*, London: E+FN Spon.

Howitt, R. and G. Lunkapis (2010), 'Coexistence: Planning and the Challenge of Indigenous Rights', in Hillier, J. and P. Healey (eds), *The Ashgate Research Companion to Planning Theory: Conceptual Challenges for Spatial Planning*, Farnham, UK: Ashgate, 109–133.

Hugill, D. (2017), 'What is a Settler-colonial City?', *Geography Compass*, 11(5), 1–11.

Jacks, T. (2019), '"Like Losing My Son": Why Trees Threatened by Western Hwy are so Sacred', *The Age*, 25 August, Melbourne.

Jackson, S., L. Porter, and L. Johnson (2018), *Planning in Indigenous Australia: From Imperial Foundations to Postcolonial Futures*, London: Routledge.

Jojola, T. (2008), 'Indigenous Planning: An emerging Context', *Canadian Journal of Urban Research*, 17(Supplement), 37–47.

King, A.D. (1976), *Colonial Urban Development: Culture, Social Power and Environment*, London: Routledge and Kegan Paul.

King, A.D. (1990), *Urbanism, Colonialism and the World Economy: Cultural and Spatial Foundations of the World Urban System*, London: Routledge.

Koh, A. and K. Freitas (2018), 'Is Honolulu a Hawaiian Place? Decolonizing Cities and the Redefinition of Spatial Legitimacy', *Planning Theory and Practice*, 19(2), 280–283.

Koh, A. (2019), 'Decolonial Planning in North America', *Progressive City*, March. Available at: www .progressivecity.net/single-post/2019/03/04/decolonial-planning-in-north-america.

Langford, R.F. (1983), 'Our Heritage – Your Playground', *Australian Archaeology*, 16, 1–6.

Larsen, S.C. and J.T. Johnson (2016), 'The Agency of Place: Toward a More-Than-Human Geographical Self', *GeoHumanities*, 2(1), 149–166.

Legg, S. (2007), *Spaces of Colonialism: Delhi's Urban Governmentalities*, Malden, MA: Blackwell.

Livesey, B. (2019), '"Returning Resources Alone is Not Enough": Imagining Urban Planning after Treaty Settlements in Aotearoa New Zealand', *Settler Colonial Studies*, 9(2), 266–283.

Mar, T.B. and P. Edmonds (2010), *Making Settler Colonial Space: Perspectives on Race, Place and Identity*, London: Palgrave Macmillan.

Matunga, H. (2013), 'Theorizing Indigenous Planning', in Walker, R., T. Jojola, and D. Natcher (eds), *Reclaiming Indigenous Planning*, Montreal: McGill-Queen University Press.

Matunga, H. (2017), 'A Revolutionary Pedagogy of/for Indigenous Planning', *Planning Theory and Practice*, 18(4), 640–644.

McElroy, E. (2020), 'Property as Technology: Temporal Entanglements of Race, Space, and Displacement', *City*, 24(1–2), 112–129.

Mignolo, W. (2010), 'Cosmopolitanism and the De-colonial Option', *Studies in Philosophy and Education*, 29(2), 111–127.

Mignolo, W.D. (2009), 'Epistemic Disobedience, Independent Thought and Decolonial Freedom', *Theory, Culture & Society*, 26(8), 159–181.

Mignolo, W.D. (2012), *Local Histories/Global Designs: Coloniality, Subaltern Knowledges and Border Thinking*, Princeton: Princeton University Press.

Mignolo, W.D. (2015), 'Sylvia Wynter: What does it Mean to be Human?', in McKittrick, K. (ed.), *Sylvia Wynter: On Being Human as Praxis*, Durham, NC: Duke University Press.

Miraftab, F. (2012), 'Colonial Present: Legacies of the Past in Contemporary Urban Practices in Cape Town, South Africa', *Journal of Planning History*, 11(4), 283–307.

Moreton-Robinson, A. (2000), *Talkin' up to the White Woman: Indigenous Women and Feminism*, St Lucia: University of Queensland Press.

Moreton-Robinson, A. (2004), 'The Possessive Logic of Patriarchal White Sovereignty: The High Court and the Yorta Yorta Decision', *Borderlands*, 3(2), 1–9.

Moreton-Robinson, A. (2015), *The White Possessive: Property, Power and Indigenous Sovereignty*, Minneapolis: University of Minnesota Press.

Nakata, M. (2007), *Disciplining the Savages, Savaging the Disciplines*, Canberra: Aboriginal Studies Press.

Noxolo, P. (2017), 'Introduction: Decolonising Geographical Knowledge in a Colonised and Re-colonising Postcolonial World', *Area*, 49(3), 317–319.

Patrick, L. (2017), 'Indigenist Planning', *Planning Theory and Practice*, 18(4), 647–649.

Peters, E. (2005), 'Indigeneity and Marginalisation: Planning for and with Urban Aboriginal Communities in Canada', *Special Issue of Progress in Planning*, 63(4), 327–404.

Porter, L. (2006), 'Rights or Containment? The Politics of Aboriginal Cultural Heritage in Victoria', *Australian Geographer*, 37(3), 355–374.

Porter, L. (2010), *Unlearning the Colonial Cultures of Planning*, London: Routledge.

Porter, L. (2014), 'Possessory Politics and the Conceit of Procedure: Exposing the Cost of Rights under Conditions of Dispossession', *Planning Theory*, 13(4), 387–406.

Porter, L., H. Matunga, L. Viswanathan, L. Patrick, R. Walker, L. Sandercock, D. Moraes, J. Frantz, M. Thompson-Fawcett, C. Riddle, and T. Jojola (2017), 'Indigenous Planning: from Principles to Practice', *Planning Theory and Practice*, 18(4), 639–666.

Porter, L. and J. Barry (2015), 'Bounded Recognition: Urban Planning and the Textual Mediation of Indigenous Rights in Canada and Australia', *Critical Policy Studies*, 9(1), 22–40.

Porter, L. and O. Yiftachel (2019), 'Urbanizing Settler-colonial Studies: Introduction to the Special Issue', *Settler Colonial Studies*, 9(2), 177–186.

Quijano, A. (2007), 'Coloniality and Modernity/Rationality', *Cultural Studies*, 21(2–3), 168–178.

Rankin, K. (2010), 'Reflexivity and Post-colonial Critique: Toward an Ethics of Accountability in Planning Praxis', *Planning Theory*, 9(3), 181–199.

Robinson, C. (1983), *Black Marxism: The Making of the Black Radical Tradition*, London: Zed Press.

Rose, D.B. (2004), *Reports from a Wild Country: Ethics for Decolonisation*, Sydney: University of New South Wales Press.

Roy, A. (2006), 'Praxis in the Time of Empire', *Planning Theory*, 5(1), 7–29.

Roy, A. (2016), 'Who's Afraid of Postcolonial Theory?', *International Journal of Urban and Regional Research*, 40(1), 200–209.

Roy, A. (2017), 'The Infrastructure of Assent: Professions in the Age of Trumpism', *The Avery Review*, 21, 5–16.

Roy, A. (2019), 'Racial Banishment', in Antipode Editorial Collective (ed.), *Keywords in Radical Geography: Antipode at 50*, Hoboken: Wiley Blackwell, 227–230.

Rutland, T. (2018), *Displacing Blackness: Planning, Power and Race in 21st Century Halifax*, Toronto: University of Toronto Press.

Said, E. (1978), *Orientalism*, New York: Pantheon Books.

Said, E.W. (1993), *Culture and Imperialism*, New York: Alfred A. Knopf.

Simpson, L.B. (2014), 'Land as Pedagogy: Nishnaabeg Intelligence and Rebellious Transformation', *Decolonization: Indigeneity, Education & Society*, 3(3), 1–25.

Simpson, L.B. (2017), *As We Have Always Done: Indigenous Freedom through Radical Resistance*, Minneapolis: University of Minnesota Press.

Smith, L. (2004), *Archaeological Theory and the Politics of Cultural Heritage*, London: Routledge.

Smith, L.T. (1999), *Decolonizing Methodologies: Research and Indigenous Peoples*, Dunedin: University of Otago Press.

Smith, L.T. (2015), 'Imagining our Own Approaches', *Cataloging and Classification Quarterly*, 53(5–6), 473–474.

Spivak, G.C. (1990), *The Post-Colonial Critic: Interviews, Strategies, Dialogues*, edited by S. Harasym, New York: Routledge.

Spivak, G.C. (1999), *A Critique of Postcolonial Reason: Toward a History of the Vanishing Present*, Cambridge, MA: Harvard University Press.

Stanger-Ross, J. (2008), 'Municipal Colonialism in Vancouver: City Planning and the Conflict over Indian Reserves, 1928–1950s', *Canadian Historical Review*, 89(4), 541–580.

Tuck, E. and K.W. Yang (2012), 'Decolonization is Not a Metaphor', *Decolonization: Indigeneity, Education, & Society*, 1(1), 1–40.

Ugarte, M. (2014), 'Ethics, Discourse, or Rights? A Discussion about a Decolonizing Project in Planning', *Journal of Planning Literature*, 29(4), 403–414.

Wahlquist, C. and N. Bucci (2020), '"Chainsaws Tearing through my Heart": 50 Arrested as Sacred Tree Cut Down to Make Way for Victorian Highway', *The Guardian: Australian Edition*, 27 October.

Walker, R., T. Jojola, and D. Natcher (2013), *Reclaiming Indigenous Planning*, Montreal: McGill-Queen University Press.

Watson, V. (2009), '"The Planned City Sweeps the Poor Away ...": Urban Planning and 21st Century Urbanisation', *Progress in Planning*, 72(3), 151–193.

Waziyatawin, A.W. and Yellow Bird, M. (2005), 'Beginning Decolonization', in *For Indigenous Eyes Only: A Decolonization Handbook*, Santa Fe: SAR Press, 1–9.

Williams, R.A. (2020), 'From Racial to Reparative Planning: Confronting the White Side of Planning', *Journal of Planning Education and Research*, doi: 10.1177/0739456X20946416.

Winkler, T. (2018), 'Black Texts on White Paper: Learning to see Resistant Texts as an Approach Towards Decolonising Planning', *Planning Theory*, 17(4), 588–604.

Wolfe, P. (2006), 'Settler Colonialism and the Elimination of the Native', *Journal of Genocide Research*, 8(4), 387–409.

Wynter, S. (2003), 'Unsettling the Coloniality of Being/Power/Truth/ Freedom', *The New Centennial Review*, 3(3), 257–336.

Yiftachel, O. (2017), '"Terra nullius" and planning: Land, Law and Identity in Israel/Palestine', in Bhan, G., S. Srinivas, and V. Watson (eds), *The Routledge Companion to Planning in the Global South*, London: Routledge, 243–254.

Yiftachel, O. (2020), 'From Displacement to Displaceability: A Southeastern Perspective on the New Metropolis', *City*, 24(1–2), 151–165.

12. Questioning the power of normative ethics in planning

Katie McClymont

INTRODUCTION

How does the environment we live in come about? How are decisions taken which shape this? Who holds what influence and power, both over the decision-making process, and in the key capacities of owning land and development capital? Can things be done differently? How can such changes be brought about? These are all questions which are at the heart of considerations about the purpose of planning, critical (if too often unacknowledged) to its daily operations as well as matters of academic reflection and theorising. These questions raise issues of ethics – calling for articulations of both the 'right' or 'better' outcomes, and the 'correct' ways of achieving these: terms which are all contentious and value-laden. In wishing to achieve positive change, planning necessarily has to reflect on issues of normative ethics, but in so doing, questions of the way these reflections are shaped by, and shape, ideas of power are too often overlooked. This chapter aims to bring these two aspects together to explore the relationship between power and normative ethics in planning. Although both are understood as important to planning theory and practice, it is rare that the two ideas are critically brought together to explore this relationship. In so doing, the chapter aims to further debate in both.

Power is both explicit and implicit, and a positive and regressive force in planning practices and the ways in which these practices are understood. Chapters in this volume demonstrate new insight on the range and reach of these debates, but this chapter specifically highlights how the above-mentioned questions of normative ethics are rarely considered alongside these issues and debates about the role of power. It aims to demonstrate how bringing these together in critical dialogue not only highlights how normative judgements have the power to frame and delimit development outcomes, but also how normative thinking, if employed differently, can offer strategies of unsettling and reframing the scope of possible outcomes in planning battles.

To begin to make places differently, the ability to think critically and inclusively about different – and here specifically better and worse – outcomes, is an a priori need. It is not necessary to approach planning issues with a blueprint of a finalised perfected 'city', but to make places better, it is necessary to have a method and vocabulary for envisaging what this better may be (Levitas, 2013). However, to do this we need to better understand the operations of power, who has it, who claims it, who is rendered powerless and how can this be redressed? Putting it another way, these situated ethical judgements which lie at the core of planning decision-making cannot, are not and should not be neutral in light of power. If planning has the ability to bring about changes, this action is an act of power, and therefore the judgements which shape its course cannot be neutral in this respect. To understand this, it is necessary to have a more conceptually focused engagement with notions of power, bringing this into dialogue with debates about the nature and scope of normativity in planning (Winkler, 2018; Winkler and Duminy, 2016; Campbell, 2016; McClymont, 2019).

To address these questions, this chapter first returns to Lukes' (1974) classic thesis on the three faces of power; linking the ideas of how power operates in the third face to more recent debates on discourse and post-politics. It then explores the role of normative thinking in planning theory and practice, engaging with debate about different ways of framing this, noting conflicts over second and first order ideas of ethical judgement, and how this emerges and shapes debates on the attendant concept of 'the public interest' as a normative justification for planning interventions. The chapter then engages with MacIntyre's (1998, 2007 [1981]) work on virtue ethics and Levitas' (2013) *Utopia as Method* to develop a way in which normative reasoning challenges the unspoken structuring of decision-making in a way which acknowledges how this structuring is an inherent part of the third face of power. It then uses this tentative framework to explore a local planning dispute to see how this understanding of power and normative ethical judgement could offer new ways in reframing the debates.

POWER AND NORMATIVE ETHICS

> [I]f only there had been a fight, then something might have been accomplished. (Crenson, 1971: 76–77, cited in Lukes, 1974: 43)

To begin this argument, I am first going to turn to Steven Lukes' classic 'Power: a Radical View'. Although now over forty years old, the text still offers a coherent and compelling account of power, and one which I will argue can complement and enrich some more recent debates about power, discourse and post-politics (see also Chapter 3 by Mäntysalo). By refer-ring back to Lukes' account rather than simply engaging with these more recent theoretical developments, this chapter aims to showcase the relevance of this conceptual engagement for planning practice. By using Lukes' account, the power of nondecisions and shaping of interests – that which cannot even be formulated as an alternative by those in whose interests it may be – can be seen on a trajectory from the more 'standard' understandings of how power and decision-making operate which remains the majority view amongst practitioners (Murphy and Fox-Rogers, 2015; Lauria and Long, 2017; Campbell and Marshall, 2000).

I will not dwell in too much detail on the first and second faces of power, but merely set these out as a useful backdrop to demonstrate the insights of the third face in relation to the more standard way this is conceived in planning practice (as noted above). Lukes first sets out the view of power held by his contemporary pluralists who see power as something observ-able: power operating when, out of two hypothetical groups with different views clash: one gets their way, and one does not. In planning, this could be an appeal decision wherein both parties have valid grounds for their positions, but only one can win in as much as getting the outcome they desire. Lukes then outlines the second face of power; seeing it as a criticism of assumptions inherent within this. Drawing on the work of Bachrach and Baratz (1962, cited in Lukes, 1974), he discusses how the mobilisation of bias works to exclude certain issues from the agenda. Unlike in the first face, where power operates overtly and viably when one group wins and another loses, the second face of power demonstrates that power operates to stop this overt show of itself coming to the fore in the guise of debate or conflict. This is the way the 'game' of decision making is set up, the way certain issues and topics are considered valid concerns, and other ones are not. In this, it can be that certain groups therefore do not lose in the explicit way they would via the framing of the first face, but their wishes/needs are crushed/remain unacknowledged because they were not able to raise them as legitimate concerns in the decision-making forum. In planning terms, from an English perspective, this could be issues which fall outside of the remit of 'other material considerations'. The planning system sets up its own rules (the mobilisation of bias at an institutional level) and then causes and issues which are beyond this set-up are written out of legitimate debate. This in itself is an act of power, normalised and made unquestionable as such, by its institutional and legal status.

Lukes maintains that these two faces are different dimensions of the same understanding of power: power in both of these faces is something observable. Even if objectors' views are deemed beyond the scope of the debate, and therefore invalid, they can still be expressed, are still visible, articulated interests. The third face deals with how power operates in less visible ways and rather than just ruling certain interests and views beyond the scope of debate, power operates to make such interests and views almost unthinkable. Power operates by the powerful 'influencing, shaping or determining his [*sic* – the powerless] very wants ... the most effective and insidious use of power is to prevent such conflict arising in the first place' (Lukes, 1974: 23). It is not even that certain interests are excluded from the debate, certain interests are prevented from either being formed or expressed in any coherent manner. This is demonstrated in Gaventa's classic study of Appalachian mining valleys, in the way that established interests manipulate the consciousness of the newly formed mining associations and emergent unions, not by saying their interests will not be listened to, but instead by reshaping their agendas. This was seen in how the dissemination of 'new information was to shift the emphasis of conflict from relatively costly issues of unemployment, unionization or civil rights to other highly emotive but less costly issues such as moral behaviour, patriotism and religion' (Gaventa, 1980: 109). Power that sets agendas does not merely exclude different opinions and interests, it dissolves and reconstructs them to serve its own ends.

Moreover, this operation of power can be seen at the systemic level, rather than just something employed by individual decision makers: 'the bias of the system is not sustained simply by a series of individual chosen acts, but also most importantly, by the socially structured and culturally patterned behaviour of groups, and practices of institutions' (Lukes, 1974: 21–22). The social structure is formed and maintained so as to shape issues and interests in a given way, and may be seen most readily in ongoing debates about the idea of 'unconscious bias'. This in turn makes some issues actively contentious and contendable, and others invisible and therefore beyond any explicit debate: linking back to the quote opening this section. When topics are structured in a way in which alternative interpretations are readily available, power can operate as explained in its first or second faces. When topics are presented as natural, neutral and unconstestable, power operates covertly, so potential lines of debate and disagreement become invisible; alternative positions unthinkable. Normative ethical thinking can be part of the structures of invisibility, or, as I argue in this chapter, can offer ways of challenging them by the imaginary construction of alternative, better, futures.

This framing of power has links to some post-foundationalist political theorising which draw on ideas of how discourses shape a given 'reality' – or ideological order. The writings of both Chantal Mouffe and Jacques Rancière, drawn on widely in planning theory debates (Metzger, 2018; Metzger et al., 2015) and show how agendas are set and opposition to dominant narratives and forces are shut down, not through open conflict, but through the shaping of agendas and interests. This analysis aligns with an understanding of power which speaks to Lukes' second and third faces. Mouffe's notion of agonism suggests ways in which the voices removed from a debate in the second face could and should be brought back in for the sake of democratic politics. Rancière's concept of the partition of the sensible resonates with the way interests become invisible, even to those who should hold them themselves, within the operation of the third face of power. Certain interests are given a certain position/non-position or 'no part' rendering them unsubstantiated in ways which are beyond just being voiceless and excluded. The problem herein is 'a consensual politics within which it is taken as given who and what matters … and in what ways' (Metzger, 2018: 182).

Understandings of power are key to these analyses, and by outlining their resonance with Lukes' framing, this chapter aims to explore the possible roles of normative ethics within this. As I have argued elsewhere (McClymont, 2019), there are synergies, if unacknowledged, between the motivations of post-political critiques of contemporary planning practices, and claims of 'better'. As Bond and Fougère (2018: 50, emphasis added) argue, in reflecting on their analysis of the local politics of mining and environmentalism in Aotearoa, New Zealand, there is a need for 'renewed attention to the ways in *which the ability to have agency to create progressive change* (whether in or to the planning system, or in any other respect) must be considered in the context of those hegemonic power relations that shape the ability to be heard'. Here, the importance of the links between power and normative thinking are evident. Abilities to shape agendas and deem interests not only relevant but in existence can be judged as repressive or progressive. This judgement is one of normative values, and (either) engaging (or not) with this debate – as a practitioner, academic or activist – is playing a role in arguments about better and worse, right and wrong, is and ought.

This discussion of Lukes' concept of power, and its synergies with some of the post-foundationalist inspired critiques of planning aims to do two things. First, it aims to give a structure to understand how power is largely thought about in planning practice today. From the limited research which engages directly and empirically with the views of practitioners (Murphy and Fox-Rogers, 2015; Lauria and Long, 2017; Campbell and Marshall, 2000), planners still largely see their roles (not surprisingly) as within the system in which they are working. This means it is unlikely that in their practice, the operation of power is conceived of in ways which go beyond Lukes' 'second face': more radical interpretations have the potential to unsettle the system in ways which are hard to reconcile with everyday professional work (see Freitas, 2019 for interesting insights on the balance between radical demands and systematic incorporation). This is important to note, as it demonstrates how one of the more problematic gaps between planning theory and practice comes about – through the limited understanding of the operation of power in much of planning practice, and the dislocated higher-level interpretations of reality expressed in some planning theory (cf. Tasan-Kok et al., 2016). For planning wanting to bring about meaningful change in our cities and societies, it needs to address not only how things are kept off the agenda, but how those things do not even materialise into something that could be substantiated enough to be an agenda point. Secondly, this critique needs to engage with the content of those interests which remain unformed or only partially formed and could offer different ways to reconceive a better outcome, place or society. Critique of present circumstances is implicitly normative, as discussed above (McClymont, 2019); by claiming certain events, relationships and outcomes are negative, a value judgement is placed on these. We need to first explicitly acknowledge this and then critically engage in normative thinking which also explores how things could instead be better, without losing sight of the insights developed from this engagement with ideas of power.

THE POWER OF NORMATIVE ETHICS?

This section first briefly outlines some of the debates in planning around normative ethical thinking, linking back to the discussion about power outlined above. It then goes on to present how the idea of utopia, and specifically Levitas' (2013) idea of 'Utopia as Method' is both relevant and useful here. It demonstrates how utopian imaginations, developed and debated through engagement with specific local understandings, needs and desires can offer alternative ethical formulations of shared futures which challenge the *a priori* shaping of interests, agendas and available positions inherent within the third face of power. The discussion of ethics in planning practice is a key part of planning education and central to codes of practice of professional institutes of planners across the world. Writings wrangle with the relative merits of approaches based on liberal, utilitarian and virtue ethics philosophical framings and how much the situation of norms is shaped by the global position of the thinker (Alexander, 2002; Campbell and Marshall, 2000, 2002; Campbell, 2006, 2012; Moroni, 2018, 2019; Lennon and Fox-Rogers, 2017; Lennon, 2017; Roy, 2008; Winkler and Duminy, 2016; Winkler, 2018).

Within these debates, questions are posed both about the intrinsic value of each epistemological framework, and the use that these ideas have for planning practice and practitioners. Much of the debate has centred on the problems with utilitarianism or the idea of individuals (Moroni, 2018; Campbell and Marshall, 2002) with discussion on virtue ethics, and in particular those expressed through the writing of Alasdair MacIntyre being a more recent addition to the debate (Lennon, 2017; McClymont, 2019). Moreover, this debate raises the key question of the idea of 'the public interest' in planning – a term much criticised but still central to planning's self-justification in practice and theory (Tait, 2016). The idea suggests firstly that there are shared interests within society, and secondly not only can these be identified, but they can be acted upon in planning practice, sometimes guided through systems of representative democracy. This idea of the pursuit and promotion of shared interests to be achieved through planning actions is both central to the idea of normative ethics in planning (searching to implement the 'ought') and highly problematic with reference to the above discussion of Lukes' faces of power. Key to the insidious operation of the third face of power is the (pre)shaping of interests. To identify certain actions and outcomes as being in the interest of the public is a political act, and one which uses and creates power in its operation. It claims a coherent totality of society, in which the units of assessment (the individual, the nation, the common/collective) are predefined, as are the values assigned to certain concepts (equity, sustainability, beauty). If interests are (pre)defined by the dominant forces, this can be done to suppress other possible expressions of the same population's social formation and interests, *and* to then claim that these actions being taken are in line with these pre-shaped interests. The powerful can therefore shape the expression of the interests of the powerless *and* pursue a policy agenda which re-enforces this, and its own value, by claiming to be taking actions which furthers a greater, normative good.

Challenging these ethical formulations is, on the one hand, challenging the power of normative thinking to shape agendas and formulate interests in one given way, but such challenges are also a form of normative thinking themselves. By making these critiques, there is a suggestion that the given way of arguing about or formulating the categories of ethical decision making is flawed, not only factually but ethically. As discussed above in relation to post-politics, outlining something as problematic holds within this judgement an implicit sense that things could be otherwise, and therefore better. Power may be inescapable in the realm of planning judgements and practice, but so too are judgements about the relative values of such practices.

A similar challenge is pursued by authors who question the 'order' of ethical framings and sorts of knowledge relevant for planners (Winkler and Duminy, 2016; Winkler, 2018; Davoudi, 2015). These raise different questions, but ones which comes back, at least in part, to the same core problems. The meaning of both different types of knowledge, and the categories used to define the scope of ethical positions in planning practice are neither universally agreed upon nor neutral. As Winkler (2018: 89) argues 'by neglecting the project of untangling subjective meanings from taken-for-granted social rules, we equally neglect what our planning interventions might mean to others, and what the consequences of different meanings might be for the residents who live and work in the places we plan'. The categories and constructs used by planners in their (ethical) decision making may well differ markedly from how the same issues are understood by a given population. Moreover, this process of decision making may not be viewed as involving ethical judgements so much as judgements based in practice, because 'the system' is too often accepted both on its own terms, and as something which is beyond the scope of questioning. This is not to argue that any individual planning officer has the power to work beyond the laws, policies and procedures that shape their professional life, but that they could have the power to see that the system is created and shaped by human intent, rather than a law of nature.

This outlines how such debates are relevant to practice; the way categories and evidence are used shape the debates and justify certain outcomes in ways which can be very removed from the understandings held by populations who are part of (or maybe subject to) such planning practices.

This can question the role of evidence and how both its power and ethical implications can too often be occluded: 'In the language of evidence-based planning, it implies that the evidence collected by planners can show them what to do, what policies to propose, what spatial strategies to promote or what actions to take. Yet, however thoughtful (knowing *what*) and skilful (knowing *how*) planners may be, they may still not know what *to do* when it comes to moral choices about what course of action to take' (Davoudi, 2015: 321). The way planners' judgements engage with evidence and with values is therefore of the utmost importance when considering issues of both normativity and power. To engage with these challenges, in light of the broader debates about normative ethics and power outlined above, I will turn first to Ruth Levitas' idea of 'Utopia as Method' and then to the work of Alasdair MacIntyre as a way of linking this to normative ethical thinking.

VIRTUE AND UTOPIA: NORMATIVITY RE-IMAGINED?

> The utopian experience disrupts the taken-for-granted nature of the present. (Levitas, 2013: 4)

The concept of utopia is one with which planning has strong associations, for good and for bad. From its roots in the Garden City movement, the idea of planning is fundamentally about imagining a better future with different levels of technical, social or aesthetic detail (Taylor, 1998). As Levitas documents in detail, utopia has received a bad press as either supportive or totalitarianism or a form of unsubstantiated ludicrously wishful thinking – or both. However, she goes on to reconfigure it as a means of productive, normative critique which does not limit or presuppose ideal future states, but instead develops a way of thinking differently: 'Utopia does not simply illustrate the meeting of familiar wants unmet by existing society … [i]t creates a space that enables us to imagine wanting something else, something qualitatively different' (Levitas, 2013: 113). Within this quote, utopian method can be seen as a means of challenging the way the third face of power can shape and trap both the meaning of now and the possibilities of the future. It starts on a basis of critical understanding of the status quo, but draws on the reactions and 'unfilled aspirations' that emerge more broadly from this (Levitas, 2013: 66). These are drawn upon creatively to imagine better, qualitatively different futures. It is the process of this imagining – of utopia as method – which is vital here, rather than the content of any given 'better future society'. Such static blueprints are not the aim of utopia as method – instead they are another fixing of meaning which uses the third face of power to establish its unassailability. This is demonstrated in the way that Forester (2018) identifies the possibility of normative thinking operating as such. In discussing the way planners frame decisions, he states 'planners on this well ordered, rational road have been *captured by an "imaginary"'* (Forester, 2018: 471, emphasis added). When normative thinking becomes a set of pre-prescribed desirable outcomes, it loses the ability to become a way of questioning differently or imagining disruptively – the problem is being 'captured', not the imaginary. This interplay of power and ethics is especially important in the field of planning as a necessarily future-oriented discipline: 'scientific knowledge of the future is not possible, so that our orientation to the future must be informed by socio-cultural ethics, wisdom, imagination and responsibility, and *this is a collective task'* (Levitas, 2013: 130, emphasis added).

It is now necessary to explore how this collective task of shared imagining links to normative ethics in planning. To do so, I suggest that concepts derived from the work of Alasdair MacIntyre's philosophical writings are useful here. This chapter will not expound this at any great length: although MacIntyre's work is not common in normative planning theory, it is debated in relation to ideas of the public interest and ethics in planning (see Lennon, 2017 and McClymont, 2019 for example). The aim here is to demonstrate how normative thinking can both support and challenge power structures, especially those identified in Lukes' (1974) third face. My contention is that underpinning Levitas' (2013) Utopia as Method with a normative ethics framed by MacIntyre's work presents a compelling case for critically thinking about power in planning.

MacIntyre's work is useful as it promotes the importance of normative thinking, but removes appeals to universalising abstracted categories which would pre-frame the limits of legitimate debate. He clearly states, 'there is no higher-order set of principles to which appeal can be made' (MacIntyre, 1998: 245): there is no pre-given set of right answers, defined concepts universally applicable. This ability to go beyond the boundaries of existing categories/ structures does offer something different, raising 'the possibility of asking those questions that most need to be asked' (MacIntyre, 1998: 243); questions which are likely to be locally formed, relevant to context, rather than imported from elsewhere and hence framed by external assumptions and categories which in turn can prefigure the realms of possibility. As discussed in greater depth elsewhere (Lennon, 2017; McClymont, 2019) the idea of 'better' is developed through an assessment of the qualities necessary to excel in a practice, or for a thing to achieve the necessary attributes for it to succeed. In planning, this could involve asking questions about what good (or better) housing, communities or cities look like. These qualities are internal to that practice or thing, rather than being measured by external criteria such as profit, efficiency or quantity. There is scope for such measures to be relevant, but only if relevant to the internal quality of the practice in question. Grounds for judgement are therefore derived, not exclusively but initially from the tradition of that practice: 'the standards are not themselves immune from criticism, but nonetheless we cannot be initiated into a practice without accepting the authority of the best standards realized so far' (MacIntyre, 2007 [1981]: 221). Traditions internal to a practice are therefore a starting point for making normative claims about that practice, and as such hold power – power to set the agenda and to define the scope of relevance. However, this power differs from claims to universal categories of 'freedom' or 'utility' because it is presented as a starting point of discussion of substantive qualities set within a specific context, not an abstracted and imposed framework. Moreover, it is one which challenges the method and rationale of most normative judgements in contemporary society as '(f)or liberal individualism a community is simply an arena in which individuals each pursue their own self-chosen conception of the good life, and political institutions exist to provide that degree of order which makes such self-determined activity possible' (MacIntyre, 2007 [1981]: 227). Assuming alternatively, that judgements should be made collectively, and about substantive qualities rather than freedom of choice, offers ways of normative thinking which are made largely invisible by the decision-making frameworks we currently employ. This has the power to change the terms of debate: 'questions that are thus framed in local terms are understood to have universal import' (MacIntyre, 1998: 246).

Here, the aim is to emphasise the productive synergy between this way of framing questions of normative judgement and the idea of utopia as method. Collectively imagining a better society to come can be part of articulating the value of different practices and in turn challenging the power structures which shape and delimit contemporary debates. By presenting a limited scope of issues worthy – or even possible – of discussion, but moreover presenting this as if it were exhaustive, power operates at its most sublime. Without appeals to the collective, contingent and specific, normative thinking can equally obscure other understandings and therefore reinforce dominant power structures. This relates to conceptions of interest framed by different political positions (Lukes, 1974: 34–35), and whether they are seen as explicitly articulated or manipulated into fitting a given agenda. Conceived of otherwise, normative thinking uncovers this operation of power and gives voice to these myriad alternatives.

This chapter has argued that normative thought can be a force for good; against the insidious operation of power as manifest in Lukes' third face, however, it also notes that it can be part of the problem itself, part of the shaping of agendas which presupposes possibilities and positions which people can take. Normative thinking in planning practice and theory can be the bold presentation of the 'right' way to do things: 'our imagination of planned possibilities has been undermined by the over-confident and seemingly dismissive rhetoric of our own good reasons' (Forester, 2018: 470) therefore simply reflecting the power of who gets to do the planning, their understanding of interests and desired normative outcomes. This, however, is not the only way to engage with normative questions, as the above discussion has endeavoured to demonstrate. Normative debates do not only have to be between set alternatives, fought out in varying degrees of openness, as presented in the two first faces of power: 'a ritual battle whose well defined rules, though unwritten, are widely understood' (Gaventa, 1980: 144). If normative choices are just between the set options of a pregiven agenda – post-political choices – normativity just becomes another cheerleader for the status quo: better or worse shades of what we have at present. Alternatively, if normative thinking can offer possibilities and interests – through utopia as method, and through human flourishing-reformulation practices – it can present a challenge to power's most oblique structures. To explore this further, I now draw on reflections about a case study in Bristol, UK.

BEDMINSTER GREEN: GENTRIFICATION, OVERDEVELOPMENT, GREED, DISPLACEMENT?

This section presents reflections on (proposed) developments and debates about the future of an area in South Bristol known as Bedminster Green, but also incorporating the wider neighbourhood and in particular the shopping area of East Street. This is done to explore the discussion of power and normative ethics outlined above, and to demonstrate the relevance of the framework to planning practice, rather than to present research findings. The information presented here is gathered largely from my own experience of these places, and backed up by other secondary sources. In my teaching, I aim to engage students in 'live' projects wherever possible, and in so doing, I am lucky enough to speak to several community representatives and activists in Bristol. This section therefore aims to illustrate the power of normative ethical thinking, and the way that thinking, reasoning and arguing differently can challenge established power structures or the role they have in bringing about progressive change.

To a certain extent, this exploration is quite questionable as it goes against several of the claims made above. These are my reflections, discussed only in my own head,[1] rather than situated engagement with relevant and diverse others – both about the meaning of the contemporary situation and utopian imaginings of a better shared future. However, it is meant merely as example and invitation: a provocation that even though power shapes the decisions we think can be made, there is also space and scope to think differently, even if this is not immediately apparent. It aims to make these more academic reflections something with which planners can think. These reflections here aim to provoke thinking, rather than present definitive findings based on research case studies. They highlight different ways in which normative thinking could challenge the preconceived boundaries of the acceptable field of debate in which contemporary English planning operates, or to put it another way, to challenge the operations of the third face of power. As highlighted above, I propose these interpretations as the start of a process, not a conclusion.

Bedminster Green is a large area just south of Bristol's city centre, highlighted as an area for extensive redevelopment. It is adjacent to existing residential neighbourhoods and a main, if slightly run-down district high street. There has been disagreement over the last few years about the scale, tenure and design of proposed new housing in the area, with supporters claiming it will increase housing supply in an area/city of great need, and regenerate a fading and run-down shopping parade, and opponents criticising the schemes for their lack of affordability and pressure placed on existing services such as schools, green space and medical facilities, as well as fear of creeping gentrification (Bricks, 2020; Vickers, 2021). In this sense, it is very like many planning disputes across prosperous cities in the United Kingdom if not also across the Global North. Moreover, the 'official' framings of what is at stake in planning terms is shaped by planning law and policy, within the broad remit of 'material considerations' as discussed above.

Within the first face of power, this is a dispute between those in favour, and those against the development, played out through the planning system. Those able to muster the best planning arguments (or at least best planning lawyers) will win. Within the second face, it is possible to see how certain concerns are kept off the agenda – local character, place attachment and independent business, the wish to see the area considered as a whole rather than a piecemeal selection of individual developments and some of the debates about the provision of affordable and/or high-quality residential accommodation. These are beyond the scope framed by the planning system. It deals with applications for development on their own merits on an individual basis, does not differentiate between types of shop or consider the subjective emotional attachment to the way somewhere looks and feels at a given time. These concerns are, however, clearly articulated by the pressure groups campaigning against such developments (WHaM, 2021; Bedminster Green Campaign, 2020), despite not 'counting' as planning grounds. This further supports the continued relevance of Lukes' framework, as the second face of power remains a useful analytical tool here. Objections are not irrelevant; they are made irrelevant by the systemisation of certain values and knowledges as being more important than others and subsequently reified as 'material'. These objections question the proposed outcomes on the grounds that they will be bad for the area, without necessarily having the space, scope or legitimacy to articulate what better could look like here, or why something different may be better. Normative thinking which can challenge this needs to explore how power currently excludes such reformulations by 'suppressing latent conflicts within society' (Lukes, 1974: 57): ones which could restructure or unsettle the way decisions are conceived.

It is harder to express clearly or definitively the way in which the third face of power operates within this scenario, partially because I am neither a local to this site, nor have I undertaken in-depth ethnography here, but also because this face of power is necessarily not something that can be observed in action (Lukes, 1974). However, by following some of the opinions expressed locally, alternatives which are not explicitly promoted can be discerned. Negativity towards the proposed development is expressed in terms of 'greed' (Bedminster Green Campaign, 2020), indicating normative judgements being made about the value of the motivation of actors, something which does not readily sit within planning decision making, but central to much ethical reasoning among the public as well as philosophers promoting virtue ethics. Such normative thinking could shift the realm of the debate, allowing development to go ahead only when the motivations of developers are virtuous and aimed towards the development of substantively good housing and in turn 'constructing and sustaining forms of community directly towards the shared achievement of those common goods without which the ultimate human good cannot be achieved' (MacIntyre, 2007 [1981]: xv). Just how preposterous this seems as a statement indicates how strong the power is of those who make such an argument almost unthinkable. It would mean repositioning debates about housing, and the 'housing crisis' from just a matter of numbers (or 'units') and opening up debate about the role and meaning of housing (Jarvis, 2015; Griffin et al. 2021) and turning instead to questions of quality, security, agency and entitlement, rather than market mechanism to maximise provision. Employing normative thinking to explore what the substantive good of housing should be like, and utopian method to reimagine how this could be brought about, different interests and identities, which previously had no part, could challenge the third face of power.

Other issues raised in the press coverage of the developments include the fears of people, particularly older people, for whom change to the high street may mean the loss of favourite cafes and shops (Vickers, 2021), and of the role of artists in the gentrification of the area (Bricks, 2020). These too hint at substantive values, imaginations of better, but are nevertheless beyond the scope of mainstream planning debate and decision making. Is a good community one which manages change in such a way as not to exclude and alienate those who live locally and could be displaced, emotionally if not physically by redevelopment? Is a good city one in which creative practice is promoted for its own sake, rather than to increase property values in a run-down area – focusing on ways of maintaining and promoting the value of goods internal to artistic practice rather than the external effect of making an area 'cool' and therefore marketable? Reframing debates in such a manner is not merely an academic exercise, but one which could impact on outcomes in the built environment. Moreover, understanding why such debates are not part of mainstream narratives should help reveal the structure of power which frames and limits these choices at a wider level. 'The utopian experience disrupts the taken-for-granted nature of the present' (Levitas, 2013: 4) offering instead grounds for hope, long cited by many as a founding facet of planning (see Inch et al., 2020).

CONCLUSION

> Above all, we need to understand utopia as method rather than a goal, and therefore as a process which is necessarily provisional, reflexive and dialogic. It is always suspended between the present and future, always under revision, at the meeting point of the darkness of the lived moment and the flickering light of a better world, for the moment only accessible through an act of imagination. (Levitas, 2013: 149)

In this chapter I have aimed to show the importance of considerations of power within normative ethics in planning, and how Lukes' three faces remain an important tool for critical analysis in this field, and can productively enter into dialogue with post-foundationalist challenges to the post political. I have argued that utilising ethical framings which draw on MacIntyre's work alongside the idea of utopia as method can produce a contingent, engaged normative ethics which challenges the operation of power in its third face, power which shapes not merely agendas but possibilities. A normative ethical frame, conceived thus, draws on local traditions and imaginations to explore the meaning of better in any given circumstance. It does not appeal to pre-set categories or epistemologies, but instead on understanding the role of developing different ways of thinking about values in society. There will be academic disagreement with some of the categories and concepts developed in this chapter – but that in itself is part of normative debate. It is motivated by belief in a better way of understanding what is better, by starting with engaging with the meanings and traditions of the core ideas and practices in planning such as community, cities and housing. To think about what better might 'look like' in any of these arenas, we need to think about what these such things are, substantively: we need to develop a shared understanding of what, for example, community 'is for' to be able to judge whether certain outcomes are better or worse in this field. This is neither simple nor closed as a process: it suggests that we do this *repeatedly* 'to identify its own incoherences and errors and how then to draw upon the resources of other alien and rival traditions in order to correct these' (MacIntyre, 1998: 251). However, this process of thinking about understandings and imaginings of better is valuable in itself. As Levitas states, '(a)ll utopias are flawed. The focus must be on what will be gained, something that can be glimpsed in different ways' (Levitas, 2013: 215).

To conclude, I wish to reflect more widely on what this means for the possibility of change, and limits of power. Lukes (1974) sees power as operating only when there is a possibility for something to be done differently; '(t)he future, though it is not entirely open, is not entirely closed either' (Lukes, 1974: 54). If no alternative were possible, it would not be an act of power to suppress it. In returning to Appalachia, Gaventa (2019) not only notes the power of Trumpism to shape and define the interest of local communities, but alternately notes the 'subaltern patterns of organizing and resistance' (Gaventa, 2019: 448) which draw on very different normative framings. There are other examples of different ways of doing things in practice, ways which demonstrate the possibility of alternatives, movements or organisations which challenge – or at least qualify – assumptions about the operation of power (Gibson-Graham, 2008; Freitas, 2019).

They show possibilities of better, in situ and right now, not as blueprints in either outcome or method but as the possibility reconfiguring any given scenario. These examples are not abstracted or idealised versions of 'the good', but instead enactments which unlock and disassemble in practice the tyranny of 'there is no alternative'. They are alternative, however fragmented and temporary. As well as demonstrating that there are alternative ways of being, some of these examples demonstrate alternative ways of doing, of engaging, of imagining. Direct (sometimes physical) engagement in development, as suggested in community-led and alternative housing shifts the meaning of housing (Jarvis, 2015; Griffin et al., 2020) – and hence the ground for normative judgement – to something active, and part of a wider understanding of a good life (McClymont and Sheppard, 2019). Additionally, engaging with artistic methods offers links to people's emotional attachments, rather than just reason, as a way of making proposals or changes more meaningful (Buser et al., 2020). Artistic endeavours are a key part of the utopian imagination, as Levitas (2013) demonstrates in her discussion of 'blue' in both visual art and music. Moreover, seeing creative engagements as practices with their own internal goods, rather than a means to something else, shifts and contextualises the normative values put on such practices.

The challenge is to articulate clearly or frame how these might represent something 'better', in a way which is both substantiated and open to debate. This is what I have aimed to demonstrate through the discussion of MacIntyre, and how the lens of power helps to problematise some claims to normative reasoning. Widening the focus from just what is (a) better (development), to *why* is it better asks a normative question which can make present interests which would otherwise be obscured or unformed. If there is a shortage of housing, it can be argued that building new housing is better than not, but asking why we need housing, what qualities of (good) life it supports/fulfils leads to a deeper understanding of its value and purpose, and therefore questions of type, size, cost, design and location. Power can frame interests and options to obscure the formulation of these alternatives. This is a simplistic example, but something which resonates with the wider discussion of Bedminster Green above. Exploring the relationship between power and normative ethics in planning asks questions about the way we think about the future, and the possible or desirable futures on offer. Only through such explorations can better outcomes be envisaged, and the limitations and exclusions of today be rendered visible.

NOTE

1. Apart from some very helpful comments from my colleague Hannah Hickman – and obviously expressed on paper here!

REFERENCES

Alexander, E.R. (2002) 'The Public Interest in Planning: From Legitimation to Substantive Plan Evaluation', *Planning Theory*, 1(3), 226–249.

Bedminster Green Campaign (2020) About Bedminster Green Campaign @properdemocracy /www .facebook.com/properdemocraticplan/, last accessed 16 February 2021.

Bond, S. and Fougère, L. (2018) 'Prising Open the Postpolitical Spaces of Planning Regimes: A Reply to E.R. Alexander', *Planning Theory*, 17(4), 647–652. doi: 10.1177/1473095218799991.

Bricks (2020) Episode 4 – Ben Hartley – Ruderal, 9 December 2020, Available from www.bricksbristol .org/2020/12/episode-4-ben-hartley-ruderal/.

Buser, M., Leeson, L., Rathore, M., Roy, A., and Sabnani, N. (2020) 'Interdisciplinary Research in Rajasthan, India: Exploring the Role of Culture and Art to Support Rural Development and Water Management', *Water Alternatives*, 13(3), 822–842.

Campbell, H. (2006) 'Just Planning: The Art of Situated Ethical Judgement', *Journal of Planning Education and Research*, 26(1), 92–106.

Campbell, H. (2012) '"Planning Ethics" and Rediscovering the Idea of Planning', *Planning Theory*, 11(4), 379–399, doi: 10.1177/1473095212442159.

Campbell, H. and Marshall, R. (2000) 'Public Involvement and Planning: Looking beyond the One to the Many', *International Planning Studies*, 5(3), 321–344.

Campbell, H. and Marshall, R. (2002) 'Utilitarianism's Bad Breath? A Re-evaluation of the Public Interest Justification for Planning', *Planning Theory*, 1(2), 163–187.

Davoudi, S. (2015) 'Planning as Practice of Knowing', *Planning Theory*, 14(3), 316–331. https://doi.org/ 10.1177/1473095215575919.

Forester, J. (2018) 'Hazards of Argumentation: How the Rhetoric of Good Reasons Can Narrow Attention and Undermine Planning Imagination', *Planning Theory & Practice*, 19(4), 469–473.

Fougère, L. and Bond, S. (2018) 'Legitimising Activism in Democracy: A Place for Antagonism in Environmental Governance', *Planning Theory*, 17(2), 143–169.

Freitas, C. (2019) 'Insurgent Planning', *City*, 23(3), 285–305, DOI: 10.1080/13604813.2019.1648030.

Gaventa, J. (1980) *Power and Powerlessness: Quiescence and Rebellion in an Appalachian Valley*. Urbana: University of Illinois Press.

Gaventa, J. (2019) 'Power and Powerlessness in an Appalachian Valley – Revisited' *The Journal of Peasant Studies*, 46(3), 440–456, DOI: 10.1080/03066150.2019.1584192.

Gibson-Graham, J.K. (2008) 'Diverse Economies: Performative Practices for "Other Worlds"', *Progress in Human Geography*, 32(5), 613–632.

Griffin, E., McClymont, K. and Sheppard, A. (2021) 'A Sense of Legitimacy in Low Impact Developments: Experiences and Perspectives of Communities in South-west England', *International Journal of Housing Policy* (REUJ), 22(1), 83–105, https://doi.org/10.1080/19491247.2021.1886027.

Inch, A., Slade, J. and Crookes, L. (2020) 'Exploring Planning as a Technology of Hope', *Journal of Planning Education and Research*, doi: 10.1177/0739456X20928400.

Jarvis, H. (2015) 'Community-led Housing and "Slow" Opposition to Corporate Development: Citizen Participation as Common Ground? Community-led Housing', *Geography Compass*, 9(4), 202–213.

Lauria, M. and Long, M. (2017) 'Planning Experience and Planners' Ethics', *Journal of the American Planning Association*, 83(2) 202–220, DOI: 10.1080/01944363.2017.1286946.

Lennon, M. (2017) 'On "The Subject" of Planning's Public Interest', *Planning Theory*, 16(2), 150–168.

Lennon, M. and Fox-Rogers, L. (2017) 'Morality, Power and the Planning Subject', *Planning Theory*, 16(4), 364–383.

Levitas, R. (2013) *Utopia as Method: The Imaginary Reconstitution of Society*, Basingstoke, UK and New York: Palgrave MacMillan.

Lukes, S. (1974) *Power: A Radical View*, London: Macmillan.

MacIntyre, A. (1998) 'Politics, Philosophy and the Common Good'. In Knight, K. (ed.) *The Macintyre Reader*, Cambridge: Polity, 235–252.

MacIntyre, A. (1999) *Dependent Rational Animals: Why Human Beings Need the Virtues*, London: Duckworth Overlook.

MacIntyre, A. (2007 [1981]) *After Virtue*, London: Bloomsbury Academic.

McClymont, K. (2019) 'Articulating Virtue: Planning Ethics within and Beyond Post Politics', *Planning Theory*, 18(3), 282–299.

McClymont, K. and Sheppard, A. (2019) 'Credibility without Legitimacy? Informal Development in the Highly Regulated Context of the United Kingdom', *Cities*, 97, https://doi.org/10.1016/j.cities.2019.102520.

Metzger, J. (2018) 'Postpolitics and Planning', in Gunder, M., Mandanipour, A., and Watson, V. (eds) *The Routledge Handbook of Planning Theory*, Abingdon and New York, Routledge, 180–193.

Metzger, J., Allmendinger, P. and Oosterlynck, S. (2015) *Planning against the Political: Democratic Deficits in European Territorial Governance*, Routledge: New York.

Moroni, S. (2018) 'The Public Interest', in Gunder, M., Mandanipour, A., and Watson, V. (eds) *The Routledge Handbook of Planning Theory,* Abingdon and New York: Routledge, pp. 69–80.

Moroni, S. (2019) 'Constitutional and Post-constitutional Problems: Reconsidering the Issues of Public Interest, Agonistic Pluralism and Private Property in Planning', *Planning Theory*, 18(1), 5–23.

Murphy, E. and Fox-Rogers, L. (2015) 'Perceptions of the Common Good in Planning', *Cities,* 42(B), 231–241, https://doi.org/10.1016/j.cities.2014.07.008.

Roy, A. (2008) 'Post-Liberalism: On the Ethico-Politics of Planning', *Planning Theory*, 7(1), 92–102, doi: 10.1177/1473095207087526.

Tait, M. (2016) 'Planning and the Public Interest: Still a Relevant Concept for Planners?', *Planning Theory*, 15(4), 335–343.

Taylor, N. (1998) *Urban Planning Theory Since 1945*, London: SAGE.

Tasan-Kok, T., Bertolini, L., Oliveira e Costa, S., Lothan, H., Carvalho, H., Desmet, M., De Blust, S., Devos, T., Kimyon, D., Zoete, J.A., and P. Ahmad (2016) '"Float Like a Butterfly, Sting Like a Bee": Giving Voice to Planning Practitioners', *Planning Theory & Practice*, 17(4), 621–651, DOI: 10.1080/14649357.2016.1225711.

Vickers, H. (2021) 'Bedminster's East Street is Changing for Better or for Worse', *The Bristol Cable*, Issue 24, Jan–March 2021.

Winkler, T. (2018) 'Rethinking Scholarship on Planning Ethics', in Gunder, M., Mandanipour, A., and Watson, V. (eds) *The Routledge Handbook of Planning Theory*, Abingdon, UK and New York, Routledge, 81–92.

Winkler, T. and Duminy, J. (2016) 'Planning to Change the World? Questioning the Normative Ethics of Planning Theories', *Planning Theory*, 15(2), 111–129.

WHaM (2021) Windmill Hill and Malago Community Planning Group, www.whambristol.org.uk/, last accessed 16 February 2021.

PART II

SITUATING POWER IN PLANNING

13. The public good and the power of promises in planning

Andy Inch

INTRODUCTION: EXHAUSTED PROMISES AND THE PROBLEM OF THE PUBLIC GOOD

In late capitalist societies, state and professional institutions continue to justify the exercise of planning powers through appeals to the public good:[1] the idea is that public intervention in land and property development can secure benefits in the wider interests of society. However, the authority of planners to speak as experts and the power of the state to act on behalf of any such interest have both been weakened by successive waves of criticism. From at least the 1960s onwards increasingly mistrustful publics have demanded a more direct say in decisions that affect their lives. From the political left, critics have argued that claims to plan for the public good frequently provide cover for exploitation, dispossession and the exclusion of minority groups (Sandercock, 1998).

Perhaps more damagingly, over recent decades planning has been subject to persistent attack from advocates of a neoliberal order who construe any attempt to deliberately steer societal change as an anachronism that distorts economic competition, stifles market freedoms and blocks entrepreneurial pathways to prosperity (Brown, 2015: 221). This has motivated efforts to reform the institutions and practices of state planning with a strong emphasis on limiting intervention in private property rights, effectively redefining the public good as the facilitation of market-led investment and development whilst denying any more expansive basis for public action.

The power of claims to serve the public good also face significant new challenges in an era marked by populist political challenges to democratic institutions and the rule of experts. Antagonism and political polarisation pose with renewed clarity the challenges of constructing any unitary 'public' whose shared interests might be articulated and acted upon.

As a result, the legitimacy of planning's claims to act for the public good frequently appears weak, part of a wider disenchantment with the idea that people can collectively shape their shared futures. At the same time, however, societies globally are facing a conjunction of major crises, from post-COVID-19 pandemic recovery to spiralling inequality and the climate emergency, that require new forms of planned intervention in response to the existential threats to life posed by extractive and predatory models of development. I therefore take the bind of an urgent need for concerted collective action and a concurrent exhaustion of faith in any collective power to act as a defining feature of the contemporary historical moment.

The impasse that this bind generates is related to the protracted unravelling of the neoliberal settlements which have framed dominant understandings of the good across many societies since the 1970s (Brown, 2015). Jens Beckert (2020: 322–323), for example, argues the promises of a good life on which commitment to neoliberal ideas was founded now also seem 'largely exhausted … the credibility of neoliberal imaginaries vanished' without the outlines of any successor regime having come into focus.

Moving beyond this impasse, tackling major societal crises and renewing planning as a technology of anticipatory governance all entail the 'need to resurrect a work-able notion of the public good' (Sandercock and Dovey, 2002: 152). Mindful of the problematic history and uses of the public good in planning, however, my intention is not to advocate any straightforward rehabilitation of state or professional power. Instead, in the next section I will argue for a critical engagement with the forms of power at work when claims are made about the public good in planning. I then draw particular attention to the centrality of promissory power and legitimacy in planning, founded on the ways promised futures help secure consent to be governed (Beckert, 2020). Suggesting its role and significance has been rather overlooked in planning debates, I illustrate my argument through an analysis of promissory power at work in a case that Jönsson and Baeten (2014: 55) have described as 'emblematic of neoliberal planning practices': the ongoing controversies around Donald Trump's golf course developments in the north-east of Scotland. Overall, I argue that this extreme case helps illuminate key challenges for refounding the promise of the public good in and beyond the impasse of the exhausted neoliberal present.

PLANNING AND THE PROBLEM OF THE PUBLIC GOOD

The continued status of terms like the public good, public interest and common good as key words despite pervasive criticism and the fact professionals seemingly struggle to define them (Slade et al., 2018) suggests they signify a central problematic for planning theory and practice. This is often discussed with reference to David Beetham's assertion that abandoning the concept of the public interest would mean tackling the issues it defines under another name (see Campbell and Marshall, 2002; Lennon, 2016). Accepting this, I want to suggest an understanding of the public good as a concept operating 'under erasure'[2] – a category we continue to use, but provisionally, whilst at the same time seeking to critically deconstruct, challenge, change and ultimately even surpass.

My aims in placing the concept of the public good 'under erasure' are threefold: first, to recognise the important space the term delineates without granting it any essential meaning. Second, as a reflection of contemporary realities. The idea that planning serves the public good is frequently questioned, particularly within neoliberal regimes sceptical of regulation and state direction of futures. Finally, because it recognises the term's constitutive political instability and ambivalences. If the public good somehow remains a necessary category for planning, it also remains deeply problematic. Its promises are always subject to capture and any attempt to rehabilitate its power must remain suspicious of the problematic baggage it carries and the exclusions on which its operation has often been founded. At the same time, however, power's need to legitimise decisions through appeals to the public good may also create openings through which dominant practices can be contested.

Placing the idea of the public good under erasure leads me away from any attempt to establish an abstract definition or justification for its use in the sometimes idealist terms of liberal political philosophy. Instead, accepting that contestation over the purposes and limits of legitimate public intervention is inescapable in capitalist societies, I prefer to see the term's nebulous, shapeshifting and malleable qualities as its defining feature (Tait, 2016). In this sense, I see the public good not as a fixed form but a central discursive stake in ongoing power struggles over the meaning and purpose of planning and development, invoked to both question and legitimise the authority to make decisions across various sites where it is recognised as a necessary justification. Following a broadly post-foundational understanding I therefore see the public good as an empty signifier that planning and governance processes work to give meaning.

The goal of political struggles over the purposes of planning is therefore to secure, sustain or challenge the dominance of articulations of the public good. This positions power relations at the centre of the debate, requiring analysis of the configurations of power and knowledge through which claims to the public good are recognised and come to be accepted as legitimate. At present, there seem to be two broad approaches to the question of power in existing literature on the public good in planning.

Critical scholarship has been more explicitly concerned with power as a distorting influence, exploring how the public interest justification is used to mask the naked operation of capital or obfuscate harms, exclusions and oppressions. This repressive or corrupting conception of power operating under the cover of the public good has been drawn upon to evaluate both the failings of particular articulations of the public interest and to question the wider (im)possibility of constituting either unitary publics or collective interests in pluralist societies (Davidoff, 1965; Sandercock, 1998). On the other hand, those seeking to rehabilitate the public interest have tended to explore conditions through which the power of planning to make 'situated ethical judgements' about the public interest can be restored as a legitimate form of authority (Campbell 2006; Lennon, 2016).

Reflecting wider debates in planning theory, this scholarship often distinguishes between procedural and outcome-based justifications for planning in the public interest. The former rests claims to legitimate authority on a just process that draws together the publics affected by a given issue and seeks to ensure fair deliberation in decision-making. The latter founds its claims on the outcomes of decision-making, sometimes entailing calls to restore trust in the judgements of representatives, experts and state institutions to determine the nature of the good.

In practice the authority of planning processes typically rests on a messy combination of both procedural and outcome-based sources of legitimacy, each playing an important role in justifying the uses of planning powers (and where their absence may generate legitimation crises). The realisation of either also poses distinct but equally irresolvable challenges, reflecting the essentially contested and undecidable nature of public decision-making. In the rest of this chapter, whilst continuing to hold the public good 'under erasure', I want to suggest that planning theoretical debates might usefully be supplemented by focusing on a third source of authority, based on what Jens Beckert (2020) calls promissory legitimacy.

INTRODUCING PROMISSORY POWER AND LEGITIMACY

Beckert (2020: 318) suggests that conceptions of the legitimacy of political authority should be expanded beyond established understandings of input (procedural) and output (outcome)-orientated justifications to incorporate what he calls promise-orientated or promissory legitimacy: 'that political authority gains from the credibility of promises with regard to future outcomes that political (or economic) leaders make when justifying decisions'. For Beckert

(2020) promissory legitimacy relates to what we might call promissory power and a wider need to account for the important but under-examined role perceptions of the future play in sustaining or remaking social and economic order.

Though there can be no facts about the future, actors' expectations, their fantasies, aspirations, desires and fears nonetheless play a significant role in shaping continuity and change over time. Future imaginaries therefore play an important and often under-examined role in bridging the constitutive uncertainties that define an unknowable future, coordinating action and contributing to the realisation of ways of life or political projects (Beckert, 2016). When such promises cease to be convincing, however, Beckert (2020) argues that the courses of action they justify cease to persuade people and the legitimacy of political systems suffers as a result.

To illustrate his argument Beckert (2020) suggests that the contemporary crisis of neoliberalism rests in part on the undermining of its promises of reform. He argues that promissory legitimacy played a distinctive role in establishing and sustaining the always contested and contingent neoliberal settlements that took shape from the 1970s onwards and which became truly hegemonic across the global north in the 1990s and 2000s as versions of neoliberal common-sense came to be accepted across the mainstream political spectrum (see also Chapter 20 by Marzukhi).

In this reading, neoliberal hegemony always rested in part on the expectations of future affluence it promised people (for example, through the promise of expanded homeownership in the United Kingdom, North America or Australia). Whilst versions of neoliberalism remain the default setting in many states globally, Beckert (2020) argues its legitimacy is now in question and that its promissory energies appear increasingly exhausted in the global north, not least since uneven development has entrenched inequalities so that the credibility of neoliberal promises now rings increasingly hollow (for example, to increasing numbers of the precariously housed left behind by years of rising housing costs). For Beckert (2020), the exhaustion of these promises contributes to various forms of political discontent that have destabilised the post-political regimes that prevailed in the heartlands of late capitalism before the 2008 financial crisis.

If there can be no facts about the future and fictional expectations play a key role in shaping assumptions, then how we feel about the future matters too. For Lauren Berlant (2011: 49) promises of the good life provide resources for surviving the 'impasse of living in the overwhelmingly present moment' by orientating people towards optimistic possibilities. However, attachments to such optimistic desires are always ambivalent and can be experienced and felt in multiple different ways (as hope, fear, anxiety, etc). Optimistic attachments can all too readily become 'cruel' when they persist in 'compromised conditions of possibility' (Berlant, 2011: 24) and Berlant pays particular attention to the dangers of remaining attached to promises in situations where there is little prospect of their being realised.

Berlant's reading of the ways clusters of promises act as magnets, sustaining people in ongoing relations with an 'extended present', potentially offers a corrective to Beckert's (2020) more categorical declaration of the exhaustion of neoliberal promises. Rather than simply losing their power to enchant, it suggests the attraction of promises may unravel only gradually, following potentially protracted periods of disenchantment.

The idea of promissory legitimacy supplements rather than supplanting existing understandings of input- and output-orientated legitimacy and their role in producing, sustaining and justifying the authority to govern. However, it usefully draws attention to a perhaps overlooked dimension of future-orientated, cultural power and the role it plays in securing and sustaining hegemonic understandings of the good. Below I go on to argue that promissory power (and legitimacy) have also been under-examined in debates around the public good in planning. Although Beckert (2020) takes the legitimacy of an entire conjunctural settlement as his focus, in the rest of this chapter I will explore how the idea of promissory power might help to reframe understandings of the seemingly fragile legitimacy of the public good in planning.

PROMISSORY LOGICS OF PLANNING

I am not the first to suggest planning and urban development might be productively analysed through the lens of either fictional expectations or promises. Rachel Weber (2021: 504) explores how 'urban governance rests on a foundation of expectancy and speculative future-thinking' orientated towards ever-expanding asset values, where constitutive uncertainties of capitalist urban development are managed by calculative practices, market devices and interactions amongst market actors that serve to stabilise expectations. Simone Abram and Gina Weszkalnys (2013: 3) and other contributors to their edited volume take 'the idea of the promise of a planned future at the heart of much planning activity' as a point of departure to explore how the power of plans is premised on frequently elusive promises of a better future. As a result, they argue planning can be conceived as 'a kind of compact between now and the future, a promise that may be more or less convincing to the subjects of planning, and more or less actualized' (Abram and Weszkalnys, 2013: 9).

Conceptually, Abram and Weszkalnys (2013) draw on linguistic philosophy to explore parallels between promises and plans as illocutionary speech acts, performative statements that are more than simple assertions, producing obligations and expectations about future actions on the part of both promisers and promisees. This parallel allows them to link the histories of planning to other foundational technologies, like promissory notes, that have been used to project control over the open but unknowable future inaugurated by modernity. The future-orientation suggested by the idea of the promise (where promises commit actors to a future course of action), whilst intrinsic to planning has not always been a central focus of scholarly attention in the field (Isserman, 1985; Connell, 2009). In particular I don't think its full implications for the forms of power involved in conceptions of the public good have been fully or explicitly addressed.

Acknowledging the promissory structure of planning frames situated judgements about the public good as both frequently dilemmatic and contested decisions about the future consequences of present actions, and also as performative utterances that seek to create (more or less) reasoned expectations about what could or should be in the future. For John Searle (1964) promises are 'institutional facts', existing within a system of rules that give rise to obligations, commitments and responsibilities. The existence of this system (sometimes called a convention or game) effectively enables statements of fact about what is ('they made a promise') to entail normative commitments about what ought to be ('they ought to keep their promise'). Conceived in this way, might planning systems too be imagined as (more or less successful) ways of creating 'institutional facts', capable of bridging the problematic gap between knowledge of 'what is' and situated judgements about 'what ought to be' (Campbell, 2012), binding actor networks into shared courses of action?

Plans (and decisions) seek to 'normalise' (Connell, 2009) the future, projecting paths through constitutive uncertainties about what is yet-to-be so that actors can reasonably expect to know how things will change. However, the best laid plans 'gang aft agley'.[3] They are always prone to failures, lapses and slippages due to the unforeseen and often unavoidable vicissitudes of time and the obduracy of material change. Taking seriously its promissory dimensions leads Abram and Weszkalnys (2013) to focus on the limits of planning as a future-orientated technology of power. The scope for gaps to emerge between the hopes, desires or fears articulated in plans and what comes to be is only increased by the complexity and mutability of the relational webs through which they operate. Judgements about the public good rarely result in the neat resolution of conflict, generating scope for ongoing political turbulence and challenge as repressed political energies resurface. As a result, like promises themselves, the future-orientated commitments in plans are frequently broken and always shrouded in uncertainty, perhaps particularly under neoliberal regimes where implementation relies so heavily on potentially volatile market dynamics.

Constitutive uncertainty about future outcomes heightens the importance of trust relations in planning (Tait, 2011). Planning systems, like promising as an institution, effectively operate on trust that promises to uphold the public good are offered in good faith and that every effort will be made to honour them. This creates considerable challenges for securing the legitimacy of both planning activity and the activity of planning. Where trust is absent or actors are prepared to deliberately misuse it, whether by making false promises or later reneging on commitments, there may be both direct consequences for promisees but also longer-term implications for the promiser and the legitimacy of the institution of promising.

PROMISSORY POWER AND PERSUASIVE STORYTELLING

Considering planning as a technology of promissory power may therefore help to focus attention on some key challenges involved in planning for the public good, including the future-orientation of 'situated ethical judgements', the concomitant challenges of dealing with uncertainty and the importance of trust. Beckert's (2020: 319) focus on promissory legitimacy also, however, presupposes a different meaning of promissory power as a persuasive force, generating compelling fictional imaginaries that help coordinate action by securing consent to ruling ideas and regimes since:

> By projecting their desires and fears regarding future events into these imaginaries, actors can cope with the uncertainty of the future and at the same time contribute to shaping this future.

For present purposes, this raises important questions about the role of promissory power in shaping how claims to the public good in planning come to be believed.

Judgements about the public good are often presented in quite sober terms as reasoned evaluations. But less focus has been placed on what makes arguments about the good persuasive, including the emotional and affective resonances implied by any attempt to shape the future. Plans seek to mobilise positive feelings, channelling optimism about the future. Their power is rooted in their ability to 'grip' people, shaping expectations and motivating action.

Throgmorton's (2003) exploration of planning as persuasive storytelling about the future is salutary in placing such power dynamics at the heart of contemporary planning work. He charges planners with the task of becoming persuasive storytellers. However, the idea of planning agencies as the authors of persuasive fictions may risk over-stating their power. For a start under neoliberal regimes planning often operates as a largely regulatory activity assessing the projects, and promises, of prospective developers. More generally, if societies produce dominant (if always contested) fictional images of the future, such as those Beckert (2020) identifies with neoliberalism, we must also consider how the persuasive power of plans is shaped by their fit with wider images of the good life. As Gunder's (2014) Lacanian psycho-analysis of power in planning suggests, the fantasies that sustain the work of planning agencies are always over-determined by larger ideological fictions.

In this sense we might identify dominant promises in any given culture as ideological fantasies that acquire what geographer Richard Peet (2002) describes as hegemonic depth and weight, their effectiveness judged by the extent to which they become accepted as everyday understandings. Plans and projects which align with such promises will resonate with people but anything that runs against the grain of a dominant common-sense is likely to seem out of place. Assessments of the public good in planning inevitably occur within such contexts and situated judgements about the changes they promise reflect the depth and weight of prevailing conceptions of the good.

Whilst this should not be taken to imply that planners' situated judgements (or persuasive stories) can be somehow read off from broader hegemonic formations, it is a reminder that they are not made by free-standing liberal individuals, impartial experts rationally weighing up disinterested facts, or through localised instances of inter-personal deliberation that can be bracketed off from wider social mores. Instead, paying attention to promissory power requires analysis attuned to the complex ways cultural forms of power permeate hopes, aspirations and expectations.

In this section I have argued that the idea of promissory power may contribute to understandings of planning's problematic relation to the public good by centring attention on the ways claims to the public good seek to shape expectations about an uncertain future. I will now turn to a notorious case of broken promises to further explore how promissory power can be used to understand the contested legitimacy of neoliberal planning for the public good in Scotland.

SHIFTING SANDS, BROKEN PROMISES

It sounds like the set up for a joke: 'did you hear the one about the president who promised the earth and tried to hold back the tide?' More seriously William Walton (2018) has described it as a 'great planning disaster' because of the way processes were bent for a high-profile, celebrity property developer promising to build a golf course and tourism resort 'of a scale not previously seen in the United Kingdom' (DPEA, 2008: 215). The proposal contravened plans and involved the almost certain destruction of a beautiful, protected dune system on a remote stretch of coast in north-east Scotland.[4] The trade-off presented was therefore a familiar one: damage to a sensitive natural environment in exchange for massive, but far from certain, economic investment. The speculative promises won out. Having seduced local and national political elites, they were afforded determining weight by a planning system that saw economic growth as an overriding priority and effectively equated development with the public good.

Fast forward through eleven years of persistent controversy to late 2019. The golf course has been built. Stabilising works have damaged the dynamic qualities that made the dunes worthy of protection but most of the promised jobs and investment have not materialised. Still, the local authority is doubling down on the deal. They again vote against the provisions of their own development plan, this time to grant permission for the building of a second golf course at the resort and then for 550 houses to be built.

The planning officer presents this as a step towards realising what was promised in the original proposal, its implementation delayed first by the global financial crash of 2008 and then the oil price collapse of 2014 which hit Aberdeenshire's offshore petroleum-based economy hard. Others are not so sure. A total of 2,921 objections are received against the housing proposal, including a petition with 18,722 signatories. One local councillor, Martin Ford, who had stood against the initial proposal refuses to vote this time. He argues that 'Aberdeenshire Council's standing and reputation had been damaged by being associated with the site owner', Trump International Golf Links Scotland (TIGLS) (Aberdeenshire Council, 2019).

In December 2020 the dunes formally lose their status as a Site of Special Scientific Interest (SSSI), prompting an ecologist who had advised TIGLS to tell a national newspaper:

> They should have to sign up to deliver what's in their proposal … That's where the Trump Organisation have let Scotland down. They have not delivered in terms of their economic promises. That frustrates both sides of the debate. (Quoted in Paterson, 2020: paragraph 9)

USES AND ABUSES OF THE PUBLIC GOOD IN SCOTLAND'S NEOLIBERAL PLANNING REGIME

So what can this long running saga of unfulfilled promises tell us about promissory power, legitimacy and the public good in planning?

The original controversy speaks to many key themes in existing accounts of the public good in planning. Most obviously it offers further proof (if any were needed) of the manifold ways power seeks to bends processes and outcomes to its will. From a critical perspective, the public good can seem little more than an 'alibi' (Abram and Weszkalnys, 2013:10), providing convenient cover for the naked pursuit of elite interests.

This was most apparent in the ways procedures were circumvented after the initial planning application for the golf course and resort was refused on the casting vote of Martin Ford, then chair of the council's Infrastructure Services Committee. Rather than accepting the decision as the legitimate outcome of established institutional processes and exercising their right to appeal against refusal of planning permission, TIGLS immediately reissued threats to pull their investment to an alternative site in Ireland unless it was reversed. Threats and promises have a lot in common, both are performative speech acts that aim to shape future expectations. Although they feel morally distinct, it can sometimes be hard to distinguish between them. The power of investors and developers to trade with public authorities through both promises and threats has been a prominent feature of neoliberal spatial politics.

In this case back channels of influence were quickly opened at the highest level, including to then First Minister of Scotland Alex Salmond (Wightman, 2011). In a highly unusual move, the Scottish Government then 'called in' the application before the decision could be formally registered, effectively unmaking the decision so that they could consider the application anew themselves. The alacrity with which senior members of the Scottish Government moved to open channels of communication with TIGLS (which was only fully revealed later through freedom of information requests) and the technicality on which the application was 'called in' combined to create a strong impression of institutional processes designed to uphold the public good being hurriedly bypassed. The promises were too big and the threats too real to allow due process to prevail. The decision to approve the application following a subsequent public inquiry surprised no-one and seemed to simply confirm what Libby Porter (2014) condemns as the 'conceit of procedure'. It was, after all, made by the same ministers who had engineered the extraordinary call-in in the first place.

Forums like council committees and public inquiries, where evidence is deliberated over before decisions are reached play an important role in ensuring procedural legitimacy for decisions. They are designed to enable the performance of due democratic process and scrutiny in accountable ways, including through formal roles and rituals of staging that entail the (uneven) recognition of various actors' rights to be involved in decision-making processes. In this way, however, they reflect the ambivalences of appeals to the public good. Democratic processes are seen to be required but need to be contained and therefore often function in tokenistic ways. If Martin Ford's casting vote illustrated that such procedures can at times threaten to disrupt the claims of the powerful in the name of the public good, the events which followed revealed all too clearly how they can be ignored when politically valued outcomes are threatened.

SITUATING JUDGEMENTS ABOUT PROMISED FUTURES

Procedural requirements to perform an assessment of the public good did nonetheless oblige local and then national planners and decision-makers to weigh up evidence about the prospective costs and benefits of the proposed development over time, and across various spatial scales from the local to the national. As a result it is also possible to see in this case the dilemmas involved in making situated judgements about an uncertain future. Such weighted assessments are a particularly pronounced feature of the discretionary planning systems operating across the United Kingdom where plans are not binding, and decisions are made on the merits of individual proposals brought forward by prospective developers.

Martin Ford's (2011: 46) own written account of the case provides a relatively rare, first-person reflection from the perspective of a local councillor placed in an 'extraordinary' decision-making role in this system. His summary of the decision councillors faced thoughtfully acknowledges some of the distinctive challenges involved in arriving at judgements in contexts where there can be no facts about the future and incommensurable values need to be measured against one another:

> Ultimately, the judgement councillors had to make was whether the benefits that could reasonably be expected in Aberdeenshire and Scotland outweighed the environmental damage that would be caused if the resort was built ... it was partly a measure of the relative importance of very different things to fourteen councillors acting as representatives of the wider public.

During the public inquiry considerable weight was placed on technical evidence, including an economic assessment prepared for the Council who had come out as staunch supporters of the application. Although there are necessarily limits to evidence-based policy-making about the inherently uncertain future impacts of present decisions, technical studies often seem at risk of being taken as 'facts' with the potential to predict the future.

The assumptions underlying technical assessments can be hard for non-experts to scrutinise and may therefore be seen to obscure decision-making by rendering technical what are ultimately political value judgements. Doubts were persistently raised by objectors about the projected scale of the economic benefits promised by the development and there are clearly significant incentives for those promoting development to talk up the potential benefits of schemes in the hope of influencing decision-makers. Academic studies suggest there may be significant 'optimism biases' systematically built into the professional projections produced to support proposals (Flyvbjerg, 2013).

Scottish Government planners acknowledged that the prospective economic benefits were subject to considerable uncertainty and that pursuing them would involve breaking the obligations implied by the SSSI designation (DPEA, 2008). Their recommendation to approve the development also therefore involved an investment of trust in the promises being made by TIGLS.

BROKEN, FALSE OR INFELICITOUS: HOW CAN WE TRUST IN PROMISES?

Ultimately the economic forecasts that informed the initial decision remain unproven since the proposed development has not materialised. Estimates of the investment that would be generated nevertheless proved to be powerful fictional constructs, influential in shaping the expectations of decision-makers if not in predicting future events.

The fact the proposed development remains unbuilt renders all too clear the weaknesses of a market-led planning regime that has effectively handed promissory power over to those promoting projects and which frequently lacks effective powers of enforcement to ensure that promises are kept. Working with a non-profit organisation in Scotland called *Planning Democracy* over the last ten years this is a frequent and recurring complaint of community groups, generating significant suspicion and mistrust amongst the publics whose interests the planning system claims to serve (see Yellowbook, 2017). Many become suspicious of the perverse incentives that exist for developers to over-promise, relatively safe in the knowledge that processes for monitoring and evaluating the implementation of proposals are weak. There is also a relative lack of available sanctions where promised benefits do not materialise, regardless of how this might be gradually undermining the legitimacy of the planning system amongst affected publics.

William Walton (2018) points to the way reforms to the planning system in Scotland, driven by neoliberal concerns that existing regulatory requirements were a barrier to development, have exacerbated these problems by simultaneously reducing scrutiny of proposals and the resources required to ensure promises are kept. To prevent further great planning disasters he suggests a need to rethink planning consents as a form of legal contract. In terms discussed earlier, this might be seen as a call to strengthen the power of planning decisions as 'institutional facts', binding actors to their promises.

Based on Trump's past behaviour as a property developer, Walton (2018) also questions whether the trustworthiness of an applicant for planning permission should be explicitly considered.[5] Linked to the long-standing evasion of questions of land ownership in planning (Krueckberg, 1995), the identity of landowners and developers has not traditionally been seen as a valid land-use planning concern in Scotland. This has effectively excluded important questions from the planning system's working definition of the public good, leading to a studied (and perhaps naïve) default presumption that applicants will act in good faith.

As Abram and Weszkalnys (2013) recognise, constitutive uncertainties about the future mean it can be hard to determine why planning promises go unfulfilled or, in the term they borrow from J.L. Austin, prove infelicitous. However, they also acknowledge the importance of being able to assess whether a promise is being made in good faith, and whether genuine efforts have been made to fulfil the obligations it entails. Notorious both for his 'alternative' relationship to the truth and boasts about doing whatever it takes to get his way in negotiations (Leonhardt and Thompson 2017), the involvement of Donald Trump in this case renders these questions in particularly stark terms. Were the promises that so seduced decision-makers sincere? Could they have been cynically broken or are they the unhappy outcome of always uncertain development processes? Might they yet be honoured (and would that still be judged in the public interest)?

WHAT MAKES PROMISES PERSUASIVE?

In his account of the initial decision made by the Infrastructures Services Commission, Martin Ford (2011) is careful to clarify how his thinking was guided by the legal and institutional logics that frame what is and is not considered a valid planning consideration in Scotland. He recognises that 'the scale of the application and the combination of on-going press coverage, strong objections and an intransigent applicant with vocal supporters, all put pressure on Aberdeenshire Council' (Ford, 2011: 41) but seeks to bracket these considerations out. The 'extraordinary' events that subsequently unfolded, however, show promissory power overwhelming faith in established planning procedures.

This begs the question of what made TIGLSs clearly speculative promises so persuasive to decision-makers? Optimistic projections of potential economic benefits were found to be credible and afforded determining weight in decision-making within a wider context, marked by 'a generalised belief that development is beneficial' (Jönsson, 2014: 233). It seems clear they resonated with powerful imaginaries that various actors and institutions were predisposed to value.

Within the Aberdeenshire region, O'Sullivan (2018: 243) identifies 'raw civic boosterism' amongst local business lobbies, premised in part on the desire to diversify a regional economy whose prosperity is heavily reliant on the oil and gas industries. This was powerfully reinforced by a vociferous local media who fostered a febrile atmosphere, vilifying those who voted against the proposal as 'traitors'.

Nationally, the reforms to the planning system in Scotland discussed above sought to foster a culture that was 'open for business' and would actively facilitate development (Inch, 2018). As Jönsson and Baeten (2014) persuasively argue, the willingness of a compliant government to yield to TIGLS's threats illustrates many of the key features of neoliberal planning. Under neoliberal rule, promissory power has been largely yielded to private enterprise and the seeming weakness of states and public authorities in the face of footloose global capital has been a defining feature of the entrepreneurial remaking of spatial governance.

Even before his divisive term of office in the White House all of this was powerfully embodied in the figure of Trump as a global, celebrity entrepreneur (Jönsson and Baeten, 2014). Although it elicited almost equally strong opposition from those who saw it as brash, gaudy and untrustworthy, the Trump 'brand' infused the proposal with a particular atmosphere and a charismatic power, resonating with hegemonic neoliberal imaginaries of elite wealth creation and the attraction of high net-worth tourists as a pathway to prosperity. These promises of an affluent future clearly seduced business and political elites. Organisations including VisitScotland and the Scottish Council for Development and Industry were quick to extol the proposal as an exemplar of 'the vision and innovation that will be required if Scotland is to grow in reputation and success as a tourism destination for recreation and business' (DPEA, 2008: 111).

In this way the case illustrates how situated judgements are always over-determined by the wider cultural contexts in which they are made and the imaginaries circulating within them. Certain promises are always likely to resonate with dominant or powerful ideas, lending them a persuasive power and affective grip that acts on and through peoples' understandings of the good, their aspirations and feelings about the future.

BEYOND THE CRUEL PROMISES OF NEOLIBERAL PLANNING?

In their report on the public inquiry in late 2008, government-appointed planners suggested that 'if developed, we find that the economic and social benefits could only be audited in 7–10 years, while the adverse environmental effects would build from the start of construction' (DPEA, 2008:215). What then does the decision to grant further permissions in 2019, despite the fact that only a fraction of the projected economic benefits had materialised, tell us about the promissory power of neoliberal planning?

It might be interpreted as a kind of path-dependence. Once they had conceded the principle of the development and the damage to the site's environmental qualities was done, the council was locked into its relationship with TIGLS, however infelicitous. But might it not also be interpreted, following Berlant (2011), as an increasingly cruel attachment to an optimistic promise of future affluence whose realisation looks increasingly improbable? The idea of diversifying an economy reliant on oil and gas through high-end luxury tourism, itself premised on carbon-intensive air travel and the hope that benefits from global wealth inequalities would trickle into a regional economy, never looked a great bet to many (to say the least). From the vantage of mid-2021 and a global pandemic that has shut down tourist economies it surely seems even less so, especially if Scotland is going to take promises to 'end our contribution to climate change by 2045' seriously (Scottish Government, 2020a).

Donald Trump's misadventures in Aberdeenshire offer a particularly vivid illustration of the ways the public good has been reworked under a neoliberal planning regime where development has come to define the public good to the detriment of public trust and therefore the legitimacy of a planning system. There are some tentative signs that governmental aspirations may now be moving beyond the overwhelming fixation with 'sustainable economic growth', recognising a need to begin to measure well-being and to struggle for just transitions (Scottish Government, 2020b). Still, it seems too early to tell whether the promises of neoliberal planning are truly exhausted. The struggle to rework deep-seated associations between development and the public good will not be easily won, even if the promises on which they rest seem increasingly illusory.

CONCLUSION: REFOUNDING THE PROMISE OF THE PUBLIC GOOD

I started this chapter by arguing that we may be living through an historical impasse, marked by the seeming unravelling of neoliberal hegemony and the bind caused by an urgent need for action amidst an apparent exhaustion of faith in collective agency. In this context, restoring a workable notion of the public good seems a necessary, if problematic, aspiration for planning theory and practice. Using the example of Donald Trump's golf course developments to exemplify the uses and abuses of the public good in planning, I have suggested that the term needs to be held 'under erasure', reflecting a need for permanent suspicion of the ways power works to define its meanings, and the power that can be derived from claims to plan in its name.

I have also argued that any attempt to re-establish the authority of the public good in planning needs to pay attention not just to procedural and outcome-based justifications of planning activity but also the distinctively promissory character of claims to the public good. Doing so centres attention on the future-orientation of judgements about the public good as reasoned attempts to shape expectations about an inherently uncertain and unknowable future. Thinking about planning as an often-complex set of promising relationships raises important questions about the ways plans and decisions might be strengthened as 'institutional facts', or by reconsidering the willingness of planning systems to trust in the speculative promises of landowners and developers.

More than this, however, I have argued that it invites consideration of the often-overlooked nature of promissory power in planning, who wields it and what it is that makes certain promises so persuasive. I see this as a corrective to a focus in existing scholarship on the public good as a product of well-intentioned, carefully reasoned judgements which arguably detracts from analysis of the ways wider ideological fictions grip actors, shaping and influencing their expectations and aspirations.

Over recent decades, promissory power in planning has been ceded to developers and the promoters of spectacular projects. Neoliberal promises may or may not now be exhausted. Either way, they seem incapable of responding to the conjunction of crises societies now face in ways that will enable just transitions towards liveable futures. The struggle remains, therefore, to articulate powerful and compelling new promises, capable of motivating new publics with conceptions of the good to collectively shape new futures. The forms that the public good takes in planning in the future will be shaped in significant part by the outcomes of such struggles over the persuasive power of promises.

NOTES

1. I use the term the 'public good' here as a synonym for others such as the public interest, collective or common good. For reasons of space, I bypass important debates about the statist connotations of public-ness. Whilst this raises important questions, my view is that the scale of the crises societies now face requires concerted collective action and that the state, however problematic, is the only actor capable of playing this role.
2. The term is originally from Heidegger via Derrida, my use of it here comes from Stuart Hall's writing.
3. The original Scots from the Robert Burns poem 'To a Mouse, On Turning her Up in Her Nest With the Plough' is usually translated into English as 'often go awry'. The poem continues, 'An' leave us

nought but grief and pain/ For promis'd joy!'. The links it draws between plans (or 'schemes' in the original), promises and (painful) feelings resonates with the argument here.

4. My analysis here is not based upon original empirical research and draws extensively on the work of others, supplemented by a review of recent press and official documents. In particular the following sources have been key: Ford (2011), Wightman (2011), Jönsson (2014), Jönsson and Baeten (2014), Walton (2018), O'Sullivan (2018).

5. Amidst wider investigations into Trump's financial affairs calls in the Scottish Parliament and Courts for the Government to issue an 'unexplained wealth order' to establish how the cash purchase of this site was funded may yet strengthen such calls (Reuters, 2021).

REFERENCES

Aberdeenshire Council (2019), *Aberdeenshire Council: Minutes*, 26 September, accessed 30 June 2021 at https://committees.aberdeenshire.gov.uk/committees.aspx?commid=1&meetid=19374.

Abram, S. and G. Weszkalnys (2013), 'Elusive Promises: Planning in the Contemporary World. An Introduction', in Abram, S. and G. Weszkalnys (eds), *Elusive Promises: Planning in the Contemporary World*, Oxford: Berghann Books, pp. 1–34.

Beckert, J. (2016) *Imagined Futures. Fictional Expectations and Capitalist Dynamics*, Cambridge, MA: Harvard University Press.

Beckert, J. (2020), 'The Exhausted Futures of Neoliberalism: From Promissory Legitimacy to Social Anomy', *Journal of Cultural Economy*, 13(3), 318–330.

Berlant, L. (2011), *Cruel Optimism*, Durham, NC: Duke University Press.

Brown, W. (2015), *Undoing the Demos*, New York: Zone Books.

Campbell, H. (2006), 'Just Planning: The Art of Situated Ethical Judgement', *Journal of Planning Education and Research*, 26(1), 92–106.

Campbell, H. (2012), 'Planning to Change the World between Knowledge and Action Lies Synthesis', *Journal of Planning Education and Research*, 32(2), 135–146.

Campbell, H. and R. Marshall (2002), 'Utilitarianism's Bad Breath? A Re-evaluation of the Public Interest Justification for Planning', *Planning Theory*, 1(2), 163–187.

Connell, D. (2009), 'Planning and Its Orientation to the Future', *International Planning Studies*, 14(1), 85–89.

Davidoff, P. (1965), 'Advocacy and Pluralism in Planning', *Journal of the American Institute of Planners*, 31(4), 331–338.

Directorate for Planning and Environmental Appeals (DPEA) (2008), 'Report to the Scottish Ministers: Case Reference: CIN/ABS/001', Falkirk: Directorate for Planning and Environmental Appeals.

Flyvbjerg, B. (2013), 'How Planners Deal with Uncomfortable Knowledge: The Dubious Ethics of the American Planning Association', *Cities*, 32(June), 157–163.

Ford, M. (2011), 'Deciding the Fate of a Magical, Wild Place', *Journal of Irish and Scottish Studies*, 4(2), 33–74.

Gunder, M. (2014), 'Fantasy in Planning Organisations and their Agency: The Promise of Being at Home in the World', *Urban Policy and Research*, 32(1), 1–15.

Inch, A. (2018), 'Opening for Business? Neoliberalism and the Cultural Politics of Modernising Planning in Scotland', Urban Studies, 55(5), 1076–1092.

Isserman, A. (1985), 'Dare to Plan: An Essay on the Role of the Future in Planning Education and Practice', *Town Planning Review*, 56(4), 483–491.

Jönsson, E. (2014), 'Contested Expectations: Trump International Golf Links Scotland, Polarised Visions, and the Making of the Menie Estate Landscape as Resource', *GeoForum*, 52(2014), 226–235.

Jönsson, E. and G. Baeten (2014), '"Because I am who I am and my mother is Scottish": Neoliberal Planning and Entrepreneurial Instincts at Trump International Golf Links Scotland', *Space and Polity*, 18(1), 54–69.

Krueckberg, D. (1995), 'The Difficult Character of Property: To Whom Do Things Belong', *Journal of the American Planning Association*, 61(3), 301–309.

Lennon, M. (2017), 'On the "Subject" of Planning's Public Interest', *Planning Theory*, 16(2), 150–168.

Leonhardt, D. and S.A. Thompson (2017), 'President Trump's Lies: The Definitive List', *New York Times*, 14 December, accessed 29 June 20121 at www.nytimes.com/interactive/2017/06/23/opinion/trumps-lies.html.

O'Sullivan, M. (2018), 'Planning for Growth in Scottish City-regions: 'Neoliberal Spatial Governance'?', unpublished PhD thesis, Glasgow: University of Glasgow.

Paterson, K. (2020), 'Scotland Let Down by Trump Over £1 Billion Boost Fail', *The National*, 13 December, accessed 27 June 2021 at www.thenational.scot/news/18940631.scotland-let-down-trump-1-billion-boost-fail-ex-advisor-says/.

Peet, R. (2002) 'Ideology, Discourse and the Geography of Hegemony: From Socialist to Neoliberal Development in Post-apartheid South Africa', *Antipode*, 34(1), 54–84.

Porter, L. (2014), 'Possessory Politics and the Conceit of Procedure: Exposing the Cost of Rights under Conditions of Dispossession', *Planning Theory*, 13(4), 387–406.

Reuters (2021), 'Court Action Seeks Probe of Trump's Scottish Golf Course Buys', 24 May, accessed 27 June 2021 at www.reuters.com/business/legal/exclusive-court-action-seeks-probe-trumps-scottish-golf-course-buys-2021-05-24/.

Sandercock, L. (1998), *Towards Cosmopolis*, Chichester: John Wiley & Sons.

Sandercock, L. and K. Dovey (2002), 'Pleasure, Politics, and the "Public Interest": Melbourne's Riverscape Revitalization', *Journal of the American Planning Association*, 68(2), 151–164.

Scottish Government (2020a), 'Update to the Climate Change Plan 2018–2032: Securing a Green Recovery on a Path to Net Zero', Edinburgh: Scottish Government.

Scottish Government (2020b), 'Scotland's Fourth National Planning Framework Position Statement', Edinburgh: Scottish Government.

Searle, J. (1964), 'How to Derive Ought from Is', *The Philosophical Review*, 73(1), 43–58.

Slade, D., Gunn, S. and A. Schoneboom (2018), 'Serving the Public Interest?', accessed 27 June 2021 at www.rtpi.org.uk/media/2005/servingthepublicinterest2019.pdf.

Tait, M. (2016), 'Planning and the Public Interest: Still a Relevant Concept for Planners?' *Planning Theory*, 15(4), 335–343.

Tait, M. (2011), 'Trust and the Public Interest in the Micropolitics of Planning Practice', *Journal of Planning Education and Research*, 31(2), 157–171.

Throgmorton, J. (2003), 'Planning as Persuasive Storytelling in a Global-Scale Web of Relationships', *Planning Theory*, 2(2), 125–151.

Walton, W. (2018), 'Donald Trump's Golf Resort in Aberdeenshire, Scotland: The "Greatest" Incomplete Planning Disaster in the World?', *Oslo Law Review*, 5(3), 175–196.

Weber, R. (2021), 'Embedding Futurity in Urban Governance: Redevelopment Schemes and the Time Value of Money', *Environment and Planning A: Economy and Space*, 53(3), 503–524.

Wightman, A. (2011), 'Donald Trump's Ego Trip: Lessons for the New Scotland', accessed 26 June 2021 at www.andywightman.com/docs/trumpreport_v1a.pdf.

Yellowbook Limited (2017), *Barriers to Community Engagement in Planning: A Research Study*, Edinburgh: Yellowbook Limited.

14. 'Tearing down and building up': a history, theory and practice of abolitionist housing justice in the US[1]

Hilary Malson

INTRODUCTION

In October of 2020, community organizer K.J. Brooks delivered a public comment at the Kansas City Board of Police Commissioners meeting at their precinct that went viral (Dawson 2020). Clutching the mic and glancing towards the ceiling, she declared:

> I don't want reform. I want *this building* to be turned into luxury, low-cost housing. These would make some really nice apartments to me. (K.J. Brooks, Board of Police Commissioners meeting, Kansas City, Missouri, October 27, 2020)

I open this chapter with her remarks because of the clarity of her analysis: an unapologetically abolitionist vision of housing justice. Between 2013 and 2020, the Kansas City Police Department held the seventh highest rate among US cities for civilian killings by police, with Black people dying at 4.8 times the rate as their white counterparts (Mapping Police Violence 2021). Living and organizing under these conditions led Brooks to envision a world where community safety entailed housing, not policing. In her reimagining of a safer world, poor Black people deserve luxury, rather than the spare designs reflecting the government's commitment to austerity for the poor. This audacious vision of a police-precinct-turned-low-cost-luxury-apartment is emblematic of what historian Robin D.G. Kelley calls a 'freedom dream': the poetic knowledge and understanding that the current conditions and structures of power are not inevitable, and that we can dare to imagine something different (Kelley 2002: 9). In his foundational work *Freedom Dreams: The Black Radical Imagination,* a tracing of Black liberation struggles, Kelley argues that envisioning a new way of being has historically been intrinsic to dismantling oppressive societal structures and relations, and to organizing and building new ones.

Freedom dreams are at the root of abolition, a term that geographer Ruth Wilson Gilmore defines as 'the undoing of bondage' (Gilmore 2017: 231). Her simple phrasing evokes the specific history of abolition as the movement to end chattel slavery; yet it also situates bondage as an uneven relation, rooted in the formation and subjugation of an underclass by those in power. Despite the abolition of slavery, bondage remains. In contemporary scholarship and social movements, abolition has come to refer to organizing and theorizing oriented towards dismantling the afterlives of slavery.[2]

The infrastructures, investments, and relationships that sustain prisons and policing – the set of relations conceptualized as the 'prison industrial complex' – are the principal focus of contemporary abolitionists.[3] Similar to the idea of the prison industrial complex, planning theorist Ananya Roy conceptualizes 'housing justice' as a framework for analysing the structural processes and relations that create violations to the universal right to housing (Roy 2019: 13–14). Planning is implicated in these violations, by enabling the continuation of uneven relations and deepening their entrenchment. This is evident in conflicts regarding property, wherein planning legitimizes the 'bundle of rights' that violently dispossess and exclude society's most marginalized from retaining land claims, staying sheltered, or even existing in urban space (Dorries 2017, Dozier 2019, Goodling 2020, Mitchell 2003). However, adopting an abolitionist orientation invites the field to engage in its own freedom dreaming: how might *prioritizing* 'undoing the bondage' that disempowers people – cancelling rent debts, returning unceded lands, stopping the sweeps, etc. – fundamentally transform how we plan, or even who does the planning? Thus, though most theories of abolition are grounded in analyses of institutions such as the plantation and the prison, in this chapter I suggest housing as another institution to think from, for several reasons. First, existing theories of abolition shed light on contemporary struggles for housing justice. Second, a closer look at centuries of Black Americans' struggles for social and spatial justice reveals an underexamined tradition of an abolitionist praxis of housing justice, one which can illuminate new horizons of abolition. And third, examining housing through carceral *and* abolitionist sets of relations allows scholars and practitioners alike to understand housing differently: as a site where slavery's afterlives live on, a critical node within the prison industrial complex, and a terrain of struggle where abolitionist futures are already present.

This chapter is organized into three sections. I begin by examining key conceptualizations and theories of abolition, drawing from scholars whose work is foundational: W.E.B. Du Bois, Angela Davis, Ruth Wilson Gilmore, Mariame Kaba, and Dean Spade. In the subsequent section, I trace significant conjunctures in the long struggle for Black liberation in the Americas, and reframe them through the lens of an abolitionist praxis for housing justice. In the final section, I share two contemporary case studies that inform my thinking: the encampments and takeovers of the Occupy Philadelphia Housing Authority (PHA) movement in Philadelphia, and the tenant organizing work of the Los Angeles Center for Community Law and Action (LACCLA). This analysis is grounded upon four years of participant observation as a LACCLA member, as well as recent interviews with members of both collectives. I end that section by highlighting organizing towards housing justice in other US cities, and conclude this chapter by grappling with the challenges and lessons learned in working towards housing justice with an abolitionist praxis, and how this praxis builds power at the grassroots.

KEY THEORIES OF ABOLITION: THE UNFINISHED WORK OF LIBERATION

Dominant theories of abolition are unified in their understanding that abolition is a process that requires, and enables, a new set of relations. In contrast to past and present movements to reform chattel slavery and current carceral systems, organizers working in the abolitionist vein maintain a distinctive goal: the total dismantling of dehumanizing institutions and their attendant infrastructures, alongside the creation of alternative ways of being. That dualistic process is characterized by philosopher and prison abolitionist Angela Davis as one of 'tearing down and building up' (Davis 2005: 73). In this section, I trace the work of key abolitionist theorists along a linear timeline, while knowing that the work of abolition – like history itself – is not linear. The intellects guiding public discourse on abolition explicitly engage with, and build upon, the scholarship preceding them, and so I follow that tradition here.

Contemporary abolitionist scholarship is rooted in the idea of an 'abolition democracy,' conceptualized by W.E.B. Du Bois nearly a century ago in his ground-breaking tome, *Black Reconstruction in America* (1935). In this work, he adopted a Marxist lens to revise existing historiography on the failures of Reconstruction, the fleeting experiment following the US Civil War in which ordinary Black people and the federal government alike sought to reconstruct society. Banned from most Southern archives on account of his race, Du Bois instead relied upon secondary material to construct his argument: the substantial investments of time and resources poured into creating new democratic institutions through Reconstruction programs were the first meaningful attempt at creating democracy in the US, and federal divestment was the root cause of their failures.

Du Bois called this freedom dream of a reconstructed society an 'abolition-democracy': a free society requiring not only slavery's abolition, but 'civil and political rights, education and land' as emancipation's guarantors (ibid: 239). Protecting the rights of newly freed Black people required new institutions, like the establishment of representative court systems to enforce laws and protect enfranchisement and the development of Black-serving educational institutions, including the schools known today as Historically Black Colleges and Universities (HBCUs).[4] Yet most pivotal to the Reconstruction agenda was the establishment of the Bureau of Refugees, Freedmen, and Abandoned Lands, which was centrally concerned with redistributing plantations to formerly enslaved Black people.[5] Meeting this goal would sever the power of the white planter class, while providing Black Southerners an opportunity to cultivate economic and community power (ibid: 219). As Congressman Thaddeus Stevens, architect of much Reconstruction legislation, remarked, 'can emancipation be carried out without using the lands of the slave-masters? … The great plantations must be broken up, and the freedmen must have the pieces.' This 'radical change in the relations of capital and of property in land,' to quote another legislator, was to be the urgent priority after the abolition of slavery (ibid: 198–199). As Du Bois argued, not only did Reconstruction's designers understand that emancipation demanded new institutions as its supportive scaffolding; it *required* those institutions' permanence for an abolition democracy to come to fruition.

Yet the abolition democracy envisioned during Reconstruction was foreclosed due to organized abandonment by the state itself (ibid: 670–710). A violent reign of vigilante terror effectively extinguished Black economic and political power through murder, arson, and intimidation. Reconstruction's supportive scaffolds were dismantled: anti-Klan legislation expired, Black men were systematically disenfranchised, public facilities were resegregated, and bans preventing Confederate officials from US government service were lifted. The death knell came in 1877: military forces – instated to protect Black people and enforce Reconstruction's institutions – were removed from the South. With that, white supremacy secured its hold on governance in the South. Under the 13th Amendment to the Constitution, chattel slavery was abolished alongside the legalization of enslavement for incarcerated people; and all the while, the creation of an abolition democracy remained unfinished.

As Du Bois noted, Southern capitalists organized to reduce Black labour power to 'a condition of unlimited exploitation,' and the prison became the physical form where those ambitions – of limitless exploitation – could be realized (ibid: 670). Real wages extracted by white people in power and 'psychological wages' of supremacy reaped by their poorer counterparts consolidated into the societal condition of white racial privilege, the coalition necessary to maintain total Black subjugation. Drawing from Cedric Robinson's foundational conceptualization of racial capitalism (1983), Gilmore succinctly states that 'capitalism requires inequality and racism enshrines it' (2017: 240). In the post-Reconstruction South, laws called Black Codes criminalized Black people for ordinary activities, such as publicly gathering in groups. Not only did such differentiated criminalization guarantee a legally enslaveable class of prisoners, it also gave birth to an extensive convict-leasing system for people seeking cheap sources of labour (Davis 2003: 94).[6] As Gilmore reminds us, abolition demands that we focus on the *dynamic nature* of relations, wherein socio-spatial relationships of subjugation expand and congeal into new forms that consolidate and deepen old outcomes. It is attention to the dynamic nature of relations that illuminates the plantation's transformation into the prison.[7]

Angela Davis explicitly links Reconstruction's incompletion to the expansion of prisons today, arguing that 'the prison-industrial-complex is a result of the failure to enact abolition democracy' (2005: 95). She builds upon Du Bois' argument by suggesting that subjugating Black life through these afterlives of slavery explicitly devours the 'social wealth' of Black communities: not only do prisons generate profits by exploiting captive Black labour, but incarceration also destabilizes communities, creating ongoing conditions that continually repopulate and expand prisons (2003: 16–17). To that end, her work is grounded upon the lessons Du Bois first imparted: that abolition is as much about the creation of a new society, anchored by social institutions that enable people to thrive, as it is about dismantling extractive institutions and rendering them fully obsolete. As she suggests through her conceptualization of the prison industrial complex, 'the prison is deeply structured by economic, social, and political conditions that themselves will have to be dismantled' (2005: 72). Informed by her lived experiences of incarceration, Davis argues that reforming institutions may improve their conditions, but reminds us that prison itself was a reform of capital punishment; limiting the field of possibility to working within an existing set of relations, such as the paradigm of crime and punishment, deepens the foothold of the prison as a normative solution to societal challenges (2003: 27). Abolitionist thinking invites us to imagine otherwise by envisioning a new set of relations, such as harm and repair, rather than reforming fundamentally punitive ones.

Gilmore further develops Davis' critique of reform by grounding her analyses upon André Gorz's idea of the 'non-reformist reform.' In *Golden Gulag*, her study of the political economy of the prison industrial complex in California and how the prison operates as a spatial fix for people and places rendered 'surplus,' she characterizes non-reformist reforms as those changes that 'unravel rather than widen the net of social control through criminalization' (Gilmore 2007: 242). Abolitionists must determine whether the changes they are working toward ultimately reinforce the system they seek to dismantle (such as replacing death penalties with life sentences, thereby subjecting living humans to social death and justifying the prison system's expansion to warehouse more people). Drawing boundaries around what constitutes a non-reformist reform, such as the cessation of prison construction, enables people to mobilize around, and firmly achieve, material wins on the road to abolition, even if that win is an incremental step towards prison obsolescence.

Like Du Bois and Davis, Gilmore asserts that 'abolition is a theory of change; it is a theory of social life. It is about making things' (Petitjean 2018). In recent work, she reframes the prison industrial complex as a 'carceral geography,' in recognition of the system's multi-scalar footprint, and posits that carceral geographies are countered by creating abolition geographies – a spatial elaboration of Du Bois' abolition democracy (Gilmore 2017: 238). She argues that, 'by seizing the particular capacities we have, and repeating ourselves – trying as C.L.R. James wrote about the run-up to revolutions, trying every little thing, going and going again – we will, because we do, change ourselves and the external world. Even under extreme constraint' (ibid). As I demonstrate in this chapter's case studies, unfreedoms wrought through carceral geographies are undone through the ongoing experimental place-making of an abolitionist geography.

Prison abolitionist and youth organizer Mariame Kaba approaches abolition through transformative justice. This framework, developed by anti-violence activists of colour, frames harm as a by-product of oppressive societal conditions and prioritizes transforming oppressive conditions to reduce the likelihood of further harm from occurring (Kaba 2021). Moreover, she directly addresses critiques of abolition's pragmatism by acknowledging that people harming one another is part of navigating social relations; transformative justice, however, foregrounds accountability as a response to harm, so that reparative relations replace the punitive disposability of the carceral system. The expansiveness of Kaba's vision – of a society where people's needs are met and where they experience true safety through empathic relationships with others – is grounded upon the idea of abolition as a praxis, wherein the 'undoing of bondage' is a process and a way of being that is already underway when people organize and act with accountability in daily life. Abolition relies upon those countless experiments of living together differently, taking risks and sometimes failing while trying to live in accountability with one another, and learning and transforming through that process (ibid: 175–180).

Central to the ethos of living together differently is the practice of mutual aid, which legal scholar Dean Spade emphasizes in his work on prison and border abolition. Rather than lobbying for change or being satiated by symbolism, mutual aid is the purposeful practice of providing for one another's material needs; in so doing, it resurrects the power that purportedly power-less people already have, by virtue of their relations with each other. Spade, who approaches abolition through a queer, trans, and working-class lens (in the Lordeian vein, rejecting a single-issue framing for an intersectional one), argues that mutual aid simultaneously creates survivable conditions while exposing the failures of the present order (2020: 136–137).[8] Abolition requires imagining beyond the existing system and cultivating a freedom dream of a better world, but mutual aid builds a literal pathway to it and transforms participants in the process (Bassichis et al. 2011: 36).

TRACING A TRADITION OF HOUSING JUSTICE IN BLACK LIBERATION STRUGGLES

In this section, I frame four notable moments in Black liberation struggles as demonstrative of an underrecognized abolitionist tradition of housing justice. Through this brief overview of Black Americans' centuries-long struggle to create sanctuaries for ourselves in a society developed through Black oppression, I seek to demonstrate that this struggle has required an abolitionist praxis. I do so by framing these conjunctures through four key tenets of abolition: freedom dreams, collective action, community control, and mutual aid.

Freedom Dreams: The Maroonage Tradition of Flight from Slavery

Even prior to their legal recognition as humans, enslaved Black people created safe shelter for themselves. Throughout the Americas, there are documented instances of enslaved people collectively extracting themselves from settler societies developed through racialized slavery, and establishing new settlements to live as free people. These communities, frequently known as 'maroons,' ranged in size, scale, and longevity. Some, such as Bas du Fleuve in Louisiana, lasted only a few years while maintaining contact with plantation society, while others, like those in the Great Dismal Swamp spanning the Virginia–Carolina border, may have had a more isolated existence; still others, including the famed Palmares in Brazil, developed into large, complex states that survived for generations (Price 1979, Bledsoe 2017: 40, Diouf 2016). The forms and practices developed by maroon societies varied according to their socio-environmental contexts, yet they shared an underlying principle: a collective right to self-determination, reflected in the creation of autonomous places and affirmation of Black humanity. The will to flee 'the known world'[9] of the plantation for lands beyond its reach, live there collectively with others, and develop an autonomous way of life – out of sight from, but under the permanent threat of, punishment by the slave state – is a freedom dream made manifest. Maroon communities required a radical imagination: an understanding of the impossibility of their freedom dreams, and a resolve to build towards them anyways (Bassichis et al. 2011: 36).

Collective Action: Building Free Black Towns

As Reconstruction came to an end, Black Southerners collectively organized to build towns where they might live safely. Two such mobilizations were the migrants known as Exodusters, some of whom fled to Kansas to develop the town of Nicodemus, and the Texans who stayed in place and established hamlets known as Freedom Colonies. Danielle Purifoy and Louise Seamster characterize Black towns like these as 'intentional communities, typically established by Black people, for the purpose of creating the socio-political conditions for Black freedom and autonomy' (Purifoy and Seamster 2020: 2). In the 1870s and 80s, tens of thousands of Black people from Mississippi, Tennessee, and Louisiana left behind the debts and violence of their homelands to move west. While many Exodusters homesteaded individual farms, some travelled in groups numbering more than one hundred; they worked with mutual aid organizations to collectively develop towns like Nicodemus, complete with residential lots, commercial businesses, and lodging for travellers (Painter 1976). Meanwhile, in Texas, formerly enslaved people quietly acquired thousands of acres of farmland in the generations after slavery. On these lands, which were typically sited 'in places where whites were not looking' like rural areas and the peripheries of old plantations, Black people organized autonomous agrarian settlements (Roberts 2017: 14). Planning historian Andrea Roberts' research reveals that more than 540 Freedom Colonies existed, yet they were often invisible by design: isolated enough to be left off maps, and little more than an undocumented cluster of homes and a church on a dirt road whose residents believed 'a community existed' (Roberts 2018, Sitton and Conrad 2005).[10] For residents of Nicodemus and Freedom Colonies alike, this logic of collective action afforded both the muscle power to construct housing as well as the protection that safety in numbers offered in an anti-Black society. Yet these histories indicate something else: belief in freedom as a collective project. As Kaba's father told her, 'everything that is worthwhile is done with other people' (Kaba 2021: 178).

Community Control: Community Land Trusts

The unfinished development of the abolition democracy directly birthed an important and lasting alternative housing model: the community land trust. Across the South, Reconstruction's failed promise of forty acres and a mule locked Black farmworkers into sharecropping, a tenant farming model that ensnared labourers into a relationship of indebtedness resembling slavery's power dynamics. Lawful discrimination alongside permanent indebtedness excluded Black farmers from entering the private housing market. Yet it was precisely this dilemma that led people from Georgia's rural Black Belt – so named for its fertile black soil and Black laborers, intertwined through the region's plantation history – to develop the community land trust. In 1969, local organizers with Civil Rights Movement experience established New Communities Inc. on 5,000 acres of farmland, so that Black farm workers could 'gain and retain control of basic resources in the face of extreme marginalization' (DeFilippis et al. 2018: 757). Inspired by Mexican anarchist ejidos and Tanzania's ujamaa villages, this new model of land stewardship reconfigured land and housing as assets to serve community needs, rather than privately owned sites for profit generation (Swann et al. 1972). Community agreements on re-sale restrictions ensured the trust's housing remained permanently affordable. As numerous planning scholars have noted, removing land from the hands of absentee owners and the speculative market, and transferring decision-making power to those living and labouring on it, directly disrupts feudal relationships of landlordism and holds the potential to build political power among previously marginalized people (see, for example, DeFilippis et al. 2018; Leavitt and Saegert 1990).

Mutual Aid: The Black Panther Party's Abolition Geographies

The Black Panther Party and other organizations in the Black Power movement of the 1960s and 1970s had an expansive interest in community control of institutions (similar to the community land trust advocate's interest in community control of land). Organized in Oakland in 1966, the Black Panther Party adopted a Marxist-Leninist critique of systemic American racism. In their classic *Black Power*, co-founders Kwame Ture (known then as Stokely Carmichael) and Charles Hamilton plainly articulated Davis' (1967: 42) abolitionist vision of 'tearing down and building up':

> The city planning commissions, the urban renewal commissions, the boards of education and the police departments fail to speak to [our] needs in a meaningful way. We must devise new structures, new institutions to replace those forms … There is nothing sacred about old institutions; the focus must be on people, not forms.

The Panthers garnered mass support for their ideas by implementing mutual aid programs to meet the real needs of low-income Black people. They 'served the people' through those programs: community-mobilized donations enabled the provision of free breakfast, medical care, legal aid services, and clothing (Seale 1972: 327–331). Their critique of the state's neglect of Black people can be understood as an indictment of the punitive carceral geographies that structured Black urban life; their intent in developing mutual aid programs can be understood as the creation of an abolition geography. The Panthers' mutual aid programs did not directly address housing (though they did advocate for the formation of tenant unions); what these programs did do was cultivate the power-building capacities and new societal relations of residents of cities like Oakland, through which they would maintain better lives and create better housing for themselves.[11]

SMALL VICTORIES: CONTEMPORARY CASES OF AN ABOLITIONIST HOUSING JUSTICE PRAXIS

In contemporary movements for housing justice, people are envisioning what non-extractive, humane, and reparative housing might look like, and collectively building towards these horizons. Struggles to build new forms of housing underscore the extent to which abolition is best understood as a process that transforms power relations, as well as a process through which participants doing abolitionist work are themselves transformed. I share case studies here of struggles for housing justice in Philadelphia and Los Angeles, two cities that profoundly inform my thinking. The two cities share little in common: different demographics, different major industries, even different histories of settler colonialism. Racial capitalism shapes space in both places, but along different racial lines and historical contexts (Malson and Graziani 2019: 38). But holding these two ground-level perspectives in tandem reveals important patterns of structural oppression, as well as common possibilities for building abolitionist futures. By disrupting and incrementally dismantling the power that landlords hold over tenants, challenging state provision of social housing, and cultivating marginalized peoples' power at the grassroots, these cases illustrate how an abolitionist praxis of housing justice transforms all existing relations that perpetuate the subjugation of one group for another's benefit.

Of the ten most populated US cities, Philadelphia is the Blackest and the poorest: 43.08% of its residents identify as Black, and the median household income is $47,474 – nearly $21,000 less than the nationwide median (Census 2021). While the 2021 Philadelphia Point-In-Time Homeless Count recorded 4,302 unhoused residents, more than 40,000 lots and buildings were classified as vacant – a staggering scale of abandonment it shares with other post-industrial cities irreversibly transformed by white flight, disinvestment, and racially discriminatory foreclosure practices, like Detroit, Flint, and Baltimore (Office of Homeless Services 2021, Sugrue 1996, Noterman 2020: 2). There is a long history of poor Philadelphians surviving by squatting in vacant lots; at times, squatters have been backed by elected officials, as was the case in the 1980s with Councilman John Street's vocal advocacy for squatter occupations as a means of abating the 'nuisance' of vacancies (*Squatters* 1984).

During the COVID-19 pandemic, unhoused and precariously housed people built on this tradition of occupation to organize 'takeovers' (their term for squatting) and encampments across Philadelphia (Marin 2021). As I learned through interviews with area organizers, the earliest of these actions was the low-profile movement of mothers and children into a half-dozen vacant homes owned by the Philadelphia Housing Authority (PHA) at the outset of the pandemic, so that they might safely shelter-in-place. By June, this network established a 'protest camp' on public land along a major boulevard downtown, which grew within days from a handful of people to roughly 100 unhoused residents living cooperatively in a tent city. The encampment, initially named Camp Maroon and later renamed Camp James Talib Dean (Camp JTD) to honour a deceased organizer, was explicitly political: residents banned police from the site and issued a host of demands, such as immediate cessation of sweeps (a term for removing unhoused people's property under the guise of sanitation service provision). Several Camp JTD residents split off to develop another protest camp, Camp Teddy, on a vacant PHA property. Residents and organizers of these different sites aligned with a pre-existing campaign called Occupy PHA to call attention to PHA's active role as a violent gentrifying force in the city. PHA was selling off hundreds of properties in North Philadelphia's economically depressed neighbourhoods to developers, rather than housing people in them in alignment with its mission; furthermore, it operated a private police force that surveilled and harassed residents of PHA properties and residents of nearby homes into self-evicting. During the pandemic, Occupy PHA residents stayed firm in their demands, refusing to leave their collectively created refuges until they secured material wins from the City: amnesty and permanent housing for all Occupy PHA members and the transfer of dozens of vacant PHA properties to their newly formed community land trust.

While these various encampments and takeovers were autonomous, they were interconnected, collaborative, and unified in their commitment to abolish police from housing.[12] Organizers of the different communities coordinated and supported each other's battles as they resisted violent eviction attempts and negotiated with City officials over their right to stay housed. Jennifer Bennetch, a core Occupy PHA organizer, attributed the residents' success in securing state support for the community's control of housing to their trust in one another. Pre-pandemic popular education by Occupy PHA members about PHA's private police force, rapid eviction-defence mobilization efforts during the takeovers and encampments, and coordinated mutual aid programs across the sites all cultivated the trust necessary for organizers to facilitate the residents' collective agreement with PHA and the City and transfer fifty units of housing to Occupy PHA members and their new community land trust. That small victory, to borrow the phrasing of Rasheedah Phillips, another Occupy PHA supporter, 'is significant in disrupting the notion of land ownership. It ... attacks a system that also has its roots in ownership of people and property and serfdom, and gets at some of those core facets of those institutions and dismantling them' (Phillips 2020). Another organizer with the campaign expressed scepticism with the community land trust model, rightly noting that successful efforts to legalize squatting in places like Germany and New York City haven't stopped local police from brutalizing squatters. Yet in the same breath, they observed that 'a lot of the people who were in the houses are still there a year later, and none of them were dragged out by the gestapo or whatever, so that's a win.' The abolitionist struggle for housing justice in Philadelphia continues unabated – as Bennetch remarked, 'abolition means getting rid of housing police, because after all this time I'm *still* fighting that battle, and they gotsta go!' – but collective action on the ground during the pandemic cultivated the grassroots power to transform peoples' sense of what was possible and build towards that vision.

Across the continent, a multigenerational, multiracial, and multilingual collective of more than 100 working-class people works within and beyond the law to create a community where housing-insecure people are safer, better protected, and better able to live lives of dignity. The Los Angeles Center for Community Law and Action (LACCLA) operates through a hybrid pro-bono legal clinic/tenant organizing model, where people seeking support for housing issues can receive free legal representation, under the agreement that service recipients become 'members' and remain involved with the organization.[13] What involvement means is open-ended rather than prescribed, but for many members, their entryway into community organizing begins with attending weekly Saturday meetings, where members might educate one another about new legislation, share testimonies of struggle, exchange advice, or determine how to support allied groups' campaigns. The two-hour meetings are horizontally organized, with a different member leading each meeting so that everyone develops facilita-

Source: Photo by the author, January 11, 2020.

Figure 14.1   *Beatriz Salazar, LACCLA member, facilitates a discussion on countering machismo and redistributing the organization's volunteer labour to meet gender equity goals; Chris Estrada, LACCLA organizer, kneels while taking notes*

tion skills. In my four years of LACCLA membership, as a language interpreter and Advisory Board member, I have witnessed numerous people join to fight a personal housing matter; yet many remain involved years after their cases are resolved. It is the interest in supporting one another and collectively building something better than what exists – imagining beyond what seems possible and building pathways to get there – that drives many to stay engaged.

The commitment to keeping one another safely housed, by any means necessary, has created many different strategies for our battles. Some struggles are fought in the courtroom. The most high-profile of these was a case led by the Rodriguez-Perez family, LACCLA members who fought their landlord's 62.5% rent increase; after years of appeals, it was their victory that was pivotal in successfully extending soft rent control to unincorporated areas of Los Angeles County, which restricted annual rent increases to 8% (Khouri 2019). LACCLA member Benito Flores recently observed that this small victory is better understood as a Pyrrhic victory: allowing rents to rise at all, while minimum wages are kept stagnant, is still an injustice. As Chris Estrada, a LACCLA organizer, religiously reminds members, '*hay espacio entre la ley y justicia*' – 'there is a gap between justice and the law.' With this understanding, Flores

Source: Photo by Kim Miranda, September 10, 2019.

Figure 14.2   *LACCLA members Hilary Malson, Maria Castro, Benito Flores (Reclaimer), and Kim Miranda (L–R) celebrate the LA County Board of Supervisors ruling to extend soft rent controls to unincorporated areas of LA County*

joined other housing insecure people and moved from his van into one of hundreds of vacant houses owned by the California Department of Transportation (Caltrans) in March of 2020, in a movement named Reclaiming Our Homes (ROH 2020). For decades, Caltrans violated the Roberti Act, part of which discouraged public agencies from sitting on surplus housing and deemed 'preserving, upgrading, and expanding the supply of housing available to persons and families of low and moderate income' in keeping with 'the provision of decent housing for all Californians … a state goal of the highest priority' (Roberti Act 1979). In Flores' words, 'we are not the rebels, we are the law abiding. It is the government who is acting unlawfully. We consider them stealing the land – *están robiendo las tierras*.'

Most members I know well came to LACCLA to fight harassment by their landlord. By serving illegal eviction notices, surveilling residents in and around their homes, or arbitrarily prohibiting ordinary activity that is permitted under the lease, these landlords avoid legally evicting their tenants; rather, they intend to intimidate people into self-eviction. In those cases, the strategies we use don't tend to involve the courts. Rather, we protest against landlord abuse and occupy harassed tenants' homes with them. By presenting a force of solidarity, we communicate to landlords that their tenant is not alone, which defies landlords' perception of domination. The quieter moments matter, too: believing members as they reveal abuses for the first time, or showing up at dusk to move someone's possessions off the lawn and safely store them post-eviction. These reparative actions of collective care illuminate the gaps in what our capitalist present allows and make clear to whom these abolitionist futures must be accountable. These various forms of collective support, from public direct actions to private moments of care, are essential for cultivating our senses of empowerment and of what else might be possible.

Although LACCLA and Occupy PHA are the collectives whose work most directly informs my thinking, they are but two of many doing such work. Every site of struggle is contextually specific; thus, the goals, demands, and strategies of each group is distinct. I share a selection of other collectives here to illuminate the many different ways that people are building abolition geographies.

Table 14.1   Abolitionist praxis

Organization	Abolitionist Praxis
Cooperation Jackson Jackson, Mississippi www.cooperationjackson.org	A Black-led network of cooperatives and organizers building a solidarity economy. One initiative is purchasing land to remove it from the speculative market, and create the Fannie Lou Hamer Community Land Trust, on which they plan to construct eco-village style housing cooperatives.
Kansas City Tenants Union Kansas City, Missouri https://kctenants.org/	A tenants union with a multiracial, multigenerational base of poor, working class tenants. They organized numerous successful campaigns, including the passage of a Tenants Bill of Rights through the City Council, which includes protections like a 'ban the box' provision preventing discrimination against people with criminal records.
Moms 4 Housing Oakland, California https://moms4housing.org/	Black unhoused and housing-insecure mothers organized an occupation of a vacant home owned by Wedgewood Properties in 2019. They successfully pushed Wedgewood to sell the home to the Oakland Community Land Trust, and have since focused on 'reclaiming housing for the community from speculators and profiteers.' They inspired both Reclaiming Our Homes (Los Angeles) and Occupy PHA (Philadelphia).
Root Cause Research Center Louisville, Kentucky www.rootcauseresearch.org/	Researchers with an 'Abolitionist Planning' orientation work to support autonomous tenant unions in the South. Their praxis includes working alongside tenants when conducting research and creating resources in alignment with grassroots-organized campaigns.
SMASH Miami, Florida https://smash.miami/	Residents of Liberty City, Overtown, and Little Havana, three historically Black and Latinx neighbourhoods, organized protests against building neglect, successfully transferred property ownership from slumlords to the City, and formed a community land trust to develop permanently affordable, community-controlled housing.
Unhoused Tenants Against Carceral Housing (UTACH) Los Angeles, California https://twitter.com/UTACH9	A collective of unhoused tenants organizing against the carceral structure and conditions of the City's Project Roomkey COVID-era hotels. They have: issued transformative demands to the program (such as extending the program until permanent housing is guaranteed); drawn attention to the carceral logics of surveillance and violence that unhoused people are subject to under state 'care'; disrupted narratives of service-resistance; and, reinforced their coalition's call for #HousekeysNotHandcuffs.

CONCLUSION AND FUTURES

Through the theories, histories, and case studies presented in this chapter, I sought to demonstrate that abolition is as much about an abolition from institutions of oppression, including slavery, incarceration, and policing, as it is an orientation towards freedom, created by building new institutions. As Occupy PHA reminds us in their struggles for social housing, abolition requires both the removal of policing and the transfer of control directly to residents. Without that dualistic perspective, adjustments within oppressive systems can lead to reforms that re-entrench the oppressive status quo, through mechanisms that Keeanga-Yamahtta Taylor describes as 'predatory inclusion' (Taylor 2019). Yet abolition does not eschew reality; the complexities of interpersonal relations make their way into abolitionist spaces. Both LACCLA and Occupy PHA have navigated and continue to navigate serious conflicts involving broken trust and violations amongst members. But as Mariama Kaba reminds us through the framework of transformative justice, abolition asks us to consider what non-punitive accountability might look like. What abolition affords is a process, whereby new ways of being might be imagined and practiced (Kaba 2021). Another significant takeaway is the understanding of abolition as a horizon, rather than exclusively a destination (Chua 2020: S-130). For example, most of the housing justice organizations and experiments referenced in the second section no longer exist, yet their legacies live on and continue to inform contemporary abolitionist praxes. Evidence of this is seen in the continued relevance of Du Bois' abolition democracy framework for prison abolition theorists; the heritage in Camp JTD's initial name, Camp Maroon; and the goal that many contemporary organizations have of developing their own community land trusts. The process of imagining, experimenting with, and working towards ways of being that undo bondage – like the shift from landlordism to community-controlled housing – not only cultivates a repertoire of abolitionist praxis at the grassroots, it also builds power at the grassroots that can transform the societal relations guiding how we plan.

NOTES

1. This chapter is dedicated in loving memory of Jennifer Bennetch, who passed at age thirty-six on February 17 2022 of COVID-19 complications.
2. Gina Hong, a Korean American lawyer with the multiethnic Los Angeles Center for Community Law and Action, shared this perspective on abolition as a culturally specific, yet universally relevant, concept:

    In my mind, it is one of many names for a concept … It's about self-determination for oppressed people. Abolition's unique gift comes from the organizing of specifically Black Americans that gives us an important unifying language for this vision. It's not just about tearing shit down, that's not what it is at all. It's *about* the building back up, and being ready for the end of institutions, and being able to take care of ourselves and command our reality. As someone who is in the US, and who is therefore working for and contributing to a history that Black folks in the US have been leading, the word abolition is my umbrella. If I was in the Philippines, it might have a different name. But in my opinion, it's part of the same will to freedom. (Interview with author, 2021)

3. Although the term 'prison industrial complex' is often attributed to Angela Davis and Ruth Wilson Gilmore through their many publications and work as co-founders of Critical Resistance, Davis credits activists and scholars with its conceptualization, and notes its initial printed use by social historian Mike Davis in his discussion of the rapid growth of the carceral industry in California. See Davis 2003: 84.
4. HBCUs continue to disproportionately educate Black students in the US. Despite representing only 3% of higher education institutions in the nation, in 2017–2018 HBCUs conferred 26,276 bachelor's degrees to Black students, or 13.47% of those earned by Black students at US institutions (IES 2019a, 2019b).
5. The Bureau of Refugees, Freedmen, and Abandoned Lands is known as 'the Freedmen's Bureau;' its plans to redistribute land are remembered as the promise of '40 acres and a mule.'

6. Toussaint Lossier and Dan Berger offer a three-part conceptualization of prison models, each operating with a different strategy: the Workhouse – popular in the South – wherein inmates become cheap labour sources; the Big House, characterized by its educational, religious, and therapeutic rehabilitation programs; and, the Warehouse, repositories for containing and eliminating surplus people from society (2018: 9).
7. On some Southern land, the transition from plantation to prison took place without any change in geography. Angola Plantation, so named for its enslaved labourers' African homeland, is one notable example. Angola became the Louisiana State Penitentiary, an 18,000-acre maximum-security prison farm. Most people incarcerated at the penitentiary today will die there, just as enslaved people did (ACLU 2013).
8. Audre Lorde famously declared, 'there is no such thing as a single-issue struggle because we do not lead single-issue lives.' See Lorde (1982).
9. See Jones (2003).
10. For relevant discussions on the invisible, the unknowable, and the unmappable dimensions of Black life, see Dionne Brand (2001), Katherine McKittrick (2006), Darius Scott (2019), and other scholars' contributions in Black geographies.
11. See 'Moms 4 Housing,' of this chapter, for one contemporary example of the Panthers' legacy of building community-based power in Oakland.
12. For more on struggles to abolish police from housing, see: Stop LAPD Spying Coalition's organizing against 'the stalker state' (Khan 2019); Rahim Kurwa's scholarship on nuisance calls against Section 8 voucher holders (Kurwa 2015); UCLA Luskin Institute on Inequality and Democracy research on gang injunctions as tools of racialized policing (Roy et al. 2020); and the National Welfare Rights Organization's 1960s campaigns against the surveillance of women public housing residents' private lives (Nadasen 2002, Shoenfeld 2019).
13. LACCLA, established in 2014 by lawyers Noah Grynberg and Brent Boos, is loosely modeled after Boston-based City Life/Vida Urbana's (CLVU) hybrid legal clinic/tenant organizing structure.

REFERENCES

American Civil Liberties Union (ACLU) (2013). *A Living Death: Life Without Parole for Nonviolent Offences*. Accessed online: www.aclu.org/sites/default/files/field_document/111813-lwop-complete -report.pdf. Accessed August 20, 2021.

Bassichis, Morgan, Alexander Lee, and Dean Spade (2011). 'Building an Abolitionist Trans and Queer Movement with Everything We've Got,' in Eric A. Stanley and Nat Smith (eds) *Captive Genders: Trans Embodiment and the Prison Industrial Complex*. Edinburgh, Oakland, and Baltimore: AK Press, 15–40.

Berger, Dan, and Toussaint Lossier (2018). *Rethinking the American Prison Movement*. London: Routledge.

Bledsoe, Adam (2017). 'Maroonage as Past and Present Geography in the Americas,' *Southeastern Geographer* 57 (1): 30–50.

Brand, Dionne (2001). *A Map to the Door of No Return: Notes on Belonging*. Toronto: Vintage Canada.

Chua, Charmaine (2020). 'Abolition is a Constant Struggle: Five Lessons from Minneapolis,' *Theory & Event* 23 (4 Supplement): S127–S147.

Davis, Angela Y. (2003). *Are Prisons Obsolete?* New York: Seven Stories Press.

Davis, Angela Y. (2005). *Abolition Democracy: Beyond Empire, Prisons, and Torture*. New York: Seven Stories Press.

Dawson, Brit (2020). 'Activist KJ Brooks on her Scathing, Viral Takedown of Kansas City Police,' *Dazed*. Accessed online: www.dazeddigital.com/politics/article/50965/1/activist-keiajah-kj-brooks -on-her-scathing-viral-takedown-of-kansas-city-police. Accessed August 18, 2021.

DeFilippis, James, Brian Stromberg, and Olivia R. Williams (2018). 'W(h)ither the *Community* in Community Land Trusts?,' *Journal of Urban Affairs* 40 (6): 755–769.

Diouf, Sylvia (2016). *Slavery's Exiles: The Story of the American Maroons*. New York: NYU Press.

Dorries, Heather (2017). 'Planning as Property: Uncovering the Hidden Racial Logic Underlying a Municipal Nuisance By-Law,' *Journal of Law and Social Policy* 27: 72–93.

Dozier, Deshonay (2019). 'Contested Development: Homeless Property, Police Reform, and Resistance in Skid Row,' *International Journal of Urban and Regional Research* 43 (1): 179–194.

Du Bois, W.E.B. [1992 (1935)]. *Black Reconstruction in America: 1860–1880*. New York: The Free Press.

Gilmore, Ruth Wilson (2007). *Golden Gulag: Prisons, Surplus, Crisis, and Opposition in Globalizing California*. Berkeley and Los Angeles: UC Press.

Gilmore, Ruth Wilson (2017). 'Abolition Geography and the Problem of Innocence,' in Gaye Theresa Johnson and Alex Lubin (eds) *Futures of Black Radicalism*. London and New York: Verso, 225–240.

Goodling, Erin (2020). 'Intersecting Hazards, Intersectional Identities: A Baseline Critical Environmental Justice Analysis of US Homelessness,' *Environment and Planning E: Nature and Space* 3 (3): 833–856. DOI: 10.1177/2514848619892433.

Institute of Education Sciences (IES) (2019a). 'Table 313.10. Fall Enrolment, Degrees Conferred, and Expenditures in Degree-Granting Historically Black Colleges and Universities, By Institution: 2017, 2018, and 2017–2018.' Accessed online: https://nces.ed.gov/programs/digest/d19/tables/dt19_313.10 .asp. Accessed August 20, 2021.

Institute of Education Sciences (IES) (2019b). 'Bachelor's Degrees Conferred by Post-Secondary Institutions, By Race/Ethnicity and Sex of Student: Selected Years, 1976–1977 Through 2017–2018.' Accessed online: https://nces.ed.gov/programs/digest/d19/tables/dt19_322.20.asp. Accessed August 20, 2021.

Jones, Edward P. (2003). *The Known World*. New York: HarperCollins.

Kaba, Mariame (2021). *We Do This 'Til We Free Us: Abolitionist Organizing and Transforming Justice*, Tamara K. Nopper (ed.) Chicago: Haymarket Books.

Kelley, Robin D.G. (2002). *Freedom Dreams: The Black Radical Imagination*. Boston, MA: Beacon Press.

Khan, Hamid, on behalf of Stop LAPD Spying Coalition (2019). 'Abolish the Stalker State: A Call to Action!,' in Ananya Roy and Hilary Malson (eds) *Housing Justice in Unequal Cities*. Los Angeles: UCLA Luskin Institute on Inequality and Democracy, 135–144. Accessed online: https://escholarship .org/uc/item/4kq1j0df.

Khouri, Andrew (2019). 'L.A. County Rent Control and Eviction Rules Advance for Unincorporated Areas,' *Los Angeles Times*. Accessed online: www.latimes.com/business/story/2019-09-10/la-county -supes-to-vote-on-permanent-rent-control-for-unincorporated-areas. Accessed September 10, 2019.

Kurwa, Rahim (2015). 'Deconcentration Without Integration: Examining the Social Outcomes of Housing Choice Voucher Holders in Los Angeles County,' *City & Community* 14 (4): 364–391.

Leavitt, Jacqueline, and Susan Saegert (1990). *From Abandonment to Hope*. New York: Columbia University Press.

Lorde, Audre (1982). 'Lessons from the 60s.' Lecture delivered at the Malcolm X Weekend, Howard University, Washington, DC. Published in Lorde, Audre (1984). *Sister Outsider: Essays and Speeches*. Berkeley: Crossing Press, 134–144.

Malson, Hilary and Terra Graziani (2019). 'Towards a Praxis of Housing Justice: Provocations for Reflection and Action,' in Ananya Roy and Hilary Malson (eds) *Housing Justice in Unequal Cities*. Los Angeles: UCLA Luskin Institute on Inequality and Democracy, 37–42. Accessed online: https:// escholarship.org/uc/item/4kq1j0df.

Mapping Police Violence (2021). 'Police Accountability Tool,' *Mapping Police Violence*. Accessed online: https://mappingpoliceviolence.org/cities.

Marin, Max (2021). 'Squatting for Survival in Philadelphia: What It's Like to Live in a "Takeover" House,' Billy Penn: Broke in Philly series. Accessed online: https://billypenn.com/2021/05/24/ philadelphia-vacant-homes-squatting-homeless-housing-crisis-history/. Accessed 24 August 2021.

McKittrick, Katherine (2006). *Demonic Grounds: Black Women and the Cartographies of Struggle*. Minneapolis: University of Minnesota Press.

Mitchell, Don (2003). *The Right to the City: Social Justice and the Fight for Public Space*. New York: Guilford Press.

Nadasen, Premilla (2002). 'Expanding the Boundaries of the Women's Movement: Black Feminism and the Struggle for Welfare Rights,' *Feminist Studies* 28 (2): 270–301.

Norward, Lindsay (2019). 'The Day Philadelphia Bombed its Own People: An Oral History of a 1985 Police Bombing that Changed the City Forever,' *Vox*. Accessed online: www.vox.com/the-highlight/2019/8/8/20747198/philadelphia-bombing-1985-move. Accessed June 20, 2020.

Noterman, Elsa (2020). 'Taking Back Vacant Property,' *Urban Geography*. DOI: 10.1080/02723638.2020.1743519.

Office of Homeless Services (2021). 'Point in Time and Youth Count of People Experiencing Homelessness,' City of Philadelphia Office of Homeless Services. Accessed online: http://philadelphiaofficeofhomelessservices.org/know-homelessness/pit-and-youth-count-of-people-experiencing-homelessnesss/.

Painter, Nell Irvin [1986 (1976)]. *Exodusters: Black Migration to Kansas After Reconstruction*. New York: W.W. Norton & Co.

Petitjean, Clément (2018). 'Prisons and Class Warfare: An Interview with Ruth Wilson Gilmore,' *Historical Materialism* blog, translated and republished from French original. Accessed online: www.historicalmaterialism.org/index.php/interviews/prisons-and-class-warfare. Accessed August 4, 2021.

Price, Richard (ed.) [1996 (1979)]. *Maroon Societies: Rebel Slave Communities in the Americas*. Baltimore: The Johns Hopkins University Press.

Purifoy, Danielle, and Louise Seamster (2020). 'Creative Extraction: Black Towns in White Space,' *Environment and Planning D: Society and Space* 0(0): 1–20. DOI http://dx.doi.org/10.1177/0263775820968563.

Reclaiming Our Homes (2020). *Reclaiming Our Homes*. Accessed online: https://reclaimingourhomes.org/. Accessed March 2020.

Roberti Act (1979). Article 8.5, Surplus Residential Property [54235-54239.3], Title 5, Chapter 5. Accessed online: https://leginfo.legislature.ca.gov/faces/codes_displayText.xhtml?lawCode=GOV&division=2.&title=5.&part=1.&chapter=5.&article=8.5. Accessed August 17, 2021.

Roberts, Andrea (2017). 'Documenting and Preserving Texas Freedom Colonies,' *Texas Heritage* 2: 14–17.

Roberts, Andrea (2018). 'Performance as Place Preservation: The Role of Storytelling in the Formation of Shankleville Community's Black Counterpublics,' *Journal of Community Archaeology and Heritage* 5 (3): 146–165.

Robinson, Cedric [2000 (1983)]. *Black Marxism: The Making of the Black Radical Tradition*. Chapel Hill: University of North Carolina Press.

Roy, Ananya (2019). 'Housing Justice: Towards a Field of Inquiry,' in Ananya Roy and Hilary Malson (eds) *Housing Justice in Unequal Cities*. Los Angeles: UCLA Luskin Institute on Inequality and Democracy, 13–19. Accessed online: https://escholarship.org/uc/item/4kq1j0df.

Roy, Ananya, Terra Graziani, and Pamela Stephens (2020). 'Unhousing the Poor: Interlocking Regimes of Racialized Policing.' The Square One Project's Roundtable on Justice Policy. Accessed online: https://challengeinequality.luskin.ucla.edu/2020/08/25/unhousing-the-poor/. Accessed August 9, 2021.

Scott, Darius (2019). 'Oral History and Emplacement in 'Nowhere at All': The Role of Personal and Family Narratives in Rural Black Community-Building,' *Social & Cultural Geography* 20 (8): 1094–1113.

Seale, Bobby (1972). 'Black Panther Party Programs – Serving the People,' in Susan Fainstein and Norman Fainstein (eds) *The View From Below: Urban Politics and Social Policy*. Boston, MA: Little, Brown and Company, 327–333.

Shoenfeld, Sarah (2019). 'The History and Evolution of Anacostia's Barry Farm.' DC Policy Center. Accessed online: www.dcpolicycenter.org/publications/barry-farm-anacostia-history/#_ftnref37. Accessed June 15, 2020.

Sitton, Thad, and James H. Conrad (2005). *Freedom Colonies: Independent Black Texans in the Time of Jim Crow*. Austin, TX: University of Austin Press.

Spade, Dean (2020). 'Solidarity Not Charity: Mutual Aid for Mobilization and Survival,' *Social Text 142* 38 (1): 131–151.

Squatters: The Other Philadelphia Story (1984). Movie. Accessed online: https://archive.org/details/squatterstheotherphiladelphiastory. Accessed August 24, 2021.

Sugrue, Thomas (1996). *Origins of the Urban Crisis: Race and Inequality in Post-war Detroit*. Princeton: Princeton University Press.

Swann, Robert S., Shimon Gottschalk, Erick S. Hansch, and Edward Webster (1972). *The Community Land Trust: A Guide to a New Model for Land Tenure in America*. Cambridge, MA: Center for Community Economic Development.

Taylor, Keeanga-Yamahtta (2019). *Race for Profit: How Banks and the Real Estate Industry Undermined Black Homeownership*. Chapel Hill: UNC Press.

Ture, Kwame, and Charles V. Hamilton [1992 (1967)]. *Black Power: The Politics of Liberation*. New York: Vintage Books.

15. Planning, informality and power

Mona Fawaz

INFORMALITY AND POWER: A FRAMEWORK

The contrast between imagined planning's ordered futures and the everyday realities of urban populations in numerous cities around the world has pushed planners to articulate approaches to addressing *unruly* realities. By *unruly*, I point to those realities that do not conform to the rules set by city planners and governing bodies. These realities correspond to urban quarters often tagged as *unplanned* or *unregulated* where land occupation may not respect legal property rights, lot subdivisions may not conform with zoning regulations, and building development does not meet the standards of building laws (Fernandes and Varley, 1998). Such realities also correspond to markets where transactions are unrecorded, workers are unprotected, and displays and/or exchanges occur on the street, outside areas allocated officially for commercial activities (Portes et al., 1989).

In most cities of the Global South, the fact that everyday urban realities rarely conform to the set laws that attempt to regulate them has dominated planning research for decades. Case studies documenting markets and low-income settlements across Latin America, East Asia, the Middle-East and/or Africa have consistently shown cities to grow outside the modern imaginary of planners. Early research on this form of housing was mostly anchored in Latin America where terminologies such as *favelas*, *barrios*, or *villa miseria* entered the lexicon of planning as of the 1960s. It translated in the reading of similar neighbourhoods across the cities of the South. Similar modes or urbanization have been documented in the United States, where *colonias* have replicated the patterns of illegal lot subdivisions and servicing documented earlier across the border in Mexico (Ward, 2010; Mukhija and Loukaitou-Sideris, 2015), while in numerous American, European, and Australian cities, scholars have also described substandard building conditions, illegal subdivision of apartments, and overcrowding in apartment units, in violation of housing building, safety, or fire codes (Kennedy, 2002; Devlin in: Porter et al., 2011). More recently, planning theorists have pointed to the fact that unruliness, or transgression of planning rules is also widely practiced by the high-heeled (Weinstein, 2008) and studies have expanded to document these practices and investigate how they mesh with the modalities of urban governance (Roy, 2009; Banks et al., 2020).

In order to explain the discrepancy between the imagined planned realities, on the one hand, and actual realities, on the other, the mainstream of planning has repeatedly called on the terminology of *informality* to designate urban settlements or labour markets. The ubiquity of this terminology however conceals radically different conceptions and uses of the term, as well as considerably different approaches to accounting for and interrogating power in the production and organization of such neighbourhoods. Early formulations of this challenge approached informality as an aberration and consequently sought to explain *why* it was occurring. These formulations rarely accounted for power, although the visions of order that they consistently adopted set the benchmarks on the basis of which those deemed *informal* could be criminalized and their homes eradicated. Other strands in the planning literature have embedded in their interpretation of informality a consideration of power differentials. To some, informality is a label that justifies the power to exclude, it is imposed by powerful state actors and serves to govern inequitably. To others, informality is a mark of resistance or potentially an affirmation of the right to the city, undeniably a sign of the power to transgress and imagine otherwise. This chapter reviews the multiple scholarly trends that have approached informality, focusing on how each has conceptualized power. It concludes by proposing an approach that weaves together readings of informality as a window to understanding everyday power as embedded in everyday urban negotiations and the recognition that planning has to wrestle and cohabitate with these multiple forms of informality – and consequently power – rather than eradicate or ignore them.

INFORMALITY: SURVIVAL AND TRANSIENCE

A review of the planning literature shows that within this body of knowledge, informality is typically embedded in two tropes: *survival* and *transience*. The oldest of the two tropes, survival, locates informality in the context of a struggle of individuals conducting menial and small-scale work that allows them to survive in substandard conditions. This was, for example, the case of the widely cited early International Labour Organization reports of the 1970s that are credited for coining the term *informality* in relation to markets (Hart, 1973; Peattie, 1987).[1] Extended to the framework of housing, informality is seen as the condition of housing where 'people have to step outside of the law in order to survive and secure shelter and income' (Watson in: Porter et al., 2011: 151). Devlin in: Porter et al. (2011) calls these activities 'instances of the urban poor, under conditions of extreme inequality, producing the urban in ways that help them survive day-to-day in the city, even if these survival strategies violate local laws regulating urban space' (p. 145).

There are multiple versions of the *survival* trope. In many cases, survival is equated with misery, deprivation, and potentially marginality – particularly in the early literature (Hardoy and Satterthwaite, 1989). In other versions, survival takes an appreciative tone, recognizing the ingenuity and creativity of low-income city dwellers who demonstrated an entrepreneurial spirit and the desire to integrate the rest of the city if given the opportunity, since, in Perlman's words, 'They have the aspirations of the bourgeoisie, the perseverance of pioneers, and the values of patriots' (Perlman, 1976: 243). Taken up again by a recent debate in the field of architecture, the survival trope also points to strategies of recycling waste to survive, showing how informal communities reuse *waste* to produce quarters where they can survive (Cruz, 2014; Brillembourg and Klumpner, 2005, also see Varley 2013).

Transience, the second trope, explains the discrepancy between planners' expectations and actual realities as a provisional or temporary condition that will naturally end when the realm of planning extends over the city. Informal settlements, it was thought, would be permanently erased once modernization completes its cycle. It is indeed the expectation of improvement that also encourages residents temporarily to accept poor conditions. 'For long periods of time,' Caldeira (2016: 5) writes, 'people inhabit spaces that are clearly precarious and unfinished, but with the expectation, frequently realized, that the spaces will improve and one day look like wealthier parts of the city'.

Widely championed by the advocates of self-help housing in the 1970s (then the terminology used for informal settlement), the trope of transience describes an incremental building process that responds better to the needs of rural migrants whose budgets and needs evolve as their settlement in the city consolidates. In its most radical version, informality allows for an open-ended process of urban settlement that consolidates in a form that fits best the needs of city dwellers. If housing is seen *as a verb*, Turner and Fichter (1972) famously argued, then housing should be assessed according to its trajectory of becoming rather than how well it fits modern building standards. Ample evidence of the initiative of informal settlement dwellers and their ability to consolidate their neighbourhoods fostered a powerful position by international organizations that encouraged city authorities to *tolerate* buildings and neighbourhoods that do not fit modern standards and/or introduce upgrading strategies that could support the efforts of those building their homes through self-help. The lesson, then, was in incrementalism as the solution. The message continues to find echoes in the work of site and service projects, but also the interventions of a handful of acclaimed architects who see in incrementalism a viable design solution to the challenge of affordable housing – as most famously with the work of the firm Elemental in Chile.

Several versions of the transience argument have been articulated over the course of the past five decades of scholarship, and not all see informal settlements and labour with the same favourable eye. While anarchists like John Turner saw in informality a freedom to build a better adapted solution, a transitional phase in which city dwellers developed their homes incrementally, others saw in the transience of informality the remaining element of a savage, vernacular, or pre-modern world destined for erasure once planning measures are finally adopted. Such depictions were prevalent in post-colonial literature and in recent discourses of neoliberal urban policy-makers that consistently 'presume that informal populations will disappear naturally as cities and countries advance through teleological stages of development' (Sheppard et al., 2020; 394).

Both survival and transience have in common the assumption that it is possible, perhaps even inevitable, that planning will extend its scope over urban territories with the unstoppable development process (Benjamin, 2008). As such, the trope allows planners to address informality as an aberration and to depict laissez-faire urban management as a temporary concession since the normal course of development will eventually set the pace and eradicate this undesirable reality. The tropes also make it possible to limit planning interventions to attempts to *fix*, *upgrade*, *improve*, or sometimes *erase* neighbourhoods, markets, or practices considered informal, in other words, to *formalize* them. Thus, the bulk of planning theory responding to informality has been essentially concerned with the *regularization* of informal practices (Durand Lasserve, 1998).

Decades later, it is evident that the assumption that informality is transient or can be confined to a mere survival strategy does not stand the test of time. Rather than expanding its scope over cities, planning as the public exercise of ordering space and providing services has considerably reduced its scope (and ambitions) across the world. A few decades ago, it may have been possible to tag such development as exceptional and confine them to the unusual condition of a handful of cities in the Global South, typically also plagued by the compounded weights of wars, colonization, and more. The body of research in urban studies has nonetheless piled the evidence against this assumption: Planners now admit that most cities grow through incrementally added floors and rooms that do not observe building standards, unrecorded rental contracts, evictions or protections secured by neighbourhood strongmen rather than the police force, and only small pockets of well-regulated development. As such, unruliness is no longer easy to explain through transience of the sheer temporary need for survival. Instead, informality has maintained its central role in the scholarly literature by locating unruliness at the intersection of power and planning. In the next sections of this chapter, I show first how informality has been depicted as the outcome of state exclusion and, second, as a transgressive exercise by state dwellers resisting this exclusion.

INFORMALITY: THE TAG OF EXCLUSION

In attempting to infuse consideration for power in the consideration of urban informality, scholars have problematized the central role of the state in systematically excluding and criminalizing large populations groups tagged as *informal*. The main arbitrator of what counts, then, as desirable, is the state that defines property laws, building guidelines, and urban regulations. 'Informality,' Portes et al. (1989: 11–37) wrote, 'lies within the scope of the state, rather than outside it … It is the power of the state that will define what is formal and what is not'. This distinction, moreover, reflects the biases embedded in the structures of state governance such as modern ideals, classed distinctions, racial or ethnic preferences are reproduced through planning law. Consequently, informality is tied to particular, geographically and historically situated constellations of power that are reproduced through the regulatory bodies that decide what will count as *inside* the law and what will not, at a specific moment. In capitalist systems, processes of accumulation by dispossession render capitalist development possible and they produce informality as their constitutive outside (De Sousa Santos, 1977; Al-Sayyad and Roy, 2004).

In this reading of informality, planning is a central culprit. Rather than the fostering of orderly or desirable cities, planning is a tool in the hands of powerful state agencies which can be deployed to exclude those deemed undesirable and/or shape the city in forms that serve the interests of the powerful, particularly capital. The binary reading of the city into formal and informal quarters, orderly and unorderly, white and black, civil and uncivil areas, reflects an imposed hierarchy in which entire urban quarters (labelled informal) are de-facto criminalized. In other words, informality is given a negative connotation as it is placed in binary opposition with a desirable formal. Through this process, planning plays a central role in offering the seemingly objective guise of science to justify exclusion. Thus, Watson argued, planning has introduced 'a dominant and persistent planning rationality which … sets standards of "normality" regarding "proper" living environments in clean, orderly, and "modern" cities' (Watson in: Porter et al., 2011: 151). Against this normality, informality became an emblem of *dis-orderliness* in Watson's words, or again a reality attached to 'unregulated, uncontrolled, messy and inefficient settlement and use of land … positioned as fundamentally different from the ordered, regulated, efficient notions of planned land use and settlement. Informality becomes the "other" to planning's ordered, neat spaces' (Porter et al., 2011: 116).

As of the 1970s, critiques of state regulations as exclusionary came from multiple poles across the political spectrum. Radical voices defending self-help housing denounced the *state-centrist* biases of housing models that imposed inadequate building standards (Turner and Fichter, 1972; Hardoy and Satterthwaite, 1989). The problem, Turner argued based on his work in Lima, lay in planning frameworks that upheld unrealistic, sometimes undesirable standards and consequently stigmatized and excluded self-help quarters. Although Marxist critics disagreed considerably with Turner's position, arguing that his pro-self-help stand justified the poor conditions in which working class urbanites were forced to dwell (Burgess,

1982), they concurred with the critiques of state standards, pointing to the dominance of class interests in the formulation of state law and its translation into the exclusion and criminalization of lower income groups for whom access to adequate housing was impossible in the capitalist economies. 'In a capitalist society,' De Sousa Santos wrote, 'the State legal system is in general an instrument of class domination' (De Sousa Santos, 1977; 5).

Since then, numerous studies have documented the biases embedded in urban regulations and models of property rights, arguing that planning agencies are sometimes directly responsible for the production of illegality, as laws and master plans are passed to alter the status of lands and buildings, criminalizing existing developments or, conversely, legalizing what was deemed irregular. In Beirut (Lebanon), my research showed that the development of peripheral neighbourhoods predated the adoption of building and zoning regulations. Regulations were in fact introduced decades after construction had happened, and they were sometimes deliberately designed to criminalize the presence of communities deemed undesirable. By for instance designating areas where low-cost housing was developing as high-end single home housing, planners sought to curtail the expansion of this form of housing. Although they often failed to stop the development, given the dire need for housing, they appended a tag of illegality on poor people's homes (Fawaz, 2004; Deboulet and Fawaz, 2011). Similarly, speaking of Delhi in India, Bhan argued that what many describe as the 'unplanned' is the 'outcome of state planning' (Bhan, 2013; 59). Plans 'determine and limit', he wrote, and they 'determine spatial patterns of settlement and inhabitation that are "unplanned" and "chaotic"' (p. 59). Still in India, Johnston showed the entanglement of class, caste and violence attached to the classifications of legality that serves the municipal authority to exclude the (indigenous) Baoris community from the city of Ahmedabad (Johnston, 2014), while in Turkey, Kuyucu (2014) shows similar practices vis-à-vis the Romany communities of Istanbul. This critique is clearly not confined to a specific geography, with for example Blomley (2007) showing that land use codes in San Francisco undermine the survival strategies of the urban poor and deny those informally housed thinking and acting subjectively, reframing them instead as offending objects (see also Sheppard et al. 2020).

In turn, the classification of building into legal and illegal quarters has important repercussions for the lives of those who are tagged with informality because it subjects them to the violence of state actions, justifying their neglect, sometimes eviction. Roy (2009) and Yiftachel (2009) have described such interventions as systems of valuation in which informality works to insert unequal worthiness to neighbourhoods that are governed inequitably or to workers whose labour can be organized in levels of flexibility, with some forced into more precarious or insecure employment while others remain stable. Thus, individuals whose labour and/or housing is labelled as *informal* may at any time find their presence and/or labour criminalized as *outside the law*. This criminalization may first materialize with seemingly benign mechanisms whereby informal urban quarters are omitted from official city maps where they appear as green areas and/or open spaces (Rolnik, 1996; Yonder, 1998). Their existence in the city happens 'off the books' (Devlin in: Porter et al., 2011: 144). With time, such erasures translate into exclusion from direly needed services and facilities, justified because of their *illegality*, their occupation of *public land*, or the fact that they threaten public health or security, ultimately reproducing and exacerbating pre-existing inequalities (Watson in: Porter et al., 2011; Johnston, 2014). Worse, the tag of informality can mobilize the aggressive arm of the planning apparatus and expose the residents of these neighbourhoods to bulldozing, since a so-called *illegal* status justifies eviction, particularly when the spaces they occupy become desirable locations for the implementation of public projects such as urban renewal (Kuyucu, 2014), roads and highways (Fawaz, 2004; Deboulet and Fawaz, 2011), or large-scale sports facilities as has been well documented in the case of the World Cup and Olympic Games (Broudehoux, 2007; Rolnik, 2013; Freitas, 2017). Even when it does not lead to eviction, the tag of informality will manifest itself in 'grey-spacing' entire urban quarters (Yiftachel, 2009), generating areas occupied by migrants or minority groups who dwell in substandard temporary arrangements, partially beyond the gaze of the state.

In problematizing further the role of the state, scholars have expanded the notion of informality from a tag attached to urban quarters to a mode of governance, one that allows the flexibility of inclusion and exclusion within the prerogatives of the ruling classes and the needs of the capitalist economy. Indeed, not only do states have the power of exclusion, but they also can deploy flexible forms of inclusion that determine, in turn, who has the right to the city and for how long (Roy, 2005). Informality is thus a political regime of governance which suspends claims over the right to the city, services, and decent living and allows for governing liberalized cities in ways that fit the needs of capital (Johnston, 2014). The neoliberal turn in urban governance has intensified this form of governance. As of the 1980s, displacements abounded to make way for urban renewal projects developed under the banners of preservation, order, or reform (Kuyucu, 2014; Lombard and Huxley in Porter et al., 2011; Briggs, 2011; Rukmana in: Porter et al., 2011). Through these projects, rights once granted to labour and/or residents were flexibly revoked, through processes described by Roy as 'un-mapping' where deliberate legal ambiguities and arbitrary administrative decisions are deployed, as documented in Calcutta (Roy, 2004), Ahmedabad (Johnston, 2014), and numerous other cities. What may have been *tolerated* or considered a de-facto recognition of an albeit truncated right to housing is thus reduced to a temporarily tolerated presence filling the need for cheap labour needed to support the lifestyle of the richer classes with drivers, nannies, cleaners, and others (Caldeira, 2001; Sassen 2001).[2] Similar trends have also been documented vis-à-vis peddlers and other informal sellers whose presence, once tolerated in numerous cities across the world, was retagged as an eyesore by municipal authorities eager to attract an imagined tourist economy and support its infrastructure (Rukmana in: Porter et al., 2011).

Conversely, neoliberalism has also expanded the discretionary power of the state to *regularize* excluded populations, particularly when they could be re-engaged as possible clients or taxpayers.[3] Best identified with the De Soto thesis (2000), planning interventions that consist of *titling* (through sales or other means) grant land ownership (and private exchange rights) to residents who have benefited from de-facto use rights on specific property (Krueckeberg, 2004). This form of regularization does not necessarily entail the right to receive urban services, since the latter also have to be paid for. However, the titling process allows city authorities to streamline all forms of property claims into the single model of freehold. Based on the liberal-economist model of property, these policies have been deployed in numerous national contexts (e.g., Tanzania, Mexico, India) where the formalization of land tenure has been shown as an exercise to restructure property relations to facilitate accumulation and control (Lombard and Huxley in: Porter et al., 2011; Gilbert, 2012). As such, informality becomes the domain of selective market inclusion rather than mere exclusion (Roy, 2005).

Not all readings of informality however focus on the disempowerment of those tagged illegal. In parallel to denouncing the exclusion of state structures, numerous scholars have argued that informal practices also embody acts of resistance by those excluded from state structure. In the next section, the chapter turns to these arguments.

INFORMALITY AS A MODE OF RESISTANCE

In its most radical reading, informal land occupation and/or work is the enactment of the right to the city as formulated by the French radical thinker, Henri Lefebvre (1968; 1974; see also Chapter 2 by Olsson and Besussi). This transgression is a political act in which individuals challenge the oppressive rules of the state and/or capitalism and actualize their presence in the city through direct occupation and labour (Fawaz, 2009; Shields, 1998; Lefebvre, 1968). This *right to the city*, as famously coined by Lefebvre, differs distinctively from other uses of the term that frame the terminology of rights through a state-based entitlement. Rather, for Lefebvre, the right to the city can only actualize when stakeholders recognize their own power and take back the authority that they were forced to relinquish to state and/or the market institutions (Purcell, 2014; Fawaz, 2009a). By occupying land that is not purchased through the market and affirming claims over the city outside the channels defined by state agencies, informal settlement dwellers are enacting a radical agenda of political change.

Lefevbre's influential thinking has inspired numerous articulations of this proposal. Aside from recognizing agency in the act of self-help, as seen in the early documentation of these neighbourhoods (Turner and Fichter, 1972), scholars have infused political intent in the acts of city dwellers engaged in squatting and/or illegal building (e.g., auto-construction in Latin America). In its basic formulation, the act of building is a resistance to the oppressive colonial project and modern standards.[4] It may also be simply an affirmation of one's right to be present and visible in the city, as in the growing body of literature documenting the agency of urban refugees and their critical participation in city-making (Chatty, 2016; Fawaz et al., 2018). Thus, Harb et al. (2017) speak of *entrepreneurs* while Fawaz et al. (2018) outline the strategies of food delivery drivers who affirm their visible presence in the city by navigating its quarters.

The extent to which acts of transgression, however, translate into political action that defies state authority differs from one context to another and from one interpretation to another. The best-known translation of the act of squatting into an alternative political vision is perhaps embodied in Holston's (2009) notion of *insurgent citizenship* in which residents in the auto-constructed peripheries of Brazilian cities confront regimes of inequality and enact through self-help strategies their right to be in urban centres and access urban services. For Holston (2009), the difficulties encountered by those who had resorted to *auto-construction* politicized their demands and made them the core issues of their grassroots organization, building movements that demanded inclusion and recognition. Taking this argument one step further, Caldeira (2016) defines acts of squatting as *experiments in politics and democracy* and argues that new modes of politics through practices are producing new kinds of citizens, claims, and contestations. These readings parallel an array of concepts, all of which infuse political intent in the transgressive action of squatters and illegal builders. Among the best known are *occupancy urbanism* (Benjamin, 2008) or *invented participation* (Miraftab and Wills, 2005), both of which refer to a repertoire of radical planning in which illegal hook-ups and resistance of eviction forms the basis of community-based activism where disadvantaged groups contest their exclusion. Others have also pointed to the *recognition* gained when, for example, informal workers gain entitlement to labour protection despite their illegal status. Thus, Banks et al. (2020) have noted the extension of urban services to informal settlements or the success of informal workers in securing pension benefits in Brazil as important modalities of reclaiming rights despite the informal tag. This amounts, for Miraftab and Wills (2005), into arenas of action where citizenship is practiced, rather than bestowed or granted. Ultimately, these authors see in the transgressive practices of social movements or grassroots organizations a citizenship actualized through new discourses of rights that experiment with new forms of local governance and formulate new approaches to social policy, planning, law, and citizen participation (Holston, 2009). These practices, Caldeira (2016) and Holston (2009) argue, are in direct connection between the informal building practices and the protests that have filled the streets of several cities in recent years, such as Istanbul (El-Kazaz, 2013; Tugal, 2013), Sao Paulo (Caldeira, 2016), and Cairo (Ismail, 2014).[5]

Not all scholars, however, agree to the political potential of these actors. Perhaps no less political in the intent, but nonetheless without vocal confrontation nor a claim over citizenships, squatters in the Middle East, for Bayat (2013), or rather those urban dwellers to which he refers as the 'urban disenfranchised' in Cairo and Teheran pursue their 'their quiet daily struggles and 'refigure new life and communities for themselves and different urban realities on the ground in Middle Eastern cities through direct actions in the very zones of exclusion' (p. 5). These actions amount, in Bayat's terms, to a *quiet encroachment* that is neither guided by ideology nor organized through officially recognized movements (Bayat, 1997). Similarly, Varley (2002) points to political cooptation and contexts rife with inequities and discrimination.

UNDERSTANDING THE CITY AS THE SITE OF POWER STRUGGLES

Most of the conceptions of informality covered in this chapter focus their reading of power on the state/city-dweller nexus. Most cities however grow outside the imagination of planners, and the structures of power that organize them cannot be limited to those of the state. Neither are the institutions and rules that organize cities' everyday lives limited to those of the formal state system. In this last section, I propose to reflect on how planning, power, and informality can be considered in a de-centred approach where everyday urban struggles occur without a necessary mediation of state law and public agencies, in the plethora of negotiations that characterize the processes through which the urban majorities access shelter and basic needs in most urban contexts around the world (Simone, 2011). The focus for planners is no longer in explaining why urbanization deviates from a standard norm. Rather, the production of the urban is approached as a continuously negotiated process among a wide array of actors whose practices and positions reflect the diversity of institutions and norms that regulate the making of the urban. In this context, planners may approach informality as a 'site of critical analysis' (Banks et al., 2020) or a resource for approaching contemporary urbanization (McFarlane, 2012), a frame through which to explore the multiple, provisionary or permanent arrangements that actors negotiate at the local, municipal and national scales (Mukhija and Loukaitou-Sideris 2015). Seeing informality as a site of critical analysis diverges attention towards the institutions and rules through which numerous urban actors secure, consolidate, negotiate access and distribution of resources.

To make this point, I begin with the common recognition that the organization of everyday life in urban contexts across the world rarely revolves solely around the state and its agencies. As city dwellers seek to access shelter, work, and other daily necessities, they negotiate access to a house, services, or a job with an employer, a landlord, and/or other providers without necessarily going through state institutions or relying on state laws to regulate their activities.[6] Instead, widespread evidence points to the deep embeddedness of everyday life in thick networks of social relations such as kinship, geographic proximity, national belonging, or religious belief. These networks connect individuals and groups and allow them to organize, collaborate, or coordinate activities according to sets of norms that are enforced through informal institutions and practices (Merry, 1984). For example, one's reputation may act as an informal institution that serves to secure interactions as individuals rely on social networks to gather information about an individual and secure the reassurance needed to conduct a transaction instead of relying on an official market rating or a contract. In this context, state laws and institutions do not serve as a basis for all agreements. Rather, state laws can take the form of a reference, more or less followed, distorted, and adapted, but also potentially dismissed, depending on numerous historical and geographic contingencies (Varley, 2002; Fawaz, 2009b; de Sousa Santos, 1977; Razzaz, 1994).[7] Without being actively involved in transaction regulations, state institutions, such as a court of law, can also be used for deterrence power to keep the other party in check (Fawaz, 2009b; Benjamin, 2008; Van Gelder, 2010; De Sousa Santos, 1979; Razzaz 1994). Furthermore, the boundaries between formal and informal (with regard to land tenure) are blurred (De la Cueva, 1987; Benton, 1994) as opposed to the default dichotomist view that assumes that land tenure, building practices, or economic transactions either reside completely inside or entirely outside the law (Van Gelder, 2010). In sum, multiple regulatory bodies often imbued with cross-references provide evolving benchmarks and/or reference when needed and most urban quarters around the globe grow regulated by such arrays of conflicting, overlapping, complementing, blurred or contradictory regulatory bodies and institutions.

Just like state institutions, social institutions and the rules they sanction are rife with power differentials that affect social actors in distinctive form. The latter, furthermore, are not passive recipients locked in structural relations. They also deploy their own energy to acquire (social, symbolic, or economic) capital that allows them to reposition themselves within the hierarchies where they conduct their everyday transactions (Bourdieu, 1979; Fawaz, 2008). Still, such hierarchies are often difficult to challenge. Thus, one's status as a refugee or migrant workers –often tagged as an illegal presence – imposes a weaker negotiation position and ultimately less power to secure an advantageous outcome. Similarly, in patriarchal societies, women tend to find themselves consistently at a disadvantage, although they are constantly renegotiating their positions (Ghannam 2002).

To clarify these points, let us look at the studies of informal urbanization which I conducted in Beirut's peripheries two decades ago (Fawaz 2008, 2009b). These studies clearly illustrated the embeddedness of informal urban development in local power hierarchies. By tracing the rise of several groups of developers in Beirut's largest informal settlement over four decades, I showed how each generation of developers had secured its penetration and control over the land and housing market by cultivating an array of social networks that connected these developers to powerful actors during the period when they managed to rise in the neighbourhood's social hierarchies and impose themselves as *the developers*. Social networks were of multiple nature, and included tribal family networks, religious networks, but also bridging networks connecting residents or developers to influential social agents (within/outside state institutions). Thus, during the 1960s, control over the land and housing markets necessitated connections with local planning agents and members of the local police station, at a time when the young nation state was being established and the rule of law was relatively enforced. Although developers broke the law in selling land and engaging in illegal building development, they secured their position and the protection of the land and housing market through networks that connected them particularly to public agents. The tides however changed during the years of civil war, when connections with local militias became necessary, empowering another generation of developers to penetrate and control the market. As such, every generation of informal land developers that took charge worked with the power hierarchies that organized the territories at the time of their operation. In parallel, the study showed that for residents to be able to acquire shelter in the neighbourhood with acceptable risk, they also had to secure some level of power. From the standpoint of the homebuyers, it was – in their words – 'being backed', or having the ability to leverage local power and impose one's entitlement over others that mattered. Backing was similarly secured by social networks that could translate into social capital when connections to sufficiently influential actors were secured. Thus, social networks translated into forms of power, such as 'negotiation power' when residents were able to secure delay in payment or lower costs. They also translated into 'retaliation power', when buyers were able to find reliable recourse if they perceived an informal developer was in default, consequently enforcing the terms of an agreement or a more favourable compromise (Fawaz, 2009b). Finally, by tracing multiple shelter transactions in these informal settlements, I showed that the relative power of actors entering transactions was not fixed. Rather, actors constantly sought to improve their relative positions in the social hierarchies by forging new sets of relations that could secure better outcomes for their transactions (e.g. lower costs for residents or more leeway, eliminating police raids or competition for developers). While these forms of organization are context specific to Beirut and its transforming history, their deep embeddedness in local histories and geographic, social, political, and cultural realities are mirrored in other contexts where similar practices are observed.

In sum, cities are not designed by planners or state actors alone. Herrle and Fokdal (2011) argue that if many cities are still functioning despite the weakness of their governments, it is due to the presence of such *clandestine factors* that maintain economic progress. They point to the fact that cities are the product of more than one group of planners or politicians, but rather that they are produced by a range of actors in which illegal groups often play an equally important role as the legal ones. These *collective actors* negotiate on the power play in the city, even when such negotiations do not occur face to face. Thus, one can read urbanization as the product of more or less coordinated labour that intersects within spaces where a wide range of actors with divergent interests and powers interact. These negotiated processes are not merely actions/reactions or direct influence, nor do they result in optimal equilibrium. As such, they can only be studied as a collection of informal practices, processes, and institutions that planners have to engage with. In other words, informality allows us as planners to widen our understanding of urban production and recognize the continuous transformation (or becoming) of urban contexts (Simone, 2011), to remain open to the multiplicity of institutions and rules that organize the city, and to the ever changing power differentials that organize them.

A CONCLUSION FOR NOW

A few decades ago, Lisa Peattie (1987) critiqued the concept of informality as obfuscating a proper reading to the city. In a widely cited essay, Peattie argued for dropping a term that was more confusing than useful. Decades later, I recall Peattie noting in one of our conversations that 'informality' was still used because it responded to the need for planners to describe a ubiquitous and persistent reality. This persistent reality, I believe, is a recognition that despite planners' best aspirations, cities are mostly shaped outside their control and the long-term trajectories that urbanization takes escapes their most sophisticated forecasting. The turn in the theorization of informality from a site of resistance and/or exploitation to a site of study provides planners with an interesting opening that allows them to consider their position within the discussed hierarchies. These conversations should necessarily recognize that cities are sites of power struggle among unequal actors, where law is often deployed as a site of contestation and a strategy of governance by those who can control it, rather than the reflection of an objective order or higher justice. Similarly, these conversations should reject the binary reading that social norms and informal regulations are either emancipatory or criminal. Only when planners are able to recognize their limited power to influence the future of cities, and when they begin to study, observe, and account for power in the contexts where they design their interventions, can they hope to engage constructively with the complexity of today's urbanization.

NOTES

1. It was in 1972 that the phrase 'informal sector' was coined in an International Labour Organization report titled 'Employment, incomes and equality' about labour in Kenya. The authors of the report used 'informal', while speaking of 'employment in a productive, economically efficient and profit-making, sector of the economy though small in scale and limited by simple technologies, little capital and lack of links with the other ("formal") [*sic*] sector'.
2. This argument recalls early Marxist critiques of self-help housing that denounced pro-self-help arguments as providing a convenient excuse for those who wanted to evade the responsibility on the capitalist class to provide adequate shelter for low-income city dwellers. By celebrating self-help as an adequate form of housing provision, Burgess (1982) famously argued, planners were perpetuating the oppression of a working class who was denied the right to adequate housing and confined instead into substandard conditions. The tolerance of informality, in other terms, provides justification for planning agencies and state authorities to deny these working-class residents the right to adequate housing and acts instead as a substitute to adequate redistributive housing policy.
3. This follows a tradition in which the selective inclusion was often conducted as a favour for the purpose of accumulating votes in exchange for favours (Varley 2002).
4. In recent years, architects have also seen in informal building acts of resistance to the state, with Brillembourg (2004) for example arguing that the architecture of the barrios in Caracas defies the rectilinear order of the colonial city and the deluded utopia of modern planning, what he describes as the 'oppressively axial colonial urbanism' (p. 81). In his words, the morphology of the barrios 'represents the anti-state' (pp. 80–81).
5. These points are however widely contested as a celebration of 'subaltern' urbanism, as in Roy's Slumdog Urbanism, for example (Roy, 2011).
6. Furthermore, the role and position of state law and its impacts on informal regulations varies from one context to another. In many contexts, weak legal systems mean that state agencies do not have a monopoly of power and the enactment of legal rules is sidestepped in favour of other forms of regulations. As such, 'many actions that are formally governed by official law in reality take place outside its regulatory reach' (Van Gelder 2010, p. 242).
7. It is noteworthy that the distinction between what counts as formal and what does not is often hard to delineate. Not only do state agencies, as pointed above, shift the boundaries for what counts as legal/ not, but there are also numerous continuities across transactions and neighborhoods that prevent a harsh delineation of urban quarters.

REFERENCES

AlSayyad, N. and Roy, A. (2004). 'Urban Informality: Crossing Borders', in Roy, A. and AlSayyad, N. (eds) *Urban Informality: Transnational Perspectives from the Middle East, Latin America and South Asia*. Lanham, MD: Lexington Books, pp. 1–6.

Banks, N. Lombard, M., and Mitlin, D. (2020). 'Urban Informality as a Site of Analysis', *The Journal of Development Studies* 56(2): 223–238.

Bayat, A. (1997). *Street Politics: Poor People's Movements in Iran*. New York: Columbia University Press.

Bayat, A. (2013). *Life as Politics*. Stanford, CA: Stanford University Press.

Benjamin, S. (2008). 'Occupancy Urbanism: Radicalizing Politics and Economy beyond Policy and Programs: Debates and Developments', *International Journal of Urban and Regional Research* 32(3): 719–729.

Benton, L. (1994). 'Beyond Legal Pluralism: Towards a New Approach to Law in the Informal Sector', *Social and Legal Studies* 3: 223–242.

Bhan, G. (2013). 'Planned Illegalities Housing and the "Failure" of Planning in Delhi: 1947–2010', *Economic and Political Weekly* 48(24): 58–70.

Blomley, N. (2007). 'How to Turn a Beggar into a Bus Stop: Law, Traffic, and the "Function of the Place"', *Urban Studies* 44(9): 1697–1712.

Bourdieu, P. (1979). *La Distinction*. Paris: Editions de minuit.

Briggs, J. (2011). 'The Land Formalisation Process and the Peri-urban Zone of Dar es Salaam, Tanzania', *Planning Theory and Practice* 12(1): 115–153.

Brillembourg, A. and Klumpner, H. (2005), 'Imagine the New City', in Brillembourg, A., Feireiss, K., and Klumpner, H. (eds) *Informal City: Caracas Case*. Munich: Prestel, pp. 248–259.

Brillembourg, C. (2004), 'The New Slum Urbanism of Caracas, Invasions and Settlements, Colonialism, Democracy, Capitalism and Devil Worship', *Architectural Design* 74(2): 77–81.

Broudehoux, A.M. (2007). 'Spectacular Beijing: The Conspicuous Construction of an Olympic Metropolis', *Journal of Urban Affairs* 29(4): 383–399.

Burgess, R. (1982). 'Self-help Housing Advocacy: A Curious Form of Radicalism. A Critique of the Work of John FC Turner', in Ward, P. (ed.) *Self-Help Housing: A Critique*. London and New York: Alexandrine Press, Mansell Publishing Ltd, pp. 55–97.

Caldeira, T. (2001). *City of Walls: Crime and Segregation in São Paulo*, Berkeley: University of California Press.

Caldeira, T. (2016). 'Peripheral Urbanization: Autoconstruction, Transversal Logics, and Politics in Cities of the Global South', *Environment and Planning D: Society and Space* 35(1): 3–20.

Castells, M. and Portes, A. (1989). 'World Underneath: Origins, Dynamics, and Effects of the Informal Economy', in Portes, A., Castells, M., and Benton, L. (eds) *The Informal Economy: Studies in Advanced and Less Developed Countries*. Baltimore: Johns Hopkins University Press, pp. 11–37.

Chatty, D. (2016). 'Refugee Voices: Exploring the Border Zones between States and State Bureaucracies', *Refuge: Canada's Journal on Refugees* 32(1): 3–6.

Collier, D. (1976). *Squatters and Oligarchs: Authoritarian Rule and Policy Change in Peru*, Baltimore: John Hopkins University Press.

Cruz, T. (2014). 'The Informal as Inspiration for Rethinking Urban Spaces: Architect Teddy Cruz Shares 5 Projects', Online Ted Blog at: https://blog.ted.com/architect-teddy-cruz-shares-5-projects/ last visited on February 9, 2022.

Deboulet, A. and Fawaz, M. (2011). 'Contesting the Legitimacy of Urban Restructuring and Highways in Beirut's Irregular Settlements', in Davis, D. and Libertun de Duren, N. (eds) *Cities and Sovereignty: Identity Politics in Urban Spaces*. Bloomington: Indiana University Press, pp. 117–151.

De la Cueva, A.A. (1987). 'Low-Income Settlements and the Law in Mexico City', *International Journal of Urban and Regional Research* 11(4): 522–542.

De Soto, H. (2000). *The Mystery of Capital: Why Capitalism Triumphs in the West and Fails Everywhere Else*. New York: Basic Books.

Durand-Lasserve, A. (1998). 'Law and Urban Change in Developing Countries: Trends and Issues', in Fernandes, E. and Varley, A. (eds) *Illegal Cities, Law and Urban Change in Developing Countries*. London: Zed Books, pp. 233–257.

El-Kazaz, S. (2013). 'It's about the Park: A Struggle for Turkey's Cities'. Available at: www.jadaliyya.com/pages/index/12259/it-is-about-the-park_a-struggle-for-turkey%E2%80%99s-cities, last visited February 9, 2022.

Fawaz, M. (2004). 'Strategizing for Housing: An Investigation of the Production and Regulation of Low-income Housing in the Suburbs of Beirut', doctoral dissertation, Massachusetts Institute of Technology.

Fawaz, M. (2008). 'An Unusual Clique of City-Makers: Social Networks in the Production of a Neighborhood in Beirut (1950–75)', *International Journal of Urban and Regional Research* 32(3): 565–585.

Fawaz, M. (2009a). 'Neoliberal Urbanity and the Right to the City: A View from Beirut's Periphery', *Development and Change* 40(5): 827–852.

Fawaz, M. (2009b). 'Contracts and Retaliation: Securing Housing Exchanges in the Interstice of the Formal/Informal Beirut (Lebanon) Housing Market', *Journal of Planning Education and Research* 29(1): 90–107.

Fawaz, M., Gharbieh A., Harb, M., and Salame, D. (eds) (2018). *Refugees as City Makers*. Beirut: Social Justice and the City Program (IFI, AUB).

Fernandes, E. and Varley, A. (eds) (1998). *Illegal Cities: Law and Urban Change in Developing Countries*. London: Zed Books.

Freitas, C.F.S. (2017). 'Undoing the Right to the City: World Cup Investments and Informal Settlements in Fortaleza, Brazil', *Journal of Urban Affairs* 39(7): 953–969.

Ghannam, F. (2002). 'Gender and the Struggle over Public Space', in *Remaking the Modern: Space, Relocation, and the Politics of Identity in a Global Cairo*. Berkeley: University of California Press.

Gilbert, A. (2012). 'De Soto's the Mystery of Capital: Reflections on the Book's Public Impact', *International Development Planning Review* 34(3): V.

Hardoy, J.E. and Satterthwaite, D. (1989). *Squatter Citizen, Life in the Urban Third World*. London: Earthscan Publications.

Hart, K. (1973). 'Informal Income Opportunities and Urban Employment in Ghana', *Journal of Modern African Studies* 11(1): 61–89.

Herrle, P. and Fokdal, J. (2011). 'Beyond the Urban Informality Discourse: Negotiating Power, Legitimacy and Resources', *Geographische Zeitschrift* 99(1): 3–15.

Holston, J. (2009). 'Insurgent Citizenship in an Era of Global Urban Peripheries: Insurgent Citizenship in an Era of Global Urban Peripheries', *City & Society* 21(2): 245–267.

Ismail, S. (2014). 'Infrastructures of Oppositional Action', in Parnell, S. and Oldfield, S. (eds) *The Routledge Handbook on Cities of the Global South*. London: Routledge, pp. 269–280.

Johnston, C. (2014). 'Politics in the Informalizing Metropolis: Displacement, Resettlement and Unstable Negotiations in Uncivil Ahmedabad: Politics in the Informalizing Metropolis of Ahmedabad', *International Journal of Urban and Regional Research* 38(2): 539–557.

Kennedy, D. (2002). 'Legal Economics of the US Low-Income Housing Markets in Light of "Informality" Analysis', *Law & Society Review* 4:71: 71–98.

Krueckeberg, D. (2004). 'The Lessons of John Locke or Hernando de Soto: What If Your Dreams Come True?', *Housing Policy Debate* 15(1): 1–24.

Kuyucu, T. (2014). 'Law, Property and Ambiguity: The Uses and Abuses of Legal Ambiguity in Remaking Istanbul's Informal Settlements: The Uses and Abuses of Legal Ambiguity in Istanbul's Informal Settlements', *International Journal of Urban and Regional Research* 38(2): 609–627.

Lefebvre, H. (1968). *Le Droit à La Ville (The Right to the City)*. Paris: Anthropos.

Lefebvre, H. (1974). *La Production de l'Espace (The Production of Space)*. Paris: Antropos.

McFarlane, C. (2012) 'Rethinking Informality: Politics, Crisis, and the City', *Planning Theory & Practice* 13(1): 89–108.

Merry, S.E. (1984), 'Rethinking Gossip and Scandal', in Black, D. (ed.) *Toward a General Theory of Social Control*. New York: Academic Press, pp. 271–302.

Miraftab, F. and Wills, S. (2005). 'Insurgency and Spaces of Active Citizenship: The Story of Western Cape Anti-Eviction Campaign in South Africa', *Journal of Planning Education and Research* 25: 200–217.

Mukhija, V. and Loukaitou-Sideris, A. (2015). 'Reading the Informal City: Why and How to Deepen Planners' Understanding of Informality', *Journal of Planning Education and Research* 35(4): 444–454.

Peattie, L. (1987) 'An Idea in Good Currency and How It Grew: The Informal Sector', *World Development* 15(7): 851–860.

Perlman, J. (1976). *The Myth of Marginality: Urban Poverty and Politics in Rio De Janeiro*. Berkeley: University of California Press.

Porter, L., Lombard, M., Huxley, M., Ingin, A.K., Islam, T., Briggs, J., Rukmana, D., Devlin, R., and Watson, V. (2011). 'Informality, the Commons and the Paradoxes for Planning: Concepts and Debates for Informality and Planning Self-made Cities: Ordinary Informality? The Reordering of a Romany Neighbourhood –The Land Formalisation Process and the Peri-Urban Zone of Dar es Salaam – Tanzania Street Vendors and Planning in Indonesian Cities – Informal Urbanism in the USA: New Challenges for Theory and Practice Engaging with Citizenship and Urban Struggle through an Informality Lens', *Planning Theory & Practice* 12(1): 115–153.

Portes, A., Castells, M., and Benton, L.A. (eds) (1989). *The Informal Economy: Studies in Advanced and Less Developed Countries*. Baltimore: Johns Hopkins University Press.

Purcell, M. (2014). 'Possible Worlds: Henri Lefebvre and the Right to the City', *Journal of Urban Affairs* 36(1): 141–154.

Razzaz, O.M. (1994). 'Contestation and Mutual Adjustment: The Process of Controlling Land in Yajouz, Jordan', *Law and Society Review* 28(1): 7–39.

Rolnik, R. (1996). 'Urban Legislation and Informal Land Markets – The Perverse Link, Paper given at the joint seminar on "Informal Land and Housing Markets"', Lincoln Institute of Land Policy and Department of Urban Studies and Planning at MIT, Cambridge, USA.

Rolnik, R. (2013). 'Ten Years of the City Statute in Brazil: From the Struggle for Urban Reform to the World Cup Cities', *International Journal of Urban Sustainable Development* 5(1): 54–64.

Roy, A. (2004). 'The Gentleman's City: Urban Informality in the Calcutta of New Communism', in Roy, A. and Alsayyad, N. (eds) *Urban Informality: Transitional Perspectives from the Middle East, Latin America, and South Asia*. Lanham, MD: Lexington Books, pp. 147–170.

Roy, A. (2005). 'Urban Informality: Toward an Epistemology of Planning', *Journal of the American Planning Association* 71(2): 147–158.

Roy, A. (2009). 'Why India Cannot Plan its Cities?', *Planning Theory* 8(1): 76–87.

Roy, A. (2011). 'Slumdog Cities: Rethinking Subaltern Urbanism', *IJURR* 35(2): 223–238.

Santos, B.D.S. (1977). 'The Law of the Oppressed: The Construction and Reproduction of Legality in Pasargada', *Law & Society Review* 12: 5–126.

Sassen, S. (2001). *The Global City. New York, London, Tokyo*. Princeton, NJ: Princeton University Press.

Sheppard, E., Sparks, T., and Leitner, H. (2020). 'World Class Aspirations, Urban Informality, and Poverty Politics: A North–South Comparison', *Antipode* 52(2): 393–407.

Shields, R. (1998) *Lefebvre, Love and Struggle*. London: Routledge.

Simone, A. (2011). 'The Surfacing of Urban Life: A Response to Colin McFarlane and Neil Brenner, David Madden and David Wachsmuth', *City* 15(3–4): 355–364.

Tuğal, C. (2013). 'Resistance Everywhere: The Gezi Revolt in Global Perspective', *New Perspectives on Turkey* 49: 157–172.

Turner, J.F.C. and Fichter, R. (1972). *Freedom to Build: User Control of the Housing Process*. New York: MacMillan Company, Collier-Macmillan Lim.

Van Gelder, J.L. (2010). 'Tales of Deviance and Control: On Space, Rules, and Law in Squatter Settlements', *Law & Society Review* 44(2): 239–268.

Varley, A. (2002). 'Private or Public: Debating the Meaning of Tenure Legalization', *International Journal of Urban and Regional Research* 26(3): 449–461.

Varley, A. (2013). 'Postcolonialising Informality?' *Environment and Planning D: Society and Space* 31(1): 4–22.

Ward, P.M. (2010). *Colonias and Public Policy in Texas and Mexico: Urbanization by Stealth*. Austin: University of Texas Press.

Watson, V. (2009). 'Seeing from the South: Refocusing Urban Planning on the Globe's Central Urban Issues', *Urban Studies* 46(11): 2259–2275.

Weinstein, L. (2008). 'Mumbai's Development Mafias: Globalization, Organized Crime and Land Development', *International Journal of Urban and Regional Research* 32(1): 22–39.

Yiftachel, O. (2009). 'Theoretical Notes on "Gray Cities": The Coming of Urban Apartheid?' *Planning Theory* 8(1): 88–100.

Yonder, A. (1998) 'Implications of Double Standards in Housing Policy: Development of Informal Settlements in Istanbul, Turkey', in Fernandes, E. and Varley, A. (eds) *Illegal Cities*. London: Zed Books, pp. 55–68.

16. Planning, power, and uneven development: a rent gap perspective[1]

Ernesto López-Morales

INTRODUCTION

Explaining underdevelopment has been a recurring topic for international studies. 'Third world,' 'dependency,' and 'unequal exchange' are categories of general use to account for an alleged incapacity of peripheral regions to achieve the productivity and living standards of the so-called global north (Biel, 2000). Historically, capitalism has expanded its parasitic character at an increasingly planetary scale (Brenner, 2014), while the idea of conceiving capitalism's development within an isolated region is materially impossible. From its inception, capitalism has drawn on a triple structure: first, domestic markets in the dominant countries; second, an economic system that links these markets; third, a global accumulation system that exploits 'southern' countries and prevents them from developing their local markets, thus preserving their exploitation (Biel, 2000). However, underdevelopment theories tend to be situated only on the international macroeconomic scale, thus making the geographical dimensions of uneven development not completely explored in all possible ways (Smith, 1984).

Entire regions represent opportunities to extract raw materials, labor force, use value (Brenner, 2014), or cheap land (Smith, 1979). For Hayes and Zaban (2020), an 'increase in transnational mobility helps to globalise rent gaps, making lower-income spaces accessible to higher income demand from higher "latitudes" of the global division of labour.' Agglomerating investment in space and leaving adjacent territories undeveloped (Vigar et al., 2005) is the core feature of the 'splintering urbanism' thesis (Graham and Marvin, 2001). Smith (1984) argued that a theory of uneven development must integrate space and social process at different levels as a fundamental change of perspective. While theorists have conceptual problems to achieve this integration, capital seems to achieve it every day in every practice since capital produces space in its image and likeness. This spatial/social integration is essential, as capital creates space in general and produces scales that give it coherence.

Since Smith (1979), the rent gap analysis dissects the political economy of privately led redevelopment. It explains fundamental issues for urban governance such as land value capture (Smolka, 2013, using different terms, though), ecological effects derived from land exploitation and residential displacement (Preis et al., 2020), foreign investment in derelict historical areas (Hayes and Zaban, 2020), and the like. Many cities show 'valleys' in their land value curves due to a continued lack of capital investment in often rundown historical areas. After a time, a rent gap appears as the disparity between the 'capitalized ground rent' (CGR) devalued by the current use of dilapidated land, and a 'potential ground rent' (PGR), increased by the new improvements in the surrounding area or the entire city. The rent gap means an economic pressure for a site that has become increasingly inadequate to its 'highest and best' use. This 'site' can be a building, an infrastructure, a neighborhood, or even the homes of specific types of users who do not hold or represent enough payment capacity under new market conditions, and so they are prone to be displaced (Wachsmuth and Weiser, 2018). The rent gap model assumes a sequence of causal connections that range from the long-lasting devaluation of a plot or entire area to the full exploitation of that potential rent. As an explanatory principle of urban capitalist redevelopment, the rent gap allows a comparison between different paths of urban redevelopment in different cities.[2]

The rent gap model has been criticized for its economistic perspective that allegedly disregards institutional, social, cultural, and political factors (Bernt, 2016); also, some neoclassical economists concluded that the standard neoclassical concept of land-use succession was more coherent than the rent gap to explain urban redevelopment (Bourassa, 1993). However, as Kallin (2020) argues, scholars should not lose sight of the model's fundamental purpose, which is a matter of rights and the power relations that inherently underpin uneven capitalist urban development. As Clark and Pissin (2020: 4) claim, critiques 'claiming grounds for rejection of the rent gap theory generally display poor understanding of it more than sound reasons for abandoning it.' Following Krijnen (2018: 2041), the rent gap should not be understood as an 'all-explanatory variable for urban change because, while the rent gap is a necessary condition for renewed capital investment in the built environment … to occur, it is an insufficient explanation of the process itself. This runs contrary to the charge of economic determinism.'

Under its many possible forms, the capture of rent gaps in urban areas is a crystal-clear example of the intersectional and conflictive arena between planning, power, and uneven development, particularly under state-oriented capitalism (López-Morales, 2016; Lai and Zhang, 2016; He, 2007; Shih et al., 2019). According to Preis et al. (2020: 3), 'rent gaps are shaped by legal structures, public policies and the social and political dimensions of economic power, all of which have been affected by shifting patterns of transnational capital investment and urban governance.' So-called 'state entrepreneurial environments and *ad hoc* urban planning' (Harvey, 1989) are essential tools to increase potential ground rents – namely, to increase the rent gap (Hackworth, 2007; López-Morales et al., 2012) to the interests of the private holders of capital and land. In the US, the powers for delineating planning goals are shared – 'in conscious or unwitting partnership' (see Preis et al., 2020: 3) – between private agents and the State. Other examples of state–private coordination in the rent gap extraction include cases from China, Lebanon, Chile, Scotland, Brazil, Sweden, and Taiwan (He, 2007; Krijnen, 2018; López-Morales, 2016; Kallin, 2020; Almeida et al., 2020; Clark and Pissin, 2020; Shih et al., 2019). This chapter addresses some of these cases. In an extremely competitive worldwide economic context, what rules is capitalists' power to extract exchange value from urban land, though not necessarily to produce the same urban image at the same scale in every place (Krijnen, 2018).

A famous phrase attributed to Lenin asserts that war is the extension of economic competition. Many military conflicts arise in areas that offer valuable commodities, namely oil, gas, water, minerals, urban rents, etc. However, when the maximized rent-seeking capitalist exploitation of land comes to a city or a neighborhood, the most obvious conflicts arise from the constant displacement pressure that unwealthy (also termed 'unresilient') land users experience (Marcuse, 1985; Slater, 2018), besides other environmental adverse effects. Often large developers or investors acquire land for renovation relatively cheaply, because of the 'oligopsonistic'[3] power the concentrators of wealth exert on the State and the economy (Christophers, 2019; López-Morales, 2016), especially those agents who represent the 1% and 0.1% of elites (Clark and Pissin, 2020), even in areas where land users are 'supposed' to receive better payments or compensation for the land they own or occupy. The rent gap also explains how and why the intensification of urban renewal in certain areas leaves the remaining space undeveloped, vast territories that do not meet basic housing conditions, perpetuating housing scarcity and assuring there will be enough devalued land to exploit as economic opportunities for subsequent rounds of renovation. This is part of the cyclical character of capitalism (Smith, 1984).

Either via strictly authoritarian and centralized planning (He, 2007; Lai and Zhang, 2016), or in a relatively chaotic laissez-faire market (Krijnen, 2018), or by piecemeal privatization of formerly state-owned housing assets (Kallin, 2020), in all cases, the rent gaps are planned to assure uneven urban conditions in favor of the capitalist maximized extraction of potential rents. For Lefebvre (2003), urban rent remains the primary income for capitalism.

The following three sections shortly theorize about uneven development and land rent. The following two sections address the rent gap as an example of uneven development and explain the role that state planning plays in rent gap formation and accumulation at the 'highest and best use,' being Shenzhen, China and Taipei, Taiwan, excellent examples of state-planned rent gaps. The following section discusses hegemonic ways of naturalizing rent gap exploitation and the racialized and environmental implications that capitalist uneven urban development generates. Along with New York, the drastic renovation of Mexico City's broad central area portrays this situation sharply. The conclusions convey possible responses to landed-profit-oriented uneven development.

UNEVEN DEVELOPMENT AT INTERNATIONAL SCALE

The rise of capitalism is the history of its geographical expansion. Capitalism reflects the victory of its unbridled forms of exploitation over existing areas of the world, imposing 'modernizing' – or in more contemporary terms, 'developmentalist' – impulses. However, despite the political costs and social resistance against the expanding capitalism, the exploitation of the modern/traditional dualism, or the urban/rural divide, has strategic advantages for capital: on the one hand, capitalism initially negates traditional economies, social knowledge, and socio-political structures found in specific peripheries, excluding them from the dominant economic flows; on the other hand, capitalism subsequently exploits these conditions precisely because of their non-monetary or underpaid character (e.g. work by women, children, local indigenous peoples or ethnic minorities; exploitation of rural land, urban peripheries or villages, etc.). Marx referred to the extraction of use-value from non-commodified spaces and its conversion to pure exchange value as 'primitive' or 'original' accumulation (Glassman, 2006); in other words, a way to elevate capital's rate of return from 'infinite' nature (see also Chapter 1 by Murphy and Fox-Rogers).

Classical economics treated nature as 'otherness,' a borderline of economic development or, in its vicissitudes, as the cause of crises, but never as a central element of economic theory (Smith, 1984). Marx was aware of the problems derived from a dualistic conception of nature. So he integrated nature and society through a metabolic relation of production of nature and, under capitalism, surplus accumulation by a minority, and the legalized slavery of the majority besides the abuse of non-commodified environments.

W.W. Rostow (1971) argued that incorporating non-capitalist territories into capitalist global markets should not be rejected. This linear-evolutionary process naturalized the international division of labor and justified the role peripheral countries play as primary commodity exporters while their economy supposedly 'takes off.' However, many saw a tendency towards a deterioration in terms of trade suffered by peripheral countries (Prebisch, 1949), and behind this deterioration, the so-called 'Dependency Theory' (Cardoso and Faletto, 1979; Marini, 1973) saw an unequal exchange by which the periphery transfers surplus value to the center.

Global uneven development during the inter-war and post-second war periods contradicted Rostow's teleology regarding successive development phases. Development discourses in southern countries during much of the twentieth century were oriented to increasing domestic production under the premise of promoting a sequence of accumulation–take-off–trickle-down. Therefore, international policies imposed early stagnation moments to reduce local consumption aiming to assure accumulation, while many peripheral states were implementing import substitution industrialization (ISI) policies. However, after World War II, ISI policies did not involve sustainable development or narrow the gap between industrialized and low-development countries. Instead, they represented the beginning of a new phase of international funding at rates so high that they would hardly allow requiting external debt but installed new forms of post-war imperialism, namely the IMF and the World Bank (Biel, 2000). Since the 1970s, the neoliberal context brought a technological handover that would further exacerbate dependence, the marginalization of 'unofficial' economic sectors, and concealed environmental damage.

To analyze capitalism's uneven development by conceiving north–south exploitative relations is an epistemological and ontological task. Capitalism makes sense – it means accumulation through inter-regional exploitation (Smith, 1984). However, as a product of this ontology, most dependency-like theses suffer from certain limitations: nation states stifled as structures without self-determination, dependent on the needs of capital; a role of the individual and social actors 'produced' by these structures; determinism in understanding the historical development of the global development process; and the teleological idea that capitalism will sooner or later exhaust its margins of maneuver, rather than mutate into a new era of financialized accumulation (Lapavitsas, 2014). Nor did dependency theorists see urban land commodification at the forefront of capitalism's contradictions in today's rapidly urbanizing world and the myriad unpredictable outcomes from urban land rent exploitation that have emerged.

LAND RENT UNDER CAPITALISM

Intrinsically, uneven development is the domination of a social class by another class that occupies a different place on earth and has a radically different class consciousness (Marcuse, 1964). The tension between 'differentiation' and 'equalization' cannot be more evident. At a global scale, the subaltern strata live far away from the owners of capital, but they sometimes exist near one another in neighboring districts within cities. Urban segregation is a sociological term to refer to uneven development, namely, the geographical expression of class contradiction and social polarization. Uneven development is just the chaotic nature of capital expressing itself in space. The social struggle for equalization, namely the claim for access to housing or urban resources in certain undeveloped territories, represents a threat to the rentier elite's control of a particular form of scarcity that benefits them (Christophers, 2019).

In urban capitalism, land, as part of nature, is increasingly commodified but always in the process of being shaped, reshaped, and challenged by a class's spatial practices whose identities and actions undermine the comparatively more homogeneous pre-capitalist city (Katznelson, 1993). Rent is consequently the rationing device for the commodification of land, required by all its inhabitants for multiple uses. In some countries, like the UK, rent is derived from a title to land (i.e. landed property), and this title changes hands infrequently. In other countries, particularly in the so-called global south, land property changes more dynamically. For instance, in places where the poor informally seize devalued land as *favelas*, *slums*, *gece-kondu*, etc., the State later 'regularizes' that land via titling policies or other 'developmentalist' planning strategies that incorporate those places as part of the urban land market. In all cases, rent is a productive means (Smith, 1984) and a financial asset (Harvey, 1989).

More importantly, though, rent is the excess payment the owner of an asset receives for that asset's monopolistic nature, namely, scarcity (Christophers, 2019). In a geographical sense, centrality is a scarce attribute. From Von Thünen's rent model to Alonso's rent-bid model to Neil Smith's rent gap theory, closeness to urban centers is essentially a matter of social dispute on land. Urban land is, by definition, scarce, and its appropriation is monopolistic (Topalov, 2003). For instance, the particularly ambiguous legal status of Shenzhen's encroached villages amidst the fast pace of urban expansion gave villages' owner-residents enormous bargaining power with the State until the law was changed precisely to curb that power (Lai and Zhang, 2016). We see this case further below.

Land rent can be theoretically understood as the future payment for a plot of land. However, unlike other commodities, rent in its natural state costs nothing to be produced – it just means unearned income to its owner (Clark and Pissin, 2020). Rent emerges as capitalism expands and the economic and legal laws affecting that land change. The transaction costs of land use imply the commodification of nature and all life embedded in a specific space, and its extraction means land transformation into an economic asset. In fact, in Marx's words, rent only comes to exist when commodified and appropriated by a parasitic landowning bourgeoisie (Marx, 1995). Still, the situation has changed, as currently, rent appropriators range from landowners to investors to land developers to real estate speculators. Notwithstanding that classical theorists have explained that rent value is produced by physical characteristics, in Marx's categories, rent starts with nature's social transformation (Smith, 1984).

DIFFERENTIAL RENTS: DIALECTICS BETWEEN EQUALIZATION AND POLARIZATION

Differences in land productivity produce differential land rents. A first form of rent is Differential Rent I, explained by Marx as the surplus generated by the social work performed on a piece of land with better productivity. Due to the intensity of the capital invested on land and the capitalist class's capacity to technically transform the natural properties of land (or space), Differential Rent II emerges to solve the naturally formed unevenness of land 'productivity.' In classical Marxism, both types of rent, I and II, are to be accumulated by a landlord or a landowning parasitic class (Borisov et al., 1965; Marx, 1995). As noted above, in today's rapidly urbanizing world, rent is accumulated by different actors at an increasingly global scale (Hayes and Zaban, 2020).

In cities, land's natural characteristics are less important, while the social agency produced around it by the needs and interests of capital are far more crucial. In some cases, landowners' power can be decisive in determining a certain level of rent since land property allows them to hold back this resource, creating artificial scarcity, until they receive a positive return above all the differential rents (Topalov, 2003). Unlike agricultural space, in urban spaces, the capitalists' goal is not to equalize land's exploitation for reasons of extracting all the value contained as a form of productive rent, but to artificially intensify urban land exploitation at its best and highest use in certain 'central' areas (Marshall, 1961), thus always leaving remaining areas undeveloped.

Differential rents in the city are artificially created. According to classical interpretations (e.g. Von Thünen's model), land rent is determined by a land plot's distance from a central marketplace. In Ricardo's model, rent is increased by the productivity of a piece of land compared to an unproductive plot. William Alonso's bid-rent and land-use distribution model follows Von Thünen's logic, maintaining distance from the center as a rent-generator mechanism (Alonso, 1964). However, in the city, the creation of differential rent is far more complicated, as other factors intervene, such as distance from different centers in the city, building regulations, floor area ratios (FAR) or residential density allowed by planning ordinances, besides advantages in infrastructure nearby, and in general, everything that generates externalities in urban space and can be obtained as a benefit by the capitalist developer (Krijnen, 2018).

Under capitalist rule and from a class perspective, rent percolates upwards in an ascendant way, but not downwards; it transfers money from low- or middle-income groups to the dominant bourgeoisie, transiting from differential 1, 2 and monopoly rent, ending finally in financial spheres. If, as Marx (1995) noted, during the Industrial Revolution, money was transferred from a productive bourgeoisie to a landlord class, after the Urban Revolution in the second half of the twentieth century (Lefebvre, 2003), rent is extracted from rented land or buildings, rather than from a productive process. From a geographical perspective, the modern mechanisms of class-monopoly rent need to operate in constrained markets (to generate scarcity; Christophers, 2019), these being one of the leading producers of urban spatial fragmentation. The exploitation of rent needs to happen in segmented niches, usually spatially constrained sub-markets, to assure enough scarcity within them. This exploitation polarizes rather than equalizes urban space.

THE RENT GAP AS URBAN UNEVEN DEVELOPMENT

Based on systematic observations of urban land rent variations (unexplained by Alonso's bid-rent curves), Neil Smith (1979) proposed that the massive 'back to the city' movement and the 'revitalizing' inner-city areas seen in North America and Western Europe were less an effect of conspicuous cultural preference of a 'returning' suburban bourgeoisie and more due to the existence of increased potential ground rent (potential benefit to developers) and a lowered ground rent (actual present land rent value) yielded in those areas (Smith, 1979), namely, rent gaps. Hence the rent gap represents the dialectical interplay between decline and 'regeneration.' It was the monopolized urban rent which produced – in conjunction with the fixity of the capital invested in land (the initial construction and its successive improvements) and its long turnover period – the cycles of devaluation and decline experienced in the inner city. When Neil Smith came up with this idea, few people had doubts about gentrification as a 'culturally motivated' force led by Brownstoners, yuppies, or other elite cultural groups (Slater, 2018). Instead, the rent gap moved the epistemic observation of gentrification to the politico-economic realm, to see how urban capitalism inherently represents a battle of contrary forces, the rent gap that:

prevents redevelopment from occurring until invested capital has lived out its economic life [and] the long turnover period of capital invested in the built environment can discourage investment as long as other sectors of the economy with shorter turnover periods remain profitable. The early industrial city presented just such a barrier by the later part of the nineteenth century, eventually prompting suburban development rather than development in situ. (Smith, 1979: 541)

In global south cities, where welfare states hardly existed and the largest parts of cities lack adequate infrastructure, new transport facilities (López-Morales et al., 2019; Smolka, 2013; Bocarejo et al., 2013) or 'floating' Transferable Development Rights (Shih et al., 2019) increase the land's attributes of centrality, and hence raise the potential ground rent (PGR). However, the rent gap realization comes exclusively from development that involves an intensity of fixed capital investment designed to accommodate land's potential use.

Theoretically, both the CGR and PGR start at the same level when a plot is first developed. However, since surrounding urban development conditions change over time, allowing 'better' and 'higher' possible uses, the value of the buildings fixed to the site constitute a stumbling block to those possibilities. The building has come to a point where it no longer corresponds to the changed context, given that urban development under new conditions of capital investment pushes up a site's potential land rent to a certain level correlated to a greater intensity of capital investment and/or a 'higher' type of use. Hence, the rent gap constitutes an economic pressure for a site that has become increasingly inadequate to its 'highest and best' use artificially set by an economic environment (Smith, 1979). Previous improvements to land would become obsolete, and the currently capitalized land rent would decline. Eventually, an economic pressure emerges, impelling the site towards redevelopment with higher intensity and type of use (Clark, 1995; Hammel, 1999).

PLANNING THE RENT GAP

The State exerts power to reduce the uncertainty of land-use competition through planning controls and the provision of infrastructure and market subsidies (López-Morales et al., 2019). State institutions and regulations, a 'superstructure' made by the ruling class, aim to maintain this existing organization intact while allowing growth and accumulation, avoiding cyclical crises, and controlling social discontent. This process rests upon the nature of capitalism, and its ideological, economic, and political principle of private freedom, regulated by the exertion of class power (Jessop, 2002).

Eric Clark (1995: 1497) argues that the tension between actual and potential rents is far from being 'clinically clean of ties to power in social contexts nor of ties to the imagery of agents.' In fact, the opposite is true. For the appropriation of the rent gap, the State and private owners and investors have specific roles. A wide-open rent gap is a necessary yet not sufficient condition for urban renewal, with the public sector's intervention being an important factor. For instance, in historically deprived neighborhoods, an intricate pattern of property rights might exist, and it is difficult for developers to put together sufficient land and properties to make their involvement worthwhile. World cases vary according to different geographical, political, and legal settings, although it is not unusual to see fragmented structures of property ownership amidst so-called 'informal areas' that turn the occupier into an inappropriate vehicle for exploiting a devalued neighborhood at its highest and best land use (Lees et al., 2016) because when renewal implies much broader scales, the role of small-scale agents seems unsound.

Further, urban redevelopment is not purely dependent on injections of capital in areas of increased rent gap but on market analysts and property surveyors, besides speculation, luck, political influences (Krijnen, 2018) and, in general, class resistance, configuring altogether complex and regionally unique social systems of spatial transformation. Nonetheless, what is probably more decisive amidst the current globally widespread neoliberal forms of land redevelopment (Smith, 2002; Hayes and Zaban, 2020) is the active intervention of the State, seeking to create the economic conditions and processes for assuring reinvestment in disinvested areas, and make them so alluring for investors and helpful in enhancing urban competitiveness and promoting city images.

Following Harvey (2005), neoliberalism, paradoxically based on the discourse of state-free markets, finds its central contradiction when an elite of state technocrats exerts intensive power towards the liberalization of space. Ostensibly benign entrepreneurial ideology transpires from those guidelines that allegedly seek to restock the profitability of the outmoded former historical areas, developing newer, more adaptive, healthier, more sustainable, greener, more walkable, cleaner, 'gender-inclusive' mechanisms to make the built environment more flexible and attractive for the investment criteria of the flowing property market capital.

Besides, several planning mechanisms undermine capitalized ground rents (CGR) for a specific time. Redlining can be either a private bank aiming to devalue specific areas (Aalbers, 2006), or a state policy that prevents low-rise redevelopment by owner-residents (López-Morales et al., 2012), or even systemic contexts under certain conditions that momentarily depress the land rent, like a war (Krijnen, 2018). Below, I offer two contemporary examples that show direct links between rent gap and planning. One comes from Shenzhen, in the People's Republic of China, and the other from Taiwan.

Shenzhen's Village Encroachment and the Rent Gap

Shenzhen's urban expansion started after China's 1978 major economic and political reforms. By that time, Shenzhen's cropland covered 355 km^2, and hundreds of thousands of peasants subsisted working that land (Hao et al., 2011). When urbanization and industrialization took place at a massive scale, urban expansion (at a rate of 6 km^2 per year) implied considerable agricultural land loss and encroachment on rural land and the villages where the peasants lived; thus, many of them sought alternative means of income. As the city's booming economy attracted millions of migrant workers, this created an increasing demand for housing which the formal housing sector in the city could not satisfy, but local villages did ('informally'). Soon, petty village owners demolished and replaced their traditional one- or two-storey dwellings with concrete-built dwellings of up to four storeys and rented the newly built extra rooms to migrant workers to capitalize the land rent. We can call this process a 'first-stage rent gap.' The total floor area of Shenzhen's villages almost doubled from 54 million m^2 in 1999 to 106 million m^2 in 2004, while the area occupied by urban villages expanded from 73 km^2 to 94 km^2, for a city of current 13 million people. In 2005, migrants (euphemistically referred by the State as the 'floating population') living in urban villages numbered about 4.69 million, close to 14 times the number of indigenous villagers at the time (Hao et al., 2011).

Village residents had the legal right to receive rent payments (CGR) for their housing, a right that was unavailable to urban residents and migrants. Such was the most valuable resource to finance low-scale, dense housing construction in villages. This rent was not enforced by regulations, given the villages' ambiguous legal urban/rural situation. Instead, the ready supply of residential space helped suppress housing prices, so villages were fully open to rural migrants who found low-paying jobs and lived as an urban underclass. Following Smith (1979), villagers' relatively low CGR was enough to allow some capitalization but not enough to amass fortunes. By the 2000s, the State aimed to expand official redevelopment to the villages (let us call this process a 'second-stage rent gap') because,

> in urban villages [located within the city boundary], the official rural status of peasants and the collective land ownership largely protects them from the intervention of urban planning control. Urban village collectives or villagers can obtain approval for construction relatively easily from township- or village-level authorities, or even start building houses without submitting any application … However, as the village is adjacent to other villages or formal urban areas, land use is often chaotic and uncoordinated at a larger scale. For example, factories of an urban village that are purposely constructed away from the village's residential areas at the periphery could appear to be positioned next to dwellings of an adjacent neighborhood. Besides, due to the absence of formal regulation and planning, urban villages often only provide infrastructures and a living environment at the minimum standard. Compared to the formal residential neighborhoods, most urban villages are associated with relatively unsuitable land use, low-quality housing construction, severe infrastructural deficiencies, and a deteriorated urban environment … The informal status and poor quality of the urban village housing determines that they operate as a sub-standard, niche market for low-income housing, with extremely low rents compared to nearby formal housing. As the architectural style of houses and the village layout may also account for a considerably lower floor area ratio than that obtainable with high-rise apartment buildings, urban villages are generally very attractive prospects for redevelopment (Hao et al., 2011: 219–222).

By 2009, in order to facilitate land redevelopment and support future urban growth, the Shenzhen Government established new institutional arrangements for land redevelopment. Compared with state-led redevelopment during 2004–2009, China's newly established institutional arrangements conferred more recognition on potential market players by endowing development rights to the diversified de facto landowners, including villagers. He (2018: 29) notes how gentrification naturally emerged from this process, involving 'creative and cultural industry clusters, loft living, and mega-events.' As Lai and Zhang (2016) described, the de facto landowners and other potential market players had the right to develop land parcels in their villages but on the condition that all the parties should reach agreements to organize an 'urban renewal unit,' namely, single projects at a larger scale. This scheme looks fairer than a simple story of capitalists swindling landowners and stealing their right to land. However, post-2009 institutional arrangements redefined the relationship between the State and villagers and modified their property rights over communal land to make room for expensive high-rise redevelopments under a scenario of a scarcity of cheap land. Although this is not a clear case of rent gap-related displacement, it still represents the commodification of formerly rural land by centralized state power.

The Rent Gap as 'Floating' Transfer Development Rights in Taiwan

In Taiwan, Shih et al. (2019) illustrate the 'floating' Transfer of Development Rights (TDR) that has existed for around forty years, a private-to-private compensation system that benefits landowners in designated areas of the city with land-use restrictions. According to this system, there are sending zones where zoning regulations cap the redevelopment potential, namely land designated for transport infrastructure, green spaces, and facilities, as the most important land uses. Also, there are broad receiving zones that encourage compact and higher density development – within these zones, developers choose where to apply the TDR as an extra floor area ratio. Moreover, a trading mechanism means transforming TDR into monetary value to be transferred from the sending to the receiving zones.

Although the sending zones are strongly regulated, the receiving zones are less regulated and commonly unprepared to receive the extra floor area ratios (extra density). The law stipulates that a receiving zone must be physically feasible; namely, there must be infrastructure capable of accommodating higher density development. However, this condition is not always observed because, in Taiwan, the maximized rent-gap-oriented 'floating TDR' policy has allowed high-density redevelopment to occur precisely in areas where the land price is the lowest possible, namely, relatively peripheral areas with the poorest rate of transport service provided. In the end, Taiwanese planners have reduced control of where the higher density projects would occur in the city, in an environmentally unsustainable way. As Shih et al. (2019) note, since the early 2000s, around 3,800 development projects have utilized TDR in Taiwan, and these have generated more than 800 hectares of buildable floor area over existing FAR regulations.

The 'floating TDR' is a highly deregulated policy that maximizes market flexibility in determining high-rise and high-density development. Expensive real estate redevelopment occurs in receiving zones where the State has not yet prepared that land to receive such a high density. However, the potential development value (potential ground rent) is very high due to the FAR reinforced by the application of 'floating TDR.' Thus, this policy is about spatially mobilizing the rent gap according to powerful developers' sovereign spatial allocation decisions, turning this allegedly redistributive policy into a form of chaotic maximized capital accumulation. Shih et al. (2019: 838) induce a rule that seems to apply not only in Taiwanese cities but also everywhere:

> the slower the land price increased in the past, the more likely it is that the developer will proceed with TDR development in that location in the future. Since TDR density bonuses increase the economic rent a development project can generate, gravitating toward locations with such a preexisting condition of slower land price appreciation further enlarges the rent gap that the development project may eventually capture.

RENT GAP GOES RACIALIZED: HEGEMONY, DISCIPLINING AND DISPLACEMENT

We have seen that since capitalist urban redevelopment's motivation is rooted in the quest for rent gap profit, urban renewal comes not in spaces where it is socially needed but where it is financially needed. As a highly speculative business dependent on extremely volatile finance capital (Christophers, 2019; Lapavitsas, 2014), capitalist urbanism imposes interdictory laws on urban space and other forms of authoritarian state practices (Flusty, 2001) wherever these are required. For capitalist goals, often low-income occupants must not be visible. In many places, strategies of entrepreneurial redevelopment generally draw on zero-tolerance policies, and physical and societal forms of discipline are present in several forms of architectural design, CCTV, private security, and a range of legal impositions, as a means to inculcate acceptable patterns of behavior under the imposed new commerce and new aesthetics (Gaytan, 2016). Reclaiming public spaces for those groups that possess economic value as producers and/or consumers, virtually excluding others who belong to subjugated social groups and live in the less valuable space of the city, is an important social repercussion of rent gap exploitation.

Preis et al. (2020) analyze four different displacement-analysis metrics applied to Boston, in the United States, to identify seven districts with the highest probability of gentrification-induced displacement, and these areas show higher indices of racially Black populations. In New York, Wachsmuth and Weisler (2018) identify that an emerging new type of Airbnb-related rent gap (where the rent gap is not realized by demolishing the previous infrastructure but by displacing former long-term tenants and making the occupancy turnover rate faster) rises in a more pronounced way in Black neighborhoods than the city's average. On the other hand, Airbnb hosts who are racially White consistently earn a larger share of revenue on Airbnb than the average share of the city's population.

For the case of Mexico, anthropologist Pablo Gaytán, a university professor and housing activist in Mexico City, conceived the polysemic concept of 'whitening by dispossession' (WBD) which many people use to refer to recent urban changes in historically devalued central areas. Inspired by David Harvey's idea of accumulation by dispossession, WBD means the aesthetic whitening of the new buildings erected in the old quarters of the city, the racial whitening of the users of the central city, the money laundry (*blanqueado de divisas*) that takes place as long as the city redevelops, and more importantly, WBD entails a diminished right to the city for the thousands of deprived *vecinos* who live in central redeveloping areas.

The broad central area of Mexico City finds its historical origins in the late nineteenth century, part of the first extension of the colonial city when many rural areas were intended to settle affluent urban socio-economic groups (and their 'indigenous' servants). Neighborhoods like La Roma (the setting of the Oscar-winning movie by Alfonso Cuarón), La Condesa, Hipódromo and Juárez are among the most renowned examples (Salinas, 2014). Because of the Revolution in 1910, there were tensions between the White oligarchy and the masses of newly empowered peasants, mestizos, and indigenous people. This tension made central spaces unsafe for the oligarchs and their managerial classes, many of whom gave away their properties and moved out. Until the 1980s, there were thousands of hidden indigenous communities living in the heart of Mexico City, and there are still a few gathered all over the place. Gaytán (2016) explains how the current reclamation of central urban space and decent housing conditions by indigenous groups continues their historical struggle up to the present.

During the 2000s, State agencies performed hundreds of overt or covert expulsions of street vendors from the central streets (Delgadillo et al., 2015). The removal of indigenous groups from public spaces is also reminiscent of the highly racialized stratification in Latin America since colonial times (Echeverría, 2007; Gaytán, 2016). The State managed urban 'whitening' of the central city not just to change the skin color of urban users but also to impose the image of a new super-futuristic architecture, a spectacular 'hygienic cleansing' of the built environment conducted by powerful private actors to support the 'touristification' of central areas and historical centers (López-Morales et al., 2021). This spatial normalization eliminates important rooted cultural activities, like eating in the streets (a transversal cultural institution in Mexican public spaces), informal cultural expressions, and the right of poor men and women to work in the city. The City of Mexico's urban normalization attracts new users who move around using an efficient, clean, technological (and more expensive) public transportation system. All of this fosters a latent conflict with those who are supposedly backward, conflictive, dirty, primitive, and indigenous or Black (Gaytán, 2016; Glassman, 2006).

Capitalism's renewed spatiality implies the establishment of 'a new morality by referring to the "good community" and it thereby attempts to engineer behavior and social norms' (Bernd and Helms, 2003: 1848). Capitalism simplifies the social and economic chains that lie behind urban space and stigmatizes the local population with insubordination when they do not respond to macroeconomic revivals. Capitalist redevelopment installs a prophetic and dystopian image of urban malaise in the old city quarters, or the imposition at any cost of the notion of the superiority of some forms of middle-class lifestyle, even if the old environment generates more benefits to the low-income inhabitants than the supposedly more beneficial mixed communities (López-Morales, 2015).

Rachel Weber (2002) used the concept of 'urban blight' to refer to the practice of identifying and targeting, through quasi-scientific methods, the most interesting areas for private redevelopment, using biological or medical metaphors referred to 'cancers' or 'ulcers.' Blighting is, therefore, a primary justification (or a hegemonic facilitator) for rent-gap exploitation via symbolic land devaluation before redevelopment. With the laudable purpose of 'healthy' cities, the moral implications of blight blur the boundaries between private and public responsibility since destruction becomes a prioritized goal. Blight and potential ground rent are not irreconcilable antinomies but part of the same chain of capitalist devaluation, destruction, and renovation.

CONCLUSIONS

This chapter has analyzed the intersection between urban planning, power, and capitalist land redevelopment. The chapter's brief theorization covered from uneven international development to the rent gap, a generic model of capitalist urban redevelopment that integrates both the causes and effects of land devaluation and the subsequent commodification and accumulation of a potential rent as part of the same cyclical process. As David Harvey (2010; in Slater, 2018: 125) claims, the rent gap is 'a singular principle power that has yet to be accorded its proper place in our understanding of not only the historical geography of capitalism but also the general evolution of capitalist class power.'

Center and periphery become mutually dependent upon the geographical expansion of capitalism, in a similar way that urban decay and renewal are time-connected phenomena, two stages of the continuous destruction of *demodé* fixed capital and its replacement by renewed, technological, and hegemonic expressions of finance capital in city spaces that yield the highest economic return. International-scale developmentalism and urban entrepreneurialism respond to the same goal of continuously incorporating peripheral regions to sustain capitalism's survival. In the highly segregated cities of the global south, the affluent urban areas where the 1% elites live represent centers of command and control in the same guise that dominant countries rule and impose their modernizing agendas over developing countries.

Imposing rent-seeking renewal in old city quarters or barely developed peripheries is an effect of always-expanding capitalism. It entails the deliberate acceleration of the devaluation of building values to lower capitalized ground rents (CGR) and increase potential ground rents (PGR). Nonetheless, if the rent gap created is to be accumulated by private developers, state powers and different ad hoc policies are required to protect the unequal concentration of private capital in targeted regions of the city. Therefore, maintaining an aggressive blighting stance regarding the surrounding territories, vilifying old city aesthetics and their generally lower-income inhabitants might accelerate these territories' real decay if this stance is materialized in actual devaluation policies or the lack of urban maintenance policies in places where social needs are the highest. In sum, although the eventual existence of a rent gap is not a sufficient condition for urban redevelopment to take place, as Shenzhen's hundreds of villages-in-the-city clearly show, it is a very necessary condition for it, besides the exertion of state powers and planning policies to make the rent gap accumulation feasible.

An important step towards solving urban inequalities is to place the rent gap discussion at the center of the debate about urban development. Some commentators argue that a redistributive land value capture (of the rent gap) affords the equalization of uneven urban development in a city (Smolka, 2013); others advance political agendas of defeating the commodification of land use value by social struggle and resistance (Smith, 2002). In either case, the rent gap denudes capitalism's inherently anarchic working, and systematic study of the rent gap may suggest possible ways to develop 'theory and practice concerned with how to make rent gap theory not true' (Clark and Pissin, 2020: 4) – in other words, a research agenda to make land available for human needs besides the preservation of nature, not a commodity for capitalization by the few.

NOTES

1. Findings presented in this chapter are derived from the author's research project titled: Fondecyt ANID Code #1210972.
2. Comparing rent gap cases seems more meaningful than the intellectually limiting quarrel regarding the limits of gentrification theory (Clark and Pissin, 2020).
3. A market situation in which each of a few buyers exerts a disproportionate influence on the market (Merriam-Webster Dictionary. www.merriam-webster.com/dictionary/oligopsony).

REFERENCES

Aalbers, M. (2006) When the Banks Withdraw, Slum Landlords Take Over: The Structuration of Neighbourhood Decline through Redlining, Drug Dealing, Speculation and Immigrant Exploitation. *Urban Studies*, 43(7), 1061–1086.

Almeida, C., Giannotti, M. and de Almeida, C. (2020) Dynamic Modeling to Support an Integrated Analysis Among Land Use Change, Accessibility and Gentrification. *Land Use Policy*. https://doi .org/10.1016/j.landusepol.2020.104992.

Alonso, W. (1964). *Location and Land Use: Toward a General Theory of Land Rent*. Cambridge: Harvard University Press.

Bernd, B. and G. Helms (2003) Zero Tolerance for the Industrial Past and Other Threats: Policing and Urban Entrepreneurialism in Britain and Germany. *Urban Studies*, 40(9), 1845–1867.

Bernt, M. (2016). Very Particular, or Rather Universal? Gentrification through the Lenses of Ghertner and López-Morales. *City: Analysis of Urban Trends, Culture, Theory, Policy, Action*, 20(4), 634–644.

Biel, R. (2000) *The New Imperialism: Crisis and Contradictions in North/South Relations*. London: Zed.

Bocarejo J., Portilla I. and Pérez M (2013) Impact of Transmilenio on Density, Land Use, and Land Value in Bogotá. *Research in Transportation Economics*, 40(1), 78–86.

Borisov, O.S., V.A. Zhamin and M.F. Makárova (1965), in Vidal, A. (ed.) *Diccionario de Economía Política*. www.eumed.net/cursecon/dic/bzm/index.htm.

Bourassa, S.C. (1993) The Rent Gap Debunked. *Urban Studies*, 30(10), 1731–1744.

Brenner, N. (2014) *Implosions/Explosions: Towards a Study of Planetary Urbanization*. Berlin: Jovis.

Cardoso, F.H. and Faletto, E. (1979) *Dependencia y desarrollo en América Latina: ensayo de interpretación sociológica*. Mexico: Siglo Veintiuno.

Choy, L.H., Lai, Y. and Lok, W. (2013) Economic Performance of Industrial Development on Collective Land in the Urbanization Process in China: Empirical Evidence from Shenzhen. *Habitat International*, 40, 184–193.

Christophers, B. (2019) The Rentierization of the United Kingdom Economy. *EPA: Economy and Space*. DOI: 10.1177/0308518X19873007.

Clark, E. and Pissin, A. (2020) Potential Rents vs. Potential Lives. *Environment and Planning A*. DOI: 10.1177/0308518X20971308

Clark, E. (1995) The Rent Gap Re-examined. *Urban Studies*, 32(9), 1489–1503.

Delgadillo, V., Díaz-Parra, I. and Salinas, L. (2015) *Perspectivas del estudio de la gentrificación en México y América Latina*. Mexico: UNAM.

Echeverría, B. (2007) Imágenes de la 'blanquitud', in Echeverría, B., Lizarazo, D. and Lazo, P. (eds) *Sociedades icónicas: Historia, ideología y cultura en la imagen*. Mexico: Siglo XXI.

Flusty, S. (2001) The Banality of Interdiction: Surveillance, Control and the Displacement of Diversity. *International Journal of Urban and Regional Research*, 25(3), 658–664.

Gaytán, P. (2016) Espacio público: entre el yosmart y la invención urbanita. *Metapolítica*, 20(95), 49–55.

Glassman, J. (2006) Primitive Accumulation, Accumulation by Dispossession, Accumulation by 'Extra-economic' Means. *Progress in Human Geography*, 30(5): 608–625.

Graham, S. and S. Marvin (2001) *Splintering Urbanism: Networked Infrastructures, Technological Mobilities and the Urban Condition*. London and New York: Routledge.

Hackworth, J. (2007). *The Neoliberal City: Governance, Ideology, and Development in American Urbanism*. Cornell: Cornell University Press.

Haila, A. (2016) *Urban Land Rent*. West Sussex: Wiley-Blackwell.

Hammel, D.J. (1999) Re-establishing the Rent Gap: An Alternative View of Capitalised Land Rent. *Urban Studies*, 36(8), 1283–1293.

Hao, P., Sliuzas, R. and Geertman, S. (2011) The Development and Redevelopment of Urban Villages in Shenzhen. *Habitat International*, 35, 214–224.

Harvey, D. (1974) Class-Monopoly Rent, Finance Capital and the Urban Revolution. *Regional Studies*, 8(3–4), 239–255.

Harvey, D. (2005) *A Brief History of Neoliberalism*. New York: Oxford University Press.

Harvey, D. (2019) *The Enigma of Capital and the Crisis of Capitalism*. London: Profile Books.

He, S. (2007) State-sponsored Gentrification under Market Transition: The Case of Shanghai. *Urban Affairs Review*, 43(2), 171–198.

Jessop, B. (2002) Liberalism, Neoliberalism, and Urban Governance: A State-Theoretical Perspective. *Antipode*, 34(3), 452–472.

Hayes, M. and Zaban, H. (2020) Transnational Gentrification: The Crossroads of Transnational Mobility and Urban Research. *Urban Studies*, 57(15), 3009–3024.

Kallin, H. (2020) In Debt to the Rent Gap: Gentrification Generalized and the Frontier of the Future. *Journal of Urban Affairs*. https://doi.org/10.1080/07352166.2020.1760720.

Katznelson, I. (1993) *Marxism and the City*. London: Oxford University Press.

Krijnen, M. (2018) Beirut and the Creation of the Rent Gap. *Urban Geography*, 39(7), 1041–1059.

Lai, Y. and Zhang, X. (2016) Redevelopment of Industrial Sites in the Chinese 'Villages in the City': An Empirical Study of Shenzhen. *Journal of Cleaner Production*, 134, 70–77.

Lapavitsas, C. (2014) *Profiting Without Producing: How Finance Exploits Us All*. London and New York: Verso.

Lees, L., Shin, H. and López-Morales, E. (2016) *Planetary Gentrification*. Cambridge: Polity.

Lefebvre, H. (2003) *The Urban Revolution*. Translated by Robert Bononno from the original French publication, *La Révolution urbaine* (1970 edition). Minneapolis, MN: University of Minnesota Press.

López-Morales, E. (2011) Gentrification by Ground Rent Dispossession: The Shadows Cast by Large-scale Urban Renewal in Santiago de Chile. *International Journal of Urban and Regional Research*, 35(2), 330–357.

López-Morales, E. (2015) Gentrification in the Global South, *CITY*, 19(4), 557–566.

López-Morales, E. (2016) A Multidimensional Approach to Urban Entrepreneurialism, Financialization, and Gentrification in the High-Rise Residential Market of Inner Santiago, Chile, *Research in Political Economy*, 31, 79–105.

López-Morales, E., Gasic, I. and Meza, D. (2012) Urbanismo Pro-Empresarial en Chile: políticas y planificación de la producción residencial en altura en el pericentro del Gran Santiago. *Revista INVI*, 28(76), 75–114.

López-Morales, E., Sanhueza, C., Espinoza, S., Órdenes, F. and Orozco, H. (2019) Rent Gap Formation Due to Public Infrastructure and Planning Policies: An Analysis of Greater Santiago, Chile. 2008–2011. *Environment and Planning A*. https://journals.sagepub.com/doi/abs/10.1177/0308518X19852639.

López-Morales, E., Ruiz-Tagle, J., Santos Junior, O., Blanco, J. and Salinas Arreortúa, L. (2021) State-Led Gentrification in Three Latin American Cities, *Journal of Urban Affairs*, https://doi.org/10.1080/07352166.2021.1939040.

Marcuse, H. (1964) *One Dimensional Man*. London: Ark.

Marcuse, P. (1985) Gentrification, Abandonment and Displacement: Connections, Causes and Policy Responses in New York City. *Journal of Urban and Contemporary Law*, 28, 195–240.

Marini, R.M. (1973) *Dialéctica de la dependencia*. Mexico: Ediciones Era.

Marshall A. (1961) *Principles of Economics*. London: Macmillan.

Marx, K. (1995) Capital – Volume Three: The Process of Capitalist Production as a Whole. In Marxists Internet Archive (ed.). www.marxists.org/archive/marx/works/1867-c1/.

Prebisch, R. (1949) El desarrollo económico de la América Latina y algunos de sus principales problemas. *El Trimestre Económico*, 16(63(3)), 347–431.

Preis, B., Janakiraman, A., Bob, A. and Steil, J. (2020) Mapping Gentrification and Displacement Pressure: An Exploration of Four Distinct Methodologies. *Urban Studies*. DOI: 10.1177/0042098020903011.

Rostow, W.W. (1971) *Politics and the Stages of Growth*. Cambridge: Cambridge University Press.

Salinas, L. (2014) Transformaciones urbanas en el contexto neoliberal. La colonia Condesa en Ciudad de México: un proceso de gentrificación. *Ci[ur] Cuadernos de Investigación Urbanística*, No. 93, March–April, Madrid.

Shih, M., Chiang, Y.-H. and Chang, H. (2019) Where Does Floating TDR Land? An Analysis of Location Attributes in Real Estate Development in Taiwan. *Land Use Policy*, 82(2019), 832–840.

Slater, T. (2018) Rent Gaps. In Lees, L. and Phillips, M. (eds) *Handbook of Gentrification Studies*. Cheltenham, UK and Northampton, MA, USA: Edward Elgar, pp. 119–133.

Smith, N. (1979) Toward a Theory of Gentrification: A Back to the City Movement by Capital, Not People. *Journal of the American Planning Association*, 45(4), 538–548.

Smith, N. (1984) *Uneven Development: Nature, Capital and the Production of Space*. New York: Basil Blackwell.

Smith, N. (2002) New Globalism, New Urbanism: Gentrification as Global Urban Strategy. *Antipode*, 34(3), 427–450.

Smolka, M. (2013) *Implementing Value Capture in Latin America: Policies and Tools for Urban Development*. Cambridge, MA: Lincoln Institute. www.lincolninst.edu/sites/default/files/pubfiles/implementing-value-capture-in-latin-america-full_1.pdf.

Topalov, C. (2003) 'Traditional Working-Class Neighborhoods': An Inquiry into the Emergence of a Sociological Model in the 1950s and 1960s. *Osiris* (18), 212–233.

Vigar, G., Graham, S. and Healey, P. (2005) In Search of the City in Spatial Strategies: Past Legacies, Future Imaginings. *Urban Studies*, 42(8), 1391–1410.

Wachsmuth, D. and Weisler, A. (2018) Airbnb and the Rent Gap: Gentrification through the Sharing Economy. *Environment and Planning A*, 50(6), 1147–1170.

Weber, R. (2002) Extracting Value from the City: Neoliberalism and Urban Redevelopment. *Antipode*, 34(3), 519–540.

17. Power in planning from a Southern perspective

James Duminy and Vanessa Watson

INTRODUCTION

That urban and planning scholarship has undergone a 'Southern turn' is now an established refrain (Bunnell, 2015; Croese, 2018; Galland and Elinbaum, 2018; Schmid et al., 2018). In considering how power has been cast within theoretical discussions that express a desire to 'see from the South' (Watson, 2009), here we distinguish between work in planning studies, specifically, and that falling within a broader ambit of urban and geographical studies. The genealogies of the Southern turn in planning and urban studies have overlapped, fed into each other, and are part of the same broader movement and critique. However, given the focus of this volume, our particular concern is Southern thought in Anglophone planning scholarship and what is distinctive about its approaches to examining and understanding power.

In general, planning scholarship comprises diverse subfields, and is always shifting in its foci, instruments, and objectives. In the same way, Southern-inspired work in planning has diverse genealogies, influences, and emphases. As a result, in this chapter we will avoid depicting Southern planning scholarship as a homogenous and unchanging 'canon'. Rather, it is a dynamic *perspective* that has changed over time, partly in response to both external and internal critiques. While many of the original works to self-identify with a Southern perspective tended to offer high-level conceptual and critical arguments around the need for new knowledge bases suitable for planning practice in different parts of the world, more recent work has engaged in greater detail with what is needed to actually generate that knowledge. The chapter seeks to map out some of those developments in a non-definitive and exploratory manner. We point to three different (yet interrelated) lines of critical inquiry that characterize the Southern perspective, each of which has particular implications for thinking about and understanding power in planning. We first consider Southern critiques of the global geographies of planning knowledge and practice that are fundamentally shaped by legacies of colonialism and underdevelopment. We then discuss the Southern scholarly emphasis on theorizing planning with and through *place*. Finally, we reflect on Southern interest in the study of actually existing planning practices, and in praxis as a mode of generating knowledge and theorizing.

It is challenging to write authoritatively about Southern discourses and theorizations of power in planning for at least two reasons. One is that many scholars have not explicitly located themselves or their work within a tradition of 'Southern theory'. Reflecting the broad diversity of its influences and contributors, the Southern perspective is, in many cases, not something that self-identifies as *Southern*. Many scholars from Latin America, for example, would likely hesitate to classify their critical efforts within a Southern tradition, even if there are important exceptions (Fix and Arantes, 2021). Given the field's diversity and eclecticism, the difficult task of assembling and identifying key axes of Southern thought and scholarship has often fallen to those who are not its key progenitors (Duminy et al., 2014; Lawhon and Truelove, 2020).

A second difficulty is that a key impetus behind the Southern perspective is a fundamental critique of the nature, formation and uses of 'theory'. An overriding suspicion of generalizing and universalizing frameworks in favour of descriptions of 'the everyday' or more recognizably meso-level theoretical propositions (Yiftachel, 2006; Watson, 2008, 2016) necessarily enjoys an uneasy relationship with efforts to synthesize and pinpoint cross-cutting themes and arguments (Harrison, 2014). Nonetheless, it is the case that some scholars have identified themselves and their work in a Southern oeuvre. That, and the fact that the task of making sense of diverse insights and critical lines of sight is intrinsically edifying, make the task worthwhile. Yet we will also show that a Southern perspective is helpful in pointing to the preconditions and power relations that make it necessary for some scholars, such as ourselves, to speak *for* the South.

The chapter proceeds in five parts. The first considers the controversial question of what we talk about when we talk about the 'Global South', tracing the genealogies of various regional terminologies and offering our understanding of the term. The second focuses on a critique of power as it produces and shapes global networks and pathways of planning knowledge. The third discusses Southern perspectives on power in planning that emphasize the importance of thinking from and through *place*. The fourth section examines how an impulse to theorize from planning *practice* informs particular notions of power in Southern scholarship. We conclude with reflections on the failure of the Southern perspective to deconstruct Northern hegemony and suggest that, despite the shortcomings of Southern critiques, emerging forms of radical planning scholarship might productively engage with some of the latter's key concerns.

WHAT IS THE GLOBAL SOUTH?

There has been considerable debate as to whether or not the term 'Global South' is appropriate or useful. Distinguishing between particular framings of the Global South would be one way to map out the differences existing within an emerging and dynamic Southern perspective. We begin by explaining three different (developmental) categorizations of world regions as these in turn have shaped Southern theorizing and perspectives.

The terms 'developed' and 'developing' countries have been used by agencies such as the World Bank for many decades. Using a measure of Gross National Income per capita the world was divided into low- and middle-income countries (developing countries) and high-income, or developed, countries. The term 'underdeveloped areas' was first used in the inaugural address of US President Harry Truman in 1949, referring to those parts of the world which needed to 'catch up' with advanced industrialized countries, and assuming a linear path of economic growth and modernization would achieve this. However, in the 2016 World Development Indicators Report the decision was made to phase out the terminology of developed and developing countries due to the significant dissimilarity existing within each of these groups. The terms were replaced instead with regional groupings based on geographic coverage. Despite this recognition, the more recent Sustainable Development Goals still make use of the term 'developing countries'.

First coined by Alfred Sauvy in 1952, the geopolitical category 'Third World' originally suited the expectation among newly independent (post-colonial) countries of their growing role and importance within international affairs – an expectation secured at the Bandung Conference of 1955 (Solarz, 2012). The Third World came to reference a political coalition of countries with common experiences of colonialism and imperialism, which could exert political pressure on the First World (advanced industrialized economies) to counter interference and to recognize the need for global equity. The Second World at this time referred to countries (then) aligned with communist and socialist ideologies. Increasingly, the term Third World came to refer more generally to poor and developing countries, despite the high levels of economic heterogeneity found within the group. It, too, is now used less frequently as the original normative stance of the coalition against the First World has tended to disintegrate with the growth of regional inequalities and the rapid economic growth experienced by countries such as China and India.

The terms Global North and Global South, in contrast to those described above, could be described as post-developmental given their use as alternatives or critiques in relation to the two previous positions. However, there are ongoing debates on the meanings of these terms – does Global South stand as a metaphor for poor and colonized parts of the world? Is it a perspective on, or critique of, processes of imperialism and colonialism, and the inequalities brought about by globalization? Or should the term refer to a geographical South? And if so, does the term Global South-East better reflect the geo-political positioning of these parts of the world?

For Ananya Roy (2014: 11) the Global South is a *concept-metaphor* 'located at the intersection of entangled political geographies of dispossession and repossession'. However, here the term does not imply a single and stable 'location' but rather defines a temporal category signifying economic and geopolitical realignments, and the emergence of what she terms the Asian Century. As metaphor, the term Global South can also stand for processes of decoloniality, postcolonialism, or neo-colonialism. For Dados and Connell (2012: 13) the Global South may be metaphor, but for more than underdevelopment: 'It references an entire history of colonialism, neo-imperialism, and differential economic and social change through which large inequalities in living standards, life expectancy, and access to resources are maintained; and opens new possibilities in politics and social science'.

A number of authors use the term Global South to suggest a perspective or critique of EuroAmerican hegemony of theoretical production, the parochialism which underlies it, and the universality which it assumes. In an important early contribution to the field, Yiftachel (2006: 212) argued that it was time to conceptualize planning from the perspectives of the global 'South-East' in a manner 'not premised on the material and political settings of the dominant regions of the "North-West", from which most leading theories emerge'. He qualified this to say that deploying the term was not an attempt to set up binary categories but rather to designate 'zones' in a conceptual grid that draws attention to the main loci of power and identity. Later Comaroff and Comaroff (2012) suggested that theorizing from the Global South can offer privileged insights into the workings of the world at large: while the project of modernity has always been a North–South collaboration, it is in the Global South that the impacts of this relationship have been most starkly felt. Or, as Roy (2009: 820) puts it, 'perhaps the distinctive experiences of the cities of the Global South can generate productive and provocative theoretical frameworks for all cities'.

There has been much debate over whether or not the term Global South refers to a *geographical region*. In other words, can it be argued that contexts of the Global South are empirically different in terms of demography, poverty, informality, or otherwise? This approach has its roots in the 1980 Brandt Report which defined the South as a world region. A number of Southern urban and planning theorists have felt strongly that the Global South should not be defined geographically, as this could potentially give rise to artificial conceptual binaries between North and South while assuming levels of homogeneity within the Global South (and North) that simply do not exist. For instance, Leitner and Sheppard (2016) support what they call a fractal, rather than regional or topographical, geography by defining the South as those living precariously regardless of where they reside.

However, there have also been strong arguments in favour of empirical specificity and hence the need for some kind of geographical definition of the Global South. Simone and Pieterse (2017: x) employ a 'majoritarian' argument to define cities of the Global South as those where 'the majority hold spatial, economic, political, and ecological vulnerability'. Bhan (2019) supports this majoritarian position as a counter to the context-blind and universalizing modes of theorizing apparent in much planning scholarship to date. For him, planning practice, especially, needs to be based on a deep understanding of complex urban realities, and this 'requires rooting oneself in an empirical specificity' (Bhan, 2019: 3). His response to the argument of Leitner and Sheppard (2016), that the South can be *anywhere*, is that such a view certainly draws attention to relational and moving peripheries, and that Southern questions can undoubtedly be asked of the peripheral spaces, populations, and activities of cities everywhere. Nonetheless, Bhan (2019: 4) holds that there are empirical realities marking a Southern location, and the South is therefore both a *relational project* and an *empirical geography*.

An emphasis on the South as being, at least in part, an actually existing geographical entity defined by its empirical characteristics leads to a key argument of the chapter – that *place* and the *materiality of space* matter in important ways for the objectives and tasks of those writing from a Southern perspective. We discuss the implications of this point for our understandings of power in the third section of this chapter. In the following section, however, we consider first how Southern planning scholars have thought about the political relations and processes that frame global patterns of knowledge production, distribution, and consumption.

THE GLOBAL GEOPOLITICS OF PLANNING KNOWLEDGE AND PRACTICE

Early forays into planning scholarship that self-identified with a Southern perspective often tended towards high-level critiques, provocations, or challenges of 'conventional' (Northern) modes of theorizing and institutional dominance in planning (Yiftachel, 2006; Miraftab, 2009; Roy, 2009; Watson, 2009). They demanded, in one way or another, a recalibration of planning knowledge to be more suited to the emerging realities of the South as a region that is increasingly dominant economically, demographically, culturally, and otherwise. Those critiques drew upon earlier work that recognized the inadequacy of consensus-based and communicative models of planning (Yiftachel and Huxley, 2000; Flyvbjerg, 2004), the conflicting rationalities and deep differences that shape planning in Southern contexts (Watson, 2003, 2006), and the significance of ethnic divisions and power in planning (Yiftachel and Yacobi, 2003). They expressed diverse inspirations from postcolonial, subaltern, feminist, and other critical traditions of planning thought that had taken root in the 1980s and 1990s in the wake of a recognizably 'radical' planning movement that worked to undermine the image of the neutral technocratic planner (Miraftab, 2009). They also drew upon critiques, external to the immediate field of planning, of the intellectual frames used to examine and narrate Southern cities and urbanisms, which generated calls to imagine new modes of 'writing a world of cities' from the starting perspective of 'peripheral' cities (Robinson, 2002, 2011; Mbembe and Nuttall, 2004; Simone, 2004; Harrison, 2006).

A key trope of these early calls to 'see from the South' was the critique of the global geo-politics of planning knowledge (Mignolo, 2002). This work has drawn from a rich tradition of postcolonial and decolonial diagnosis of the privileging of EuroAmerican categories and nar-ratives of historical analysis; a critique of Europe as the 'sovereign theoretical subject' around which all other histories oscillate (Chakrabarty, 1992). Many planning scholars associated with the Southern perspective have thus started from a recognition of how power relations – many tracing a colonial genealogy – shape the discourses, languages, and tools of planning thought (Harrison, 2006). That they face the dilemma of thinking both *with* and *against* the EuroAmerican canon is a foundational and immanent imperative and challenge of their work.

Planning scholars have posited various modes of 'border thinking' as a strategy to manage this dilemma; a 'decentred' search for 'interstices' (Harrison, 2006) and the in-between spaces that cut, subvert, and productively hybridize universal thought with the emplaced realities of the South to identify multiple modernities and rationalities (Pieterse, 2010; Agyemang and Morrison, 2018). In this focus and approach, the Southern perspective shares much with modes of critique more recently styled as decolonial (Winkler, 2018). Substantively, it implies conceptual and empirical care for 'the quotidian, mundane practices and routines' of Southern places; uncovering their ordinary 'cityness' as a necessary precondition for generating 'more relevant' knowledge (Pieterse, 2010: 210).

If a desire to 'provincialize' Northern urban and planning studies has formed a basic intellectual impulse of the Southern perspective (Lawhon et al., 2016; Leitner and Sheppard, 2016), its translation in academic practice has sometimes focused on the roles of powerful institutions, linked to dominant modes of capital accumulation, in shaping the production, networks, and flows of planning knowledge. This work has helpfully highlighted a particular domain and form of power: the systems of research finance, education, publication, language, and dissemination that structure and delimit global flows of planning ideas and practices, defining what is deemed universal and legitimate, or parochial and illegitimate. It goes without saying that more and better resourced researchers, institutions, and journals, which dominate English-language planning scholarship, are located in a small number of countries in the Global North. One result is that geographical patterns of research and publication are skewed away from the places that are increasingly the global centres of gravity for settlement and change (Mabin, 2001).

A second outcome relates more closely to the core craft of academic writing. Many scholars in the South face pressures from their institutions to publish in mainstream high-impact jour-nals, often without much or anything by way of financial support or an empirical research base from which to draw. And doing so generally requires facing up to the indignation of journal reviewers that key (read Northern) debates have not been addressed (Home, 2018; Lawhon and Truelove, 2020). Those scholars who do find themselves in fortunate positions of institu-tional and financial comfort are often invited or forced into a position where they are expected to 'speak for' the South, potentially enjoining a degree of generalization that runs counter to their instincts or the principles of a Southern critique. The resourcing issue also manifests itself in the way that a mere handful of better-off institutions may emerge as (perceived) centres and gatekeepers of legitimate Southern scholarship and theorization.

A somewhat different emphasis on the roles of universities in perpetuating Northern lenses and preoccupations points to the nature of curricula and teaching, and the pedagogical and methodological imperatives necessary to produce situated bodies of planning knowledge and competencies (Odendaal, 2012; Watson and Odendaal, 2013; Duminy et al., 2014). That perspective focuses less on how academic publication is circumscribed by the biases of journals and publishing houses, and more on the modalities of teaching and learning. Some of this work has been informed by critiques of models of learning focused on the acquisition of rule-based context-independent knowledge (Flyvbjerg, 2004). Instead, this work has highlighted the importance of models of learning more attuned with a social constructivist and humanistic emphasis on personal experience, analogical modes of reasoning, and problem-based learning. While such an approach would arguably be important for planning students everywhere, engaged as they are in a practical field, in Southern contexts there is the added benefit of avoiding the replication of rule-governed theoretical knowledge that is informed by Northern models of spatial and professional urbanism with aspirations of universalism (Duminy et al., 2014; Siame, 2016). In this strand of critique, the Southern perspective highlights learning as a principal process of knowledge generation, and diagnoses modes of teaching delivery, assessment, and acquisition as surfaces along which Northern biases are reproduced.

In recent years scholars have drawn our attention to complex dynamics in the global geographies of knowledge and practice. Some have pointed to the processes of 'worlding' through which Southern cities reference one another and compete for prominence; processes that involve variegated circuits of ideas, expertise, practices, and models of development and governance (Simone, 2001; Roy, 2011; McCann, Roy and Ward, 2013; Vainer, 2014; Franco and Ortiz, 2020). Others have highlighted how exchanges of planning knowledge have become more geographically complex with the increasing significance of South–South learning represented and enabled by the rise of institutions like the IBSA (India, Brazil, South Africa) Dialogue Forum and the BRICS (Brazil, Russia, India, China, South Africa) partnership (Harrison, 2015; Tomlinson and Harrison, 2018). Still others have examined the influence of international developers in transferring models of urban development between Southern contexts, pointing to the complex power dynamics that shape how projects are taken up and implemented in particular settings (Ballard et al., 2017; Brill and Reboredo, 2019; Ballard and Harrison, 2020). In this work, the focus is on the dynamic and multiscalar power relations (governmental, private sector, cultural, symbolic) that drive and shape the production, mobility, and deployment of planning knowledge and practices.

For over two decades a diverse and diffuse network of planning scholars have laboured to elaborate the critical and substantive ethos of the Southern perspective. Despite those efforts, Northern canons and institutions remain dominant in planning thought and scholarship, even if one finds book volumes that kindly reserve a chapter for scholars to speak from and of 'the South'. The issue of the biases of journal reviewers aside, it is nonetheless the case that publishing houses are acutely aware of the market opportunities presented by planning students and scholars in Southern settings. There is a demand for work addressing the realities of these places. In some cases, this acts as an incentive for scholars to locate their work in a Southern perspective and tradition, even if their empirical focus is a single region, country, or city. Again, this can produce unwanted pressure to generalize to other contexts; at the same time, it may limit the potential to make legitimate generalizations to a more global planning scholarship as Southern theory becomes intellectually 'ghettoized'. In this respect, the very existence of this chapter is an artefact of that which the Southern perspective has sought to critique. It demonstrates too the dilemma of thinking and writing from that perspective, of working with and against the power relations that underpin the geopolitics of knowledge.

This seam of work, comprising high-level conceptual debates and critiques that centre on the geopolitics of knowledge, is extant. Yet in its evolution the Southern perspective has also inspired other areas and foci of analysis. We discuss these in the following sections, beginning with a reflection on Southern epistemological modalities that highlight the significance of thought that emerges from situated engagements with *place*.

THINKING POWER FROM CONTEXT AND PLACE

If a strategy and modality of critical scholarship linked to the spatial metaphor of 'the border' was an early position associated with the Southern perspective, then more recent scholarship has sought to relocate the starting point of our thinking from the peripheral frontier to the centre. A key trope of recent Southern work on planning is the need to consider what changes, in the ways that we ask questions and understand planning phenomena, when we think about such things from and through a particular *place* (Bhan, 2019). The emphasis here is not so much on the interstices and hybridities that emerge at the margins, but rather the holistic pictures that emerge when one attempts to 'write the world' from a particular position-in-location (Mbembe and Nuttall, 2004).

Such an impetus emerged, in part, from longstanding critiques of the universalist aspirations of Northern planning theory in conjunction with calls for the crafting of 'meso-level' planning theories that are 'fit-for-purpose' for particular issues and locations of the South. It has been further encouraged by critiques of the anti-realist ontologies that are seen to underpin planning theory, undermining planning's core historical concern with the 'materiality of space' (Beauregard, 2012; Harrison, 2014). For planning scholars working through a Southern perspective, as for many others, *place matters* in significant ways (Bhan, 2019). It matters not only as planning's central object of analysis and intervention, but also as a starting point and methodological mechanism for disrupting unequal global geographies of knowledge.

A place-centred Southern perspective reorients our understanding of power in planning away from place-less abstractions of power, or the notion that power operates similarly everywhere and may be accurately described by typically grand and 'muscular' Northern discourses such as bio/necropolitics or Capitalism. Again, this perhaps provides an impetus for more descriptive accounts of the situated ordinariness of planning settings that avoid political themes and questions altogether. Yet few Southern planning scholars would settle for a body of work that claims for itself little more than idiographic fidelity to the 'everyday'. That tension has seen the emergence of productive methodological experiments that seek to account for, and reflect on the respective limitations of, everyday ethnographies alongside the macro-scale processes that give rise to precarity (Cirolia and Scheba, 2019). Here power is diffuse and distributed – emerging through the material and social capillarities of everyday life in their connections to multiple circuits and scales of power. The emphasis and approach is somewhat different to older instantiations of 'structure and agency' research in planning (Healey and Barrett, 1990). The conceptual and methodological starting point is a single place, and the move is one of reading out wider structural processes and relations of power in a manner akin to the individualizing comparison or case study. The gesture is to locate understandings of power in a place while building an explanatory structure outwards, in centrifugal fashion, keeping wider empirical processes under critical scrutiny in order to avoid their reification (Robinson, 2016).

In that sense, such practices can be described as the methodological correlate of empirical studies of Southern city 'worlding'.

The notion that a place-centred perspective on power requires some methodological reorientation or refinement is reflected in sustained arguments for the importance of case study methodologies for building theory in planning (Flyvbjerg, 2006). Some of this work has explicitly located itself within a Southern perspective (Duminy et al., 2014; Watson, 2014b). Here the case study is seen not only as a means of generating valuable empirical knowledge on under-researched settings with the potential to inform phronetic experiential judgements (Flyvbjerg, 2004), but also as a preeminent opportunity to inductively articulate new directions of theoretical propositioning to form part of an avowedly global scholarly dialogue (Robinson, 2016). In that sense, case study methodologies offer a corrective to global imbalances in knowledge production and a potential means of rendering a North–South theoretical binary redundant. It is a vision that accords well with a rejection of deductive theorizations of power – the use of grand explanatory theory to 'read off' local phenomena – in favour of more analogical modes of reasoning (Barnett, 2020). With the latter perspective, the status of the 'theoretical' is 'closer to a sense of shared vernacular than to the production of generalizing theoretical frameworks' (Barnett, 2020: 12). An emphasis on the primacy of context and place within understandings of power in planning reflects a mode of intellectual work that is more akin to the 'casuistry' associated with disciplines like law and medicine rather than explanatory theory (Barnett, 2020).

If attention to the centrality of place and the 'materiality of space' is a characteristic of a Southern perspective on power, then a close corollary is a recognition of the existence of diverse modes of situated planning practice. In the following section we discuss how Southern planning scholars have recognized the potential of *practice* as a source of learning and intellectual insight related to power.

LEARNING AND THEORIZING FROM AND FOR PRACTICE

Calls for planning theory to emerge from an engagement with practice are neither new nor specific to Southern thinking. The 1980s and 1990s were replete with arguments promoting a closer linkage between planning theory and practice, as part of a broader post-positivist shift in the discipline (Allmendinger, 2002) emphasizing the socially constructed ways in which planning norms and practices are produced and legitimated.

Donald Schön (1983) originally developed an interest in how professionals learn through doing rather than by drawing on abstract rules or theories. Building on this perspective, John Forester (1989) weaved insights derived from Jürgen Habermas and critical pragmatism to highlight the ways public professionals collaborate in practice. The term 'communicative planning', linked to these ideas, focused on the social relations which connect actors together and the dynamics of these relations in planning practice. In a similar vein, 'collaborative planning' drew on the practical work of planners within institutions, and considered how the institutional context shapes plan-making (Healey, 1997). Both these strands of planning theory drew on Habermasian communicative theory and his understanding of how power operates in and through processes of dialogue. In what he termed the 'life-world' (or public sphere), separate from and outside 'the system' of formal economy and government, Habermas believed it was possible for rational and inherently democratic human beings to reach consensus and coordinate action. If these processes of dialogue could be inclusive, empathetic, and open, and if power differences between participants could be neutralized, then the outcomes of such processes could be considered valid (Habermas, 1990a, 1990b). Basic to this position is an assumption of universal citizenship, where differences between actors occur mainly at the level of speech or ideas and can be overcome through argumentation.

Where Southern planning theory departs from these positions is in the concept of power which shapes understandings of practice-theory engagement, as well as in the assumptions of universality – of the nature of citizenship and of the prevalence of liberal democracy. The early work of Bent Flyvbjerg (2004) was integral to this shift. While he did not locate his position within a Southern perspective, his critique of Habermasian concepts of power (from a primarily Foucauldian position), and his challenge of the universalist assumptions active in planning theory by insisting on the importance of practice and context, influenced a number of Southern planning theorists. Moreover, Flyvbjerg's argument that power cannot be wished away, and that technically or democratically produced planning solutions can be countered by the *realrationalität* of power, has shifted acknowledgement, especially in Southern planning theory, of the relevance of both conflict and collaboration.

Likewise, Oren Yiftachel's long-term activist involvement in the conflict between the Israeli state and Palestinian settlements led him to challenge Habermasian assumptions of consensus-seeking and the search for inherently democratic planning processes (Yiftachel and Huxley, 2000).[1] Yiftachel (2006) contested the communicative rationality existing in conflict-ridden societies and called on planning theorists to think and conceptualize 'from the South-East'. His development of new planning concepts (such as ethnocracy) from his planning practice, and his argument in favour of new global 'vantage points' for planning theory located outside of EuroAmerican regions, was highly influential in the development of Southern planning theory.

In subsequent developments of Southern planning theory, the concept of learning and theorizing from context – from place and from practice – has been foundational. Many of these new ideas have been rooted in case studies or practical experiences involving activists and the work of non-governmental organizations (NGOs). Practices could also involve planners in the form of individuals or groups operating outside of the state, but here the concept of 'who plans' can be broadened to include any person engaged in intentional, goal-directed action. It could be argued that a key characteristic of Southern planning theory is its oppositional nature – in relation to both locally and globally dominant planning policies and practices (see also Chapter 15 by Fawaz). Two strands of developing planning scholarship illustrate how theorizing from practice and context has become a feature of Southern theory.

The first strand is insurgency and insurgent planning (see also Chapter 10 by Sletto). This has roots in research carried out in the 1980s in the city of Brasilia by urban anthropologist James Holston (1989). Holston's (2009) work highlights the territorialization of power and violence alongside the emergence of new paradigms of citizenship in the urban peripheries, all of which impact directly on any form of planning, law, and administration. In these new 'hybrid spaces of citizenship', rights talk is used by social movements to achieve political ends, justifying 'illegal' criminal actions and land or building invasions as the legitimate claiming of deserved rights from an 'illegitimate' state that has withheld them. More recently the concept has been developed by Faranak Miraftab (2009) to suggest insurgency as both 'invited' and 'invented' spaces of citizen action.

Miraftab (2020) draws on the practices of two subordinate groups as key actors – one group involved in struggles for sanitation services in a South African township and the other for housing and land in a Brazilian city. In these examples, groups operate in both invited and invented 'spaces of action as interstitial spaces of power in poor communities and as practices of citizenship from below' (Miraftab 2020: 437). Invited spaces (of action) are those legitimized by donors and the state, and can include formal and electoral channels as attempts to contain grassroots claims. Invented spaces (of action) are formed through the collective actions of the poor to confront and challenge the state and to destabilize the status quo. These spaces are not in binary opposition but 'stand in a mutually constituted, interacting relationship' (Miraftab 2020: 437). In the struggle over sanitation in Cape Town, for example, activist groups shifted between strategies: collecting data on toilet availability to present to officials in invited spaces, while also throwing faeces in public spaces to create new invented spaces of insurgency. These practices are a long way from the ideals of collaborative planning, yet a collaborative approach might be used as a tactic to gain visibility and advantage in everyday struggles. The nature of planning theory emerging from a study of such practices likewise stands in stark contrast to previously prevailing ideas of planning.

A second and related strand of Southern planning theory arising from a close engagement with practice is that concerned with processes of 'coproduction'. This has often involved engagements between citizens and the state, usually through the mediation of NGOs such as Slum Dwellers International and the Asian Coalition of Housing Rights. Documenting the practices of social movements reveals how they seek to improve the living conditions of their constituencies by engaging with the state in ways that vary between some kind of collaboration and direct protest. Diana Mitlin (2008: 339) describes coproduction as a political strategy used by citizen groups and social movement organizations to 'enable individual members and their associations to secure effective relations with state institutions that address both immediate basic needs and enable them to negotiate for greater benefits'. Mitlin (2008) draws on Foucauldian concepts of governmentality and state power to understand the strategic aspects of coproduction. Collective practices by civil society groups allow them to counter the tactics of individualization that operate through the state. Community groups are then able to challenge particular modes of governmentality and particularly the concepts, techniques, and rationalities through which services are delivered by the state. Mitlin (2008: 357) suggests this represents a 'governmentality from below' or a form of 'counter-governmentality' arising from shared poverty and everyday politics.

The concept and practice of coproduction has been drawn into discussions of planning theory (Watson, 2014a) as well as into numerous reported case studies on Southern contexts. In one case of coproduction in Kampala (Uganda), state–society engagement progressed beyond deliberation to the actual implementation of planning and service delivery (Siame, 2018). This research reflected 'a microanalysis of happenings, the structure and agency of power, conflict, collaboration and the meaning of change' (Siame 2018: 226) within and between the various arms and sectors of the state, within upgrading communities, and within and between the mediating NGO, state, and community. This case and others show that there are 'many areas of conflict in coproduction processes, and that conflicts are useful in maintaining a balance between municipal service improvement and achieving shifts in power between the state and society' (Siame 2018: 232). Using this understanding, the NGO and community groups continually and consciously repositioned planning as both a collaborative and conflicted process.

However, more work needs to be done within insurgent and coproduction planning research to understand the complex and multifaceted nature of power at work in such processes. Foucault's position that power is embodied and enacted rather than being a capacity that is possessed, that power constitutes agents rather than being deployed by them, and that power can be productive as well as repressive, suggests that both state and society can be divided and act in contradictory ways. Ngwenya and Cirolia (2020), for example, argue that 'conflicting rationalities' operate not only between state and society but also within them. In their case study of Cape Town, conflicts emerged between the levels of government, their departments, and their technical and political arms, as well as within communities with respect to the nature of their housing demands and the role the state should play in addressing those demands. Similarly, with respect to Kampala, Lindell and colleagues (2019) describe conflicts in negotiations between and within sections of the state and the leaders of street vendor associations, who made efforts to exclude certain street vendors from taking up places in a market as they feared the competition this would create. In the coproduction literature 'communities' are often assumed to be homogenous and cohesive, acting together in the interests of the poor. Yet power may also be exercised through parallel or overlapping processes of clientelism, generally regarded as ubiquitous in Southern cities, in which groups or individuals receive public benefits from politicians in exchange for votes or bribes. This often takes place through political 'brokers' in informal settlements where leaders forge ties with politicians in order to secure community benefits. Powerful actors can also be exploitative, locking poor communities into dependency relationships, exercising control through violence, or offering protection in return for payment (Deuskar, 2019). Without further research it cannot be assumed that such processes do not also occur alongside, or within, the tactics and practices of coproduction and insurgency.

Scholars of coproduction are well aware that power relations may exist in many different forms within processes of state–civil society engagement. However, many stop short of highlighting power as a central object of analysis and theoretical elaboration. Indeed, an impulse to recognize the emplaced complexities of power and political relations at work in Southern planning processes does not always lend itself to neat theoretical applications and contributions. That scholars writing from a Southern perspective may undertake 'uncritical' engagements with the concept of power perhaps reflects their reluctance to rely on grand Northern theorists of power whose ideas, it is suspected, may not travel so compatibly to different kinds of settings and problems. If such scholars are sometimes uncritical, this may be because their work is located within a broader tension between idiographic and nomothetic modes of analysis – a tension that has long underpinned debates around how to research in, and develop authentic representations of, Southern contexts (Mafeje, 1981).

CONCLUSION

This chapter has sought to chart three distinct yet interrelated lines of critical insight into the ways that power is expressed within Southern planning scholarship. We have argued that the Global South is both a relational project and an empirical geography, and that views of power in planning associated with the Southern perspective are notable for their emphasis on thinking from and through both *place* and *practice*. Those emphases raise a series of conceptual and methodological questions that have been addressed in a variety of ways and through diverse influences. Our exploratory reflection on how power has been placed within planning knowledge has not sought to be definitive; it is necessarily a work-in-progress, like the Southern perspective itself.

We have noted and accepted our own complicity in the dilemma and seeming contradiction of critiquing broad theoretical claims while attempting to distil key principles and propositions of a diverse intellectual and geographical field. Yet, we would suggest, one of the principal values of a Southern perspective is the capacity to diagnose why scholars, like ourselves, are faced with such dilemmas in the first place: the predicament of undoing placeless generalizations while seeking to generalize, of critiquing the EuroAmerican canon while using Northern concepts, of avoiding the master's voice while speaking for the South.

In some respects, it seems that the Southern perspective in planning may have already ridden the crest of its wave, always from a position of epistemic marginality. Critical discussions in planning and other disciplines are increasingly interested in the ideas and tools of decoloniality and more avowedly race-based traditions of critique (Winkler, 2018; Kimari and Ernstson, 2020). That new generation of decolonial scholarship is generating important insights, and there are interesting examples of cross-fertilization with work that is more explicitly Southern in orientation (Porter and Yiftachel, 2019). Yet although the genealogies of postcolonial and Southern perspectives in planning have much in common with self-styled decolonial ways of thinking, particularly in their emphasis on the geographies of knowledge as shaped by colonial legacies of power (Winkler, 2018), it is nonetheless noticeable that some of the key insights emerging from self-described Southern scholarship may be overlooked. In many respects, it is clear that the Southern perspective has not done enough. It has secured a place in our edited volumes of planning research, but it has neither displaced the hegemonic position of Northern planning theory nor appealed to the frustrations and aspirations of young planners and citizens of the South, and we recognize our place and role in that failure.

At the same time, we would humbly suggest that the next generation of critical planning scholars would do well to retain some of the insights discussed in this chapter. That might include an awareness of how certain discourses of power (including strong culturalist versions) obscure other forms of political relation and domination in planning. It might include expressing a degree of conceptual and methodological care for the emplaced case as a launchpad for theoretical contribution, by contrast with deductive applications of grander theory-driven claims that may not resonate quite so well with settings geographically and historically removed from current centres of theoretical elaboration. It might, too, encompass a keen awareness of how uncritical circulations and applications of (even self-styled radical) theoretical knowledge may work to produce new, perhaps unintended, geographies and kinds of epistemological hierarchy. It is in a spirit of care for the subject of planning, and from a demand for more just and equitable futures, that we extend this invitation for a productive engagement with critique in and of the South.

NOTE

1. Also see Watson (2003) on the limitations of communicative rationality in planning theory based on a case study of 'conflicting rationalities' in Cape Town.

REFERENCES

Agyemang, F.S.K. and N. Morrison (2018), 'Recognising the Barriers to Securing Affordable Housing Through the Land Use Planning System in Sub-Saharan Africa: A Perspective from Ghana', *Urban Studies*, 55 (12), 2640–2659.

Allmendinger, P. (2002), 'Towards a Post-positivist Typology of Planning Theory', *Planning Theory*, 1 (1), 77–99.

Ballard, R., Dittgen, R., Harrison, P. and A. Todes (2017), 'Megaprojects and Urban Visions: Johannesburg's Corridors of Freedom and Modderfontein', *Transformation: Critical Perspectives on Southern Africa*, 95 (1), 111–139.

Ballard, R. and P. Harrison (2020), 'Transnational Urbanism Interrupted: A Chinese Developer's Attempts to Secure Approval to Build the "New York of Africa" at Modderfontein, Johannesburg', *Environment and Planning A*, 52 (2), 383–402.

Barnett, C. (2020), 'The Strange Case of Urban Theory', *Cambridge Journal of Regions, Economy and Society*, 13 (3), 443–459.

Beauregard, R.A. (2012), 'Planning with Things', *Journal of Planning Education and Research*, 32 (2), 182–190.

Bhan, G. (2019), 'Notes on a Southern Urban Practice', *Environment and Urbanization*, 31 (2), 639–654.

Brill, F. and R. Reboredo (2019), 'Failed Fantasies in a South African Context: The Case of Modderfontein, Johannesburg', *Urban Forum*, 30 (2), 171–189.

Bunnell, T. (2015), 'Antecedent Cities and Inter-referencing Effects: Learning From and Extending Beyond Critiques of Neoliberalisation', *Urban Studies*, 52 (11), 1983–2000.

Chakrabarty, D. (1992), 'Postcoloniality and the Artifice of History: Who Speaks for "Indian" Pasts?', *Representations*, 37, 1–26.

Cirolia, L.R. and S. Scheba (2019), 'Towards a Multi-scalar Reading of Informality in Delft, South Africa: Weaving the "Everyday" with Wider Structural Tracings', *Urban Studies*, 56 (3), 594–611.

Comaroff, J. and J.L. Comaroff (2012), *Theory From the South: Or, How Euro-America is Evolving Toward Africa*, Boulder, CO and London: Paradigm Publishers.

Croese, S. (2018), 'Global Urban Policymaking in Africa: A View from Angola through the Redevelopment of the Bay of Luanda', *International Journal of Urban and Regional Research*, 42 (2), 198–209.

Dados, N. and R. Connell (2012), 'The Global South', *Contexts*, 11 (1), 12–13.

Deuskar, C. (2019), 'Clientelism and Planning in the Informal Settlements of Developing Democracies', *Journal of Planning Literature*, 34 (4), 395–407.

Duminy, J., Andreasen, J., Lerise, F., Odendaal, N. and V. Watson (eds) (2014), *Planning and the Case Study Method in Africa: The Planner in Dirty Shoes*. Basingstoke, UK: Palgrave Macmillan.

Fix, M. and P.F. Arantes (2021), 'On Urban Studies in Brazil: The Favela, Uneven Urbanisation and Beyond', *Urban Studies*, 59 (5), 893–916, doi: 10.1177/0042098021993360.

Flyvbjerg, B. (2004), 'Phronetic Planning Research: Theoretical and Methodological Reflections', *Planning Theory & Practice*, 5 (3), 283–306.

Flyvbjerg, B. (2006), 'Five Misunderstandings about Case-study Research', *Qualitative Inquiry*, 12 (2), 219–245.

Forester, J. (1989), *Planning in the Face of Power*. Berkeley: University of California Press.

Franco, I.D. and C. Ortiz (2020), 'Medellín in the Headlines: The Role of the Media in the Dissemination of Urban Models', *Cities*, 96, 102431. doi: 10.1016/j.cities.2019.102431.

Galland, D. and P. Elinbaum (2018), 'A "Field" under Construction: The State of Planning in Latin America and the Southern Turn in Planning', *disP – The Planning Review*, 54 (1), 18–24.

Habermas, J. (1990a), *Moral Consciousness and Communicative Action*. Cambridge, MA: MIT Press.

Habermas, J. (1990b), *The Theory of Communicative Action*. Cambridge, MA: MIT Press.

Harrison, P. (2006), 'On the Edge of Reason: Planning and Urban Futures in Africa', *Urban Studies*, 43 (2), 319–335.

Harrison, P. (2014), 'Making Planning Theory Real', *Planning Theory*, 13 (1), 65–81.

Harrison, P. (2015), 'South–South Relationships and the Transfer of "Best Practice": The Case of Johannesburg, South Africa', *International Development Planning Review*, 37 (2), 205–224.

Healey, P. (1997), 'Situating Communicative Practices: Moving Beyond Urban Political Economy', *Planning Theory*, 17, 65–82.

Healey, P. and S.M. Barrett (1990), 'Structure and Agency in Land and Property Development Processes: Some Ideas for Research', *Urban Studies*, 27 (1), 89–104.

Holston, J. (1989), *The Modernist City: An Anthropological Critique of Brasilia*. Chicago: University of Chicago Press.

Holston, J. (2009), 'Dangerous Spaces of Citizenship: Gang Talk, Rights Talk and Rule of Law in Brazil', *Planning Theory*, 8 (1), 12–31.

Home, R. (2018), 'Conference Report: Second African Urban Planning Conference, Lisbon 7–8 September 2017', *Planning Perspectives*, 33 (2), 293–294.

Kimari, W. and H. Ernstson (2020), 'Imperial Remains and Imperial Invitations: Centering Race Within the Contemporary Large-scale Infrastructures of East Africa', *Antipode*, 52 (3), 825–846.

Lawhon, M., Silver, J., Ernstson, H. and J. Pierce (2016), 'Unlearning (Un)located Ideas in the Provincialization of Urban Theory', *Regional Studies*, 50 (9), 1611–1622.

Lawhon, M. and Y. Truelove (2020), 'Disambiguating the Southern Urban Critique: Propositions, Pathways and Possibilities for a More Global Urban Studies', *Urban Studies*, 57 (1), 3–20.

Leitner, H. and E. Sheppard (2016), 'Provincializing Critical Urban Theory: Extending the Ecosystem of Possibilities', *International Journal of Urban and Regional Research*, 40 (1), 228–235.

Lindell, I., Ampaire, C. and A. Byerley (2019), 'Governing Urban Informality: Re-working Spaces and Subjects in Kampala, Uganda', *International Development Planning Review*, 41 (1), 63–84.

Mabin, A. (2001), 'Contested Urban Futures: Report on a Global Gathering in Johannesburg, 2000', *International Journal of Urban and Regional Research*, 25 (1), 180–185.

Mafeje, A. (1981), 'On the Articulation of Modes of Production: Review Article', *Journal of Southern African Studies*, 8 (1), 123–138.

Mbembe, A. and S. Nuttall (2004), 'Writing the World from an African Metropolis', *Public Culture*, 16 (3), 347–372.

McCann, E., Roy, A. and K. Ward (2013), 'Assembling/Worlding Cities', *Urban Geography*, 34 (5), 581–589.

Mignolo, W. (2002), 'The Geopolitics of Knowledge and the Colonial Difference', *The South Atlantic Quarterly*, 101 (1), 57–96.

Miraftab, F. (2009), 'Insurgent Planning: Situating Radical Planning in the Global South', *Planning Theory*, 8 (1), 32–50.

Miraftab, F. (2020), 'Insurgency and Juxtacity in the Age of Urban Divides', *Urban Forum*, 31, 433–441.

Mitlin, D. (2008), 'With and Beyond the State – Co-production as a Route to Political Influence, Power and Transformation for Grassroots Organizations', *Environment and Urbanization*, 20 (2), 339–360.

Ngwenya, N. and L.R. Cirolia (2020), 'Conflicts between and Within: The "Conflicting Rationalities" of Informal Occupation in South Africa', *Planning Theory and Practice*, 22 (5), 691–706, doi: 10.1080/14649357.2020.1808237.

Odendaal, N. (2012), 'Reality Check: Planning Education in the African Urban Century', *Cities*, 29 (3), 174–182.

Pieterse, E. (2010), 'Cityness and African Urban Development', *Urban Forum*, 21 (3), 205–219.

Porter, L. and O. Yiftachel (2019), 'Urbanizing Settler-colonial Studies: Introduction to the Special Issue', *Settler Colonial Studies*, 9 (2), 177–186.

Robinson, J. (2002), 'Global and World Cities: A View from Off the Map', *International Journal of Urban and Regional Research*, 26 (3), 531–554.

Robinson, J. (2011), 'Cities in a World of Cities: The Comparative Gesture', *International Journal of Urban and Regional Research*, 35 (1), 1–23.

Robinson, J. (2016), 'Thinking Cities through Elsewhere: Comparative Tactics for a More Global Urban Studies', *Progress in Human Geography*, 40 (1), 3–29.

Roy, A. (2009), 'The 21st-century Metropolis: New Geographies of Theory', *Regional Studies*, 43 (6), 819–830.

Roy, A. (2011), 'Urbanisms, Worlding Practices and the Theory of Planning', *Planning Theory*, 10 (1), 6–15.

Roy, A. (2014), 'Worlding the South: Towards a Post-colonial Urban Theory', in S. Parnell and S. Oldfield (eds), *The Routledge Handbook of Cities of the Global South*. Abingdon, UK and New York: Routledge, pp. 9–20.

Schmid, C., Karaman, O., Hanakata, N.C., Kallenberger, P., Kockelkorn, A., Sawyer, L., Streule, M. and K.P. Wong (2018), 'Towards a New Vocabulary of Urbanisation Processes: A Comparative Approach', *Urban Studies*, 55 (1), 19–52.

Schön, D.A. (1983), *The Reflective Practitioner*. New York: Basic Books.

Siame, G. (2016), 'The Value and Dynamics of Community-based Studio Projects in Planning Education in the Global South', *Berkeley Planning Journal*, 28 (1), 40–67.

Siame, G. (2018), 'Co-production as an Alternative Planning Approach in the Cities of the South: The Case of Kampala (Uganda)', *Urban Forum*, 29, 219–238.

Simone, A. (2001), 'On the Worlding of African Cities', *African Studies Review*, 44 (2), 15–41.

Simone, A. (2004), 'People as Infrastructure: Intersecting Fragments in Johannesburg', *Public Culture*, 16 (3), 407–429.

Simone, A. and E. Pieterse (2017), *New Urban Worlds: Inhabiting Dissonant Times*. Cambridge, UK and Medford, MA: Polity Press.

Solarz, M.W. (2012), '"Third World": The 60th Anniversary of a Concept that Changed History', *Third World Quarterly*, 33 (9), 1561–1573.

Tomlinson, R. and P. Harrison (2018), 'Knowledge of Metropolitan Governance in the South', *International Journal of Urban and Regional Research*, 42 (6), 1127–1139.

Vainer, C. (2014), 'The Coloniality of Urban Knowledge and City Models', in S. Parnell and S. Oldfield (eds), *The Routledge Handbook on Cities of the Global South*. Abingdon, UK and New York: Routledge, pp. 48–56.

Watson, V. (2003), 'Conflicting Rationalities: Implications for Planning Theory and Ethics', *Planning Theory & Practice*, 4 (4), 395–407.

Watson, V. (2006), 'Deep Difference: Diversity, Planning and Ethics', *Planning Theory*, 5 (1), 31–50.

Watson, V. (2008), 'Down to Earth: Linking Planning Theory and Practice in the "Metropole" and Beyond', *International Planning Studies*, 13 (3), 223–237.

Watson, V. (2009), 'Seeing from the South: Refocusing Urban Planning on the Globe's Central Urban Issues', *Urban Studies*, 46 (11), 2259–2275.

Watson, V. (2014a), 'Co-production and Collaboration in Planning – The Difference', *Planning Theory & Practice*, 15 (1), 62–76.

Watson, V. (2014b), 'The Case for a Southern Perspective in Planning Theory', *International Journal of E-Planning Research*, 3 (1), 23–37.

Watson, V. (2016), 'Shifting Approaches to Planning Theory: Global North and South', *Urban Planning*, 1 (4), 32–41.

Watson, V. and N. Odendaal (2013), 'Changing Planning Education in Africa: The Role of the Association of African Planning Schools', *Journal of Planning Education and Research*, 33 (1), 96–107.

Winkler, T. (2018), 'Black Texts on White Paper: Learning to see Resistant Texts as an Approach Towards Decolonising Planning', *Planning Theory*, 17 (4), 588–604.

Yiftachel, O. (2006), 'Re-engaging Planning Theory? Towards "South-eastern" Perspectives', *Planning Theory*, 5 (3), 211–222.

Yiftachel, O. and M. Huxley (2000), 'Debating Dominance and Relevance: Notes on the "Communicative Turn" in Planning Theory', *International Journal of Urban and Regional Research*, 24 (4), 907–913.

Yiftachel, O. and H. Yacobi (2003), 'Urban Ethnocracy: Ethnicization and the Production of Space in an Israeli "Mixed City"', *Environment and Planning D: Society and Space*, 21 (6), 673–693.

18. Queer perspectives on planning and power
Petra Doan and Ozlem Atalay

INTRODUCTION

This chapter utilizes queer theory to examine the relationship between planning, power, and the LGBTQ community at a global scale. We draw on experiences in cities in both North America (Atlanta) and the Middle East (Istanbul, Turkey) to illustrate the ways that power in conjunction with the planning process is often used to displace LGBTQ communities. Both cities share a progressive urban imaginary linked to their spatial locations. Atlanta has been called the capital of the New South, grafting many northern transplants or return migrants to its distinctive southern roots. Istanbul's strategic location on the Bosphorus that divides Europe from Asia, merges European culture with a more traditional Middle Eastern base. The resulting mixture of intersectional geographies (north-south and east-west) provides a haven for non-conforming populations (including LGBTQ people) seeking respite from more conservative regions. Nevertheless, each city is dominated by a heteronormative power structure that seeks to impose its own definition of modernity and urban redevelopment. This chapter will explore the ways that LGBTQ populations in these cities resist that dominating heteronormative power drawing on a queer set of strategies that explicitly incorporate diverse and insurgent communities and seek to transform the narrow discursive frameworks used by the existing power structure to justify redevelopment at the expense of queer and non-conforming populations. Accordingly, we name this queer power of resistance 'queer insurgency' that in these places enables LGBTQ individuals to resist top-down planning.

Both Atlanta and Istanbul have mobilized neoliberal gentrification schemes to dominate previously queer-friendly neighbourhoods or gayborhoods. The actions of both cities illustrate the strong link between hetero-patriarchal power and planning practice, and yet the larger socio-political contexts are quite different, providing contrasts that highlight the nuances and limitations of queer power. Historically LGBTQ individuals and groups have used different methods to resist hetero-normative power. Some groups use homo-normalization efforts (e.g. emphasizing the value of the pink (queer) dollar or other efforts to normalize queerness). Others use identity-based liberation approaches that have resulted from lengthy internal struggles for power/control within the LGBTQ community itself. Both of these approaches have been criticized, the first as a variety of assimilation and the second as narrowly divisive and limiting. Accordingly, this chapter will focus on two additional tactics: queer insurgency strategies and discourse-shifting efforts. In queer insurgencies excluded individuals and organizations take a 'stand' and assert their agency by intervening to disrupt formal processes from which they would otherwise be excluded. In discourse shifting, queer groups use various techniques to reframe the dominant neo-liberal discourse that both prioritizes capital accumulation and frames non-normative sexuality and identity as harmful. The examples described below illustrate several different instances of how this reframing occurred.

UNDERSTANDING POWER

The concept of power is associated with words such as authority, control, influence (Bell et al., 1969; Uphoff, 1989), but there is no single definition that is widely accepted. The way we define or theorize power depends on the questions we ask and the context of the analysis. A classic definition of power by Weber is 'the probability that one actor within a social relationship will be in a position to carry out his own will despite resistance' (Weber, 1947 in Uphoff, 1989: 299). Dahl (1957: 203) expands the concept of power to include relations between people such that 'A has power over B to the extent that he can get B to do something that B would not otherwise do.' The subjects in this definition could be individuals, groups, offices, governments, states, or any type of organization.

In the context of urban planning, problematization of power has been linked to issues of technical expertise and knowledge since the 1970s. Technical knowledge is often used in a top-down, hegemonic fashion to frame the critical issues to be decided often with little or no consideration of wider community inputs. In subsequent decades, the 'communicative turn' in planning shifted the discipline and practice away from a narrow focus on scientific and technical knowledge towards a broader recognition of the usefulness of deliberation, communication and consensus building to create more just decision-making processes in planning (Forester, 1989; Healey, 1997; Innes and Booher, 2010). This new approach recognizes that planners not only serve the state and provide information to the politicians for them to make their decisions among alternatives, but they also bring different groups and voices together to find solutions to complex problems in the postmodern world (see also Chapter 9 by Legacy).

The Habermasian basis for the communicative rationality idealized in collaborative dialogues in the pursuit of more equitable decision-making processes assumes that the 'power of the better argument' enables actors to come to agreement about what is true and right among diverse voices (Habermas, 1984 in Healey, 1997: 54). However, these have been criticized for minimizing inequalities of power and knowledge (Huxley, 2000; Neuman, 2000; Tewdwr-Jones and Allmendinger, 1998) and its power blindness (Flyvbjerg, 1998; Flyvbjerg and Richardson, 2002).

These classic definitions suggest a one-way, straightforward impact of power, with one side controlling and dominating the other(s). However, critical theorists argue that power itself is better conceptualized in terms of relationships, rather than the possession of individuals. Yet, this approach continues to view power as coercive, insidious, or repressive (Waite, 2016). In contrast, Miraftab (2006, 2009) highlights the importance of expanding our understanding of who is involved in power relations. She argues that informal networks outside of the formal participatory structures governing plan-making or policymaking processes are a means of insurgent power. These strategies have been called insurgent strategies, as policies of radical inclusion increase the breadth of communities able and willing to participate in planning processes. A key element of insurgent planning is the recognition that there are a variety of powerful actors at the grassroots including: residents, community organizations and activist movements who are able to challenge traditional frameworks and assumptions about power and planning (see also Chapter 10 by Sletto).

Queer Resistance to Heteronormative Power

Strategies to resist heteronormative power have been widely debated in the LGBTQ community. For instance, Foucault (1979) argued that the assimilation strategy of some gays and lesbians required them to become self-regulating to police themselves and their visible behaviours to appear 'normal' to gain access to power usually reserved for the heterosexual elite. Liberation-based strategies were based on the premise that it was the 'the momentous shift to industrial capitalism that provided the conditions for homosexual and lesbian identity to emerge' (John d'Emilio, 1983: 11). Indeed, this historiographic understanding of repression was linked to capitalism's need to repress and contain sexuality so that it did not interfere with the labour force (Corber and Valocchi, 2003). Ultimately, identity-based strategies (gay and lesbian liberation movements), recognized as separatist movements that were intent on making their identities visible as a means of challenging the status quo raised problematic issues. Jagose (1996: 81) suggests that 'Foucault questions the liberationist confidence that to voice previously denied and silenced lesbian and gay identities and sexualities is to defy power and hence induce a transformative effect.' In effect, identity movements simply reinforced the oppressive social structures they were intended to overturn.

However, according to Foucault (1980: 95), power is always present, but 'where there is power, there is resistance, and yet consequently, this resistance is never in a position of exteriority in relation to power.' Sullivan (2003: 42) argues that Foucault's understanding of power is better seen as a 'network of relations rather than something one group owns and wields to control another.' In essence, a queer perspective on power recognizes that it is through discourse that hegemonic power is used to shape our understandings of key issues, but that very discourse can be undermined through acts of resistance. Understanding the difficulties of challenging the discourse is critical for queer understandings of power. Foucault (1985) himself recognized and validated the importance of this struggle:

> If the discourse can be co-opted, that is not because it is vitiated by nature, but because it is inscribed in a process of struggle. Indeed, the adversary pushing, so to speak, on the hold you have over him in order to turn it around, this constitutes the best valorization of the stakes and typifies the whole strategy of struggles. As in judo the best answer to your opponent's maneuver never is to step back, but to re-use it to your advantage as a base for the next phase (Foucault 1985: 2, cited in Halperin 1995: 114).

The interplay between political activism and theoretical advances in queer theory are closely linked as the above quote from Foucault suggests. In the early 1990s the actions of groups like ACT UP (AIDS Coalition to Unleash Power), Queer Nation, PUSSY (Perverts Undermining State Scrutiny), Transsexual Menace, Lesbian Avengers, Transgender Nation helped to shape the evolution of queer theory and the way it is practiced. The resistance practiced by these groups used a variety of strategies, or what Foucault would recognize as judo holds to resist heteronormative power.

Queer theorists recognized the contested and contingent nature of subjectivity and used that deconstructive approach to re-shape the very questions under discussion. The emergence of this queer approach to challenging heteronormative power was partly based on strategies to destabilize the process, thereby undermining the distinctions used to fuel the intolerance that drives heterosexualized power. Sedgwick (1990: 9–10) suggests that deconstruction of basic identity categories is an important component in demonstrating 'that categories presented in culture as symmetrical binary oppositions – heterosexual/homosexual, in this case – actually subsist in a more unsettled tacit relation.' Queer theorists recognize the intersectional nature of exploitations – racism, homophobia, transphobia (Sullivan, 2003). But since queer itself is an indeterminate term, queer theory is not linked to a particular identity or set of identities, but rather one that reflexively indicates marginalized status of an indeterminate nature. Accordingly, queer approaches emphasize ephemerality, questioning of identities, as well as challenging power structures based on fixed assumptions.

ATLANTA CASE

In the city of Atlanta heteronormative power is epitomized by a broad coalition linking the largely white business community with well-established African American religious and political leaders that found common ground in promoting urban redevelopment through infrastructure investment and urban renovations intended to show off Atlanta as a modern city for the Olympic Games in 1996 and that impetus continued in the aftermath (Keating, 2001). This urban regime also stimulated the gentrification of Peachtree Street along the western edge of the traditional Midtown gayborhood that had a detrimental impact on this openly queer neighbourhood, forcing several LGBTQ institutions to close and replacing them with high rise condominiums (Doan and Higgins, 2011).

The impact of these prior developments coloured responses to subsequent efforts by the City of Atlanta to clean up *immoral* behaviour (sex work) and *indecent* land uses (adult enterprises) and provoked a queer storm of controversy that illustrate a very queerly inflected set of responses. Doan (2015) has described these two measures as an overreach by municipal officials responding to neighbourhood voices from the Midtown Ponce Security Association about prostitution in Midtown and neighbourhood groups near Cheshire Bridge Road about plans to *clean up* that corridor. The good news is that neither effort was successful, but it is the ways in which the resistance was organized that is the theme of this chapter.

There are clear elements of a very queer resistance strategy evident in both efforts. The queer backlash involved a much broader range of LGBTQ constituents than the A list gays who were responsible for much of the early gentrification in the Midtown neighbourhood. Young queer-identified individuals quickly organized, creating new organizations that appear to have been somewhat ephemeral, but were quite successful in halting these efforts. A critical element of their efforts involve resistance to the City's effort to characterize both policy changes as attempts to *clean up* areas that were plagued by immoral activities that discouraged families and reduced property values. The success of both efforts was linked to their ability to reframe this discourse.

Stay Out of Areas of Prostitution (SOAP) Policy

At night, the streets of Midtown, Atlanta's traditional gayborhood, sometimes attract young people of colour seeking to support themselves through sex work. The fact that these young men were also cross-dressed caused considerable upset amongst those gentrifiers who came because of the urban redevelopment and not the gayborhood. These newer residents were the most invested in *cleaning up the area* to make it *family* friendly. They created an organization called the Midtown Ponce Security Association (MPSA) that documented these 'incursions' with regular security briefings, describing the threat posed by a 'gang of transvestite prostitutes' (MPSA, 2013). One member of the MPSA regularly drove around at night and photographed the young sex workers, afterwards posting their images on the MPSA website (Nourae, 2008).

After numerous complaints from residents about prostitution, johns, and drugs in their neighbourhoods, including the influential backers of the MPSA, Atlanta Police Chief George Turner made a proposal for a new directive, called *Stay Out of Areas of Prostitution* (SOAP) (McWilliams, 2013). This proposed regulation directed that anyone convicted of solicitation of a sexual act in addition to paying any court-ordered fines and jail time, must in the future stay out of 'Areas of Prostitution' as defined each year by the Atlanta Police Department for at least 165 days. For a second offence the perpetrator would pay larger fines, do longer jail time, and be banned from the city limits for 120 days. Although the SOAP ordinance did not specify Midtown, the MPSA got very involved and urged everyone in the Midtown Neighborhood Association to show their support of the SOAP Ordinance by attending the February 2013 city council meeting. Doan (2015) has described the efforts to implement this policy as examples of racist and transphobic interference.

The local response of the LGBTQ community to the proposed SOAP ordinance provides an example of the way that queer power dynamics can be deployed to resist an unwanted and harmful municipal policy. A coalition of young queer activists as well as long-time LGBTQ Midtown residents emerged to resist this policy. The organizations that became involved included: Georgia Equality, JustUSATL, La Gender, Southerners on New Ground (SONG), Social Justice Guild at First Existentialist Congregation, Trans(forming) and Trans Individuals Living Their Truth. Members of this coalition recognized the importance of reframing the discourse used by the MPSA and reflected in proposed policy. Instead of treating this as an issue of recidivist criminal activity (repeated arrests for prostitution) the group chose to highlight discrimination that these individuals faced. They collectively wrote a letter to the City Council opposing the ordinance and arguing that the effort was:

> … rooted in homophobia, transphobia, and racism. We fall prey to a myriad of allegations that are baseless simply because we are viewed as 'different.' It is a result of lifelong discrimination that we are forced into underground economies and are subject to the most egregious forms of violence, bullying and marginalization. By and large, engaging in sex work is an act of survival, not of choice. (as quoted in Bagby, 2013a)

At the same time other established LGBTQ Midtown residents sent a similar letter suggesting that the MPSA had inappropriately used force against transgender sex workers. They argued that the city refrain from stigmatizing and banishing these individuals, and instead focus on helping these women find other gainful employment.

> We live and work in Midtown, one of the areas most mentioned in this conversation. The news seems obsessed with a few people's claim that there are condoms and syringes littering our sidewalks. This is simply not true … As Midtown residents and business owners, we want to make it clear that they [the MPSA] do not speak for the entire neighborhood and, in fact, the vast majority of us would much prefer to see the Council lead with solutions to help these women leave the streets for good. Please do not allow this terrible policy to be enacted in the name of Midtown residents and businesses. (as quoted in Hennie, Feb 27, 2013)

In effect this even broader coalition of queers undermined attempts to narrowly identify and stigmatize sex workers. The breadth of the coalition and their claims that such policies were rooted in a deep-seated bias against a highly marginalized community had an impact and the ordinance was tabled.

Cheshire Bridge Road Re-zoning Proposal

The success of the coalition organized to defeat the SOAP ordinance likely inspired a similar coalition to rise up and protest a different municipal policy, this time proposed changes to the zoning designation for the Cheshire Bridge Road corridor. Cheshire Bridge Road is just north of the traditional Atlanta gayborhood, known as Midtown, and contains an eclectic mix of businesses, including some that could be characterized as 'adult enterprises.' In 1999 the City of Atlanta used its Livable Cities Initiative to sponsor a study of this corridor with the partic- ipation of neighbourhood groups, some local businessmen, and developers interested in the area (City of Atlanta, 1999). Subsequently, in 2013 this area was targeted by a member of the Atlanta City Council who claimed that neighbourhood residents were eager for the city to 'do something' because they considered it a blighted area with strip clubs, porn shops, massage parlours, and gay bars. This attempt to use zoning to control sex in the public eye is similar to what Warner (1999) describes as Mayor Giuliani's use of a 'new politics of privatization' (p. 153) to clean up Greenwich Village and other areas where sex-oriented businesses were visible.

The neighbourhoods adjacent to Cheshire Bridge Road (Woodland Hills and Lindridge-Martin Manor) were developed after the Second World War to provide modest housing for the large number of returning veterans. The strip itself became commercialized in the 1960s, and many of the initial residents relocated to suburbs further away from downtown. There is little histor- ical data on the types of businesses on Cheshire Bridge, but Chenault and Braukman (2008) suggest that in 1971 a gay bar called the Sweet Gum Head opened and provided popular weekly drag shows, making this area attractive to LGBTQ individuals. Indeed the 1999 Cheshire Bridge Report noted an increase in the number of individuals and childless couples moving into the area during the 1980s, though the Report makes no mention of the sexual orientation of these new residents.

The 1999 Cheshire Bridge Road study recommended changing the zoning of the corridor to 'neighborhood commercial' which the City of Atlanta uses in other dense commercial areas adjacent to residential areas to limit the kinds of businesses which can be in that zone. The pro- posed changes were anticipated to make the area more attractive for heterosexual families by removing the visual blight of the existing 'adult enterprises' by producing a 'delightful street featuring shade trees, outdoor cafes, fountains, public art, and an eclectic mix of restaurants, neighborhood businesses and specialty stores' (City of Atlanta, 1999: ii).

The Report described the area as a seedy red-light district and provided a list of adult enter- prises including strip clubs, shops that sold/rented X-rated videos (some of them specialized in gay materials), as well as several well-known gay clubs. This classification system used in this report reflects several implicit biases since there were no typical 'red light district' businesses such as brothels and the inclusion of gay clubs is not usually considered an adult enterprise any more than any bar is an adult-oriented business. LGBTQ residents and patrons of these various establishments were clearly aware of the rather prurient bias entailed by these inconsistencies and that may have heightened their angry response.

Initially the Atlanta City Council decided to accept the recommendations of the Cheshire Bridge Study, by re-zoning the area into two almost adjacent neighbourhood commercial designations (NC-4 and NC-5) with a small industrial district in the middle. The new zoning also specified a list of non-conforming uses, including auto repair shops, car washes, and adult enterprises, although existing enterprises were permitted to stay (grandfathering), even if they did not conform to the newly adopted standard.

Subsequently, in 2012 a gay city council member, Alex Wan, with strong ties to the real estate community decided that the zoning for this corridor should be amended to remove the grandfathering granted to con-conforming uses. This use of planning power influenced by the real estate industry illustrates Hillier's (2000) contention that power operates through formal and informal networks. This proposal provoked a storm of controversy. *The Georgia Voice*, an LGBTQ newspaper, called this debate, 'the Battle for Cheshire Bridge.'

In response to this attempted re-zoning, many activists came together and reflected wide-spread anger from these disenfranchised groups. They developed a strategy aimed at queering the process, by repudiating the 'blight' issue and reframing the terms of the debate. Some of the organizers began to highlight the issue as one of basic economics since the proposed policy would force successful businesses to close, putting their workers out of a job. Many of these soon to be out of work employees were encouraged to attend the public meeting. In addition, other groups also sought to change the terms of the argument, by arguing that they had chosen to live in the area precisely because it was a diverse and sex-positive area. Others criticized the neoliberal gentrification aspects of the proposed change and reminded the audience of what had happened in Midtown several years earlier.

The economic argument was framed as an attempt by the city to impose a 'taking' both on property owners, but also on the patrons who enjoyed using these businesses. When the Zoning Board met to consider the proposal to revise the Cheshire Bridge Zoning code, many people showed up to protest. This meeting was described by a reporter from WABE a local television station as follows:

> Employees of the strip clubs filled entire rows and held protest signs. Zoey Hughes, a local resident and a former dancer at one of the strip clubs along the street, said she likes the neighborhood the way it is. 'I don't want to be in the PTA, I don't want to be a homeowners association member, I don't want children. I moved to Cheshire Bridge, I moved to Atlanta to be who I wanted to be without some soccer mom telling me who I could be.' (Shapiro, 2013)

A queer social media website Q Atlanta also had a Facebook group with lots of commentary as well. One commentator identified the assimilationist strategy of the zoning changes, saying:

> some elements of LGBT Atlanta citizens do not want to be assimilated and a few courageous ones refuse to do so. I did write something to Alex Wan and basically called him a traitor to LGBT Atlantans esp [*sic*] the ones who voted for him that do not mind going out to see some porn at the video booth arcades or taking in some strippers etc.

Another resident of the neighbourhood added:

> I live one block off of Cheshire Bridge and have been here for 17 years. Is CB Rd the 'cleanest' or 'neatest' road in Atlanta. No. But for all the 'unsavory' businesses there is little crime and a lot of funky color. I don't want my neighborhood to turn into another cookie cutter community. A lot of the character is gone from Midtown and has been replaced by the same crap you'd find in the burbs. I'm

all for paving roads, smooth sidewalks, and better infrastructure. But I object to wiping out valid (and successful) businesses because they don't fit someone's ideal.

Another commentator expressed deep concern that this change would stimulate significant gentrification in the area.

> Cheshire Bridge, in my view, became the new Midtown several years ago after the second wave of gentrification in Midtown entered full swing, displacing the working class homosexuals who fixed up the place. So, do we, the gay community, allow *The Jungle* and *The Heretic* to go the same way as *Backstreet*? Do we allow another community to be yuppified, buppified, and sterilized – forcing us, the gays who wish to party, to some industrial area in the outskirts like Mr. Wan envisions, perhaps Fulton Industrial, where we can dance the night away in one of the worst pollution hotspots in all of the metro Atlanta area? (Cardinale, 2013)

The anger expressed by Cardinale, the editor of the Atlanta Progressive News, was widely shared. An article in *Georgia Voice*, an Atlanta-based LGBTQ publication described the presence of a queer coalition group *Queer Up! Atlanta* that emerged as an organizing force for the resistance. This group coalesced around a coalition based on the owners and employees of the queer-themed adult businesses as well as the other businesses that had been grandfathered and were at risk from the proposed zoning changes. But the coalition also attracted other young queer individuals who felt the loss of queer spaces in nearby Midtown due to gentrification and were willing customers of the gay porn shops and bars. The article cites the group's Facebook page (no longer active) describing itself as follows:

> QUEER UP! Atlanta is a collective of young, queer activists-in-the-making committed to dismantling the oppressive forces of heterosexist ideologies, uplifting marginalized communi-TEAs and the intersections that arise – all with a Southern twang – while unapologetically throwing glitter in the faces of the normative, y'all! In the vein of our fore-queers, who led such efforts as 'MondoHomo' and 'GlitterBomb Atl', we aim to cultivate a progressive, inclusive movement in HOT-lanta and the greater Southern community. (Georgia Voice Editors, 2013)

When this zoning change was reviewed by the Atlanta City Council, Queer UP Atlanta circulated a petition and a flyer urging queers in the community to show up and tell the Atlanta City Council to vote no on the Cheshire Bridge Zoning Proposal. The flyer provided the details of the meeting place and time and resulted in many queer-identified people showing up to the council meeting. Ultimately, the attempt to change the zoning and force non-conforming businesses to close did fail (Bagby, 2013b). This decision was partly due to the energetic voices organized in this queerly diverse coalition, but also to the successful reframing of the discourse away from 'family values' towards the economic well-being of small businesses, the attractiveness of sex-related businesses for many residents, and the importance of preventing the loss of more queer spaces in Atlanta.

ISTANBUL

The following case material is drawn from the first-hand experiences of one of the authors in the Gezi uprising, as well as an extensive review of documents and academic articles about the Gezi protests. The case highlights the difficulties that ensue when urban planning decisions are taken in authoritarian ways that include virtually no public participation. A queer reading of the Gezi Uprisings highlights the usefulness of insurgent coalition-building as well as the subtle reframing of development discourse that occurred as an emotionally charged 'Gezi Spirit' erupted among the participants. These insurgent queer solidarities triggered a shift in the discourse and a fundamental reframing of both the process and outcome of an urban planning intervention.

Background on Gentrification in Beyoglu and Gezi Park

Beyoglu is one of the most accepting neighbourhoods in Istanbul for marginalized communities. The wide variety of housing, employment and entertainment options have attracted numerous marginalized groups including LGBTQ individuals (Atalay and Doan, 2020a; Selek, 2001; Ozbay and Savci, 2018). Near the centre of Beyoglu lies Gezi Park which is one of the last remaining green areas in Istanbul and has long been a popular venue for LGBTQ activities. The proposed project for the Gezi Park was one of the key elements in the Turkish government's neoliberal policy to encourage urban redevelopment through gentrification in the district. The city was planning to turn this green space into a replica of the old Ottoman barracks including a shopping mall, hotel, and luxury apartment units, but their attempt to begin construction activities in the summer of 2013 triggered the Gezi protests. Initially these protests began by drawing protestors to Gezi and subsequently to Taksim, and finally demonstrations spread to other parks and streets across the country. In this section, we present a discussion of the underlying reasons for the Gezi uprisings along with urban planning interventions that built the path to the protests.

When Adalet ve Kalkinma Partisi (AKP; Justice and Development Party) came into power in 2002, the party platform included a human rights discourse, because the AKP wanted to promote an image of a moderate Islamic political party to facilitate Turkey's membership of the European Union (EU). However, once the AKP consolidated its grasp through the adoption of constitutional amendments in 2010 and its third electoral victory in 2011, both then Prime Minister Erdogan and his party, the AKP became more explicitly authoritarian and willing to intervene in the daily lives of the public as well as to restructure cities and public lands across the country. This dictatorial prime minister and his now openly conservative Islamist party moved away from its moderate and pluralist democratic roots to begin discursive interventions intended to micromanage the daily lives of its citizens by restricting the right to abortion, specifying the number of kids families should have, establishing internet censorship, and banning the consumption of alcohol (Unan, 2015).

In another arena, the AKP passed urban planning legislations such as the urban Renewal and Preservation Law (2005) and the Disaster Act (2012), that gave the local municipalities enormous capability to implement state-led gentrification processes in urban areas as well as national government to privatize natural resources and public lands. The Mass Housing Development Administration of Turkey (TOKI) gained enormous power through the AKP years and its projects displaced many disadvantaged groups from their neighbourhoods to build new housing units for middle- or higher-income groups. These AKP projects are a stark illustration of 'the corporatization, commodification, and privatization of hitherto public assets [that] have been signal features of the neoliberal project' (Harvey, 2006: 35).

Located in the centre of Istanbul, Beyoglu has experienced significant neoliberal redevelopment projects. The enactment of the Renewal and Preservation Law in 2005 enabled the government to build the large Demiroren Shopping Centre whose scale and design were completely out of character for the historic Istiklal Street. This early redevelopment was the first of a variety of other planned projects including plans to redevelop the historic and much-loved Emek Movie Theatre that triggered public concern for the erasure of the character of the building and the history that was embodied within it (Yasar, 2019). The public–private partnership process used for the Tarlabasi urban renewal project was tainted by the fact that the bid winner, Calik Holding, had close ties to the AKP and the prime minister (Islam and Sakizlioglu 2015). These unpopular redevelopments set the stage for the proposed Gezi Park project and the public's immediate response.

Gezi Park and the area where it is located, Beyoglu, have always had critical importance for queers because the district has been home to LGBTQ individuals and couples who were attracted by its welcoming character and open door to minorities and marginalized groups over a long period of time. Furthermore, Gezi Park was historically used for cruising by queers who used the park for sex work or socializing with others from a diverse array of classes, ethnicities, ideologies, genders, and sexualities (Erol, 2018; Ozbay and Savcı, 2018). In 1987, long before the Gezi protests, the steps of the park were the site of a hunger strike by the transgender people, protesting police brutality and unbearable living conditions.

Because the Beyoglu district was known to be friendly towards LGBTQ people, it is likely that reputation is one of the reasons the area became a special target for redevelopment. For instance, Yasar (2019) suggests the AKP focus on Beyoglu was clearly an attempt to change the social and cultural make-up of the area through *social engineering*. These redevelopment projects were partly intended to *cleanse* of the area of the *degenerate* populations, as well as *dangerous* and *illicit activities* by marginalized communities including the LGBTQ population. While these changes have made the district more convenient for conservative and international consumers, Beyoglu as the *home* of the LGBTQ community has started becoming less attractive to sexual dissidents. Urban planning scholar Murat Cemal Yalcintan explains the hidden intent behind the projects going on in the district as a desire 'to suppress dissident cultures that had been flourishing in and around Beyoglu's various streets and local establishments …' (Yalcintan 2012 cited in Yasar 2019: 52). Obviously, these planning processes or projects had little concern for the public interest and were neither collaborative nor participatory. Although the initial spark for the Gezi protests was the illegal entry of bulldozers into Gezi Park to take down trees on midnight of May 27, it was the heavy-handed interference of the authoritarian government and the prime minister in the physical and social public life that brought so many members of the public to join the uprisings. The LGBTQ community played a critical role in the protests, not only to defend the park and the district from neoliberal restructuring but also to make public witness of their very existence.

Queer Insurgencies

In this section, we analyse and elaborate on the uprisings from the queer power perspective. First, we discuss the role of the LGBT Blok that formed during the protests in the park and note the emergence of solidarities among the protestors. We then discuss the reframing of the overall discourse that came to be known as the Gezi spirit.

One of the critical features of the Gezi protests was the development of an impromptu coalition that brought together people from all walks of life. Participants included Turkish nationalists along with Kurds who usually do not get on well together, people from different ethnicities, chanting football fans, religious groups such as non-capitalist Muslims next to LGBTQs, mothers who were at first worried for their kids but later found themselves attending the protests, youth, young professionals, working class people – basically people from all different backgrounds (Arat, 2013; Zengin, 2013). The solidarity that emerged among these diverse groups lasted throughout the uprisings.

An LGBT Blok was established among various queers including members of nonprofit LGBT organizations as well as independent queers attending the protests (Savci, 2021). The Blok established a space in the middle of the park, in solidarity with the other tents in the area which provided food, emergency care, and books free to read. Money had no function within this environment. Ozbay and Savci (2018) note that a kind of 'queer commons' emerged that was reminiscent of other queer spaces in the area including 'certain bathhouses, parks, and fairly cheap adult movie theatres' that were slowly being closed due to neoliberal restructuring (p. 516). However, in contrast to the privately operated bathhouses and movie theatres which were only open to those who could afford them (usually men), the Gezi commons included a diversity of genders and sexualities.

But the presence of the queer community did more than provide physical support to the protests; they also changed the very discourse involved. It was the bravery of LGBTQ people willing to lie down in front of the police barricades or stand in the front line of the protests that visibly disrupted the stigma of *fagness* which usually carried connotations of *softness* in Turkish society. Queers in the park also intervened in the use of sexist and homophobic language. While chanting next to football fans, they warned the protestors not to use derogatory sexist curses such as *fags (ibne in Turkish)* or *son of a b*tch (O.C. in Turkish)* while chanting against the prime minister or governmental officials. Instead, the LGBTQ protesters introduced a new way of protesting drawing on queer slang and humorous slogans full of love such as *nerdesin, askim? Burdayim, askim! (where are you, my love? I am here, my love!), direniyoruz ayol! (we are resisting ayol!), yasak ne ayol?! (What is prohibition ayol?!), ay resmen devrim, ayol! (this is literally a revolution, ayol!)*. Savci (2021: 137) argues that using queer vernacular helped to queer 'the protest style and attitude of hypermasculinized, teargas-mask wearing, barricade-building bodies, redefining the subject of revolution.' While such slogans spread across the crowds, it was not only queers but also all the other protestors were chanting *where are you my love? I am here, my love!* In a sense, through voicing the love, they were deconstructing the language and attitude of a government which had built its rhetoric around hate and divisiveness and its negative reflections on society (Savci, 2021).

There were two principal effects for queer people from this outpouring of solidarity, resistance, affection, and compassion. First, along with the other protestors, LGBTQ people were able to create a viable and insurgent counter-public (Fraser, 1990; Warner, 2002) that worked to save their queer space, Gezi Park, from a top-down, exclusionary planning intervention. This uprising was undertaken by residents outside of so-called formal processes through 'an affective and intimate economy of encounters, touches, and dialogues that have opened bodies and lives to new, unpredictable becomings' (Zengin, 2013: n.p.). From the perspective of the LGBTQ community, what was lived in the Gezi was a queer insurgency that altered both the process and the outcome of a planning intervention.

The other victory for them was a very important shift in the discourse surrounding queerness. Through the actions of LGBTQ protestors and the shift in vernacular that was adopted by the crowd, queers became more visible following the uprisings. The LGBTQ community gained broader public awareness across Turkey. Partial evidence for this shift lies in the record attendance at Pride Parades held in 2013 and 2014 in Taksim, Beyoglu. In a sense, queers both physically and socially claimed back what the government had tried to take, erase, and convert. They not only rescued the park but also found creative ways of expressing themselves to the broader public which resulted in gaining more visibility and support. What we observed during Gezi protests was more than trying to reach ideal speech conditions, it was also the existence of actions; sharing of emotions, humour and their manifestations as art, slogans, performances that contributed to the outcome, the survival of the park and hitherto unimagined solidarities among participants which resulted in the queer commons and Gezi Spirit (Cidam, 2017; Dagtas, 2016; Eslen-Ziya et al., 2019).

POTENTIAL FOR URBAN PLANNING

> ... recognizing the urban requires a revolutionary imagination. It requires a habit of thinking in terms of urgent utopia. To see the present urban, we must be willing to imagine and demand a possible world, even if that world is impossible under the conditions that exist now. For Lefebvre, the urban constitutes a revolution, but one that requires millions of everyday acts of resistance and creation. (Henri Lefebvre, 1970, *La Revolution Urbaine*, as cited by Purcell, 2013: 151)

In both the Atlanta and Istanbul cases we find evidence of increasing sophistication in the use of queer power. In both cases LGBTQ activists were able to assemble broad insurgent coalitions to protest the policies and redevelopment interventions. But more importantly in each case, they were able to engage directly with the discourse that the neoliberal regimes were using to justify the changes and interventions. By shifting the urban imaginary in critical ways these queer insurgencies were able to reframe the issues in ways that undermined the hegemonic power of the urban authorities. This Foucaultian type of resistance to power is derived from the survival tactics which the LGBTQ community has developed over the years in the face of a long history of oppression and exclusions. In Atlanta they appealed to fairness and economic justice for sex workers as well as employees of strip clubs and porn shops as well as reframing the 'family values' discourse in favour of a more inclusive message that we all have value. In Istanbul they used humorous and affectionate vernacular to reframe the Islamic 'family values' mobilized by the regime and demonstrated the importance of action and emotions during such times.

If concerns about basic justice are not acknowledged and rights to the city are blocked (Lefebvre, 1991 [1974]) then, justice and rights may need to be demanded by 'going beyond the state' (Purcell, 2013: 143). What queers across various classes, ethnicities, genders, and sexualities demonstrated was the importance of encounter spaces for them as much as the concerns of redistributive and recognitional policies (Fincher and Iveson, 2008). As Freitas (2019: 302) argues, 'we must scrutinize the practices and strategies of the excluded groups, because they are the ultimate source of any substantive change in power relations. Being able to learn from these emancipatory practices of vulnerable groups might thus serve as an exercise of de-colonizing the imagination of alternative development modes.' There is a value in these queer insurgencies that can be useful in guiding urban planning practices.

The Anti-SOAP coalition, Queer Up Atlanta, and the Gezi Uprisings were just a part of the millions of (everyday) acts of resistance and creation where the public, and those who are excluded from formal ways of collaboration and participation have been jolted awake and rose up against not only exclusionary practices of urban governance but also the discriminatory discourses used by authoritarians to control marginalized people.

In the Atlanta case, the LGBTQ community learned from the Redevelopment of Peachtree Street and its disastrous impact on the Midtown gayborhood and came together to protect their collective rights to claim space and to survive as marginalized businesses and workers in a more sex-positive environment. In the Istanbul case, the uprisings helped people to realize their own power in altering the destiny of a public space in the city as well as creating a dream-like space where collective resources and emotions were shared through the queer commons 'created along with the spirit of mutual care' (Savci, 2021: 137). In a sense, we observed the public acting, protesting the situation, and intervening in the process resulting in the cancellation of the project and survival of the park. The lived experience of activists in both cases reflects the tenets of insurgency and insurgent planning (Freitas, 2019; Holston, 2008; Laskey and Nicholls, 2019; Lopes de Souza, 2014, 2016; Miraftab, 2009; Sandercock, 1998), along with queer critiques of neoliberalism and its effects on city building processes (Hanhardt, 2013) as well as queerness' 'rejection of a here and now and insistence on potentiality or concrete possibility for another world' (Muñoz, 2019: 11). Based on her study of insurgent planning in Fortelaza, Brazil, Freitas (2019: 286) states that 'insurgency is not a formal/rigid condition of a given set of practices but rather a fluid and complex attitude that responds to the shifting nature of power with the current state/civil society relations' and it is 'a necessary counter-hegemonic process that aims at changing the current structure of power reliant on the system of beliefs and values associated with neoliberalism' (Freitas, 2019: 289). Miraftab (2009) also defines insurgent planning as practices against the neoliberal specifics of dominance which are counter-hegemonic, subversive, and imaginative.

In both cases harsh municipal policies and redevelopment plans were resisted and overturned. The Atlanta decisions were reversed by developing powerful insurgent pressure within the system, whereas the less democratic planning process for Gezi Park needed more radical and immediate solutions than communicative and/or participatory planning practices can provide.

In a similar vein to what Lefebvre defines or imagines with the *right to the city* as an open project toward a horizon beyond the present capitalist and state-bureaucratic society, which is yet to come (in Purcell 2013), Muñoz (2019: 1, 99) sees queerness as an ideality which is not yet here but felt 'as the warm illumination of a horizon imbued with potentiality … standing against capitalism's ever expanding and exhausting force field of how things are and will be.' However, Muñoz (2019) does not leave us with an unknown future, he claims the future is in the present where certain performances of queer citizenship accommodate and anticipate a more visibly queer world. Inspired by the queer commons and Gezi Spirit as performances of queer citizenship, we suggest the tactics applied in the Gezi protests can be a queer insurgent way of doing planning. If we can capture similar synergies of subaltern politics for planning processes, we can both transcend the unbalanced power relations and overcome exclusionary processes in the pursuit of a concrete utopia.

REFERENCES

Arat, Y. (2013). Violence, Resistance, and Gezi Park. *International Journal of Middle East Studies*, 45(4), 807–809, https://doi.org/10.1017/S0020743813000962.

Atalay, O. and Doan, P.L. (2020). Making Lesbian Space at the Edge of Europe: Queer Spaces in Istanbul. *Journal of Lesbian Studies*, *24*(3), 255–271, doi:10.1080/10894160.2019.1683700.

Bagby, D. (2013a). LGBT Advocates Help Put Atlanta's 'Banishment Ordinance' on Hold. *The Georgia Voice*. March 1, 2013. Accessed March 13, 2013 at: www.thegavoice.com/news/atlanta-news/5897 -lgbt-advocates-help-put-atlantas-banishment-ordinance-on-hold.

Bagby, D. (2013b). Atlanta City Council Votes Against Outlawing Adult Businesses on Cheshire Bridge Road. *The Georgia Voice*. June 3, 2013. Accessed June 5, 2013 at: www.thegavoice.com/news/atlanta -news/6326-atlanta-city-council-votes-against-outlawing-adult-businesses-on-cheshire-bridge-road.

Bell, R., Edwards, D.V., and Wagner, R.H. (1969). *Political Power: A Reader in Theory and Research*. New York: Free Press.

Cardinale, Matthew (2013). Counterpoint: Save Cheshire Bridge from Alex Wan and the Gentrifiers, *The Georgia Voice*. February 15, 2013. Accessed March 13, 2013 at: www.thegavoice.com/opinion/ columnists/5854-counterpoint-save-cheshire-bridge-from-alex-wan-and-the-gentrifiers.

Chenault, W. and Braukman, S. (2008). *Images of America: Gay and Lesbian Atlanta*. Charleston, SC: Arcadia Publishing.

Cidam, C. (2017). Unruly Practices: Gezi Protests and the Politics of Friendship. *New Political Science*, *39*(3), 369–392, https://doi.org/10.1080/07393148.2017.1339413.

City of Atlanta (2007). Peachtree Corridor Task Force, Final Report. Atlanta: Department of Planning, Development, and Neighbourhood Conservation.

City of Atlanta (1999). Cheshire Bridge Road Study. Atlanta: Department of Planning, Development, and Neighbourhood Conservation.

Corber, Robert and Stephen Valocchi (2003). Introduction. In R. Corber and S. Valocchi (eds), *Queer Studies: An Interdisciplinary Reader*. Oxford: Blackwell, pp. 1–17.

D'Emilio, John (1983). *Sexual Politics, Sexual Communities*. Chicago: University of Chicago Press.

Dagtas, M.S. (2016). 'Down with Some Things!' The Politics of Humour and Humour as Politics in Turkey's Gezi Protests. *Etnofoor*, *28*(1), 11–34.

Dahl, R.A. (1957). The Concept of Power. *Behavioral Science*, *2*(3), 201–215, https://doi.org/10.1002/ bs.3830020303.

Doan, P.L. (ed.) (2011). *Queerying Planning: Challenging Heteronormative Assumptions and Reframing Planning Practice*. Aldershot, UK: Ashgate Publishing.

Doan, P.L. (2014). Regulating Adult Business to Make Spaces Safe for Heterosexual Families in Atlanta. In P. Maginn and C. Steinmetz (eds), *(Sub)Urban Sexscapes Geographies and Regulation of the Sex Industry*. London: Routledge.

Doan, P.L. (2015). Planning for Sexual and Gender Minorities. In M. Burayidi (ed.), *Cities and the Politics of Difference: Multiculturalism and Diversity in Urban Planning*. Toronto: University of Toronto Press.

Doan, P.L. and Higgins, H. (2011). The Demise of Queer Space? Resurgent Gentrification and LGBT Neighborhoods. *Journal of Planning Education and Research*, *31*, 6–25.

Erol, A.E. (2018). Queer Contestation of Neoliberal and Heteronormative Moral Geographies During #occupygezi. *Sexualities*, *21*(3), 428–445.

Eslen-Ziya, H., McGarry, A., Jenzen, O., Erhart, I., and Korkut, U. (2019). From Anger to Solidarity: The Emotional Echo-chamber of Gezi Park Protests. *Emotion, Space and Society*, *33*, 100632, https:// doi.org/10.1016/j.emospa.2019.100632.

Fincher, R. and Iveson, K. (2008). *Planning and Diversity in the City: Redistribution, Recognition and Encounter*. Basingstoke, UK and New York: Macmillan International Higher Education.

Flyvbjerg, B. (1998). Habermas and Foucault: Thinkers for Civil Society? *The British Journal of Sociology*, *49*(2), 210–233, https://doi.org/10.2307/591310.

Flyvbjerg, B. and Richardson, T. (2002). Planning and Foucault: In Search of the Dark Side of Planning Theory. In P. Allmendinger and M. Tewdwr-Jones (eds), *Planning Futures: New Directions for Planning Theory*, London: Routledge, pp. 44–62, available at: www.researchgate.net/publication/ 244609075_Planning_and_Foucault_In_Search_of_the_Dark_Side_of_Planning_Theory.

Forester, J. (1989). *Planning in the Face of Power*. Berkeley, CA: University of California Press.

Foucault, Michel (1979). *Discipline and Punish: The Birth of the Prison*. A. Sheridan (trans.). New York: Vintage.

Foucault, Michel (1980). *The History of Sexuality: Volume 1: An Introduction*. R. Hurley (trans.). New York: Vintage.

Foucault, Michel (1985). 'An Interview with Michel Foucault,' *History of the Present* (February 1985). Translated from an article in *Les Nouvelles Littéraires*, March 17. 1975, quoted in Keith Gandal, 'Michel Foucault: Intellectual Work and Politics'. *telos*, *1986*(67), 121–134.

Fraser, N. (1990). Rethinking the Public Sphere: A Contribution to the Critique of Actually Existing Democracy. *Social Text*, *25/26*, 56–80. JSTOR, https://doi.org/10.2307/466240.

Freitas, C.F.S. (2019). Insurgent Planning? Insights from Two Decades of the Right to the City in Fortaleza, Brazil. *City*, *23*(3), 285–305, https://doi.org/10.1080/13604813.2019.1648030.

Friedmann, J. (1998). Planning Theory Revisited*. *European Planning Studies*, *6*(3), 245–253, https://doi.org/10.1080/09654319808720459.

Georgia Voice Editors (2013). Queer Up! Atlanta Wants to Keep Cheshire Bridge Adult Businesses, Auto Body Shops Safe, *Georgia Voice*, May 2, 2013. Accessed https://thegavoice.com/community/organizations/queer-up-atlanta-wants-to-keep-cheshire-bridge-adult-businesses-auto-body-shops-safe/.

Gunder, M. (2003). Passionate Planning for the Others' Desire: An Agonistic Response to the Dark Side of Planning. *Progress in Planning*, *60*(3), 235–319, https://doi.org/10.1016/S0305-9006(02)00115-0.

Habermas, J. (1984). *The Theory of Communicative Action: Vol 1: Reason and the Rationalization of Society*. London: Polity Press.

Halperin, D.M. (1995). *Saint Foucault: Towards a Gay Hagiography*. Oxford: Oxford University Press.

Hanhardt, C.B. (2013). *Safe Space: Gay Neighborhood History and the Politics of Violence* Durham, NC: Duke University Press.

Harvey, D. (2006). Neo-Liberalism as Creative Destruction. *Geografiska Annaler. Series B, Human Geography*, *88*(2), 145–158.

Healey, P. (1997). *Collaborative Planning: Shaping Places in Fragmented Societies*. London: Macmillan.

Hennie, M. (2013). 'Midtown's Sex Workers Safe from Exile – For Now.' *Project Q*, February 27, 2013. Accessed April 4, 2013 at: www.projectq.us/midtowns-sex-workers-safe-from-banishment-for-now/.

Holston, J. (2008). *Insurgent Citizenship: Disjunctions of Democracy and Modernity in Brazil*. Princeton: Princeton University Press.

Huxley, M. (2000), The Limits to Communicative Planning. *Journal of Planning Education and Research*, *19*(4), 369–377, https://doi.org/10.1177/0739456X0001900406.

Innes, J. and Booher, D.E. (2010). *Planning with Complexity*. New York: Routledge.

Islam, T. and Sakızlıoğlu, B. (2015). The Making of, and Resistance to, State-led Gentrification in Istanbul, Turkey. In L. Lees, H.B. Shin, and E.L. Morales (eds), *Global Gentrifications: Uneven Development and Displacement*. Bristol: Policy Press, pp. 245–262.

Jagose, A. (1996). *Queer Theory: An Introduction*. New York: New York University Press.

Karakayalí, S. and Yaka, Ö. (2014). The Spirit of Gezi: The Recomposition of Political Subjectivities in Turkey. *New Formations*, *83*(83), 117–138, https://doi.org/10.3898/NeWf.83.07.2014.

Keating, L. (2001). *Atlanta: Race, Class, and Urban Expansion*. Philadelphia: Temple University Press.

Laskey, A.B. and Nicholls, W. (2019). Jumping Off the Ladder: Participation and Insurgency in Detroit's Urban Planning. *Journal of the American Planning Association*, *85*(3), 348–362, https://doi.org/10.1080/01944363.2019.1618729.

Lopes de Souza, M. (2014). Towards a Libertarian Turn? Notes on the Past and Future of Radical Urban Research and Praxis. *City*, *18*(2), 104–118, https://doi.org/10.1080/13604813.2014.896644.

Lopes de Souza, M. (2016). Lessons from Praxis: Autonomy and Spatiality in Contemporary Latin American Social Movements. *Antipode*, *48*(5), 1292–1316, https://doi.org/10.1111/anti.12210.

McWilliams, J. (2013). 'Atlanta Proposes Controversial Crackdown on Prostitution.' *The Atlanta Journal – Constitution*, February 11, 2013. Accessed April 4, 2013 at: www.ajc.com/news/news/atlanta-proposes-controversial-crackdown-on-prosti/nWLnX/.

Midtown Ponce Security Alliance (2013). Transvestite Prostitutes on our Watch List, March 3, 2013. Accessed March 28, 2013 at www.midtownponce.org/p4462.html.

Miraftab, F. (2006). Feminist Praxis, Citizenship and Informal Politics: Reflections on South Africa's Anti-eviction Campaign. *International Feminist Journal of Politics*, *8*(2), 194–218, https://doi.org/10.1080/14616740600612830.

Miraftab, F. (2009). Insurgent Planning: Situating Radical Planning in the Global South. *Planning Theory*, 8(1), 32–50, https://doi.org/10.1177/1473095208099297.

Muñoz, J.E. (2019). *Cruising Utopia, 10th Anniversary Edition: The Then and There of Queer Futurity*. New York: NYU Press.

Neuman, M. (2000), Communicate This! Does Consensus Lead to Advocacy and Pluralism? *Journal of Planning Education and Research*, 19(4), 343–350, https://doi.org/10.1177/0739456X0001900403.

Nouraee, A. (2008). One Man's Battle against Midtown Prostitutes and their Johns, *Creative Loafing*, January 16, 2008. Accessed March 28, 2013, http://clatl.com/atlanta/one-mans-battle-against-midtown-prostitutes-and-their-johns/Content?oid=1271636.

Ozbay, C. and Savci, E. (2018). Queering Commons in Turkey. *GLQ: A Journal of Lesbian and Gay Studies*, 24(4), 516–521, https://doi.org/10.1215/10642684-6957870.

Purcell, M. (2013). Possible Worlds: Henri Lefebvre and the Right to the City, *Journal of Urban Affairs*, 36(1), 141–154.

Sandercock, L. (1998). *Making the Invisible Visible: A Multicultural Planning History*. Berkeley and London: University of California Press.

Savci, E. (2021). *Queer in Translation: Sexual Politics under Neoliberal Islam*. Durham, NC: Duke University Press.

Sedgwick, E. Kosofosky (1990). *Epistemology of the Closet*. Berkeley: University of California Press.

Selek, P. (2001). *Maskeler suvariler gacılar: Ulker Sokak: Bir alt kulturun dıslanma mekani*. Ankara: Ayizi Kitap.

Shapiro, Jonathan (2013). Zoning Board Rejects Plan to Remove Adult Businesses from Cheshire Bridge, But Measure Still Alive, WABE News, Atlanta, May 9, 2013. Accessed: www.wabe.org/zoning-board-rejects-plan-remove-adult-businesses-cheshire-bridge-measure-still-alive/.

Sullivan, Nikki (2003). *A Critical Introduction to Queer Theory*. New York: New York University Press.

Tewdwr-Jones, M. and Allmendinger, P. (1998), Deconstructing Communicative Rationality: A Critique of Habermasian Collaborative Planning. *Environment and Planning A: Economy and Space*, 30(11), 1975–1989, https://doi.org/10.1068/a301975.

Unan, A.D. (2015). Gezi Protests and the LGBT Rights Movement: A Relation in Motion. In A. Yalcintas (ed.), *Creativity and Humour in Occupy Movements: Intellectual Disobedience in Turkey and Beyond*. Basingstoke, UK: Palgrave Macmillan UK, pp. 75–94, https://doi.org/10.1057/9781137473639_5.

Uphoff, N. (1989). Distinguishing Power, Authority and Legitimacy: Taking Max Weber at His Word by Using Resources-Exchange Analysis, *Polity*, 22(2), 295–322, https://doi.org/10.2307/3234836.

Waite, I.A. (2016). Planning, Power, Politics: Urban Redevelopment in Istanbul. Doctorial dissertation, University of California Los Angeles, https://escholarship.org/uc/item/04f489ff.

Warner, M. (1999). *The Trouble with Normal: Sex, Politics, and Ethics of Queer Life*. Cambridge, MA: Harvard University Press.

Warner, M. (2002). Publics and Counterpublics. *Public Culture*, 14(1), 49–90.

Weber, M. (1947). *The Theory of Social and Economic Organization*. A.M. Henderson and T. Par (trans.). New York: Oxford University Press (original work published 1922).

Yalcintan, M. (2012). Soylular Beyoglu'ndan ne istiyor? [What do gentrifiers want from Beyoglu?] Radikal 2, February 12. Retrieved March 10, 2020 at: www.radikal.com.tr/radikal2/soylular-beyoglundan-ne-istiyor-1078521/.

Yasar, Z. (2019). 'Emek Is Ours, Istanbul Is Ours': Reimagining a Movie Theater through Urban Activism. *The Velvet Light Trap*, 83, 46–59.

Zengin, A. (2013). What is Queer about Gezi? Hot Spots, *Fieldsights*, October 31. https://culanth.org/fieldsights/what-is-queer-about-gezi.

19. Feminist planning in the face of power: from interests and ideologies to institutions and intersections

Leonora C. Angeles

INTRODUCTION

Feminist theory is eclectic, permeable, and easily wedded to various conceptions of power, ideologies and practices, including planning. Unlike planning theory, which has expressed uncertainty in its lack of endogenous theories (Allmendinger 2002: 78), feminist theorizing stands on solid philosophical foundations, inspiring power expressions within global feminist political movements. Planners could no longer ignore the challenge, visibility and analytical power contributions of feminist theorizing and politics in their practice. Coinciding with the 'second wave' global women's movement, the 1970s marked the decade planning practice has paid greater attention to women and gender issues at national and international levels. It would, however, be wrong to assume that feminist planning ideas did not exist prior to the emergence of gender planning practice and nineteenth-century 'first wave' suffragists and later waves of women's movements. These historical social movements had their own 'barefoot' planners and planning strategists – precursors of advocacy, social mobilization and empowerment planning within feminist communities of practice – making their work and achievements possible. However, the formalization of community, city and international planning work using a feminist theoretical lens or institutionalized feminist planning has a much more recent, well-defined history spanning the last fifty years.

Historically, the institutionalization of feminist planning has been multiscalar, multisectoral work. Local community-based feminist action (think of the 1890s women's suffrage rallies and the 1960s 'consciousness raising' sessions) inspired national and international institutional efforts in the post-war period. Since the 1970s, efforts radiating from international circles of power – notably the United Nations and the US Congress – mobilized global resources channelled to official national governments' women's machineries, intermediary non-government organizations, community-based organizations, and academic research. Feminist planning practitioners at all government levels were nurtured and trained in these interconnected, overlapping circles of engagement. The cross-fertilization of planning and feminist theories, well established in academic literature, has led to related practices in gender and development, gender equity planning, diversity planning, cross-cultural/multicultural, advocacy and empowerment planning since the 1980s. By the 1990s, Indigenous, Black and Intersectional Feminist theories have also enriched planning theory and practice in academic and political spaces.

Planners have translated aspects of feminism's liberating and emancipatory potentials into 'real' (read material) projects, policies, plans and programs. In turn, feminist theory has shaped planning practice, values and ethics in at least four ways: (1) exposing the limits of positivist empiricist epistemologies and methodologies in planning by incorporating gendered lived experiences and feminist standpoint theory; (2) demonstrating how intersectional identities and layers of inequalities, oppression and exclusion manifest in socio-spatial, economic and political relationships; (3) signifying the importance of gender and other intersectional identities in symbolic representation in planning language and communication; and (4) changing the discourses on the determinants, drivers, and domains of planning ethics, values, and publics.

This chapter examines the intellectual and praxiological genealogy of feminist planning praxis in relation to how feminist analyses of power have shaped the planning field. The first section deals with the interface between planning and feminist theories, values, power and ethics. The second examines how feminist planning has been institutionalized and practised as a specialized technocratic professional planning subfield. The third traces the genealogy and integration of intersectional feminist analyses of power in various planning domains.

FEMINIST AND PLANNING THEORIES IN THE FACE OF VALUES, POWER AND ETHICS

Politics and power analytics are at the heart of the cross-fertilization of feminism, feminist praxis, and planning theory and practice. This cross-fertilization is fraught with analytical tensions and practical conflicts, given their own internal disagreements over foundational ideological influences, values, claims and assumptions about the world (Sandercock and Forsyth 1992; Snyder 1995).

The take-off point in most historical and theoretical discussions on planning to address the 'woman question' is the experience of white middle class women in Western industrialized countries. Western feminism, as it developed in the United States, Canada, Australia, New Zealand, and Europe, seeks to analyse women's position under industrial capitalism. Western women were not the only ones who had fought for women's emancipation and empowerment throughout history, but their experiences have been privileged in archival practices and academic writings.

With the observed universality of gender inequality and sex-gender systems asymmetry around the world, one might expect that these would result in common global responses among women. In fact, stubborn patriarchal traditions require women's complicity in their own oppression. And while many feminists and allies have historically attacked misogyny and articulated ideas on women's rights and empowerment, feminist planning, or the conscious translation of feminist ideas into organized action was not, however, universal or a natural skill for all women, or for all feminists. Some women and some feminists in fact have fraught relations with the professional planning field implicated with colonial and neoliberal state developmentalist projects. Moreover, ideological, class, sexual orientation, and other cleavages of differences between women divide them along diverse political and ideological traditions; nuances within left-wing, centrist or right-wing politics; economic policy preferences; and influences of religious or symbolic nationalist cultures.

Feminism shares with planning ethics and norms associated with resource redistribution, equity, justice and ending racism, sexism and other forms of oppression (Davidoff 1978). It is no historical coincidence that planning theorist Paul Davidoff's (1965) theory of advocacy planning paradigm, predicated upon the concept of pluralism, emerged when feminist theorizing within women's movements was asking parallel questions to Davidoff's questions,

'Who is the client? Who is the stakeholder or the constituent?' and these questions entered into professional planning usage. Feminists in the 'second wave' of the turbulent 1960s and 1970s were likewise asking, who speaks for women, particularly the poor, the disenfranchised, and minorities? Why can't they speak for themselves? Why don't they have voice and power? Directing these parallel questions back to planners, Piven (1970) asked, ultimately, 'Whom does the advocate planner serve?' What advocacy planning and feminist advocacy share are their self-reflexive practice, normative ethics, and cognition of power constraints and possibilities.

Normative planning ethics beyond narrow 'incrementalist' versus 'rational comprehensive' planning interests benefit from feminist ethics, helping planners decide on a desirable, caring and empathetic society free from oppression (Hendley 1994: 123). There are at least eight main planning-relevant approaches to addressing the question of women's and gender oppression, roughly equivalent to feminist theories, which developed within varied (e.g. Western and non-Western) contexts: (1) liberal feminism (Friedan 1973; Wendell 1987; Abbey 2011); (2) traditional Marxism (Burnham and Louie 1985; Dunayevskaya 1981, 1985; Vogel 1983); (3) radical (lesbian) feminism (Firestone 1971; Greer 1971; Millet 1970); (4) socialist feminism (Rowbotham, Segal and Wainwright 1981; Sargeant 1981); (5) Indigenous feminism (Green and Bourgeois 2017; Hernández Castillo 2002, 2010); (6) Black feminism (Collins 1990, 1996; hooks 1981); and (7) ecofeminism (Shiva and Mies 1993; Salleh 2017; Warren, Warren, and Erkal 1997); and (8) 'Third World' post-colonial or post-development feminism (Grewal and Kaplan 1994; Mohanty 1988, 2003; Saunders 2005).

Each of these approaches differ in their analysis of (1) oppression's sources and origins; (2) how oppression is perpetuated; (3) institutional, state and other forms of power; (4) planning directions or proposed solutions to oppression; and (5) prescriptions for women's movements' relationships to institutions such as state agencies, social movements or political parties (Jaggar 1983). In terms of state institutional power, there are pro-state and anti-state feminists from various ideological camps with their own claims over state power legitimacy, authority, and dynamics in state–civil society relations (Brodie 1996), made more complicated by how we remap gender and reconceptualize social, power and (re)production under contemporary globalization (Brodie 2003; Griffin-Cohen and Brodie 2007).

In brief, liberal feminists believe gender oppression and subordination manifest in social discrimination against women and female-identified bodies because of sexist socialization and socially prescribed sex roles (Friedan 1973, Wendell 1987). Planning against oppression begins with reforms in sex-role socialization within the family, schools, legal systems, and state support to improve women's social, political and economic status. Radical feminism argues that patriarchal oppression is the primary cause of women's and other forms of oppression, requiring separatist, sometimes anti-male, strategies (Firestone 1971; Greer 1971; Millet 1970). It has been a 'much maligned, caricatured and misrepresented theory' (Robinson 2003), given its association with lesbian feminism which has emerged as being integral to radical feminist theory in challenging heteronormativity and heterosexuality as oppressive institutions of sexual power.

Traditional Marxists analyse class power and capitalist exploitation through labor surplus extraction to argue for class struggle's primacy in eliminating all forms of oppression. Traditional Marxist feminists believe in the importance of women in class struggles as oppressed working-class members (Burnham and Louie 1985; Dunayevskaya 1981, 1985; Vogel 1983). Socialist feminists combine analyses of patriarchal and capitalist class power as the sources of gender-based oppression (Burris 1982; Hartsock 1983; Rowbotham, Segal and Wainwright 1981; Sargeant 1981). They challenge sexism and patriarchal systems of oppression, but using Marxist analysis, see patriarchal power, not as a separate analytical category, but shaped by, and functional to, capitalist political economy and patriarchal socialist states (Stacey 1983).

Black and Indigenous feminisms react against Western feminists' neglect of colonial violence and its legacies of racism at the structural roots of women's oppression (Suzack, Huhndorf, Perreault and Barman 2010). In particular, mainstream white, middle-class liberal feminists often ignore the realities of Indigenous, Black African, and working-class women's lives (Collins 1990, 1996; Dorries and Harjo 2020; hooks 1981; Fox-Genovese 1996). Indigenous feminists in particular emphasize the Indigenous roots of feminist values of gender equality and justice, inspiring women's exercise of formal and informal power within and outside their communities. Their political organizing comes in various forms, such as harnessing the power of arts and cultural representation (Huhndorf 2021), and in diverse contexts from the Global North (Green and Bourgeois 2017; Knobblock and Kuokkanen 2015; Nickel 2017; Trask 1996) to the Global South (Hernández Castillo 2002, 2010; Jain 2011).

Postmodern and postcolonial feminism borrow from postmodern and postcolonial critiques of modernist/imperialist projects, critical of grand narratives and absolute truths and taking unitary, homogeneous views on social reality.

Poststructuralist and postmodern theories reject positivist claims of universal truths, essentialism, rationality in progress and totalizing top-down structures of power (Grewal and Kaplan 1994; Saunders 2005). They problematize objectivity, and standardized evaluation of knowledge claims and power as malleable and social worlds, identities, and ideologies as discursively constructed. They disagree with feminist researchers who privilege women's experiences and feminist standpoint, arguing that there is no objective reality known by feminists or anyone else, since knowledge is perspectival and partial. The feminist perspective does not necessarily have epistemological privilege, in the same vein masculine and elite standpoints claim to have such privilege. They problematize 'experience' as authoritative evidence, emphasizing instead the discursive constructions and effects of individual experiences and interpretations. This discursive-linguistic turn in analysis, or emphasis on the relation of meaning and discourse to power, identity, and society, enabled poststructuralist (and postmodern) feminists to criticize the totalizing notion of a monolithic 'women's experience' and 'feminist standpoint.'

Postcolonial feminists, mostly Third World scholars based in the North, analyse colonial and imperial power shaping feminist politics and research (Mohanty 1988, 2003; Nagar 2002). Like Black feminists in the West, postcolonial feminists problematize mainstream feminist analysis and politics largely based on hegemonic white US middle-class women's experiences and their complicity and participation in imperialist projects and practices. Like postcolonial feminist analysis critical of white imperial feminism, associated with neoliberalism, post-development feminist thinking views 'development,' particularly development aid, as largely a Western, self-serving imperialist project to be rejected in favour of decolonial, more humane, just and people-centred solutions to poverty and inequality (Parpart 1993; Saunders 2005). Postdevelopment writing therefore interpreted development (and by extension, development planning) as 'a particular vision and intervention' with its own 'regime of knowledge, truth and power that is not necessarily empowering or rewarding for many of those on the receiving end' (Sidaway 2007: 346).

Ecofeminism draws inspiration from Indigenous women's knowledge and practices and other strands of feminist theories. It shares postcolonial and postdevelopment feminists' critique of 'catch-up' development planning and (neo)liberal feminists' emphasis on skills in protecting local livelihoods. It shares many assumptions with Socialist and Marxist feminists, particularly their challenges to the postmodern penchant for relativism and capitalist commodification, which homogenizes cultures and perpetuates capitalist patriarchal systems by treating women's bodies and nature as resources to be exploited, packaged, and marketed. As Ariel Salleh noted in the Foreword to 2014 edition of the classic 1993 book by Vandana Shiva and Maria Mies:

> Ecofeminism is the only political framework I know of that can spell out the historical links between neoliberal capital, militarism, corporate science, worker alienation, domestic violence, reproductive technologies, sex tourism, child molestation, neocolonialism, Islamophobia, extractivism, nuclear weapons, industrial toxics, land and water grabs, deforestation, genetic engineering, climate change and the myth of modern progress. (Shiva and Mies, 2014: i)

The above categorization of feminist theories is based on how people situate themselves in relation to one another. Feminists, especially in the Western context, employ these categories to differentiate their ideological positions. Not all feminists however would claim adherence to these theories or their theoretical presuppositions. Some feminist planners might disagree with certain ideas attributed to each theoretical position and their planning or action implications. Some who believe in their basic ideological presuppositions might not even call themselves feminists or feminist planners.

Feminist theories are multiplicitous and malleable with varying conceptions of power dynamics, social relations and ethical-moral positions. They differ in their explanation of how power operates in society, of the bases or evidence of the 'woman' or 'gender' question relative to other questions around class, race, nation, or justice. They also have conflicting or competing visions of 'good social change' or a 'good alternative society.' Differences in their analysis and visions reflect in their bitter criticisms of each other, sometimes without realizing how theoretical and practical weaknesses of one approach may be the other's strength (Jaggar, 1983). Since the early 1990s, at least in the West, 'second wave' liberal, radical, Marxist, socialist feminists have been challenged by 'third wave' feminism, sometimes called postfeminism,

As practical people, feminist planners informed or influenced by any combination of feminist and planning theories as feminist planning ethics share many commonalities drawn from various influences. These commonalities include the emphasis on holistic approaches, care and empathy, alongside if not above rights and justice; the desire to balance responsibilities, freedom, obligations and accountability to multiple stakeholders; and cooperative problem solving through mediation and negotiation (Hendler 1994; Ritzdorf 1992). In revisiting her famous essay 'Under Western Eyes,' (Mohanty 1988), Chantal Talpade Mohanty argues for a more differentiated analysis of power relations in (de)colonization. She argues that current globalization processes necessitate a move away from 'geographical and ideological binarisms' such as the distinction between 'Western' and 'Third World' feminist practices, given their commonalities, and focuses instead on what she calls 'an anticapitalist transnational feminist practice – and on the possibilities, indeed on the necessities, of cross-national feminist solidarity' (Mohanty 2003a: 506, 509). This echoes what Black Feminist theorist Patricia Hill Collins (1990) called 'dialogical standpoint theory.' Predating Intersectionality

Theory, Feminist Standpoint Theory argues '*the* one marginal, critical standpoint does not exist and thus advocates a critical dialogue between positions' leading 'to the identification of similarities in perspectives that result in politics of solidarity between standpoints and hence to a de-centring of dominant discourses and knowledge claims' (Schurr and Segebart, 2012: 148).

Such combined Black and Postcolonial Feminist thinking has informed feminist planners and policy analysts cognizant of their ethical standpoints in asking planning-related questions from feminist perspectives. Feminist political philosopher Iris Marion Young (1992) long ago noted the potentially powerful synergy between feminism and planning:

> Feminism and planning will serve each other best … if they dig down into the sort of problems of women-centred change … What would it mean to organize cities and suburbs so that parents spend less time driving? How can the environment of streets, parks, train stations, etc. be made safer for women and discourage harassment? Can planners devise safer alternatives to malls and basketball courts as teenage hangouts? Can the process of planning away open public spaces be reversed so people can meet and mingle safely, and watch from the edges? What incentives can be developed for reducing the gender coding of occupations? How can the dependence of industrial economies on military production and serving a military machine be severely reduced without jettisoning workers from the workforce and without gender bias in retraining efforts?

Young's questions, especially the last, echo visions of an alternative society, urban design, transportation systems and safety in public spaces from socialist feminist perspectives. But in a capitalist economy that increasingly marginalizes social(ist) democracy, dominated by neoliberal ideologies since the 1970s, liberal feminist analytical tools and planning approaches won, prospered, and hitherto integrated in local, national and international circles of institutionalized state and global power.

FEMINIST PLANNING AND INSTITUTIONAL POWER

Feminist planning is nothing without agency, institutional embodiments and institutional power analysis. Feminist theories providing analytical insights on power and power relations in institutional settings have shaped institutionalized planning practices, particularly in urban and international development spaces. Feminist planners deal with power dynamics and power structures, particularly within capitalist planning bureaucracies, in two main historical strands.

The first strand consists of how liberal feminist planning has considered contextual gender relations ideologies and interests through combined institutional, socio-spatial, and political economic analysis, best exemplified in gender-based empowerment, recognized as one of the key elements of international development discourse. Evolving from the earlier welfare approach dominant in the 1950s, the need to address women's concerns and issues has entered community and international development theory and practice under the rubric of Women in Development (WID). Following the 1972 Percy Amendment declaring 10 percent of international development aid be channelled to women's programs and projects, WID became popular in the 1970s until the mid-1980s. WID gained momentum following the declaration of the International Women's Development Decade in 1975, leading to the establishment of national governments' women's machinery in the form of ministries, departments, commissions, or agencies in many countries in the Global North and South (Moser 2012). Feminist planners within these bureaucracies are sometimes called state feminists or 'femocrats.' State feminism refers to the institutionalization of feminist policy agenda, or the use of state-level mechanisms and policy instruments to improve women's situation (Angeles 2003). Alongside WID-based state feminism came discourses on participatory development enshrining people's participation and empowerment as development planning objectives (Chambers 1994; Guijt and Shah, 1998).

A gender analytical lens applied to empowerment planning discourse, shifted the focus from women's welfare to women's empowerment, embodied in the mid-1980s shift from WID to Gender in Development (GID) or Gender and Development (GAD). This shift from WID to GAD is not without controversy for various reasons, among them, the highly contested concept of 'gender' as a social construction especially in cultures mainly recognizing biology, or biological sex, as bases for gender differences; the implicit recognition that while all women's issues are gender issues, not all gender issues concern only women; and the diversion of much-needed resources from women to men, now assumed to have roles to play in gender-based empowerment (Baden and Goetz 1997). Ideological and operational shifts also marked variations in the way feminist planners conceptualized power in structural-institutional and discursive ways – from the liberal, neo-liberal to orthodox Marxist, Foucauldian, ecofeminist, and socialist – especially in feminist academic and praxis-related discourses.

GAD popularized the marriage of feminist and planning theories based on empowerment theorizing, enabling gender and empowerment discourses mainly through the professionalization and technicalization of gender-relevant planning. The practice came in analytical approaches and tools, with their varied planning guidebooks, handbooks, guidelines and techniques such as Gender Budgeting (GB), Gender Budget Audits (GBA), Gender Impact Assessment (GIA), Gender Equality Planning (GEP), Gender-Based Analysis (GBA), Gender Mainstreaming (GM) and Gender-Based Empowerment (GBE). GBE, influenced by empowerment (planning) theory builds on nearly three decades of WID and GID/GAD approaches used in national development planning and international development co-operation (Moser 2012). GAD relied on liberal feminism and a liberal conception of states and state power as able to resolve competing interests and claims through political bargaining and competition within liberal democratic institutions such as political parties, electoral systems and planning bureaucracies. As a hybrid planning principle drawing from liberal, socialist, Indigenous, Black and postcolonial feminist analyses, GBE focuses not on women-as-target-group, but problematizes gender relations, conflict, power, and social structures. GEP and GBE are well-recognized elements of national and international development discourses targeting institutional structures and practices that perpetuate gender and other forms of inequality based on race, class, age, and sexuality. Like GID/GAD and its dominant tool of gender mainstreaming, GBE views gender equality as a development goal, which targets institutional structures and practices that perpetuate gender and other forms of inequality. In this vein, one might argue GBE is the philosophical and operational precursor to Intersectional Feminist Analysis.

The second contemporary strand coming out of this 'empowerment turn' in feminist planning, coinciding with the general 'cultural turn' and 'affective turn' in the social sciences, has also influenced planning theory and practice. As explained in the next section, intersectionality or intersectional feminist analysis, although common in applied social research in social work and education since the 1990s, has only belatedly penetrated urban planning practice. However, community development planning in Global South contexts has already grappled with the complexity of power relations that act in multidirectional 'rock-paper-scissor' dynamics or in intersecting relations of power, identities, oppression and privilege. The rise of using

Participatory Rural Appraisal (a.k.a. Participatory Reflection and Action) tools for knowledge generation and more inclusive participatory planning was one such attempt to capture local knowledge, increase local ownership and local resource generation, and empower local people in their own development processes (Chambers 1994; Kapoor 2002). Although power relations have also persisted in participatory development planning processes (Cooke and Kothari, 2001; Guijt and Shah, 1998), it can be argued that participatory planning methods and participatory action research since the 1970s had paved the way for more complex interrogation and conceptualization of intersectional dimensions of power relations and social identities.

Despite initial fears that shifting from WID to GID/GAD/GBE would displace women from mainstream development planning, producing many productive tensions, it is now increasingly recognized in many circles that women-only initiatives and a gender mainstreaming focus are not contradictory but rather complementary to the goal of gender equality (Walby 2005). The terms women's empowerment and/or gender-based empowerment highlight the agential aspect of empowerment. Empowerment could only be achieved by individuals, such as women, men, children and transgendered peoples; and collectivities, such as social movements, social groups, and communities, not by social categories and constructs such as gender. Women's empowerment is therefore a form of empowerment based on gender, or gender-based empowerment. It requires a restructuring of gender relations; a rearrangement of rights, responsibilities and privileges allocated to women and men; and the support and transformation of institutions. Policy makers and development planners need to pay attention to individual, rather than household-based recipients of social and economic interventions addressing gender inequality, since '(m)ale and female goals within nuclear and inter-generational households are typically pursued not by playing out cooperative plans, but rather through institutionalized inequalities' (Bruce and Dywer, 1988: 19). In other words, it is not institutions that act, but rather individuals and people within institutions who act, or face constraints to planning and other forms of action leading to their (dis)empowerment.

At the international development level, comparative gender-disaggregated country and regional data collection and analyses are important for multiscalar planning interventions. Complementing the Human Development Index (HDI) is the Gender Development Index (GDI), which was sharpened by more focused measures of gender equality gap through the Gender Empowerment Measure (GEM). GEM provides insights into the economic, legal and social aspects of the gender gap by measuring the degree of inequality between men and women in the following areas: (1) economic participation and opportunity – outcomes on salaries, participation levels and access to high-skilled employment; (2) educational attainment – outcomes on access to basic and higher level education; (3) political empowerment – outcomes on representation in decision-making structures; and (4) health and survival – outcomes on life expectancy and sex ratio.

Steeped in liberal feminist assumptions about the roots of gender inequality that is silent about capitalism and patriarchal institutions, gender equality planning in many parts of the world has resulted in the form of 'governance feminism' where feminist knowledge has become governmentalized (Prügl 2011). Gender equality planning becomes a managerialist discourse that limits the possibilities for gender equality negotiations, thus creating 'legal and liberal bio-power geared toward the production of new selves' (Prügl, 2011: 80). In the Global South, perhaps the most well-documented effects appear in academic and practitioner literature on how microfinance targeting women has created new forms of consumerism and desires as participating neoliberal citizen subjects in market-based entrepreneurship (Rankin

2001; Speak 2012). In the Global North, the biopower of neoliberalism has also transformed citizenship, feminist knowledge formation, and subjectivities complicit in neoliberal forms of governance (Prügl, 2011, 2015).

Planning and its foundational 'development thinking is steeped in social engineering and the ambition to shape economies and societies, which makes it an interventionist and managerial-ist discipline. It involves telling other people what to do – in the name of modernisation, nation building, progress, mobilisation, sustainable development, human rights, poverty alleviation and even empowerment and participation (participatory management)' (Pieterse 2000: 182). Gender equality planning in this light is a form of managerial developmentalism or planning for social engineering. However, Ikävalko and Kantola (2017) argue that this 'persuasive and pervasive' critique of gender equality planning and its reproduction of neoliberal biopower which shapes organizational practices, produces incentives, activates diversity and difference, and acts upon the subjectivities of individuals, leaves 'little theoretical and empirical space for accounts of feminist resistance that might take place in gender equality work' (245). Borrowing from Foucault's works on different modalities of exercising power – repressive, disciplinary, and biopower 'takes charge of life' through technologies for managing popula-tions. They argue that promoting gender equality as a 'common good' has effectively silenced or pre-empted 'opposing or different voices in advance' a form of 'neoliberal disciplining' generating both 'feminist resistance' and 'resistance to feminism in gender equality work,' a distinction based on Foucauldian concepts of power and resistance where 'the two are con-ceptualized as deeply intertwined' (Ikävalko and Kantola, 2017: 246).

Studying the European Union (EU), for example, Verloo (2006) argues there are planning-related tendencies at EU level that assume an unquestioned similarity of inequalities. In failing to address these at the structural level, EU planners fuel the political competition between inequalities, thus necessitating constructive ideas for a more comprehensive way of addressing multiple inequalities (Verloo 2006). Given the above contentious outcomes of institutionalized feminist planning mechanisms, often accused of association with white imperial feminism unwittingly or intentionally serving neoliberal capitalist agendas, feminist scholars turn to intersectionality as an alternative, progressive, more comprehensive and holistic framework promising to address the weaknesses of dominant technocratic feminist planning in the last fifty years.

INSTITUTIONALIZING INTERSECTIONAL ANALYSIS IN PLANNING

Intersectionality theory or intersectional analysis originated in a critique of legal doctrine's confining approach to subject formation (Crenshaw 1989, 1991). Since the 1990s, it has been adopted nationally and internationally outside of legal scholarship to explain how fields of power operate and interact to produce hierarchy for any limitless combination of identities (Cho 2013). Tracing intersectionality to 1970s socialist feminist (Gordon 2016) and Black feminist theories (Combahee River Collective 1986), contemporary intersectionality recog-nizes multiple forms of domination while refusing to rank them in importance.

Intersectionality, considered a central tenet of 'fourth wave' feminist thinking (Daum 2019: xxi), has been defined in many ways, including: 'the mutually constitutive relations among social identities' (Shields 2008); 'the interactivity of social identity structures such as race, class, and gender in fostering life experiences, especially experiences of privilege and oppression' (Gopaldas 2013); 'the primary analytic tool that feminist and anti-racist scholars deploy for theorizing identity and oppression' (Nash 2008); 'the relationships among multiple dimensions and modalities of social relations and subject formations as a central category of analysis' (McCall 2005); 'analytic approaches that simultaneously consider the meaning and consequences of multiple categories of identity, difference, and disadvantage' (Cole 2009); 'the interaction of multiple identities and experiences of exclusion and subordination' (Davis 2008); and 'the recognition of multiple interlocking identities, defined by relative sociocultural power and privilege, which constitutes a vital step forward in research across multiple domains of inquiry' (Parent, DeBlaere, and Moradi 2013). These varied definitions have their respective differing emphases on intersecting elements and axes of differences (e.g. identities, subjectivities, lived experience, social relations, relations of oppression). However, they share common interests in how these elements and axes ultimately connect with power, privilege and positionality.

Since the early 2000s, major cities in Northern industrialized countries have incorporated intersectional analysis in their work, replacing an earlier penchant for gender-based analysis and gender mainstreaming. Intersectionality is now considered a useful analytical framework for city planners, decision-makers, and policy-makers to help them gain a better understanding, access, and skilled intervention as regards the world's complexities and people's lives, as their own lives. It has already proved to be a useful analytical tool or framework to think about and develop strategies to address equity, fairness, justice, diversity, inclusion, and other goals by focusing on the intersection of identities (e.g. class, gender, race, ethnicity, linguistic, sexuality, ability, religion, nationality, etc.). These intersectional identities shape layers and degrees of oppression and marginalization as people experience city spaces, services and policies, requiring intersectional planning approaches.

Inequalities often consist of different layers of social exclusion, where gender, sexuality, class, race and age intersect to produce different subject formation, modes of oppression and privilege, as well as forms of domination and resistance. An intersectional approach raises questions as to how different power relations risk strengthening each other, thereby contributing to making certain groups specifically exposed to exclusion. Intersectional analysis helps breaks down the divide between scholarship-activism; planning-advocacy-activism; critical inquiry-praxis-planning (Bilge, 2013; Hill Collins and Bilge, 2016). The implication for planners is that:

> We also need to speak several languages for intersectionality is everywhere, and it is polyglot: it speaks the language of activism, community organizing, as much as it speaks the language of academia, or of institutions. It speaks to young people through social media and popular culture and through established journals and conferences … Practitioners and activists are often frontline actors for solving social problems that come with complex social inequalities, a social location that predisposes them to engage intersectionality as critical praxis. Teachers, social workers, parents, policy advocates, university support staff, community organizers, clergy, lawyers, graduate students, and nurses often have an up-close and personal relationship with violence, homelessness, hunger, illiteracy, poverty, sexual assault, and similar social problems. For practitioners and activists, intersectionality is not simply a heuristic for intellectual inquiry but is also an important analytical strategy for doing social justice work. (Hill Collins and Bilge, 2016: 9, 39)

Critics of intersectionality claim it is 'too vague,' 'too abstract' or 'too ambivalent' to be called a theory (Nash 2008; Townsend-Bell 2014). Others argue the opposite and prefer its open-endedness as the hallmark of a 'good theory' (e.g. Davis 2008). Based on their engagement with postcolonial feminism through participatory action research and intersectionality, Schurr and Segebart (2012) reasoned:

> It is the ambivalence and vagueness of the concept of intersectionality that makes it a productive tool to decolonise development research and practice in alignment with feminist postcolonialism. This vagueness opens up possibilities for a creative engagement with the concept in order to identify inclusions and exclusions along intersecting identity categories. (Schurr and Segebart 2012)

Complex human problems require complex analyses like intersectionality frameworks, and feminists lost no time debating the analytical, methodological and practical power tensions that the theory has generated. Some intersectional researchers use Black women as 'quintessential intersectional subjects' (Nash 2008) and thus have marginalized intersectionality by conceptualizing race and gender in fixed and static ways, thus misdescribing Crenshaw's original articulation (Cabardo 2013). Carbado (2013) critiques colourblind intersectionality and gender-blind intersectionality to show how formal equality frameworks in law and civil rights advocacy produce and entrench normative racial and gender identities.

Intersectional insights and frameworks are practised in a multitude of highly contested, complex, and unpredictable ways (Cho, Crenshaw and McCall 2013), raising many dilemmas and debates (Nash 2008; Walby, Armstrong and Strid 2012). For example, comparing debates on intersectional racism in Britain in the 1980s and around the 2001 UN World Conference Against Racism, Yuval-Davis (2006) raised four analytical issues in conceptualizing the interrelationships of gender, class, race and ethnicity and other social divisions: (1) the relative helpfulness of additive or mutually constitutive models of intersectional social divisions; (2) the different analytical levels at which social divisions need to be studied, (3) their ontological base and their relations to each other, and (4) the appropriate intersectional methodological approach for engaging in aid and human rights work in the South.

As a malleable and permeable framework, intersectionality has been applied to various planning domains – from climate change and prison reform to public health, and immigrant justice. As cities grapple with the complexity of climate change impacts, an intersectional analysis of climate change examines relations among humans and between humans and nature, and integrates insights from various academic fields to help illuminate how different individuals and groups relate differently to climate change, due to their situatedness in power structures based on context-specific and dynamic social categorizations (Kaijsel and Kronsell, 2014).

Intersectionality-Based Policy Analysis (IBPA) for example has been applied to Canadian health policy through collaboration developed using a participatory process involving researchers, practitioners, users of health services, and other stakeholders (Hill Collins and Bilge, 2016: 41). Given the increasing overrepresentation of racialized people within prisons in multi-ethnic and multiracial countries, intersectionality has also been useful in planning reforms in the criminal justice system through intersectional critiques of mass incarceration (Hill Collins and Bilge, 2016: 41). Intersectionality has also been used to analyse institutional power relations between cities and racialized LGBTQ+ communities (Bergersen, Klar and Schmitt 2018; Parent, DeBlaere, and Moradi 2013). It has been used in examining immigrant women's health (Bowleg 2012), labor and engagement with the uneven impacts of globalization intruding into the micro-world of families and households in multi-sited transnational spaces (Flippen 2014; Tungohan 2016; Viruell-Fuentes, Miranda, and Abdulrahim 2012).

Dhamoon (2011) identifies five key considerations for adopting and mainstreaming intersectionality, with implications for planning: (1) language and concepts used; (2) the complexities of difference and how to navigate this complexity; (3) the choice of focusing on identities, categories, processes, and/or systems; (4) the model used to explain and describe mutually constituted differences; and (5) the principles that determine which interactions are analysed. In the process of mainstreaming intersectionality, it is crucial to frame intersectionality as a form of social critique so as to foreground its radical capacity to attend to and disrupt oppressive vehicles of power (Dhamoon 2011).

There are increasing numbers of examples of how intersectional analysis has made a difference, or not, in social development and urban spatial planning through its conceptualization of social power and power relations. Intersectionality allows for more nuanced perspectives on disability, showing how stereotypical attitudes, social stigma, discrimination and neglect of people with disabilities require planning for preferential support services and socio-psychological interventions within a larger inclusiveness framework (Pal 2011). Intersectional disability discourses among youth in schools experiencing intersecting forms of oppression, dis/abilities, and social identity constructions can significantly improve young adults' experiences with education and schooling (Hernández-Saca, Gutmann Kahn, and Cannon 2018). In contrast, a lack of empathy and intersectional perspectives in policing, public safety planning, and transition shelter services exacerbates cisnormative and heteronormative stereotyping, homophobia, transphobia, discrimination and marginalization towards gender-diverse bodies and communities (Angeles and Roberton 2020; Pyne 2011; see also Chapter 18 by Doan and Atalay).

CONCLUSIONS

Differential planning contexts in the face of power within and outside formal institutions, with their gendered practices and norms, shape various forms of resistance and exercise of power. Intersectional feminist analysis has enabled solidarity and agency across and beyond social categories, illustrating how power relations, ideologies, structures, and ideological-structural categorizations may be reinforced, but also challenged and renegotiated. Feminist planners operating at various scales and institutional sites have shown how the renegotiation, facilitation, and resolution of conflicts and power dynamics are dialogic. They may occur not only at the individual and collective levels, in highly visible forms of public activism but also at the micro, subtle, routine, and everyday forms of struggles and resistance 'from above' (e.g. state feminists) and 'from below' (e.g. community activists).

Investigating the interconnectedness of socio-economic, political and environmental changes within human societies requires an intersectional approach that stays clear of traps of neocolonialisms, power essentialisms and reductionisms, which weakened earlier generations of feminist theories. Intersectional feminist planning frameworks are promising not only for their practical applications in health policy, social services, urban development, and other planning domains but also in their analytical critique of how gender-focused equality planning measures, and their measurements, have unwittingly served neoliberal capitalist agendas by seeing sexism and gender inequality, and more recently, racism and racial inequality, as fetters to further economic growth, that need resolution through gender equality (or equity, diversity and inclusion) planning.

Gender equality planning might be viewed as similar to other critical approaches to development by dealing with development's 'dark side' – sexism, gender injustice and inequality. It parallels how dependency theory raises global inequality; alternative development, the lack of popular participation; human development, lack of investment in people, and post-development, the underlying motives of development, all requiring repudiation and rejection (Pieterse 2000: 176). What intersectional feminist thinking and planning enables is the imagination of multiple centres of intersecting power relations of oppression and privilege. Thus, it is able to integrate academic research informing various modalities of power politics – from community activism to self-organizing and planning capacities of the oppressed, without letting elites, states and city, national and international planning institutions 'off the hook.' It shares postcolonial and post-development critiques and observations about the 'dark side' of development, without rejecting development and planning altogether. Only time will test and prove the analytical power, praxiological effectiveness and longevity of intersectional feminism in transforming planning praxis.

REFERENCES

Abbey, R. 2011. *The Return of Feminist Liberalism*. Durham: Acumen Publishing.
Allmendinger, P. 2002. Towards a Post-positivist Typology of Planning Theory. *Planning Theory*, 1(1): 77–99.
Angeles, L.C. 2003. Creating Social Spaces for Transnational Feminist Advocacy: The Canadian International Development Agency, the National Commission on the Role of Filipino Women and Philippine Women's NGOs. *The Canadian Geographer*, 47(3): 283–302.
Angeles, L.C. and Roberton, J. 2020. Empathy and Public Safety in the City: Examining LGBTQ2+ Voices and Experiences of Intersectional Discrimination. *Women's Studies International Forum*, 78, 102313.
Baden, S. and Goetz, A.M. 1997. Who Needs [Sex] When You Can have [Gender]? Conflicting Discourses on Gender at Beijing. *Feminist Review*, 56(1): 3–25.
Bergersen, M., Klar, S., and Schmitt, E. 2018. Intersectionality and Engagement among the LGBTQ+ Community. *Journal of Women, Politics & Policy*, 39(2): 196.
Bilge, S. 2013. Intersectionality Undone: Saving Intersectionality from Feminist Intersectionality Studies. *Du Bois Review*, 10(2): 405–424.
Bowleg, L. 2012. The Problem with the Phrase Women and Minorities: Intersectionality-an Important Theoretical Framework for Public Health. *American Journal of Public Health*, 102(7): 1267–1273.
Brodie, M.J. 1996. *Women and Canadian Public Policy*. Toronto and London: Harcourt Brace.
Brodie, J. 2003. Globalization, In/Security, and the Paradoxes of the Social. In I. Bakker and S. Gill (eds), *Power, Production and Social Reproduction*, London: Palgrave Macmillan, pp. 47–65.
Bruce, J. and Dwyer, D. 1988. Introduction. In D. Dwyer and J. Bruce (eds), *A Home Divided: Women and Income in the Third World*. Stanford: Stanford University Press, pp. 1–19.
Burnham, L. and Louie, M.C.Y. 1985. *The Impossible Marriage: A Marxist Critique of Socialist Feminism*. Oakland, CA: Institute for Social and Economic Studies.
Burris, V. 1982. The Dialectic of Women's Oppression: Notes on the Relationship Between Capitalism and Patriarchy. *Berkeley Journal of Sociology*, 27: 51–73.
Carbado, D.W. 2013. Colorblind Intersectionality. *Signs*, 38(4): 811–845.
Carbado, D.W., Crenshaw, K.W., Mays, V.M., and Tomlinson, B. 2013. Intersectionality. *Du Bois Review: Social Science Research on Race*, 10(2): 303–312.
Chambers, R. 1994. The Origins and Practice of Participatory Rural Appraisal. *World Development*, 22(7): 953–969.
Cho, S., Crenshaw, K.W., and McCall, L. 2013. Toward a Field of Intersectionality Studies: Theory, Applications, and Praxis. *Signs*, 38(4): 785–810.

Combahee River Collective. 1986. *The Combahee River Collective Statement: Black Feminist Organizing in the Seventies and Eighties*. New York: Kitchen Table: Women of Color Press.

Crenshaw, K. 1989. 'Demarginalizing the Intersection of Race and Sex: A Black Feminist Critique of Antidiscrimination Doctrine, Feminist Theory and Antiracist Politics.' *The University of Chicago Legal Forum*, 140: 139–167.

Crenshaw, K. 1991. 'Mapping the Margins: Intersectionality, Identity Politics, and Violence Against Women of Color.' *Stanford Law Review*, 43(6): 1241–1299.

Cole, E.R. 2009. Intersectionality and Research in Psychology. *American Psychologist*, 64(3): 170–180.

Collins, P.H. 1990. *Black Feminist Thought: Knowledge, Consciousness and the Politics of Empowerment*. Boston: Unwin Hyman.

Collins, P.H. 1996. What's in a Name? Womanism, Black Feminism, and Beyond. *The Black Scholar*, 26(1): 9–17.

Collins, P.H. and Bilge, S. 2015. *Intersectionality*. London: Polity Press.

Cooke, B. and Kothari, U. (eds). 2001. *Participation. The New Tyranny?* London: Zed.

Daum, M. 2019. *The Problem with Everything: My Journey Through the Culture Wars*. New York: Gallery Books.

Davidoff, P. 1965. Advocacy and Pluralism in Planning. *Journal of the American Institute of Planners*, 31(4): 331–337, http://dx.doi.org/10.1080/01944366508978187.

Davidoff, P. 1978. The Redistributive Function in Planning: Creating Greater Equity among Citizens of Communities. In R. Buchell and G. Sternlieb (eds), *Planning Theory for the 1980s*. New Brunswick, NJ: Centre for Urban Policy Research.

Davis, K. 2008. Intersectionality as Buzzword: A Sociology of Science Perspective on what Makes a Feminist Theory. *Feminist Theory*, 1: 67–85.

Dhamoon, R.K. 2011. Considerations on Mainstreaming Intersectionality. *Political Research Quarterly*, 64(1): 230–243.

Dorries, H. and Harjo, L. 2020. Beyond Safety: Refusing Colonial Violence Through Indigenous Feminist Planning. *Journal of Planning Education and Research*, 40(2): 210–219.

Dunayevskaya, R. 1981. *Rosa Luxemburg: Women's Liberation and Marx's Philosophy of Revolution*. Brighton, UK: Harvester Press.

Dunayevskaya, R. 1985. *Women's Liberation and the Dialectics of Revolution: Reaching for the Future*. Atlantic Highlands, NJ: Humanities Press International.

Firestone, S. 1971. *The Dialectics of Sex. The Case for Feminist Revolution*. New York: Bantam Books.

Flippen, C.A. 2014. Intersectionality at Work: Determinants of Labor Supply among Immigrant Latinas. *Gender & Society*, 28(3): 404–434.

Fox-Genovese, E. 1996. *'Feminism is Not the Story of My Life': How Today's Feminist Elite has Lost Touch with the Real Concerns of Women*. New York: Doubleday, Anchor Books.

Friedan, B. 1973. *The Feminine Mystique*. London: Penguin.

Gordon, L. 2016. 'Intersectionality,' Socialist Feminism and Contemporary Activism: Musings by a Second-Wave Socialist Feminist. *Gender & History*, 28(2): 340–357.

Gopaldas, A. 2013. Intersectionality 101. *Journal of Public Policy & Marketing*, 32(1): 90–94.

Green, J. and Bourgeois, R. 2017. *Indigenous Feminism*. Halifax: Fernwood Publishing.

Greer, G. 1971. *The Female Eunuch*. New York: Bantam Books.

Grewal, I. and Kaplan, C. 1994. *Scattered Hegemonies: Postmodernity and Transnational Feminist Practices*. Minneapolis: University of Minnesota Press.

Griffin-Cohen, M. and Brodie, J. (eds). 2007. *Remapping Gender in the New Global Order*. London: Routledge.

Guijt, I. and Shah, M.K. (eds). 1998. *The Myth of Community. Gender Issues in Participatory Development*, London: Practical Action.

Hartsock, N.C.M. 1983. *Money, Sex and Power: Towards a Feminist Historical Materialism*. New York: Longman,

Hendler, S. 1994. Feminist Planning Ethics. *Journal of Planning Literature*, 9(2): 115–127.

Hendler, S. 2005. Towards a Feminist Code of Planning Ethics. *Planning Theory & Practice*, 6(1): 53–69.

Hernández Castillo, A. (2002). Zapatismo and the Emergence of Indigenous Feminism. *NACLA Report on the Americas*, 35(6): 39–43.

Hernández Castillo, R.A. (2010). The Emergence of Indigenous Feminism in Latin America. *Signs: Journal of Women in Culture and Society*, 35(3): 539–545.

Hernández-Saca, D.I., Gutmann Kahn, L. and Cannon, M.A. 2018. Intersectionality Dis/ability Research: How Dis/ability Research in Education Engages Intersectionality to Uncover the Multidimensional Construction of Dis/abled Experiences. *Review of Research in Education*, 42(1): 286–311.

Hill Collins, P. and Bilge, S. 2016. *Intersectionality*, Cambridge: Polity Press.

hooks, b. 1981. *Ain't I a Woman? Black Women and Feminism*. Boston, MA: South End Press.

hooks, b. 1984. *Feminist Theory from Margin to Center*. Boston, MA: Southend Press.

Huhndorf, S.M. (2021). Scenes from the Fringe: Gendered Violence and the Geographies of Indigenous Feminism. *Signs: Journal of Women in Culture and Society*, 46(3): 561–587.

Ikävalko, E. and Kantola, J. 2017. Feminist Resistance and Resistance to Feminism in Gender Equality Planning in Finland. *European Journal of Women's Studies*, 24(3): 233–248.

Jaggar, A.M. 1983. *Feminist Politics and Human Nature*. Brighton, UK: Harvester Press.

Jain, J. 2011. *Indigenous Roots of Feminism: Culture, Subjectivity and Agency*. New Delhi and Thousand Oaks, CA: Sage Publications.

Kaijser, A. and Kronsell, A. 2014. Climate Change through the Lens of Intersectionality. *Environmental Politics*, 23(3): 417–433.

Kapoor, I. 2002. The Devil's in the Theory: A Critical Assessment of Robert Chambers' Work on Participatory Development. *Third World Quarterly*, 23(1): 101–117.

Knobblock, I. and Kuokkanen, R. 2015. Decolonizing Feminism in the North: A Conversation with Rauna Kuokkanen. *NORA-Nordic Journal of Feminist and Gender Research*, 23(4): 275–281.

McCall, L. 2005. The Complexity of Intersectionality. *Signs*, 30(3): 1771–1800.

Millet, K. 1970. *Sexual Politics*. New York: Ballantine Books.

Mohanty, C. 1988. Under Western Eyes: Feminist Scholarship and Colonial Discourses. *Feminist Review*, 30(1): 61–88.

Mohanty, C.T. 2003a. 'Under Western Eyes' Revisited: Feminist Solidarity through Anticapitalist Struggles. *Signs: Journal of Women in Culture and Society*, 28(2): 499–535.

Mohanty, C.T. 2003b. *Feminism without Borders. Decolonizing Theory, Practicing Solidarity*. Durham, NC: Duke University Press.

Moser, C. 2012. *Gender Planning and Development: Theory, Practice and Training*. London: Routledge.

Nagar, R. 2002. Footloose Researchers, 'Traveling' Theories, and the Politics of Transnational Feminist Praxis. *Gender, Place and Culture*, 2: 179–186.

Nash, J.C. (2008). 'Re-Thinking Intersectionality', *Feminist Review*, 89(1): 1–15. https://doi.org/10.1057/fr.2008.4.

Nickel, S.A. (2017). 'I Am Not a Women's Libber Although Sometimes I Sound Like One': Indigenous Feminism and Politicized Motherhood. *American Indian Quarterly*, 41(4): 299–335.

Pal, G.C. 2011. Disability, Intersectionality and Deprivation: An Excluded Agenda. *Psychology and Developing Societies*, 23(2): 159–176.

Parent, M.C., DeBlaere, C., and Moradi, B. 2013. Approaches to Research on Intersectionality: Perspectives on Gender, LGBT, and Racial/ethnic Identities. *Sex Roles*, 68(11): 639–645.

Parpart, J. 1993. Who Is the 'Other'? A Postmodern Feminist Critique of Women and Development Theory and Practice, *Development and Change*, 3: 439–446.

Pieterse, J.N. 2000. After Post-development. *Third World Quarterly*, 21(2): 175–191.

Piven, F.F. 1970. Whom Does the Advocate Planner Serve? *Social Policy*, 1(1): 32–35.

Prügl, E. 2011. Diversity Management and Gender Mainstreaming as Technologies of Government. *Politics & Gender*, 7(1): 71–90.

Prügl, E. 2015. Neoliberalising Feminism. *New Political Economy*, 20(4): 614–631.

Pyne, J. 2011. Unsuitable Bodies: Transpeople and Cisnormativity in Shelter Services. *Canadian Social Work Review/Revue canadienne de service social*, 28(1): 129–137.

Rankin, K.N. 2001. Governing Development: Neoliberalism, Microcredit, and Rational Economic Woman. *Economy and Society*, 30(1): 18–37.

Ritzdorf, M. 1992. Feminist Thoughts on the Theory and Practice of Planning. *Planning Theory*. 7/8: 13–19.

Robinson, V. 2003. Radical Revisionings? The Theorizing of Masculinity and (Radical) Feminist Theory. *Women's Studies International Forum*, 26(2): 129–137.

Rowbotham, S., Segal, L. and Wainwright, H. 1981. *Beyond the Fragments: Feminism and the Making of Socialism*. Boston, MA: Alyson Publications.

Salleh, A. 2017. *Ecofeminism as Politics: Nature, Marx and the Postmodern*. London: Zed Books.

Sandercock, L. and Forsyth, A. 1992. A Gender Agenda: New Directions for Planning Theory. *Journal of the American Planning Association*, 58(1): 49–59.

Sargeant, L. (ed.). 1981. *Women and Revolution: A Discussion of the Unhappy Marriage of Marxism and Feminism*. Boston, MA: Southend Press.

Saunders, K. (ed.). 2005. *Feminist Post-development Thought: Rethinking Modernity, Post Colonialism and Representation*. London: Zed Books.

Schurr, C. and Segebart, D. 2012. Engaging with Feminist Postcolonial Concerns through Participatory Action Research and Intersectionality. *Geographica Helvetica*, 67(3): 147–154.

Shields, S.A. 2008. Gender: An Intersectionality Perspective. *Sex Roles*, 59(5): 301–311.

Shiva, V. and Mies, M. 1993, 2014. *Ecofeminism*. London: Zed Books.

Sidaway, J.D. 2007. Spaces of Postdevelopment. *Progress in Human Geography*, 31(3): 345–361.

Snyder, M.G. 1995. Feminist Theory and Planning Theory: Lessons from Feminist Epistemologies. *Berkeley Planning Journal*, 10(1): 91–106.

Speak, S. 2012. Planning for the Needs of Urban Poor in the Global South: The Value of a Feminist Approach. *Planning Theory*, 11(4): 343–360.

Stacey, J. 1983. *Patriarchy and Socialist Revolution in China*. Berkeley: University of California Press.

Suzack, C., Huhndorf, S.M., Perreault, J., and Barman, J. (eds) (2010). *Indigenous Women and Feminism: Politics, Activism, Culture*. Vancouver: UBC Press.

Townsend-Bell, E. 2014. Ambivalent Intersectionality. *Politics & Gender*, 10 (1): 137.

Trask, H.K. 1996. Feminism and Indigenous Hawaiian Nationalism. *Signs: Journal of Women in Culture and Society*, 21(4): 906–916.

Tungohan, E. 2016. Intersectionality and Social Justice: Assessing Activists' use of Intersectionality through Grassroots Migrants' Organizations in Canada. *Politics, Groups, and Identities*, 4(3): 347–362.

Verloo, M. 2006. Multiple Inequalities, Intersectionality and the European Union. *European Journal of Women's Studies*, 13(3): 211–228.

Vogel, L. 1983. *Marxism and the Oppression of Women: Toward a Unitary Theory*. Leiden: Brill Press.

Viruell-Fuentes, E.A., P.Y. Miranda, and S. Abdulrahim. 2012. More than Culture: Structural Racism, Intersectionality Theory, and Immigrant Health. *Social Science & Medicine*, 75(12): 2099–2106.

Walby, S., J. Armstrong, and S. Strid. 2012. Intersectionality: Multiple Inequalities in Social Theory. *Sociology*, 46(2): 224–240.

Walby, S. 2005. Gender Mainstreaming: Productive Tensions in Theory and Practice. *Social Politics: International Studies in Gender, State & Society*, 12(3): 321–343.

Warren, K.J., Warren, K., and Erkal, N. (eds). 1997. *Ecofeminism: Women, Culture, Nature*. Bloomington: Indiana University Press.

Wendell, S. 1987. A (Qualified) Defense of Liberal Feminism. *Hypatia*, 2(2): 65–93.

Young, I.M. 1992. Concrete Imagination and Piecemeal Transformation. *Planning Theory*, 7/8: 59–62.

Yuval-Davis, N. 2006. Intersectionality and Feminist Politics. *European Journal of Women's Studies*, 13(3): 193–209.

20. Neoliberalism and power

Marlyana Azyyati Marzukhi

INTRODUCTION

This chapter delineates the emerging modes of governance that have caused neoliberalism to thrive. Drawing on the French philosopher Michel Foucault's (1980) work on governmentality and power, the chapter articulates and provides insight into governance practice and power relations to further theoretical understanding of the tension created by neoliberalism's hegemony and how planning practices have reshaped decision making. Accordingly, the term 'governance' is used to refer to emerging trends in the governing process that determine the way in which society is being governed in the twenty-first century (Gualini, 2010; Healey, 2010). This understanding elucidates how neoliberalism reflects the logic of the market to a greater extent than it does social and environmental needs, thus harming democracy in the planning processes of most countries around the globe. This decreased focus on social and environmental needs reflects the reconceptualised role of planners in the twenty-first century. Foucault's (1980) notion of governmentality, which embodies a set of practices and ways of thinking relating to virtues of the market, was adopted by the research conducted for this chapter to analyse the planning practices by which actions, strategies and techniques are shaped and shifted towards a neoliberal order. This practice also enables reflection on what appears to be Foucault's conception of power that discerns the act to resist freely; that is, his idea that when there is no form of resistance, power itself is absent. Instead it becomes outright oppression and domination. This notion of power needing resistance to exist suggests that a consultative planning approach can both challenge and reinforce the dynamics of power relations by (un)intentionally reorienting decision making towards a neoliberal agenda.

This chapter begins by providing crucial understanding of how neoliberalism has emerged as the dominant ideology in governance practice globally, by structuring the logic of social and environmental affairs to advocate capitalist market logic.

NEOLIBERALISM AND GOVERNANCE: SETTING THE CONTEXT

For five decades, a great deal of research has focused on globalisation and its dependency on, or even interchangeability with, the term 'neoliberalism' (Baeten, 2018; Fainstein and Campbell, 2012). Neoliberalism or the process of neoliberalisation (Olesen, 2014; Peck et al., 2009; Purcell, 2009) is considered a 'socio-economic and political doctrine … an independent belief system regarding the issues of state regulation of the economy' (Pervova, 2020: 2). The current processes of globalisation have undergone a shift towards market-led development through which the proliferation of neoliberalism has defined the landscape of urban development by facilitating the emergence of global market values embedded in capitalism. This emergence of global market values occurs through the transfer of much of the state's authority to a new governing process that is articulated through certain rationalities, leading to the triumph of market control over the democratic process (Dean, 2010; Gunder and Hillier, 2009). In this neoliberal system, the objective is to maximise profit for wealth creation in a market economy (Bellanca, 2013; Van de Klundert, 2013). A central element of capitalism is the ability of the economic system to promote economic growth, measured by gross domestic profit per capita as the determinant of economic progress and success (Gunder and Hillier, 2009).

The idea of neoliberalism originally emerged in the 1940s (Harvey, 2005) and was famously embraced in the era of Ronald Reagan in the United States and Margaret Thatcher in the United Kingdom from the late 1970s (Clifford and Tewdwr-Jones, 2013; Fainstein and Campbell, 2012; Sanyal et al., 2012; Tasan-Kok, 2012) and then 'exported across the globe by the World Bank and International Monetary Fund (IMF)' (Turner et al., 2013: 483). The post-2008 recession government bailouts of corporations, bank privatisation and the austerity policies being imposed in many countries worldwide demonstrate the '*modus operandi* of neo-liberalism' (Aalbers, 2013b: 1087). These neoliberal practices have facilitated the emergence of the global capitalist order by shifting from a 'logic of sovereignty to a logic of regulation in defining political power' as a result of neoliberal demands (Gualini, 2010: 79). This most recent world financial crisis led to the proliferation of 'neoliberal discourses and policy formu-lation ... [that] mask evidence of a more deeply rooted transformation of policies, institutions and spaces' (Peck et al., 2013: 1091). In fact, following the crisis, Aalbers (2013a: 1055) claimed that what 'we are beginning to see is perhaps a new phase of neoliberalism, certainly on an ideological level' (see also Gunder, 2010).

Despite the recession of 2008, researchers such as Baeten (2012) and Peck et al. (2013) claimed that neoliberalism continues to expand and evolve in diverse ways that reshape the socioeconomic landscape of countries around the world. Today, neoliberalism is being debated more than ever with the emergence of Trumpism (Weinman and Vormann, 2021). Donald Trump's victory operates from the understanding of popular sovereignty that posits resistance to white supremacy and the defiance of immigrants' rights (Roy, 2019). Trumpism presented the politics of spectacle through mass media that 'continues to dazzle, horrify and destabilise as much as to solidify and control the population in new ways' (Miller, 2021: 3).

Importantly, such perspectives demonstrate how neoliberal ideological reform has involved a rethinking of the role of the state (Haughton and Allmendinger, 2013; Haughton et al., 2013). As Sager (2013: 11) stated, 'there is neoliberal pressure to shift from planned solutions drawn up in bureaucratic hierarchies to solutions implemented in competitive or contested markets'. Thus, neoliberalism is associated with a process of governance transformation that inevitably aligns with the economic agenda (Haughton and Allmendinger, 2013; Olesen, 2014; Peck et al., 2013; Pervova, 2020). It seems that governance around the globe has reached a point where new forms of governance now control planning processes through a consultative approach among the actors that reveals a profound shift towards economic development being the prior-ity in any planning. This shift in priority in planning is considered part of a problem that may lead to effective planning practices (Gunder, 2014).

This new mode of governance fundamentally reflects the evolution of governance and demonstrates how and why governance frames the conduct of other actors in the planning process (Healey, 2012b; Hillier, 2015). This situation of planning practice by neoliberal inter-est foregrounds concern about the way in which the 'governors' and the 'governed' conduct themselves in particular situations. At its worst, the neoliberal agenda may produce political, economic and social instability (Kumi et al., 2014; Swyngedouw, 2009; Van de Klundert, 2013) and lead to what Lovering (2009: 3) described as a 'neoliberal disaster'.

Further, the changing nature of governance has led to changes in fundamental factors of social organisation, such as the relationship between the state and society, and is now revealing important trends, including what has been described as the disappearance or decline of democracy (Gualini, 2010; Swyngedouw, 2014). This decline is seen in the strategic interactions between actors in their efforts to frame reality in response to neoliberalism's dominance, further limiting public resistance. In this sense, planning acknowledges that neoliberalism may affect how governance practices achieve the goals of managing public perceptions of economic development. This premise leads to the consideration of the paradox of governance instruments that favour the powerful over the powerless, stabilise decisions, and shape the conduct of planning practices as 'common sense' by rationalising a growth-first approach. The imbalances of power in this situation may consolidate the acceptance of pro-growth planning, suggesting the hegemonic position of neoliberalism.

To conduct an in-depth examination of neoliberalism and power, this chapter consults the works of the post-structuralist Foucault (1980, 1994) that are concerned with notions of governmentality and power (see also Chapter 4 by Pløger). Governmentality refers to a set of practices and ways of thinking that are designed to achieve objectives of market-based solutions through the process of governing (Dean, 2010). This chapter will elucidate the approach of governmentality to create a more comprehensive understanding of the regimes of practice between the state, society and the market, according to which actions, strategies and tactics have been shaped and shifted towards a neoliberal order (Duineveld et al., 2013; Lelandais, 2014; Swyngedouw, 2005, 2009, 2015). Governmentality implies the exercise of power through politicising the practice of managing the acceptance of decision making by public and dictating a shift in planning towards upholding and advancing market values (Gunder, 2010a). Here, power is concerned with what defines a reality that permits the act of freedom to challenge this power.

However, if those who are acted upon cannot resist, then power is absent (Flyvbjerg, 1998a; Gunder and Mouat, 2002). As Flyvbjerg (1998b: 229) has argued, the 'greater the power, the greater the freedom in this respect, and the less need for power to understand how reality is "really" constructed'. In this sense, attempts to make sense of 'reality' delineate the restrictions and possibilities of governance to steer and manage decisions towards specific objectives. This theory about how governing works in relation to power, resistance and reality draws on the notion of Foucauldian governmentality that reflects the exercise of power in the form of conduct that is deeply rooted in a mode of action (Foucault, 2007). Such an understanding of governmentality in the study of power is essential in providing perspective on how governance, markets and society evolve and continuously restructure the regime of governance practice (Beunen et al., 2015; Van Assche et al., 2014a). This transformation process 'involves "rules of behaviour" as well as the political–ideological commitment to fight for collective affairs and public interests' (Pløger, 2001: 224). This calls attention to the 'conduct of conduct' of the actors in relation to the notion of governmentality.

In this globalised era, governance practice has become 'a new technology of government that mirrors Foucault's notion of governmentality' (Gualini, 2010: 7), which can enable us to understand and analyse the effects of neoliberalism (Clifford and Tewdwr-Jones, 2013; Giroux, 2017; Pervova, 2020; Rosol, 2014). The theories of Foucault are core to the study of governmentality, which he defined as the 'art of government' that exercises power in societies that are concerned with certain ends (Dean, 2010: 27; Foucault, 2007), and which Gunder and Hillier (2009: 5) refer to as the 'art of affect'. The notion of governmentality emerged from

Foucault's lecture series in the 1970s and was originally concerned with ways of thinking and exercising of power in relation to certain societies (Cadman, 2010; Jessop, 2009; Rosol, 2014). In this lecture series, Foucault created the term 'by combining the verb *to govern* with the noun *mentality*'[1] (Blakeley, 2010: 132). Use of the term has advanced to a broader definition that refers to the practice of governance that became a phenomenon in the late 1990s (Dean, 2010; McKee, 2009). Foucault (1994: 318) defined this practice as follows:

> more or less regulated, more or less conscious, more or less goal-orientated, through which one can grasp the lineaments both of what was constituted as real for those who were attempting to conceptualise and govern it, and of the way in which those same people constituted themselves as subjects capable of knowing, analysing, and ultimately modifying the real.

In short, the practice of governance describes the new mode of governing that has been mobilised to achieve certain objectives through the notion of 'mentalities'. This idea of 'mentalities' suggests the use of imagination (Dean, 2010), fantasy (Gunder, 2014), spectacle (Miller, 2021) and metaphor (Van Assche et al., 2014a) to shape people's preferences within a discursive (Schon and Rein, 1994) or ideological frame (Gunder and Hillier, 2009). Thus, the practice of governance becomes significant in generating and facilitating market-oriented values in the public psyche; this practice has even normalised the public interest to suit contemporary ideas and development. Blakeley (2010: 132) provided the most practical and realistic description of the engagement of neoliberalism with governmentality:

> [n]eoliberalism denotes both a new rationality of government and a new set of techniques or 'technologies' for governing which underpin this new articulation between the state, civil society and the market.

Importantly, the field of urban planning may be considered part of the discourse on neoliberalism and governmentality. Indeed, the ideas of governmentality continue to have relevance that reflects the repertoire of planning practice in the twentieth century (Allmendinger and Haughton, 2012; Duineveld et al., 2013). In fact, this form of governmentality is considered to redefine and restructure planning in theory and practice (Tasan-Kok and Baeten, 2012). This ambivalent position of planning has become more problematic and complex as a result of the broader effects of neoliberalism (Raco, 2012).

Death (2010: 249) argued that the 'degree to which acts of resistance [in the planning process] destabilise or reinforce existing power relations' defines the practice of governance that is solely concerned with the economic agenda. This is further reflected in the regimes of governance in relation to power and resistance that illuminate the challenges for planning in the dominant forms of neoliberal global governance. Thus, it is important to note that, Foucault's interpretation of power relations may effectively lead to a change in practice.

THE MANIFESTATION OF POWER RELATIONS: SOME CRUCIAL SIGNS

This section discusses the different manifestations of power as conceptualised by Foucault to enable examination of planning practices in the contemporary neoliberal world. Reflecting on power, Flyvbjerg (2001: 107) argued the following:

Power is needed to limit power. Even to understand how publicness can be established we need to think in terms of conflict and power. There is no way around it. It is a basic condition for understanding issues of exclusion and inclusion in a democracy.

Power is generally associated with 'something which a group of people or an institution possesses and ... power is only concerned with oppressing and constraining [the powerless and has] the ability to force them to do things which they do not wish to do' (Mills, 2003: 33–35). Traditionally, power is considered 'located in a dense field of distinctions and in relation to many other terms [such as] authority, domination, legitimacy, jurisdiction, violence, government, coercion, control, capability, capacity, ability, force, and so on' (Dean, 2013: 2). Thus, causal power is traditionally understood as something negative that is associated with repressive acts engaged in by the agent who possesses the power (McKee, 2009).

However, rather than conceiving power as something that can be possessed and controlled, Foucault develops an understanding of power relations that differs from this traditional concept of oppression and domination. Foucault endeavours to reinterpret power in relation to governmental form, by which power 'takes effect not by disciplining or controlling individuals but in the form of conducting conduct, particularly by encouraging certain forms of conducting the self' (Foucault, 2007 [1978], cited in Rosol, 2014: 6). Foucault holds that a situation in which the public cannot act freely represents 'domination' rather than 'power' (Gunder and Mouat, 2002; Torfing, 2009). Weber (1978, cited in Jenkins, 2009) defined this lack of ability to act freely as 'authority' and Gramsci (1971: 120, cited in Davies, 2013: 8) argued that it involves 'military and civil coercion'.

Foucault (1988, cited in Gunder and Mouat, 2002: 128–129) observed the following:

[w]e must distinguish the relationships of power as strategic games between liberties – strategic games that result in the fact that some people try to determine the conduct of others – and the states of domination, which are what we ordinarily call power and, between the two, between the games of power and the states of domination, you have governmental technologies.

Thus, Foucault (1982a) believes that the question of how power is exercised is more important than the question of who has the power. This perspective means that attempts to make sense of 'reality' delineate the restrictions and possibilities of governance to steer and manage decisions towards specific objectives, which evolve the objects in a manner that relies on power relations. Power is everywhere and always present (Blakeley, 2010). Drawing on Foucault, a dictum of Gunder and Mouat (2002: 131) can be used as a springboard: 'planning as a regime of governmentality often strives to stifle resistance'. That is, power relations have been governmentalised.

Importantly, the power relationship can only exist when there is less manipulation and no domination, and where citizens have the capacity to resist and act freely (Gunder and Mouat, 2002). When such a situation exists, 'power produces, it produces reality; it produces domains of objects and rituals of truth' (Foucault, 1991: 194). In fact, these notions of power 'are discursive strategies that not only intend to shape and reshape truth, but also to alter positions of power' through discourse (Buenen et al., 2015: 139). Discourse is important because it defines the basis of the social order and how it affects power relations that form the conduct of governance. Foucault interpreted discourse as 'multiple and sets of ideas and metaphors embracing both text and practice' (Sharp and Richardson, 2001: 196). Importantly, the power relations arising from discourse can be transmitted 'by means of a language, a system of signs, or any other symbolic medium' (Foucault, 1982a: 786). The perspectives of power that operate within communicative planning[2] are significant because they 'can underpin and stabilise rules, policies, and plans directly' (Van Assche et al., 2015: 23). Further, this practice entails adopting a manifestation of power that allows the 'form of struggle among actors for the recognition, acceptance with respect, and valuation of ... identities until all actors possess an equal chance to participate' in the planning processes (Hillier, 2002: 67). This idea of power enabling the equal chance to participant is captured in the phrase 'where there is power, there is resistance' (Foucault, 1998: 95). Foucault (cited in Flyvbjerg, 2001: 102) reflects on how power can be exerted without domination:

> [t]he problem is not of trying to dissolve [relations of power] in the utopia of a perfectly transparent communication, but to give ... the rules of law, the techniques of management, and also the ethics ... which would allow these games of power to be played with a minimum of domination.

This shows how communicative planning through power dynamics can ultimately articulate and reveal the tensions that emerge between rhetoric and reality in the way that actors are constituted (Beunen et al., 2015). It does this in a manner that shows how governance practices deploys ways of thinking, or the use of governance tools, to shape and legitimise the consultative planning process within the power relationships of governance by 'producing docile citizens that accept the norms and expectations of government as part of the ethical governance of themselves' (Gunder and Mouat, 2002: 130). Therefore, understanding the Foucauldian interpretation of power relations reveals how frames are constructed to be capable of shaping decision making as representing 'common sense'. In this context, power defines a reality in which the resistance shapes a decision 'by making it more real, for more people, within more and different networks' (Duineveld et al., 2013: 23). At this point in the reasoning process, it becomes evident that the strategic interactions between actors in the framing of reality further limit public resistance. By understanding power relations through communication, the 'tension points' that can improve the practice of governance can be identified and used to effect significant change (Flyvbjerg et al., 2012).

COMMUNICATIVE DISCOURSE

The communicative discourse has spread to many parts of the world (Healey, 2012, 2013) and has gained traction as a new paradigm of planning theory and practice in the twenty-first century (Gunder, 2010a). This discourse represents an attempt to promote the idea of consensual engagement among actors in setting planning agendas and actions within the democratic planning process. As Albrecht (2010: 228) stated:

> [governance and planners] must acknowledge that there are multiple publics and that planning and governance in a new multicultural era requires a new kind of multicultural literacy and a new kind of democratic politics, which is more participative, more deliberative and more agonistic.

Albrecht's (2010: 228) perspective draws attention to the ongoing tensions in planning that demand more participatory involvement to achieve balanced and sustainable development. In addition, this perspective draws attention to the central conflict of participatory democracy that exists between the everyday struggles of actors, particularly in the planning process.

This is because the consultative process 'can expand the scope and impact of decisions in an organisation and can grant an impact on the making of collectively binding decisions in the community' (Beunen et al., 2015: 9). As noted, this participatory arena has demonstrated the issues concerning power relations through communication. This also accords with Aitken's (2010: 253) argument that meaningful communication 'requires empowerment of participants and thus any evaluation of participatory activities considers where power is found and how this is deployed'. The importance to participation of 'where power is found and how it is deployed' is reflected in the idea that becoming 'democratic is ... a process by which people reclaim their own power' (Purcell, 2013: 92).

However, what Albrecht (2010: 228) described as a new kind of 'multicultural literacy' and 'democratic politics' can be considered to represent a range of approaches to consultative practices. In particular, such varied assumptions lead to ideological shifts and changes as underlying factors in broader interactions of social change. These changes are manifested through changes in concepts or ideologies that relate to the 'real' meaning, interpretation and implementation. This practice increases understanding of why a consultative process that commands agreement in the formal arena seeks to be manoeuvred through control of, and arrangement within, this consensual setting (Healey, 2012a). Thus, the original objectives of planning to produce political, economic and social stability are not fully achieved, which threatens the legitimacy of the consultative process (Versteeg and Hajer, 2010). It seems that communication efforts are inherently employed as a way to limit the exercise of power in the planning process. This communicative role reflects Neuman's (2003: 84) view that people 'do shape their own destiny, but not under conditions of their own choosing'. That is, public opinion has been mostly unable to influence the dynamics of institutional change and institutional settings in which market-led development has always been argued to have priority over social needs. In fact, almost twenty years ago, Flyvbjerg (1998a) provided practical evidence from the City of Aalborg, Denmark that demonstrated how power saturates everyday practice and how planning through the mechanism of power adopts a strategy that shapes decisions in favour of dominant market interests. Flyvbjerg (1998a) termed this strategy 'realrationalitat'. Thus, what is in question here is how planning can shift a 'formal rationality' to a 'realrationalitat' within the dynamics of power relations in which 'power defines what counts as rationality and knowledge, and thereby what counts as reality' (Flyvbjerg, 1998a: 227).

Given this dynamic view of power relations in the consultative processes, consultative practice may demonstrate how power imbalances are manifested, revealing the rhetoric and reality about the planning process's democratic nature. As Huxley (2013: 1537) states:

> [w]hat discourses did it [communication] enter into and enable in order to become 'sayable' and taken for granted in different conditions? What solutions did it provide and for whom? What configurations of power did it reinforce or undermine? What tensions and contradictions did it resolve or engender?

These questions highlight the co-option of democratic rhetoric to confer market-based logic on planning practice. In the process, public involvement is legitimised through governance mechanisms in which communication may only neutralise existing power relations, rather than challenge them. As Bailey (2010: 324) noted:

> [t]he duty to promote democracy and the duty to involve may simply represent top-down directions that are largely cosmetic if authorities only implement the letter of the law or if citizens are unwilling or unable to engage fully in the process.

Significantly, these arguments imply the value of incorporating power relations into participatory debates (Holgersen, 2015). Sharp and Richardson (2001) argue that the knowledge exchange that occurs within communication is a way of achieving acceptance of the 'truth'. Indeed, Gunder (2006: 211) contended one decade ago that 'discourses are made to vie, often without success, to be the one dominant truth that gives the only possible meaning to our empty and ambiguous but contested terms of identification'. Consequently, 'existing statutory and legislative rules [as] democratic hallmarks' are used to understand how the consultative process frames, facilitates and formalises planning decisions (Legacy et al., 2014: 28).

Such uses of communication demonstrate that a consultative manner in planning practice is not always desirable because it has contradictory potential effects on the public's capacity for resistance (Brownill and Parker, 2010). Consequently, the underlying premise of participation poses a far more critical challenge to planning, one that can both test and reinforce the dynamics of power relations. For example, drawing on Foucauldian perspectives, Duineveld et al. (2013) demonstrated how planning practices in the Dutch city of Groningen use strategies and tactics as technologies of governing. Through this approach, the state seeks to ensure that the public feel empowered. However, in reality, the citizenry has continued to feel marginalised. Such examples demonstrate that the statutory planning system exemplifies a form of domination imposed through the use of the consultative process.

Further, as argued in this chapter, neoliberalism maintains the dominance of some groups over others. To some extent, this has led to unintended consequences that have resulted in conflict and tension among the various actors involved. It is worth noting that when a marginalised group struggles to gain access to be heard, a 'movement made up of allied groups seeking broad transformation of existing power relations' is advocated (Purcell, 2009: 159); this leads to an agonism (Bond, 2011; Hillier, 2007). Purcell (2009, 2011, 2013) provided insight into the relationship between neoliberalism and democratic governance, thereby demonstrating how this relationship has resulted in many public protests in major countries such as Greece and Spain, and in Arab uprisings in Egypt, Syria and Yemen. These protests stem from the possibility of resistance that 'captures the close relationships between protests and the forms of government they oppose' (Death, 2010: 236).

Indeed, as Purcell (2009) claimed, planning practice is often arranged to command agreement in governance, but instead such practice largely marginalises the public in the process. In particular, this critical perspective on planning practice illustrates that consultative processes are fraught with potentially conflicting arguments because 'considerable power rests with the decision-maker and his/her subjective judgement' (Aitken, 2010: 252). Importantly, as Foucault (1988, cited in Gunder and Mouat, 2002: 129) observed, if 'there is no scope for resistance, then only domination and oppression may occur resulting in violence and victimisation on those acted against', and between the two (i.e. domination and [Foucauldian] power) are regimes of governmentality applied through governmental technologies. These governmental technologies can enable certain forms of conduct to be directed to and lead to agreement and normalisation (Baeten, 2018; Dean, 2010; Gunder, 2010a). Foucault advances this idea by viewing power as something that is not owned but exists 'only when it is put into action' (Foucault, 1982b: 219), and by arguing that power can only occur 'when those acted upon are free to exert power back – resist' (Gunder and Mouat, 2002: 129).

Thus, it is important to examine how neoliberalism has influenced governance practice through the use of 'technologies of governing' in planning.

GOVERNMENTAL TECHNOLOGIES

This section explores the role of policy instruments (e.g. planning policies, legislation and guidelines) to provide an overview of the profound effect of neoliberalism on the decision-making process through the rationale that underpins neoliberalism and governance practices. Significantly, with the understanding of Foucault's conceptualisation of power relations comes an understanding of the proliferation of planning practices that institute society and far-reaching policing tactics in the consultative process. Therefore, this section clarifies how governmentality is able to control and guide resistance through an explicit or implicit process that allows decision making to occur in a way that permits those acted upon no element of choice to resist.

There is a broad body of empirical evidence on neoliberal governance demonstrating that the use of governmental reason has been a failure in regulating public interest (Eraydin, 2012; Fox-Rogers and Murphy, 2015). Haughton et al. (2013: 230–231) provided practical evidence from England to demonstrate how the new form of governmentality in the neoliberal era has led away from a 'presumption in favour of development' to a 'presumption in favour of *sustainable development*'. In their empirical research examining New Zealand's Resource Management Act of 1991, Gunder and Mouat (2002: 124) demonstrated that this theoretically consultative legislative structure produced 'symbolic violence and institutional victimisation [which] allows no element of choice, or freedom to resist, for those acted upon'. Analysing the democratic consultative process in Norway, Pløger (2001: 230) revealed how the use of law (i.e. the Norwegian Planning and Building Act of 1985) can play a directorial role in a decision-making process that favours 'those who in one way or other have either some kind of *strength-of-will* or some kind of formal institutional power'. Similarly, Fox-Rogers and Murphy (2015) investigated the nature of legislative change in Ireland, and found that such change favoured development capital over the interests of the public. Aalbers (2013b: 1085) also argued that although 'there is now a lot of talk about more regulation, much of it may be beneficial to the neoliberal agenda'. Moreover, in their empirical analysis in the context of the capital city of Canada, Ottawa, Andrew and Doloreux (2012: 1302) illustrated the relationship between economic development and social revival on the city-region scale, finding that governance 'tends to reproduce the silos of compartmentalized modern society' through the use of a legislative framework. Bahmanteymouri (2020: 9) provided practical evidence from Perth, Australia that demonstrated how the desire to provide affordable housing and infrastructure in Ellenbrook urban development was only 'neoliberal fantasy that framed housing policies and urban development policies ... to prevent speculative increases in [land] price'. In particular, the development was 'redirected from filling the lack to speculative activities on land and maximisation of surplus-value and inevitably surplus-enjoyment' (p. 14).

A study by Tasan-Kok and Baten (2012: 206) addressed the question of 'how planners respond to the overruling profit principle in land allocation and to, what is left of, non-profit driven development' to show the adherence to the hegemony of neoliberalism in planning. Flyvbjerg (1998a) advanced this perspective in relation to planning practices by providing practical evidence from the City of Aalborg, Denmark (as discussed in the above section). Further, in the past two decades, Forester (1999) has drawn attention to the paradox of neoliberalism among planners. Associated with the emergence of neoliberal globalisation, in Malaysia, planners have often needed to justify their actions to ease public tension and to prevent the public from questioning authority. This has been coupled with concerns for using the concept of sustainable development in planning policy or legislative mechanisms to justify their decisions and actions that facilitate economic development (Marzukhi, 2020). In addition, the case studies of Eshuis and Edwards (2013: 1066) suggest that, in the Netherlands, responses to neoliberalism, have shown how other governance strategies – such as branding – have been widely applied as 'a form of spin that prevents the public from gaining a proper understanding of their government's policies'. In many respects, such views reflect the ideological shift of planning practice to a position that supports economic growth and capital accumulation.

These case studies have found a reason to question whether these emerging themes, such as sustainable development and legislative framework, have significantly influenced the governance practice that seems to command agreement in the planning process.

CONCLUSION: WHAT REALLY MATTERS?

This chapter delineates a neoliberalism that invades everything, including planning. The chapter also aimed to present an account of neoliberalism as governmentality through examining the relationship between actors that occurs in the context of the 'conduct of conduct'. Given the uncertainty of future outcomes in planning practice, the nature of practice tends to be related to risk and ambiguity embedded in the outcome of a recursive power dynamic. Thus, using Foucault's insights on governmentality and power provides useful insight into how the practice of governance can influence and shape the planning process.

Arguably, planning concepts and ideology mainly contribute to this framing of practice, enabling planners to restructure and reshape 'ways of thinking, ways of valuing, and ways of acting' in the planning processes (Healey, 2006: 29; see also Gunder and Hillier, 2009). Thus, according to Beunen et al. (2015: 9), participation has fundamentally expanded the 'scope and impact of the decision in an organisation, [and] can grant an impact on the making of collectively binding decisions in the community'. Specifically, the focus is on the dialogue by which participants in planning practice 'come to know what is in their own best interest' (Sager, 2013: 27). These interactions between the state and the public affect the rationale of the state's actions and highlight a significant form of participation that emphasises the dynamic practices of governance, where the rights of all concerned parties are generally acknowledged (Blakeley, 2010; Brownill and Parker, 2010). As Bond (2011) has pointed out, the consultative process also reveals the effects of power relations and demonstrates how democratic practices are thoroughly stifled to favour certain rationalities.

Therefore, planning must adapt to a rapidly changing world to survive (Friedmann, 1993). This need to adapt is particularly important because planning plays a crucial part in arranging the 'order of power' by 'structuring the possible field of action' in the decision-making process (Pløger, 2001: 227). Thus, as a result of neoliberalism's emphasis on capital accumulation, planning in the neoliberal era may lead to political, economic and social instability, as well as environmental pollution and periodic collapse in market processes (Healey, 2012b; Hillier and Healey, 2010; Kumi et al., 2014; Van de Klundert, 2013). Gunder (2010a: 308) believed planning has become 'the ideology of contemporary neoliberal space'.

As discussed, ideological beliefs related to planning are then created to legitimise the acts of governance. This is achieved through using governmental technologies that have been permeated by the nexus of neoliberal market practices to the disadvantage of public interests

(Gunder, 2006; Raco, 2016). In particular, neoliberalism represents the art of governmentalisation by forming consensus and agreement among actors, which is achieved through communicative discourse. This, of course, calls into question the role of planners and how the planning profession in the neoliberal era needs to be transformed so that it embodies and reflects democratic principles.

In sum, planners 'are particularly well-placed to engage in such an ethics of care and responsible action' in the neoliberal era, but they often operate within the constraints of bureaucratic procedures (Clifford and Tewdwr-Jones, 2013: 215; see also Fainstein and Campbell, 2012; Gunder and Hillier, 2009; Sager, 2013). As Harper and Stein (2006: 263) stated, planning is supposed to be a democratic process; thus, it may turn out to 'have undercurrents that serve certain [elite] interests other than those it purports to serve'. This dilemma is further complicated by and reflected in the decisions that planners make because these decisions often relate to the struggles and challenges facing groups that increasingly have no options for resistance.

This way of governing has come to be regarded as the reason why planners embody the institutional form of power relations in their practices (Pløger, 2001). This embodiment provides the reason to believe that planning practice has reshaped and reoriented planning process in ways that reinforce the operation of power. In fact, the notion of governance, which has been influenced by the roles of the state, the market and civil society, is a matter of urban and regional planning (Gunder et al., 2018; Porter et al., 2013; Sanyal et al., 2012). Thus, the way in which neoliberalism articulates the tensions of power struggles between forms of governance and social order succeeds (or does not succeed) in facilitating the capital accumulation and social cohesion of the country, and then creates a 'regime of truth' in the planning process. As Dean (2013) and Foucault (2007), among others, have pointed out, these specific kinds of power relations deploy ways of thinking (or use of governmental technologies) to shape and legitimise the decision-making process through the logic of neoliberal mantras with which planning is directly engaged.

Indeed, power can politicise practice (Gunder, 2010a); therefore, it is important to determine how power relations and forms of resistance are connected, and how such regimes are contested. What is particularly relevant is that the exercise of power by governance 'can produce as much acceptance as may be wished for [among the actors]' (Foucault, 1982a: 789) and can 'control the shape and degree of resistance precisely through the notion of the private autonomous individual' and for governmental reasons (Clifford, 2001: 121). Notably, it is the articulation of governance practice, power and discourse within the hegemonic agenda of neoliberal that demonstrated how neoliberalism is implanted and implemented through the consultative process that marks this new mode of governing. This, of course, has direct implications for today's governance practices that conform to neoliberalism.

Indeed, understanding the planner's role in governance has significant implications for the consultative process given that planning occurs in the public domain (Friedmann, 1987). For Van Assche et al. (2012: 999), the evolution of planners' roles in the sphere of planning implies that roles are seen as the 'catalysts and modifiers' of further transformation. As seen through the lens of Foucault's interpretation of power, what can be done is to ensure that planners are aware of what is occurring and that they are able to 'speak up' and be honest about the force of neoliberalism as a basis for their actions (Grange, 2014; 2016). An important implication of this is that the influences on the decision-making process by the actors 'can be observed in a positive or negative way' (Van Assche et al., 2014a: 35). After all, any fearless speech that focuses on the practices and mentalities of planners should be closely connected to planners' professional commitment. The recognition of this practice is essential if planners are to create a power relationship in the consultative process that enhances democracy and mitigates the problems embedded in and caused by neoliberalism's dominant ideology.

NOTES

1.   The word 'governmentality' was originally used by Roland Barthes (1957).
2.   The term 'communicative planning' refers to a consultative process that reflects how actors (i.e. planners and other stakeholders) behave, communicate and reach agreements in decision making.

REFERENCES

Aalbers, M.B. (2013b), 'Neoliberalism is Dead … Long Live Neoliberalism!', *International Journal of Urban and Regional Research*, 37 (3), 1083–1090.

Aitken, M. (2010), 'A Three-dimensional View of Public Participation in Scottish Land-use Planning: Empowerment or Social Control?', *Planning Theory*, 9 (3), 248–264.

Albrechts, L. (2010), 'More of the Same is Not Enough! How Could Strategic Spatial Planning be Instrumental in Dealing with the Challenges Ahead?' *Environment and Planning B: Planning and Design*, 37 (6), 1115–1127.

Allmendinger, P. and G. Haughton (2012), 'Post-political Spatial Planning in England: A Crisis of Consensus?', *Transactions of the Institute of British Geographers*, 37 (1), 89–103.

Allmendinger, P and G. Haughton (2013), 'The Evolution and Trajectories of English Spatial Governance: "Neoliberal" Episodes in Planning', *Planning Practice & Research*, 28 (1), 6–26.

Allmendinger, P. and Haughton, G. (2014), 'Post-political Regimes in English Planning', in J. Metzger, P. Allmendinger and S. Oosterlynck (eds), *Planning Against the Political*, New York and London: Routledge, pp. 29–54.

Andrew, C. and Doloreux, D. (2012), 'Economic Development, Social Inclusion and Urban Governance: The Case of the City-Region of Ottawa in Canada', *International Journal of Urban and Regional Research*, 36 (6), 1288–1305.

Baeten, G. (2012), 'Normalising Neoliberal Planning: The Case of Malmö, Sweden', in T. Tasan-Kok and G. Baeten (eds), *Contradictions of Neoliberal Planning*, Dordrecht: Springer, pp. 21–42.

Baeten, G. (2018), 'Neoliberal Planning', in M. Gunder, A. Madanipour and V. Watson (eds), *The Routledge Handbook of Planning Theory*, New York: Routledge, pp. 105–117.

Bahmanteymouri, E. (2020), 'A Lacanian Understanding of Urban Development Plans under the Neoliberal Discourse', *Planning Theory*, 3 (1), doi: 10.1177/1473095220981118.

Bailey, N. (2010), 'Understanding Community Empowerment in Urban Regeneration and Planning in England: Putting Policy and Practice in Context', *Planning, Practice & Research*, 25 (3), 317–332.

Barthes, R. (1957), *Mythologies*, Paris: Les Lettres nouvelles.

Bellanca, N. (2013), 'Capitalism', in L. Bruni and S. Zamagni (eds), *Handbook on the Economics of Reciprocity and Social Enterprise*, Cheltenham, UK and Northampton, MA, USA: Edward Elgar, pp. 59–67.

Beunen, R., Van Assche, K., and Duineveld, M. (2015), *Evolutionary Governance Theory: Theory and Applications*, Cham, Switzerland: Springer.

Blakeley, G. (2010), 'Governing Ourselves: Citizen Participation and Governance in Barcelona and Manchester', *International Journal of Urban and Regional Research*, 34 (1), 130–145.

Bond, S. (2011), 'Negotiating a "Democratic Ethos": Moving Beyond the Agonistic–Communicative Divide', *Planning Theory*, 10 (2), 161–186.

Brownill, S. and Parker, G. (2010), 'Why Bother with Good Works? The Relevance of Public Participation(s) in Planning in a Post-collaborative Era', *Planning, Practice & Research*, 25 (3), 275–282.

Cadman, L. (2010), 'How (Not) to be Governed: Foucault, Critique, and the Political', *Environment and Planning D, Society and Space*, 28 (3), 539.

Clifford, B. and Tewdwr-Jones, M. (2013), *The Collaborating Planner? Practitioners in the Neoliberal Age*, UK: The Policy Press.

Clifford, M. (2001), *Political Genealogy after Foucault*, London: Routledge.

Davies, J. (2013), 'Rethinking Urban Power and the Local State: Hegemony, Domination and Resistance in Neoliberal Cities', *Urban Studies*, 51 (15), 3215–3232.

Dean, M. (2010), *Governmentality: Power and Rule in Modern Society* (2nd ed.), London: Sage.

Dean, M. (2013), *The Signature of Power: Sovereignty, Governmentality and Biopolitics*, Thousand Oaks, CA: Sage.

Dean, M. (2014), 'Rethinking Neoliberalism', *Journal of Sociology*, 50 (2), 150–163.

Death, C. (2010), 'Counter-conducts: A Foucauldian Analytics of Protest', *Social Movement Studies*, 9 (3), 235–251.

Duineveld, M., Van Assche, K. and R. Beunen (2013), 'Making Things Irreversible. Object Stabilization in Urban Planning and Design', *Geoforum*, 46, 16–24.

Earle, L. (2010), 'Housing, Citizenship, and the Movimento Sem Teto of Sao Paulo', paper presented at the Cities Academic Seminar, University of Cape Town, South Africa, 15 April.

Eraydın, A. (2012), 'Contradictions in the Neoliberal Policy Instruments: What is the Stance of the State?', in T. Tasan-Kok and G. Baeten (eds), *Contradictions of Neoliberal Planning*, Dordrecht: Springer, pp. 61–77.

Eshuis, J. and Edwards, A. (2013), 'Branding the City: The Democratic Legitimacy of a New Mode of Governance', *Urban Studies*, 50 (5), 1066–1082.

Fainstein, S.S. and Campbell, S. (2012), 'Introduction: The Structure and Debates of Planning Theory', in S.S. Fainstein and S. Campbell (eds), *Readings in Planning Theory*, Malden, MA and Oxford: Blackwell Publishing Ltd, pp. 1–20.

Flyvbjerg, B. (1998a), *Rationality and Power*, Chicago: University of Chicago Press.

Flyvbjerg, B. (1998b), 'Habermas and Foucault: Thinkers for Civil Society', *The British Journal of Sociology*, 49 (2), 210–233.

Flyvbjerg, B. (2001), *Making Social Science Matter: Why Social Inquiry Fails and How it Can Succeed Again* (S. Sampson trans.), Cambridge: Cambridge University Press.

Flyvbjerg, B. (2012), 'Why Mass Media Matter and How to Work with Them: Phronesis and Megaprojects', in B. Flyvbjerg, T. Landmann and S. Schram (eds), *Real Social Science: Applied Phronesis*, Cambridge: Cambridge University Press, pp. 95–121.

Forester, J. (1999), *The Deliberative Practitioner*, Cambridge, MA: MIT Press.

Foucault, M. (1980), 'Truth and Power', in C. Gordon (ed.), *Power/Knowledge*, Brighton, UK: Harvester Press, pp. 107–133.

Foucault, M. (1982a), 'The Subject and Power', *Critical Inquiry*, 8 (4), 777–795.

Foucault, M. (1982b), 'How is Power Exercised', in H.L. Dreyfus and P. Rabinow (eds), *Michel Foucault: Beyond Structuralism and Hermeneutics*, Chicago: The University of Chicago Press, pp. 216–226.

Foucault, M. (1991), *Discipline and Punish: The Birth of the Prison*, Harmondsworth, UK: Penguin.

Foucault, M. (1994), *Michel Foucault: Power. Knowledge. (Selected Interviews and Other Writings 1972–1977)* (Colin Gordon ed.), New York: Pantheon Books.

Foucault, M. (1997), 'What is Critique?', in S. Lotringer and L. Hochroth (eds), New York: Semiotext (e), pp. 191–211.

Foucault, M. (1998), *The Will to Knowledge: The History of Sexuality*, Vol. I, USA: Vintage.

Foucault, M. (2007), *Security, Territory, Population: Lectures at the College de France, 1977–1978* (G. Burchell trans.). Basingstoke, UK: Palgrave Macmillan.

Friedmann, J. (1987), *Planning in the Public Domain: From Knowledge to Action*, Princeton: Princeton University Press.

Friedmann, J. (1993), 'Planning Theory Revisited', *European Planning Studies*, 6 (3), 245–253.

Fox-Rogers, L. and Murphy, E. (2015), 'From Brown Envelopes to Community Benefits: The Co-option of Planning Gain Agreements under Deepening Neoliberalism', *Geoforum*, (67), 41–50.

Giroux, A.H. (2017), *The Terror of Neoliberalism: Authoritarianism and the Eclipse of Democracy*, New York: Routledge.

Göhler, G. (2009), 'Power to and Power Over', in S.R. Clegg and M. Haughard (eds), *The Sage Handbook of Power*, London: Sage, pp. 27–39.

Grange, K. (2014), 'In Search of Radical Democracy: The Ideological Character of Current Political Advocacies for Culture Change in Planning', *Environment and Planning A*, 46, 2670–2685.

Grange, K. (2016), 'Planners – A Silenced Profession? The Politicisation of Planning and the Need for Fearless Speech', *Planning Theory*, 15 (1), 1–21.

Gualini, E. (2010), 'Governance, Space and Politics: Exploring the Governmentality of Planning', in J. Hillier and P. Healey (eds), *The Ashgate Research Companion to Planning Theory: Conceptual Challenges for Spatial Planning*, Aldershot, UK: Ashgate Publishing Limited, pp. 57–85.

Gunder, M. (2006), 'Sustainability Planning's Saving Grace or Road to Perdition?', *Journal of Planning Education and Research*, 26 (2), 208–221.

Gunder, M. (2010a), 'Planning as the Ideology of (Neoliberal) Space', *Planning Theory*, 9 (4), 298–314.

Gunder, M. (2010b), 'Making Planning Theory Matter: A Lacanian Encounter with Phronesis', *International Planning Studies*, 15 (1), 37–51.

Gunder, M. (2014), 'Fantasy in Planning Organisations and their Agency: The Promise of Being at Home in the World', *Urban Policy and Research*, 32 (1), 1–15.

Gunder, M. (2014), 'Fantasy in Planning Organisations and their Agency: The Promise of Being at Home in the World', *Urban Policy and Research*, 32 (1), 1–15.

Gunder, M. and Hillier, J. (2009), *Planning in Ten Words or Less: A Lacanian Entanglement with Spatial Planning*, Aldershot, UK: Ashgate Publishing Limited.

Gunder, M., Madanipour, A. and Watson, V. (2018), *The Routledge Handbook of Planning Theory*, New York: Routledge.

Gunder, M. and Mouat, C. (2002), 'Symbolic Violence and Victimisation in Planning Processes: A Reconnoitre of the New Zealand Resource Management Act', *Planning Theory*, 1 (2), 124–145.

Harper, L.T. and Stein, S.M. (2006). *Dialogical Planning in a Fragmented Society: Critically Liberal, Pragmatic, Incremental*. New Brunswick, NJ: Transaction Publishers.

Harvey, D. (2005), *A Brief History of Neoliberalism*, Oxford: Oxford University Press.

Haughton, G. and Allmendinger, P. (2013), 'Spatial Planning and the New Localism', *Planning Practice & Research*, 28 (1), 1–5.

Healey, P. (2006). *Collaborative Planning: Shaping Places in Fragmented Societies* (2nd ed.), New York: Palgrave Macmillan.

Healey, P. (2010), *Making Better Places: The Planning Project in the Twenty-First Century*, London: Palgrave Macmillan.

Healey, P. (2012a), *Communicative Planning: Practices, Concepts and Rhetorics*, Cambridge, MA: MIT Press.

Healey, P. (2012b), 'Re-enchanting Democracy as a Mode of Governance', *Critical Policy Studies*, 6 (1), 19–39.

Healey, P. (2013), 'Circuits of Knowledge and Techniques: The Transnational Flow of Planning Ideas and Practices', *International Journal of Urban and Regional Research*, 37 (5), 1510–1526.

Hillier, J. (2002), *Shadows of Power: An Allegory of Prudence in Land-Use Planning*, London: Routledge.

Hillier, J. (2007), *Stretching Beyond the Horizon: A Multiplanar Theory of Spatial Planning and Governance*, Aldershot, UK: Ashgate Publishing Limited.

Hillier, J. and Healey, P. (eds) (2010), *The Ashgate Research Companion to Planning Theory: Conceptual Challenges for Spatial Planning*, Aldershot, UK: Ashgate Publishing Limited.

Hillier, J. (2013), 'Are We There Yet?', *Urban Policy and Research*, 31 (1), 1–3.

Hillier, Jean (2015), 'Transformation Processes: Introduction to Part IV', in J. Hillier and J. Metzger (eds), *Connections: Exploring Contemporary Planning Theory and Practice with Patsy Healey*, Aldershot, UK: Ashgate Publishing Limited, pp. 329–340.

Holgersen, S. (2015). 'Spatial Planning as Condensation of Social Relations: A Dialectical Approach', *Planning Theory*, 14 (1), 5–22.

Huxley, M. (2013), 'Historicizing Planning, Problematizing Participation', *International Journal of Urban and Regional Research*, 37 (5), 1527–1541.

Inch, A. (2015), 'Ordinary Citizens and the Political Cultures of Planning: In Search of the Subject of a New Democratic Ethos', *Planning Theory*, 14 (4), 404–424.

Jenkins, R. (2009). 'The Ways and Means of Power: Efficacy and Resources', in S.R. Clegg and M. Haughard (eds), *The Sage Handbook of Power*, London: Sage, pp. 140–156.

Jessop, B. (2009), 'The State and Power', in S.R. Clegg and M. Haughard (eds), *The Sage Handbook of Power*, London: Sage, pp. 367–382.

Kumi, E., Arhin, A.A. and Yeboah, T. (2014), 'Can Post-2015 Sustainable Development Goals Survive Neoliberalism? A Critical Examination of the Sustainable Development–neoliberalism Nexus in Developing Countries', *Environment, Development and Sustainability*, 16 (3), 539–554.

Legacy, C., March, A. and Mouat, C. (2014), 'Limits and Potentials to Deliberative Engagement in Highly Regulated Planning Systems: Norm Development within Fixed Rules', *Planning Theory & Practice*, 15 (1), 26–40.

Lelandais, G.E. (2014), 'Space and Identity in Resistance against Neoliberal Urban Planning in Turkey', *International Journal of Urban and Regional Research*, 38 (5), 1785–1806.

Lovering, J. (2009), 'The Recession and the End of Planning as we Have Known it', *International Planning Studies*, 14 (1), 1–6.

Marzukhi, M.A. (2020), 'Sustainability Discourse in Participatory Planning: The Case of Malaysia', *International Journal of Urban Sustainable Development*, 12 (2), 236–250.

McKee, K. (2009), 'Post-Foucauldian Governmentality: What Does it Offer Critical Social Policy Analysis?', *Critical Social Policy*, 29 (3), 465–486.

Miller, C.J. (2021), *Spectacle and Trumpism: An Embodied Assemblage Approach*, Bristol: Bristol University Press.

Morris, P. (2009), 'Power and Liberalism', in S.R. Clegg and M. Haughard (eds), *The Sage Handbook of Power*, London: Sage, pp. 54–69.

Olesen, K. (2014), 'The Neoliberalisation of Strategic Spatial Planning', *Planning Theory*, 13 (3), 288–303.

Peck, J., Theodore, N. and Brenner, N. (2009), 'Neoliberal Urbanism: Models, Moments, Mutations', *SAIS Review of International Affairs*, 29 (1), 49–66.

Peck, J., Theodore, N. and Brenner, N. (2013), 'Neoliberal Urbanism Redux?', *International Journal of Urban and Regional Research*, 37 (3), 1091–1099.

Pervova, L.I. (2020), *Neoliberalism, Social Policy and Welfare in Developing Countries (Russia, India and South Africa)*, Cambridge: Cambridge Scholars Publishing.

Pløger, J. (2001), 'Public Participation and the Art of Governance', *Environment and Planning B: Planning and Design*, 28, 219–241.

Porter, L., Martí-Costa, M., Torvà, M.D., Cohen-Bar, E., Ronel, A., Rogers, D. and Gibson, C. (2013), 'Finding Hope in Unpromising Times: Stories of Progressive Planning Alternatives for a World in Crisis/Ncoliberal Planning is not the Only Way: Mapping', *Planning Theory & Practice*, 14 (4), 529–529.

Purcell, M. (2009), 'Resisting Neoliberalisation: Communicative Planning or Counter-Hegemonic Movements', *Planning Theory*, 8 (2), 140–165.

Purcell, M. (2011), 'Neoliberalisation and Democracy', in S.S. Fainstein and S. Campbell (eds), *Readings in Urban Theory*, Malden, MA and Oxford: Blackwell Publishing Limited, pp. 42–54.

Purcell, M. (2013), 'A New Land: Deleuze and Guattari and Planning', *Planning Theory & Practice*, 14 (1), 20–38.

Raco, M. (2012), 'Neoliberal Urban Policy, Aspirational Citizenship and the Uses of Cultural Distinction', in T. Tasan-Kok and G. Baeten (eds), *Contradictions of Neoliberal Planning. Cities, Policies, and Politics*, Dordrecht: Springer, pp. 43–59.

Raco, M. (2016), 'Mass Privatisation and the Changing Nature of Governance in the UK', in M. Bevir and Rhodes, R.A.W. (eds), *Rethinking Governance: Ruling, Rationalities and Resistance*, London and New York: Routledge, pp. 50–69.

Rosol, M. (2014), 'On Resistance in the Post-political City: Conduct and Counter-conduct in Vancouver', *Space and Polity*, 18 (1), 70–84.

Roy, A. (2010), 'Informality and the Politics of Planning', in J. Hillier and P. Healey (eds), *The Ashgate Research Companion to Planning Theory: Conceptual Challenges for Spatial Planning*, Aldershot, UK: Ashgate Publishing Limited, pp. 87–107.

Roy, A. (2019), 'The City in the Age of Trumpism: From Sanctuary to Abolition', *Environment and Planning D: Society and Space*, 37 (5), 761–778.

Sager, T. (2013), *Reviving Critical Planning Theory: Dealing with Pressure, Neo-Liberalism, and Responsibility in Communicative Planning*, New York: Routledge.

Sanyal, B., Vale, L.J. and Rosan, C.D. (eds) (2012), *Planning Ideas That Matter: Livability, Territoriality, Governance, and Reflective Practice*, London: The MIT Press.

Schon, D.A. and Rein, M. (1994), *Frame Reflection: Toward the Resolution of Intractable Policy Controversies*, New York: HarperCollins Publisher.

Sharp, L. and Richardson, T. (2001), 'Reflections on Foucauldian Discourse Analysis in Planning and Environmental Policy Research', *Journal of Environmental Policy and Planning*, 3 (3), 193–209.

Swyngedouw, E. (2005), 'Governance Innovation and the Citizen: The Janus face of Governance-beyond-the-state', *Urban Studies*, 42 (11), 1991–2006.

Swyngedouw, E. (2009), 'The Antinomies of the Postpolitical City: In Search of a Democratic Politics of Environmental Production', *International Journal of Urban and Regional Research*, 33 (3), 601–620.

Swyngedouw, E. (2010), 'Apocalypse Forever? Post-political Populism and the Spectre of Climate Change', *Theory, Culture & Society*, 27 (2-3), 213–232.

Swyngedouw, E. (2014), 'Where is the Political? Insurgent Mobilisations and the Incipient "Return of the Political"', *Space and Polity*, 18 (2), 122–136.

Swyngedouw, E. (2015), 'Insurgent Urbanity and the Political City', in M. Mostafavi (ed.), *Ethics of the Urban: The City and the Spaces of the Political*, Zurich: Lars Müller Publishers.

Tasan-Kok, T. and Baeten, G. (eds) (2012), *Contradictions of Neoliberal Planning: Cities, Policies, and Politics*, Dordrecht: Springer.

Tilly, C. (2009), 'Power and Democracy', in S.R. Clegg and M. Haughard (eds), *The Sage Handbook of Power*, London: Sage, pp. 70–88.

Torfing, J. (2009), 'Power and Discourse: Towards an Anti-foundationalist Concept of Power', in S.R. Clegg and M. Haughard (eds), *The Sage Handbook of Power*, London: Sage, pp. 108–124.

Turner, M., O'Donnell, M., Suh, C. and Kwon, S. (2013), 'Public Sector Management and the Changing Nature of the Developmental State in Korea and Malaysia', *The Economic and Labour Relations Review*, 24 (4), 481–494.

Van Assche, K., Salukvadze, J. and Duineveld, M. (2012), 'Speed, Vitality and Innovation in the Reinvention of Georgian Planning Aspects of Integration and Role Formation', *European Planning Studies*, 20 (6), 999–1015.

Van Assche, K., Beunen, R. and Duineveld, M. (2014), *Evolutionary Governance Theory: An Introduction*, Heidelberg: Springer.

Van Assche, K., Beunen, R. and Duineveld, M. (2015), 'An Overview of EGT's Main Concept', in R. Beunen, K. Van Assche and M. Duineveld (eds), *Evolutionary Governance Theory: Theory and Applications*, Cham, Switzerland: Springer, 19–33.

Van de Klundert, T. (2013), *Capitalism and Democracy: A Fragile Alliance*, Cheltenham, UK and Northampton, MA, USA: Edward Elgar.

Versteeg, W. and Hajer, M. (2010), 'Is this How it is, or is this How it is Here? Making Sense of Politics in Planning', in J. Hillier and P. Healey (eds), *The Ashgate Research Companion to Planning Theory: Conceptual Challenges for Spatial Planning*, Aldershot, UK: Ashgate Publishing Limited, pp. 159–182.

Weinman, M.D. and Vormann, B. (2021), 'From a Politics of No Alternative to a Politics of Fear: Illiberalism and Its Variants', in B. Vormann and M.D. Weinman (eds), *The Emergence of Illiberalism: Understanding a Global Phenomenon*, New York: Routledge.

21. The emerging autonomous smart city and its impacts on planning and power relations in late capitalism

Elham Bahmanteymouri and Mohsen Mohammadzadeh

INTRODUCTION

> We ourselves are utterly enmeshed in technological systems, which shape in turn how we act and how we think. We cannot stand outside of them; we cannot think without them. (James Bridle, 2018: 2)

Over the last decades, the rapid advancement of information communication technologies (ICTs) and cybernetics has radically transformed contemporary cities and our everyday lives. Urban development led by the application of ICTs has appeared as an important discourse in both academia and practice, including planning (Hollands, 2015). Adherents of the use of advanced technologies in cities generally ratiocinate that these technologies provide new solutions to urban problems such as controlling traffic congestion, mitigating pollution and climate change, and improving efficiency (Yigitcanlar et al., 2018; Bouzguenda et al., 2019). Some believe that these new technologies can reverse or mitigate the adverse effects of rapid urbanisation, industrialisation, and consumerism (Taamallah et al., 2017; Trindade et al., 2017; Wiig, 2015). Although the justification for the pervasive usage of ICTs in cities is often associated with environmental concerns, investigation of ICT projects and their outcomes in cities reveals that 'only marginal attention is paid to these [environmental] concerns' (Yigitcanlar et al., 2018: 145). ICT projects often contribute to improving efficiency and economic growth. Some researchers maintain that ICT technological advancements should be considered in the context of capitalism, that is, techno-capitalism (Suarez-Villa, 2012), particularly in response to the failures of global neoliberalism (Bahmanteymouri and Farzaneh 2020). Consideration should be given to how urban digitalisation, and later automation, has reinforced the new stage of techno-capitalism and its mechanism of power.

Urban digitalisation is 'a decision that has multiple consequences: social, political, economic, and natural, the composite of which may decide the human trajectory' (Suarez-Villa, 2012: 2). Martin Heidegger, as one of the most influential philosophers in the twentieth century, argues in his work *The Question Concerning Technology* (2013: 4 [1954]) that '[e]verywhere we remain unfree and chained to technology, whether we passionately affirm it or deny it. But we are delivered over to it in the worst possible way when we regard it as something neutral.' Technology functions beyond human control. Heidegger suggests the concept of enframing to explain that 'social dimensions of technological systems belong to the essence of technology' (Feenberg, 2012: 17). Urban automation is inherently a political process. Based on the Žižekian perspective, this chapter investigates the normalising role of techno-capitalist ideology, the planner's subjectivity, and enframing planning knowledge based on techno-scientific approaches.

The advanced ICTs that are omnipresent in cities have given rise to notions such as the smart city (Hollands, 2008; Wiig, 2015), smart urbanism (Luque-Ayala and Marvin, 2019; Marvin et al., 2015), and other related concepts, such as the networked city (Graham, 2005; Tierney, 2019), the digital city (Ishido, 2002), and the intelligent city (Komninos, 2002). These concepts 'often link together technological informational transformations with economic, political and socio-cultural change' (Hollands, 2008: 305). These techno-scientific notions refer to cities that are often perceived as major labs in which smart gadgets, sensors, and the Internet of Things (IoT) collect a large amount of data (i.e. Urban Big Data) from all aspects of the cities and their residents' everyday lives (Cowley and Caprotti, 2019). The smart city has become even more topical with the recent success of urban artificial intelligence (UAI), machine learning algorithms (MLAs), and digital twinning (DT) – computer-based virtual simulation of both manufactured and living things – in creating self-directed agency based on predictions produced from autonomous self-learned analysis of Big Data sets focused on urban activities and interactions. Urban automation omits, or at least limits, the role of human actors, including planners, from the process of urban data collection, analysis, and generating outcomes. Urban artificial intelligence (UAI) drafts urban plans and policies based on urban Big Data that potentially attenuates the role of communicative/collaborative, advocacy, and radical planning in challenging the hegemonic power relations of techno-capitalism.

Kitchin, et al. (2019) argue that the adoption of smart city technologies across a range of urban domains results in new urban technocracy, technocratic governance, and city development. This new technocratic governance is embedded in 'instrumental rationality' (Mattern, 2013) and 'solutionism' (Morozov, 2013). Kitchin (2014: 9) explains that:

> The drive towards managing and regulating the city via information and analytic systems promotes a technocratic mode of urban governance which presumes that all aspects of a city can be measured and monitored and treated as technical problems which can be addressed through technical solutions.

Thus, urban problems can be solved or better managed through urban digitalisation, and later automation. 'Instrumental rationality provides a logical way to determine the optimal available means to accomplish a given goal' (Alexander, 2000: 245). Marcuse (1989 [1958–1959]) argued that 'technological rationality' can be considered as a component of a control apparatus for further domination. Similarly, Delanty and Harris (2021: 4) contend that:

> Modern technological rationality, manifest in industrial capitalism, is based on convenience, efficiency, standardization; it leads to adjustment and atomization, and the loss of personal autonomy. Technological rationality erodes critical rationality … Technology is presented as both a means of social control and an ideology in itself. It is an ideology in the sense that the pervasive spread of technological rationality makes impossible the conception of an alternative society or way of thinking.

Urban automation, as the next stage of urban digitalisation, redefines the role of planning to encompass an urban technocratic and solutionist approach to running cities (Kitchin, et al., 2019). The urban technocratic approach claims that 'planning can be a scientific enterprise with the associated kudos and respectability that accompanies it. It also provides a simple and highly structured view of the world' (Almendinger, 2009: 54). Urban automation enframes planning knowledge and practice as a component of urban technocracy based on its instrumental rationality. Planning will consequently lose its critical rationality, particularly at the subjective level, that enables it to challenge the existing mechanism of power.

The new emerging technologies are significantly transforming the operation of power (Bridle, 2018). The pervasive 'presence of digital, interactive technologies in urban environments, households and as citizens' personal devices will optimise patterns of consumption and communication, and assert the centrality of interactive Big Data – as real-time streams and cumulative patterns – in perfecting urban dynamics and governance' (Krivý, 2018: 9). The advancements of UAI, MLA, and DT have generated new capacities to compile urban Big Data in real-time, allowing efficient solutions without human interaction. Thus, smart cities 'understand themselves and thereby govern themselves' (Chandler, 2015: 844). However, these technologies can be also used for controlling and manipulating populations in their understandings, perceptions, and behaviours. Over thirty years ago, Deleuze developed the concept of 'societies of control' as personified by the datified 'dividual' rather than the individual. This theory was later utilised in planning theory by Krivý (2018). Subsequent thinkers have further developed these critical concerns, perhaps best articulated, at least from a Foucaultian perspective, by Vanolo's *smartmentality* (Vanolo, 2014) and Malette and Gabrys's *environmentality* (Malette, 2009; Gabrys, 2014). Since then, academics including Bär et al. (2020) and Grossi and Pianezzi (2017) have investigated the ideological dimensions of urban digitalisation. 'Reading these accounts of the transformation of technology and its extension into the inner realms of subjectivity, there is a certain fatalistic sense of technological determinism at work, akin to the "iron cage" of rationalization described by Weber' (Delanty and Harris, 2021: 8). Marcuse (2013) uses the term 'technical *a priori*' to explain how technology shapes subjects and their understanding of the world. This chapter investigates how urban digitalisation, and later automation, reinforces the hegemonic power relations in techno-capitalist cities through enframing planners' subjectivity and their knowledge. The chapter seeks to complement such studies with an ideology analysis method informed by Žižek's (1989) concept of ideological deconstruction, thereby adding a conceptual repertoire to planning.

The rest of this chapter is structured in three sections. The following section deploys a post-structural approach derived from Žižekian ideological deconstruction, particularly the conceptualisation of the relationship between the known and the unknown, to investigate why planners, at both individual and institutional levels, often adapt, uphold, and pervasively utilise urban automation. The subsequent section explains how techno-rationality depoliticises planning knowledge and practice. The final section concludes the chapter by considering what urban automation means for planning, particularly its power relations in late capitalism.

URBAN AUTOMATION: WHAT ARE THE KNOWN AND THE UNKNOWN?

Žižekian ideological deconstruction presages the smart city structured in a fantasy that reinforces the hegemonic ideology and its power relations in techno-capitalism. In this section, we use Žižek's ideas on knowledge to consider what planners know and do not know about urban automation and its impacts on power relations in late capitalism. This formulation assists in investigating why planners often promote urban automation as a smart city initiative despite (un)consciously knowing that such a smart city initiative could exacerbate the existing uneven mechanism of power in late capitalism.

Žižek is a Lacanian-Marxist who has challenged contemporary society's social, cultural, and political conditions in late capitalism. Žižek (1989, 1991, 2006, 2011, 2017) engages with and then re-interprets traditional Marxist concepts, adding the idea of 'ideological fantasy' to the concept of ideology. For Žižek, ideology is no longer the Marxist belief that 'they do not know it, but they are doing it' but is instead 'they know that, in their activity, they are following an illusion, but still they are doing it' (Žižek, 1989: 30). For example, planners often know that the full realisation of a smart city and urban automation would reinforce societal control apparatuses and strengthen existing capitalist power relations, yet they actively engage in developing and implementing smart city initiatives. Žižek focuses on 'how ideology is sustained by the complex relations between ideas and practices, and in particular between people's beliefs, actions, and knowledge' (Krips, 2018: 340). Žižek (2006) critically conceptualises the relationship between the known and the unknown as *'known-knowns'*, *'known-unknowns'*, *'unknown-unknowns'*, and *'unknown-knowns'*. Žižek contends that these combinations, although axiomatic, ideologically shape humans', including planners', beliefs, and subsequently inform their decisions and actions.

Known-knowns are the 'things we know that we know' (Žižek, 2006: 132); that is, they are what people perceive as their knowledge about themselves and the world. However, as MacDonell (1986: 79) argues, 'no form of knowledge is objective or neutral'. Foucault in *Power/knowledge* (1988) contends that knowledge is socially and politically constructed. For Žižek (1991), the dominant ideology regulates knowledge, or constructs known-knowns, to obscure the numerous inconsistencies in social reality. Foucault uses the term 'apparatus' to describe a formation that aims to respond to an urgent need at a particular historical moment. The apparatus is 'always inscribed in a play of power, but it is also always linked to certain coordinates of knowledge which issue from it but, to an equal degree, condition it' (Gordon, 1980: 196).

As planners, we should recognise that knowledge of urban automation has been generated by techno-capitalism and that knowledge supports techno-capitalist formation to respond to the failures of neoliberal markets. Technology as a discourse comprehends the capacity of shaping social and political relations (Fischer, 2010). Gunder and Hillier (2009: 8) argue that:

> [n]arratives or discourses are sets of sentences constituting speeches, arguments, and conversations that have become institutionalised into a particular way of thinking … [These] narratives, such as planning narratives, contain explanations and claims justifying 'truths,' values and beliefs, i.e., they claim legitimacy as knowledge and set the boundaries of acceptability.

Discussion on urban automation, particularly in the smart city, has become prevalent in planning discourse over the last decades. 'Digital technologies mark both new and changing affordances and new discourses about social [and power] reality' (Delanty and Harris, 2021: 10). Techno-capitalism works, and meanwhile reinforces, instrumental rationality in which human subjects often perceive techno-scientific knowledge as the only legitimate 'regime of truth' and reality, or as Žižek defines it, the subject's known-knowns. Khakee et al. (2000: 776) argue that 'reality is socially constructed and that there is a multiplicity of causes and effects'. By overstating the capacity of scientific knowledge to control both natural and social phenomena, techno-scientific knowledge is often perceived as the most legitimate and accurate knowledge to explain reality. Planning knowledge is largely shaped based on hegemonic discourses and narratives such as smartness, resilience, and efficiency in the flows of information within the autonomous smart city. Urban automation largely enframes planning knowledge based on 'technological rationality' that is perceived as the most economically efficient and scientifically accurate response to urban problems. 'Technological rationality' is a component of the control apparatus that reinforces the hegemonic power relations of late capitalism that 'is being both technologically driven while being an expression of something more pervasive, namely instrumental rationality' (Delanty and Harris, 2021: 3).

Urban automation often occurs under the banner of the smart city. Like other prevalent terms in planning such as the sustainable city (Gunder and Hillier, 2009), the resilient city (DeVerteuil and Golubchikov, 2016), the creative city (Barreto, 2018), the liveable city (Hamraie, 2020), among the others, there is no consensus as to what the smart city actually signifies. According to Gunder and Hillier (2009: 1):

> The smart city and all these terms 'are mere "empty signifiers", meaning everything and nothing – comfort terms – all things to all people. These desirous states of living and being, which most of us would aspire towards and, accordingly, attempt to shape our cities to achieve, are often illusions, attained, at best, with limited success'.

The term 'smart city' emanates from two prevalent, pre-developed concepts in planning: Smart Growth and New Urbanism (Hollands, 2008). Gunder and Hillier (2009: 83) argue that Smart Growth and New Urbanism are empty signifiers that have been largely utilised in planning to 'shift the benefits and costs relating to urban spatial development'.

The 'smart city' as an empty signifier is 'strictly speaking, a signifier without the signified' (Laclau, 1996: 36). The term 'smart city', like other similar 'empty signifiers', is interpreted vaguely, inconsistently, and often in a confused manner based on the hegemonic ideology and its norms, values, and discourses. 'The premise is that most mainstream discourses implicitly assume that smart city projects will empower and improve the lives of citizens. However, their role is often ambiguous' (Vanolo, 2016: 26). The concept of the smart city is often deployed in planning as a justificatory narrative (de Jong et al., 2015). Bunders and Varró (2019: 145) maintain that the ambiguity of the 'smart city' concept generates an opportunity to interpret it 'as a development concept that urban stakeholders strategically invest in making cities more sustainable, efficient, and competitive, as well as liveable'. León and Rosen (2020: 498) argue that the smart city 'is contributing to urban transformations by turning cities into digital geographies optimized for capital accumulation'.

Techno-capitalism reinforces technological and technocratic rationality that neutralises urban automation as a natural evolutionary stage of civilisation. Hatch (2012) compares urban automation (smart city) with electrification, which underlines the evolutionary nature of technological advancement and its influence on contemporary cities and urban planning. Komninos et al. (2019: 4–5) consider

> urban automation as an expression of 'evolutionary processes … characterized and affected by essential diversifications in the capacity of societies to generate technical innovations that are suitable to their needs … to achieve a leading position within the global context, to attract more funds and inward investment.

The tangible achievements of urban automation reinforce smart city initiatives around the world. For example, '[d]uring the pandemic, the coronavirus successfully partnered with the digital industry to speed up the digitalisation of society, in education, health services, and public surveillance' (Kunzmann, 2020: 22). The response to the COVID-19 pandemic has been intertwined with different layers of the smart city. Urban automation has become vital for citizens and private and public sectors by providing opportunities such as remote working, online shopping, trace tracking, e-service, and e-government.

Miller and Hoel (2002: 16) argue that 'the word "smart" carries a universally popular connotation'; it is difficult to argue against the notion of the "smart city", as its opposite would presumably be the "dumb city". Urban automation imposes 'a new moral order on the city by introducing specific technical parameters to distinguish between the "good" and "bad" [or dumb] city' (Vanolo, 2014: 883). Smart city initiatives often aim to provide advanced digital infrastructure for local industries, businesses, and citizens that is prerequisite for improving ecological and economic efficiency (Albino et al., 2015). Indeed, for some, utilising urban digital technologies has become a moral and ethical action for urban betterment (Datta and Odendaal, 2019). The moral and 'respectable' attitude towards the smart city is one of determinism where 'there is no place for asking why the new technology is necessary, who benefits from it, or whether it diverts resources from more important endeavors' (León and Rosen, 2020: 500). Some believe that this imperative is another phase in the evolution of the city as a 'growth machine', which is also termed the 'innovation machine' (Florida et al., 2017). This is characterised by the emergence of local coalitions 'assembled around urban technology as an unquestioned good' (Shearmur and Wachsmuth, 2019: 177).

Further, the smart city is implemented as a city marketing component and through place branding strategies (Kolotouchkina, and Seisdedos, 2018). Looking smart and being considered a smart city is crucial for strengthening global city competition and increasing a city's rank in the international smart-city rankings (Kunzmann, 2020; Bär et al., 2020). Creating a smart image can attract tourists and local/international investors (financial capital) and a global creative class (human capital) to the city during late capitalism (Kolotouchkina and Seisdedos, 2018).

The optimistic rhetoric and dominantly 'respectable' image of the smart city helps in promoting the utilisation of emerging technologies such as UAI, MLAs, and DT, among others, to address urban issues (Austin et al., 2020; Cugurullo, 2020; Nikitas et al., 2020). Urban 'artificially intelligent (UAI) entities are taking the management of urban services as well as urban governance out of the hands of humans, operating the city in an autonomous manner' (Cugurullo, 2020: 1). MLAs can classify, cluster, identify relationships and irregularities in Big Data, and learn the structure of large-scale grids and their attributes (Austin et al., 2020). Picon (2018: 270) argues that 'the smart city belongs partly to the imagination': a condition which makes the incarnations of this urban ideal hard to identify. Austin et al. (2020: 2) define digital twinning as:

> a cyber component that mirrors the physical urban system through real-time monitoring and synchronization of urban activities. Appropriate software and algorithms will work to provide superior levels of urban performance (e.g., in urban mobility, energy efficiency), urban planning (e.g., zoning), and resilience (e.g., through strategies of control and risk management).

DT provides complementary support for UAI and MLAs to gather, compile, and visualise urban Big Data. From a technological point of view, UAI, MLAs, and DT 'are part of a broader process of development which is now culminating in the passage from automation to autonomy' (Cugurullo, 2020: 10). Zhang and Wu (2019) argue that UAI, MLAs, and DT are radically changing urban governance and planning domains by becoming autonomous decision and planning makers in the autonomous city.

Known-unknowns are those 'things that we know we don't know' (Žižek, 2006: 132). These are identified gaps in knowledge. 'Something is uncertain if it is unknown or cannot be known' (Abbott, 2005: 237). These voids are recognised as sources of uncertainty. Uncertainty has always been part of nature's ongoing processes, and the future has always been complex and indeterminate. 'The future is the great unknown' (Abbott, 2005: 237). However, known-unknowns reveal the limitations of (perceived) knowledge in addressing the agents of stability in the future. The recognition of knowledge limitations largely affects decision-making by including unpredictability and unknowability in any consideration. Critical thinkers have therefore challenged techno-scientific utopian perspectives as the dominant way of thinking (Feenberg, 2012). In the planning domain, 'despite the heavy reliance in traditional planning on scientific knowledge, it was not exclusively a technocratic exercise' (Khakee, et al., 2000: 776). The recognition of known-unknowns therefore requires decision-makers, including planners, to deploy adaptable dynamic plans and policies such as strategic plans instead of solid plans, which are largely derived from natural science (Khakee, 1991). Yet, the knowledge gap should be investigated at the subjective level. Particularly under the influence of post-positivism, planners are informed that complete knowledge does not exist. Yet, 'knowledge is ideological when it becomes involved in power knowledge regimes … The interpellated subject is "captured" by the ideological discourse in order to act politically in the name of a specific system of knowledge' (Maesse and Nicoletta, 2021: 2). Techno-capitalism, as the hegemonic ideology, and its discourse define what should be considered a knowledge gap, or what should be prioritised for further investigations. Planners often attempt to address the knowledge gap based on technological and scientific approaches (Davoudi, 2015). Known-unknowns compel the adoption of new technologies such as UAI and MLA in contemporary cities. 'Technologies are rarely completely known or completely unknown; over time, they show themselves to be more or less effective' (Christensen, 1985: 64). There is increasing planning literature on the smart city and urban automation that discusses their potential consequences from technical/practical and critical perspectives and their ability to alter unknowns to knowns.

Unknown-unknowns are those 'things we don't know we don't know' (Žižek, 2006: 132). These are mostly beyond current human knowledge. Crucially, Freud's 'name for the "unknown unknowns" is trauma, the violent intrusion of something radically unexpected, something the subject was absolutely not ready for, and which it cannot integrate in any way' (Žižek, 2011: 292). Beck (2006: 335) adds that:

> If catastrophes are anticipated whose potential for destruction ultimately threatens everyone, then a risk calculation based on experience and rationality breaks down. Now all possible, more or less improbable scenarios have to be taken into consideration; to knowledge, therefore, drawn from experience and science, there now also has to be added imagination, suspicion, fiction, fear.

For instance, the COVID-19 pandemic is perceived as an unknown-unknown that 'has caught Governments, cities, regions, and planners on the wrong foot. Nobody was prepared or knew how to react' (Kunzmann, 2020: 20). Grant (2020: 569) argues that the COVID-19 pandemic largely 'challenges the ways we think about planning'. Under the hegemony of techno-capitalism, the pandemic has reinforced urban automation and smart city initiatives. The most advanced smart cities, such as Singapore, are ranked as resilient against the pandemic because they have successfully controlled the pandemic and its impacts by regulating social activities based on constant digital social tracking (Das and Zhang, 2020; Costa and

Peixoto, 2020). These smart cities also provide adequate digital infrastructure for both public and private sectors to operate remotely, vital for economic growth during lockdowns. The pandemic is strengthening the smart city and urban automation, hence the perceived value of Vanolo's (2014) smart mentality. Kunzmann (2020: 22) states that '[r]esistance to smart urban digitalisation, whether applied by public authorities, semi-public utilities or private corporations, will be much weaker. Individual convenience will outweigh privacy concerns. It is the most obvious experience in neoliberal times during the COVID-19 pandemic.' Kunzmann (2020: 22) concludes that 'smart city strategies will undoubtedly see a further boom in all cities that are already promoting smart-city development in one way or the other'.

Unknown-knowns refer to 'the things we don't know that we know' (Žižek, 2006: 132). This concept is directly embedded in the Freudian unconscious. 'From a psychoanalytical point of view, the unconscious is exactly about a knowledge which doesn't know itself; it is not some deep-buried unknown secret, it is the self-evident lying at the very surface' (DeVos, 2009: 225). For Žižek, unknown-knowns, or the unconscious, often determine people's decisions and inform their actions. Žižek (2006: 138) stresses that 'unknown-knowns are the disavowed beliefs, suppositions, and obscene practices we pretend not to know about, although they form the background of our public values'. Žižek (2008: 66) observes that the informing role of unknown-knowns in shaping our decision-making is largely ignored:

> These disavowed beliefs and suppositions [unknown-knowns] are the ones that prevent us from really believing in the possibility of the catastrophe, and they combine with the 'unknown-unknowns.' The situation is like that of the blind spot in our visual field: we do not see the gap, the picture appears continuous.

Hegemonic ideology often prevents us from becoming aware of these 'unknown-knowns' (Žižek, 2008). In planning, as elsewhere, unknown-knowns are largely disavowed realities concerning the adverse social and political impacts of urban automation – the realities that inform actors' decisions and their actions.

There is a growing body of critical literature that challenges the dominant discourse and optimistic attitude towards smart cities and urban automation (Bär et al., 2020; Hollands, 2015, 2008; Greenfield, 2017; Vanolo, 2014, 2016; Luque-Ayala and Marvin, 2019; Kitchin, 2015). These critiques can be broadly categorised into two main streams:

The first stream mainly focuses on the technical and practical limitations of smart-city initiatives, such as the challenges related to the quality of collected Big Data, data management, analysis and interpretation (Batty, 2013), and cybersecurity and privacy (Doku and Rawat, 2019; Kitchin, 2014). These technical concerns have often informed critical studies that investigate the practical challenges of urban automation.

The second stream adopts different critical standpoints, viewing the smart city as a panopticon (Klauser et al. 2014; Robb and Deane, 2021), datacracy (Radfahrer and Da Cunha Pasqualin, 2017), technopoly (Bloom and Sancino, 2019), and privatopia (Voordijk and Dorrestijn, 2019), among others. These concepts are also largely empty signifiers that inherently fail to explain the complexity of smart-city initiatives and their impacts on contemporary cities. Critical thinkers have questioned the 'smart' in smart cities from different perspectives. Holland (2008), as well as Hemment and Townsend (2013), among others, challenge urban digitisation as a top-down process that tends to neglect the actual needs of residents. Indeed, this 'top-down technology-driven smart city may be a threat to democratic liberties and rights and democracy' (Voordijk and Dorrestijn, 2019: 14). Some researchers consider that the smart city includes a process that is neoliberalising urban space. Major international ICT and technology corporations such as IBM, Cisco, Siemens, NEC, and Huawei promote and often finance urban digitalisation, later urban automation. Wiig (2015) notes that IBM's Smarter Cities has influenced local policy making in Philadelphia.

International corporations often define, finance, and technologically support smart-city projects, plans, and policies based on public–private partnership contracts. Thus, it is quite possible that the market-driven development of smart cities will reinforce the privatisation and marketisation of urban space in late capitalism (Hollands, 2008; Vanolo, 2014; Krivý, 2018). Some have argued that the smart city and urban automation have become an ideology that aligns with, or complements, neoliberalism as the hegemonic ideology (Grossi and Pianezzi, 2017; Bär et al., 2020; León and Rosen, 2020). Suarez-Villa (2012) argues that the major international ICT and technology corporations have authoritarian power over technology that creates a new era of capitalism, which he terms techno-capitalism. The impact of the ICT corporates is not limited to mere collaboration with governments based on their common interests, rather, they significantly influence society, state policy, and consequently planning practice. The international ICT corporations play a crucial role in shaping residents, including planners' knowledge, by controlling the flows of information as well as reinforcing the power relations which most 'people are not on top of' (Bridle, 2018: 8).

The second stream also provides a critical understanding of the impacts of automated smart cities on planning and power derived from UAI, MLAs, and DT. Greenfield (2017: 8), in his book *Radical Technologies*, states that 'allegedly disruptive technologies' such as UAI, MLAs, and DT, often 'leave existing modes of domination mostly intact'. The pervasive usage of UAI, MLAs, and DT in cities is 'not an abrupt phenomenon, but rather part of a long-standing process of technological development and a politico-economic agenda which together are enabling the transition from automation to autonomy' (Cugurullo, 2020: 2). The autonomous smart city, or urban automation, has multiple social, political, economic, and natural consequences that define the human trajectory. The autonomous smart city and its impacts on planning should be considered in the context of techno-capitalism. Mosco (2019: 23) argues that:

> the political battles over smart cities often come down to the ability of technology companies to expand their power by becoming real estate dealmakers and developers, who invest in digital technologies that offer new stores of profitable data on the behaviour of people and the performance of things.

Indeed, international ICT corporates have become urban infrastructure providers and real estate developers involved in urban development policies and planning through this very process of urban automation. Thus, it is widely known that international ICT corporations play a vital role in reinforcing top-down power relations to maximise their benefits in techno-capitalism.

The impacts of the urban autonomous smart city on power relations and the planning discipline continue to be well studied and are now often taught in planning programmes. Planners know that smart city initiatives 'have been used as rhetorical devices to legitimise the reproduction [and reinforcement] of existing power relations, ideologies, and political economies' under techno-capitalism (Cugurullo, 2020: 2). Planners know urban automation is not neutral; instead, it often operates based on black box algorithms developed by international ICT corporations. As the enframed subjects become entangled in the hegemony of techno-capitalism and its technological rationality, planners mostly adhere to the autonomous smart city's illusion of being a techno-utopia. Sarewitz (2020: 18) argues that:

> Planning 'must face its own uncomfortable knowledge. We find ourselves in a crisis of cognitive dissonance: though [America] remains the world's leader in science and technology by almost any measure, the widely shared benefits that such leadership was supposed to deliver to society seem to be drifting farther from reach.

Planners often know the consequences of urban autonomation, but they disavow this knowledge by supporting smart-city initiatives. 'A central challenge for a contemporary critical theory of technology would be to research the impact of technology on the subject's capacity, [including planners] for critique, for non-instrumental thought, and the new cognitive capacities required to flourish in digital neoliberalism' (Delanty and Harris, 2021: 17).

Urban automation is an inherently political phenomenon. The autonomous smart city fundamentally influences the mechanisms of power in cities. Several academics have critically challenged the concept of the autonomous smart city. Although planners often know that urban automation potentially reinforces the existing uneven power relations in capitalist cities, they actively implement smart city initiatives and urban digitalisation. Understanding how techno-capitalism depoliticises planning is fundamental for investigating the power relations in the autonomous smart city.

HOW DOES URBAN AUTOMATION DEPOLITICISE PLANNING?

Technology has previously been thought of as neutral so as to remove it from political controversy (Feenberg, 2012). Yet, as early as 1954, Martin Heidegger questioned the pervasive usage of technology in industrial capitalism by investigating its adverse impacts on human subjectivity and understanding of the world. Heidegger (2013 [1956]) argued that technology is not only an instrument but a way of understanding the world. Heidegger believed that technology 'forms a culture of universal control. Nothing escapes it, not even its human makers' (Feenberg, 2012: 3). For Heidegger, this techno-culture has enframed human subjectivity and our understanding of the world. Delanty and Harris (2021: 4) argue that 'technological rationality erodes critical rationality'. Technology functions as an 'iron cage' that prevents the human subject, as unknown-knowns, from discerning alternatives beyond technological solutions or from challenging the hegemonic mechanism of power (Marcuse, 2013).

Foucault discusses the 'modes of objectification which transform human beings into subjects' through power relations (Daldal, 2014: 161). He recognises three types of objectification of people in modern society: (1) objectification by producing the subject through scientific paradigms; (2) objectification through 'dividing practices' [such as the smart or dumb city]; (3) the self-subjectivising of the person who 'learns to call himself the subject of some practice' such as a planner (Daldal, 2014: 161). Like Heidegger, Foucault questions the role of science and technology in the objectification of humans in modern society. Derived from Foucault's concept of governmentality, Gabrys' (2014; 32) concept of environmentality argues that smart city residents have 'become sensing nodes … or citizen sensors … a modality of citizenship that emerges through interaction with computational sensing technologies used for environmental monitoring and feedback'. The residents simultaneously have become a component of 'an automated behavioural sensor and transgressed as an environmental vector' (Krivý, 2018:

16). Based on predefined algorithms, UAI uses urban Big Data to conduct social sorting of residents based on their recorded behaviours, or even their financial status such as 'Social Credit Scores' (Kostka, 2019). Self-tracking applications constantly inform the residents about their ranks, which define their eligibility to use urban amenities and access places.

Patrício (2017) argues that surveillance technologies affect our emotions and moral behaviour. Smart city residents are normalised as docile bodies based on the new disciplinary mechanism. Urban automation strengthens the existing control apparatus through reinforcing biopolitics. Urban digitalisation generates a range of visual Big Data from the smart city and its residents, collected from various CCTVs and visual materials from online social media platforms. Any misbehaviour and disorder can be observed and punished in real-time, and the record is stored permanently in the system. Robb and Deane (2021: 297) argue that the smart city panopticon is a 'city that is empowered by this technology to monitor, control and oppress in an "Orwellian" fear of the ever-watching panopticon'. Residents should be controlled as docile bodies in techno-capitalist cities. Planners increasingly utilise DT to visualise collected Big Data for policy making and planning, despite knowing that DT generates a virtual version of urban reality. DT inherently cannot visualise the power relations that are crucial in analysing the production of space. Planners, as unknown-knowns, often perceive these images as a reality for policy making and planning because of their efficiency (Ketzler, et al., 2020). Planners generally know that urban automation expands the hegemonic power relations of capitalism, yet they deny this reality under the influence of technological rationality.

Based on Foucault's definition of power, governmentality can be seen as 'not only the product of active agents applying force and sovereignty to the bodies of the subjected (as it basically was up to the 18th century) but rather the product of discursive tactics of professionals who use scientific surveillance techniques to normalise social behaviour' (Vanolo, 2014: 885). Governmentality generates a self-management mechanism whereby normalised subjects' behaviour is based on the dominant discourse, norms, and values. Pali and Schulenburg (2019: 872) argue that governmentality (regarded as the 'conduct of conduct') 'involves how subjects form their identities through processes of government – processes that encourage and suppress actions by drawing a line between what is acceptable and what is unacceptable, between what is strange and suspicious and what is not'. Several scholars have used governmentality to investigate how the production of the smart city transforms urban governmentality by generating a new paradigm of knowledge, norms, and values (Vanolo, 2014; Ho, 2017; Kitchin et al., 2020). For Klauser et al. (2014: 869), contemporary governmentality essentially comprises 'software-mediated techniques used to regulate and manage urban systems'. Similarly, Vanolo (2014: 894) conceptualises 'smartmentality' as the 'production and circulation of knowledge, rationalities, subjectivities, and moralities suited to the management of the smart city'. Under the banner of the smart city, a new paradigm of urban identity, norms, and values is produced whereby '[ci]ties are made responsible for the achievement of smartness – i.e., adherence to the specific model of a technologically advanced, green, and economically attractive city, while "diverse" cities, those following different development paths, are implicitly reframed as smart-deviant' (Vanolo, 2014: 889).

To normalise smart people/citizens' behaviours, the major international ICTs have invested in school digitalisation as a component of their global smart city programmes, such as IBM via 'Smarter Education' and Microsoft via 'Educated Cities'. Smart people/citizens, including planners, are often perceived as vital components of shaping the smart city (Albino et al. 2015; Hollands, 2015). Smartmentality generates a new set of moral and ethical values that inform residents' behaviour. Residents should willingly participate in the 'quantified-self', 'self-surveillance', and 'self-optimisation' as ethical behaviour. Self-surveillance is perceived as an ethical and moral action because it is presented mostly as an evidence-based, objective, and value-neutral mechanism. These new norms and values shape planners' identity in their role of working, living, interacting within the smart city. Planners should be 'skilled computational actors who can assist in programming and coding the technologies that will facilitate the flow, analysis, and visualization of urban data' (Williamson, 2015: 4). UAI and MLA provide advanced 'analysis, predictions, and recommendations … [and] such tools and services are often framed in terms like "a good life", "sustainable lifestyle", "healthy living", and "individual responsibility"' (Klauser et al., 2014: 879). 3). Planners often promote urban automation because it is objectified through 'dividing practices' as a good planning practice and reflects constructed known-knowns in techno-capitalism.

Following Foucault, Deleuze (1995) developed the concept of 'societies of control', referring to the initial deployment of ICT technology and its impacts on the power mechanism in post-industrial societies. Deleuze (Negri and Deleuze 1995: 174) argues that '[w]e're moving toward control societies that no longer operate by confining people but through continuous control and instant communication'. The coding mechanism breaks down the disciplinary duality of the individual and the mass. 'The individual is becoming a *"dividual"* whilst the mass is reconfigured in terms of data, samples, and markets … disciplinary individuals produced quantifiable and discrete amounts of energy, *"dividuals"* are caught up in a process of modulation' (Santilli, 2007: 56). In contrast to disciplinary society, 'control is exerted by inducing action rather than restricting it, or, more precisely, by "curating" a networked terrain within which action is nurtured' (Krivý, 2018: 19). The integrated network of control constantly modulates individuals' interactions, desires, and attitudes within a society of control: while the individual signifies a complete, whole person, the dividual is partial, fragmented, and incomplete. Control de-emphasises, or even abandons, the quest to train, moralise, reform, and remake the individual. It relinquishes the dream of an all-encompassing normalised society. 'Smart cities subsume a heterogeneous range of techniques and efforts aimed at governing through code' (Klauser et al., 2014: 870).

For Deleuze, networked communication is the new instrument of control. Patton (2006: 27) argues that,

> Technology is social in the sense that it is not the material object that determines whether an axe serves as a tool or a weapon but the collective assemblage or machine in which it functions: not the technical machine, itself a collection of elements, but the social or collective machine, the machinic assemblage that determines what is a technical element at a given moment, what is its usage, extensions, comprehension, etc.

Residents' subjectivity is largely shaped through their interactions and communications with other nodes, human and non-human, in the smart city. Residents are not just data producers; rather, they, as communication nodes, constantly receive and consume data. AI and algorithms sort, regulate, and direct the flows of data to the residents. Krivý (2018:10) argues that 'in the society of control, it is impossible to think, not because communication is disallowed but precisely because there is no outside to infinitely differentiating communication'. Human subjectivity is entangled within this autonomous mechanism and its network which 'is a power relationship, and most people are not on not on top of it' (Bridle, 2018: 8). In techno-capitalism, planning's known-(un)knowns are shaped based on 'a certain understanding of the world that, thus reified, is capable of achieving certain effects in that world' (Bridle, 2018: 13). The autonomous smart city codifies the individual's data in real-time. UAI and MLA compile the 'dividual' data alongside other data as Big Data to offer various options, and DT virtually visualises the most efficient options.

The transformation of power relations is consequently changing planning as a political practice in the autonomous smart city. Urban automation has essentially become the centre of planning and policy making in the autonomous smart city (Zhang and Wu, 2019; Cugurullo, 2020). Yet planners, among others, often adhere to the hegemonic techno-utopian illusion as an 'ideological fantasy' and disavow critical knowledge as an unknown-known (Žižek, 1989).

CONCLUSION

Urban automation is inherently a complex and multi-layered political phenomenon that has developed within the context of neoliberal globalism. This chapter has taken several critical steps towards understanding the autonomous smart city, particularly in its implications for planning and the power relations in cities. We explained that smart city advocates largely promote 'techno-utopian' imaginaries, fantasies, and illusions. Cugurullo (2020: 1) states that autonomous smart cities and their AI, ML, and Big Data 'are taking the management of urban services as well as urban governance out of the hands of humans, operating the city in an autonomous manner'. Based on technological rationality, smart city advocates believe that the elimination of human [including planner] errors and their interests in the city operation will increase the system's efficiency and reliability.

Similar to Feenberg (2012: 86), we argued that 'technological development is constrained by cultural norms originating in economics, ideology, religion, and tradition'. The chapter elucidated that based on instrumental rationality and capitalist economic efficiency, capitalism operates ideologically through decoding and recoding power relations, regulations, and disciplinary discourses within planning institutions. The international ICT corporations are the primary digital urban infrastructure providers, real estate investors, urban planners, and policy-makers. These major companies often collect Big Data to sell as a commodity in the market, to control the flows of information in the connected society, and to provide the required software and urban algorithms vital for the autonomous smart city operation. The chapter elaborated that the autonomous smart city embodies the corporatisation of urban areas that exacerbate and reproduce social gaps and urban inequalities. Urban automation eventually reinforces the hegemony of capitalism and its top-down power relations as techno-capitalism. Techno-capitalism as the hegemonic ideology significantly shapes planners' subjectivity, both knowns and unknowns, that consequently informs their decisions and actions. The adverse implications of the autonomous smart city are largely known in the planning discipline. However, planners often disavow this knowledge as an unknown-known and actively participate in expanding techno-capitalism and its power relations. Ultimately, we believe that disclosing this knowledge is an ethical requirement that impacts the knowledge and practice of the planning discipline and should be taken into consideration in our policy analysis and plan making.

REFERENCES

Abbott, J. (2005). 'Understanding and Managing the Unknown', *Planning Education and Research*, 24(3), 237–251.

Albino, V., Berardi, U., and Dangelico, R. (2015), 'Smart Cities: Definitions, Dimensions, Performance, and Initiatives', *Journal of Urban Technology*, 22(1), 3–21.

Alexander, E. (2000). 'Rationality Revisited: Planning Paradigms in a Post-Postmodernist Perspective', *Journal of Planning Education and Research*, 19(3), 242–256.

Allam, Z. and Dhunny, Z. (2019). 'On Big Data, Artificial Intelligence and Smart Cities', *Cities*, 89(June), 80–91.

Amin, A. and Thrift, N. (2002). *Cities: Reimagining the Urban*, Cambridge: Polity.

Austin, M., Delgoshaei, P., Coelho, M., and Heidarinejad, M. (2020). 'Architecting Smart City Digital Twins: Combined Semantic Model and Machine Learning Approach', *Journal of Management in Engineering*, 36(4), 040200261-13.

Bahmanteymouri, E. and Farzaneh, H. (2020). 'Airbnb as an Ephemeral Space: Towards an Analysis of a Digital Heterotopia', in S. Ferdinand, I. Souch, and D. Wesselman (eds), *Heterotopia and Globalisation in the Twenty-First Century*, New York: Routledge, pp. 131–146.

Bär, L., Ossewaarde, M., and Van Gerven, M. (2020). 'The Ideological Justifications of the Smart City of Hamburg', *Cities*, 105(October), 1028111-9.

Barreto, L.M. (2018). 'Make Live and Let Die: Why Creative People are not so Creative to Solve Social Problems?', *Global Politics Review*, 4(2), 29–49.

Batty, M. (2013). 'Big Data, Smart Cities and City Planning', *Dialogues in Human Geography*, 3(3), 274–279.

Beck, U. (2006). 'Living in the World Risk Society', *Economy and Society*, 35(3), 329–345.

Bloom, P. and Sancino, A. (2019). *Disruptive Democracy: The Clash between Techno-Populism and Techno-Democracy*. London: SAGE Publications Limited.

Bina, O., Inch, A., and Pereira, L. (2020). 'Beyond Techno-utopia and its Discontents: On the Role of Utopianism and Speculative Fiction in Shaping Alternatives to the Smart City Imaginary', *Futures*, 115(102475), 1–14.

Bouzguenda, I., Alalouch, C., and Fava, N. (2019). 'Towards Smart Sustainable Cities: A Review of the Role Digital Citizen Participation Could Play in Advancing Social Sustainability', *Sustainable Cities and Society*, 15(101627), 1–27.

Bridle, J. (2018). *New Dark Age: Technology and the End of the Future*. London: Verso.

Bunders, D. and Varró, K. (2019). 'Problematizing Data-driven Urban Practices: Insights from Five Dutch "Smart Cities"', *Cities*, 93(October), 145–152.

Chandler, D. (2015). 'A World Without Causation: Big Data and the Coming of Age of Posthumanism', *Millennium: Journal of International Studies*, 43(3), 833–851.

Christensen, K. (1985). 'Coping with Uncertainty in Planning', *The American Planning Association*, 51(1), 63–73.

Costa, D. and Peixoto, J. (2020). 'COVID-19 Pandemic: A Review of Smart Cities Initiatives to Face New Outbreaks', *IET Smart Cities*, 2(2), 64–73.

Cowley, R. and Caprotti, F. (2019). 'Smart City as Anti-planning in the UK', *Environment and Planning D: Society and Space*, 37(3), 428–448.

Cugurullo, F. (2020). 'Urban Artificial Intelligence: From Automation to Autonomy in the Smart City', *Frontiers in Sustainable Cities*, 2(38), 1–14.

Daldal, A. (2014). 'Power and Ideology in Michel Foucault and Antonio Gramsci: A Comparative Analysis', *Review of History and Political Science*, 2(2), 149–167.

Das, D. and Zhang, J. (2020). 'Pandemic in a Smart City: Singapore's COVID-19 Management through Technology and Society', *Urban Geography*, 41(8), 1–9.

Davidson, M. (2010). 'Sustainability as Ideological Praxis: The Acting out of Planning's Master-signifier', *City*, 14(4), 390–405.

Datta, A. and Odendaal, N. (2019). 'Smart Cities and the Banality of Power', *Environment and Planning D: Society and Space*, 37(3), 387–392.

Davoudi, S. (2015). 'Planning as Practice of Knowing', *Planning Theory*, 14(3), 316–331.

de Jong, M., Joss, S., Schraven, D. et al. (2015). 'Sustainable–smart–resilient–low carbon–eco–knowledge Cities; Making Sense of a Multitude of Concepts Promoting Sustainable Urbanization', *Journal of Cleaner Production*, 109(special issue), 25–38.

Delanty, G. and Harris, N. (2021). 'Critical Theory and the Question of Technology: The Frankfurt School Revisited', *Thesis Eleven*, 164(1). 1–21.

Deleuze, G. (1992). 'Postscript on the Societies of Control', *October*, 59(Winter), 3–7.

DeVerteuil, G. and Golubchikov, O. (2016). 'Can Resilience be Redeemed? Resilience as a Metaphor for Change, Not against Change', *City*, 20(1), 143–151.

Doku, R. and Rawat, D. (2019). 'Big Data in Cybersecurity for Smart City Applications', in R. Doku and D. Rawat (eds), *Smart Cities Cybersecurity and Privacy*, Amsterdam: Elsevier, pp. 103–112.

Duan, L., Lou, Y., Wang, S., Gao, W., and Rui, Y. (2018). 'AI-Oriented Large-Scale Video Management for Smart City: Technologies, Standards, and Beyond', *IEEE MultiMedia*, 26(2), 8–20.

Feenberg, A. (2012). *Questioning Technology*, London and New York: Routledge.

Fischer, E. (2010). 'Contemporary Technology Discourse and the Legitimation of Capitalism', *European Journal of Social Theory*, 13(2), 229–252.

Foucault, M. (1971). 'Orders of Discourse', *Social Science Information*, 10(2), 7–30.

Foucault, M. (1972). *Archaeology of Knowledge*, New York, Pantheon Books.

Foucault, M. (1982). 'The Power and Subject', *Critical Inquiry*, 8 (Summer), 777–795.

Foucault, M. (1991). *Discipline and Punish*, London: Vintage Books.

Friedmann, J. (1987). *Planning in the Public Domain: From Knowledge to Action*, Princeton: Princeton University Press.

Friedmann, J. (2011). *Insurgencies: Essays in Planning Theory*, New York: Routledge.

Florida, R. (2002). *The Rise of the Creative Class and How It's Transforming Work, Leisure, Community and Everyday Life*, New York: Basic Books.

Florida, R., Adler, P., and Mellander, C. (2017). 'The City as Innovation Machine', *Regional Studies*, 51(1), 86–96.

Gabrys, J. (2014). 'Programming Environments: Environmentality and Citizen Sensing in the Smart City', *Environment and Planning D: Society and Space*, 32(1), 30–48.

Gordon, C. (1980). *Power/knowledge*, New York: Pantheon.

Graham, S. (2005). 'Strategies for Networked Cities', in L. Albrechts and S. Mandelbaum (eds), *The Network Society – A New Context for Planning*, London: Routledge, pp. 95–109.

Grebosz-Krawczyk, M. (2020). 'Place Branding (R)Evolution: The Management of the Smart City's Brand', *Place Branding and Public Diplomacy*, 17(1), 1–12.

Greenfield, A. (2017). *Radical Technologies: The Design of Everyday Life*, London and New York: Verso.

Grossi, G. and Pianezzi, D. (2017). 'Smart Cities: Utopia or Neoliberal Ideology?', *Cities*, 69 (September), 79–85.

Gunder, M. (2003), 'Passionate Planning for the Others' Desire: An Agonistic Response to the Dark Side of Planning', *Progress in Planning*, 60(3), 235–319.

Gunder, M. (2010). 'Planning as the Ideology of (Neoliberal) Space', *Planning Theory*, 9(4), 298–314.

Gunder, M. and Hillier, J. (2007). 'Planning as Urban Therapeutic', *Environment and Planning: A*, 39(2), 467–486.

Gunder, M. and Hillier, J. (2009). *Planning in Ten Words or Less: A Lacanian Entanglement with Spatial Planning*, Farnham, UK: Ashgate.

Hamraie, A. (2020). 'Alterlivability: Speculative Design Fiction and the Urban Good Life in Starhawk's Fifth Sacred Thing and City of Refuge', *Environmental Humanities*, 12(2), 407–430.

Hatch, D. (2012). 'Smart Cities: are Futuristic Metropolises Good Investments?', *CQ Researcher*, 22(27), 1–24.

Ho, E. (2017). 'Smart Subjects for a Smart Nation? Governing (Smart) Mentalities in Singapore', *Urban Studies*, 54(13), 3101–3118.

Hollands, R.G. (2008). 'Will the Real Smart City Please Stand Up? Intelligent, Progressive or Entrepreneurial?', *City*, 12(3), 303–320.

Hollands, R. (2015). 'Critical Interventions into the Corporate Smart City', *Cambridge Journal of Regions, Economy and Society*, 8(1), 61–77.

IBM. (2021). 'Smarter Planet'. Retrieved January 10, 2021, from www.ibm.com/smarterplanet/us/en/.

Ishido, T. (2002). 'Digital City Kyoto', *Communications of the ACM*, 45(7), 78–81.

Ketzler, B., Naserentin, V., Latino, F., Zangelidis, C., Thuvander, L. and Logg, A. (2020). 'Digital Twins for Cities: A State of the Art Review', *Built Environment*, 46(4), 547–573.

Khakee, A. (1991). 'Scenario Construction for Urban Planning', *OMEGA*, 19(5), 459–446.

Khakee, A., Barbanente, A. and Borri, D. (2000) 'Expert and Experiential Knowledge in Planning', *Journal of the Operational Research Society*, 51(7), 776–788.

Kitchin, R. (2014). 'The Real-Time City? Big Data and Smart Urbanism', *GeoJournal*, 79(1), 1–14.

Kitchin, R. (2015). 'Making Sense of Smart Cities: Addressing Present Shortcomings', *Cambridge Journal of Regions, Economy and Society*, 8(1), 131–136.

Kitchin, R., Coletta, C., and McArdle, G. (2020). 'Governmentality and Urban Control', in K.S. Willis and A. Aurigi (eds), *The Routledge Companion to Smart Cities*, London: Routledge, pp. 109–122.

Kitchin, R., Coletta, C., Evans, L., Heaphy, L., and MacDonncha, D. (2019). 'Smart Cities, Algorithmic Technocracy and New Urban Technocrats', in M. Raco and F. Savini (eds), *Planning and Knowledge*, Bristol: Policy Press, pp. 199–212.

Klauser, F., Paasche, T. and Söderström, O. (2014). 'Michel Foucault and the Smart City: Power Dynamics Inherent in Contemporary Governing Through Code', *Environment and Planning D: Society and Space*, 32(5), 869–885.

Kolotouchkina, O. and Seisdedos, G. (2018). 'Place Branding Strategies in the Context of New Smart Cities: Songdo IBD, Masdar and Skolkovo', *Place Branding and Public Diplomacy*, 14(2), 115–124.

Komninos, N. (2002). *Intelligent Cities: Innovation, Knowledge Systems and Digital Spaces*, London: Spon Press.

Komninos, N., Kakderi, C., Panori, A., and Tsarchopoulos, P. (2019) 'Smart City Planning From an Evolutionary Perspective', *Journal of Urban Technology*, 26(2), 3–20.

Kostka, G. (2019). 'China's Social Credit Systems and Public Opinion: Explaining High Levels of Approval', *New Media & Society*, 21(7), 1565–1593.

Krips, H. (2018). 'Ideology and its Pleasures: Althusser, Žižek and Pfaller', *Continental Thought & Theory: A Journal of Intellectual Freedom*, 2(1), pp. 333–367.

Krivý, M. (2018). 'Towards a Critique of Cybernetic Urbanism: The Smart City and the Society of Control', *Planning Theory*, 17(1), 8–30.

Kuecker, G. and Hartley, K. (2020). 'How Smart Cities Became the Urban Norm: Power and Knowledge in New Songdo City', *Annals of the American Association of Geographers*, 110(2), 516–524.

Kunzmann, K. (2020). 'Smart Cities after COVID-19: Ten Narratives', *Disp-The Planning Review*, 56(2), 20–31.

Lazzarato, M. (2006). 'The Concepts of Life and the Living in the Societies of Control', in M. Fuglsang and B.M. Sorensen (eds), *Deleuze and the Social*, Edinburgh: Edinburgh University Press, pp. 171–190.

León, L. and Rosen, J. (2020). 'Technology as Ideology in Urban Governance', *Annals of the American Association of Geographers*, 110(2), 497–506.

Luque-Ayala, A. and Marvin, S. (2019). 'Developing a Critical Understanding of Smart Urbanism', in T. Schwanen and R. van Kempen (eds), *Handbook of Urban Geography*, Cheltenham, UK and Northampton, MA, USA: Edward Elgar, pp. 210–224.

Lynch, C. (2020). 'Contesting Digital Futures: Urban Politics, Alternative Economies, and the Movement for Technological Sovereignty in Barcelona', *Antipode*, 52(3), 660–680.

MacDonell, D. (1986). *Theories of Discourse: An Introduction*, New York: Wiley-Blackwell.

Maesse, J. and Nicoletta, G. (2021). 'Economics as Ideological Discourse Practice: a Gramsci-Foucault-Lacan Approach to Analysing Power/knowledge Regimes of Subjectivation', *Journal of Multicultural Discourses*, 16(2), 1–20.

Malette, S. (2009). 'Foucault for the Next Century: Eco-governmentality', in S. Binkley and J. Capetillo (eds), *A Foucault for the 21st Century: Governmentality, Biopolitics and Discipline in the New Millennium*, Newcastle upon Tyne: Cambridge Scholars Publishing, pp. 221–239.

Marcuse, H. (1982 [1941]). 'Some Implications of Modern Technology', in A. Arato and E. Gebhardt (eds), *The Essential Frankfurt School Reader*, New York: Continuum.

Marcuse, H. (1989 [1958–9]). 'From Ontology to Technology: Fundamental Tendencies of Industrial Society', in S.E. Bronner and D. Mackay Kellner (eds), *Critical Theory and Society*, London: Routledge, pp. 54–63.

Marcuse, H. (2013). *Towards a Critical Theory of Society: Collected Papers of Herbert Marcuse, Volume 2*, New York: Routledge.

Martinez, D. (2011). 'Beyond Disciplinary Enclosures: Management Control in the Society of Control', *Critical Perspectives on Accounting*, 22(2), 200–211.

Marvin, S., Luque-Ayala, A., and McFarlane, C. (eds) (2015). *Smart Urbanism: Utopian Vision or False Dawn?*, London and New York: Routledge.

Mattern, S. (2013). Methodolatry and the Art of Measure: The New Wave of Urban Data Science. Design Observer: Places. 5 November 2013. http://designobserver.com/places/feature/0/38174/. Accessed 11 February 2021.

Meerow, S. and Newell, J. (2019). 'Urban Resilience for Whom, What, When, Where, and Why?', *Urban Geography*, 40(3), 309–329.

Morozov, E. (2013). *To Save Everything, Click Here: Technology, Solutionism, and the Urge to Fix Problems that Don't Exist*, New York: Allen Lane.

Miller, J. and Hoel, L. (2002). 'The "Smart Growth" Debate: Best Practices for Urban Transportation Planning', *Socio-Economic Planning Sciences*, 36(1), 1–24.

Mohammadi, M. and Al-Fuqaha, A. (2018) 'Enabling Cognitive Smart Cities Using Big Data and Machine Learning: Approaches and Challenges', *IEEE Communications Magazine*, 56(2), 94–101.

Mohammadzadeh, M. (2014). 'The Neoliberalism City Fantasy: The Place of Desire and Discontent', Doctoral dissertation, ResearchSpace@Auckland.

Mosco, V. (2019). *The Smart City in a Digital World*, Bingley, UK: Emerald Group Publishing.

Negri, A. and Deleuze, G. (1995). 'Control and Becoming', in *Negotiations 1972–1990*, trans. Martin Joughin, New York: Columbia University Press , pp. 169–76.

Nikitas, A., Michalakopoulou, K., Njoya, E. and Karampatzakis, D. (2020). 'Artificial Intelligence, Transport and the Smart City: Definitions and Dimensions of a New Mobility Era', *Sustainability*, 12(7), 1–19.

Pali, B. and Schuilenburg, M. (2019). 'Fear and Fantasy in the Smart City', *Critical Criminology*, 27(14), 1–14.

Patrício, C. (2017). 'Smart Cities and the Re-Invention of the Panopticon', in C. Smaniotto Costa and K. Ioannidis (eds), *The Making of the Mediated Public Space*, Lisbon: Universitarias Lusófonas, pp. 55–64.

Patton, P. (2006). 'Order, Exteriority and Flat Multiplicities in the Social', in M. Fuglsang and B.M. Sorensen (eds), *Deleuze and the Social*, Edinburgh: Edinburgh University Press, pp. 21–38.

Picon, A. (2018). 'Urban Infrastructure, Imagination and Politics: From the Networked Metropolis to the Smart City', *International Journal of Urban and Regional Research*, 42(2), 263–275.

Rawat, D. and Ghafoor, K.Z. (eds) (2018). *Smart Cities Cybersecurity and Privacy*, Cambridge: Elsevier.

Robb, L. and Deane, F. (2021). 'Smart Cities as Panopticon: Highlighting Blockchain's Potential for Smart Cities through Competing Narratives', in B.T. Wang and C.M. Wang (eds), *Automating Cities*, Singapore: Springer, pp. 297–317.

Santilli, P. (2007). '8 Culture, Evil, and Horror', *American Journal of Economics and Sociology*, 66(1), 173–193.

Sarewitz, D. (2020). 'Unknown Knowns', *Issues in Science and Technology*, 37(1), 18–19.

Shearmur, R. and Wachsmuth, D. (2019). 'Urban Technology: The Rise of "The Innovation Machine"', *Plan Canada*, 59(1): 175–179.

Söderström, O., Paasche, T., and Klauser, F. (2014). 'Smart Cities as Corporate Storytelling', *City*, 18(3), 307–320.

Suarez-Villa, L. (2012). *Technocapitalism: A Critical Perspective on Technological Innovation and Corporatism*, Philadelphia: Temple University Press.

Taamallah, A., Khawaja, M., and Faiz, S. (2017). 'Strategy Ontology Construction and Learning: Insights from Smart City Strategies', *International Journal of Knowledge-Based Development*, 8(3), 206–228.

Tabachnick, D.E. (2004). 'Techne, Technology, and Tragedy', *Techné: Research in Philosophy and Technology*, 7(3), 90–111.

Tierney, T. (2019). 'Networked Urbanism: Definition, Scholarship, Directions', in S. Chattopadhyay and J. White (eds), *The Routledge Companion to Critical Approaches to Contemporary Architecture*, New York: Routledge, pp. 270–286.

Townsend, A. (2013). *Smart Cities: Big Data, Civic Hackers, and the Quest for a New Utopia*, New York and London: W.W. Norton & Company.

Trindade, E., Hennig, M., Moreira da Costa, E., Marques, J., Bastos, R., and Yigitcanlar, T. (2017). 'Sustainable Development of Smart Cities: A Systematic Review of the Literature', *Journal of Open Innovation: Technology, Market, and Complexity*, 3(11).

Vanolo, A. (2014). 'Smartmentality: The Smart City as Disciplinary Strategy', *Urban Studies*, 51(5), 883–898.

Vanolo, A. (2016). 'Is There Anybody Out There? The Place and Role of Citizens in Tomorrow's Smart Cities', *Futures*, 82(September), 26–36.

Voordijk, H., and Dorrestijn, S. (2019). 'Smart City Technologies and Figures of Technical Mediation', *Urban Research & Practice*, 14(1), 1–26.

Walters, W. (2006). 'Border/Control', *European Journal of Social Theory*, 9(2), 187–203.

Wiig, A. (2015). 'IBM's Smart City as Technoutopian Policy Mobility', *City*, 19(2–3), 258–273.

Williamson, B. (2015). 'Educating the Smart City: Schooling Smart Citizens Through Computational Urbanism', *Big Data & Society*, 2(2), 1–13.

Yang, F., and Xu, J. (2018). 'Privacy Concerns in China's Smart City Campaign: The Deficit of China's Cybersecurity Law', *Asia & the Pacific Policy Studies*, 5(3), 533–543.

Yavuz, M., Cavusoglu, M., and Corbaci, A. (2018). 'Reinventing Tourism Cities: Examining Technologies, Applications, and City Branding in Leading Smart Cities', *Journal of Global Business Insights*, 3(1), 57–70.

Yigitcanlar, T. (2016). *Technology and the City: Systems, Applications and Implications*, New York: Routledge.

Yigitcanlar, T., Kamruzzaman, M., Buys, L., Ioppolo, G., Sabatini-Marques, J., da Costa, E.M., and Yun, J.J. (2018). 'Understanding "Smart Cities": Intertwining Development Drivers with Desired Outcomes in a Multidimensional Framework', *Cities*, 81(November), 145–160.

Zhang, F. and Wu, F. (2019). 'Rethinking the City and Innovation: A Political-economic View from China's Biotech', *Cities*, 85(February), 150–155.

Žižek, S. (1989). *The Sublime Object of Ideology*, London: Verso.

Žižek, S. (1991). *For They Know Not What They Do*, London: Verso.

Žižek, S. (2006). 'Philosophy, the "Unknown Known," and the Public Use of Reason', *Topi*, 25, 137–142.

Žižek, S. (2008). 'Nature and its Discontents', *SubStance*, 37(3), 37–72.

Žižek, S. (2011). *Living in the End Times*, New York, Verso.

Žižek, S. (2017). *The Courage of Hopelessness: Chronicles of a Year of Acting Dangerously*, London: Penguin UKDT.

22. Power in regulatory planning processes: searching for the third face of power

Yvonne Rydin

INTRODUCTION

The focus of this chapter is the regulatory process within planning systems, that is the point where consent for development is authorized. This is less about anticipating and delineating where development should happen and what form it should take, as with plan-making, and more about responding to specific development proposals when they arise. Regulation takes a variety of forms in different countries according to political ideology, institutional arrangements within the planning profession and government, and the legal system. Rather than detailing this variety, this chapter looks conceptually at the different ways that power can operate through regulation in these varying contexts, seeking to develop a broader framework for understanding power within regulatory processes. It takes a Foucauldian approach, as set out in Lukes' third face of power and is, further, influenced by the material turn in planning studies seeking to understand how socio-material relations generate power.

The first section details this third face of power, thus situating this chapter within the range of contributions in the *Handbook*. It then considers the key question of how regulatory decisions and actions are rendered legitimate, before going on to consider regulation in the context of trends towards governmentality as a mode of governing, and explicitly considering the materiality of regulation. In all these aspects, the power of discursive framing identified by Foucault is apparent. Having set the broader theoretical framework, the chapter then looks at specific ways that power operates through discursive dimensions of regulatory processes considering the role of knowledge and evidence, of classification and categorization, and of silences. It concludes with a consideration of power and inequality in regulatory outcomes and what form options for reform might take.

The approach of this chapter deliberately begins from analysis of the micro-dynamics of regulation, looking at how the details of regulatory practice make a difference. This is not to dismiss more structural approaches that situate regulation within national or even global economic and political dynamics. However, it does seek to demonstrate the value of this more fine-grained approach and to argue that it brings something distinctive and insightful to the analysis.

CONCEPTUALIZING POWER

Lukes first provided his framework for alternative understandings of the concept of power in terms of three faces in 1974, updating this with a fuller consideration of the third face in 2005; this provides a convenient starting point for considering alternative approaches to analyzing power (see also Chapter 3 by Mäntysalo). The first face concerns the overt use of power by one actor to get another actor to do something or refrain from doing something. It is intentional and observable with power vested in the resources that the actor can command. Hence, regulation would be seen as the power that is exercised through the resource of controlling development consent and this resource would vest with lawyers, planners and/or politicians, those who are charged with confirming that development consent has or has not been granted. Furthermore, this power would be exercised over the development proponent. This is a view of regulation that many planners and developers are content to buy into, planners to justify their professional role in exercising power in the public interest and developers and landowners to complain that they are being over-regulated and thus it should be easier to obtain the consent that permits their profit-making activities or enhances the utility and value of their property.

The second face of power covers non-decision-making, as it was termed by Bachrach and Baratz (1962). It looks at the way the power is exercised, again by identifiable actors, in order to control the policy agenda and to keep certain issues off that agenda. So, in the case of planning regulation it might concern what gets regulated and what falls outside regulation, what issues are considered during regulation, and which are not included in decision-making. But – to distinguish it from the third face discussed next – power is here invoked in the process of determining the regulatory agenda. It helps understand the lobbying that goes on, typically at the national scale, about the scope of regulation and the power that different stakeholders exercise in shaping this scope.

For example, recent and ongoing policy changes in England are expanding the scope of permitted development rights, that is development that can occur without the need for explicit planning consent (Clifford, 2022). This is enabling the change of use of premises between business activities and also the conversion of commercial premises such as offices for housing, often producing low-quality homes. A second-face-of-power perspective would look at the way that the actors who benefit from these changes, principally developers and businesses, have pressed central government for them and used various political and governmental connections, possibly through the ruling Conservative Party, to achieve them. It would also look at how the lobbying power of the planning profession was weaker by comparison. However, the second face has less to say about the day-to-date operation of regulation and how power operates through these everyday regulatory practices. This is where the third face comes in.

The Foucauldian basis of the third face is made clearer in Lukes' 2005 edition of *Power*, as is the radically different approach to the exercise of power it puts forward. Power is no longer something that vests with one or more actors and is linked to the resources they control. Rather power is something that is emergent from relationships between actors and is an explanation of how agency occurs. The planner does not exercise power over the developer through the control of granting (or, alternatively, not granting) planning consent in various institutional ways. Rather the planner and the developer (and also other actors such as politicians, landowners and local communities) are connected through sets of relationships that extend before and beyond the regulatory moment, even though they coalesce in that moment. Through studying the connections between these actors, a particular perspective on regulation emerges that has implications for understanding the consenting of development projects.

To be clear, this is not a governance perspective which takes actors and sees them in networks of relationships, mutually using their resources on the basis of acknowledged inter-dependencies (Rhodes, 1997). Rather the emphasis is on the way that change emerges from the multiple connections that actors are enmeshed in and, while these instances of connections exist at particular points in space and time, they are also shaped by flows at different scales and over time. To clarify this in terms of regulatory planning, the moment of regulation involves actors local to the site of the proposed development but also at regional, national and even international scales; these will be across governmental bodies (local, regional and national governments as well as agencies at all these scales), private companies (developers, infrastructure providers, property owners), non-governmental organizations (covering a variety of interest and values) as well as less organized or bounded groups. As the number of such bodies involved in regulation grows, it is not possible to pinpoint the actor–actor connections along which resources flow as a cause of action; rather the collectivity generates such action.

This collective agency arises from the interconnection of various flows between actors, but Lukes' third face follows Foucault in pointing to the particular role of discourse in shaping relationships and hence outcomes (see also Chapter 4 by Pløger). The influence of circulating discourses arises from how they frame the taken-for-granted in everyday intercourse so that routine practices do not get questioned but rather, repeatedly circulating over time, become embedded. These discourses are established as common sense and exercise influence through their widespread acceptance. Those that question such discourses are positioned as outsiders and mavericks; not relevant. In this way, the prevailing norms around what should and should not be considered as relevant to planning regulation does not just derive from a national agenda set by the first and second faces of power but becomes internalized in routinized regulatory practice and accepted as the only way in which to do planning regulation. Power operates through the routinized way that planning regulation occurs and the way that everyday practices reproduce those routines. A developer or their consultant seeking to get development approval, whether through a specific consent or varying a particular ordinance or drawing up a zoning plan, will have regard to the way that this has worked in the past. They will seek to understand the taken-for-granted of regulation and draw up plans and strategies accordingly. The accepted ways of getting consent imply certain relationships being strengthened, certain procedures being followed in specific ways and, above all, certain arguments being made.

Since regulation is about why a development should be permitted to go ahead, about the form in which it should be permitted or the extent to which it complies with existing policies, ordinances and zoning rules, regulatory processes centrally involve the making and assessing of arguments about these issues, a process which involves the use of various resources (such as money, social capital and authority) but is, above all, discursive. An energy infrastructure project is granted consent or not because of the myriad ways in which the energy company, the different layers of government, the nature conservation and environmental protection bodies, consultancies, NGOs (non-governmental organizations) and local residents and companies put forward arguments. Some of these arguments will be ruled irrelevant while others will fit within the accepted framing of regulatory practice. Arguments about impacts on nationally and internationally important natural landscapes will be relevant; those about the impact on this person's livelihood or that person's view of the countryside will not be. Arguments about the contribution to energy security will be relevant; those about alternative energy pathways which might be more sustainable are not. Each planning system will frame the acceptable and the irrelevant in different ways but they are always important in determining regulatory outcomes.

The importance of discourse within regulation is given a further twist by Hajer's idea of a discourse coalition (1995). This suggests that the power of collective groups of actors can operate in different ways. There is the more conventional first-face approach that sees actors come together in coalitions to pool resources and amplify their power, but Hajer also suggests that actors can have their influence on outcomes enhanced through sharing a circulating discourse even if they never meet or strategize together or share resources; in line with the third face of power, it might be better to say that that they collectively benefit from certain outcomes associated with the circulation of a discourse that they articulate. The fact that they are all using a common discourse reinforces the power of that discourse as it circulates and has impacts on outcomes. Thus, say, a common discourse around the importance of supporting economic growth, when shared by developers and planners, has considerable impact on the quantum and pattern of urban development that is permitted with distributional consequences (Rydin, 2013).

The emphasis on discourse is a central example of how power operates in a dispersed way. For here power is emergent from relationships between actors; on specific occasions and in specific places, it is contingent on the particular sets of relationships in those places and at those times. There are flows within society more broadly that enter into these particular sets of relationships and thus operate across specific contingent circumstances. Power is, therefore, dispersed but also ever present. It is part of the flows that exist within societies, that coalesce in particular ways at particular points to generate agency and outcomes. It can never be escaped from and, in one sense, all are oppressed by such power. Planning regulation may comprise repeated instances of these particular points of coalescence but these instances are set within circulating discourses constituting what regulation is and also what it should be. The way that some actors benefit more than others from such dispersed patterns of power operating through regulation is an issue this chapter returns to later, alongside consideration of how resistance to ever-present flows of power is possible.

REGULATION AND LEGITIMACY

If power is ever-present within regulatory processes, how do more or less legitimate regulatory outcomes emerge? Addressing this issue requires attention to the concept of legitimacy but in a regulatory context. The legitimacy of a local plan, which is given considerable attention within planning literature, is different to that of a development consent. Eyal (2019; see also Rydin, 2022) pinpoints the distinctive character of regulation in the way that regulatory practice relates to a particular proposal and that consideration of that proposal is time-limited; a decision needs to be made within a certain time-frame on whether the development should go ahead or not. However, as emphasized above, such consideration of proposals is also repeated over time. Whether a development proposal is considered in depth on a case-by-case basis as in England, or judged against an ordinance for compliance as in United States or is the object of a detailed local plan that constitutes a form of zoning ensuring consent and implementation as in Sweden, these are all practices that, in each case, require closure in terms of a decision or action.

On this basis, Eyal recasts legitimacy in terms of the twin requirements of validity and defensibility. Thus, a legitimate development consent is one that is regarded as valid and can be defended against challenge. The idea of being perceived as valid goes back to the importance of the circulating discourses shaping communication and decisions. But the notion of defensibility points to the opportunities that exist within regulatory systems for formalized challenges to decisions on development consent. A legitimate consent is, therefore, one that will be upheld upon challenge. A planning system would struggle to maintain legitimacy as a whole if development consents (or denials of consent) were repeatedly and successfully challenged.

The specific form in which challenges are permitted and resolved and by whom vary from system to system. In some cases, only the developer can appeal against the refusal of development consent; in others, a third party such as an NGO or local residents can appeal against grant or confirmation of such consent. But the essence of such challenges – and hence of the legitimacy of regulatory planning – is the building up of a consistent set of arguments about valid and invalid challenges, that is a discourse of what counts as a robust basis for regulatory action and is accepted as such. Thus, we have layered discursive networks around regulatory practices in relation to development proposals and also around challenges to those practices. Where there are limited challenges and a strong connection between these layers, then the regulatory system may be considered legitimate; where the challenges escalate or there is a disconnect between the layers, then the legitimacy of the regulatory system may be considered fragile. For example, challenges may come not only from questioning regulatory decisions and actions but also from side-stepping regulation completely. Where there is extensive so-called informal development, this is a challenge to formal regulation. Or, in another example, legitimacy is also in question if the argumentation in support of regulatory practices is not mirrored when challenges are considered but is rather replaced by forms of corruption (exchanging development consent for money or other favours) or by overriding reference to political ideology.

REGULATION AND GOVERNMENTALITY

Another aspect of Foucauldian thinking that has received considerable attention is the idea of governmentality, particularly as developed by Miller and Rose (2006). This suggests a mode of governing offered as an alternative to prevailing ideas of governance in which networks, collaboration, social capital and stakeholder involvement are all given prominence. Again, taking a non-actor-centred approach, governmentality looks at how the framing of governing involves a variety of actors taking on responsibility for the state project of governing through their own actions; this has been termed self-responsibilization (Raco and Imrie, 2000). Here the discourses surrounding governing shift the locus of governing so that citizens, communities and other stakeholders see it as their own role to deliver the project's goals. A key way in which this happens is through the deployment of governmental technologies which can take a variety of forms, although attention has particularly been directed to the use of statistics and other means of constructing information.

Applying this to the situation of planning regulation involves consideration of how the state project of regulating urban development – however this is framed in particular circumstances – is being achieved by non-state actors seeing it as their role to meet the expectations of regulated development and, indeed, other relevant policy objectives. It further suggests a search for the governmental technologies that enable this to happen. We could point here to the internalization of regulatory policies and guidelines so that they are complied with before and even independently of regulatory requirements. Where developers take on board regulatory expectations as a matter of course, not simply as a strategic move in the game of getting planning consent, then there has been self-responsibilization. This might relate to site selection, design features but also the offer of planning gain (a benefit to the wider community) as part of the overall development project.

The question then becomes: what governmental technologies play a role in delivering such outcomes? How do governmental expectations of new developments become widely accepted by developers? We could point here to a wide range of ways in which ideas of best practice are presented and circulated: models, manuals, toolkits, suggested design templates, recommendations for how to achieve certain performance levels, building and development accreditation schemes such as BREEAM (BRE Environmental Assessment Method) and LEED (Leadership in Energy and Environmental Design). Through the widespread use of such artefacts, each with an embedded script about the development, the expectations of planning regulation become entrenched before the regulatory moment occurs. It is, therefore, important to understand the norms of regulation and how they are discussed, replicated and transmitted in forms outside of the formal exchange between development proponent and local planning authority. Building and development certifications have proved to be particularly significant ways in which regulatory expectations and development proposals have been brought into line, through the detailed nature of such schemes with their credits earned, weighted and aggregated by consultant assessors following substantial manuals producing by Green Building Councils or cognate organizations (Sullivan et al. 2014).

These expectations do not just fall on non-state actors though. Where there are expectations of planning regulation that cross scales of government, the idea of governmentality can be used to understand the subtle and dispersed ways in which local planning regulation is aligned to central government agendas through the use of governmental technologies. An example of this is the way in which calculations of development land supply are used in England to direct new urban development to sites that meet market criteria and promote market-led urban change. Here local planning authorities engage, as part of routine practices of plan-making, in calculations of the need for new urban development – particularly housing – and then match this with a selection of sites which engagement with market developers tells them would support viable development. The discourse of land supply (itself a neo-classical economic term) is imbued with assumptions about developers determining market viability for sites and, further, identifying sites themselves that they can readily buy from landowners or already own. In this way, a market-led approach is inherent in the planning discourses around land supply and the specific calculative practices for quantifying that land supply over a given period of time. This aligns local planning practice when allocating and regulating housebuilding with a pro-growth central government planning agenda (Freire Trigo 2022, Rydin 2022, Layard, 2019).

REGULATION AS SOCIO-MATERIAL ASSEMBLAGES

The notion of governmental technologies has already highlighted the role that specific artefacts – capturing best practice for development design or calculations of housing land supply – can play in promoting self-responsibilization within planning regulation. This is only a limited example of the role that artefacts play in planning regulation and of the way that such regulation is materially constituted. This builds on the idea of power within regulation as emergent from relationships between actors to suggest that regulation constitutes a set of socio-material assemblages (DeLanda, 2006). Such an assemblage brings together, in specific situations, not only social actors but also a variety of material features. Among these can be included the materiality of the site, the development and the surrounding environment, the materiality of planning practice in terms of spaces and venues for that practice and the embodied nature of that practice, and the materiality of the numerous artefacts that are involved in planning.

The fact that developments occur in particular places means that the regulation of such development has to take account of the character and features of the site and the locale. This further means that regulation cannot just be a desk-exercise but, at some point, needs to involve planners going out to visit, see, traverse and investigate such sites and locales. For example, in the case of major wind farms in England, regulation falls to a national agency, the Planning Inspectorate who provide one or more inspectors to act as the Examining Authority, considering evidence and making a report to central government on whether development consent should be granted or not and subject to which conditions. A key but often under-appreciated element within this regulatory process is the engagement of the Examining Authority with the site and locale through multiple site visits, both accompanied and unaccompanied. These provide an opportunity for the Examining Authority to assess some of the evidence *in situ* and come to their own judgements, based on their embodied experience of the physicality of the site and local environment (Rydin et al., 2017).

Again, one can consider the materiality of the venues in which regulatory practices play out. These may be planning department offices, local authority council chambers, and town hall meeting rooms. But they may also venture out into settings for stakeholder and community consultation and take place in hotels and conference venues, school halls, community centres, shopping centres, parks and streets. Looked at in detail, it can be seen how the nature of public consultation activities depends, say, on material features of the places in which they take place: the size and shape of the room, the way that flipcharts, pens and models can be deployed in that room, and even the possibilities for engaging over pizza, tea, coffee and biscuits within that space (Rydin and Natarajan, 2015).

These examples relate to the material world through which planners and other key social actors move during the course of regulation, but planning is also an arena in which artefacts circulate, many, many artefacts (Hull, 2012). Within planning regulation, specifically, one can point to the numerous artefacts – virtual, paper, 3D – that are involved in the procedures of determining development consent. To take the English case, a planning application produces and involves engagement with online forms, notices, plans, certificates and documents from the applicant together with reports, minutes, legal agreements and decision notices from the local planning authority and a variety of responses to consultation from government agencies, communities and other stakeholders. There may be maps, designs and physical models as well as virtual simulations of various kinds. The form of these artefacts makes a difference as each has a specific embedded script which suggests how they should be read and how they can contribute to interaction: artefact to social actor and artefact to artefact (Rydin, 2022). In this way, artefacts contribute to the interplay of discourses and shape the relationships both between social actors and with other material aspects of the regulatory assemblage.

Having set out this broader theoretical framework for considering regulation and power from a Foucault-inspired perspective, the next three sections consider specific ways in which discourse shapes the practice of regulation, looking at knowledge, classification or categorization and silences.

KNOWLEDGE AND EVIDENCE-BASED REGULATION

In so far as regulation presents itself as a rational process led and legitimated by evidence about the development project and its likely impacts, then knowledge framed as evidence is centrally important to regulation. Such evidence is a form of knowledge and it is a key tenet of the Foucauldian approach that knowledge and power are inter-connected, even co-constituted. The generation and circulation of confirmed knowledge is a central way that power operates in post-Enlightenment societies. Thus, in seeking to understand power, it is necessary to understand knowledge and this is as true of planning regulation as other societal processes. By referring to 'knowledge framed as evidence', this acknowledges that knowledge is socially constructed (Raco and Savini, 2019). The social construction of knowledge is a process of putting forward knowledge claims and then warranting them so as to selectively recognize some of those claims as knowledge. This process is shaped by prevailing discourses and the institutional arrangements for generating and accrediting knowledge. This can occur within universities, research institutes, government agencies or private companies, as far as generation of knowledge claims is concerned, although accreditation usually has regard to more specific institutions such as academic disciplines, peer review journals and governmental committees and is judged by prevailing scientific criteria (natural, technological, social).

It is now widely acknowledged within planning studies that knowledge does not only reside in accredited forms of expertise but can also arise from a variety of lay or community sources (Rydin, 2007). This means that regulation does not only have regard to evidence from sources arguing that their claims are accredited by accepted scientific standards. It is increasingly asserted within planning practice more broadly that regulation also should consider how local communities or local NGOs should be able to present their lived experience as a form of experiential knowledge and be able to use a variety of media to convey that experiential knowledge. However, it often remains the case that within regulatory instances such knowledge claims are treated with less weight than the more conventional scientifically framed claims. Thus, for example, a sleep or traffic diary completed by local residents will not convince regulators about the noise impacts of a development unless the residents are able to present their evidence in the usual form of accredited knowledge claims, say, a report on decibels measured. And, further, even if the evidence is presented as a report with tables and graphs (rather than anecdotes and stories) and the methodology rendered explicit, then such evidence is subjected to forensic examination on the same terms as the accredited knowledge claims, say, examining how, where and when noise was measured. The local residents have to be prepared to defend their report of their experiential knowledge for it to count fully. This can be difficult for local residents and adversely affects residential communities without access to professional or scientific expertise to support them (and disproportionately benefits those with such access) (Lee et al., 2018).

Producing defensible knowledge can be easier for those local NGOs who have access to more widespread data collection opportunities and possibly more expertise in presenting evidence in standardized and defensible forms. Thus, wildlife NGOs who have conducted comprehensive systematic surveys of green spaces or bird sightings over time may have their evidence treated as more admissible within regulatory deliberations than the more apparently ad hoc information from residents. In addition, the citizen science movement is facilitating local communities in producing evidence in forms that will be admissible in regulatory arenas and carry more weight there than individual representations (Hecker et al., 2018). Here, universities and NGOs work with local residents, providing them with monitoring technology and data-collecting protocols to enable them to record evidence about, say, air pollution that could then influence regulatory action about new industrial developments or road-building schemes.

This is part of a broader shift towards a 'new mode of knowledge production' (Gibbons et al., 1994) in which the so-called users of knowledge are involved in the processes by which that knowledge is generated. This covers the generation of policy-relevant knowledge for policy makers but also the involvement of corporate actors in knowledge they may need in their commercial activities. For planning regulation, this might concern the way that a government ministry or local municipality works with professional planning bodies and a university department or consultancy to produce knowledge about how regulation works, with a view to recommending and making reforms. But it could also cover the involvement of developers and construction companies in co-producing building and development certification schemes, say, for safety, health or sustainability, alongside expert bodies. For example, the production of BREEAM, an internationally-renowned sustainability standard, involves the English BRE (an ex-government agency, now a not-for-profit body that incorporates considerable technical expertise on construction) alongside experts within universities and research institutes. But it also involves companies that will be using BREEAM to assess their developments and, thereby, hoping to ease the path to development consent; BREEAM is often used within planning regulation, at least in England, to establish what counts as a sustainable building.

Contemporary studies of the processes by which knowledge is generated and accredited go beyond the social institutions involved to consider also the socio-materiality of these processes. This is emphasized by Actor-Network Theory (Latour, 2005; Rydin and Tate, 2016), which has been influential in how the analysis of knowledge claims is conducted. Within Actor-Network Theory, knowledge is seen as emergent from relationships that are socio-material, that is the materiality of the world enters into knowledge construction. This emphasizes the materiality of what otherwise appear to be uniquely social processes, of the laboratory, the field site, the modelling software and hardware. But, significantly, it also emphasizes the role of the material world in validating a knowledge claim – or not (Latour, 1999). The materiality of the world resists certain constructions so that not all representations are considered equally valid or defensible. Data about the material world is typically collected to assess different constructions of knowledge but there are multiple ways in which that materiality can be represented through 'data' and considerable uncertainties in judging how far a certain representation is acceptable. Scientists may point to the uncertainties inherent in the statistics; lay people may point to the discrepancies with lived experience. These views of the academy and the community may be in tension or complement each other. The processes by which challenges to specific knowledge claims are addressed and then settled are part of the social construction of legitimate knowledge claims and some of this occurs within regulatory processes.

In regulation, the consenting process depends on an assessment of knowledge claims put forward about the site, the development and the project's impacts. This is central to the idea that the regulatory act is not corrupt or politically motivated but rather a response to information or evidence. Some knowledge claims are institutionalized as a particular form of assessment, such as Environment Impact Assessment or Health Impact Assessment or Landscape Character Assessment. The artefacts representing the consolidation of knowledge claims from such assessments can be important reference points in regulation. They may be used as valid support for the decision or judgement about consent, but they can also become key points of debate within regulation, particularly where the project is large or complex or is debated in a public arena with the involvement of multiple stakeholders. In such cases, attention can be focused on knowledge that has been black boxed (Rydin, 2019).

Black boxing refers to a process whereby the detail of how a particular knowledge claim is generated remains hidden and the emphasis falls onto the outputs, the key conclusions or determined facts. Thus, in the regulation of wind farms the likely impact of turbines on bird population is a key issue that may affect the granting of consent. This impact is in the future and inherently uncertain but considerable efforts have been made by university academics, consultancies and government agencies such as Natural England to model this. Modelling is complicated because the dynamics by which birds are killed by turbines is not fully understood, particularly when one is considering specific bird species given that different species behave differently. So, this phenomenon of bird strike is modelled using available (and partial) data and the results – in terms of likely numbers of birds killed per annum and impact on overall bird population for different species – are presented as inputs into regulatory discussions. Modelling evidence may be presented by the developer and other parties; different models may produce different results or similar results using different assumptions and algorithms. The emphasis, though, is on the outcomes of modelling, the summary results. Some stakeholders, such as communities and NGOs, may seek to extend the debate, to open up the black box and debate how these knowledge claims are derived in more detail, questioning the reliance on such outputs.

However, opening up the black boxes of knowledge within regulatory contexts can be problematic. This is due to the time-limited nature of regulation. While the timescale for resolving debates about such knowledge claims within the academy will be extensive (usually years), the demands of planning regulation require a resolution within a period of weeks and months at the most. This suggests that resolution cannot arise from additional research or movement towards a scientific consensus according to the peer-reviewed criteria of acceptable scientific knowledge. Rather, as Jasanoff (2004) argues, regulatory processes present a different benchmark for acceptable knowledge; the knowledge claim needs to be sufficiently robust for the regulatory purpose but does not need to meet the more extended requirements for peer-reviewed scientific knowledge. This often keeps the black box closed, without attention to the details of how knowledge was generated, a closure that is itself powerful.

CLASSIFICATION AND CATEGORIZATION

The time-limited nature of regulation together with the involvement of multiple stakeholders, often in different organizations, results in another feature, namely the search for simplification of the complexities of a development proposal occurring in a particular location. If the details of the development, the location and/or the impacts can be so simplified then this reduces the pressures of time on regulation. A key way in which such simplification occurs is through the discursive act of putting the development, the site and/or the impacts into a category or classification. For example, in the English planning system land uses are put into use classes and then planning regulation is linked to those classes. Some shifts between classes require regulatory decision; others do not. Currently it has been part of the Conservative central government agenda to reduce the need for explicit planning consent by allowing buildings to move between certain use classes or by creating new broader use classes. This opens up the possibility for businesses or occupiers to change activity and for developers to re-purpose premises for a different use; the use of revised classification systems carries with it agency and hence power.

Categories are also used for protection of sites from development on the basis of historic heritage, archaeological remains, culturally significant monuments or edifices, landscape value and many kinds of nature conservation rationale. These sites can vary from one building and its curtilage to large areas covering many hectares. In each case, the value of the building or site or wider environmental context will have been justified by a prior assessment and then captured in a line or shading on a map and an associated descriptor indicating the degree of value and hence the degree of desired protection from urban development proposals. Many such assessments are longer-term, established at one point in time to guide plan-making and regulatory activity going forward. Thus, in England, planners can look to mappings of Conservation Areas, Listed Buildings, Local Nature Reserves, National Nature Reserves, Areas of Outstanding Natural Beauty, and many other categories to guide regulatory decision-making. Either these designations denote that certain kinds of development should not occur within these boundaries or they suggest specific requirements for how planning regulation should be conducted, suggesting mitigation measures for the impacts of development or restrictions on the form of that development. This will impact on the relationships between actors within the regulatory moment and how power emerges through those relationships.

Such classification and categorizations may also be generated as part of the development proposal and the regulation of that development proposal. Thus, a landscape assessment of a local authority area can form part of the consideration of a development proposal which might impact on that local landscape. The developer, their consultant or the planning authority could use this to identify the places and locations that are at higher or lower risk of negative impact from that development and then argue the overall merits of the project on this basis. Mitigation measures could be suggested, debated and/or required on the basis of such categorizations. For example, if the development of an energy centre is visible from a categorized area of landscape value then the extent of visibility or impact will be considered and tree-planting may be suggested to reduce that impact. If the categorization of landscape value is at the lower end of the spectrum used, this may count in favour of the development on regulation; while if the landscape value is categorized as high, this may count against it. In all these cases, there is no need to further question the value of the landscape; that has been established by the classification and attention can turn to whether development is permissible and/or whether mitigation measures are required. The classificatory artefact becomes a governmental technology, shaping interactions and outcomes in certain directions. It, therefore, becomes important to understand the detail of such classification to understand how power flows through planning regulation.

As well as guiding and easing regulation by simplifying the assessment of the site, the development and/or the impacts to a category, these classifications also enable these assessments to circulate more readily between different stakeholders and organizations involved in the regulatory process. The original justifications for declaring a set of roads and buildings as a conservation area or deciding that a particular river and its river banks forms a local nature reserve do not need to circulate among all actors. This means that these justifications do not need to be made legible for all these actors in their different contexts. Rather – as with black-boxed evidence – the emphasis is on the summary outcomes, the classifications, the categorizations, and the associated designations. All organizations and stakeholders involved

in the regulatory process can appreciate the implications of such categorizations and classifications even if they do not fully understand how they were arrived at.

The term given to an artefact that circulates in this way among actors and organizations is
a boundary object. Originally coined to analyse the circulation of knowledge about biological
taxonomies in museum contexts (Bowker and Star, 1999), this term is useful in discussing regulation where many actors are involved and may need to either jointly discuss an assessment of
a site or project or wish to contest each other's assessment of said site or project. The boundary
object becomes the medium for carrying summary judgements made during the regulatory
process from actor to actor for confirmation or for challenge. Insofar as the classifications and
categorizations carry legitimacy (i.e. are considered valid and defensible), then they become
a shorthand for discussion and debate within regulatory arenas. If they are challenged for their
legitimacy, the black box of the classificatory system and of the categorization process is then
potentially opened up for re-examination. However, the time involved in such challenges may
lead to resistance to such re-examination and a strong rationale for reinforcing the legitimacy
of these boundary objects and the classification and categorizations that they carry within their
scripts.

This emphasizes again how artefacts – here boundary objects carrying classifications across
organizations and between actors – are implicated in the relationships of planning regulation
and, thus, how they shape outcomes. These artefacts are implicated in agency within planning
regulation and are thus powerful in specific circumstances.

THE ROLE OF SILENCES

One final key aspect of planning regulation to consider is the exclusion of things. While the
planning profession prides itself on an ability to synthesize knowledge of many different
issues that shape urban change and consider a wide range of different aspects of specific development proposals within regulation, being completely comprehensive is not possible. There
are cognitive limits to taking on board additional factors and, within the time-constrained
settings of regulatory actions, there are also pragmatic limits as to what can be considered. In
addition, regulation within a planning system reflects the political and ideological agendas of
that planning system and this will result in the prioritization of some issues over others. For
these reasons, it is important to be alert to the silences within planning regulation as within
planning more broadly (Davoudi et al. 2020).

Silence is a way of diverting attention away from certain actors, issues and solutions and
towards others. It can, therefore, be a powerful way of structuring regulation. It is a form of
non-decision making but operates through the third face of power, not from the pressure from
one or more actor(s) to keep something off the planning regulation agenda. It is part of the
DNA of regulatory practice itself. It is inevitable that regulatory attention will be partial but
the way in which attention is directed has significant impacts. If decisions around housing
development do not consider the social groups that will get access to that housing, the tenure
of that housing and the price or rents that it will be offered at, then these are powerful silences.
It means that opportunities to contain and direct market-led development may be missed and
the ability of a planning system to generate more housing that meets the needs of particular
social groups will be limited. Or, in another example, if the carbon emissions associated with
a development proposal are not identified and counted (activating a governmental technology

here), then they cannot influence regulatory outcomes with powerful implications for environmental sustainability. Requiring a life-cycle assessment or embodied carbon account means that this becomes an issue for consideration within regulatory deliberations; it may not always result in a different regulatory decision but it raises that as a possibility.

In this way, the presence and use of governmental technologies as artefacts, the classifications and black-boxed outputs that they generate, represent and justify, and the silences that arise from the patterns of such use are significant within the socio-material assemblages of regulation and the micro-practices that activate such assemblages. Thus, they carry power through the relations of the assemblage as enacted through regulatory practices.

IMPACTS, INEQUALITIES AND AVENUES FOR REGULATORY REFORM

The idea of dispersed power operating through socio-material assemblages of planning regulation can help explain why certain outcomes occur in specific cases. It can unearth the more hidden, silent and taken-for-granted aspects of regulatory practice and highlight the role they play – in conjunction with other elements of the assemblage – in producing these outcomes. This approach lends itself to in-depth analysis of specific cases, looking beyond the surface story of discourses that can be readily heard to understand the implications of those discourses and the way that the circulation of artefacts within regulatory processes shapes discourses, silences and outcomes.

Adopting a dispersed view of power does not mean acceptance of the idea that all are equally oppressed by the operation of that power. Clearly there are significant inequalities involved in urban development and the way that dispersed power generates outcomes is implicated in these inequalities. It does, however, become more difficult to pinpoint specific actors as responsible for those inequalities. Rather there are a number of relationships through which power flows and that come together to generate these outcomes, relationships between social actors but also involving non-social elements. Each case of regulation needs to be understood in terms of the specific sets of relationships involved; after that, repeated patterns of relationships and outcomes across regulation cases can be identified. The repeated outcomes will show the inequalities that are associated with regulatory processes. They are likely to point to more embedded relationships. They can show how the discourses, silence, knowledge claims, and modes of classification *inter alia* shape socio-material relationships so as to systematically privilege some actors and disadvantage others.

The relevance of this perspective for reform of regulation is that it does not pick out powerful and less powerful actors and seek to address inequality through redistributing resources. Rather it suggests an attention to the detailed use of language within regulation and the specific form and function of artefacts (Rydin, 2022). It suggests that positive reforms may be achieved by considering how the black boxes of accepted knowledge claims can be challenged and on what bases, and how other forms of knowledge can become accepted. It looks to challenge of classifications or categorization that may be implicated in unequal outcomes and it proposes attention to the silences that focus attention within regulation in particular ways, with consideration of how unrecognized issues could come to the fore within regulation. Furthermore, it suggests that new forms and types of artefact within planning regulation could restructure relations of power by introducing new discourses and knowledge claims and shaping the detail of how legitimate decisions are taken within planning regulation and how agency emerges within the consenting of development. Such reform needs to look for the small entry points into the socio-material assemblages of regulation to disrupt existing, repeated patterns and general new patterns of power with different outcomes.

This may seem less attractive than identifying powerful actors who can be rendered less powerful and looking to structural changes, say through national policy and legislation. It is indeed more challenging to change planning regulation through multiple points of entry to prevailing practices, artefacts and situation-contingent sets of relationships. However, without such attention, apparently easier ways to achieve change may be subverted by the ongoing flows of power around regulatory practices and institutions and for this reason, these flows demand our attention.

REFERENCES

Bachrach, P. and M.S. Baratz (1962), 'Two Faces of Power', *The American Political Science Review* 56 (4), 71–95.

Bowker, G. and S.L. Star (1999), *Sorting Things Out: Classification and its Consequences*, Cambridge, MA and London: MIT Press.

Clifford, B. (2022), 'Planning Deregulation, Material Impacts and Everyday Practices: The Case of Permitted Development in England', in Y. Rydin, R. Beauregard, M. Cremaschi and L. Lieto (eds), *Regulation and Planning: Practices, Institutions, Agency*, New York: Routledge.

Davoudi, S., D. Galland and D. Stead (2020). 'Reinventing Planning and Planners: Ideological Decontestations and Rhetorical Appeals', *Planning Theory* 19 (1), 17–37.

DeLanda, M. (2006), *A New Philosophy of Society: Assemblage Theory and Social Complexity*, London: Continuum.

Eyal, G. (2019), *The Crisis of Expertise*, Cambridge: Polity Press.

Freire Trigo, S. (2022), 'Creating Land through the Regulatory Process. The Case of Brownfield Land in England', in Y. Rydin, R. Beauregard, M. Cremaschi and L. Lieto (eds), *Regulation and Planning: Practice, Institutions, Materiality*, New York: Routledge.

Gibbons, M., C. Limoges, H. Nowotny, S. Schwartzman, P. Scott and M. Trow (1994), *The New Production of Knowledge: The Dynamics of Science and Research in Contemporary Societies*, London: Sage Publications.

Hajer, M.A. (1995), *The Politics of Environmental Discourse: Ecological Modernization and the Policy Process*, Oxford: Clarendon Press.

Hecker, S., M.E. Haklay, A. Bowser, Z. Makuch, J. Vogel and A. Bonn (2018), *Citizen Science*, London: UCL Press.

Hull, M. (2012), *Government of Paper: The Materiality of Bureaucracy in Urban Pakistan*, Berkeley, CA: University of California Press.

Jasanoff, S. (ed.) (2004), *States of Knowledge: The Co-Production of Science and Social Order*, London and New York: Routledge.

Latour, B. (1999), *Pandora's Hope: Essays on the Reality of Science Studies*, Cambridge, MA: Harvard University Press.

Latour, B. (2005) *Reassembling the Social: An Introduction to Actor-Network-Theory*, Oxford: Oxford University Press.

Layard, A. (2019), 'Planning by Numbers: Affordable Housing and Viability in England', in M. Raco and F. Savini (eds), *Planning and Knowledge: How New Forms of Technocracy Are Shaping Contemporary Cities*, Bristol: Policy Press, pp. 213–224.

Lee, M., L. Natarajan, S. Lock and Y. Rydin (2018), 'Techniques of Knowing in Administration: Co-production, Models, and Conservation', *Journal of Law and Society* 45 (3), 427–456.

Lukes, S. (1974), *Power: A Radical View*, London: Macmillan.

Lukes, S. (2005), *Power: A Radical View*, 2nd edn, Basingstoke, UK: Palgrave Macmillan.

Miller, P. and N. Rose (2006), 'Governing Economic Life', *Economy and Society* 19 (1), 1–31.

Raco, M. and R. Imrie (2000), 'Governmentality and Rights and Responsibilities in Urban Policy', *Environment and Planning A* 32 (12), 2187–2204.

Raco, M. and F. Savini (eds), *Planning and Knowledge: How New Forms of Technocracy Are Shaping Contemporary Cities*, Bristol: Policy Press.

Rhodes, R.A.W. (1997), *Understanding Governance: Policy Networks, Governance, Reflexivity and Accountability*, Maidenhead, UK: Open University Press.

Rydin, Y. (2007). 'Re-examining the Role of Knowledge within Planning Theory', *Planning Theory* 6 (1), 52–68.

Rydin, Y. (2013), *The Future of Planning*, Bristol: Policy Press.

Rydin, Y. (2019), 'Silences, Categories and Black-boxes: Towards an Analytics of the Relations of Power in Planning Regulation', *Planning Theory* 19 (2), 214–233.

Rydin, Y. (2022), 'Artefacts in Dialogue: Regulatory Planning and the Search for Legitimacy', in Y. Rydin, R. Beauregard, M. Cremaschi and L. Lieto (eds), *Regulation and Planning: Practice, Institutions, Materiality*, New York: Routledge.

Rydin, Y. and L. Natarajan (2015), 'The Materiality of Public Participation: The Case of Community Consultation on Spatial Planning for North Northamptonshire, England', *Local Environment* 21 (10), 1243–1251.

Rydin, Y. and L. Tate (eds) (2016), *Actor Networks of Planning: Exploring the Influence of ANT*, Abingdon, UK and New York: Routledge.

Rydin, Y., L. Natarajan, M. Lee and S. Lock (2017), 'Artefacts, the Gaze and Sensory Experience: Mediating Local Environments in the Planning Regulation of Major Renewable Energy Infrastructure in England and Wales', in M. Kurath, J. Ruegg, J. Paulos and M. Marskamp (eds), *Rethinking Planning: Tracing Artefacts, Agency and Practice*, Basingstoke, UK: Palgrave.

Sullivan, L.J., Y. Rydin, C. Buchanan and J. Twigg (2014), 'Neighbourhood Sustainability Frameworks – A Literature Review', USAR Working Papers 001, London, UK: Centre for Urban Sustainability and Resilience, UCL.

23. Power of, on and in planning

Kristof Van Assche, Raoul Beunen and Martijn Duineveld

INTRODUCTION

Power is a topic that has gained a fair amount of traction in planning literature. The importance of power is reflected in the literature that foregrounds the political character of planning practices (Flyvbjerg, 1998b; Swyngedouw et al., 2002), in writings on planning managing conflicting interests and perspectives (Pløger, 2004, 2021; Gunder and Hillier, 2009; Hillier, 2002), and in work on the possibilities and limits for planners to make a difference (Buchan et al., 2019; Grange, 2012; Miraftab, 2009). Power is conceptualised and analysed in many ways, as there are conflicting discourses on power, and because those conflicts are part of ongoing strategising for a dominant position of specific perspectives and approaches in planning theory.

The work of Michel Foucault, who explicitly focused on power relations and the functions of expertise in society and governance, figured most prominently in the thinking of the power theorists in planning since the 1990s (Foucault, 1970, 1975, 1980). The Foucauldian ideas of power fundamentally differ from traditional approaches that revolve around a privileged access to truth, because of the underlying idea of a social, discursive, construction of reality. Still, the older, traditional approaches linger on, visible in a search for science-based forms of planning that claim to offer generalisable approaches and solutions to practical problems (Hillier, 2002). The Foucauldian angle is also different from approaches that attribute power to specific actors and understand it as something that is or can be possessed. Rather it stresses the relational nature of power and the entanglement with knowledge, as in configurations of power/knowledge that Foucault labelled discourses. Furthermore it stresses that power should not be seen a-priori in a negative light, as for Foucault power is a productive force that shapes and is nested in social structures, discourses, knowledge, subjects and so on (Van Assche et al., 2017; see also Chapter 4 by Pløger).

Planning in the Foucault-inspired perspective is inherently political, implying that planning can no longer present itself as a value-neutral and/or scientific endeavour (Flyvbjerg, 1998a). Planning operates in an evolving governance context, with contested and shifting forms of state power, shifting expectations about how planning should be organised, and about what it can contribute (Beunen et al., 2015; Van Assche, Beunen, et al., 2014). All these aspects are influenced by power dynamics within a society and itself constitutive of the power of planning (Gunder and Hillier, 2009; Hajer, 1995; Hillier, 2002). Planning takes place in a fragmented society, marked by networks mixing state and non-state actors, and all of these can use or oppose planning (Booher and Innes, 2002; Marquardt, 2017; Munro, 2000; Rydin, 2010). Power and knowledge are intimately entwined in any institutionalised form of planning. They influence each step of the planning process, from the definition of issues, actors and procedures to the forms of reinterpretation in implementation, and the strategic uses of maintenance and neglect (Ferguson, 1994; Gunder, 2010; Scott, 1998; Van Assche, Verschraegen, et al., 2021a).

To deepen our understanding of the mutual relations between planning and power we present a framework for analysing the positionality of planning and power in an evolving governance context. We therefore distinguish power in planning and power of planning, and we connect the steering attempts of planning with its attempts to know itself and the world it aspires to intervene in (Peters, 2017; Pløger, 2021; Van Assche, Verschraegen, et al., 2021b). We also pay attention to the influence of society on planning, on planning systems and practices, and speak there of power on planning. Power of planning, we will argue, cannot be understood without reference to power on planning and power in planning, and power in all these forms can only be comprehended as interwoven with knowledge, as part of ever-changing power/knowledge configurations.

POWER AND CONTINGENCY

In the further elaboration on the relations between planning and power, we start from a broad definition of planning as the coordination of policies and practices affecting spatial organisation (Van Assche and Verschraegen, 2008). This definition enables us to look at a wide variety of planning perspectives, practices, and aspirations. Planning is thus not limited to a specific sector, discipline, or administration that is labelled 'planning', but it is a system that is constituted by an ever-changing set of coordinated actions by a diversity of actors.

Power is, at this initial stage of definition, and in line with much of the Foucauldian-inspired planning literature, conceptualised as something that is always present and consists of 'relations that exist at different levels, in different forms; … power relations are mobile, they can be modified, they are not fixed once and for all' (Foucault, 1997: 291–292). It should be understood 'as the multiplicity of force relations immanent in the sphere in which they operate and which constitute their own organisation; as the process which, through ceaseless struggles and confrontations, transforms, strengthens, or reverses them; as the support which these force relations find one other, thus forming a chain or a system, or on the contrary, the disjunctions and contradictions which isolate them from one another' (Foucault, 1998: 92). Power produces some discourses, realities, knowledge, subjects, objects and values, and pushes others into the background (Foucault, 1998: 81–102; see also Foucault, 1994).

Leaning on the work of Alain Pottage (1998), who combined in novel ways the work of Deleuze, Luhmann, Foucault and Latour in power analysis, and also leaning directly on Luhmann, Deleuze and Foucault, we emphasise the potential role of contingency as a cornerstone concept of a theory of power and planning. Contingency brings attention to the ways in which elements and structures emerge from ongoing social processes. 'In place of ontological substances and structures, "emergence" deals instead with structures, processes and theories that produce themselves out of their own contingency' (Pottage, 1998: 3). Within such a perspective reality consists of events. Over time, recursive repetition of events leads to new structures, with both elements and structures, both objects and subjects, to be considered products of transformation and starting points for further transformation (Pottage, 1998, 2004). This bring the perspective close to Deleuze's concept of the fold (Deleuze, 1993), Lacan's idea of a gap (Žižek, 2003, 2012), or Luhmann's differentiation and de-paradoxification (Luhmann, 1989, 1995, 2012), as the creation of discontinuities that need continuous reproduction to stabilise temporarily. The focus on recurring sets of events or communications creates an evolutionary understanding of social systems, in which power is a driving force.

This theory of contingency, of emergent elements and processes furthers Foucault's notions of power and that allows a conceptualisation of power that is 'clearly and unequivocally distinguished from "sovereign" or "repressive" power' (Pottage, 1998: 25). Power can have two distinct meanings in this conceptualisation. First of all, it is the fuel of the universe and second as the potentiality emerging in relations between individuals and structures. In this perspective, Foucault's (1994: 238) later assertion that 'power comes from power', and his argument that power always exists in a relation, appears more meaningful. Power in process, is power that needs to be reproduced in a recursive manner, from one event to the next one. It allows seeing power as a relational effect and brings attention to the performative effects of particular attribution of power to objects or subjects (cf. Allen, 2003; Kooij, 2014; Van Dam et al., 2015). It also allows for understanding the performative effects of post-event ascriptions, the inextricable relationship between decisions made and the understandings of the world on which they rely, and the different ways in which path-, inter- and goal dependencies influence the course of events (Van Assche, Beunen, et al., 2014). This idea of contingency relates to the ways in which societies deal with chance and risk in order to gain control over the course of events (Hacking, 1990; Luhmann, 1989). Such a perspective is gaining ground in complexity theories and is used to put forward novel insights in the working, effects and limitations of steering attempts in disciplines like economics, law, and public administration (MacKenzie et al., 2007; Teubner, 1989; Walker et al., 2008).

The concept of contingency also draws attention to the emergent and ever-changing character of a planning system in relation to its environments (Van Assche, Beunen, et al., 2014). Structures and elements, subjects and objects, in planning and governance all evolve in a manner that relies on power (Foucault, 1975, 1976, 1994). In policy and planning, this entails that it is precisely in the continuous interaction between objects and subjects, between elements and structures, between discourses and materialities, that realities are changing (Jentoft, 2017; Oliveira and Hersperger, 2018). Materiality plays an important role in planning, but what matters most is how that materiality is understood in social systems, or more particularly the discourses that constitute these social systems (Van Assche et al., 2017). We stress that neither Foucault nor Luhmann, although both radical constructivists, would argue that there is nothing outside the text. It is only that almost everything people understand is discursively structured, and it is this discursively structured understanding that drives the organisation of societies and the evolution of governance. Such evolutionary understanding, that highlights the notion of contingency, gives a sharper delineation of the positionality of planning in society and of the possibilities and limitations to influence that society from a certain position.

POWER IN, ON AND OF PLANNING

For the further elaboration of power and planning we distinguish three foci of attention: power in planning, power on planning, and power of planning. Power in planning refers to the mechanisms of power that mark the planning system itself. Understanding power in planning is about understanding the relations in the planning system. Power on planning refers to the influence of broader society on the relations in the planning system. Power of planning refers to the impacts of planning discourses and planning practices on society and its physical environment. This impact can entail literal implementation and partial implementation, but also includes various political, economic, social and cultural effects. For each focus point, we will highlight contributions from different lines of research to the understanding of each relation.

Power in Planning

Within the context of planning, power relations define the strategic interactions between actors, as well as the definition of actors, issues, realities, problems, methods and solutions (cf. Ferguson, 1994; Hillier, 2002). Power is omnipresent in the construction of possible and desirable futures in the planning system. It is reflected in micro- and macro-relations, strategies, tactics, institutions, knowledge, and in the framing of what is real, possible and desirable (Gunder and Hillier, 2009).

The planning system needs an image of the outside world to operate on, as well as tools to implement decisions, plans, and policies in that outside world. This image is always a reduction of the complexity of the outside world. Complexity theory (e.g. Beunen and Van Assche, 2013; Chettiparamb, 2006; De Roo and Silva, 2010; Innes and Booher, 2010) and social systems theory (e.g. Valentinov, 2014; Van Assche and Verschraegen, 2008) argue that this reduction of complexity enables the planning system to reproduce itself and to interact with society at large, while at the same time it obscures many features of that larger reality. This is similar to Foucault's observation that the selectivity of discourse at once opens up reality and closes alternative interpretations (Foucault, 1969, 1975). Internal complexity is needed to accommodate a model of the outside world that is subtle enough to operate upon, but on the other hand, an established model becomes quickly entrenched and easily obscures alternative planning options and strategies (Luhmann, 1990).

In other words the focusing of attention creates a grip on the world but in the long run, by necessarily closing off other understandings (and their institutionalisation), the trade-offs can be less understanding, and effective steering and control (c.f. Alvesson and Spicer, 2016; Latour, 1996). Society, and hence planning systems, are thus constituted in the confrontations between different versions of the world (c.f. Peters, 2017; Peters and Pierre, 2019). Power shapes and reflects these confrontations, and ongoing power dynamics influence which perspectives and views become dominant and which remain marginalised (Brownill and Bradley, 2017; Pløger, 2021; Sarmiento and Tilly, 2018). This is what Chantal Mouffe (2000, 2005) has referred to as the 'political', something which she distinguishes from 'politics' to show that 'political' is an inextricable part of the world, while 'politics' refers to way in which we deal with this. It is useful to make this distinction in order to understand that 'conflict between different interests, values, and norms is inescapable' and should be seen as a productive force in the processes of planning (Pløger, 2004: 87).

Power on Planning

The external influences on the planning system cannot be discussed without reference to its internal mechanics. If one tries to grasp the array of influences of society at large on the planning system, and consider the multiplicity of potential relations between planning and society, it makes sense to draw on theories giving importance to complexity and evolution, such as institutional economics, social systems theory and Evolutionary Governance Theory (Beunen et al., 2015; Van Assche, Beunen, et al., 2014). Again, it is important to stress that planning here should be understood broadly as the coordination of policies and practices affecting spatial organisation and certainly not be limited to planning as a governmental domain.

Planning requires a level of complexity that is not only capable of producing somewhat predictable effects, but also of stabilising itself for a while. Institutionalisation and the formation of dedicated governmental organisations could contribute to that stabilisation, and this could take place under the label 'planning' or by many different other names (Cleaver and Whaley, 2018; Sarmiento and Tilly, 2018). It is furthermore very possible that a planning department is only assigned very specific tasks, while other departments play a pivotal role in the discussions about spatial developments. The power on planning can never be fully grasped if one limits the study to the department or professionals bearing the label planning.

Just as important is a thorough understanding of the temporal dimension (Pierson, 2004; Van Assche, Beunen, et al., 2014). The evolution of planning systems is ongoing and the power on planning is an important mechanism in that evolution. Actors in the planning system, as well as the role of planning in society and the role of government in society will keep changing (Gunder and Hillier, 2009). This irrevocably changes the effects of society on planning, but also the effects of planning in society. Disappointments in society with particular forms of planning, or with a political party, with an ideology, with a certain lifestyle tied to images of collective identity, or events that are felt as traumatic and pasts that are reinterpreted, can all cause shifts in the planning system and the position of planning in society, and thus affect the dynamics of power there (Brownill and Bradley, 2017; Friedmann, 1971; Gunder, 2010; Peters and Pierre, 2019; Wildavsky, 1979).

Here one could refer to the more recent planning reforms that take place in various Western European countries (Allmendinger and Haughton, 2013; Niedziałkowski and Beunen, 2019; Olesen and Carter, 2018). These reforms reflect shifts in the political landscape in which parties favouring smaller government and market-based solutions gain prominence. A significant part of the legitimation of the reforms came from discourses in which planning was characterised as a bureaucratic obstacle for economic development or even sustainability transitions (Allmendinger, 2016; Broto and Westman, 2019). These reforms had a profound effect on the organisation of planning, on the roles and responsibilities of planning organisations, on the expertise that is considered relevant, and hence the form of planning that is possible (Metzger et al., 2014; Sager, 2020). Interestingly the reforms often created a planning system that to a much greater degree reflects the negative image put forward to legitimise reforms, limited to procedural checks and balances, with few possibilities for more creative forms of design, and much more dependent on private parties such as real estate developers in the implementation of plans (Lennon and Moore, 2019). A consequence of these reforms is a significant loss of planning powers due to deregulation and loss of planning possibilities and planning systems even more susceptible to critiques: a negative spiral that is difficult to breach.

Shifts in planning also have direct implications for the types of knowledge that play out in the internal games of the planning system. Each form of planning is interwoven with particular discourses and specific forms of knowledge. If planning is seen as a scientific endeavour, based on empirical studies of the socio-material environment, this requires different expertise than focusing only on stakeholders' processes or legal procedures. Actors within the planning system identify with certain discourses, either scientific or otherwise, and in other cases they deploy these discourses to maintain or improve their position in the system (see for example Hoch, 1992; Friedmann, 1998, 2008). Changes in society directly or indirectly affect the forms of knowledge that can play out within the planning system, either adopted by actors in the system, or by adding and removing actors (Gunder, 2010; Hardy, 1991; Kiernan, 1983).

Power of Planning

As noted above, the power of planning in society, as in the effects of planning in society, must be considered to be extremely varied. The assessment of these effects cannot be reduced to a set of categories produced within the planning system (Allen and Cochrane, 2010; McFarlane, 2009). To understand the impact of planning in society, it is useful to remember that although the overt function of planning is coordination, the success of planning hinges on the dissemination of its articulations in society, that is: the distribution and acceptance of concepts, strategies, forms, and materialities (Oosterlynck et al., 2010; Van Assche et al., 2012; Van Wymeersch et al., 2020). Hence Luhmann's (1997) famous assertion that planning is possible if people are used to being planned.

'Steering' and 'implementation' look different in this unfolding perspective. Our integrated perspective helps in establishing a middle ground between cynical apprehension of steering attempts and blind belief in the possibilities of steering (Allmendinger, 2016; Van Assche et al., 2020; Van Assche, Verschraegen, et al., 2021b). Indeed, actions can have effects that are predictable to a certain degree, but an interpretation of effects as results of steering remains just that: an interpretation (Luhmann, 1990) (Luhmann, 1995). Power in this sense, as Grange (2012), drawing on Dryberg, has argued, should be understood as that which authorises the retroactive construction of the ability, authority or identity to plan, as if this was a presupposed capacity, possible to posit in the subject (see also Allen, 2003; and Seidl's 2016 argument on organisational strategy).

A further reduction of steering ideology into one concept of 'implementation' only makes it more difficult to observe the process of linkages between players, objects, and knowledges that can produce effects (Ferguson, 1994; Scott, 1998; Wildavsky, 1979). A related ideology, compounding the opacity, is that of politics (and planning as a helper) as the centre of society, enabling it to have a full and 'objective' overview of society and public interests, improving its changes to successfully intervene in society (Deleuze and Guattari, 1987; Luhmann, 1990). Thus, some assumptions of steering, implementation and politics, compound to veil the view of the functioning of the assemblages from within. This combination of machining and veiling the machining is a classic trope of post-structuralism but can appear now as grounded in a more generally applicable theory of power, and the link with distributed agency makes a balanced reassessment of steering in planning easier.

Lacanian-inspired research in planning (Gunder and Hillier, 2007; Hillier and Gunder, 2005; Wood, 2009) and beyond (Žižek, 2003, 2004, 2012) can help us to grasp why these steering ideologies persist and why they inspired successive phases of overconfidence and lack of confidence in the power of planning (c.f. Metzger et al., 2014; Sager, 2020). The imaginaries of planners, the planning community, and the community at large can resonate in patterns that are hard to predict, with different desires competing, sometimes attenuating, sometimes magnifying each other (Hillier, 2017). Yet, if planners consider this, there is still a danger of assuming that what makes the planner more powerful is good for the community, so strategies to advocate for more planning are considered legitimate in advance (Hoch, 1992; (Fischler, 2000; Grange, 2012; Gunder, 2010).

An empowering role in society could better be described as a continuous vigilance, in making society sensitive to new combinations of powers, actors, values, objects and places. We believe that the specific simplifications of the world pertaining to high modernist ideologies (Scott, 1998) indeed created a powerful position for planning in society. It also created a tendency to de-politicise planning activities, since consensus and assumed neutrality allow for expert prominence (Hoch, 1992; Wildavsky, 1979). This de-politicisation made it susceptible to critiques and substantial reforms of planning systems, which also produced a nostalgia with many planners for days of prominence, and a continuous identity crisis. Both the ideological underpinnings of planning and its cognitive limitations are forgotten over and over again, and cognitive closure makes it harder to adapt. Friedmann (1971: 251) noted that 'Wisdom has it that to be a good planner is to be acutely aware not only of what our work can reasonably be expected to accomplish, but also what it cannot; as professionals, we have to be aware of our cognitive limitations'.

A more profound reflection on the powers in, on and of planning and the role of underlying ideologies might make it easier to accept that for some places and problems spatial planning might not be the most appropriate answer and that where planning does emerge, it might be without planners bearing the label 'planner' (Abbott, 2012). Labels such as 'urban design', 'place branding' and 'policy integration' all embrace a certain form of spatial coordination and might in some places be a more useful way to enhance or revive planning than the label 'planning' itself.

PLANNING AND GOVERNANCE

In the previous paragraphs, the concept of governance has been mentioned many times, and this is no coincidence. Our perspective on power in/and/of planning makes most sense if planning is placed in governance systems and those governance systems in communities they are serving. The planning system then naturally entertains relations with other parts of the governance system and with the community whose space it is organising.

Since our initial work on power, planning and contingency (Van Assche, Duineveld, et al., 2014), this line of work has been productive in further elucidating both the embedding of planning in communities and the roles and forms of power at play. In dialogue with critiques of planning on the left and on the right (or from somewhere else), we became more convinced that an understanding of planning and governance as radically co-evolutionary (see for example Beunen and Patterson, 2016; Cleaver and Whaley, 2018; Hillier, 2017; Oliveira and Hersperger, 2018; Van Assche et al., 2017) allows us better to understand how planning, as spatial coordination, can emerge in governance systems, how power relations emerge around particular forms of planning which can stabilise them, erode them, or transform them, either strategically or unintentionally.

Power in the planning system can come from many sides, as we pointed out, and an evolutionary governance perspective highlights the importance of changing contexts in which the planning system is trying to define itself and retain a position. As new coordination problems emerge in society, partly driven by changing worries and values, planning systems must adapt and the actors, institutions, and forms of knowledge in the system close to the new values, topics and associated forms of organisation will result in new strategies (Broto and Westman, 2019; Brownill and Bradley, 2017). Even without strategising taking place in the system, new coordination problems might be picked up by external actors, inside and outside governance, as potential drivers for a reinvention of planning, endowing them with more power internally (see Lennon and Moore, 2019; McGuire and Hutchings, 2006). Relevant examples are urban design (Abd Elrahman and Asaad, 2021; Gunder, 2011), climate adaptation (Grafakos et al., 2019; Runhaar et al., 2018), or heritage planning (Stegmeijer et al., 2021; Van Knippenberg et al., 2021), all topics that require spatial coordination that can either be organised via an existing planning system, or become an arena in which other actors and disciplines take the lead in planning endeavours.

Power on planning becomes more prominent in an evolutionary governance perspective, as planning is more unambiguously understood as a domain of governance. Planning is indeed the coordination of space. That means, in a governance context, the coordination of other domains of governance, and the question is to what extent they want to be coordinated, let alone subjugated to an overarching perspective defined by planners (Allmendinger, 2016; Oosterlynck et al., 2010; Van Wymeersch et al., 2020). Changes in governance, frequent in democratic systems, and certainly democratic systems under stress, continuously put pressure on the activity of coordination, on the types of planning which are possible. Long-term perspectives might be argued for by newly prominent fields and disciplines (including resilience thinking, the consolidating field of climate adaptation expertise), but those long-term perspectives, and the implied forms of coordination and policy hierarchy, might not be linked to planning (Van Assche, Duineveld, et al., 2021; Van Assche, Verschraegen, et al., 2021b). Changes in what is really possible can antedate formal changes by years, so sharp observation of practices, of informal rules, and observation of shifting relations beyond the planning system are therefore important in attempting to grasp the shifting potential of planning (Beunen and Lata, 2021; Niedziałkowski and Beunen, 2019).

Power of planning then, as pointed out earlier, emerges out of the interplay of the two other forms of planning, and if the external and unstable factors receive more emphasis in an evolutionary governance perspective, this means that the iterative character of power relations has to be emphasised to a greater degree. It means that the power of planning can never be taken for granted, even if actors in the system remain entirely convinced that the system is good, essentially works, just needs a tweak, just needs to overcome an obstacle – a combination of naturalisation and teleological thinking very common in planning, policy, administration (see observations in Metzger et al., 2014; Sager, 2020; Scott, 1998). If big societal challenges could in principle use more involvement of planners, and citizens are also convinced of this, then the imaginaries of planners ought to catch up with the complexity sketched above. Planners could then play the role of critics of governance and community, when they are expected to do something but are not allowed to or capable of it, or when the expectations are far below what they could do to pursue accepted common goods (Marquardt, 2017; Peters and Pierre, 2019). The power of planning can be significantly reduced by governments favouring laissez-faire policies and using planning reforms to deregulate and decentralise the planning system (Boddy and Hickman, 2018; Olesen and Carter, 2018).

The Foucauldian concept of power/knowledge retains its utility in this more governance-oriented perspective of power and planning. In fact, we argue, it shows itself more fully in its utility. The access to governance, to collectively binding decisions, thus to the collective, makes governance inherently attractive for strategists seeking to give power to their ideas and/or themselves. Beyond strategising, evolving governance transforms the distribution of knowledges in governance and in society. With that it transforms the position of particular forms of expertise, particular narratives and perspectives. Power positions in and around planning change even without strategising, and, in understanding this process, it is still useful to rely on Foucault, and to see that shifting power relations in governance go through power/knowledge interactions (Van Assche et al., 2017). Planning here is both more vulnerable and potentially more powerful than other domains of governance since, when planning actually does what it claims to do, the coordinating function in the organisation of space makes it possible for planning knowledge to entrench itself in space, in daily life, in other governance domains, in the long run. At the same time, this exercise of coordination power is exceedingly difficult, as both planning theory and practice discover over and over again.

DISCUSSION AND CONCLUSION

Distinguishing between power in, on, and of planning is useful to explore and disentangle the different foci of attention in the debates about planning and power, and to integrate different strands of thought for the analysis of planning in society. It allows us to see planning as a system within society where power relations constitute the possibilities, the forms, and the potential impact of planning. The positionality of planning in a particular case is to be understood as the result of a coupled evolution of planning, governance, and society. Power of and power on planning are to be analysed as two sides of the same coin, as the dual force driving the evolution. Power in planning is framed by that duality. The mechanics of power in planning can be deduced from the specific entwining of the two other aspects of power. Changes in the relationship between power of and power on planning are bound to affect power in planning, while changes in the power landscape in planning itself only have wider effects if mediated by a particular position of planning in society.

Remaining within the same perspective, one can also account for power in the narrower sense, as the potential to get things done, in planning, and for planning in society. This potential exists but is subjected to the mechanics of contingent reproduction of society and its elements described above. Power as the potential to influence is continuously reshaped (McGuire and Hutchings, 2006). The configuration of potentialities is both the outcome as well as the precondition for the recursive operations of power. Just as the subjects, their values, and the power attributed to them, can only be understood as 'folds', or temporary discontinuities and densities in the fabric of reality, the power relations between subjects are subjected to the same processes of self-transformation. Cause, effect, intentionality and its cohesive version, rationality are considered ascriptive and a posteriori in character.

The idea that planners can know, either in advance or during the process, what is good for a community or what is the best procedure to get there, is a trace of a modernist configuration of power. The stress on contingency and evolution in no way diminishes the potential power of planning, but it does undermine the hopes of ever stabilising a planning system or of ever perfectly tying it to a community. Planning will always change. This point, both critical and hopeful, emerges from our integrated perspective on power that stresses emergence, continuous reconstruction, distributed agency, and a homology between power on planning and power of planning. It can help in finding a middle ground between radical deconstructions of planning as oppressive or an obstacle for change and development completely disconnected from the life in communities, and, on the other hand, overly optimistic expectations regarding the steering power of planning and a perfect fit with a community.

REFERENCES

Abbott, J. (2012). *Green Infrastructure for Sustainable Urban Development in Africa*. Earthscan.

Abd Elrahman, A.S., and Asaad, M. (2021). Urban Design and Urban Planning: A Critical Analysis to the Theoretical Relationship Gap. *Ain Shams Engineering Journal*, 12(1), 1163–1173.

Allen, J. (2003). *Lost Geographies of Power*. Blackwell Publishers.

Allen, J., and Cochrane, A. (2010). Assemblages of State Power: Topological Shifts in the Organization of Government and Politics. *Antipode*, 42(5), 1071–1089.

Allmendinger, P. (2016). *Neoliberal Spatial Governance*. Routledge.

Allmendinger, P., and Haughton, G. (2013). The Evolution and Trajectories of English Spatial Governance: 'Neoliberal' Episodes in Planning. *Planning Practice & Research*, 28(1), 6–26.

Alvesson, M., and Spicer, A. (2016). *The Stupidity Paradox: The Power and Pitfalls of Functional Stupidity at Work*. Profile Books.

Beunen, R., and Lata, I.B. (2021). What Makes Long-term Perspectives Endure? Lessons from Dutch Nature Conservation. *Futures*, 126, 102679.

Beunen, R., and Patterson, J. (2016). Analysing Institutional Change in Environmental Governance: Exploring the Concept of 'Institutional Work'. *Journal of Environmental Planning and Management*, 1–18.

Beunen, R., and Van Assche, K. (2013). Contested Delineations: Planning, Law, and the Governance of Protected Areas. *Environment and Planning A*, 45(6), 1285–1301. https://doi.org/10.1068/a45284.

Beunen, R., Van Assche, K., and Duineveld, M. (2015). *Evolutionary Governance Theory: Theory and Applications*. Springer.

Boddy, M., and Hickman, H. (2018). 'Between a Rock and a Hard Place': Planning Reform, Localism and the Role of the Planning Inspectorate in England. *Planning Theory & Practice*, 19(2), 198–217.

Booher, D.E., and Innes, J.E. (2002). Network Power in Collaborative Planning. *Journal of Planning Education and Research*, 21(3), 221–236.

Broto, V.C., and Westman, L. (2019). *Urban Sustainability and Justice: Just Sustainabilities and Environmental Planning*. Zed Books Ltd.

Brownill, S., and Bradley, Q. (2017). *Localism and Neighbourhood Planning: Power to the People?* Policy Press.

Buchan, R., Cloutier, D.S., and Friedman, A. (2019). Transformative Incrementalism: Planning for Transformative Change in Local Food Systems. *Progress in Planning*, 134, 100424.

Chettiparamb, A. (2006). Metaphors in Complexity Theory and Planning. *Planning Theory*, 5(1), 71–91.

Cleaver, F., and Whaley, L. (2018). Understanding Process, Power, and Meaning in Adaptive Governance. *Ecology and Society*, 23(2).

De Roo, G., and Silva, E.A. (eds) (2010). *A Planner's Encounter with Complexity*. Ashgate.

Deleuze, G. (1993). *The Fold: Leibniz and the Baroque*. University of Minnesota Press.

Deleuze, G., and Guattari, F. (1987). *A Thousand Plateaus: Capitalism and Schizophrenia*. Continuum.

Ferguson, J. (1994). *The Anti-politics Machine: 'Development', Depolicization, and Bureaucratic Power in Lesotho*. University of Minnesota Press.

Fischler, R. (2000). Communicative Planning Theory: A Foucauldian Assessment. *Journal of Planning Education and Research*, 19(4), 358–368. https://doi.org/10.1177/0739456x0001900405.

Flyvbjerg, B. (1998a). Habermas and Foucault: Thinkers for Civil Society. *British Journal of Sociology*, 49(2), 210–233.

Flyvbjerg, B. (1998b). *Rationality and Power: Democracy in Practice*. University of Chicago Press.

Foucault, M. (1969). *L'archéologie du savoir*. Éditions Gallimard.

Foucault, M. (1970). *The Order of Things*. Pantheon Books.

Foucault, M. (1975). *Surveiller et punir*. Gallimard.

Foucault, M. (1976). *Histoire de la sexualité. Tome 1: La volonté de savoir*. Paris: Gallimard.

Foucault, M. (1980). *Power/Knowledge: Selected Interviews and Other Writings, 1972–1977*. Pantheon Books.

Foucault, M. (1994). *Power. Essential Works of Foucault 1954–1984*. Volume 3. The New Press.

Foucault, M. (1997). *Ethics: Subjectivity and Truth; The Essential Works of Michael Foucault, 1954–1984*. London.

Foucault, M. (1998). *The Will to Knowledge. The History of Sexuality: Volume 1*. Penguin Books.

Friedmann, J. (1971). The Future of Comprehensive Urban Planning: A Critique. *Public Administration Review*, 31(3), 315–326.

Friedmann, J. (1998). Planning Theory Revisited*. *European Planning Studies*, 6(3), 245–253. https://doi.org/10.1080/09654319808720459.

Friedmann, J. (2008). The Uses of Planning Theory: A Bibliographic Essay. *Journal of Planning Education and Research*, 28(2), 247–258.

Grafakos, S., Trigg, K., Landauer, M., Chelleri, L., and Dhakal, S. (2019). Analytical Framework to Evaluate the Level of Integration of Climate Adaptation and Mitigation in Cities. *Climatic change*, 154(1), 87–106.

Grange, K. (2012). Shaping Acting Space: In Search of a New Political Awareness Among Local Authority Planners. *Planning Theory*, 12 (3), 225–243.

Gunder, M. (2010). Planning as the Ideology of (Neo-liberal) Space. *Planning Theory*, 9(4), 298–314.

Gunder, M. (2011). Commentary: Is Urban Design Still Urban Planning? An Exploration and Response. *Journal of Planning Education and Research*, 31(2), 184–195. https://doi.org/10.1177/0739456x10393358.

Gunder, M., and Hillier, J. (2007). Planning as Urban Therapeutic. *Environment and Planning A*, 39(2), 467.

Gunder, M., and Hillier, J. (2009). *Planning in Ten Words or Less. A Lacanian Entanglement with Spatial Planning*. Ashgate.

Hacking, I. (1990). *The Taming of Chance* (Vol. 17). Cambridge University Press.

Hajer, M.A. (1995). *The Politics of Environmental Discourse: Ecological Modernization and the Policy Process*. Clarendon.

Hardy, D. (1991). *From Garden Cities to New Towns: Campaigning for Town and Country Planning, 1899–1946* (Vol. 1). Taylor & Francis.

Hillier, J. (2002). *Shadows of Power: An Allegory of Prudence in Land-use Planning*. Routledge.

Hillier, J. (2017). Cat-alysing Attunement. *Journal of Environmental Policy & Planning*, 19(3), 327–344.

Hillier, J., and Gunder, M. (2005). Not Over Your Dead Bodies! A Lacanian Interpretation of Urban Planning Discourse and Practice. *Environment and Planning A*, 37(6), 1049–1066.

Hoch, C.J. (1992). The Paradox of Power in Planning Practice. *Journal of Planning Education and Research*, 11(3), 206–215.

Innes, J.E., and Booher, D.E. (2010). *Planning with Complexity: An Introduction to Collaborative Rationality for Public Policy*. Routledge.

Jentoft, S. (2017). Small-scale Fisheries within Maritime Spatial Planning: Knowledge Integration and Power. *Journal of Environmental Policy & Planning*, 19(3), 266–278.

Kiernan, M.J. (1983). Ideology, Politics, and Planning: Reflections on the Theory and Practice of Urban Planning. *Environment and Planning B: Planning and Design*, 10(1), 71–87.

Kooij, H.-J. (2014). Object Formation and Subject Formation: The Innovation Campus in the Netherlands. *Planning Theory*, 14(4), 339–359, 1473095214527278.

Latour, B. (1996). *Aramis, or, the Love of Technology*. Harvard University Press.

Lennon, M., and Moore, D. (2019). Planning, 'Politics' and the Production of Space: The Formulation and Application of a Framework for Examining the Micropolitics of Community Place-making. *Journal of Environmental Policy & Planning*, 21(2), 117–133.

Luhmann, N. (1989). *Ecological Communication*. University of Chicago Press.

Luhmann, N. (1990). *Political Theory in the Welfare State*. Mouton de Gruyter.

Luhmann, N. (1995). *Social Systems*. Stanford University Press.

Luhmann, N. (1997). *Die Gesellschaft der Gesellschaft*. Suhrkamp.

Luhmann, N. (2012). *Theory of Society, Volume 1. Cultural Memory in the Present*. Stanford University Press.

MacKenzie, D., Muniesa, F., and Siu, L. (eds) (2007). *Do Economists Make Markets? on the Performativity of Economics*. Princeton University Press.

Marquardt, J. (2017). Conceptualizing Power in Multi-level Climate Governance. *Journal of Cleaner Production*, 154, 167–175.

McFarlane, C. (2009). Translocal Assemblages: Space, Power and Social Movements. *Geoforum*, 40(4), 561–567.

McGuire, D., and Hutchings, K. (2006). A Machiavellian Analysis of Organisational Change. *Journal of Organizational Change Management*, 19(2), 192–209.

Metzger, J., Allmendinger, P., and Oosterlynck, S. (2014). *Planning Against the Political: Democratic Deficits in European Territorial Governance*. Routledge.

Miraftab, F. (2009). Insurgent Planning: Situating Radical Planning in the Global South. *Planning Theory*, 8(1), 32–50.

Mouffe, C. (2000). *The Democratic Paradox*. Verso.

Mouffe, C. (2005). *The Return of the Political* (Vol. 8). Verso.

Munro, L. (2000). Non-disciplinary Power and the Network Society. *Organization*, 7(4), 679–695.

Niedziałkowski, K., and Beunen, R. (2019). The Risky Business of Planning Reform – The Evolution of Local Spatial Planning in Poland. *Land Use Policy*, 85, 11–20.

Olesen, K., and Carter, H. (2018). Planning as a Barrier for Growth: Analysing Storylines on the Reform of the Danish Planning Act. *Environment and Planning C: Politics and Space*, 36(4), 689–707.

Oliveira, E., and Hersperger, A.M. (2018). Governance Arrangements, Funding Mechanisms and Power Configurations in Current Practices of Strategic Spatial Plan Implementation. *Land Use Policy*, 76, 623–633.

Oosterlynck, S., Van den Broeck, J., Albrechts, L., Moulaert, F., and Verhetsel, A. (2010). *Strategic Spatial Projects: Catalysts for Change*. Routledge.

Peters, B.G. (2017). Management, Management Management Everywhere: Whatever Happened to Governance? *International Journal of Public Sector Management*, 30(6).

Peters, B.G., and Pierre, J. (2019). Populism and Public Administration: Confronting the Administrative State. *Administration & Society*, 51(10), 1521–1545.

Pierson, P. (2004). *Politics in Time: History, Institutions, and Social Analysis*. Princeton University Press.

Pløger, J. (2004). Strife: Urban Planning and Agonism. *Planning Theory*, 3(1), 71–92.

Pløger, J. (2021). Politics, Planning, and Ruling: The Art of Taming Public Participation. *International Planning Studies*, 26(4), 426–440.

Pottage, A. (1998). Power as an Art of Contingency: Luhmann, Deleuze, Foucault. *Economy and Society*, 27(1), 1–27.

Pottage, A. (2004). The Fabrication of Persons and Things. In A. Pottage and M. Mundy (eds), *Law, Anthropology and the Constitution of the Social. Making Persons and Things*. Cambridge University Press, pp. 1–39.

Runhaar, H., Wilk, B., Persson, Å., Uittenbroek, C., and Wamsler, C. (2018). Mainstreaming Climate Adaptation: Taking Stock About 'What Works' from Empirical Research Worldwide. *Regional Environmental Change*, 18(4), 1201–1210.

Rydin, Y. (2010). Actor-network Theory and Planning Theory: A Response to Boelens. *Planning Theory*, 9(3), 265–268.

Sager, T. (2020). Populists and Planners: 'We are the People. Who are You?' *Planning Theory*, 19(1), 80–103.

Sarmiento, H., and Tilly, C. (2018). Governance Lessons from Urban Informality. *Politics and Governance*, 6(1), 199–202.

Scott, J.C. (1998). *Seeing Like a State: How Certain Schemes to Improve the Human Condition Have Failed*. Yale University Press.

Seidl, D. (2016). *Organizational Identity and Self-transformation. An Autopoietic Perspective*. Routledge.

Stegmeijer, E., Veldpaus, L., and Janssen, J. (2021). Introduction to *A Research Agenda for Heritage Planning*: The State of Heritage Planning in Europe. In Stegmeijer, E. and Veldpaus, L. (eds), *A Research Agenda for Heritage Planning*. Edward Elgar Publishing, pp. 3–20.

Swyngedouw, E., Moulaer, F., and Rodriguez, A. (2002). Large Scale Urban Development Projects and Local Governance: From Democratic Urban Planning to Besieged Local Governance. *Geographische Zeitschrift*, 89(2–3), 69–84.

Teubner, G. (1989). How the Law Thinks: Towards a Constructivist Epistemology of Law. *Law & Society Review*, 23(5), 727–758.

Valentinov, V. (2014). K. William Kapp's Theory of Social Costs: A Luhmannian Interpretation. *Ecological Economics*, 97, 28–33.

Van Assche, K., Beunen, R., and Duineveld, M. (2012). Performing Success and Failure in Governance: Dutch Planning Experiences. *Public Administration*, 90(3), 567–581. https://doi.org/10.1111/j.1467 -9299.2011.01972.x.

Van Assche, K., Beunen, R., and Duineveld, M. (2014). *Evolutionary Governance Theory: An Introduction*. Springer.

Van Assche, K., Beunen, R., Duineveld, M., and Gruzmacher, M. (2017). Power/knowledge and Natural Resource Management: Foucaultian Foundations in the Analysis of Adaptive Governance. *Journal of Environmental Planning and Policy*, 19(3), 308–322.

Van Assche, K., Beunen, R., Gruezmacher, M., and Duineveld, M. (2020). Rethinking Strategy in Environmental Governance. *Journal of Environmental Policy & Planning*, 22(5), 695–708.

Van Assche, K., Duineveld, M., and Beunen, R. (2014). Power and Contingency in Planning. *Environment and Planning A*, 46(10), 2385–2400.

Van Assche, K., Duineveld, M., Gruezmacher, M., and Beunen, R. (2021). Steering as Path Creation: The Art of Managing Dependencies and Reality Effects. *Politics and Governance*, 9(2), 369–80

Van Assche, K., and Hornidge, A.-K. (2015). *Rural Development: Knowledge and Expertise in Governance*. Wageningen Press.

Van Assche, K., and Verschraegen, G. (2008, November 1, 2008). The Limits of Planning: Niklas Luhmann's Systems Theory and the Analysis of Planning and Planning Ambitions. *Planning Theory*, 7(3), 263–283. http://plt.sagepub.com/cgi/content/abstract/7/3/263.

Van Assche, K., Verschraegen, G., and Gruezmacher, M. (2021a). Strategy for Collectives and Common Goods. Coordinating Strategy, Long-term Perspectives and Policy Domains in Governance. *Futures*, 128, 102716.

Van Assche, K., Verschraegen, G., and Gruezmacher, M. (2021b). Strategy for the Long Term: Pressures, Counter-pressures and Mechanisms in Governance. *Futures*, 131(102758).

Van Dam, R., Duineveld, M., and During, R. (2015). Delineating Active Citizenship: The Subjectification of Citizens' Initiatives. *Journal of Environmental Policy & Planning*, 17(2), 163–179.

Van Knippenberg, K., Boonstra, B., and Boelens, L. (2021). Communities, Heritage and Planning: Towards a Co-Evolutionary Heritage Approach. *Planning Theory & Practice*, 23(1), 26–42.

Van Wymeersch, E., Vanoutrive, T., and Oosterlynck, S. (2020). Unravelling the Concept of Social Transformation in Planning: Inclusion, Power Changes, and Political Subjectification in the Oosterweel Link Road Conflict. *Planning Theory & Practice*, 21(2), 200–217.

Walker, Edward T., Martin, Andrew W., and McCarthy, John D. (2008). Confronting the State, the Corporation, and the Academy: The Influence of Institutional Targets on Social Movement Repertoires. *American Journal of Sociology*, 114(1), 35–76.

Wildavsky, A. (1979). *Speaking Truth to Power: The Art and Craft of Policy Analysis*. Little, Brown and Co.

Wood, S. (2009). Desiring Docklands: Deleuze and Urban Planning Discourse. *Planning Theory*, 8(2), 191–216.

Žižek, S. (2003). The Rhetorics of Power. *Diacritics*, 31(1), 91–104.

Žižek, S. (2004). What Can Psychoanalysis tell us About Cyberspace? *The Psychoanalytic Review*, 91(6), 801–830.

Žižek, S. (2012). *Organs Without Bodies: On Deleuze and Consequences*. Routledge.

24. A post-postmodernist perspective on power in planning: situating practices and power

Ernest R. Alexander

INTRODUCTION

This chapter is about power in planning, when 'planning is what planners do' (Vickers, 1968), and it focuses on planning practices. There are different views about power in planning, as this book shows. Here I will suggest that these views often relate to different kinds of planning theories, which are for and about different planning practices. In the editors' spirit of 'multiple ... perspectives', the chapter's approach follows from the author's[1] position, one that I call post-postmodernist (Alexander, 2000).

Post-postmodernist Position

My position is post-postmodernist because, like my postmodernist colleagues, I am critical of modernism's naïve positivism; but, finding their ensuing relativism problematic,[2] my epistemology tends toward critical realism. Sharing their progressive agenda (Alexander, 2008), my vaguely social democratic ideology rejects simple generalisations, for example privatisation vs. public. I believe that 'the devil is in the detail', and complex issues need detailed institutional analysis and design (Alexander, 2017).

As a planning academic, I have a positive view of planning – possibly biased by personal engagement and interest. In this view, planning evolved from a modernist rational-scientific practice into a postmodern stage when planning was seen as the link between knowledge and action (Friedmann, 1987) and planning practice as collective enactment of the social construction of knowledge. A post-postmodernist perspective sees planning as diverse knowledge-based practices engaged in the social *co*-construction of knowledge. These planners are not modernist technocrats, nor postmodern mobilizers, mediators or policy entrepreneurs in communicative planning processes, but professionals integrating their expert knowledge with other engaged participants' mutual knowledge in planning for collective action.

This chapter goes on to tell how conceptions and enactment of different kinds of planning practices relate to conceptions and exercise of power in planning. Beginning with a brief exposition of planning practices and a summary discussion of power, it continues with a review of how planning theories changed over time with evolving concepts of planning practices and power. These are presented in three stages: modern, postmodern and post-postmodern.

Planning Practices

The sociology of knowledge defines different kinds of practice. In one sense practice is descriptive: what people do in a set of activities linked by common understandings and abilities, for example cooking practices or teaching practices are what people do when they are cooking or teaching. In another sense practice is also normative: practice as 'institution of meaning' in knowledge-centred practices (Schatzki, 2001: 48–53). Knowledge-centred practices are 'epistemic' practices, demanding knowledge of their epistemic objects (Knorr-Cetina, 1999). Thus neurosurgeons' epistemic object is the human brain, the epistemic objects of macroeconomics are national economies, and chefs' epistemic object is food – from sauces to pastries, depending on their specialisations.

Defining planning has been difficult: maybe 'Planning is a funny field …' (Chapin 2015: 315) is the best definition we can get. Though planning has always been called a practice (Vickers, 1968; De Neufville, 1983), can we talk about planning as *a* practice? The answer is: no – none of the planning we know fits these definitions as *the* practice of planning. But sociology of knowledge definitions imply three kinds of planning practices: (1) Generic 'planning' – what people do when they are planning; (2) Knowledge-centred planning practices: for example, spatial planning, environmental-, transportation- or e-planning; (3) Real-life planning: planning practices in specific contexts, from advocacy planning for a Colombian barrio to transportation planning for the EU Trans-Europe Network, and enacted practices in general contexts: colonial, insurgent or Southern planning (Alexander, 2022).

Power

This book offers a comprehensive discussion of power, with analyses from different perspectives, so this is just a summary review to anchor the chapter's discussion. For our purposes we can identify three dimensions of power: Type – the kind of power referred to; Purpose – what does the agent use power for; Level – what is the level or scope of influence of the referenced power.

Type of power: There are two kinds of power, which differ in their sources and agency.

1. Positional power: A person's or group's (social unit) position or role can give them power to affect others' behaviour/actions and influence outcomes. In a social or organisational hierarchy his position (e.g. elected officials, officers in government/public agencies, organisational managers/executives) may give him legitimacy or authority over others. Another source of positional power can be an actor's strategic position in a social or organisational network, giving her control of needed resources: funds, property, equipment etc. These positions give their holders other bases of power: coercion and incentives-rewards. Holders of positional power can also control information, giving them informational influence, while information as knowledge is the base of expert power (French and Raven, 1959; Raven, 2008).
2. Hegemonic power: While the agent exercising positional power can be an individual or a social unit (a group acting collectively as a quasi-individual), hegemonic power is systemic. Hegemonic power is how some elements in a society affect the thoughts, behaviour and actions of others, or even of the whole society. Through hegemonic power an ideology serving particular interests becomes a society's dominant hegemonic culture, for example capitalism in modern societies (Gramsci, 1971), neo-liberalism in Western democracies (Laclau and Mouffe, 1985), or party-led state capitalism in China today.

Purpose: Power can be exercised for different purposes. Conventional views of power focus on *constraining power*: an agent's power to prevent others' actions or to set limits to their behaviour and the scope and results of their actions. Essentially, this is the power to stop others from doing something they might otherwise do. Legal and regulatory prohibitions are a widespread exercise of authoritative constraining power. The use of force, sanctions, punishment or threats to prevent or limit another's possible actions is an exercise of coercive constraining power; informed readers can easily recognize cases and examples. Domination through hegemonic power to establish social norms setting the boundaries of acceptable beliefs, behaviour and actions is also constraining power.

But power can also be positive. Positional power holders can invoke authority and deploy resources directly or indirectly to initiate or effect behaviour and actions; social norms can stimulate beneficial behaviour and encourage positive actions, if one subscribes to the dominant interest or adopts the hegemonic ideology.[3] This is *enabling power*; though often neglected, it is no less important than constraining power (Guerrero and Andersen, 2011).

Levels: Various kinds of power can be exercised at different levels of a society. Lukes (2005) calls them 'dimensions' of power. At the lowest level is individuals' or interest groups' *power in direct competition or conflict* to affect their desired outcomes. This is often related to their positional power. The next dimension is the power to frame the discourse or set the terms or rules for conflict or competition. This has been called *agenda-setting power* (Bachrach and Baratz, 1962). At the highest level is *hegemonic power* over actors' and groups' perceptions. Hegemonic power affects outcomes through actors' adaptation to or acceptance of their perceived reality.

There is another aspect of power that qualifies the above review: the legitimacy of the exercised power. Much of the discussion of power in the recent and current literature – from political philosophy to planning theory – is critiquing power, implicitly or explicitly labeling it as illegitimate. Conversely, the possibility and potential of legitimate power is neglected (Westin, 2022).

The legitimacy of power is a central feature of Westin's conceptual framework for his analysis of power in communicative planning theory. This identifies three basic types of power: 'Power to' (:) – agents' dispositional ability to act; 'Power with' (:) – agents' power to act in concert; and 'Legitimate and illegitimate power over' (:) – agents' power to get other actors to do what they otherwise would not have done … legitimate or illegitimate 'according to local or universal criteria' (Westin, 2022).

'Power over' clearly includes many of the forms of power introduced above. One is positional power over others, whether by the position holder's authority or control of resources these actors need, to direct their behaviour and actions as actual or potential incentives, rewards or sanctions. Another is information-knowledge power, which lets experts influence other actors through their authoritative advice and essential information. Finally, hegemonic power is also 'power over': power to constrain peoples' and groups' behaviour and actions through their norms and perceptions that set the limits of the acceptable, and enabling power that encourages and legitimizes behaviour and actions that conform to or promote the desirable.

Reflective readers can easily recall examples of all these in the planning practices reviewed above. In some recollected cases one can usually distinguish between legitimate and illegitimate uses of planners' 'power over'. Is environmental planners' positional and expert power over plan applicants in California when reviewing their EISs for project approval legitimate? Most right-thinking respondents (i.e. those who are not extreme libertarians or anarchists) would answer: yes, confirming the hegemonic power of a liberal democratic regime.[4]

At the other extreme, planning powers deployed by colonial regimes (Porter, 2010) or ethnocratic polities[5] to oppress 'the others' – minorities, aboriginals and disadvantaged groups

– are clearly illegitimate, even though their planning systems are established by law. Between these poles, representing planners' powers and distinguishing between the obvious 'good' and 'bad guys', lies a large grey area where the legitimacy of planning powers is debatable, and may be decided 'according to local or universal criteria' which may in turn be contested.

Determining these criteria is such a complex problem that Westin (2022) apparently (and wisely) saw it as a minefield he'd better not enter, and so do I. This issue of legitimacy engages intellectuals, scholars and researchers in many fields and disciplines. 'Local criteria' are often addressed as political and discussed in political philosophy, sociology, political science and policy sciences, public administration and planning theory.[6] 'Universal criteria' involve norms, values and knowledge, which are debated in philosophy (under ethics and epistemology), political philosophy (e.g. ideologies), sociology and law.[7]

PLANNING THEORIES: EVOLVING CONCEPTS OF PLANNING PRACTICES AND POWER

Modern

Planning theory: Rationality was the ideal model for modern planning theory as it evolved, and rational planning was the dominant planning paradigm. Understood as instrumental rationality, this was often translated into simplistic prescriptions for planning processes and methods, seeing planning as a linear means–ends decision-making process and planners' knowledge as science-based technical expertise (Beauregard, 2020: 7–8, 9–10, 21–23).

Later, more nuanced understanding applied Weberian rationality in planning theory, recognizing substantive rationality with proposals for participative goal setting and value analysis, and acknowledging the limits of instrumental rationality (Alexander, 2000). This was reflected in prescribed planning methods (e.g. supplementing prevailing benefit–cost analysis with more complex multi-criteria evaluation methods (Alexander, 2006a). Throughout this stage, prevailing planning theory, methods and prescribed practices were based on modernist positivist-scientific epistemology, and planning practice was the application in action of scientific knowledge and theory through rational methods and appropriate technology.

Planning practice: The modernist planner was a credentialed professional, whose education and experience made him[8] an expert in his field. Practising planners had positional power, though it was limited. One base of their positional power was expertise: expert power through their professional knowledge, information, skills and practical experience. Planners' professional expertise was accepted as benign: enabling power to propose good policies and effective projects for their polity, and make plans that would benefit their community.

Planners' positional constraining power should also be benign. This is what statutory planning systems are for: to invoke state and local government planners' legitimate authority in their official positions. Land use regulation and development control to avoid the adverse effects of 'free market'-led development is one obvious example. Another is planners' power through environmental regulations to limit agents' harmful actions and require them to mitigate the expected damaging effects of planned projects and operations.

But planners' position also limits their power: they are only 'decision makers'; politicians and elected officials, not professional experts, are the 'decision takers' (Friend and Jessop, 1969). Politicians do not always have to follow the advice of their professional planning staff, and often they do not. This limit to planners' enabling power was seen as a problem; there were two kinds of response. One was the creation of City Planning Boards/Commissions with non-political citizen members, initiated by the reform movement c. 1900 in an attempt to divorce scientific-professional planning from political corruption and widespread municipal graft (Reps, 1965). The other was among planning theorists and scholar-practitioners, who began to address – and agonize over – the relationship between politics and planning. This began with Walker's (1941) structural-functional analysis, and was followed by political science oriented planning theorists Altschuler (1965), Rabinovitz (1969), Allensworth (1975) and (most recently) with Flyvberg's (1998) Foucaultian personal case study.

Modernist rational planning has its personification: its archetype is Rexford G. Tugwell (1891–1979), a prominent figure in US planning history. Tugwell was the epitome of the modern professional planner; though his career predated planning professionalization (he was educated as an economist) it ended appropriately teaching graduate planning at the University of Chicago. The son of a prosperous upstate New York farmer-businessman, Tugwell first appeared on the national stage as one of Roosevelt's 'Brains Trust', a group of young advisors at the beginning of the New Deal. When Roosevelt created the Resettlement Administration (RA) he made Tugwell its first director.

Tugwell launched and directed the RA's Greenbelt program, his best-known achievement, which planned and built three new towns before it was halted by legal and congressional opposition.[9] Later he served as the first director of the New York City Planning Commission under Mayor LaGuardia, and as Governor of Puerto Rico, where he established the PR Planning Urbanization and Zoning Board in 1942. An ardent advocate of planning, he even proposed planning as 'the fourth power of government' in a reformed US Constitution (Tugwell, 1954). Tugwell was self-confident and assertive to the point of arrogance, making many enemies. This limited his effectiveness, and he came to be seen as a political liability, leading to his removal from his RA position (Namorato, 1988). Mistakenly labeled a socialist, Tugwell saw central planning as a way to save capitalism by mitigating destructive market competition (Chichester, 2011).

Critiques: Planning theory began to question the rational paradigm, when its problems were exposed by related disciplines and social sciences. Rationality was redefined as an ideal model, its literal application in practice incompatible with the limits of human knowledge and action (Beauregard, 2020: 25–26). Instead, political scientists, economists, decision- and planning theorists proposed bounded rationalities: satisficing (Simon), incrementalism (Lindblom), mixed scanning (Etzioni) etc. (Alexander, 1992: 47–51). Research revealing the subjectivity of science discredited the validity of the positivist-scientific epistemology behind modern rational planning, planning theory and practice, leading to postmodern planning theory and practice.

Critics of *planning practice* decried the professional planner for misuse of his expertise. Modern rational planners' power was not benign, on the contrary. They were blind technocrats, willing agents of capitalist neo-liberal hegemonic power to serve their social elites' political establishment.[10] Planners used their positional powers (state authority and professional expertise) to advance profitable projects and development and oppress minority and deprived groups, as shown in 1960s critiques of US urban renewal (Gans, 1962; Anderson, 1965). In its 'dark side', modern planning power supports authoritarian, colonialist and ethnocratic regimes (Yiftachel, 1993).

Postmodern

Planning theory: Postmodern epistemology is a radical departure from modernist positivism. Responding to critiques (above), postmodern thought (including planning theory) is based on hermeneutic epistemology that calls subjective interpretations of reality 'true', denying the objective truth of any single empirical reality. The social construction of knowledge implies that planning is a collective endeavour to apply knowledge to action.

At the same time, planning theory dismissed 'classic' rationality. The limits of instrumental rationality made it counterproductive for methods, and refocusing interest on discourse and communication instead of decisions and action made substantive rationality irrelevant. Now Habermas' communicative rationality inspired planning theorists' thinking. Communicative collaborative practice is the new mainstream prevailing planning paradigm. Later, theorists proposed other (post-structuralist) paradigms: agonism (Mouffe), becoming (Deleuze-Guattari) etc. (Alexander, 2018; Beauregard, 2020).

Planning practice: Planning defined as the link between knowledge and action (Friedmann, 1987) has no epistemic object. This planning is generic 'planning' practice, done by everyone who is planning. Critiques of modern positivist epistemology deprivileged systematic scientific knowledge; 'planning' is something anyone can do, and no reason why everyone cannot do it well. Epistemological and sociological objections combined with critiques of modern planners' actions and impacts (see above) to demonize the professional planner and question his expertise.

Discussion of the social construction of knowledge was mainly concerned with integrating 'lay' experiential and appreciative knowledge into planning, decision making and political processes.

Planners' enactment of communicative collaborative practice involves participation and interaction with other actors engaged in the social construction of knowledge for collective decisions and action. Now a central concern of planning is peoples' participation and empowerment of disadvantaged and marginalized groups and minorities to affect decisions, change outcomes and transform societies. The planner adopts the role of facilitator, mediator, mobilizer, visionary or policy entrepreneur, rather than the knowledgeable expert, for an effective participatory planning process.

Power in the postmodern stage of planning is usually related to 'planning' practice. In a (sometimes implicitly) normative discussion of power, planners are expected to use their positional power (role, authority) to empower disadvantaged actors, marginalized groups and dissident interests in the planning process. Through insurgent planning, oppositional planners can deploy their expert power to raise consciousness and mobilize (Foucauldian) resistance to prevailing hegemonic power. Book chapters here also present current planning theory analysis of power from a generic 'planning' practice perspective, some expounding 'imported' (e.g. neo-Marxist and post-structuralist) concepts, some from particular (e.g. Southern, feminist, queer) perspectives.

Critiques: Current postmodern *planning theory* offers no clear definition or explanation of what planning is: 'planning is a funny field' (Chapin, 2015: 315) looks like the best we can do. References to planning practice abound (e.g. De Neufville, 1983), as in 'communicative practice' (Beauregard, 2020: 54–56). But this is without a clear conception of practice in general or understanding of planning practice (or practices) in particular (Alexander, 2022).

Postmodern views of *planning practice* are also questionable. There is a contradiction between prevailing planning theory and academic planning practice studies' concept of planning practice, and real-world planning practices. Postmodern planning practice is essentially generic 'planning': people engaged in planning as collective social construction of knowledge for action. In reality, most of the people called planners are professional practitioners enacting specialized planning practices in relevant institutional settings.

Planning and power are discussed from a generic 'planning' orientation, analysing power in society in general from different philosophical, ideological and sectoral perspectives. With postmodern ambivalence on professionalization, little attention is paid to planners' power (or lack of power) in their roles as professional planners. This ambivalence takes two forms. One is denial of these roles' validity with the devaluation of scientific-systematic knowledge and professional expertise. Also, planners' positional power in their professional roles is seen as negative, based on modern planners' practices and their impacts (see above). In postmodern planning theory discussion of planning and power has a normative focus, with planners as 'moral agents' using their positional power to resist hegemonic power and transform society.

Post-postmodern

Planning theories and practices: The post-postmodern stage involves the elaboration and revision of two postmodern concepts. In the sociology of knowledge, the model of socially constructed knowledge has been elaborated to become the social *co-construction* of knowledge. In planning theory, the definition of planning as a practice demands revision according to current practice theory, to thinking of planning *practices*.

Researchers engaged in the study of knowledge, curious about how the social construction of knowledge really happens, found a variety of practices that produce our recognized fields of knowledge and adopted technologies. These are knowledge-centred practices of communities with a common interest engaged in a collective undertaking: scientific research, technology development and professional practice in fields ranging from medicine to planning and public policy. In these communities scientists and professionals interact with the other participants in a cooperative process researchers called: the co-production of knowledge. Deconstructing the postmodern generalization of social production of knowledge, co-production of knowledge is a post-postmodern concept.[11] In co-production of knowledge the interactions between experts (scientists, professionals and technicians), contributing knowledge in their specialized domains, and other actors with their knowledge contributions are detailed, in an integrative process producing socially valid knowledge for action. Today's planners, then, are not modern technocrats, but post-postmodern professionals in knowledge-centred practices.

Practice theory defines different kinds of practice. One sense of practice is descriptive: what people do in a set of activities linked by common understandings and abilities, for example healing, banking or planning practices are what people do when they are healing, banking or planning. In another sense practice is normative: practice as 'socially recognized forms of activity, done on the basis of what members learn … capable of being done well or badly, correctly or incorrectly' and endowing their 'membership with the power to perform' (Barnes, 2001: 19-20). These are 'epistemic' practices, each with its epistemic object (Knorr-Cetina, 1999). Thus physicians' epistemic object is the human body, economists' is the economy, high-energy physicists' is subnuclear particles, and spatial planners' is human life and activities in space.

Postmodern planning theorists, educators and planners have always thought about planning as a practice (De Neufville, 1983; Sandoval, 2020: 129). But can we talk about planning as *a* practice, in either of the senses suggested above? The post-postmodern answer is: no; but there is planning as diverse practices.

Sociology of knowledge definitions suggest three kinds of planning practices: (1) Generic 'planning' practice: what people do when they are planning.[12] (2) Knowledge-centred planning practices: recognized (something) planning for example spatial planning, environmental-, transportation- or community development planning. (3) Real planning practices. These include (something) planning in specific contexts, from regional ecosystem planning for the Hardanger reindeer preserve, Norway, to transportation planning for the Shanghai municipality-metropolitan area; and 'planning' enacted in general (form, space and time) contexts, from (historical or contemporary) colonial-, through informal and insurgent- to Southern planning (Alexander, 2022). Now planning practitioners are not rational technocrats, nor communicative mobilizers or mediators, but professional (something) planners pooling their expert knowledge with other participating actors' knowledges in the social co-production of knowledge for action that is post-postmodern planning.

Power in planning practices: In the post-postmodern stage we are in, how is power manifest in societies that are planning's subjects and environments, and how do planners deploy and experience power in their practices? The first question is beyond my competence: the answer demands a comprehensive critique of the whole range of postmodern theories and expositions on power in societies (some of which are included in this book) and presenting a significantly different alternative. Anyway, a general post-postmodern discussion of power in society is well beyond the scope of this chapter.

To answer the second question, we need to address it to the planning practices identified above. For (generic) 'planning' practice: how would a post-postmodern discussion of 'planners'' power diverge from the postmodern exposition presented above? Bearing in mind that the subject 'planner' is anyone engaged in planning something, it is hard to distinguish this issue from the more general question of power in society, which was posed before.

In their knowledge-centred planning practices (as urban, environmental, community development or transportation planners), professional planners may have positional power. Their power may take different forms depending on its source. A planners' legitimacy or authority (by her position or role in the institutional context of her activity) can give her positional power to influence involved actors' behaviour and actions.

Power is intrinsically neutral. Like technology, whether it is harmful or benign depends on how it is deployed (by whom and to what purposes), what are its effects, and whether it is recognized as legitimate or not. Evaluating legitimacy is usually subjective, and conclusions often differ (except in clear and extreme cases) according to observers' ideologies and values.[13] Planners' positional power is no exception, and many critics associate planners' abuse of their positional power with technocratic planning in state bureaucracies supporting exploitative capital in neo-liberal regimes, and planning destroying poor and minority communities to promote development for local growth regimes.[14]

Planners' positional power can also be benign. A planner's position may give him power to transform societal-institutional networks and change other parties' power relations. This can be enabling power through institutional design, redesign or reform to empower disadvantaged groups and excluded interests by raising transparency, increasing representation, and enabling public participation and citizen control of common resources.

It can be constraining power (often through planners' regulatory authority) to oppose elites' dominant interests, for example developers and speculators in land-property markets. But we must recognize the limits of professional planners' positional power. Post-postmodern planning (like modern and postmodern planning) is constrained in its particular context: an institutional environment that reflects prevailing political and societal cultures, and where planners' role is often more advisory (decision 'makers') than as executive 'decision takers'.

Another source of planners' power is their expertise that gives them informational-knowledge based power. Post-postmodern planners acting in their professional roles (rather than just as mobilizers or mediators) have enabling power through their specialized knowledge-centred practices. These planners can contribute their knowledge, information and experience to planning that involves the social co-construction of knowledge, enabling the integration of other actors' systemic, appreciative and experiential knowledges in interactive planning processes.

Professional planners' informational-knowledge based power, drawing on their expertise, can promote a progressive agenda in different ways, depending on their working contexts. Their professional knowledge and experience can produce better policies and plans, and enable the design of participative planning processes that empower involved communities, include disadvantaged groups and recognize marginalized interests. Practising in a supportive regime, these planners' advice to decision makers will enable their plans' adoption and implementation of participative planning processes. Working in less supportive contexts, planners' knowledge still gives them enabling power to resist oppressive hegemonic power, for example acting as 'guerillas in the bureaucracy' (Needleman and Needleman, 1974). In insurgent planning, radical planners deploy the same enabling power, working with community activists to co-produce successful counterplans (Huq, 2020).

DISCUSSION

Conclusions

With the evolution of planning and planning theory over time, in successive periods different views emerged of planning and planning practice. In each of these periods – roughly labelled as modern, postmodern and post-postmodern – these views are linked to different perspectives on power in planning, and changing evaluation of power as good or bad.

Planning theorists' ideas of planning have been vague, but they (and planners) have always recognized planning as a practice. What has changed over time is our view of planning practice – or practices. Modern planners were viewed (and identified themselves) as professional experts, applying their science-based knowledge to plan rationally for a better future and regulate development in the public interest. Postmodernists no longer trusted professional planners, but saw them as oppressive technocrats serving capitalist hegemonic power. The postmodern planner engages in communicative practice, in the role of mobilizer, mediator or policy entrepreneur, as appropriate, participating in the social construction of knowledge for collective action that is postmodernist planning.

The post-postmodern approach modifies the postmodern paradigm to a more nuanced concept: the social *co*-construction of knowledge. This implies knowledge-centred practices in science, technology, professional and other fields. Following postmodern practice theory, planning is a multiscalar set of diverse practices, made up of three kinds of planning practices:

generic 'planning' – planning that everyone does, and anyone can do; planning practices: the knowledge-centred 'something' (e.g. spatial) planning practices we know; real planning in specific contexts, for example metro-regional planning for Stockholm or 'Southern' insurgent planning in Rio de Janeiro. The post-postmodern planner is not a technocrat, communicator or social-change agent, but an expert in his field – contributing her knowledge to the social *co*-construction of knowledge for collective action that is post-postmodernist planning.

The evolution of planning and planning theory from modern through postmodernism to an emerging post-postmodernism also changed prevailing views of power in planning. Modern planners and planning theorists saw power in a positive light, and regretted limitations (political and institutional) on the powers of planning. Planners' positional and informational power, as professional experts, allowed them to plan better communities, cities and regions and enabled the adoption of their plans, promoting and controlling development in the public interest. The power of modern planning was the authoritative (often verging on authoritarian) application of scientific knowledge *for* (not with) the subjects of plans: members of communities, neighbourhood residents, citizens and all those affected by planning policies and decisions.

Postmodernists' critique of scientific knowledge radically changed views of power in general, and of power in planning in particular. Generally, power was seen as negative, with intellectual discourse focusing on hegemonic power and resisting its oppression. Postmodernist planning theorists follow this trend in presenting institutionalized planning as an agent of (usually capitalist or neo-liberal) hegemonic power. This complemented postmodernist critiques of modern planning practice that labeled planners as insensitive technocrats whose plans and projects devastated neighbourhoods and divided communities.

These critics threw the baby out with the bathwater. Focusing on the negative side of power in society, they neglected its positive potential: the deployment of enabling and constraining power for legitimate ends to benefit society. The post-postmodern implications of these findings are discussed next.

Implications

Today, discussion of power in planning usually refers to planning theorists' 'planning', and reflects the prevailing critical attitude towards power in society. But we should be talking about power in planning: planners' power in recognized planning practices (spatial, environmental, community development or transportation planning) and engaged in real-world planning. In this approach planners are no longer presumptuous modern technocrats or communicative postmodern mobilizers, mediators or social-change agents, but post-postmodern professionals engaged the social *co*-construction of knowledge that is planning.

Recognizing this as planners' role and planning practices can moderate current critiques of power in planning in two ways. One is retreat from the critical focus on power (mainly hegemonic power) in society; the other is adopting a less negative view of planners and recognizing the positive potential of planning practices.

Positive power in planning takes various forms, both as enabling and constraining power. Planners' positional power and the informational power of their expertise can enable beneficial actions, from producing policies, plans, programmes and projects that improve peoples' lives and their environment, through purposeful strategic interaction to ensure their adoption, to taking action (e.g. allocating needed resources) in their implementation. A planner's position in legitimate authority or nodal influence in social or institutional networks can empower her to initiate or promote social change through institutional design (Alexander, 2006b). In this way his enabling power can ensure transparency and increase participation (especially of disadvantaged and marginalized groups) in planning, administrative and political processes, leading to better decisions and outcomes. Here enabling power in planning is positive, deployed to enhance effectiveness, equity and social justice.[15]

Constraining power in planning can also be positive. Planners' positional power in legitimate authority is exercised to constrain actors' behaviour and prevent actions expected to have negative impacts. Spatial planners engaged in land use planning and development control at national, regional and local levels deploy constraining power, as do planners engaged in environmental planning and regulation.

Through statutory planning, zoning codes and planning and building regulations, planners' constraining power prevents undesirable development, channels development to conform to plan designations and achieve policy goals (such as sustainability), protects open space and conserves natural and cultural assets and environmental resources. The constraining power of regulatory planning is also an important tool for public intervention in the 'free' land-property market to restrain speculative development and avoid its negative impacts on housing equity and environmental justice (Alexander, 2014).

In environmental planning and regulation too, planners' constraining power has positive effects. Requiring and evaluating planning and project proposals' Environmental Impact Statements (EIS) in deliberating on their approval minimizes negative environmental impacts and promotes mitigation of unavoidable effects. Environmental regulation prohibiting air, land or water pollution can effectively influence the location of activities and land uses, for example applying air quality standards to constrain or prevent industrial location, limiting deterioration of (or even enhancing) environmental quality and promoting sustainability.

How, then, can we engage in constructive discourse on power in planning? My above review suggests some answers. One: make the planning practice that is the subject of the discussion the (knowledge-centred and real) *planning* we know, rather than the 'planning' theorists love. Another: think less about negative power, with fewer expositions on hegemonic power in all its aspects and exhortations of resistance, and pay more attention to positive power – in particular, the potential of enabling and constraining power in planning. This leads to the third answer: developing useful normative prescriptions for planners: how to acquire, keep and deploy positive power in planning.

NOTES

1. Elderly (86) white (Jewish) conventional (married + 2) male; for more detail see Alexander (2017).
2. Like Plato's famous 'Cretan liars' paradox, Lyotard's postmodernist slogan: 'There is no metanarrative' is self-contradictory.
3. This is, of course, contestable (cf. the current debate over liberal democracies' vs. China's party-led regime's responses to the COVID-19 pandemic) and raises the issue of legitimate or illegitimate power that is discussed below.
4. Foucauldians might qualify their positive answer with a (typically) critical reservation: provided that the planners' considerations were sufficiently responsive to the demands of environmental justice.
5. Israel (Jewish) is the prominent example in the planning literature (Yiftachel, 2006), but the archetype was 'white' (apartheid) South Africa. In contemporary Africa ethnocracies (perpetuating historical rivalries) are still widespread, e.g. Shona (vs. Ndebele) in Zimbabwe and Tutsi (vs. Hutu) in

Rwanda, and arguably exist in Asia, e.g. Bamar in Myanmar, Han in China and Yamato in Japan. Of course, all the subjects of the above examples will (legitimately) dispute that they are ethnocracies.

6. Following my above reservation, no citations are offered here.
7. An example (from these fields) of how values can form perceptions of legitimacy, is the conflict between universal values (human rights, equity, rule-of-law) and communitarian values: solidarity, loyalty to family, friends, community, country (patriotism) (Walzer, 1990).
8. The pronoun is intentional: most planners then were male.
9. The Greenbelt program is a classic case of modern planning: three new towns were planned and built based on Howard's 'Garden City' concept. These new communities were successful in providing low-cost housing in attractive living environments (Corden, 1977), as I can personally confirm. As a long-time resident of Milwaukee, I learned that housing in Greendale, WI was still sought after and highly valued (relative to its size and amenities) in the Milwaukee metropolitan area.
10. There are too many references in the last three decades' planning literature to cite them here.
11. Co-production has two (loosely related) meanings. The one used here (from the sociology of knowledge) refers to the integration of expert and non-expert domains of knowledge in the sciences and as professional expertise e.g. medicine and engineering (Jasanoff, 2004). Another (in the policy sciences) refers to the collaborative production of public services between public officials, professionals, bureaucracies, communities, and civil society, which also involves co-production of knowledge in planning, policy and program design (Albrechts, 2013; Bovaird et al. 2014).
12. 'Planning' is not a knowledge-centred practice, because it has no epistemic object. This is obvious if we review the 'objects' definitions have associated with (generic) planning, e.g. knowledge and action, decisions, the future, rational choice.
13. See pp. 369–70 above.
14. The reference to regimes is no accident; for an illustration of the link between regime and planning evaluation see Alexander (2010) which evaluates planning under different regimes in British-controlled mandatory Palestine and the Israeli-occupied Palestinian West Bank.
15. Informed readers can think of examples in countries they know. US cases that come to my mind are Federal mandatory participation requirements for urban revitalization projects, equity planning in Cleveland, OH, and EPA institutionalized environmental justice (Schryer, 2018; Krumholz, 1982; EPA, 2020).

REFERENCES

Albrechts, L. (2013) Reframing Strategic Spatial Planning by Using a Coproduction Perspective. *Planning Theory* 12(1): 46–63.

Alexander, E.R. (2000) Rationality Revisited: Planning Paradigms in a Post-Postmodernist Perspective. *Journal of Planning Education & Research* 19(3): 242–256.

Alexander, E.R. (2006a) Evolution and Status: Where Is Planning Evaluation Today and How Did It Get Here? In Alexander, E.R. (ed.) *Evaluation in Planning: Evolution and Prospects*. Aldershot, UK: Ashgate, pp. 3–17.

Alexander, E.R. (2006b) Institutional Design for Sustainable Development. *Town Planning Review* 77 (1): 1–27.

Alexander, E.R. (2008) Between State and Market: A Third Way of Planning. *International Planning Studies* 13(2): 119–132.

Alexander, E.R. (2010) Planning, Policy and the Public Interest: Planning Regimes and Planners' Ethics and Practices. *International Planning Studies* 15(2): 143–162.

Alexander E.R. (2014) Land-property Markets and Planning: A Special Case. *Land Use Policy* 41(2): 533–540.

Alexander E.R. (2017) Perspective: Chance and Design: From Architecture to Institutional Design. *Journal of the American Planning Association* 83(1): 93–102.

Alexander, E.R. (2018) How Theory Links Research and Practice – 70 Years' Planning Theory: A Critical Review. In Sanchez, T.W. (ed.) *Planning Knowledge and Research*, New York: Routledge pp. 7–23.

Alexander E.R. (2022) On Planning, Planning Theories and Practices: A Critical Reflection. *Planning Theory* 21 (2): 181–211.

Allensworth, D.T. (1975) *The Political Realities of Urban Planning*. New York: Praeger.

Altschuler, A. (1965) *The City Planning Process: A Political Analysis*. Ithaca, NY: Cornell University Press.

Anderson, M. (1965) *The Federal Bulldozer: A Critical Analysis of Urban Renewal*. Cambridge, MA: MIT Press.

Bachrach, P. and Baratz, M.S. (1962) Two Faces of Power. *The American Political Science Review* 56(4): 947–952.

Barnes, B. (2001) Practice as Collective Action. In T.R. Schatzki, K. Knorr-Cetina and E. von Savigny (eds) *The Practice Turn in Contemporary Theory*. New York: Routledge pp. 17–28.

Beauregard, R.A. (2020) *Advanced Introduction to Planning Theory*. Cheltenham UK and Northampton, MA, USA: Edward Elgar.

Bovaird, T., Van Ryzin, G.G., Loeffler, E. and Parrado, S. (2014) Activating Citizens to Participate in Collective Co-production of Public Services. *Journal of Social Policy* CJO2014, doi:10.1017/S004729414000567.

Chapin, T. (2015). Notes from the Review Editor. *Journal of the American Planning Association* 81(4): 315.

Chichester, S.A. (2011) Make America Over: Rexford Guy Tugwell and his Thoughts on Central Planning. MA (History) paper. Lynchburg, VA: Liberty University. https://digitalcommons.liberty.edu/egi/ retrieved 14/2/21 20:20.

Corden, C. (1977) *Planned Cities: New Towns in Britain and America*. Beverly Hills, CA: Sage.

De Neufville, J.I. (1983) Planning Theory and Practice: Bridging the Gap. *Journal of Planning Education & Research* 3(1): 35–45.

EPA (2020) EPA Annual Environmental Justice Progress Report FY 2020. Washington DC: US Environmental Protection Agency. epa.gov/environmentaljustice/annual-environmental-justice-progress-reports.

Flyvberg, B. (1998) *Rationality and Power: Democracy in Practice*. Chicago: University of Chicago Press.

French, J. and Raven, B.H. (1959) The Bases of Social Power. In Cartwright, D. (ed.) *Studies in Social Power*. Ann Arbor, MI: Institute for Social Research, pp. 150–167.

Friedmann, J. (1987) *Planning in the Public Domain*. Princeton NJ: Princeton University Press.

Friend, J.K. and Jessop, W.N. (1969) *Local Government and Strategic Choice*. London: Tavistock.

Gans, H.J. (1962) *The Urban Villagers: Group and Class in the Life of Italian-Americans*. New York: Free Press.

Gramsci, A. (1971) *Selections from the Prison Notebooks*. Trans. and ed. Q. Hoare and G. Nowell Smith. London: Lawrence and Wishart.

Guerrero, L.K. and Andersen, P.A. (2011) *Close Encounters: Communication in Relationships* (3rd edn). Thousand Oaks, CA: Sage.

Huq, E. (2020) Seeing the *Insurgent* in Transformative Planning Practices. *Planning Theory* 19(4): 371–391.

Jasanoff, S. (2004) Ordering Knowledge, Ordering Society. In S. Jasanoff (ed.) *States of Knowledge: The Co-Production of Science and Social Order*. London and New York: Routledge, pp. 13–45.

Knorr-Cetina, K. (1999) *Epistemic Cultures: How the Sciences Make Knowledge*. Cambridge, MA: Harvard University Press.

Krumholz, N. (1982) A Retrospective View of Equity Planning Cleveland 1969–1979. *Journal of the American Planning Association* 48(2): 163–174.

Laclau, E. and Mouffe, C. (1985) *Hegemony and Socialist Strategy: Towards a Radical Democratic Politics*. London: Verso.

Lukes, S. (2005) *Power: A Radical View* (2nd edn). London: MacMillan.

Namorato, N. (1988) *Rexford G. Tugwell: A Biography*. New York: Praeger.

Needleman, M.L., and Needleman, C.E. (1974) *Guerillas in the Bureaucracy: The Community Planning Experiment in the United States*. New York: Wiley.

Porter, L. (2010) *Unlearning the Colonial Cultures of Planning*. London: Routledge.

Rabinovitz, F.F. (1969) *City Politics and Planning*. New York: Atherton Press.

Raven, B.H. (2008) The Bases of Power and the Power/interaction Model of Interpersonal Influence. *Analyses of Social Issues and Public Policy* 8(1): 1–22.

Reps, J.W. (1965) *The Making of Urban America: A History of City Planning in the United States.* Princeton, NJ: Princeton University Press.

Sandoval, G.F. (2020) Notes from the Review Editor. *Journal of the American Planning Association* 86(1), 129–130.

Schatzki, T.R. (2001) Practice-mind-ed Orders. In Schatzki, T.R., Knorr-Cetina, K. and von Savigny, E. (eds) *The Practice Turn in Contemporary Theory.* New York: Routledge, pp. 42–55.

Schryer, S. (2018) *Maximum Feasible Participation: American Literature and the War on Poverty.* Palo Alto, CA: Stanford University Press.

Tugwell, R.G. (1954) The Place of Planning in Society: Seven Lectures. San Juan, PR: Office of the Government Planning Board.

Walzer, M. (1990) The Communitarian Critique of Liberalism. *Political Theory* 18(1): 6–23.

Westin, M. (2022) The Framing of Power in Communicative Planning Theory: Analysing the Work of John Forester, Patsy Healey and Judith Innes. *Planning Theory* 21(2): 132–154.

Vickers, Sir G. (1968) *Value Systems and Social Process.* New York: Basic Books.

Wikipedia (2019) en.wikipedia.org/wiki/planning, accessed 15/11/2019.

Yiftachel, O. (1993) Planning and Social Control: Exploring the 'Dark Side'. *Journal of Planning Literature* 12(2): 395–406.

Yiftachel, O. (2006) *Ethnocracy: Land and Identity Politics in Israel/Palestine.* Philadelphia, PA: University of Pennsylvania Press.

25. Planning, media, and power

Jaime Lopez and Lisa Schweitzer

INTRODUCTION

Planners in the twenty-first century, just like everybody else, find themselves and the issues they work on scrutinised in the media more than ever before. The media have always been important to planning and development, but digital technologies and new media have changed planning and development politics. In earlier decades, planners could, for the most part, assume that their projects and professional activities would enjoy favourable press unless the projects included blatant financial scandals or powerful opposition. However, new media have created opportunities for more dissent and more viewpoints on development that both expand and threaten the possibilities for planning. This chapter discusses these changes and what they portend for planning.

Before we launch our discussion, we should clarify a couple of points. Planners have written extensively about the promises of new communications technologies as a means to engage publics and to make cities 'smarter,' in tandem with sensing and automation technologies. We shall set aside the latter to focus on the former. New communications technologies boost the opportunities for planning and data science applications. For our purposes, we are still interested in new media as a mechanism for information creation, presentation, and dissemination about planning and development rather than their potential in technical analysis. These are sufficiently important pathways to power.

The second clarification concerns our fundamental assumptions about planning and media as concurrently occurring within and influencing urban politics. Our perspective examines the role that media play in planning as a form of political communication about development, futures, and places. Therefore, our discussion is somewhat limited to western media and planning. We hope to identify factors that scholars and practitioners might find useful in analysing their own contexts.

This chapter covers three major components of media that shape contemporary planning. The first section defines different general forms and structures of modern media and how that media has changed over the past thirty years with digital technologies. The second discusses how new media has altered planning and places. The penultimate section discusses misinformation and disinformation and their effects on planning, while our last section wraps up the discussion with some possibilities for research and practice.

MEDIA AND MEDIATISATION

First, media requires some defining. Throughout, we shall use the term 'media' to refer to all forms of media, including what communication specialists call the 'legacy' and 'new' media (Stroud, 2011). Legacy media, sometimes called 'traditional' media, are the information outlets that have been around for decades, such as television, radio, and the oldest media, print.

Much of the legacy media are targeted at general, mass media markets. However, we should not overlook the importance of niche market outlets in the legacy media, such as Black-owned newspapers, radio, and television, as well as legacy media outlets that serve immigrants and ethnic enclaves. New York, for example, has over 100 ethnic newspapers that have a readership of just under 3 million (Center for Community and Ethnic Media, 2013). Legacy media typically have some institutional structure that professionalises their content selection and presentation, such as editors and fact-checkers.

New media, by contrast, are those that grew from digital technologies and especially Web 2.0. (Davis and Owen, 1998). New media include the now familiar social media sharing sites like Facebook, Twitter, and Instagram and blogs, video-sharing platforms, and new apps. Changes in digital and computing technology have made the creation and dissemination of information content much more straightforward, cheaper, and in general, faster than with legacy media. New media rely much less on traditional structures of owners, publishers, producers, and editorial boards. As a result, new media both democratise and destabilise the information environments in which planners work. Information environments refer to the information available to individuals about the people and institutions engaged in planning to influence discussions and decisions about specific places.

Though often framed as competing, legacy and new media tend to work together (Wired Staff 2017). Significant overlap exists between legacy and new media, and while the distinction matters, we should not treat them as rigid categories. Perhaps nothing exemplifies this overlap more than documentary film – a longstanding legacy media tool that new technology opened up to millions of new content producers on platforms like YouTube and TikTok.

The traditional roles associated with media in politics are threefold and related. First, the media plays a 'watchdog' role, checking and reporting political actors and their actions (Francke, 1995). Second, media serve as an agenda-setter for framing and directing public attention and discussion around issues (Boydstun, 2013). In the case of new media, that agenda-setter role involves offering new fora for political expression. Third and finally, media can foster community creation or division, helping people find common political goals and values and solidify political identities (May, 2000).

Media expansion through digital technologies has made media markets far more competitive than in prior decades. Commercial pressures lead to incendiary stories that garner the most attention. Further, while platforms proliferate, similar content is dispersed widely. Media power remains at least somewhat concentrated in a small number of old and new media corporations, just with different framings designed to appeal to audiences that want information presented their way (McChesney, 2015).

Media-sharing through social networking platforms like Facebook has amplified niche media's ability to engage with broader audiences. Sharing, in turn, has multiple and significant potential effects on information dissemination. Sharing moves content from one person to another in their networks. It places information in front of audiences who might otherwise, without their peers' sharing, have been uninterested in the content (Gottfried et al., 2017; Wallsten, 2010). Peer-to-peer content sharing can also strengthen the influence that the information has on individuals who see it. Among recipients, people tend to pay more attention to information from friends and family than they do content from broadcast media, and they tend to weigh that shared content more than information from other sources (Bene, 2017; Thorson, Cotter, Medeiros and Pak, 2019). Sharers also deploy their networks differently. They will share media content that viscerally affects them, which builds on the niche and 'à la carte' nature of current media consumption (Pariser, 2011; Rossini, Stromer-Gallery, Baptista and Veiga de Oleiva, 2020). Outrage, empathy, disgust, or other strong emotions can drive media sharing, and content publishers draw on these emotions through tactics like 'clickbait' headlines (Brady, Wills, Jost, Tucker and Van Bavel, 2017). Political disinformation strategies exploit this tendency towards outrage to spread false information.

All of this competition boosted the notion of 'infotainment' over time, even though the term first appears among broadcasters as early as the 1970s (Jebril, Albaek and deVreese, 2013). These developments pose problems for planning and media. Stories, to garner attention, must entertain or provoke (Moy and Hess 2009). Some political information – and this may be especially true for planning politics – may not provoke much emotion until there is a crisis. Climate change serves as an example.

The possibilities expand for urban and planning news with national and international audiences. Legacy media have always had a substantial role in development. Molotch (1976) identifies local newspapers as among the key members of elite, pro-development coalitions in urban politics. New media have changed both the mindset and orientation of urban media content. New urban media emerged with urban studies as cities, and urban life became a general interest topic. We might trace that back to media-savvy industrial designers like Norman Bel Geddes, architects like Le Corbusier, or critics like Lewis Mumford. Still, perhaps the clearest example of urbanism and planning gaining national media prominence occurred in 1961 when a journalist from New York, Jane Jacobs, published her best-selling book *The Death and Life of Great American Cities*. With that book and its reception, Jacobs, the journalist, became a celebrity urbanist and exerted an outsized influence on planning as a profession.

Many seek to follow Jacobs to become urban media darlings, with good reason. Media attention can harness media's influence – the ability to highlight issues and contribute to positive political change (Strömberg, 2015). Planning scholar Richard Florida used his status as a celebrity urbanist to boost an outlet, *The Atlantic Cities*, with an explicit focus on planning and urbanism content. *The Guardian* newspaper followed suit.[1] *Planetizen* is a new media outlet that centres specifically on planning, rather than urbanism, and offers classes to planners on new media, such as virtual reality. Streetsblog.org is a non-profit, independent new media player that offers both urban lifestyle, development, and planning content for its major locational outlets in cities like New York and Los Angeles.

Self- and subject-promotion are only one possibility. Media can help discipline planning information as well. Bent Flyvbjerg's research on megaproject cost overruns suggests that such media can be an effective way to create a consequential public debate (Flyvbjerg, 2012). As such research has shown, the public can benefit from media's power of and on agency when it achieves, for instance, financial transparency for megaprojects. Nevertheless, despite critical media attention, planning and media can also produce pernicious outcomes if an ideal level of project transparency is compromised by subversive attempts from powerful neoliberal interests to shape public aspirations in their favour (Gunder, 2011; Schweitzer and Stephenson 2016).

With the desire to gain prominence in expanded media comes mediatisation. Mediatisation refers to the process of making individuals far more self-aware of themselves as potential media subjects and how they change their behaviour to accommodate media. Media attention in either the legacy or new media can significantly boost or harm careers in the academy and public institutions. Being willing to court media attention offers rewards like book sales for both academics and practitioners. The term 'mediatisation' itself signals a significant, potential problem: moving planners and scholars to take on the mores and norms of media to sell their projects and themselves to larger audiences. Communicating across many platforms seems like a reasonable requirement for planners, a profession whose work is inherently political. But much of what is worthy in planning is tedious rather than titillating: building relationships with people and their places, gathering information, and deliberation are all things difficult to serve up as infotainment and are also all activities that can readily fail if the parties involved are performing more for external audiences than in commitment to deliberative process (Rosen and Schweitzer, 2018).

The rewards of mediatisation, combined with an unrelenting need for content, and attention-grabbing content at that, can lead not to the diversity of perspectives required to make better public decisions but to an endless and destructive cycle around the trivial and media-ready squabbles that are not truly debates. An economist, Paul Romer, has become a media darling espousing shallow ideas about urban governance, such as the idea that 'good rules' should govern cities, as if that somehow never previously occurred to anybody engaged in urban governance before. Journalists benefit from this material because these stories circulate well and do not involve difficult writing or reporting. Media-savvy scholars and practitioners always have quips for journalists pressed to produce content.

Being the one scientist willing to cast doubt on climate change can do far more for one's career in terms of attention and citation than being one name among the many thousands of scientists in the Union of Concerned Scientists attesting to climate urgency. In a similar vein, writer Joel Kotkin has parlayed a willingness to disparage cities and planning in favour of suburbs to media platforms that increasingly publish him (and thus further anoint him) as a subject matter expert on all things urban. In this way, Kotkin became a media creation whose writing exists to lend a false credibility for niche market audiences who do not want to deal with unsustainable urbanism. Framing him as an underdog contrarian to groupthink equates Kotkin's opining with what is, in fact, a persistent, widespread consensus among experts across myriad disciplines globally that American land use and transportation practices contribute to climate disasters.

Mediatisation thus contributes to a noisy information environment where audiences can have trouble sorting the important from the trivial, the true from the false, and sophistry from carefully weighed consensus (see also Chapter 26 by Sheppard). Such information environments can be counterproductive but expanded – and diversified – media have also wrought more democratic inclusion of voices that planning has ostensibly sought, but failed, to bring into planning and development. New media, however, enables these participants to mediate planning and planners' voices, along with other professions, rather than the other way around. Black and ethnic content creators have successfully used media democratisation to challenge white supremacist institutions, including general interest media that centre whiteness in politics to capture majority audiences. Digital media technologies have enabled Black perspectives, including using cameraphones and digital media, to focus majority attention on police and white violence. In so doing, these newly mediated perspectives have challenged the role of the police and planning in harming their neighbourhoods.

Deliberative planning theories hold that planning should actively enable multiple voices into the planning process. But with new media, getting more voices speaking to the issues is no longer a role that planners need to assign to themselves.

DEMOCRATISING PLANNING INFORMATION AND PLACE REPRESENTATION

Planning tends to present public engagement solely as a formal effort, typically a state-led, state-regulated pursuit to decide by actively seeking public input within a state-controlled communication process. But this perception of participatory planning fails to recognise the complex and wide-ranging cast of participants and interactions that have ultimately influenced planning and development decisions throughout history. Traditional planning engagement theories have long offered a myopic conception of participatory planning, often tracing its origins to the mid-twentieth century despite a complex variety of informal participatory arrangements existing for centuries (Thorpe, 2017). Such historical accounts fail to acknowledge informal contributions made by myriad stakeholders (Tauxe, 1995). They also portray conventional planning engagement as a process only recognised as such when occurring within state-designed processes. Nonetheless, the overlap between new media and conventional planning engagement is apparent in the noticeable increase in visual data and storytelling tools among influential organisations such as Human Right Watch and Amnesty International (Rall et al., 2016).

New media allows for many voices, but it still does so alongside established institutions that may not share power in any meaningful way (Afzalan and Muller, 2018). Control over decisions and narratives about places still persists even when technology changes. In 1969, scholar Sherry Arnstein described a newly devised planning engagement process with her metaphor, a ladder of citizen participation, as an institutionally driven process created to provide the public with influence in decision-making (Arnstein, 1969). Public agencies commonly maintained control of public debate forums, often establishing terms and frameworks for shaping outcomes. The result was often a closed planning process (Thorpe, 2017). However, critics challenged public agency expertise, viewing formal participatory processes as those providing the illusion of engagement and legitimacy while, in reality, working to suppress conflicting stakeholder viewpoints (Davidoff, 1965; Sandercock, 1975). In addition to excluding opposing viewpoints, conventional planning engagement implemented top-down approaches with the underlying presumption that it is those with power who bestow marginalised stakeholders with the opportunity to be included (Rosen and Painter, 2019). Such a condescending view of marginalised voices is apparent today when the *International Association of Public Participation* states its empowerment goal 'to place final decision making in the hands of the public' (IAP2, 2020).

As we go from an era entirely dominated by mass communication to one where self-communication provides a voice to many, developing a sharper understanding of new potential communication opportunities and pitfalls is critical, including the reproduction and exacerbation of social inequality through the digital divide (Jenkins, 2006; Castells, 2009; 2012). Against this backdrop, cyber-optimists argue that expanding communication tools are critical for democratising participation, while cyber-pessimists warn us about the new challenges presented by new media (Trapenberg Frick, 2016). The appeal of new media as tools for civic engagement come about partially from widespread suspicions that: (a) state institutions are dysfunctional and unworthy of public trust; (b) elections have been corrupted to protect incumbents and marginalise minority and youth voices; and (c) legacy media parrots messaging controlled by fewer and fewer conglomerates (Rosanvallon and Goldhammer, 2008; Jenkins et al., 2016; Palmer, Toff, and Nielsen, 2020).

For most of the twentieth century, mass media had the unchallenged and multifaceted power to establish political, social, economic and cultural frameworks that shaped how outsiders perceived a given location. For instance, legacy media covers and, at times, sensationalises criminal activity that stigmatises Black and ethnic neighbourhoods among its consumers (Matei, Ball-Rokeach and Qiu, 2001). A burgeoning industry in 'true crime' podcasts and documentaries might help challenge these spatial perceptions – or not. In a similar vein, local media, both traditional and new, also run features on 'the hottest new neighbourhoods to buy in' that help foster real estate interest and potential displacement. Place representation among those outside communities demonstrates how media can prove instrumental to powerful interests in reinforcing spatial and racial hierarchies within capitalist real estate development.

Civic media offers a framework for understanding new media practices and the potential for political influence to counter established media influence. While it can be defined in many ways, civic media is any use of a medium that empowers a community to engage within and beyond the people, places and problems of their community. But civic media as a practice is difficult to define perhaps because civics and democracy are themselves always evolving (Vatikiotis, 2014). While what constitutes a 'good citizen' has been traditionally based on previous models of 'informed citizens' and 'dutiful citizens', alternative models of citizenship have been new for several decades (Bennett, 2008; Delli, Carpini and Keeter, 1996). Civic media's ability to foster pluralistic representations hinges on new (different) citizenship roles that emphasise self-expression, creativity, and direct action (Kligler-Vilenchik, 2017). Furthermore, examples of civic media must include social media that can help individuals find others with similar interests and policy preferences, enabling them to interact, bolster their political identities, and organise (Graham, Jackson and Wright, 2016).

Within these conceptual frameworks, new media's power lies in part within its ability to enable individuals to represent place for themselves (Shannon, 2016). These self-representations can offer spatial conceptualisations that lay the foundations for how planners identify, analyse, and approach particular geographies outside those of elite interests. New media in the twenty-first century presents people with an opportunity to counter external place representations and engage in ways that participatory frameworks such as Arnstein's ladder never fully achieved (Blue, Rosol and Fast, 2019). New media that enables participatory storytelling can be critical for delivering democratised representation by allowing marginalised voices an opportunity to shape community narratives, which, throughout planning history, have been overshadowed by a prioritisation of technocratic knowledge that has often been presented as either the dominant narrative or as the 'decontextualized applications of cold, hard logic' (Throgmorton, 1992: 28).

Media tools are widely available, and we follow transmedia producer Kamal Sinclair's conceptual categories for understanding the shifting landscape (Sinclair, 2018). Spending too much time on the particulars of any one application will quickly make our discussion obsolete, but we do want to present some potentially fruitful technologies and practices. Sinclair's categories include a wide range of practices and tools that we loosely collapse into three umbrella groups: virtual and augmented realities; interactive mapping, movies, storytelling; and collaborative design/social art practices. These overlap and interact in creative ways that can be useful for place and issue representation among professional artists, computer scientists, architects, and users in such a way that the distinction between creator/consumer of information begins to dissolve. One application, collaborative design and social art practice, develops projects through teams made of different disciplines, which offers an intersectional consideration of multiple perspectives and knowledge construction (Zahedi, Tessier and Hawey, 2017). At a basic level, participatory story media uses a variety of 'high-quality, low-cost tools' for media consumption that also invites its community members to actively take part in collecting, reporting, analysing, and sharing content (https://thestorycatchers.com.au). Co-creation media, while sharing the participatory and co-creation elements found in participatory story media, can also empower people to create supplementary content with the potential to fuse with, or expand upon, an original source, including members' own text, videos, or other material that can be shared through social media. Co-creation media's potential for delivering democratised representation, therefore, similar to new social movements, revolves around both solidarity and individuality (Castells, 2012; Poell and van Dijck, 2018).

In some contrast, crowd sourcing is the practice of obtaining needed services, ideas, or content by soliciting contributions from a large group of people for a predefined issue. Perhaps most importantly in journalism, crowd sourcing offers the possibility of delivering democratised representation in terms of having all perspectives revealed equally, thereby loosening the power of journalistic authorities to gate-keep (Sinclair, 2018). Just as citizen science has increasingly played a role in policy and urban planning scholarship, mainstream news sources have taken increasing note of citizen journalists, whose content has been used as an alternative to vox pops, opinion polls, or even editorial work, as 'the hybridization and convergence between bottom-up and top-down models of news work continues to evolve' (Deuze, Bruns and Neuberger, 2007: 335).

Multiplying voices is only one possibility. Multiplying platforms is another. Transmedia, which describes storytelling done via different platforms in both linear and nonlinear ways, is a term so often debated and analysed that its use has been significantly neglected within new media discourse, mostly as a result of multi-platform digital architectures becoming commonplace (Sinclair, 2018). Nonetheless, transmedia strikes us as being potentially very useful to planning with new media because it can enable people using multiple tools to participate in the same story creation – pieced across different platforms – rather than forcing everybody onto the same forum, technology, or platform in order to be included. Perhaps especially when engaging generations Y and Z, transmedia can be considered part of the hybrid systems of media-content circulation, representing massive potential for empowering marginalised voices without access to 'mainstream forms of distribution' (Jenkins et al., 2016).

Co-produced, interactive media also have great potential, but it would be a mistake to emphasise those and forget about the power of new media to present emancipatory and democratised information in traditional narrative forms. For some issues – particularly for those related to racial justice – media that allow for production and dissemination of finished narratives and ideas may be better. Podcasts and documentary video, for example, have enabled Black content producers to set their own agendas for idea presentation, naming for themselves racism and racist institutions, unmediated by white-dominated media and entertainment channels. Black Twitter is a socio-political phenomenon that elevates Black responses to cultural and political events in ways that expose white supremacist bias in established political media (Lee, 2017). Portland State planning professor Lisa Bates and artist Sharita Towne worked with a large group of Black artists and residents to create a project on the Black Spatial Imaginary (Bates et al., 2018). Among multiple other visions of Black history and futures, the group created a digital map and artist recreation of the Black space of Jumptown, along with its jazz clubs and residences, with over 100 structures that the City of Portland destroyed to build its Veterans Memorial Coliseum. Some media benefit from allowing expression uninterrupted by white impulses to erase, or excuse, or derail. Speaking more globally, indigenous media content producers seek to disrupt media dominated by settlers (Salazar, 2009).

DISINFORMATION

With new media, planners face an expansion of a longstanding problem – making sense of places and their futures from multiple voices with many stories. New media can increase individuals' ability to watchdog planning, frame places and issues for themselves, and formulate identities and communities dedicated to what matters to them. This democratic potential, however, can also result in non-democratic consequences, particularly when a preponderance of anti-democratic voices becomes a tyrannical majority (de Tocqueville, 2001 [1835]). As the United States experiences growing political division, such political disputes, captured more widely through new media tools used by both planners, civically engaged residents, and powerful interests, also carry the possibility of impeding planning deliberation.

Unfortunately, the same new media that have enabled more diverse and insightful place representation have enabled organising and propaganda among violent, white supremacist and misogynistic groups seeking to find larger audiences to legitimate their grievances. American author Ralph Keyes (2004) suggests that the United States has entered into a 'post-truth' era, where media performs, rather than reports, information. Debate or information reports appeal to emotions disconnected or irrelevant to the facts or details via repetition and become immune to factual rebuttal. In this political context, communication is not about informing fellow community members, political leaders, or their deliberation but about demonstrating a willingness to accept and repeat information as a sign of group membership and loyalty.

Such a political environment creates significant challenges for planning as a tool for deliberative democracy. Deliberative democracy promises to make a pathway to collective decision-making despite the pluralism of planning publics. Deliberative planning theory, and the practices of community engagement it seeks to enable, relies on participants' commitment to engage with each other in a good-faith effort to understand one another's information and perspectives. Pluralistic groups in a functioning deliberation have to share, at base, one thing in common: a faith in a loyal opposition. Loyal opposition holds that while differences of preferences and perspectives on development might exist among the members of a political community, the members of that political community regard each other as legitimate and well-meaning, even if wrong or misguided, members of the same political community with the same rights and standing as their own. When willingness to espouse information regardless of factuality becomes a standard for group membership, the act of negotiating those ideas with an opposition itself becomes an act of betrayal, not the act of an engaged democratic citizen.

New media can foster quick dismissal of opposition through conspiracism and variants thereof. Conspiracy theories are longstanding in politics; they go back as long as innuendo and information asymmetries do in human communication. Political theorists Nancy Rosenblum and Russell Muirhead (2020), however, argue that new conspiracists differ from those of the past in how they handle information. In the mid-century of American politics, conspiracies, such as the CIA assassinating US President John Kennedy, flourished on the impulse to investigate the conspiracy. The community of investigators, though fractious, used information and evidence to try to prove or disprove various theories of what happened. The unifying norm of the community was its reliance on evidence – finding it, evaluating it, and interpreting it. By contrast, Rosenblum and Muirhead (2020: 19) describe a contemporary information environment of 'conspiracism' that exists without theory or investigation: what matters is the willingness to support, or at least not contradict, the conspiracy.

PizzaGate is an excellent example of conspiracist disinformation and how politicians, media, and tech companies profit from it. In summary, the PizzaGate conspiracy holds that then-presidential candidate Hillary Clinton and former White House Chief of Staff John Podesta ran a Satanic child sex ring from the basement of a DC pizza restaurant called Comet Ping Pong.[2] The theory grew in popularity out of the imageboard website, 4chan (Aisch, Huang and Kang, 2016). For political disinformation strategists, PizzaGate was conspiracy gold because shortly before the election, FBI director James Comey announced the FBI was re-opening its investigation into Hillary Clinton's emails. Alt-right media provider Alex Jones (InfoWars) cashed in during the days before the election. Jones said in a YouTube video on November 4, 2016: 'Yeah, you heard me right. Hillary Clinton has personally murdered children. I just can't hold back the truth anymore.' That video was viewed more than 427,000 times before it was taken down.[3] (He has subsequently apologised, long after the harm was done, and he made no gesture to compensate or return his payments for the video.) The #PizzaGate hashtag rushed through bots (automated accounts that are organised in tandem to elevate information on social media platforms) in the millions as part of a coordinated political disinformation campaign (Ordway, 2017).[4] Disinformationists such as Alex Jones can enjoy large platforms not because of some free-market interest that lifts his content in platform algorithms, but because well-funded, elite interests pay platforms like YouTube to juice the number of times his video appears in their featured content.[5] Donald Trump directly benefited from the dirt sticking to his opponent. YouTube gained advertising revenues. Apple and Google both have allowed vending of apps that disseminate conspiracies that flourished among PizzaGate believers. Tech giants profit from disinformation just as they do for apps developed for weather information, and they have little reason to curtail these activities. Even legacy media benefit from the cycle through churning content.

The dissolution of media as a potential watchdog and purveyor of quality information was purposeful. Steven Bannon, a former investment banker turned media executive behind disinformation player *Brietbart News*, once argued that the real enemy of conservatism was not progressives but the media, and the way to incapacitate the media as a political force was to 'flood the zone with shit.'[6]

The recrudescent Agenda 21 conspiracies exemplify the problems that disinformation and misinformation bring to planning. Agenda 21 was a nonbinding resolution passed by the United Nations in 1992 that promoted the best practices of sustainable urban development to governments around the globe. For right-wing politicians in the western liberal democracies, this development programme helped spark conspiracies that unite their political followers toward a general disposition against sustainable development and collective action. Conservative media personality Glenn Beck wrote two books where Agenda 21 becomes environmental fascism, takes over the government, and strangles personal freedom. Much more influential politicians like sitting Senator Ted Cruz (R-TX) echoed the conspiracy, and the Republican Party condemned Agenda 21 in its 2012 platform in the United States. During this same time, state legislators in over half of the US states introduced anti-Agenda 21 legislation (Trapenberg Frick, Weinzimmer and Waddell, 2015). These ultimately failed, but they help coalesce opposition against climate planning. Deliberation about how to solve problems becomes impossible because stakeholders enter politics with the problems defined already in ways that make reconciling the concepts nearly impossible.

Regarding specific planning examples where conspiracy and disinformation have undermined projects, Trapenberg Frick (2016), for example, outlines how TEA Party interests found each other and coalesced in opposition to specific projects. We are not really addressing that kind of opposition in our argument here. The defeat of an individual bike lane or a light rail project may be unfortunate, but planning projects always have had to take their political lumps. TEA party spatial development preferences about specific projects may not be sympathetic to the sustainable urbanism that planners have, in general, embraced, but democratic deliberation cannot promise that the democratic preferences explored are always going to be pro-justice, pro-sustainability, or pro-planning. In our chapter here, we are talking not about preferences but about distinct information environments shaping political realities prior to any chance of deliberation. It is one thing to refuse to act on climate change because one thinks other things, such as employment and the economy are more important than the environment. It is quite another to refuse to even discuss climate change, let alone take serious policy action, because one thinks, sincerely, that climate change is entirely a hoax promulgated by evildoers. The former allows climate change into the policy process where others who do not share a preference for inaction can potentially persuade skeptics to come aboard. The latter hamstrings deliberation by pulling the debate away from issue importance to debating both reality and the character of others in the political community.

Certainly, these problems are longstanding: getting white Americans to seriously reflect on and deliberate white supremacy has been a long-term problem. The difference is a matter of degree. New media and mass disinformation have moved so much of the discourse away from solutions deliberation to debating the basics about reality that the already slow world of democratic deliberation falters in its face. Perhaps most important for planners to understand, the disinformation on climate change was purposeful. Powerful political officials such as Jim Inhofe and Scott Pruitt used various communications channels in recent years to spread their belief that climate change is a hoax, thereby limiting planning deliberation by significantly preventing solutions and action debate (Emanuel, 2018). One result is that, in the United States, we have excellent climate planning research and planning being done with less impact than the work merits – not because planners are not rigorous enough or pragmatic enough or any of the pejoratives usually applied to the field, but in part because climate change cannot gain enough political salience to force strong legislative action in most of the country.

PLANNING POST-TRUTH

Media have changed significantly over the past three decades, bringing both new opportunities and methods for community organising and empowerment as well as noise and disinformation. The western liberal democracies have also arrived at a demographic crossroads with increasing population diversity and its attendant democratic struggles. During that same time, planning has sustained its legitimacy through its reinvention away from a strictly technical field to one that fosters deliberative democratic practice.

Planning's orientation to deliberative democracy would seem to prepare the profession to work with people coming from such different information environments, but media availability has fostered what are, essentially, pre-political identities hostile to deliberation. Sager

(2020) identifies one collective result as 'authoritarian populism' that simultaneously rejects pluralism and planners as part of a treacherous elite in favour of an imagined, 'authentic' citizenship. In line with Nazi legal theorist Karl Schmitt, authoritarian populism recognises no loyal opposition with which one might engage in deliberation and compromise – only friends and enemies that one might embrace or reject.

Planners need to understand these changes, but we should not overstate what authoritarian populism is or ignore its longstanding roots in western politics. Racialised, white supremacist authoritarianism is not an aberration, particularly in American politics, even if the naked malfeasance represented by the Trump administration was (Toscano, 2020). Disinformation too, is a longstanding problem. But disinformation's potential reach differs quite a bit from the past due to proliferating media platforms and the connections that digital media allow. Early twentieth-century fascists like the United Kingdom's Oswald Mosley had to rely on leaflets handed out by sympathetic volunteers and mass media appearances doled out by media gate-keepers. Donald Trump, by contrast, could spread disinformation via his smartphone from his golf cart to millions of followers. And he could garner that disinformation, largely for free, from thousands of media content creators. In addition, we have to believe that the deadlocked politics that so far have resulted from mass disinformation also make authoritarianism more attractive to those who are understandably alarmed by our worsening climate crisis, mass extinction, and other markers of ecological collapse and who fear that slow, deliberative politics may not be able to catch up to these crises.

The question becomes what planning ought to do about it. Planning's response ideally recognises the need to secure its own power base through organising and advocacy for good places, cities and governance. To be less scatological than Steve Bannon, just because the zone is flooded with garbage does not mean the rest of us have to put up with it. Some new media voices rate more attention than others, just like some injustice claims or scientific facts are more valid than others. Planning can boost the media watchdogs that call out the fields' problems and address those problems, and it can boost the emancipatory potential of new media. A nice example appears in Vernon (2017) where social media documented disaster response failures. Planners can produce, promote, and elevate emerging, grassroots, civic media efforts, such as those we have highlighted throughout this chapter.

Planners can also seek, along with communications and media professionals, to de-platform those seeking to take power away from communities and incite violence. Elevating what is true, accurate, and meaningful in deliberation requires literacy across multiple domains, including media. Such a task is not easy because it requires planners to mediatise themselves, thoughtfully and ethically, along with others who promote evidence and good values. In order to do so, planning and planners have to build media into their twenty-first century theories and practices for the profession in the same way that prior generations have had to incorporate computers and other technologies. The movement towards media requires discernment and a clear normative commitment to what and whom planning serves and how to be accountable to these. It also requires a commitment to using media and data openly so that our own practices remain subject to scrutiny, critique, debate, and elevation (Schweitzer and Afzalan, 2017). Planners must understand how various media and their concomitant networked information works and create our own media practices, just like any group that hopes to wield influence (Mihailidis and Thevenin, 2013).

Yet, planning scholarship largely ignores media's influence on the profession and its stakeholders. While some scholars have considered the role of contemporary media in shaping what the public considers desirable for cities and settlements, we have found only a few research papers on media and planning to draw from for this chapter (c.f. Gunder, 2011; Flyvbjerg 2012). Publishing on the topic in the past decade has had this chapter's authors dealing with complacency about media that goes deeper than the normal hurly burly of paper reviewing. In case studies that we have published over the years, planning scholars urged us to cite only plans and official agency documents, not news stories or social media reactions about them because only the original documents are germane – not accurate (a valid concern), but *germane*. Planning reviewers have described things like television to us as 'silly.' No one who studies media seriously would say such a thing. So powerful is the magnitude of influence represented by television and film that their content has been understood as part of the 'societal curriculum,' a reminder that such media are 'pervasive, relentless and lifelong educators' (Cortes, 1992, p. 92). Television is the media technology with the greatest global reach. Nothing else is even close. Planners' willingness to discount television and other media does not establish planning as a scholarly discipline too serious-minded to waste its talents on trifles. It instead suggests a field out-of-step with political and cultural realities about media power. The evidence from media and politics research more generally gives us no reason to believe that planning or development is uniquely insulated from media influence. Planning research badly needs more empirical work on where people get their information, how they select information providers, and how that informs their orientation to planning and development. Planning's tendency to ignore or dismiss media merely weakens it and leaves Bannon's field open to those less committed to positive social outcomes.

Courting media on its own terms can be just as misguided. Planning as social marketing or public relations to create media darlings out of particular scholars, practitioners, or their projects recognises media power, but accepts media norms. These do not necessarily advance a democratic, inclusive representation or deliberation about places and futures. Unlocking the potential of media for planning requires new norms and practices in media, not just planning, so that leadership here can create a truly useful path forward.

NOTES

1. *The Guardian* is an interesting example in the urban media market, as it is a nonprofit newspaper owned by a foundation (the Scott Trust). Nonetheless nonprofits can exhibit market behaviour similar to for-profit outlets in competing for fundraising dollars and readership.
2. Interesting sidenotes: the conspiracy also demonstrates how the virtual trumps reality of physical space: the building does not have a basement. That fact, and the restaurant's silly (but fun) name serve almost as a means of hazing, of presenting people with ideas so ludicrous that their willingness to sign on and espouse the theory, despite commonsense reactions, is proof of their utter loyalty to the conspiracy group.
3. This video has been taken down, but the authors have an archived copy.
4. For more information on the use and reach of bots in disinformation, see New Technology from the arXiv (2017).
5. See Hindman (2008) for a discussion about the role that elite power plays in establishing large digital media audiences.
6. This quote was reported by writer Michael Lewis; we have been unable to find other sources for it (Lewis, 2018).

REFERENCES

Afzalan, N. and Muller, B. (2018) 'Online Participatory Technologies: Opportunities and Challenges for Enriching Participatory Planning'. *Journal of the American Planning Association* 84, 162–177.

Aisch, G., Huang, J., and Kang, K. (2016) 'Dissecting the #PizzaGate Conspiracy Theories'. *The New York Times*, December 10, 2016 [online]. Available at: www.nytimes.com/interactive/2016/12/10/business/media/pizzagate.html?_r=0 (accessed February 10, 2021).

Allcott, H. and Gentzkow, M. (2017) 'Social Media and Fake News in the 2016 Election'. *Journal of Economic Perspectives* 31(2), 211–236.

Arnstein, S. (1969) 'A Ladder of Community Participation'. *Journal of the American Institute of Planners* 35, 216–224.

Bates, L.K., Towne, S.K., Jordan, C.P., Lelliott, K.L., Johnson, M.S., Wilson, B., Winkler, T., and Bennet, W.L. (2008) *Civic Life Online: Learning How Digital Media Can Engage Youth*. Cambridge, MA: MIT Press/MacArthur Foundation.

Bene, M. (2017) 'Influenced by Peers: Facebook as an Information Source for Young People'. *Social Media + Society*. doi: 10.1177/2056305117716273.

Blue, G., Rosol, M., and Fast, V. (2019) 'Justice as Parity of Participation'. *Journal of the American Planning Association* 85(3), 363–376.

Boydstun, A.E. (2013) *Making the News: Politics, the Media, and Agenda Setting*. Chicago: University of Chicago Press.

Brady, W.J., Wills, J.A., Jost, J.T., Tucker, J., and Van Bavel, J.J. (2017) 'Emotion Shapes the Diffusion of Moralized Content in Social Networks'. *Proceedings of the National Academy of Sciences of the United States of America* 114, 7313–7318.

Brand, A.L., Corbin, C.N.E., Miller, M.J., Koh, A., Freitas, K., and Roberts, A.R. (2018) 'Race and Spatial Imaginary: Planning Otherwise'. *Planning Theory & Practice* 19(2), 254–288.

Castells, M. (2009) *Communication Power*. Oxford: Oxford University Press.

Castells, M. (2012) *Networks of Outrage and Hope: Social Movements in the Internet Age*. London: Polity.

Center for Community and Ethnic Media (2013) 'Getting the Word Out (or Not): How New York City Advertises'. City University of New York Graduate School of Journalism. http://cdn.journalism.cuny.edu/blogs.dir/601/files/2013/03/CCEMAdvertisingReport.pdf (accessed February 23, 2021).

Cortes, C. (1992) 'Who is Maria? What is Juan? Dilemmas of Analyzing the Chicano Image in US Feature Films', in Noriega, C. (ed.) *Chicanos and Film: Essays on Chicano Representation and Resistance*. New York and London: Garland Publishing, Inc., pp. 83–104.

Davidoff, P.A. (1965) 'Advocacy and Pluralism in Planning'. *Journal of the American Institute of Planners* 31(4), 8–63.

Davis, R. and Owen, D. (1998) *New Media and American Politics*. New York: Oxford University Press.

De Tocqueville, A. (2001 [1835]) *Democracy in America*, reprint edition. Signet.

Delli Carpini, M.X. and Keeter, S. (1996) *What Americans Know about Politics and Why it Matters*. New Haven, CT: Yale University Press.

Deuze, M., Bruns, A., and Neuberger, C. (2007) 'Preparing for an Age of Participatory News'. *Journalism Practice* 1(3), 322–338.

Emanuel, K. (2018) *What We Know about Climate Change*, updated edition. Cambridge, MA: MIT Press.

Flyvbjerg, B. (2012) 'Why Mass Media Matter to Planning Research: The Case of Megaprojects'. *Journal of Planning Education and Research* 32(2), 169–181. https://doi.org/10.1177/0739456X12441950.

Francke, W. (1995) 'The Evolving Watchdog: The Media's Role in Government Ethics'. *The Annals of the American Academy of Political and Social Science* 537, 109–121.

Gottfried, J.A., Hardy, B.W., Holbert, R.L., Winneg, K.M., and Jamieson, K.H. (2017) 'The Changing Nature of Political Debate Consumption: Social Media, Multitasking, and Knowledge Acquisition', *Political Communication* 34(2), 172–199. DOI: 10.1080/10584609.2016.1154120.

Graham, T., Jackson, D., and Wright, S. (2016) 'We Need to Get Together and Make Ourselves Heard': Everyday Online Spaces as Incubators of Political Action'. *Information, Communication & Society* 19(10), 1373–1389.

Gunder, M. (2011) 'A Metapsychological Exploration of the Role of Popular Media In Engineering Public Belief on Planning Issues'. *Planning Theory* 10(4), 325–343. https://doi.org/10.1177/1473095211413754.

Hindman, M. (2008) *The Myth of Digital Democracy*. Princeton, NJ: Princeton University Press.

International Association for Public Participation (2020) International Association for Public Participation [online]. Available at: www.iap2.org/mpage/Home (accessed February 23, 2021).

Jacobs, J. (1961) *The Death and Life of Great American Cities*. New York: Vintage Books.

Jebril, N., Albaek, E., and de Vreese, C.-H. (2013) 'Infotainment, Cynicism and Democracy: The Effects of Privatization vs. Personalization in the News'. *European Journal of Communication* 28(2), 105–121.

Jenkins, H. (2006) *Convergence Culture: Where Old and New Media Collide*. New York: NYU Press.

Jenkins, H., Shresthova, S., Gamber-Thompson, L., Kligler-Vilenchik, N., and Zimmerman, A. (2016) *By Any Media Necessary: The New Youth Activism*. New York: New York University Press.

Keyes, R. (2004) *The Post-truth Era*. New York: St. Martin's Press.

Kligler-Vilenchik, N. (2017) 'Alternative Citizenship Models: Contextualizing New Media and the New "Good Citizen"'. *New Media & Society* 19(11), 1887–1903. https://doi.org/10.1177/1461444817713742.

Lee, L. (2017) 'Black Twitter: A Response to Bias in Mainstream Media'. *Social Sciences* 6(1), 26.

Lewis, M. (2018) 'Has Anyone Seen the President?' *Bloomberg Opinion*, February 9 [online]. Available at: www.bloomberg.com/opinion/articles/2018-02-09/has-anyone-seen-the-president (accessed February 23, 2021).

Matei, S., Ball-Rokeach, S.J., and Qiu, J.L. (2001) 'Fear and Misperception of Los Angeles Urban Space: A Spatial-Statistical Study of Communication-Shaped Mental Maps'. *Communication Research* 28(4), 429–463.

May, L. (2000) *The Big Tomorrow: Hollywood and the Politics of the American Way*. Chicago: University of Chicago Press.

McChesney, R. (2015) *Rich Media, Poor Democracy*, 2nd edition. New York: The New Press.

Mihailidis, P. and Thevenin, B. (2013) 'Media Literacy as a Core Competency for Engaged Citizenship in Participatory Democracy'. *American Behavioral Scientist* 57(11), 1611–1622. https://doi.org/10.1177/0002764213489015.

Molotch, H. (1976) 'The City as a Growth Machine: Towards a Political Economy of Place'. *American Journal of Sociology* 82(2), 309–332.

Moy, P., Xenos, M.A., and Hess, V.K. (2009) 'Communication and Citizenship: Mapping the Political Effects of Infotainment'. *Mass Communication and Society* 8(2), 111–131.

New Technology from the arXiv (2017) 'First Evidence that Social Bots Play a Major Role in Spreading Fake News'. *MIT Technology Review*, August 7. Available: www.technologyreview.com/2017/08/07/150097/first-evidence-that-social-bots-play-a-major-role-in-spreading-fake-news/ (accessed February 15, 2021).

Ordway, D.-M. (2017) 'Fake News and the Spread of Misinformation'. *The Journalist's Resource*. Boston, MA: The Shorenstein Center on Media, Politics and Public Policy, Harvard University [online]. Available at: https://journalistsresource.org/studies/society/internet/fake-news-conspiracy-theories-journalism-research (accessed February 15, 2021).

Palmer, R., Toff, B., and Nielsen, R.K. (2020) '"The Media Covers up a Lot of Things": Watchdog Ideals Meet Folk Theories of Journalism', *Journalism Studies* 21(14), 1973–1989, DOI: 10.1080/1461670X.2020.1808516.

Pariser, E. (2011) *The Filter Bubble: How the New Personalized Web is Changing What we Read and How we Think*. New York: Penguin.

Poell, T. and van Dijck, J. (2018) 'Social Media and New Protest Movements', in Burgess, J., Marwick, A., and Poell, T. (eds) *The Sage Handbook of Social Media*. London: Sage Publications Ltd, pp. 546–561.

Rall, K., Satterthwaite, M.L., Pandey, A.V., Emerson J., Boy, J., Nov, O., and Bertini, E. (2016) 'Data Visualization for Human Rights Advocacy'. *Journal of Human Rights Practice* 8(2), 171–197. https://doi.org/10.1093/jhuman/huw011.

Rosanvallon, P. and Goldhammer, A. (2008) *Counter-democracy: Politics in an Age of Distrust*. Cambridge: Cambridge University Press.

Rosen, J. and Painter, G. (2019) 'From Citizen Control to Co-Production: Moving Beyond a Linear Conception of Citizen Participation'. *Journal of the American Planning Association* 85, 335–347.

Rosen, J. and Schweitzer, L. (2018) 'Benefits-Sharing Agreements and Nonideal Theory: The Warning Signs of Agreement Co-Optation'. *Planning Theory* 17, 396–417.

Rosenblum, N.L. and Muirhead, R. (2020) *A Lot of People Are Saying: The New Conspiracism and the Assault on Democracy*. Princeton, NJ: Princeton University Press.

Rossini, P., Stromer-Galley, J., Baptista, E.A., Veiga de Oliveira, V. (2020) 'Dysfunctional Information Sharing on WhatsApp and Facebook: The Role of Political Talk, Cross-cutting Exposure and Social Corrections', *New Media & Society* 23(8), 2430–2451. doi: 10.1177/1461444820928059.

Sager, T. (2020) 'Populists and Planners: "We are the People. Who are You"'*', *Planning Theory* 19(1), 80–103.

Salazar, J.F. (2009) 'Self-Determination in Practice: The Critical Making of Indigenous Media'. *Development in Practice* 19(4–5), 513.

Sandercock, L. (1975) *Cities for Sale: Property, Politics, and Urban Planning in Australia*. Carlton: Melbourne University Press.

Schweitzer, L.A. and Afzalan, N. (2017) 'Four Reasons Why AICP Needs an Open Data Ethic'. *Journal of the American Planning Association* 83, 161–166.

Schweitzer, L. and Stephenson, M. (2016) 'Planning, Development, and Media'. *Journal of Planning Education and Research* 36, 239–254.

Shannon, B. (2016) 'Avoiding Middle-class Planning 2.0: Media Arts and the Future of Urban Planning' dissertation submitted to the University of Southern California.

Sinclair, K. (2018) 'Categories of New Media'. *Medium.com* [online]. Available at: https://medium.com/vantage/categories-of-emerging-media-9c8d3c96004a (accessed February 23, 2021).

Strömberg, D. (2015) 'Media and Politics'. *Annual Review of Economics* 7, 173–205.

Stroud, N.J. (2011) *Niche News: The Politics of News Choice*. New York: Oxford University Press.

Tauxe, C.S. (1995) 'Marginalizing Public Participation in Local Planning: An Ethnographic Account'. *Journal of the American Planning Association* 61(4), 471–481. https://doi.org/10.1080/01944369508975658.

Thorpe, A. (2017) 'Rethinking Participation, Rethinking Planning', *Theory & Practice* 18(4), 566–582. https://doi.org/10.1080/14649357.2017.1371788.

Thorson, K., Cotter, K., Medeiros, M., and Pak, C. (2019) 'Algorithmic Inference, Political Interest, and Exposure to News and Politics on Facebook'. *Communication & Society* 24, 183–200.

Throgmorton, J. (1992) 'Planning as Persuasive Storytelling about the Future: Negotiating an Electric Power Rate Settlement in Illinois'. *Journal of Planning Education and Research* 12, 17–31.

Toscano, A. (2020) 'The Long Shadow of Racial Fascism'. *Boston Review*, 28 October [online]. Available at: http://bostonreview.net/race-politics/alberto-toscano-long-shadow-racial-fascism (accessed February 23, 2021).

Trapenberg Frick, K. (2016) 'Citizen Activism, Conservative Views and Mega Planning in a Digital Era'. *Planning Theory and Practice* 17(1), 93–118. https://doi.org/10.1080/14649357.2015.1125520.

Trapenberg Frick, K., Weinzimmer, D., and Waddell, P. (2015) 'The Politics of Sustainable Development Opposition: State Legislative Efforts to Stop the United Nations Agenda 21 in The United States', *Urban Studies* 52(2), 209–232.

Vatikiotis, P. (2014) 'New Media, Democracy, Participation and the Political'. *Interactions: Studies in Communication & Culture* 5(3), 293–307. https://doi.org/10.1386/iscc.5.3.293_1 (accessed February 23, 2021).

Vernon, P. (2017) 'The Media Today: Social Media and the Storm', *Columbia Journalism Review*. August 29 [online]. Available at: www.cjr.org/the_media_today/hurricane-harvey-social-media.php (accessed February 16, 2021).

Wallsten, K. (2010) '"Yes We Can": How Online Viewership, Blog Discussion, Campaign Statements, and Mainstream Media Coverage Produced a Viral Video Phenomenon'. *Journal of Information Technology & Politics* 7(2–3), 163–181.

Willis, J. (1987) 'Editors, Readers and News Judgement'. *Editor and Publisher* 120(6), 14–15.

Wired Staff (2017) 'Old-school Media is Pulling Way More Viewers Than You Think', *Wired*, February 2, 2017 [online]. Available at: www.wired.com/2017/02/daily-audience-numbers-for-big-media-outlets/ (accessed February 17, 2021).

Zahedi, M., Tessier, V., and Hawey, D. (2017) 'Understanding Collaborative Design through Activity Theory'. *The Design Journal*, 20(sup1), S4611–S4620. https://doi.org/10.1080/14606925.2017 .1352958.

26. Urban planning and the truthiness question

Eric Sheppard

INTRODUCTION

Urban and regional planning, at least as conceived within European and white settler societies, is an arm of the democratic capitalist state. Its purpose is to deploy state-endorsed expertise in order to realize state priorities that reflect the current state of pluralist democratic politics. As such experts, urban planners seek to create new 'facts on the ground': roads and other infrastructure, public spaces and buildings, land use zoning, and the like. Expertise and truth are thus central to a planning practice, legitimized through training and certification, that combines empirical evidence with state-of-the art understandings of socioecological processes to improve the spatial organization of society, and thereby society itself: evidence-based planning. Now that we find ourselves in a global moment where truth itself suddenly seems to be in question (Higgins, 2016), in this chapter I interrogate the implications of this for democratic urban planning.

Post-truth feels like it has become the order of the day in western democracies, with public debate focusing on grassroots skepticism about global warming, COVID-19 and the like, skepticism pushed by conservative forces to the point that liberals are ready to throw up their hands at the possibility of constructive engagement across difference. Inaugurating post-truth as the 2016 word of the year, the *Oxford English Dictionary* (2021) defines it as 'relating to or denoting circumstances in which objective facts are less influential in shaping public opinion than appeals to emotion and personal belief'.[1] In the United States, ex-President Trump's critics hanker for Joe Biden to bring a return to a normality ruled by respect for truth. As in the OED, this central rhetorical claim of the Biden administration turns on setting up a truth/false binary: objective truth vs opinion; just the facts vs emotion.

Challenging this binary, I show that truth has never been straightforwardly objective. Such objectivity is a social construct, whose contestations have shaped planning theory and practice long before Trumpism and will continue to do so. Concerns that planning is now being undermined by post-truth thus overlook compelling critiques of the 'god trick' (Haraway, 1988) of objectivity; of attempts to elevate universal rationality over situated knowledge, agonism and emotion (Mouffe, 1999; Corburn, 2003; Hoch, 2006; Baum, 2015; De Satgé and Watson, 2018).

I begin by examining this history of truth: the European enlightenment process through which specific facts came to be taken for granted as generalizable truths about the world, and objective knowledge production was deemed possible. But the truth/non-truth binary is illusory; truth is a social construction. The best we can do, perhaps, is to reach an understanding about what counts as truthiness – the quality of seeming or being felt to be true.[2] As for any social construction, however, the question of truthiness also is one of power and hegemony. *Whose* truths come to matter, and what is the process through which they gain consensus and thereby legitimacy? Turning to the post-truth moment, I examine key processes through which anti-hegemonic truth claims from the periphery, lauded by critical scholars and activists, became swamped by the right wing and xenophobic post-truth discourses that now distress us: neoliberal Globalization, digitization and platform capitalism.[3] Finally, curating a forced march through Anglophone critical planning theory, I tease out the implications of this for urban and regional planning.

THE SOCIAL CONSTRUCTION OF TRUTH

Truth has two overlapping aspects in the mainstream social and natural sciences, captured in the OED definition: agreed-on empirical statements about the world (facts) and value-free explanations of how the world works ('scientific' theories). This construction of truthiness emerged from a particular spatio-temporal conjuncture, whose influence needs to be critically interrogated: the eighteenth-century European Enlightenment, and particularly empiricism (its Anglophone variant). Seeking to displace the pre-Enlightenment consensus that society should be organized according to God's will as dictated by His representatives on Earth – itself a truth asserted about the world – Scottish and English philosophers such as John Locke, David Hume and Francis Bacon argued that direct observations of society contradict this assertion, undermining its claim to truthfulness.[4]

First, consider facts. Mary Poovey (1998) and Barbara Shapiro (2003) narrate how, in sixteenth- to eighteenth-century England, facts came to be what we take for granted today: truthful general statements about the world. At the start of this trajectory, facts described a specific, distinct event: 'matters of fact' in court cases, or the economic details in double-entry mercantile bookkeeping. Poovey and Shapiro narrate a tortuous path whereby theory-free observations, descriptions of a different world in travel writing, and facts reported in the news, entered the domain of what came to be known as science. Along the way, facts were elevated from descriptions of the particular, the peculiar and the spectacular, to generalizable empirical statements that are explainable through scientific investigation.

Second, consider theories. The epistemological goal of achieving universal, objective explanations of observed events reached its apotheosis under the paired labels of logical empiricism and positivism. Positivism began with Auguste Compte (Gregory, 1978), and was refined into logical empiricism in *fin de siècle* Vienna under the Vienna Circle philosophers. Its center of calculation relocated to Cambridge after World War II, where exiled members of the Vienna Circle joined Bertrand Russell and fellow analytical philosophers. These proponents of logical empiricism sought to revolutionize philosophy: putting philosophy in the service of science by banning metaphysics and ethics as meaningless forms of expression.[5] This meant developing *analytical statements* – universal theoretical claims argued to be true on their own terms (expressed as mathematical Aristotelian logic), that account for *synthetic statements* – empirical generalizations characterizing the world that humans experience (facts). The goal was to achieve a truthful account of the world by explaining the latter in terms of the seemingly iron-clad foundations of the former.

Taken together, the presumption that the world can be described in terms of objective uncontestable facts, accounted for through value-free analytical theories, amounted to the claim that scientists possess unique and exclusive expertise that enables them to divine truthful statements about our world. Invoking this 'foolproof method' (Curry, 1985), 1960s spatial science became the foundation for the confidence with which spatial planning set about optimizing the spatial organization of society (Scott, 1971; Openshaw, 1983). Yet this assertion of absolute truth is at best misleading (Olsson, 1972). To see this, consider again both observation and explanation.

The claim that the precepts of logical empiricism enable scientists to derive objectively truthful statements about the world has been widely critiqued, and undermined. In *A Social History of Truth* Stuart Shapin (2011) argues that what came to be accepted as truthful scientific claims in eighteenth-century England cannot be reduced to careful observations by lone scientists. Rather it was an intersubjective process, in which trust was essential for the observations of one person to become accepted as a fact by others. With scientific knowledge production dominated by male members of the Royal Society, Shapin describes how such trust was based on civility among gentlemen – seen as serious men whose word was their bond. But it was not just gender and class: David Livingstone (2003) argues that place also matters. For facts to be taken at face value as knowledge, not just beliefs, they need to travel from the places where they are constructed (laboratories, etc.) to become accepted across the world of everyday life. Obviously, for knowledge produced in the laboratories of members of the Royal Society to become generally accepted in the broader world, it helped immensely that scientists came to be accorded the expertise that is still commonly asserted under the label of science. To this day, the phrase 'science tells us that …' is commonplace discourse, asserting that science settles what counts as truth, as knowledge and not just belief, forming a basis from which we all can then move on.[6]

More broadly, the core philosophical principles of logical empiricism, advanced most influentially by Rudolf Carnap (1967) and in the social sciences by such luminaries as Karl Hempel (Hempel and Oppenheim, 1948) and David Harvey (1969), have become indefensible. Edmonds and Eidinow (2002) amusingly narrate logical empiricism's Achilles' heel: the impossibility of value-free observation. After attending a debate between Ludwig Wittgenstein and Karl Popper on a 1946 afternoon in a room at Cambridge University, the world's leading logical empiricist philosophers were unable to agree on whether they had observed Wittgenstein threaten Popper with a poker. Popper himself argued that observations are necessarily theory-laden, proposing critical rationalism and falsification as a fix for scientists' predilection to fit observations to their favorite theory (Popper, 1959). Further, the mathematician and fellow-Austrian exile Karl Gödel (1931) had already proven that mathematics itself is not an objective theory-language: that the truth or falsity of logical/analytical statements cannot necessarily be independently determined. Indeed, by the late 1960s, even as Harvey was introducing geographers to logical empiricism as the foundation for spatial science, John Passmore (1967: 57) could conclude that: 'Logical positivism, then, is dead, or as dead as a philosophical movement ever becomes'.[7]

Notwithstanding substantial, even seemingly unbridgeable, disagreements within the critical social science and critical planning communities, which range across Marxist, feminist, post-structural, critical race and decolonizing approaches, there is a shared critique of logical empiricism's claim to achieving value-free truth claims. There is no space here to rehearse in any detail the compelling feminist and social constructivist accounts of knowledge production, or to go over the 'science wars' that roiled throughout the 1990s (cf. Ashman, 2001). Yet Bruno Latour offers one way to summarize this. Latour was castigated by scientists for arguing (Latour and Woolgar, 1979; Latour, 1987) that their truths are social constructs – in many ways instigating the science wars. More recently, he has been distressed to see his skepticism about what counts as truth being used to legitimate post-truth claims made by right-wing science, climate change and vaccine skeptics (Latour, 2004). As he points out (2018: 23), 'facts remain robust only when they are supported by a common culture, by institutions that can be trusted, by a more or less decent public life, by more or less reliable media'.[8] All this suggests that the key issue is not truth but truthiness (the quality of seeming or being felt to be true).

The current concern about post-truth reflects the breakdown of such consensus as society polarizes and engagement across difference withers. But how was consensus arrived at, and what is the role of power in shaping it? Reflecting his flattened actor-network ontology, Latour pays little attention the role of power in shaping societal consensus about what counts as truth. Against this, Michel Foucault (1973 [1971]) traced the ways in which powerful discourses create consensus, what he glosses as power/knowledge, examining also how such elite discourses dramatically shift, reshaping what becomes taken for granted as truthful (Foucault, 1971 [1969]). Following Foucault and against Latour, consensus is shaped by powerful elites, and reshaped when they change their minds about what counts as truth, retaining their influence over its construction. Indeed, as Antonio Gramsci (1971) pointed out, consensus, alongside coercion, is how hegemony is realized. In this spirit Marx (1998 [1845]: 67) famously quipped: 'The ideas of the ruling class are in every epoch the ruling ideas'. It follows that when power hierarchies are challenged so is the truthiness of ruling ideas, as has been the case for emergent concerns about post-truth.

THE DISSIPATION OF TRUTH

Since the turn of the Millennium, and particularly since US President Trump came to power in 2016, there has been an extraordinary polarization of positionalities and viewpoints as to what is or is not real, what is or is not true.[9] This has occurred across geographical scales, ranging from inter-state to intra-familial conflicts and disagreements, generating a vibrant sub-field of post-truth scholarship (cf. d'Ancona, 2017; McIntyre, 2018). Latour's distress at the dissipation of consensus is now widely shared by those accustomed to shaping consensus about truthiness, as their taken-for-granted truth claims no longer seem acceptable: power hierarchies and their power/knowledge claims are in question. The emergence of this full-fledged knowledge crisis is overdetermined, but at least three longer-standing inter-related forcing factors have been identified: Globalization, the digitization of everyday life, and the platform capitalism (Srnicek, 2016; Langley and Leyshon, 2017) that has come to dominate the latter.

The 1944 Bretton Woods conference ushered in a post-1945 world dominated by US-led discourses of post-colonial capitalist Development, modernization and Globalization (supplanting inter-war counter-globalization and, before that, UK-led colonial/capitalist globalization). Under US hegemony, the consensus emerged around a capitalist Development project capable of bringing prosperity to all those who play by its rules (Gilman, 2003); thereby vitiating desires for socialist and communist alternatives (Rostow, 1960).[10] This consensus constructed a discourse – a power/knowledge – about the unique potential of capitalism that remains influential, even as its details have profoundly shifted. Until the late 1970s, the consensus was that capitalist Development required an activist nation-state whose role was to save capitalism from itself (Keynes, 1936; Mann, 2017) by mitigating its inherent socio-spatial inequalities: state-organized globalizing capitalism (Sheppard, 2016). After 1980, this was replaced by an anti-state discourse enacting neoliberal Globalization. Rather than the state being presented as saving capitalism from itself, suddenly the state was constructed as standing in the way of capitalism achieving its potential. Neoliberal Globalization was built on the free trade doctrine, free markets and democratic capitalism, gaining worldwide influence in the 1980s under the tutelage of the Bretton Woods institutions and the US Administration: the Washington Consensus. This consensus was challenged by grassroots movements across the Global South, particularly in light of the deleterious impact of 1980s structural adjustment policies. Many of those leading the rainbow revolutions that brought down the Soviet Block also imagined alternatives to capitalist Development. Yet such challenges failed to dislodge this post-1980s consensus that there is no alternative to capitalist Globalization (Sparke, 2012).

The destabilization of this neoliberal consensus about how capitalism really works that actually gained global resonance came from a different time and place – from within the regional Global North, after the Millennium. In addition to its deleterious effects on peoples and places across the Global South, Globalization also had been undermining the livelihood possibilities of members of the northern working class who had prospered since 1950 through unionized manufacturing work. From the 1970s, manufacturing disappeared from many traditional northern industrial heartlands as investment shifted to non-unionized and lower wage regions (in the US south, in southern and then eastern Europe, and in selected parts of Latin America, Asia and Africa). From the 1980s, neoliberal discourses undermined the very idea of unionization, replacing the 1945–1975 Keynesian inter-regnum of reduced socio-spatial inequalities with the current era of increasing socio-spatial inequality (Piketty, 2014 [2013]).

By the early 2000s, households and communities that previously benefited from unionized manufacturing had been suffering from economic stagnation, underemployment and lower wages for a generation. It was through resistance from these places that challenges to the 'truths' of capitalist Globalization gained resonance. The (particularly older-generation and white) residents of these regions enabled both Trump's narrow win over Hilary Clinton (undermining the neoliberal wing of the US Democratic Party), and the passing of the Brexit referendum that signalled the United Kingdom's departure from the Single Market of a neoliberalizing European Union (Baccini and Weymouth, 2021; Essletzbichler et al., 2018).

Contemporary challenges to what count as truth are not limited, however, to the economic consequences of deindustrialization and deunionization. Ongoing Globalization (in all forms) also has the cultural effect of creating a sense of loss of local control over livelihoods, cultural norms and lifestyles. Those feeling left by the wayside, rejecting Globalization discourses, have resorted to reiterating truths associated with pre-existing value systems over those of the capitalist Development consensus (Oberhauser et al., 2019). These alternatives are remarkably varied. They include religious fundamentalism (e.g., The Islamic State, US Evangelicals, Indian Hindu nationalism, and anti-Muslim Myanmar Buddhism), white supremacy and racism, identitarian movements and other variants of xenophobia, heteronormativity, masculinity, and anti-capitalist value systems (socialism, commoning). They also include the remarkable proliferation of such conspiracy theories as QAnon, which Uscinski and Parent (2014) argue are associated with feelings of disempowerment and marginalization. The coming to power of authoritarian national leaders, taking advantage of and empowering such right-wing grassroots challenges, triggered ever deeper disputes about counts as truth. We are perhaps entering an era of nationalist and authoritarian capitalism (Sheppard, 2020) in which global hegemony is in question, making it hard to construct the kind of power-laden consensus necessary to mobilize global-scale truthiness.

The emergence of Web 1.0 in the 1990s created conditions of possibility for the digitization of social life that we now take for granted. Notwithstanding persistent stark socio-spatial differences in connectivity – digital divides, more than half the global population is now on social media. Those creating the Web imagined a new world in which information flows flatten out and everyone has a voice, empowering grassroots perspectives and knowledge in ways that can challenge attempts by powerful interests to legislate what counts as truth, knowledge and appropriate behaviour. The elimination of barriers to global communication, it seemed, would augur an era in which we could engage with anyone: a global village (McLuhan, 1963) enabling a Habermasian deliberative, potentially radically democratic, public sphere (Habermas, 1974; Dahlberg, 2007). This pollyannish imaginary failed to anticipate, however, how the shifting geographies associated with online communication (Miller et al., 2021) create new barriers, even as others are broken down. Communication in the meat space of everyday life – neighborhoods, schools, workplaces, entertainment venues – forces encounters with difference. Notwithstanding socio-spatial segregation, such encounters also offer conditions of possibility for the everyday construction of equality across difference (Fincher et al., 2019). Proximity no longer structures communication in cyberspace, however. Instead, cybercommunities of like-minded participants have emerged that potentially reinforce their particular shared worldviews, insulated from having to engage with alternative perspectives and interpretations of the world. There is significant debate about the role of the Internet in shaping polarization: Boxell et al. (2017) conclude that political polarization in the United States is greater among non-Internet users. Others argue that social media are undermining democracy (Persily and Tucker, 2020), giving extremists a sense of purpose and self-worth (Bail, 2021). The really existing Internet is thus far from the flattened communications space imagined by its inventors. It has evolved its own spatially extensive power-geometries and hierarchies (Massey, 1999), shaped by powerful private and public actors and the cyber truths they popularize.

The commodification of the Internet reinforces these tendencies. On the one hand, key platform capital firms (Meta, Alphabet, Twitter, Alibaba, etc.) have grown to the point that they can exert quasi-monopoly control over social media, deploying algorithms that generate profits by assetizing personal information and selling advertising. This search for platform profits reinforces the potential for Internet polarization through a process that Shoshana Zuboff (2019) has dubbed surveillance capitalism. Zuboff has influentially argued that these algorithms prioritize radically controversial content, directing users' attention to other sites with content that reinforces their current search preferences. As Robert Frank (2021a) has put it: 'The algorithms that choose individual-specific content are crafted to maximize the time people spend on a platform. As the developers concede, Facebook's algorithms are addictive by design and exploit negative emotional triggers. Platform addiction drives earnings, and hate speech, lies and conspiracy theories reliably boost addiction'. On the other hand, state actors not only seek to reign in the influence of such monopolies but also increasingly manipulate the flow of cyberinformation to align with state-promoted narratives promoting their own versions of truthiness.

Given that truth is always in question, and that questioning received truths is central to critical scholarship and science, we should be cautious about seeking to legislate what counts as truth by simply excising post-truth narratives from public discourse. Consider the demands that Facebook, Twitter, Reddit and Google, etc., eliminate such narratives from their sites. Thomas Frank (2021b) cautions: 'The remedy for bad speech, we now believe, is not more speech, as per Justice Brandeis's famous formula, but an "extremism expert" shushing the world'. If we think of truth as a claim about the observable world, there are direct experiences that are so pervasively and inter-subjectively shared that they achieve a truth-like status – a correspondence theory of truth – that is hard to deny ('it's raining'). In most cases, however, claims to truth are interpretive; they are coherence theories of truth not correspondence theories. We may both be looking at the same information – such as the hockey-stick diagram of global heating – but see different truths in the sense of interpreting what that information means. One person may accept it as fact-like while another questions its construction – each bringing to it a contrasting theory-laden interpretive lens. Scientists also habitually engage in this. Those (like myself) who seek to build an egalitarian and diverse society, one that also treats the more-than-human world with respect, seek to advance that prospect by questioning the truth claims advanced by those advocating for an exclusionary, xenophobic and anthropocentric world. Hoping, with Martin Luther King, that the moral arc of the universe is long but bends toward justice, it is all too easy to dismiss right-wing claims as post-truth diversions from the righteous path. Such dismissal runs the danger, however, of giving them more resonance.

Adjudicating truth claims is almost always a power-laden political project: a struggle between those constituting truthiness and those seeking to deconstruct it. Considering the spatial history of this since Bretton Woods and modernization theory, US capitalist hegemony built on UK colonial/capitalist hegemony to construct capitalist Development as truthiness (with traditional planning enrolled to help states mitigate perceived market imperfections and/ or deliver public goods). In the late 1980s and particularly after the Asian financial crisis, social movements and select state institutions across the postcolony set about deconstructing this truth, pushing the World Bank and IMF to depart somewhat from the Washington Consensus (Sheppard and Leitner, 2010). Nevertheless, and notwithstanding the 2008 global economic crisis, these deconstructions – duplicated in critical Anglophone and third world social science scholarship – failed to dislodge the consensus around this truthiness. Instead, its dislodging came from the political power exerted by alienated first world populations, experiencing Globalization as undermining their livelihoods, cultural norms and racial formations (Omi and Winant, 1994). This political power was not only social but spatial – its location in western and white settler societies gave it global resonance (Sheppard, 2020). By the time this happened, social justice critiques were already being taken on board to some degree by state and capitalist institutions (affirmative action, GLBTQ+ policies, etc.), also influencing planning theory. Hence the widespread exasperation: even as longstanding globally hegemonic truth claims were beginning to take on board progressive critiques, their power to determine truthiness was being undermined by powerful northern and largely white post-truth and alternative fact counterclaims. All kinds of powerful institutions have set about denigrating and trying to dismiss right-wing truthiness, with the jury still out as to whether and how a new truthiness consensus will emerge and who it will empower.

These developments have significant implications also for urban and regional planning, whose truth claims have become increasingly critical of the status quo now being challenged from the right.

URBAN PLANNING, KNOWLEDGE AND TRUTHINESS

The field of urban planning has come a long way from the confidence exuded during its association with the illusory certainty of 1960s spatial science. Then, it was believed that planning could be based on absolute truth, achievable by hewing to the rational principles of logical empiricism (Faludi, 1973). It followed that planning could be an applied science whose practitioners deploy truthful knowledge: politicians set the agenda; planners implement it in an objective and value-free way, irrespective of their particular political inclinations. As Palat Narayanan (2020: 992) puts it: 'The plan is rendered scientific, and the irrational city and its ordinary citizens need to mend their ways of life to conform to these plans'. After this certainty was undermined, a sequence of competing urban planning paradigms have taken the stage, each based on particular alternative, post-positivist truth claims. Without attempting to be in any way comprehensive, in this section I examine some of these, teasing out the competing conceptions of truth that animate them.

Consider advocacy planning (Davidoff, 1965). Influenced by the 1960s urban protests, this paradigm emerged from a critique of logical empiricist knowledge claims. In this view, the differentiated knowledge and experiences of urban residents – reflecting their socio-spatial positionality within the city – constitute important alternative truth claims that scientific planning ignores. Seeking to legitimize and integrate such alternatives, the advocacy planner saw her task as representing residents' knowledge within the planning process: an expert intermediating between residents and urban policy. 'Davidoff viewed planning as a process to promote democratic pluralism in society, by representing diverse groups in political debate and public policy' (Checkoway, 1994: 140). This was an attempt to empower community-based truthiness against that mobilized by established planning elites.

The 1980s saw the emergence of neoliberal urban planning (Sager, 2011), seeking to empower a very different set of truth claims. 1960s scientific planning and advocacy planning both worked within a conception of capitalism that accorded the state the important role of mitigating the socio-spatial inequalities produced by unregulated commodity production and exchange. With the onset of neoliberalization, this came to be seen as a false understanding of how capitalism can deliver on its promise of prosperity for all bodies and places that conform to its principles. The new truthiness represented the state as inimical to realizing capitalism's potential. 'Much of urban public planning [came to be] seen as distortion of market mechanisms, and thus as a threat to private motivation and efficient allocation of resources' (Sager, 2011: 149). If cities were to become economically competitive, planning should not be a tool for correcting market failure but should minimize spatial regulation (Gleeson and Low, 2000: 135). Sager (2011) has compiled a list of such planning initiatives, including enterprise zones, attracting the creative class, city marketing, public–private partnerships, privatization of urban infrastructure provision and gentrification. Urban planners were relocated from planning departments, where they were subject to the mayor and council, into economic development quangos isolated from political pressure. Neoliberal truth claims elevated planners as now superior to the state: ideology-free technocrats, implementing cast-iron economic principles. As Margaret Thatcher memorably quipped: there is no alternative (Berlinski, 2011). Neoliberal truth claims were empowered, marginalizing the grassroots truths espoused by supposedly overtly politicized advocacy planners.

Drawing strength from increasingly trenchant critiques of neoliberal truth claims about capitalism, reinforced by their repeated failure to deliver on the promises of such claims, communicative planning took urban planning by storm (Innes, 1995). Influenced inter alia by Habermas' notions of communicative action and the public sphere (Mattila, 2020), the truths to be mobilized by communicative planning are rooted outside the sphere of instrumental rationality inhabited by scientific and neoliberal planning. Communicative planning is based on the principle that 'planning could be made more democratic, more legitimate, more just and more responsive to the needs of the people by enhancing the quality and quantity of communication between different groups of actors in planning: public planning officials, political decision-makers, citizen-stakeholders and the representatives of private businesses' (Mattila, 2020: 2).

Like advocacy planning, communicative planning locates the truths that matter in the everyday city rather than derivable through the application of social or economic theory: bringing these diverse participants together through practice-oriented models of communicating, learning from one another, the vision was that this would build consensus – a shared truth that can then form the basis for community-oriented planning initiatives. Unlike advocacy planning, the planner is no longer seen as a trusted and expert intermediary, tasked with putting grassroots truths in conversation with those normalized by planning technocrats. Instead, truths must be constructed directly by those outside this process. Further, this consensual truth-building should not prioritize the marginalized perspectives that advocacy planners saw themselves as empowering. The vision is that all should participate in a process through which pre-existing power hierarchies fall away during consensus-building – a form of deliberative democracy (for a critique of this vision, see McGuirk, 2001). This effectively disempowers technical expertise and instrumental rationality by empowering communicative rationality, in the expectation that this will produce a new consensual truthiness.

Finally, consider the southern turn in planning theory (cf. Connell, 2013; see also Chapter 17 by Duminy and Watson). This is based on the argument that truthiness does not just depend on pre-existing theoretical principles (scientific and neoliberal planning) and/or urban residents' grassroots truthiness (advocacy and communicative planning), but on where in the world we think from. There is now a rich body of planning scholarship reinforcing Connell's case that the distinctive realities of southern cities challenge northern convention that planning is the state-directed ordering and administration of society when such ordering breaks down. Watson (2009: 2267) calls this the rationality of 'techno-managerial and marketized systems of government administration and service provision'. Many have remarked on the failure of such ordering across cities of the post-colony; southern planning theorists argue, however, that the failure is not one of implementing this rationale, but of conventional planning theory itself.

The key issue here is argued to be the pervasiveness of informal livelihoods in southern cities. On the one hand, are the many ways in which community planning occurs in ways that exceed the state. For example, local communities set about organizing their own allocation of land to community members in ways that do not conform to state and/or capitalist market logics. More generally, everyday life, and urban morphologies and infrastructure are all deeply shaped by informal livelihood strategies in cities of the post-colony (Bayat, 2000; Benjamin, 2008; Caldeira and Holston, 2005; Caldeira, 2016; Holston, 2009; Simone, 2004, 2019). Watson (2009: 2267) calls these 'a different rationality – shaped by efforts of survival – which in turn operates with its own logics and imperatives'. She argues that such alternatives are beyond the scope of the rationalities of communicative planning (2009: 2272), and thus that planning needs to reconceptualize itself as operating at the intersection of these conflicting rationalities. Miraftab (2009: 45), like Connell, calls for insurgent planning that would decolonize 'the planning imagination by taking a fresh look at subaltern cities to understand them by their own rules of the game and values rather than by the planning prescriptions and fantasies of the West'. Highlighting the pervasiveness of informality also among elites and within the state, Roy (2009) concludes that urban planning itself necessarily fails in southern mega-cities.

It is important to acknowledge, however, that this southern turn is more than an argument that certain cities are different. The pervasiveness of informality in cities of the post-colony is not simply a contingent place-based detail of the kind that all theorizations seek to abstract from (as argued, for example, by Scott and Storper, 2015), but reflects their shared conjunctural positionality within a global periphery that still bears the marks of colonialism (Sheppard, 2014a; 2019). This southern turn also does not seek to create a binary of southern planning for southern cities and northern planning for northern cities. Rather, by making the informality of urban life visible because of its pervasiveness in the periphery it forces a rethinking of planning that is pertinent for cities everywhere (Watson, 2009; Sheppard et al., 2015; Roy, 2016). In short, the southern turn empowers the more-than-capitalist truthiness experienced by southern urban residents (Sheppard 2019), against those advanced by instrumental and flattened communicative rationality.

Thinking across this abbreviated genealogy of Anglophone urban planning paradigms, each makes particular assertions about what is truthful – about what counts as knowledge and not just belief. To select any one of these as correct would have the effect of dismissing the competing truth and knowledge claims associated with others. Indeed, this has been something of a trend as theoretical approaches have multiplied across the Anglophone critical social sciences over the past fifty years, with each new approach seeking to gain resonance by dismissing its forebears. Yet defaulting to any one approach as superior would abandon the instinct of critical thought to keep asking the hard questions. The alternative should be to engage in a constructive exchange across different truth and knowledge claims, as I elaborate below.

CONCLUDING REFLECTIONS: BEYOND THE TRUTH WARS

In this chapter, I have argued that truth is contingent: there is no absolute standard to adjudicate once and for all whether any claim is true or false. To achieve truthiness, a claim must be supported by an inter-subjective consensus validating it (Latour, 2018). Scholars from Gramsci to Foucault remind us, however, that consensus typically is not built through a flattened democratic deliberation between all members of society of the kind imagined by Habermas; it is shaped to a considerable degree by powerful forces constructing power/knowledge discourses that others then consent to. It follows that the current 'post-truth' moment is not novel, a moment where truth has been replaced by 'alternative facts'. Rather, it is a disruptive moment when long marginalized right-wing truth claims are regaining attention. Its emergence is overdetermined by how the inequalizing and disempowering nature of Globalization, the digitization of society and the algorithms of platform capitalism have come to intersect. Our distress at this particular challenge to (our) truthiness reflects legitimate concerns that making space for such truth claims bends the arc of knowledge production away from advancing social, environmental and more-than-human justice. Briefly examining the trajectory of Anglophone planning, the succession of paradigms characterizing the field since the 1970s also has been based on asserting counter-truth claims against pre-existing power hierarchies and the truthiness they validate – albeit seeking to bend the arc towards justice.

If truth claims cannot be independently resolved, the alternative is to engage conflicting claims with one another. Trevor Barnes and I dub this engaged pluralism (Barnes and Sheppard, 2010). The principle is to convene representatives of all competing sets of truth claims; those willing to take competing truth claims seriously, in an even-handed exchange of knowledge claims where each participant is positioned to learn from others on their terms and encouraged to rethink her own claims. The goal is not necessarily to arrive at a consensus; participants may still disagree when they part ways, hopefully adjusting their knowledge and truth claims as they learn from others (Longino, 2002). The devil is in the detail, of course; pre-existing power differences would need to be reversed (Young, 1990) and interpersonal exchange should countenance passion as well as logic – agonistic pluralism (Mouffe, 1999). Further, there is no pre-determined outcome – so the political consequences are also contingent.

This is a reminder that urban planning – like all knowledge production – is always a contestable political project, whose presuppositions must always be open to contestation about which truths matter. Planning is thus not reducible to best practice: the best means to realize a predefined end. Since truth claims are contestable, ends and means are both up for grabs. They are shaped by those powerful enough at any given moment to curate a societal consensus around a particular set of truth claims, but only so long as that hegemony can be maintained.

NOTES

1. See www.lexico.com/en/definition/post-truth, accessed June 29, 2021.
2. Truthiness recently has been popularized by American comedic commentator Stephen Colbert, but dates back to 1832.
3. I capitalize Globalization to distinguish the current neoliberal era from previous longer-standing phases and alternative logics of anthropocentric globalization, dating back to the exodus of homo sapiens from Africa (Sparke, 2012).
4. This empirical, Anglophone approach to establishing truth is also challenged within the European enlightenment philosophical canon. Idealism, structuralism, hermeneutics, dialectics, and post-prefixed approaches, emanating from across the English Channel, all challenge this path to truth. Yet the geopolitical influence of Britain and then the United States has enabled empiricism to diffuse worldwide as taken-for-granted best practice when it comes to determining truthfulness.
5. Notwithstanding their adherence to explaining the world as it is, logical empiricist philosophers leaned radically progressive. Like their Enlightenment forebears, they sought to deconstruct support for Austria's Catholic Hapsburg legacy. The Vienna Circle polymath Otto Neurath was influential in the planning of socialist Vienna. Russell was an anti-war activist and Fred Schaefer – the promoter of spatial science – attracted FBI surveillance for his radicalism (Sheppard, 2014b).
6. Importantly, practicing scientists would be the first to assert that they do not in fact produce settled knowledge, as science must always be in question (Polanyi, 1958; Sheppard, N., 1999).
7. By this point the term logical positivism had been largely replaced by logical empiricism, but Passmore equated the two (as others have since: Creath, 2017).
8. See also Kofman (2018).
9. Such polarizations had already characterized the science wars, including debates about whether there is a real world. As for Latour, they suddenly became elevated from abstruse academic exchanges to general social disagreement.
10. I capitalize Development to reference development trajectories that are propagated across the world as a universal best practice (Hart, 2002).

REFERENCES

Ashman, K. (ed.) (2001) *After the Science Wars*. London: Psychology Press.
Baccini, L. and Weymouth, S. (2021) Gone for Good: Deindustrialization, White Voter Backlash, and US Presidential Voting. *American Political Science Review* 115(2): 550–567.
Bail, C. (2021) *Breaking the Social Media Prism: How to Make our Platforms Less Polarizing*. Princeton, NJ: Princeton University Press.

Barnes, T. and Sheppard, E. (2010) 'Nothing Includes Everything': Towards Engaged Pluralism in Anglophone Economic Geography. *Progress in Human Geography* 34(2): 193–214.

Baum, H. (2015) Planning with Half a Mind: Why Planners Resist Emotion. *Planning Theory & Practice* 16(4): 498–516.

Bayat, A. (2000) From 'Dangerous Classes' to 'Quiet Rebels': Politics of the Urban Subaltern in the Global South. *International Sociology* 15(3): 533–557.

Benjamin, S. (2008) Occupancy Urbanism: Radicalizing Politics and Economy beyond Policy and Programs. *International Journal of Urban and Regional Research* 32(3): 719–729.

Berlinski, C. (2011) *There is No Alternative: Why Margaret Thatcher Matters*. Paris: Hachette UK.

Boxell, L., Gentzkow, M. and Shapiro, J.M. (2017) Greater Internet use is Not Associated with Faster Growth in Political Polarization among US Demographic Groups. *Proceedings of the National Academy of Sciences* 114(40): 10612–10617.

Caldeira, T. (2016) Peripheral Urbanization: Autoconstruction, Transversal Logics, and Politics in Cities of the Global South. *Environment and Planning D: Society and Space* 35(1): 3–20.

Caldeira, T. and Holston, J. (2005) State and Urban Space in Brazil: From Modernist Planning to Democratic Interventions. In Ong, A. and Collier, S.J. (eds) *Global Anthropology: Technology, Governmentality, Ethics*. London: Blackwell, pp. 393–416.

Carnap, R. (1967) *The Logical Structure of the World*. Berkeley, CA: University of California Press.

Checkoway, B. (1994) Paul Davidoff and Advocacy Planning in Retrospect. *Journal of the American Planning Association* 60(2): 139–143.

Connell, R. (2013) Using Southern Theory: Decolonizing Social Thought in Theory, Research and Application. *Planning Theory* 13(2): 210–223.

Corburn, J. (2003) Bringing Local Knowledge into Environmental Decision Making: Improving Urban Planning for Communities at Risk. *Journal of Planning Education and Research* 22(4): 420–433.

Creath, R. (2017). Logical Empiricism. *Stanford Encyclopedia of Philosophy* online. Stanford, CA: Stanford University. https://plato.stanford.edu/entries/logical-empiricism/, accessed June 29, 2021.

Curry, M. (1985) On Rationality: Contemporary Geography and the Search for the Foolproof Method. *Geoforum* 16: 109–118.

d'Ancona, M. (2017) *Post-Truth: The New War on Truth and How to Fight Back*. New York: Random House.

Dahlberg, L. (2007) The Internet, Deliberative Democracy, and Power: Radicalizing the Public Sphere. *International Journal of Media & Cultural Politics* 3(1): 47–64.

Davidoff, P. (1965) Advocacy and Pluralism in Planning. *Journal of the American Institute of Planners* 31(4): 331–338.

De Satgé, R. and Watson, V. (2018) *Urban Planning in the Global South: Conflicting Rationalities in Contested Urban Space*. Berlin: Springer.

Edmonds, D. and Eidinow, J. (2002) *Wittgenstein's Poker: The Story of a Ten-minute Argument between Two Great Philosophers*. New York: HarperCollins.

Essletzbichler, J., Disslbacher, F. and Moser, M. (2018) The Victims of Neoliberal Globalisation and the Rise of the Populist Vote: A Comparative Analysis of Three Recent Electoral Decisions. *Cambridge Journal of Regions, Economy and Society* 11(1): 73–94.

Faludi, A. (1973) *Planning Theory*. London: Pergamon Press.

Fincher, R., Iveson, K., Leitner, H. and Preston, V. (2019) *Everyday Equalities: Making Multicultures in Settler Colonial Cities*. Minneapolis, MN: University of Minnesota Press.

Foucault, M. (1971 [1969]) *The Archeology of Knowledge*. London: Tavistock.

Foucault, M. (1973 [1971]) *The Order of Things*. New York: Vintage.

Frank, R.B. (2021a) The Economic Case for Regulating Social Media. *The New York Times*, February 11. www.nytimes.com/2021/02/11/business/social-media-facebook-regulation.html, accessed May 5, 2021.

Frank, T. (2021b) Liberals Want to Blame Rightwing 'Misinformation' for our Problems. Get Real. *The Guardian*. www.theguardian.com/commentisfree/2021/mar/19/rightwing-misinformation-liberals, accessed May 5, 2021.

Gilman, N. (2003) *Mandarins of the Future: Modernization Theory in Cold War America*. Baltimore, MD: Johns Hopkins University Press.

Gleeson, B. and Low, N. (2000) Revaluing Planning: Rolling Back Neo-liberalism in Australia. *Progress in Planning* 53(2): 83–164.

Gödel, K. (1931) Über formal unentscheidbare Sätze der Principia Mathematica und verwandter Systeme I. *Monatshefte für Mathematik und Physik* 38: 173–198.

Gramsci, A. (1971) *Selections from the Prison Notebooks*. London: Lawrence and Wishart.

Gregory, D. (1978) *Ideology, Science and Human Geography*. London: Hutchinson.

Habermas, J. (1974) The Public Sphere: An Encyclopedia Article (1964). *New German Critique* (3): 49–55.

Haraway, D. (1988) Situated Knowledges: The Science Question and the Privilege of Partial Perspective. *Feminist Studies* 14(3): 575–599.

Hart, G. (2002) Geography and Development: Development/s Beyond Neoliberalism? Power, Culture, Political Economy. *Progress in Human Geography* 26(6): 812–822.

Harvey, D. (1969) *Explanation in Geography*. London: Edward Arnold.

Hempel, C. and Oppenheim, P. (1948) Studies in the Logic of Explanation. *Philosophy of Science* 15: 135–175.

Higgins, K. (2016) Post-truth: A Guide for the Perplexed. *Nature* 540(9). https://doi.org/10.1038/540009a.

Hoch, C. (2006) Emotions and Planning. *Planning Theory & Practice* 7(4): 367–382.

Holston, J. (2009) Insurgent Citizenship in an Era of Global Urban Peripheries. *City & Society* 21(2): 245–267.

Innes, J.E. (1995) Planning Theory's Emerging Paradigm: Communicative Action and Interactive Practice. *Journal of Planning Education and Research* 14(3): 183–189.

Keynes, J.M. (1936) *The General Theory of Employment, Interest, and Money*. London: Macmillan.

Kofman, A. (2018) Bruno Latour, the Post-truth Philosopher, Mounts a Defense of Science. *New York Times Magazine* 25, October 25. www.nytimes.com/2018/10/25/magazine/bruno-latour-post-truth-philosopher-science.html?, accessed May 5, 2021.

Langley, P. and Leyshon, A. (2017) Platform Capitalism: The Intermediation and Capitalisation of Digital Economic Circulation. *Finance and Society* 3(1): 11–31.

Latour, B. (1987) *Science in Action*. Cambridge, MA: Harvard University Press.

Latour, B. (2004) Why has Critique run out of Steam? From Matters of Fact to Matters of Concern. *Critical Inquiry* 30(2): 25–28.

Latour, B. (2018) *Down to Earth: Politics in the New Climatic Regime*. Cambridge: Polity Press.

Latour, B. and Woolgar, S. (1979) *Laboratory Life: The Social Construction of Scientific Facts*. Beverly Hills, CA: Sage Publications.

Livingstone, D. (2003) *Putting Science in its Place: Geographies of Scientific Knowledge*. Chicago: University of Chicago Press.

Longino, H. (2002) *The Fate of Knowledge*. Princeton NJ: Princeton University Press.

Mann, G. (2017) *In the Long Run we are all Dead: Keynesianism, Political Economy, and Revolution*. London: Verso Books.

Marx, K. and Engels, F. (1998 [1845]). *The German Ideology*. Amherst, NY: Prometheus Books.

Massey, D. (1999) Imagining Globalization: Power-geometries of Time-space. In Brah, A., Hickman, M. and Mac an Ghaill, M. (eds) *Global Futures: Migration, Environment and Globalization*. New York: St. Martin's Press, pp. 27–44.

Mattila, H. (2020) Habermas Revisited: Resurrecting the Contested Roots of Communicative Planning Theory. *Progress in Planning* 141, e100431.

McGuirk, P.M. (2001) Situating Communicative Planning Theory: Context, Power, and Knowledge. *Environment and Planning A* 33(2): 195–217.

McIntyre, L. (2018) *Post-Truth*. Cambridge, MA: MIT Press.

McLuhan, M. (1963) *The Gutenberg Galaxy*. Toronto: University of Toronto Press.

Miller, D., Rabho, L., Awondo, P., de Vries, M., Duque, M., Garvey, P., Haapio-Kirk, L., Hawkins, C., Otaegui, A. and Walton, S. (2021) *The Global Smartphone: Beyond a Youth Technology*. London: UCL Press.

Miraftab, F. (2009) Insurgent Planning: Situating Radical Planning in the Global South. *Planning Theory* 8(1): 32–50.

Mouffe, C. (1999) Deliberative Democracy or Agonistic Pluralism? *Social Research* 66(3): 745–758.

Oberhauser, A., Krier, D. and Kusow, A. (2019) Political Moderation and Polarization in the Heartland: Economics, Rurality, and Social Identity in the 2016 US Presidential Election. *The Sociological Quarterly* 60(2): 224–244.

Olsson, G. (1972) Some Notes on Geography and Social Engineering. *Antipode* 4(1): 1–21.

Omi, M. and Winant, H. (1994) *Racial Formation in the United States*. London: Routledge.

Openshaw, S. (1983) Location-allocation Techniques: Practical Methods for Spatial Planning. *Planning Outlook* 26(1): 7–14.

Palat Narayanan, N. (2020) Southern Theory without a North: City Conceptualization as the Theoretical Metropolis. *Annals of the American Association of Geographers* 111(4): 989–1001.

Passmore, J. (1967) 'Logical Positivism', in Edwards, P. (ed.) *The Encyclopedia of Philosophy*, Vol. 5. New York and London: Macmillan and Collier Macmillan, pp. 52–57.

Persily, N. and Tucker, J. (eds) (2020) *Social Media and Democracy: The State of the Field, Prospects for Reform*. Cambridge: Cambridge University Press.

Piketty, T. (2014 [2013]) *Capital in the Twenty-first Century*. Cambridge, MA: Belknap Books.

Polanyi, M. (1958) *Personal Knowledge: Towards a Post-critical Philosophy*. Chicago: University of Chicago Press.

Poovey, M. (1998) *A History of the Modern Fact: Problems of Knowledge in the Sciences of Wealth and Society*. Chicago: University of Chicago Press.

Popper, K. (1959) *The Logic of Scientific Discovery*. New York: Basic Books.

Rostow, W.W. (1960) *The Stages of Economic Growth: A Non-communist Manifesto*. Cambridge: Cambridge University Press.

Roy, A. (2009) Why India cannot Plan its Cities: Informality, Insurgence and the Idiom of Urbanization. *Planning Theory* 8(1): 76–87.

Roy, A. (2016) Who's Afraid of Postcolonial Theory? *International Journal of Urban and Regional Research* 40(1): 200–209.

Sager, T. (2011) Neo-liberal Urban Planning Policies: A Literature Survey 1990–2010. *Progress in Planning* 76(4): 147–199.

Scott, A. (1971) *Combinatorial Programming, Spatial Analysis and Planning*. London: Methuen.

Scott, A. and Storper, M. (2015) The Nature of Cities: The Scope and Limits of Urban Theory. *International Journal of Urban and Regional Research* 39(1): 1–15.

Shapin, S. (2011) *A Social History of Truth: Civility and Science in Seventeenth-century England*. Chicago: University of Chicago Press.

Shapiro, B.J. (2003) *A Culture of Fact: England, 1550–1720*. Ithaca, NY: Cornell University Press.

Sheppard, E. (2014a) Globalizing Capitalism and Southern Urbanization. In Parnell, S. and Oldfield, S. (eds) *The Routledge Handbook on Cities of the Global South*. London: Routledge, pp. 143–154.

Sheppard, E. (2014b) We have Never been Positivist. *Urban Geography* 35(5): 636–644.

Sheppard, E. (2016) *Limits to Globalization: Disruptive Geographies of Capitalist Development*. Oxford: Oxford University Press.

Sheppard, E. (2019) Globalizing Capitalism's Raggedy Fringes: Thinking through Jakarta. *Area Development and Policy* 4(1): 1–27.

Sheppard, E. (2020) What's Next? Trump, Johnson, and Globalizing Capitalism. *Environment and Planning A: Economy and Space* 52(4): 679–687.

Sheppard, E., Gidwani, V., Goldman, M., Leitner, L., Roy, A. and Maringanti, A. (2015) Introduction: Urban Revolutions in the Age of Global Urbanism. *Urban Studies* 52(11): 1947–1961.

Sheppard, E. and Leitner, H. (2010) Quo Vadis Neoliberalism? The Remaking of Global Capitalist Governance after the Washington Consensus. *Geoforum* 41(2): 185–194.

Sheppard, N. (1999) Michael Polanyi and the Philosophy of Science. *Appraisal* 2: 107–115.

Simone, A. (2004) People as Infrastructure: Intersecting Fragments in Johannesburg. *Public Culture* 16(3): 407–429.

Simone, A. (2019) *Improvised Lives: Rhythms of Endurance in an Urban South*. Cambridge: Polity Press.

Sparke, M. (2012). *Introducing Globalization: Ties, Tensions, and Uneven Integration*. New York: John Wiley & Sons.

Srnicek, N. (2016) *Platform Capitalism*. Cambridge: Polity Press.

Uscinski, J. and Parent, J. (2014) *American Conspiracy Theories*. Oxford: Oxford University Press.

Watson, V. (2009) Seeing from the South: Refocusing Urban Planning on the Globe's Central Urban Issues. *Urban Studies* 45(11): 2259–2275.

Young, I. (1990) *Justice and the Politics of Difference*. Princeton, NJ: Princeton University Press.

Zuboff, S. (2019) *The Age of Surveillance Capitalism: The Fight for a Human Future at the New Frontier of Power*. New York: Public Affairs.

Index